I0894375

AN EVOLVING VISION:
THE JAMES COLLECTION, 1997–2022

MARIN F. HANSON
CAROLYN DUCEY
PENELOPE McMORRIS

International Quilt Museum
UNIVERSITY OF NEBRASKA-LINCOLN

This publication accompanies the International Quilt Museum's *An Evolving Vision: The James Collection, 1997 – 2022* exhibition series held between March 4 and October 29, 2022.

Major funding for this publication was received from:
Creta Warner Filley Memorial Fund
Joan Laughlin, Ph.D, Endowment Fund
Mary Ann Beavers Fund for Public Programming & Outreach

International Quilt Museum
University of Nebraska-Lincoln
Lincoln, Nebraska 68583-0838
www.internationalquiltmuseum.org

 Collection object photos by: Jamie Swartz and Sarah Walcott.

ISBN: 978-1-7352784-3-8
Library of Congress Control Number: 2022932153

Designed by Ebbeka Design Co., Lincoln, Nebraska

Cover images, L - R: The "Reconciliation Quilt" by Lucinda Ward Honstain (1867, Gift of the Robert and Ardis James Foundation, IQM 2001.011.0001), "Finn," by Pauline Burbidge (1983, Ardis and Robert James Collection, IQM 1997.007.1070), and Ralli quilt (c. 1994, Patricia Stoddard Collection, Partial gift of the Robert and Ardis James Foundation, IQM 2016.012.0077).

AN EVOLVING VISION:
THE JAMES COLLECTION, 1997–2022

5

Foreword, *Leslie C. Levy*

6

1. Introduction, *Marin F. Hanson*

13

2. Classics, *Carolyn Ducey*

47

3. From the Studio, *Penelope McMorris*

77

4. New Horizons, *Marin F. Hanson*

111

The James Collection

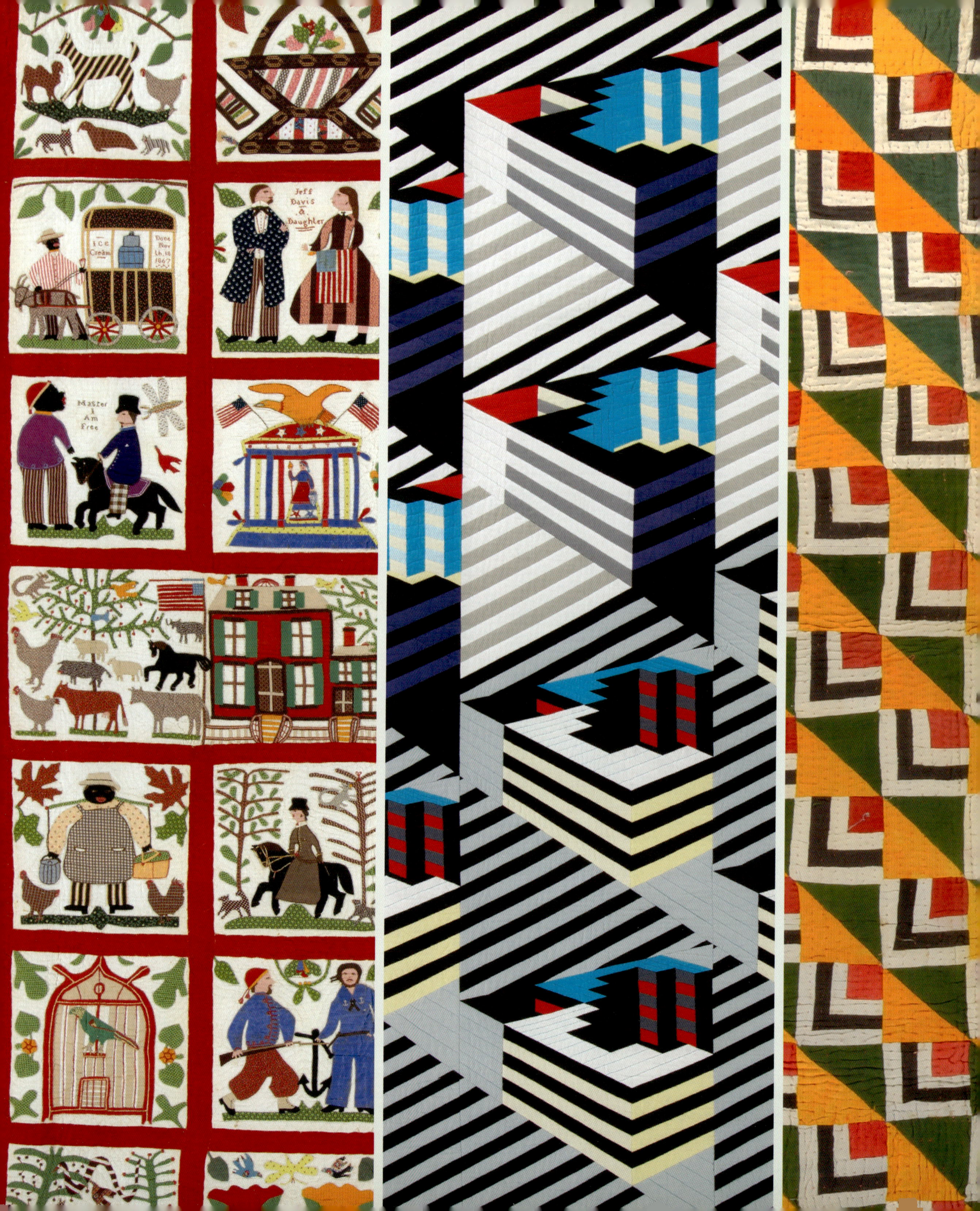
Ice Cream
Jeff Davis & Daughter
Master I Am Free

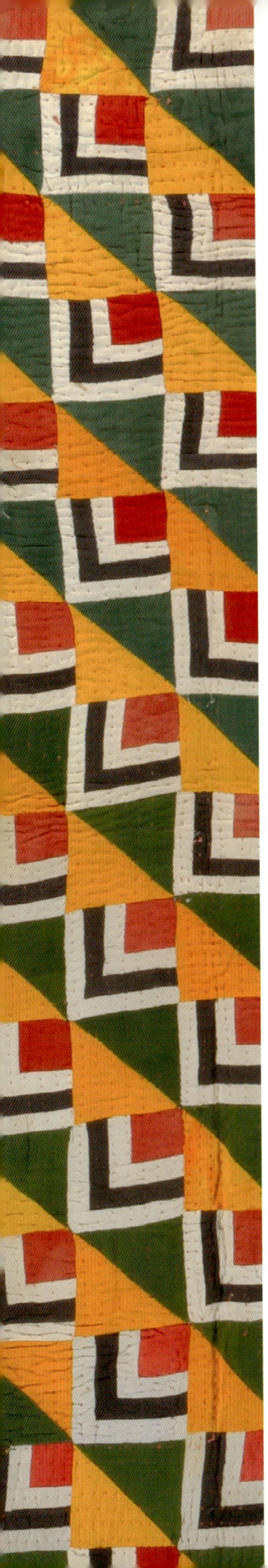

FOREWORD

An Evolving Vision: The James Collection, 1997-2022 is an International Quilt Museum (IQM) exhibition series on view from March 4 to October 29, 2022. With these exhibitions, we mark the IQM's 25th anniversary and celebrate the Ardis and Robert James Collection, the outstanding group of quilts whose donation to the University of Nebraska-Lincoln (UNL) in 1997 established our museum.

In the *An Evolving Vision* exhibitions, we highlight important pieces from various segments of the James Collection: *Classics* – stunning antique American quilts; *From the Studio* – early and innovative art pieces; and *New Horizons* – examples of quilt traditions from around the world. And in each of these chapters, we also present bonus quilts, ones we could not fit into the exhibitions but knew people would enjoy seeing featured. The back section of the book comprises a comprehensive catalog of the entire James Collection—nearly all of the over 1000 quilts that make up the original 1997 gift as well as important groups donated by the Jameses in 2006 and 2009.

An Evolving Vision documents the significance of the James Collection but also underscores the broad vision its collectors developed not only for themselves, but for the museum they so vitally helped shape. Ardis and Robert James were driven to discover, collect and document quilts of all types and origins, an endeavor they passed along to our museum a quarter century ago. They understood that by transferring their unique vision for a quilt collection to us, that it would change and expand—an evolution they and their family have supported from Day One.

Since becoming the IQM's Executive Director in 2014, I have been honored to lead the IQM team in fulfilling our mission of building a global collection and audience that celebrate the cultural and artistic significance of quilts. A key partner in pursuing our goals has been the Robert and Ardis James Foundation. From the moment the quilts came to UNL in 1997, they have encouraged and enabled the IQM to grow, both substantially and prudently. We thank them for continuing to honor the legacy of Robert and Ardis James, and we are honored to have inherited their namesakes' dream of building, studying, and sharing a world-class quilt collection. Here's to the International Quilt Museum's next 25 years!

—Leslie C. Levy
Ardis & Robert James Executive Director

CHAPTER 1

INTRODUCTION

Without the Ardis and Robert James Collection, the International Quilt Museum (IQM) would not exist. The collection's arrival at the University of Nebraska-Lincoln (UNL) 25 years ago established the IQM (known then as the International Quilt Study Center), but more than that, for the past quarter century it has formed the museum's core, its heart. In that time, the James quilts have anchored blockbuster exhibitions, inspired countless in-person and online visitors, been closely studied and documented, and acted as the seeds from which the IQM's collection has continued to grow. And with ongoing James family support, the vision of what a quilt collection—a quilt museum—could become and accomplish has expanded and evolved into what the IQM is today: the world's largest public quilt collection with over 6,000 pieces from more than five dozen countries, stewarded by an institution committed to interpreting the quilts and sharing them as widely as possible.

In 1997, after years of deliberation and negotiation, Robert and Ardis James of Chappaqua, New York donated their comprehensive 1000-piece quilt collection to UNL. They had acquired the quilts over the previous two decades in a deliberate effort to represent as fully as possible an art form—"women's art" and "people's art," as they called it—they had come to greatly admire. The couple had visited antique shops and fairs, worked with dealers and artists, cataloged each piece as it came in, and eventually, hired a curator to help document and care for the collection, which was stored and displayed in a purpose-built space above their garage.

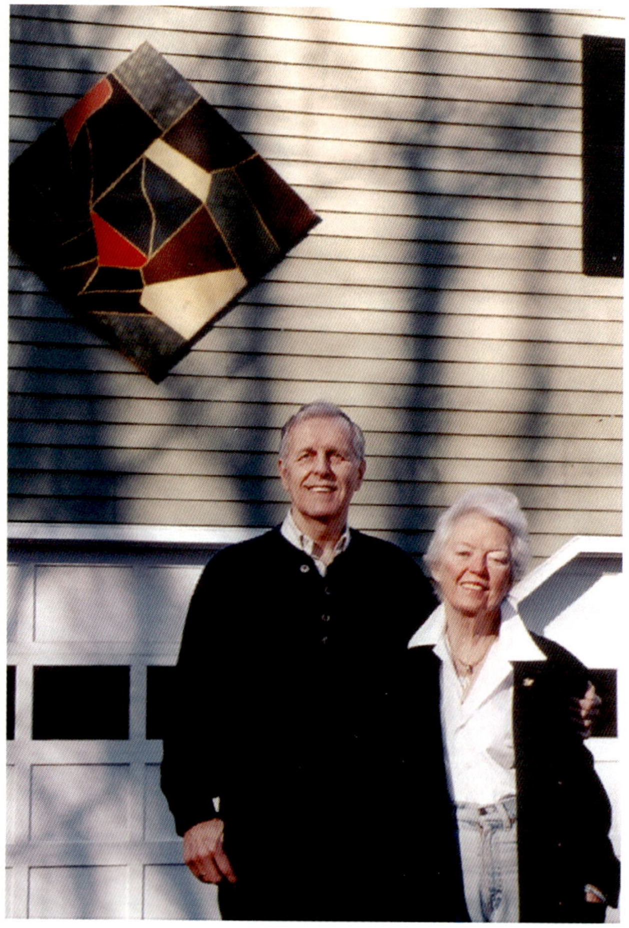

Robert and Ardis James outside of their quilt gallery/storage area at their home in Chappaqua, New York, 1990s.

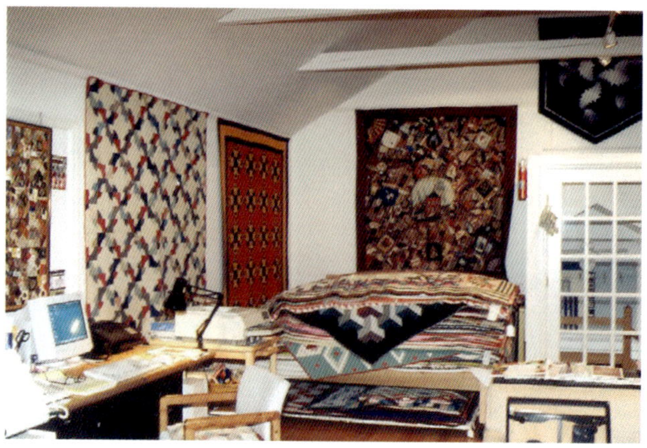

The James Collection was housed in a large room where the quilts could be rotated on display and the remainder could be viewed in several large stacks.

The collection comprised two primary groups: antique and contemporary. Robert and Ardis, both natives of Nebraska, grew up with female relatives who quilted. Additionally, Ardis made quilts herself, and for nearly a decade co-owned a fabric shop. Thus, traditional American quilts were the Jameses' point of entry for collecting. And the collection they built was exceptional, encompassing high-quality examples of the most representative American styles and patterns from the early 1800s onwards, many of which are featured in Chapter 2, "Classics." They quickly came to also understand that quilts had become a contemporary form of artistic expression and they began to add pieces made by artists who chose quilts as their medium, many of whom are represented in Chapter 3, "From the Studio." Along the way, they also acquired a smaller number of non-U.S. quilts, both in the antique and contemporary sections. During their two decades of collecting, they made great headway towards their goal of representing the history, artistry, and cultural significance of quilts.

Building the collection had been a labor of love for the Jameses, but eventually, they wanted to give the quilts to an institution that would both continue their work and expand upon it. One of the couple's explicit aims was to house the collection somewhere that would not simply preserve the quilts, but also research and exhibit them. The University of Nebraska-Lincoln was both willing and equipped to establish a study center as well as an academic program in which graduate students could earn a quilt studies degree from the Department of Textiles, Clothing and Design (now Textiles, Merchandising and Fashion Design, or TMFD). In Chapter 2, IQM Curator of Collections Carolyn Ducey describes several key research projects undertaken by curators, fellows, and students, most of which utilized the James Collection and led to interesting, and sometimes groundbreaking, findings. Some of these projects involved whole segments of the collection, while others focused on a single piece. For instance, the "Reconciliation Quilt" (Plate 2.3), arguably the museum's most famous artifact, has been researched by students and curators on many occasions, each effort leading to a greater understanding of this fascinating document of American social history.

New York Beauty, *maker unidentified, probably made in Missouri, United States, 1850-1870, Ardis and Robert James Collection, IQM 1997.007.0124.*

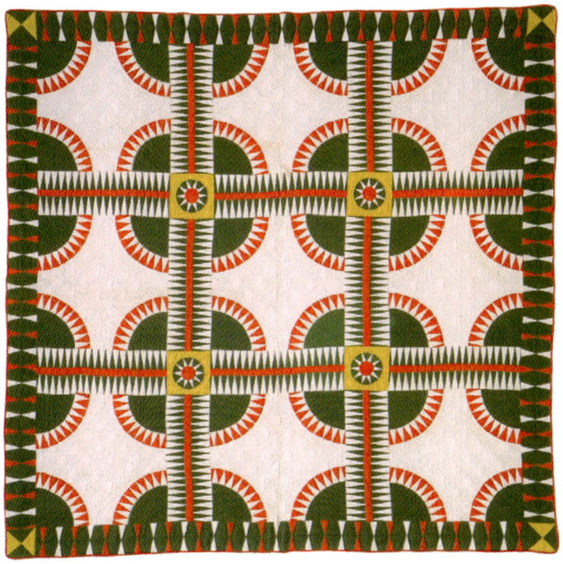

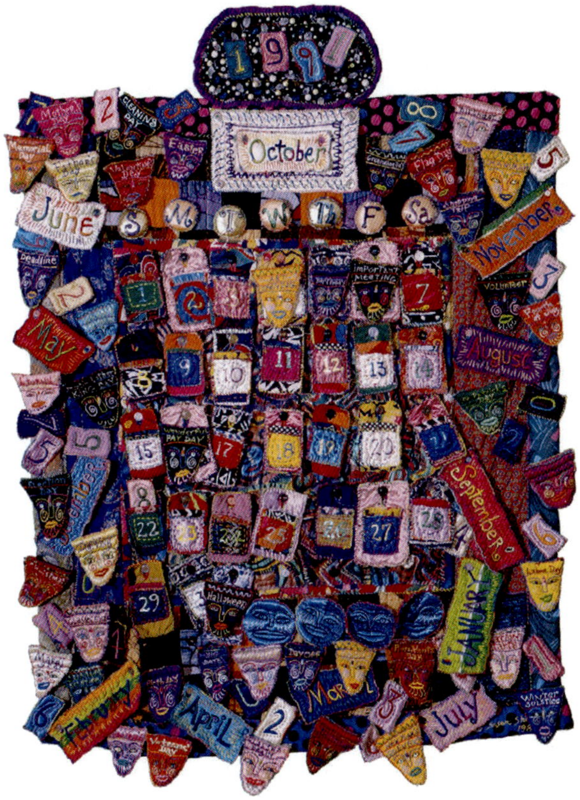

The Calendar Fetish: An Altar to Time, *by Susan Shie, Wooster, Ohio, United States, 1989, Ardis and Robert James Collection, IQM 1997.007.1087.*

A Tribute to Ardis James (2012) *consisted of works donated by the artists to the IQM in honor of Ardis James, who passed away in 2011.*

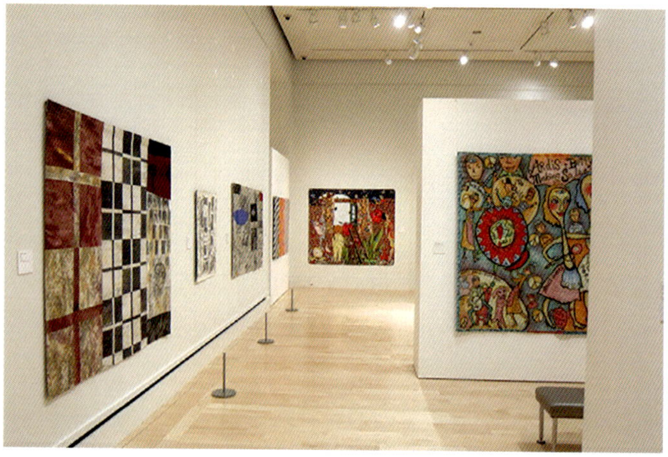

The James Collection sustained the IQM's exhibition program in its first decade, providing a seemingly endless source of quilts for diverse exhibitions such as *Sunshine and Shadow: Mennonite Quilts*; *Fanciful Flowers: Botany and the American Quilt*; and *Wild by Design: 200 Years of Innovation and Artistry in American Quilts*. In keeping with the Jameses' educational goals for the collection, exhibitions curated by graduate students became a standard element of the IQM/TMFD program and included *Modern Marvels: Quilts Made from Kits; Indigo Gives America the Blues*; *Partisan Pieces: Quilts of Political and Patriotic Persuasion*; and *Visual Systems: The Quilter's Eye*. Because it did not yet have a facility of its own, the IQM's early exhibitions were held in cultural institutions across Lincoln and Nebraska, but also in places like the Chicago Cultural Center and the Textile Museum in Washington D.C.

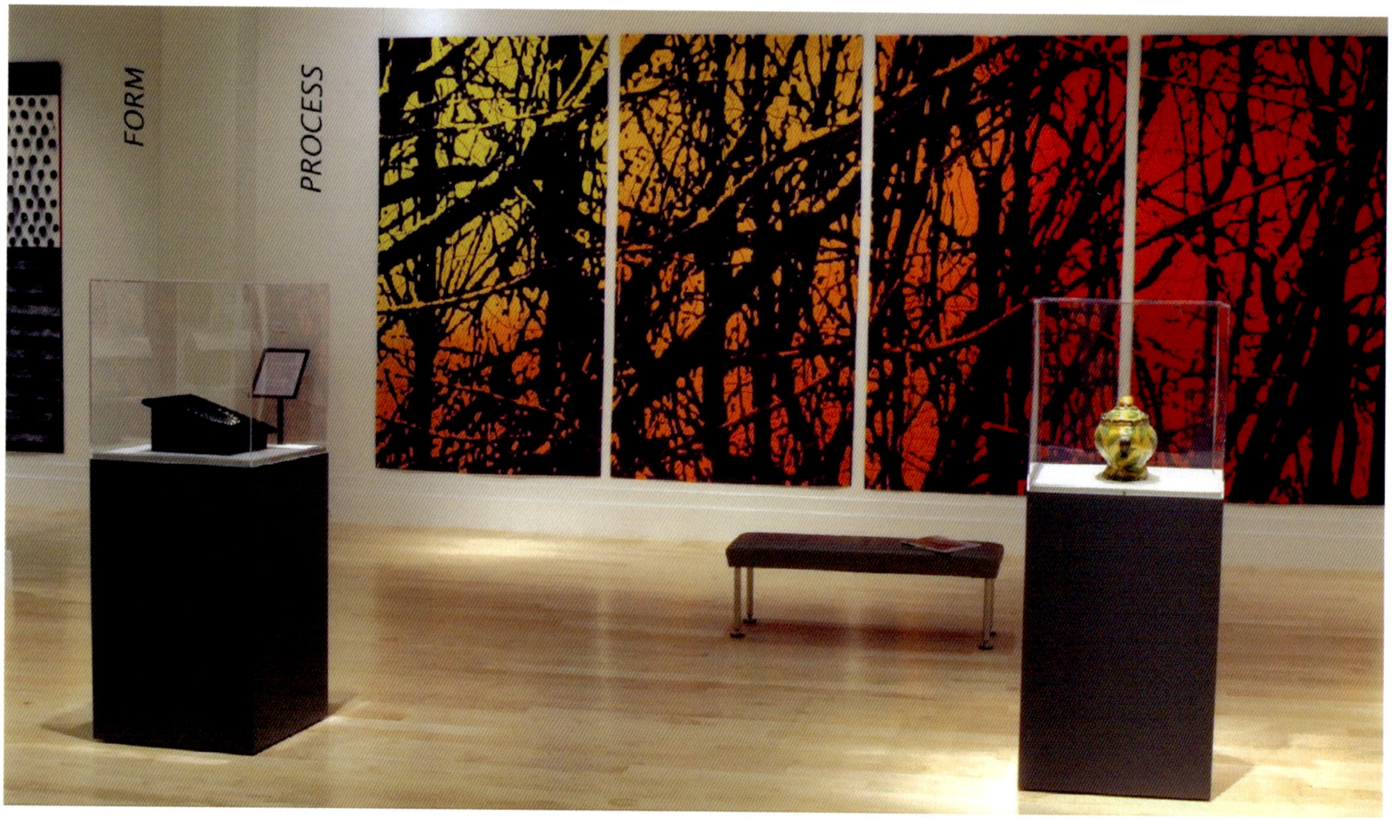

Perspectives: Art, Craft, Design and the Studio Quilt *was curated by artist and UNL professor Michael James and artist and author Sandra Sider in 2008 and featured several gems from the original James Collection as well as many later acquisitions made possible by the Robert and Ardis James Foundation.*

Once the IQM's state-of-the-art museum facility was completed in 2008—thanks to a leadership gift from the Jameses and to countless other private donations—larger and more ambitious exhibitions could be held. Studio art quilts, in particular, benefitted from the beautiful 16-foot walls on which they could now hang. In Chapter 3, independent curator Penny McMorris describes how the Jameses began collecting studio art quilts in the 1980s. McMorris eventually became their contemporary quilt advisor, helping them acquire key pieces such as Michael James's early quilt, *Aurora* (Plate 3.9) and Faith Ringgold's "*The Men: Mask Face Quilt #2*" (Plate 3.12). With McMorris's assistance, the Jameses acquired work from the most significant and influential quilt artists of the 1980s and '90s, often boosting artists' morale through the purchase of their work. Studio quilter Susan Shie stated her appreciation in a simple but heartfelt way: "I especially thank Ardis for believing in all of us." Indeed, when Ardis James died in 2011, seventeen artists donated twenty-six quilts to the IQM in her honor—symbols of respect for a true patron of the arts.

IQM Collections Manager Sarah Walcott vacuuming quilts in the Byron and Sara Rhodes Dillow Collections Work Room.

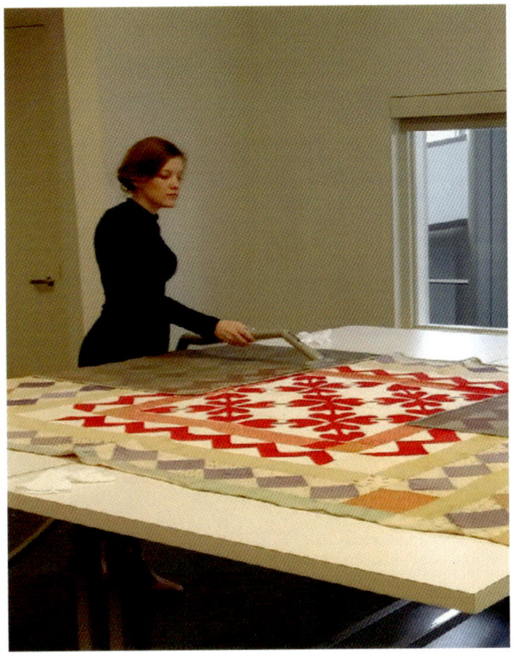

Petassoun *(whole cloth lap quilt), maker unidentified, Provence, France, c. 1850-1890, Kathryn Wilson Berenson Collection, Partial gift of the Robert and Ardis James Foundation, IQM 2005.018.0012.*

Another of the Jameses' expectations upon donating their quilts was that the new caretakers would expand the collection in intentional and significant ways. At the beginning, the museum's International Advisory Board—a group of curators, academics, artists, collectors, philanthropists, and industry professionals from all over the world—often assisted in this effort, identifying pieces and collections that might be available and a good fit for the museum. Another important development in the collection's growth was the addition of an Acquisitions Coordinator and an Acquisitions Committee. Sara Rhodes Dillow (1940-2008), an avid collector and quiltmaker with robust relationships in the quilt research world and to the quilt market, served as the first IQM Acquisitions Coordinator. Dillow helped the museum add important works such as the Wistar Family Tree Album quilt and significant collections such as the Kathryn Wilson Berenson Collection of French quilts. (In addition, the IQM is now the proud caretaker of Sara Dillow's own exceptional collection of quilts.) The Robert and Ardis James Foundation has consistently helped fund these efforts, making it feasible to acquire important quilts and quilt collections as well as representative objects from around the world.

The Acquisitions Committee, under the leadership of the current coordinator, Linda Pumphrey, continues to monitor the quilt market, liaise with collectors and artists, and give advice on how to proceed with augmenting the collection. In Chapter 4, "New Horizons," IQM Curator of International Collections Marin Hanson sketches the progress the Acquisitions Committee and the IQM curators have made, focusing particularly on the museum's global representation. The IQM has always striven to work towards Robert James's ambition for it to become the "Metropolitan Museum" of quilts—in other words, to have the best

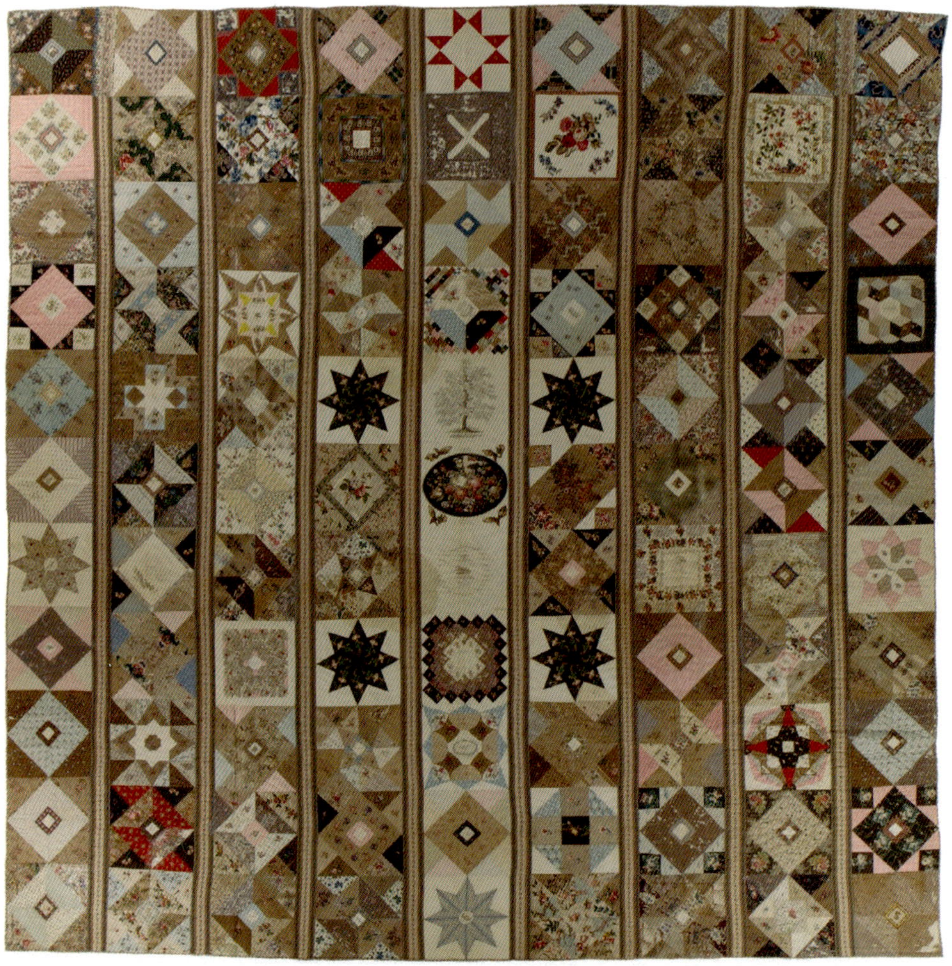

Wistar Family Tree Album, *maker unidentified, Philadelphia, Pennsylvania, dated 1842 and 1843, Gift of the Robert and Ardis James Foundation, IQM 2005.059.0001.*

collection of the most widely geographically and culturally representative quilts in the world. In 1997, only nine countries were represented in the IQM collection, but a decade later that number was 24 and by 2012 it was 45. Today, the collection has pieces from over 60 countries. Although it can be said that the goal of becoming a comprehensive museum has been reached in many ways, it is truly a never-ending quest, one that the IQM curators and Acquisitions Committee are ready and excited to continue pursuing.

The International Quilt Museum and the Ardis and Robert James Collection are inextricably linked. This bond exists not simply because the James Collection is the museum's founding collection, but because the vision its collectors formed—for discovering, collecting, researching, exhibiting, and celebrating quilts—is one that the IQM has fully embraced and continues to revisit, refine, augment, and adapt. At their core, Ardis and Robert James loved quilts for the complex, revealing, intimate objects they are—and so do we.

—Marin F. Hanson, Curator of International Collections

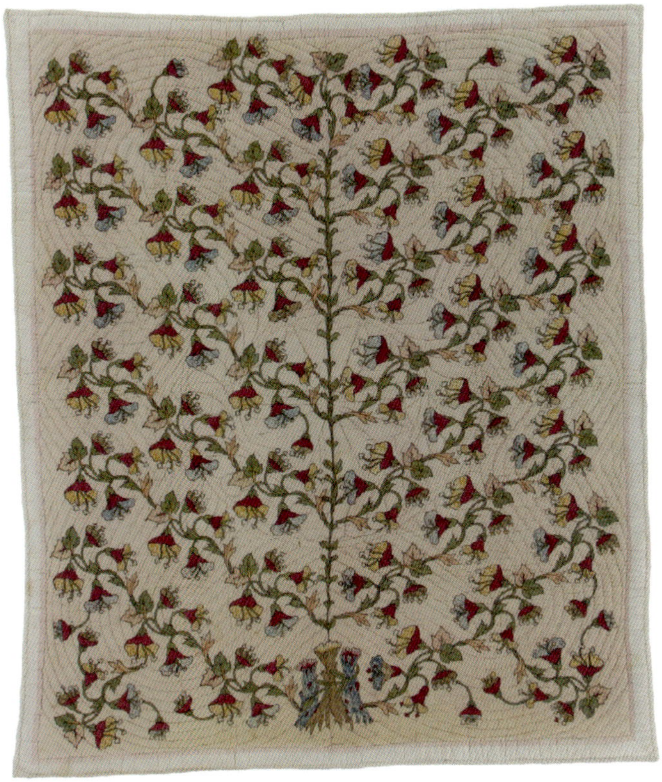

Block Printed Yorgan (Quilt), *unidentified maker, made in Turkey, 1920-1940, Gift of the Robert and Ardis James Foundation, IQM 2020.079.0003*

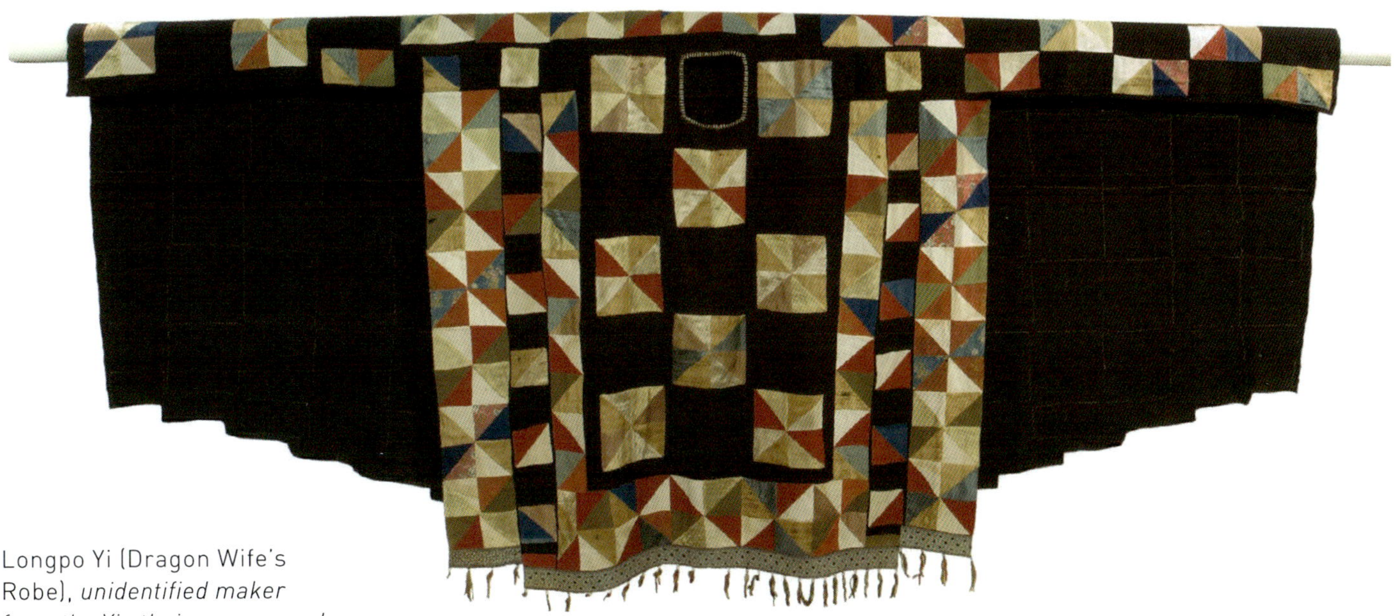

Longpo Yi (Dragon Wife's Robe), *unidentified maker from the Yi ethnic group, made in Malipo County, Yunnan Province, China, circa 1940, Gift of the Robert and Ardis James Foundation, IQM 2012.021.0001*

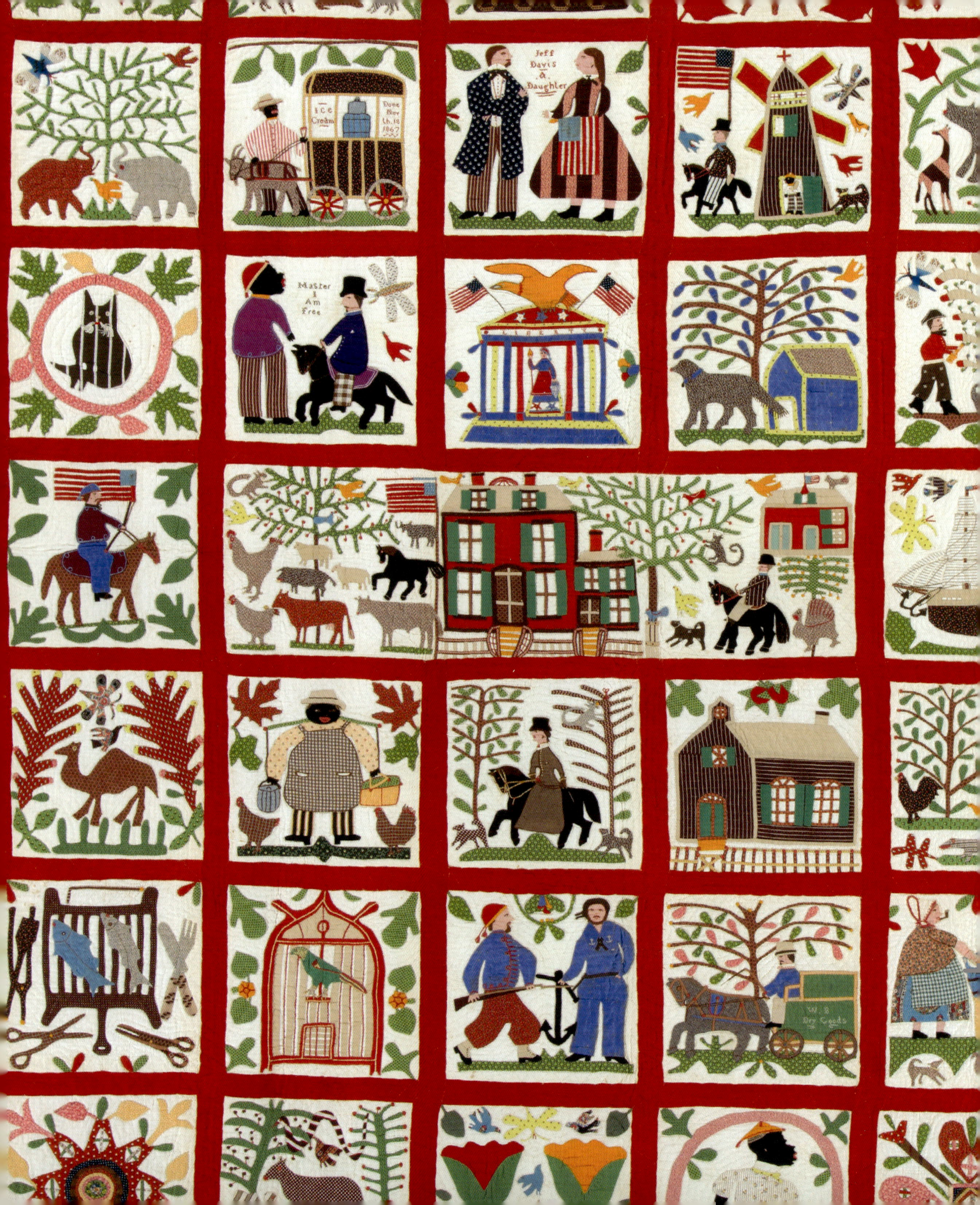
Ice Cream
Done Nov th 16 1867
Jeff Davis & Daughter
Master I Am Free
W.B
Dry Goods

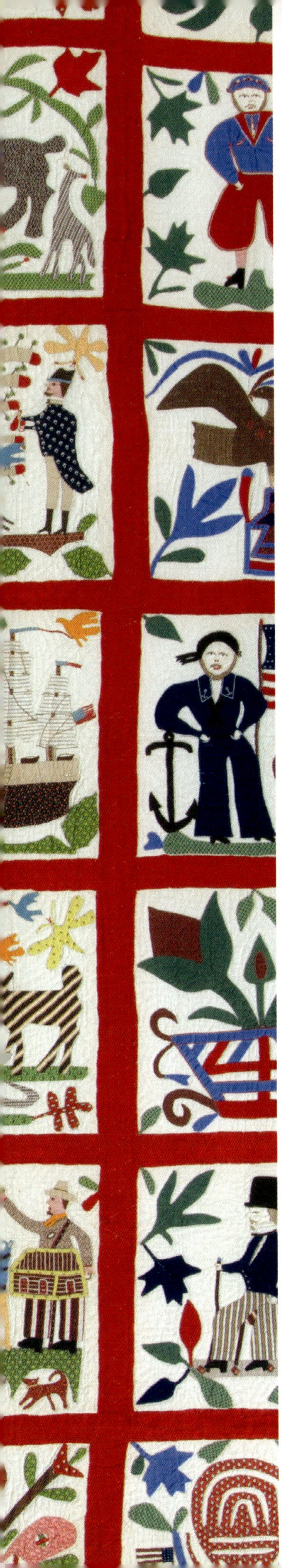

CHAPTER 2

CLASSICS

Carolyn Ducey
Ardis B. James Curator of Collections

Ardis and Robert James began collecting quilts like many of us do when building collections—without really planning to. In 1979, they selected a quilt they liked at a local antique sale, then added another the next year, and then three and then five. They realized then that they were indeed quilt collectors!

Ardis and Robert (Bob) very quickly decided to create an encyclopedic collection. They began to work with knowledgeable dealers and taught themselves about quilt history. They learned the importance of documentation, and impeccably recorded every detail they could gather about each quilt they acquired. Ardis wrote in a letter to an individual offering a quilt, "If it is convenient for you, we would appreciate some written history ... we maintain a file on each important quilt that we own, knowing how valuable this information will be to future generations." They hired a part-time curator to help with photographing, accessioning, and organizing the collection, and sought out specific and significant quilts to fill gaps in the collection. They encouraged quilt lovers and scholars to visit and to use the collection in research projects and exhibitions.

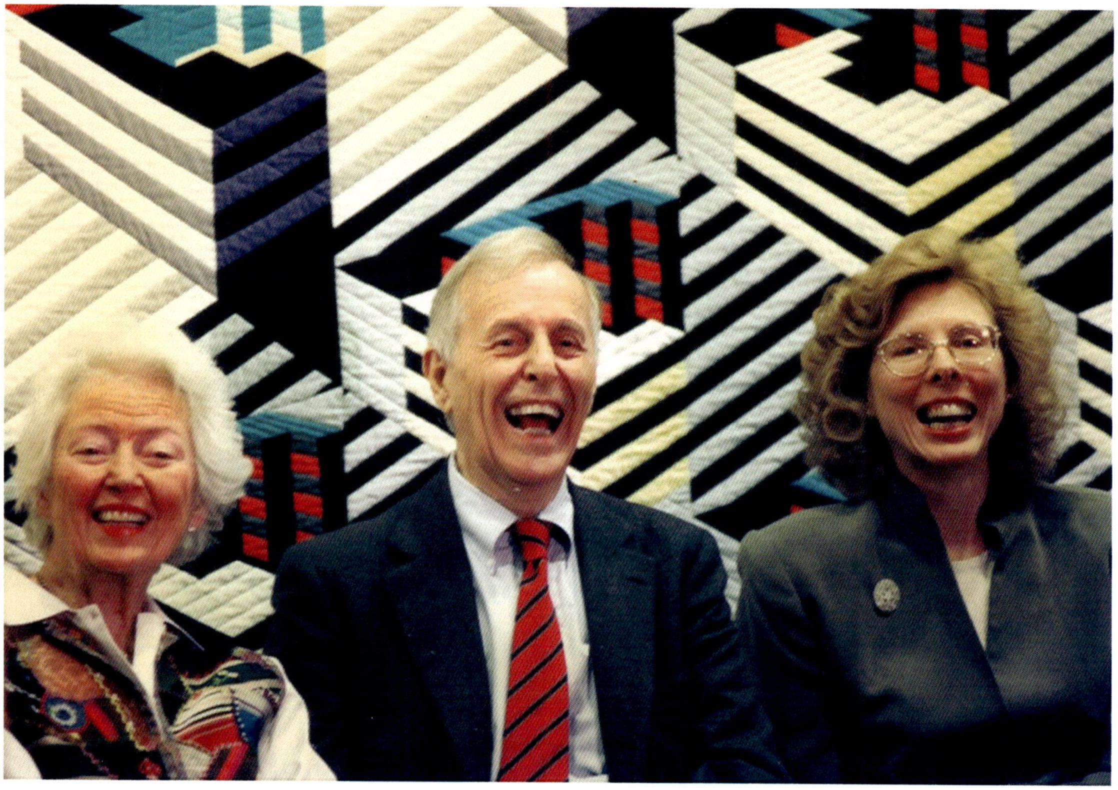

Ardis and Robert James with founding Director Patricia Crews at announcement of the James gift to the University of Nebraska, 1997.

The Jameses diligently collected all types of American quilts. By chance, in 1990, Ardis spied a lavishly embellished Crazy quilt titled "My Crazy Dream" in an antiques magazine and through phone calls and letters, found the individual looking to find it a new home. Both she and Bob were excited about the extraordinary quilt. Bob wrote: "We are crazy about *My Crazy Dream*. It is certainly one of the great quilts of its time." Penny McMorris, advising the Jameses, noted: "It is a masterpiece ... This addition would give you an extremely strong crazy quilt sub-collection" (Plate 2.1). A basket quilt with unknown provenance was the first expensive quilt the Jameses purchased. Ardis wrote, "I learned the importance of a third color. A red and green quilt is a red and green quilt—with a third color it's spectacular" (Plate 2.2). Collecting had become a genuine passion for both of the Jameses.

Sara Dillow, speaking with Ardis James and son Ralph James, late 1990s.

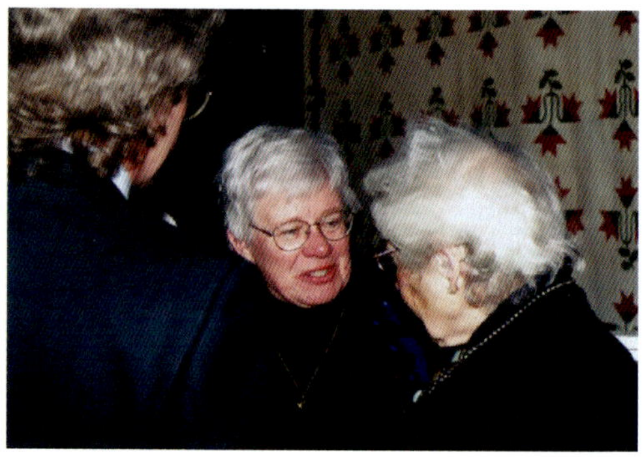

When it became apparent in the early 1990s that keeping the quilts at their home was simply not feasible, the Jameses began to search for a long-term home for their collection. In 1993, at a quilt conference, they met Patricia Crews, a textile historian and University of Nebraska-Lincoln (UNL) professor, and Sara Dillow, a quilt collector and philanthropist. Crews and Dillow recognized the potential of acquiring the collection under the umbrella of the

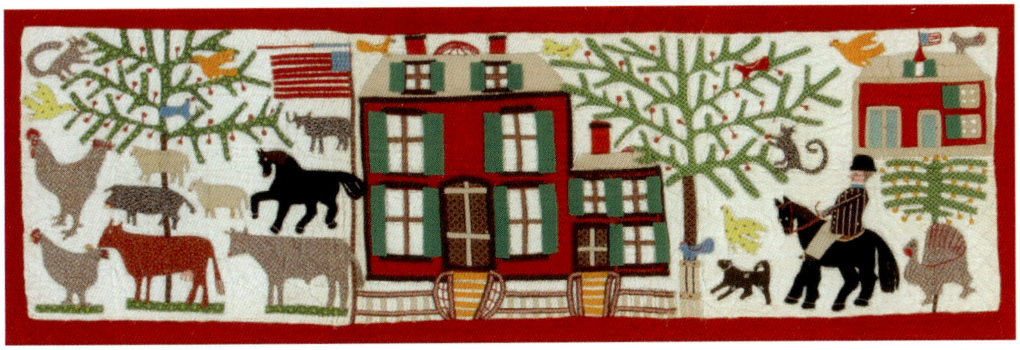

The "Reconciliation Quilt" (detail), *made by Lucinda Ward Honstain, Brooklyn, New York, United States, 1867, Gift of the Robert and Ardis James Foundation, IQM 2001.011.0001.*

UNL system. Four years later, they had convinced the university leadership to not only embrace the collection but to build a program of study as well, something the Jameses enthusiastically endorsed.

In 1997, the Jameses donated approximately 1000 quilts, valued at more than $6 million, to the university. They also pledged $1 million for the creation of the International Quilt Study Center (now the International Quilt Museum).

When the quilts arrived at the University of Nebraska-Lincoln in 1997, the groundwork was firmly in place for meeting the Jameses' goal of a comprehensive collection and academic study center. The existing History of Textiles degree was enhanced with an emphasis in quilt studies. A hybrid program of in-person and online classes offered students an opportunity to complete their degree from anywhere, with only one semester of residence in Lincoln. Founding director and professor Patricia Crews worked with quilt scholars to produce new classes for the program. Students were able to select from a wide variety of quilt genres, historical eras, and technical elements for study. Early research topics included historical developments in sewing thread manufacture that help in dating quilts; identification of Mennonite quilts and understanding their cultural significance; and aesthetic connections between Victorian-era gardening and quilt design. During the first decades of the IQM's existence, what we knew about quilts grew dramatically. Myths were debunked, new approaches and techniques were utilized, and our understanding of quiltmaking as a global art form expanded.

One quilt in particular illustrates the many ways IQM research has informed what we know about quilts. It is the jewel of the IQM collection, identified by Nancy Druckman, director of American folk art at Sotheby's Auction House, as "one of the finest pieces of Americana to come across my desk, unsurpassed in condition, composition and historical importance." Titled the "Reconciliation Quilt," it was made by Lucinda Ward Honstain of Williamsburg, Brooklyn, New York in 1867 (Plate 2.3).[1] Researched by Patricia Crews and former IQM Assistant Curator of Exhibitions Jonathan Gregory, the quilt reveals a story that encompasses national issues of military and cultural history as well as personal issues of family, daily life in Brooklyn, fantasy, and betrayal and divorce. Despite the carefully crafted imagery contained in Honstain's quilt, her story is a human story, fraught with messy details that connect us to her through our shared humanity, even when separated by more than 150 years.

Honstain created appliqué designs that reflect her experience of and reaction to the Civil War.

[1] *Descendants of Lucinda Ward Honstain donated a Tulip appliqué quilt to the IQM collection that is believed to have been made by her or her daughter Emma Bingham (Plate 2.4).*

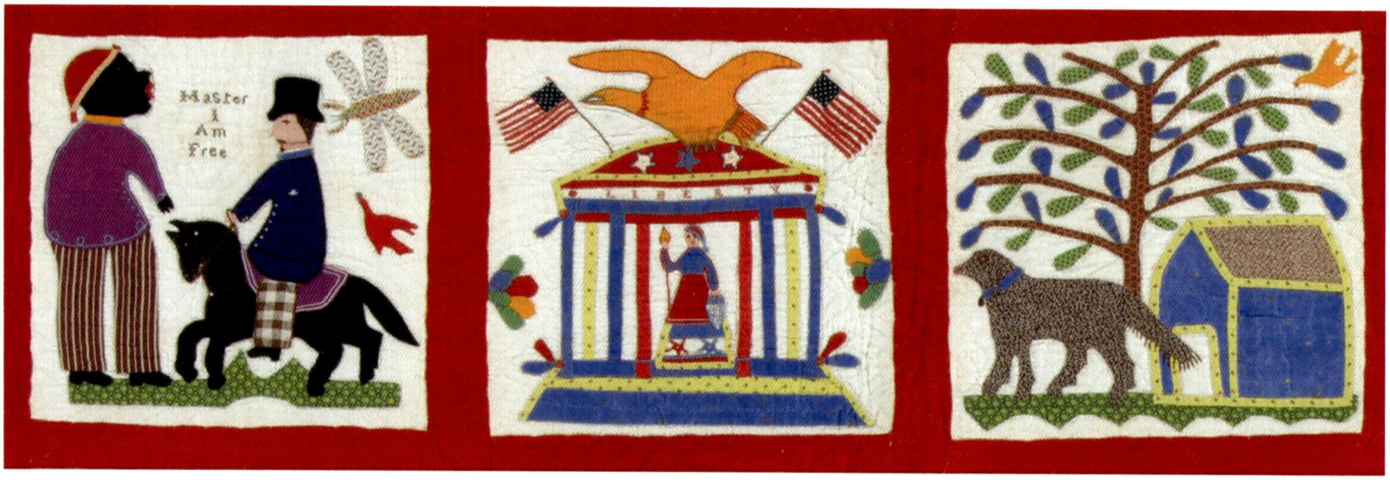

The "Reconciliation Quilt" (detail), *made by Lucinda Ward Honstain, Brooklyn, New York, United States, 1867, Gift of the Robert and Ardis James Foundation, IQM 2001.011.0001.*

A dramatic block illustrates a tall Black figure stating, "Master, I Am Free." Honstain emphasized the former slave's freedom by making him nearly twice the size of the white man opposite him. She also included images of Black people at work among her Brooklyn street scenes, perhaps a tacit statement of support for emancipation. However, her imagery also reflects the racism deeply embedded in American society: the Black figures are portrayed with exaggerated facial features.

A second block features another event linked to the Civil War. It reads "Jeff Davis and Daughter," and portrays the former president of the Confederate States of America with his daughter Margaret, holding a U.S. flag with 13 stripes. On May 13, 1867, in a gesture of reconciliation, a northern judge released Jefferson Davis on bail from Virginia's Fortress Monroe where he'd been imprisoned for two years. Perhaps Lucinda Honstain read about the Davis family's reunion and was thus inspired to depict them together holding an American flag. Here the quilt presents a somewhat contradictory note: the fact that a New Yorker would put the former president of the Confederate States on her quilt, with his daughter, humanizes him. Was Lucinda hoping to do her part in reconciling the division between North and South?

Genealogical research has added an enormous amount of information about Lucinda and her family to the quilt's record, revealing that Lucinda made the quilt during a difficult period in her life. Military records show that her husband, John, was dishonorably discharged from the military due to a violation of orders when he crossed beyond enemy lines into rebel territory and was captured. A litany of other transgressions and disturbances was documented by local newspaper: John's arrest for forgery and abandonment of his wife in 1865, his alleged dalliance with the daughter of the owner of a boarding house, a street fight between John and Lucinda and several of her friends, legal action against John and Lucinda by those to whom they owed money, and finally, the divorce of John and Lucinda in March 1866 (John remarried in Wisconsin in 1867). These events took place as Lucinda was creating appliquéd images of John in the uniform of the New York Volunteer Infantry Regiment. Even as her marital problems were published in the local paper, she evidently chose to deny the fact of her divorce, listing herself as a widow in census reports for the remainder of her life. Research using contemporary primary sources such as newspapers and census records led to the enrichment of our understanding of this important piece of American cultural history.

Other IQM research projects also resulted in advances in the field of quilt studies. Janneken Smucker and Nao Nomura's research,[2] grounded in fiber analysis and ethnographic fieldwork, dramatically changed some of the "rules" about Amish quilts. The pair examined quilts in the IQM collection to "confront unsubstantiated assumptions—most notably the idea of a classic period of Amish quiltmaking prior to 1940." Their research confirmed that many quilts presumed by experts to

[2] *At the time of this research, Smucker and Nomura, both graduates of the UNL quilt studies graduate program, were, respectively, a PhD student in the History of American Civilization and the IQM Collections Manager. Today, Smucker is a Professor of History at West Chester University, and Nomura is an Associate Professor in the Faculty of Liberal Arts at Saitama University, Japan. For more on their research, see: "From Fibers to Fieldwork: A Multifaceted Approach To Re-Examining Amish Quilts." Uncoverings: Research Papers of the American Quilt Study Group 27 (2006): 123-155.*

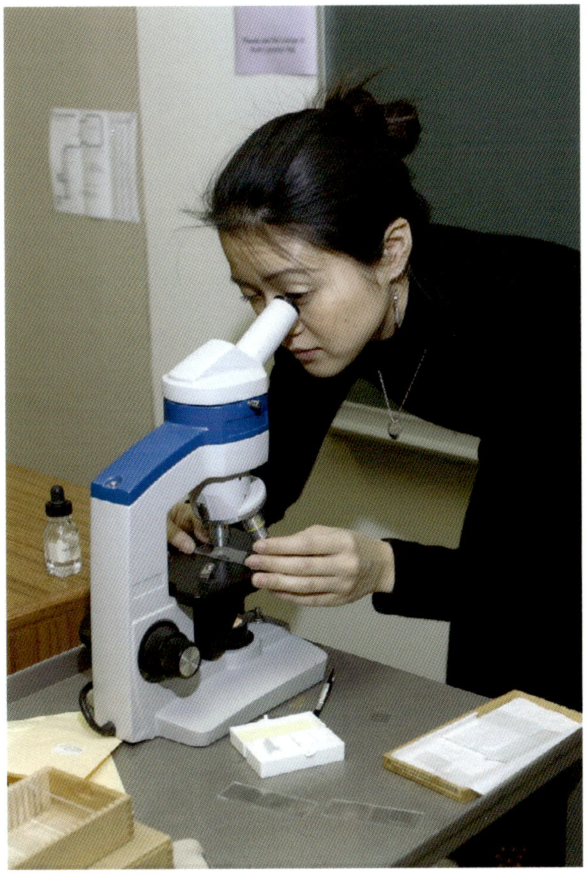

Nao Nomura, former IQM Collections Manager performs fiber microscopy.

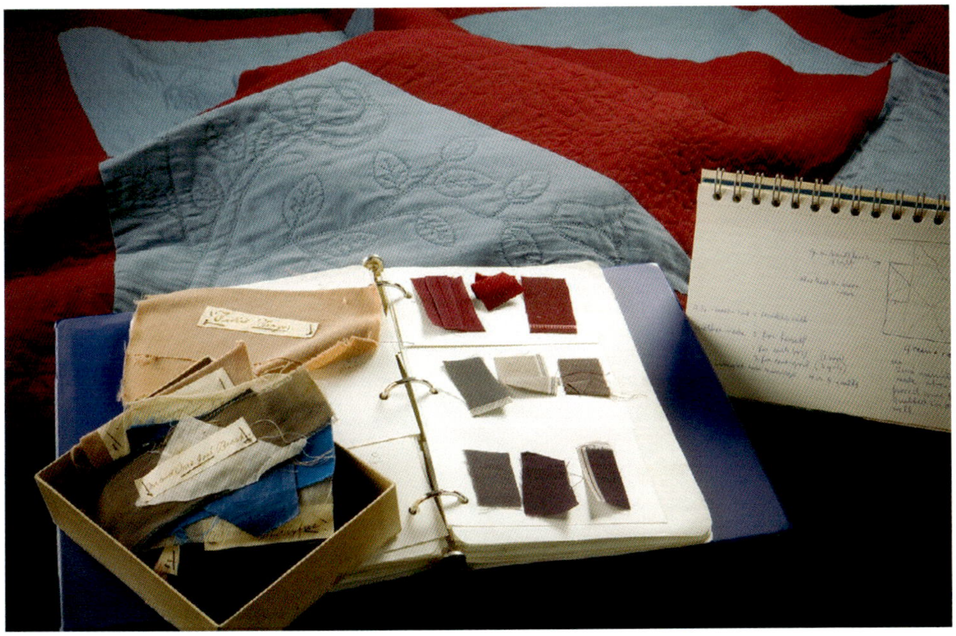

Fiber/fabric identification adds information to what we know about dating Amish quilts.

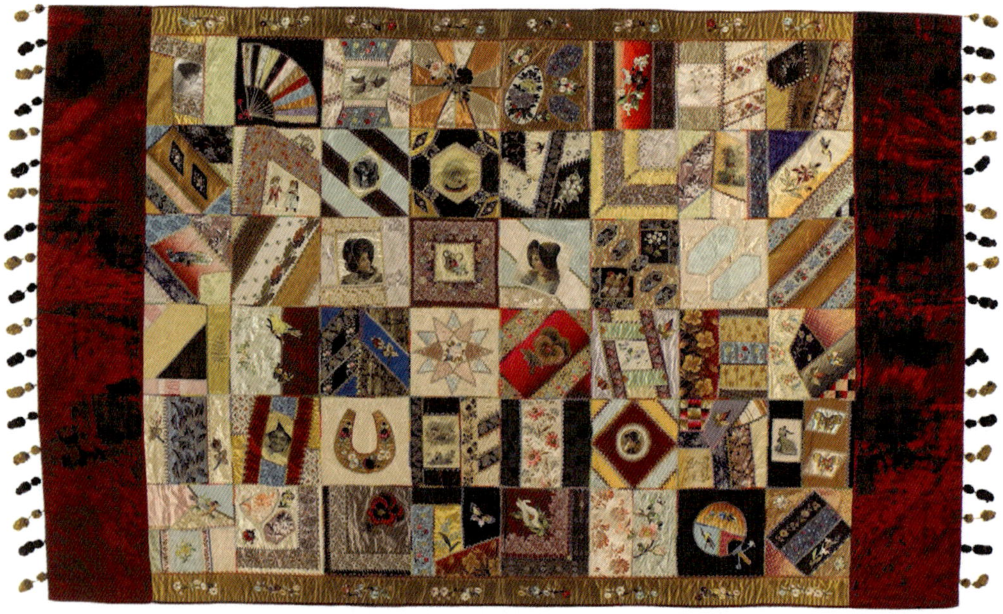

Although this Crazy quilt *is typical in its display of abundant hand embroidery, it also reveals the influence of industrial production in its ready-made, pre-embroidered decals and in the machine quilted fabric lining its back.* Crazy quilt, *maker unidentified, made in the U.S., 1885-1900, Ardis and Robert James Collection, IQM 1997.007.0698.*

be "classic" Amish quilts were made long after the commonly accepted classic period of 1920 to 1940.[3] Fiber analysis helped determine earliest possible construction dates (often several decades later than originally assigned) and genealogical records and interviews within Amish communities enabled Smucker and Nomura to find known makers and further confirm dates of construction. The pair also broached the topic of Amish quilts made more recently, often for a retail market, and raised the question of whether or not they can be classified and valued in the same way as early examples. These new discoveries and discussions helped remove myths about Amish quilts that had evolved over the years into unchallenged canon perpetuated by sheer repetition.

In preparing for the 2009 publication of *American Quilts in the Modern Age, 1870-1940*, the IQM Collections team conducted object reviews of over 600 quilts, the majority coming from the James Collection. Co-editor and current IQM Curator of International Collections, Marin Hanson, analyzed the accumulated data and both confirmed and debunked prior assumptions about "Modern Age" (late 19th- and early 20th-century) quilts. She did so within an overarching theme of modernism versus anti-modernism, identifying areas in American culture and quiltmaking that either embraced the country's rush towards technological and societal progress or shied away from it.

For instance, the commonly held assumption that machine sewing in quiltmaking dramatically increased after the Civil War, when access to sewing machines grew, was borne out by the object reviews: of the quilts made between 1865-1900, 40% contained some amount of machine stitching while that number grew to 60% in quilts made between 1901 and 1940 (prior to the Civil War, machine stitching on quilts is rare). It is unsurprising, therefore, that Emma Leonhard's entry to the "Sears Century of Progress" contest, held in conjunction with the 1933 Chicago World's Fair, contains machine sewing (Plate 2.5). On the other hand, Crazy quilts, which have often been held up as the epitome of late-Victorian handwork and thus a symbol of the rejection of industrialization, frequently

[3] *See Plate 2.11 for an Amish quilt which, despite its "classic" look, came with a family history that dates it to the late 1940s.*

have some machine stitching on them. Of the 64 Crazy quilts examined, a surprising 73% were constructed at least partially with a machine (albeit often in less visible areas). Having access to a large and diverse sample of quilts enabled Hanson to reach more nuanced conclusions about quilts made between the Civil War and World War II.[4]

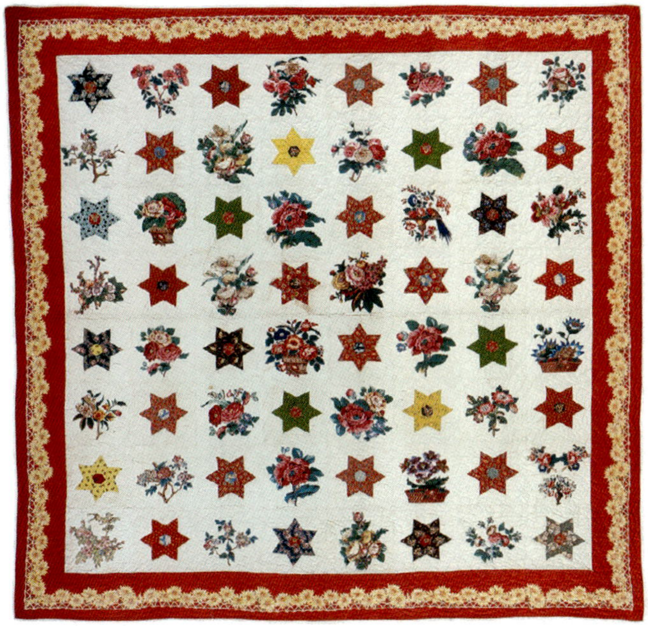

A Colonial Revival reinterpretation of the mid-19th-century pattern Gunn is examining in the photo below. Star and Chintz Album, *maker unidentified, possibly made in Pennsylvania, 1935-1955, Ardis and Robert James Collection, IQM 1997.007.0387.*

As she too conducted research for *American Quilts in the Modern Age, 1870-1940*, contributing author and University of Akron professor Virginia Gunn built upon her previous studies of the Colonial Revival's impact on quiltmaking. She described the late 19th- and early 20th-century decorative movement this way: "The Colonial Revival style ... was a romanticized, not a pure, interpretation of the past" in which "old-fashioned styles became the new fashion." In examining the IQM collection, Gunn identified several of these "new-fashioned" quilts, clarifying dates for pieces that dealers had misidentified as being older than they were. She noted differences in fabric choices, overall sizes, dye characteristics, and quilting designs, all of which pointed to quilts being re-interpretations of pre-Civil War styles and patterns. In her *American Quilts in the Modern Age* chapter, Gunn also presented rich context for understanding such quilts as Olive Emily McClure's English Rose variation (Plate 2.6). McClure updated a traditional mid-19th-century rose pattern by stylizing the flowers and softening the color palette from bold red and green to a more modern pink and yellow, as well as a greyed green sometimes called Depression Green. As Gunn noted, "Olive's interpretation is certainly contemporary, showing that in her seventies she still embraced new ideas." Gunn's invaluable research and interpretation helps us make sense of a period of American quiltmaking when everything old was new again.[5]

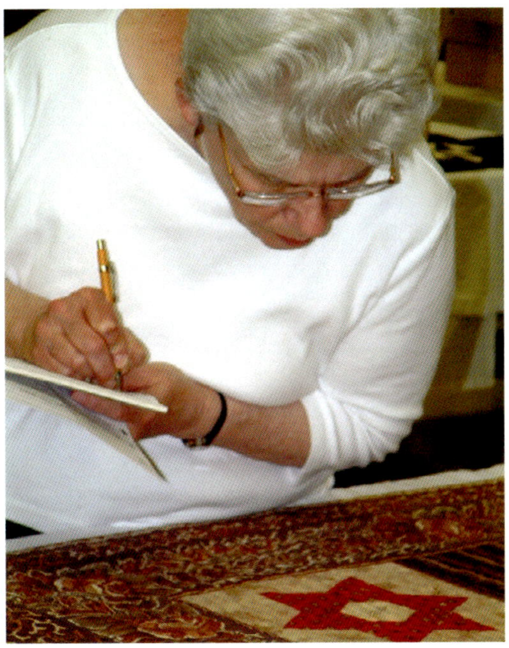

Virginia Gunn examines a c. 1844 James Collection quilt.

[4] *To read more of Hanson's analysis, see: "Modern, Yet Anti-Modern: Two Sides of Late-Nineteenth and Early-Twentieth Century Quiltmaking." Uncoverings: Research Papers of the American Quilt Study Group 29 (2008): 106-135.*

[5] *For more of Gunn's analysis of the IQM's Colonial Revival quilts, see: "Perfecting the Past" (Chapter 5) in Marin Hanson and Patricia Cox Crews,* American Quilts in the Modern Age, 1870-1940, *University of Nebraska Press (2009), 226-302.*

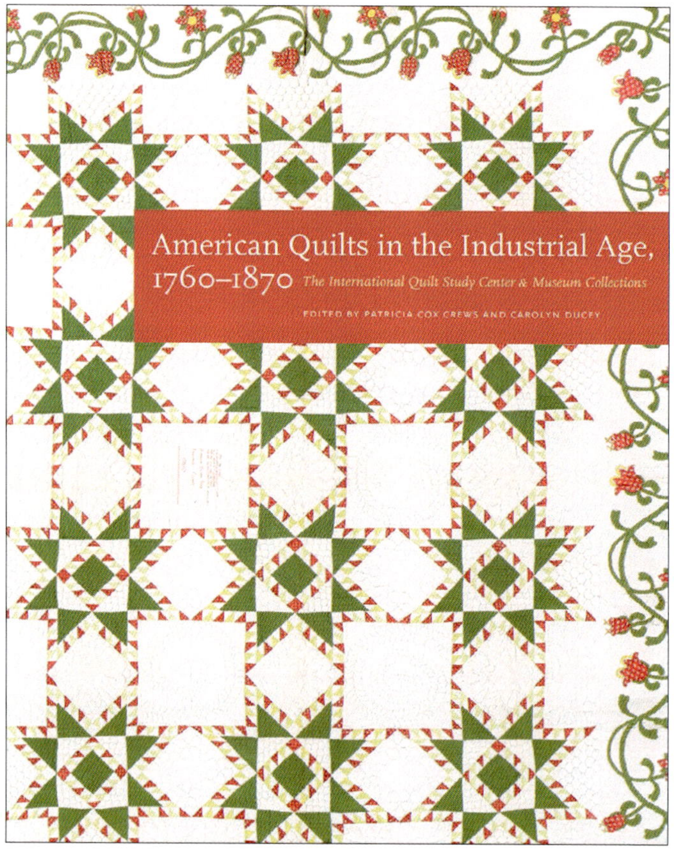

American Quilts in the Industrial Age, *1760-1870, edited by Patricia Cox Crews and Carolyn Ducey. Much of the research on the IQM's early quilts was featured in this comprehensive publication.*

Identification of regional quilt styles and discoveries of "sister" quilts (i.e. family pieces that had previously not been linked) have enhanced our understanding of American quilt history. Regional quilt styles researched utilizing the IQM collection include 18th-century whole cloth quilts from Philadelphia, chintz quilts of the Delaware River Valley, appliquéd Baltimore Album quilts (Plate 2.12), inscribed quilts of Lehigh and Berks Counties in Pennsylvania, and folk art album quilts of Miami Valley, Ohio. In the case of "sister" quilts, IQM researchers have often used a combination of genealogy and online databases to find links between individuals who inscribed their names on fabric 100 or more years ago. In the case of the prolific "Grandma" Carpenter of Lancaster County, Pennsylvania, research revealed that a group of quilts attributed to her were instead made by two neighbors who likely worked alongside her and in her style (Plate 2.7). All three women embroidered their initials in large and ornate embroidery and used the same fabric combinations and quilting designs. Each discovery of regional and individual links provides a greater understanding of the transmission of patterns among friends and neighbors and the communities of women who worked together to create quilts.

The presence of inscribed names on quilts can also give us fascinating clues about makers and their quilts. In the case of Mercy Jane Bancroft, who made a Friendship Block quilt in the 1850s and '60s (Plate 2.8), diligent research by former UNL graduate student Melissa Jurgena led to the discovery of the quiltmaker's diaries. The diary entries focused primarily on details of Bancroft's professional life as a traveling seamstress. Through these writings, we learn that she made clothing for many of the women named on the quilt. Also inscribed, Rachel Trundle's elaborate Bethlehem Star quilt (Plate 2.9) celebrates friendship, reading, "When friendship once is rooted fast, It is a plant no storm can sever." Trundle's niece, Lillian Dickerson, whose name is on the reverse, inherited the masterpiece quilt. The information uncovered about these makers and recipients fleshes out our perceptions of nineteenth century women.

With a large and diverse group of quilts like the James Collection, close examination and comparison can yield new and exciting knowledge. Through a steady stream of research, publications, and exhibitions, the IQM's curators, students, and scholarly collaborators have expanded and enriched the field of quilt studies, unveiling fascinating stories and connections that show links across time and space. With each new discovery, the James Collection takes on even greater significance.

Today, the IQM's encyclopedic collection, launched by Ardis and Robert James's founding gift of about 1000 quilts, now numbers more than 6000. It will continue to grow as the IQM pursues its aim of representing the breadth and depth of quiltmaking around the globe. The IQM collection, the ever-expanding extension of the James Collection, has become the most significant quilt collection in the world in its first 25 years—the next 25 will be even better!

***Note: Plates 2.1 – 2.10 appear in the exhibition,* An Evolving Vision: Classics.**

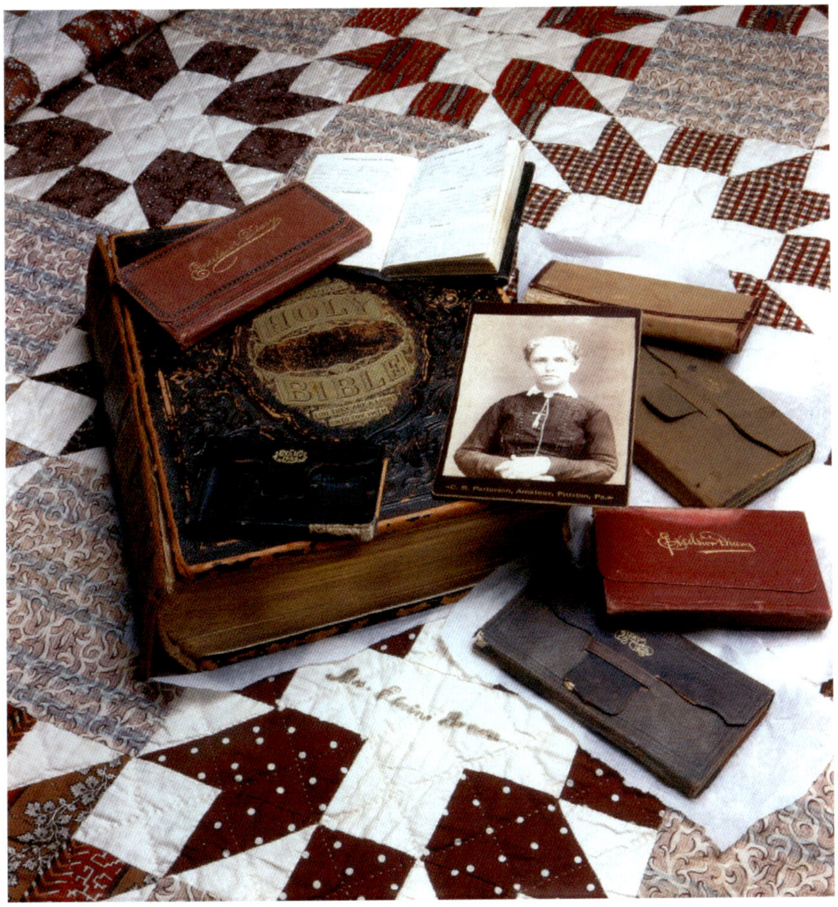

Mercy Jane Bancroft Blair's diaries and family Bible were found during a research trip to her former home.

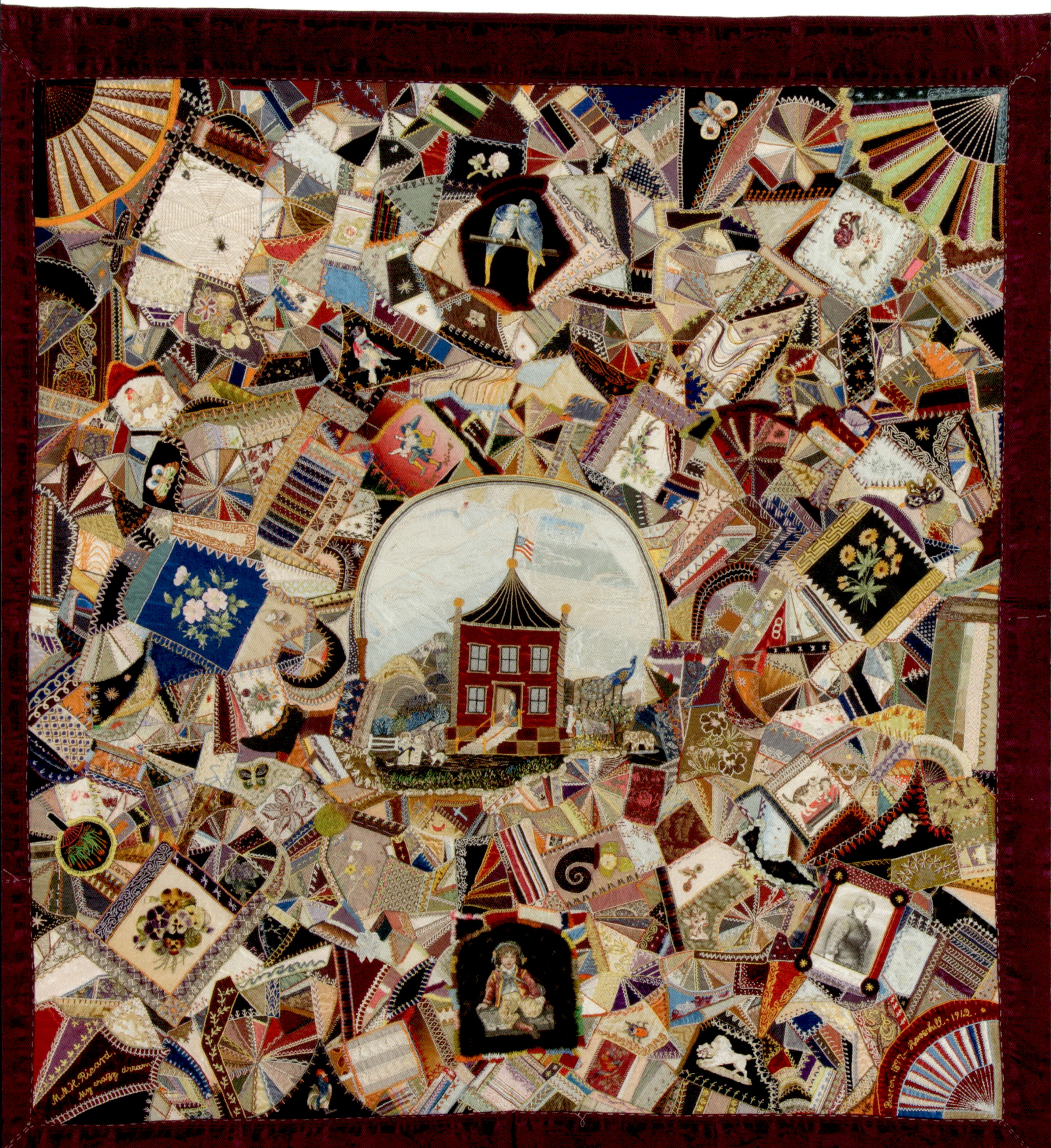
M.M.H. Ricard.
My crazy dream.
Boston. 1877 – Haverhill. 1912.

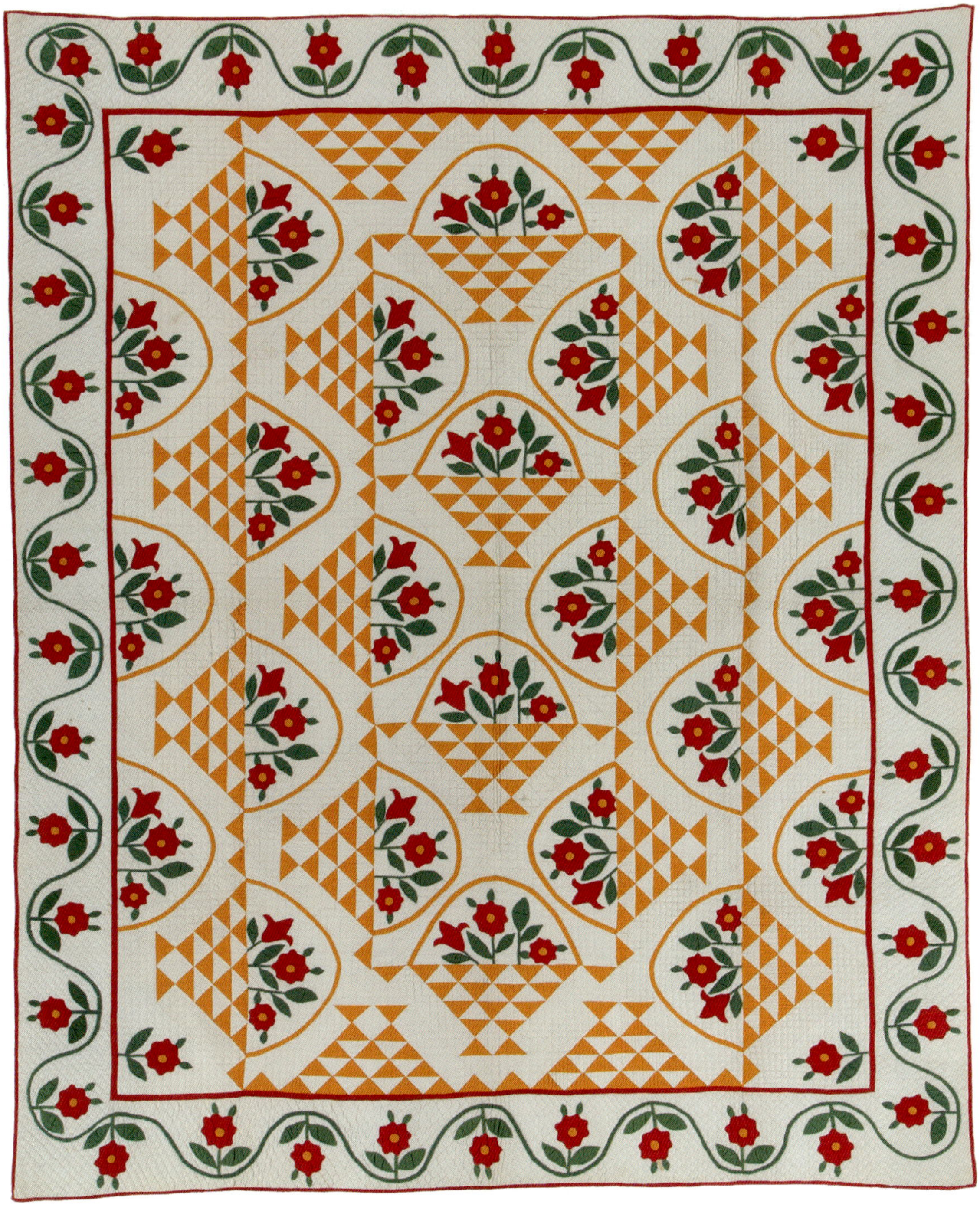

2.2

Basket of Flowers

Maker unidentified
Made in the United States, 1880-1900
Cotton; hand pieced, appliquéd, and quilted
104 x 83 in.

Ardis and Robert James Collection, IQM 2009.039.0038

2.1

My Crazy Dream

Mary Hernandred Ricard
Boston and Haverhill, Massachusetts, 1877-1912
Silk; Hand pieced (foundation)
74 x 68.5 in.

Ardis and Robert James Collection, IQM 1997.007.0541

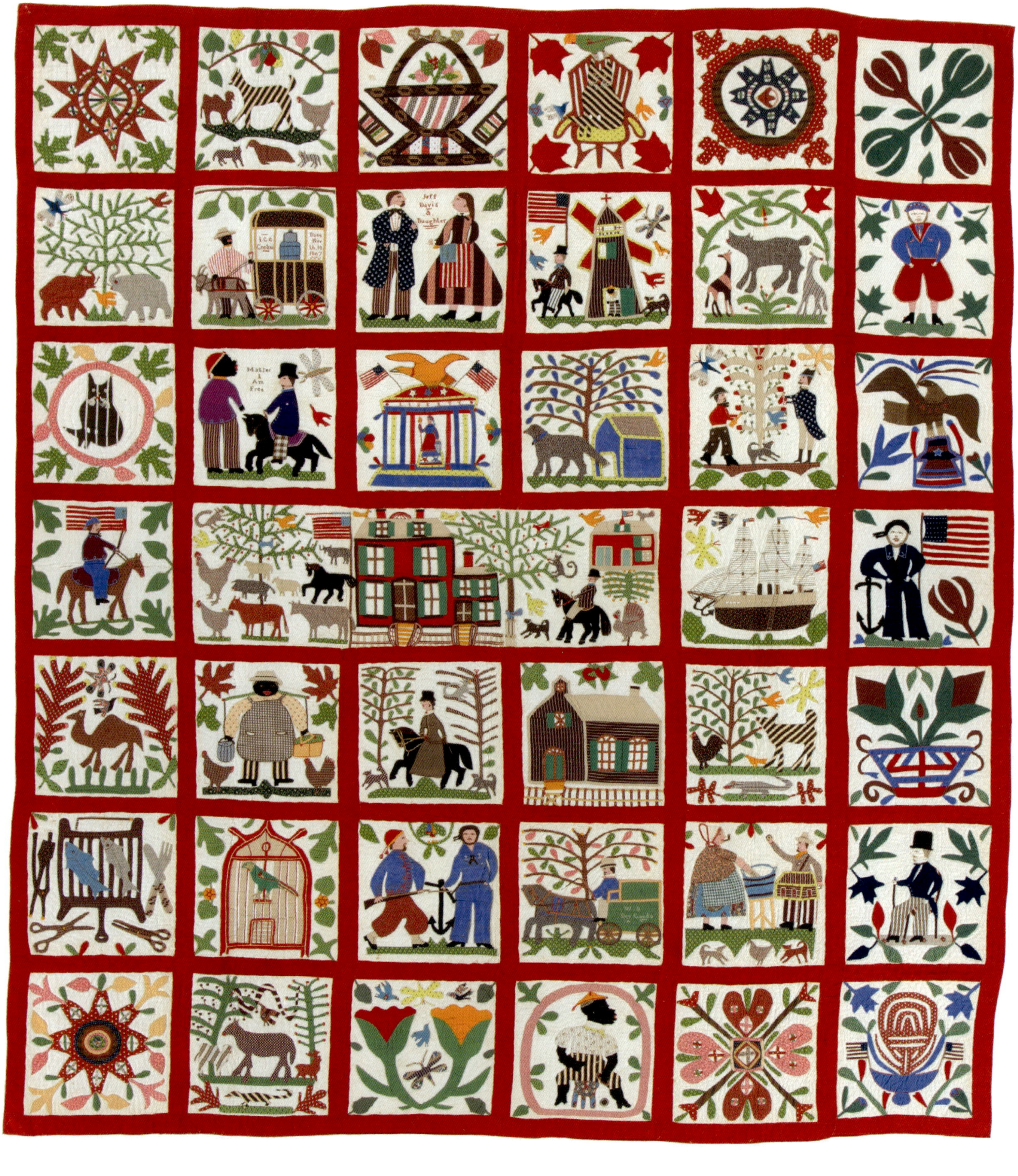
Ice Cream
Jeff Davis & Daughter
Master I Am Free

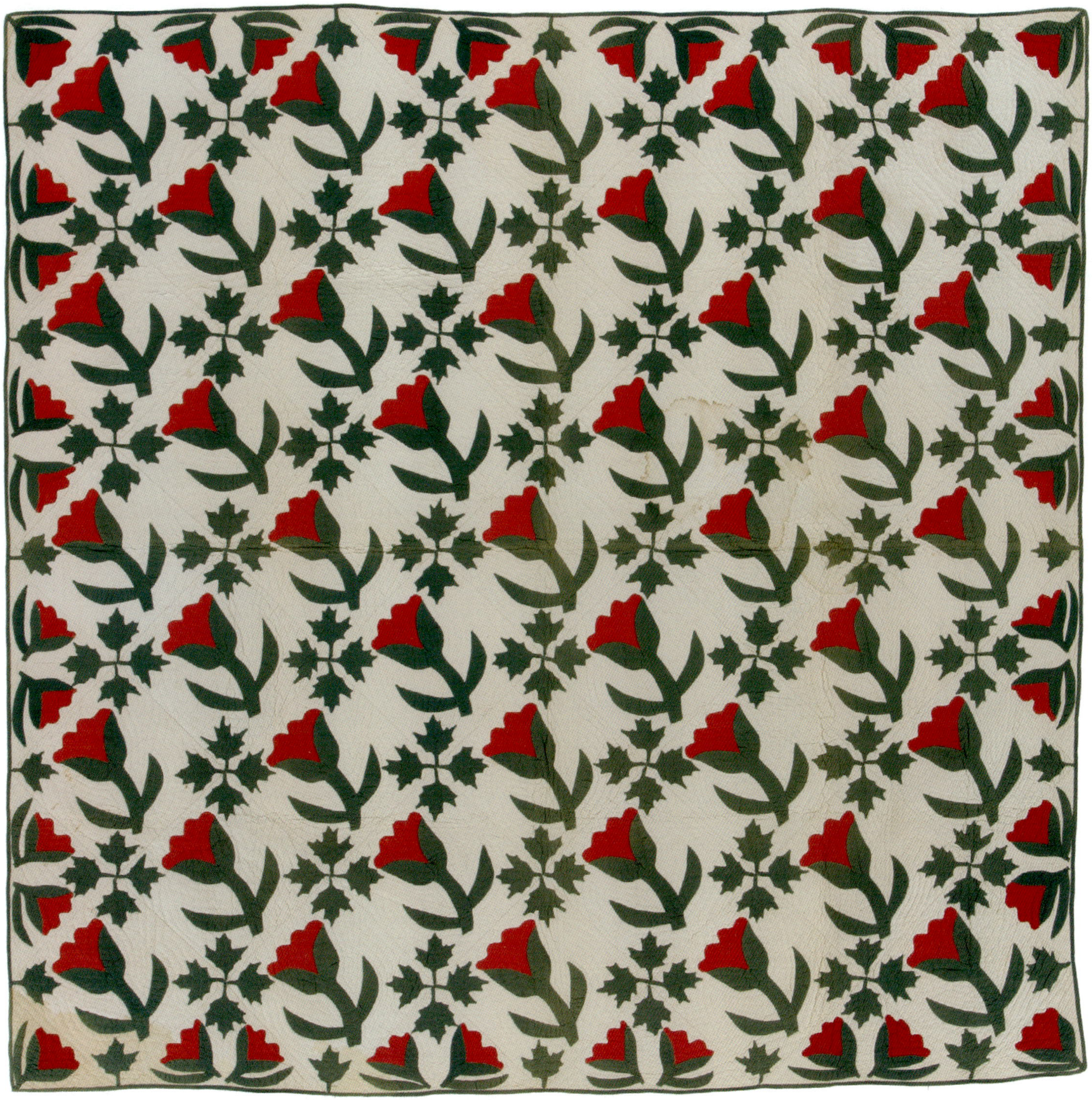

2.3

Reconciliation Quilt

Lucinda Ward Honstain
Brooklyn, New York, 1867
Cotton; hand appliquéd, pieced and quilted
97 x 84.5 in.

Gift of the Robert and Ardis James Foundation, IQM 2001.011.0001

2.4

Lucinda's Tulip

Lucinda Ward Honstain or Emma Bingham
Brooklyn, New York, 1860-1880
Cotton; hand appliquéd, pieced and quilted
77 x 76.5 in.

Gift of Madeline Ricards, IQM 2001.012.0001

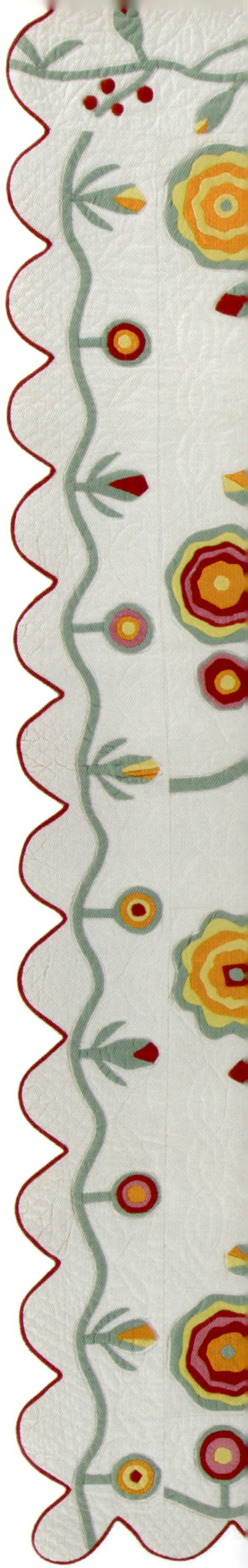

2.6

English Rose variation

Olive McClure Cook
Anna, Illinois, 1939
Cotton; hand appliquéd, embroidered, and quilted
88 x 86 in.

Ardis and Robert James Collection, IQM 1997.007.0669

2.5

From 1833 to 1933

Emma Leonhard
Virginia, Illinois, c. 1933
Cotton; hand appliquéd, machine pieced, hand quilted
86.5 x 78 in.

Ardis and Robert James Collection, IQM 1997.007.0368

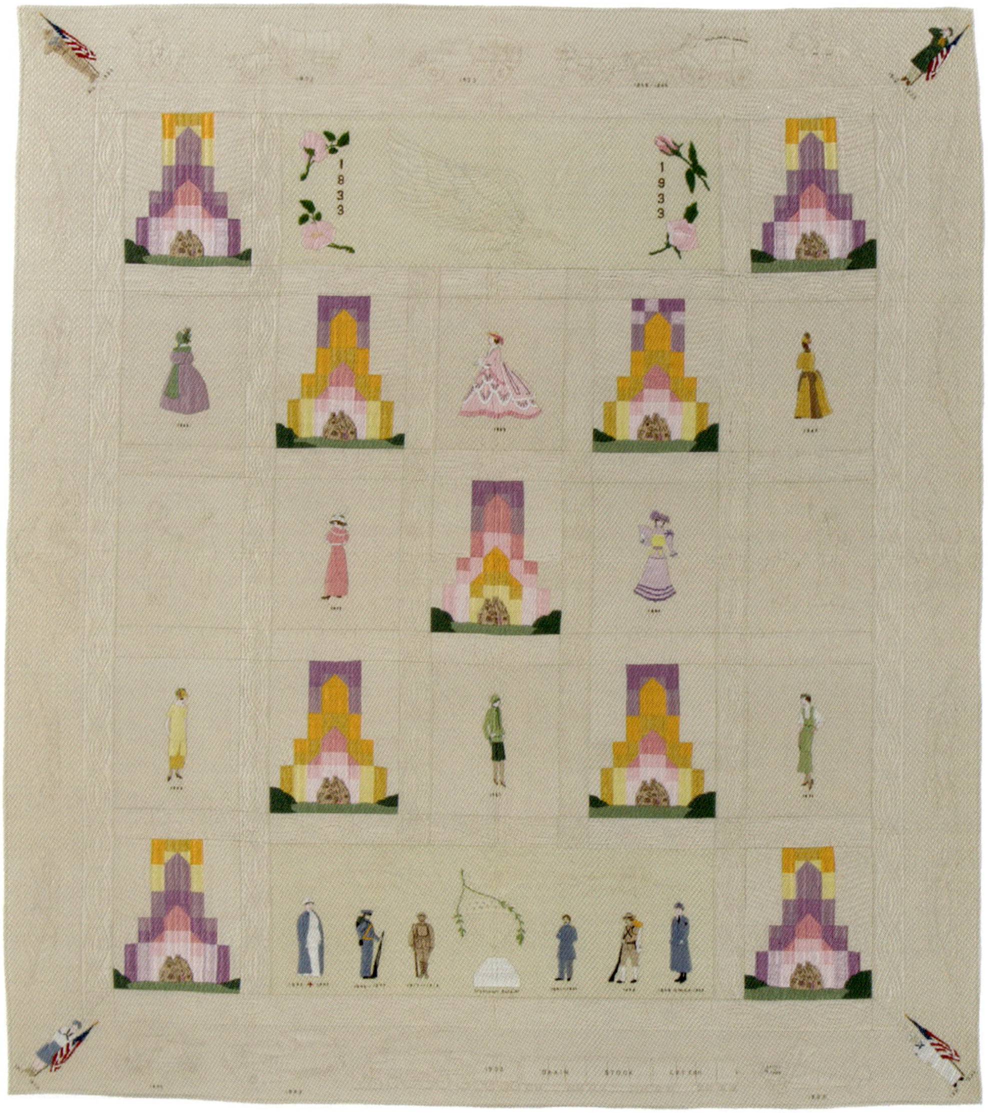

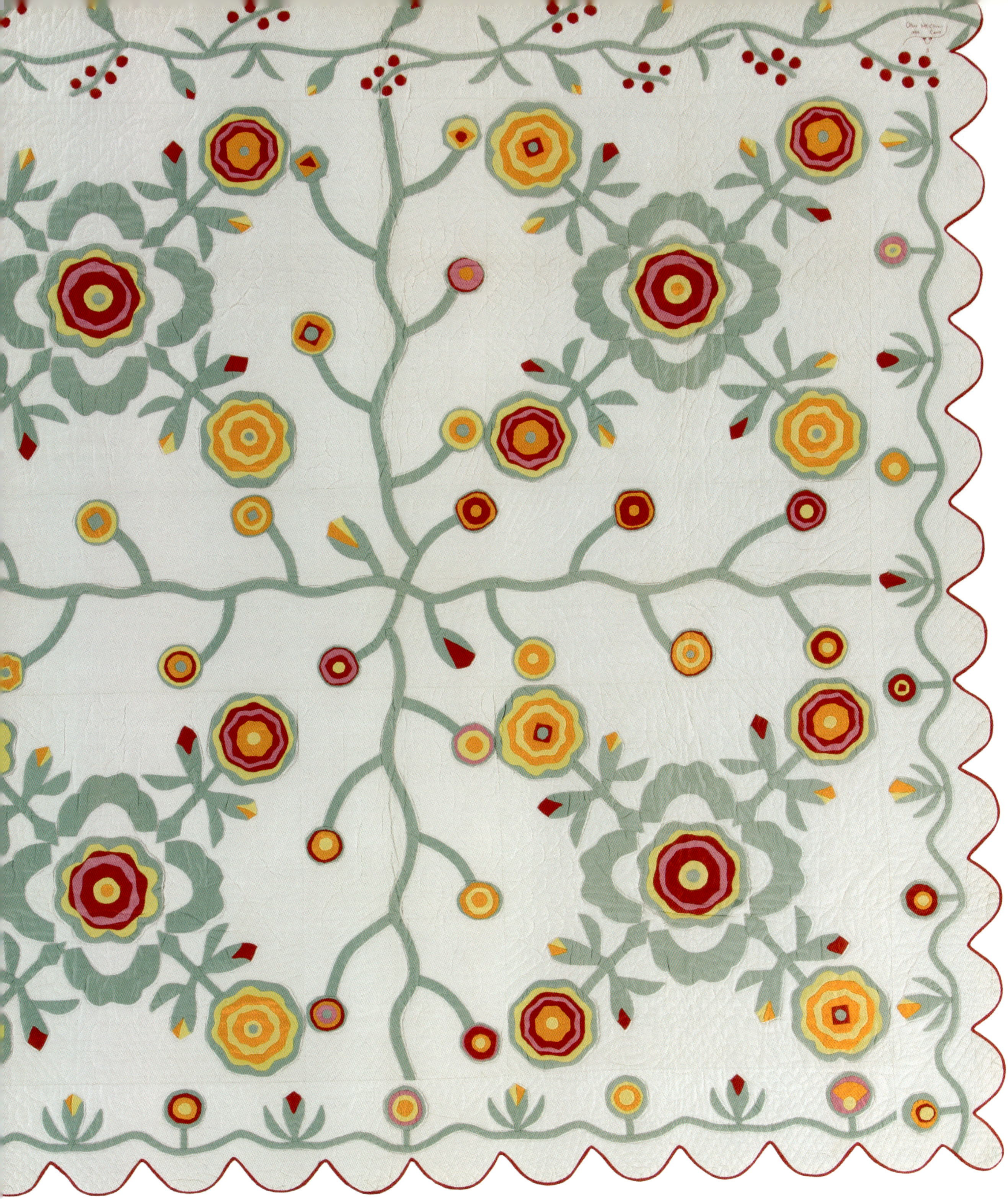

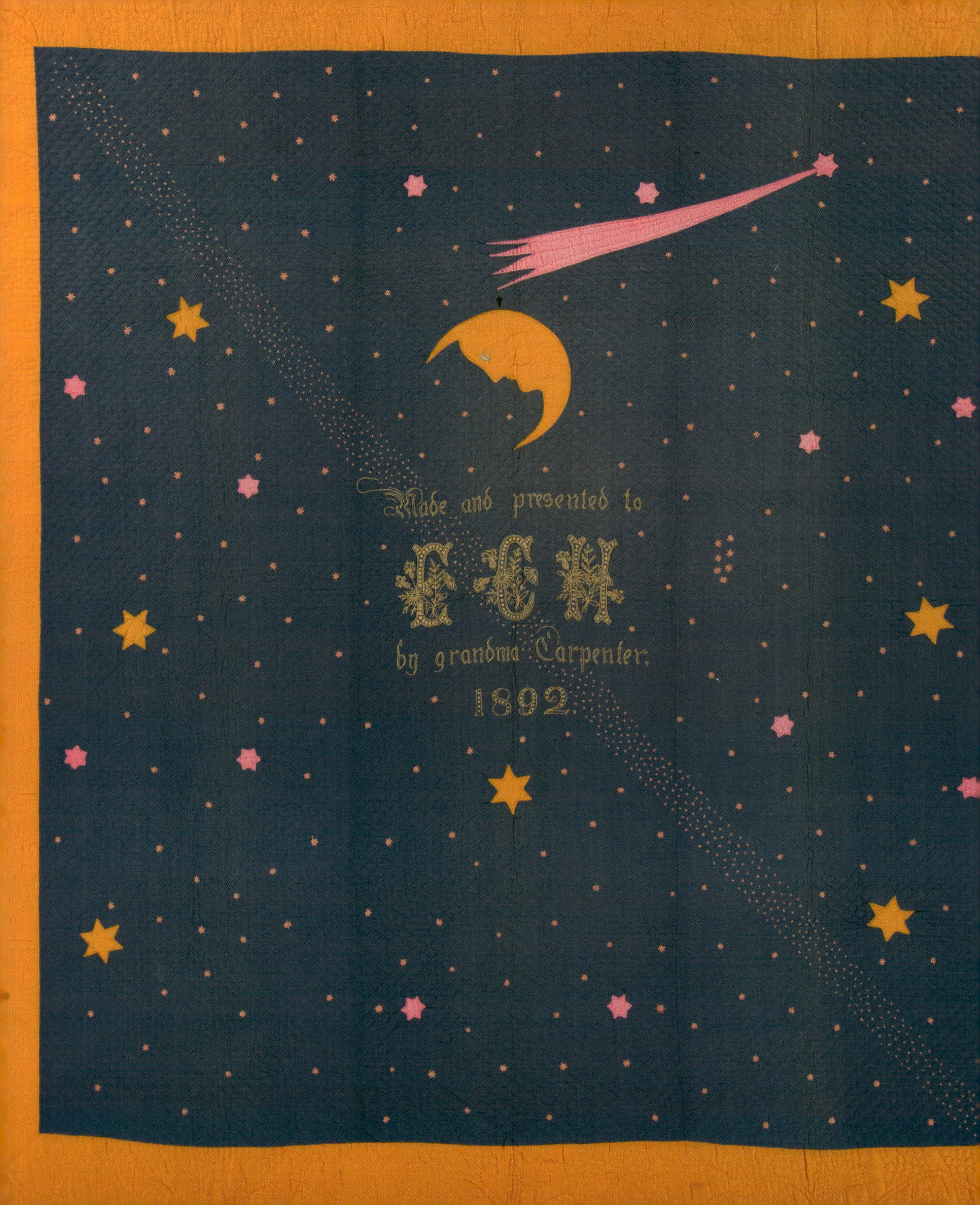
Made and presented to
ECH
by grandma Carpenter.
1892.

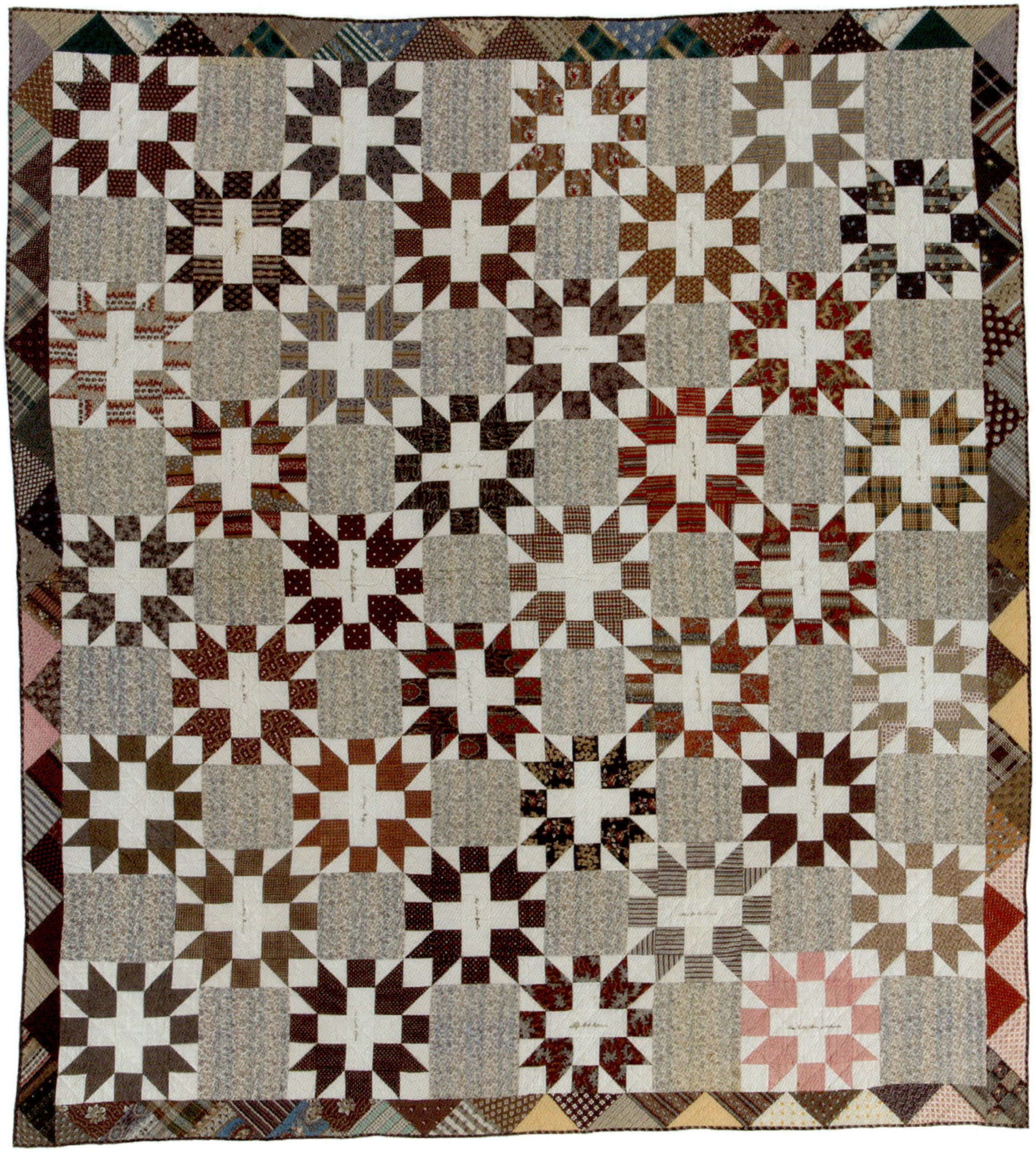

2.8

Friendship Block

Mercy Jane Bancroft Blair
South Apalachin, New York, 1855-1863
Cotton; hand pieced and quilted
90 x 79 in.

Ardis and Robert James Collection, IQM 1997.007.0852

2.7

Star and Comet

Harriet Miller Carpenter
Lancaster County, Pennsylvania, 1892
Cotton; hand appliquéd and quilted
94 x 85 in.

Ardis and Robert James Collection, IQM 1997.007.0264

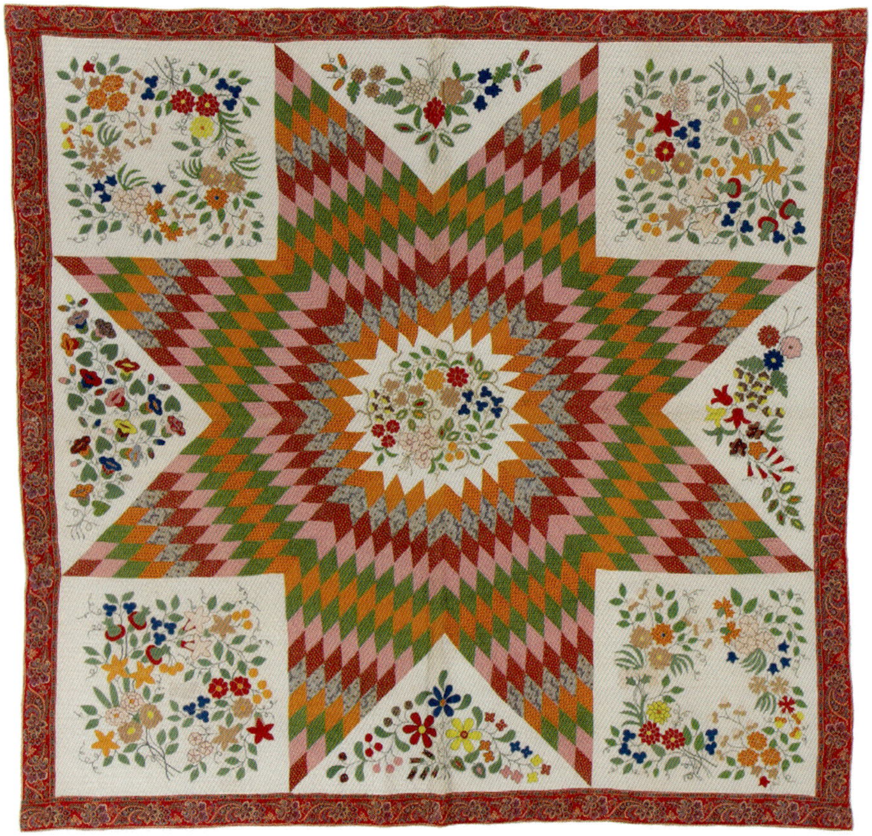

2.9

Star of Bethlehem

Rachel K. Trundle
Mt. Auburn, Maryland, 1855-1865
Cotton; hand pieced, embroidered, and quilted
94.5 x 95 in.

Ardis and Robert James Collection, IQM 2009.039.0042

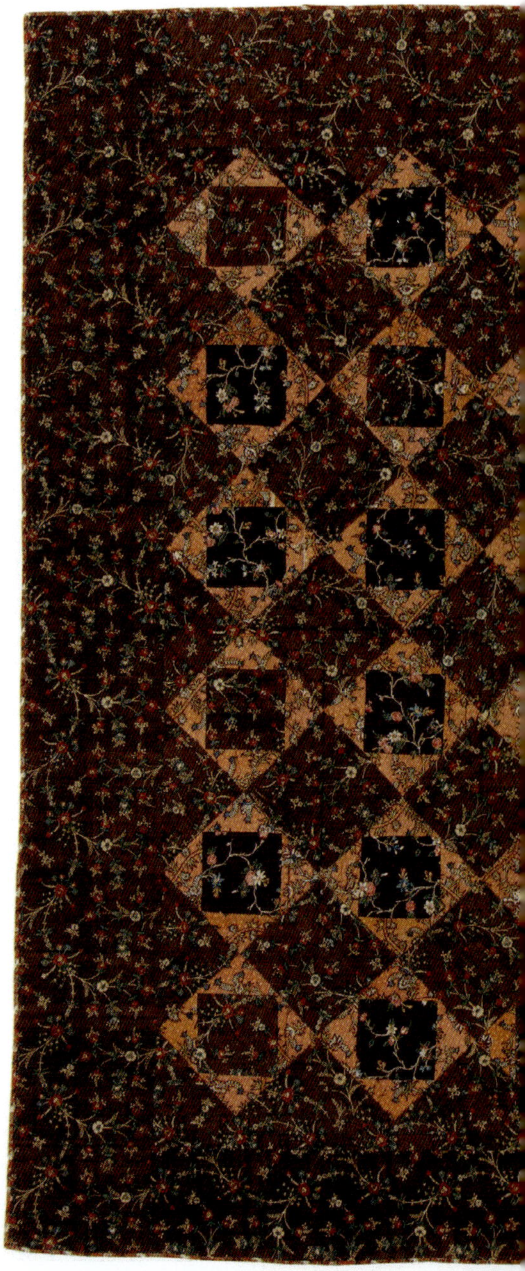

2.10

Square in a Square with Toile back

Maker unidentified
Possibly made in Berks County, Pennsylvania, 1810-1830
(toile backing fabric, c. 1775)
Cotton; hand pieced and quilted
84 x 71 in.

Ardis and Robert James Collection, IQM 1997.007.0428

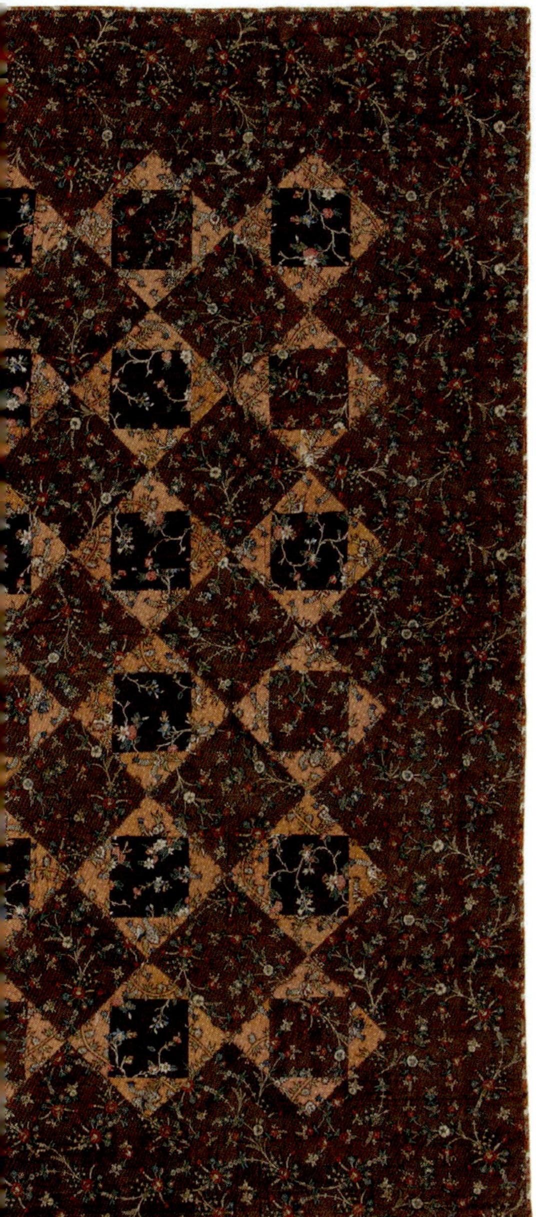

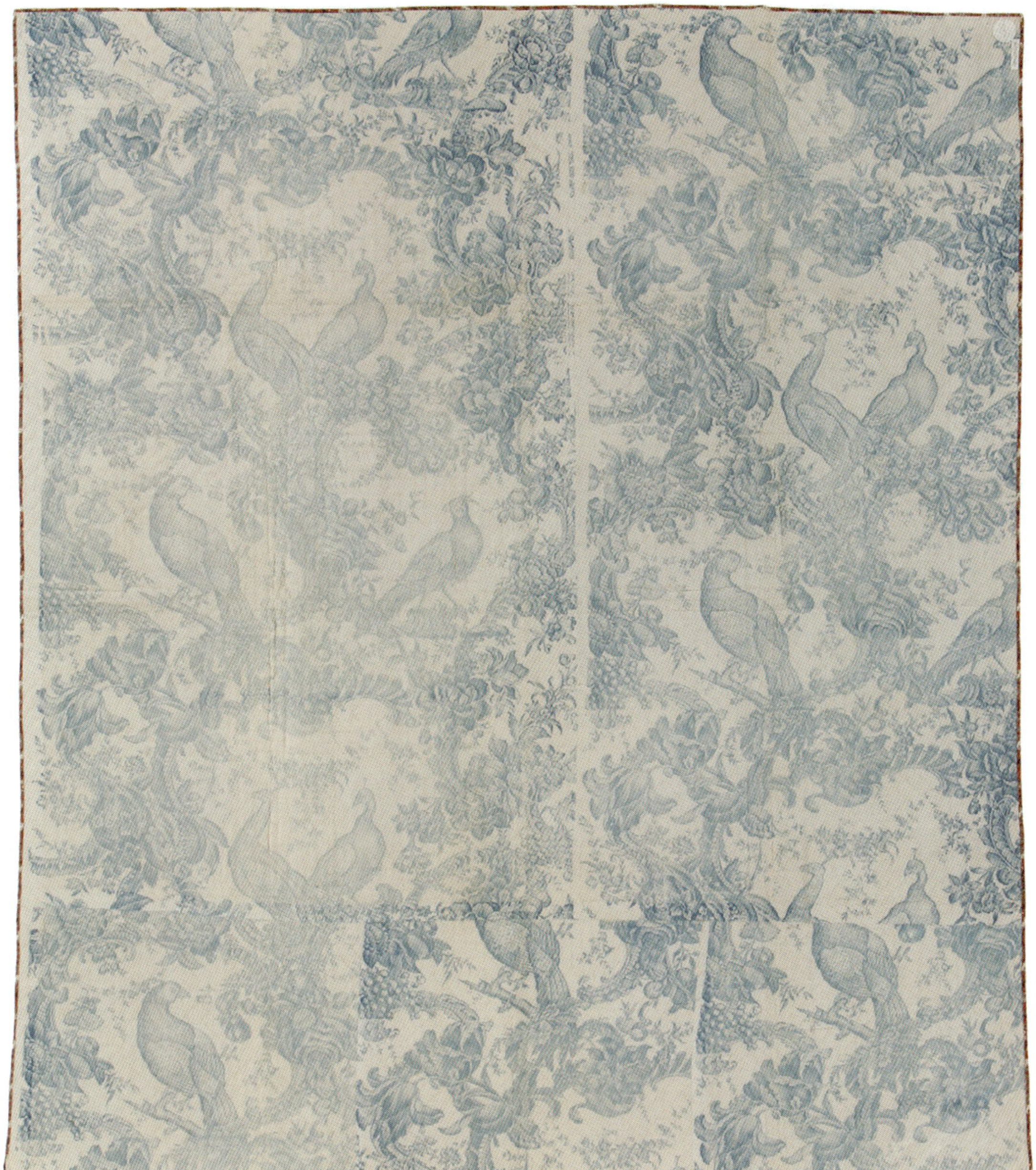

2.11

Basket

Possibly made by Mrs. Yost Miller
Holmes County, Ohio, 1940-1960
Cotton; machine pieced and quilted
73 x 87 in.

Ardis and Robert James Collection, IQM 1997.007.0224

2.12

Album

Maker unidentified
Baltimore, Maryland, 1850
Cotton; hand appliquéd, embroidered, and quilted
106.5 x 107 in.

Ardis and Robert James Collection, IQM 1997.007.0319

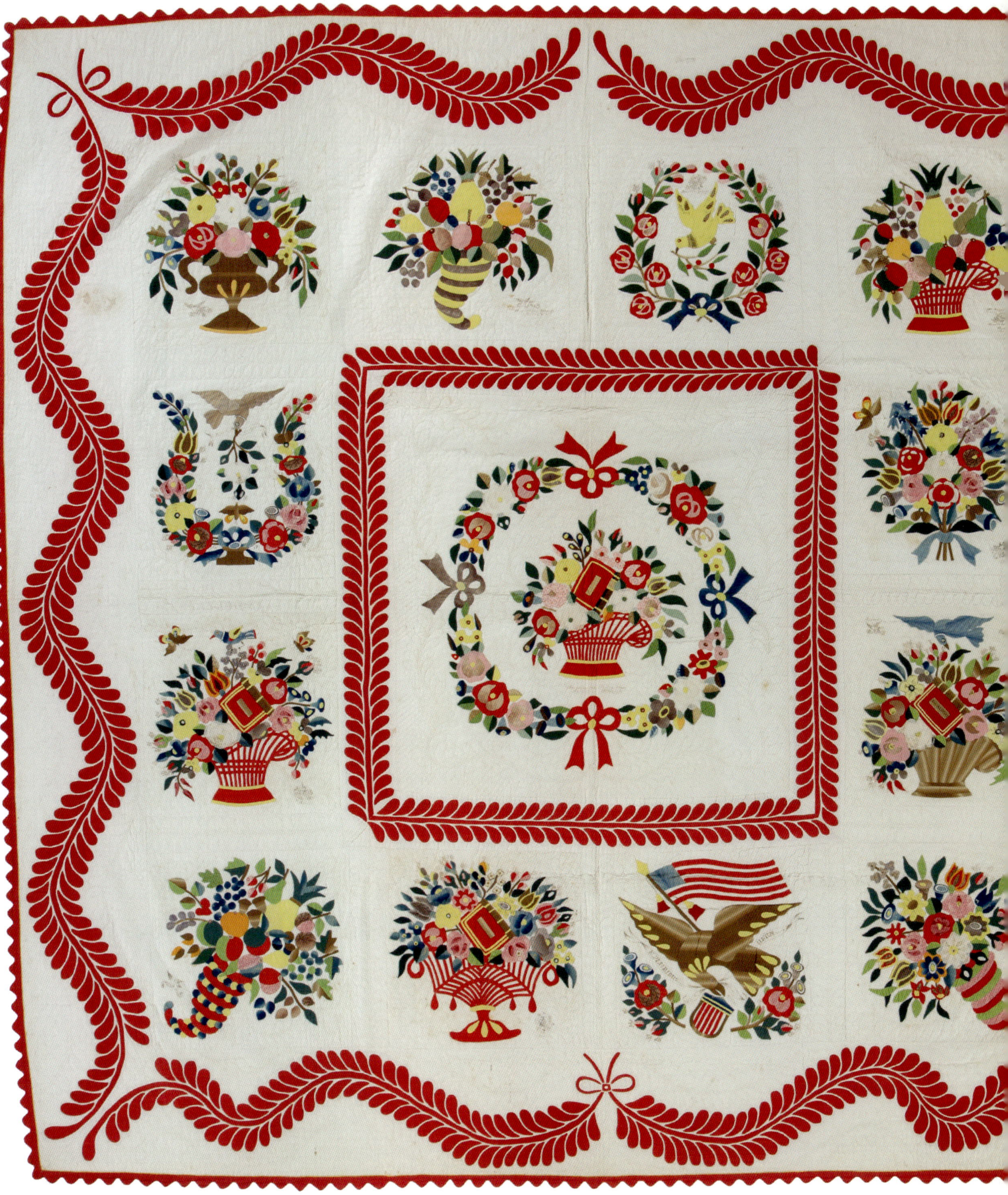

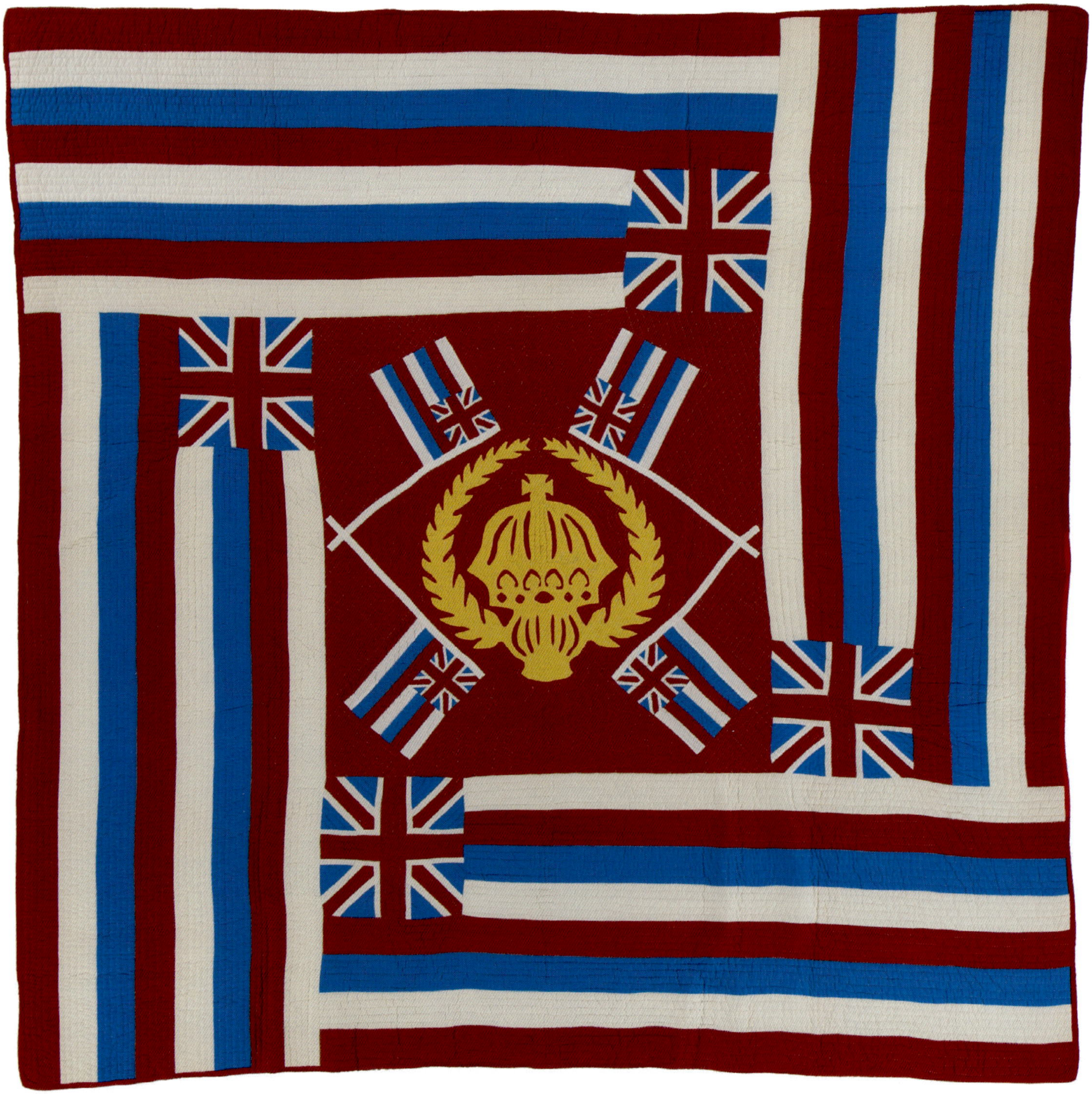

2.13

Hawaiian Flag

Marie E. Akana
Hawaii, c. 1955
Cotton; hand appliquéd and quilted
98.5 x 97.5 in.

Ardis and Robert James Collection, IQM 1997.007.0099

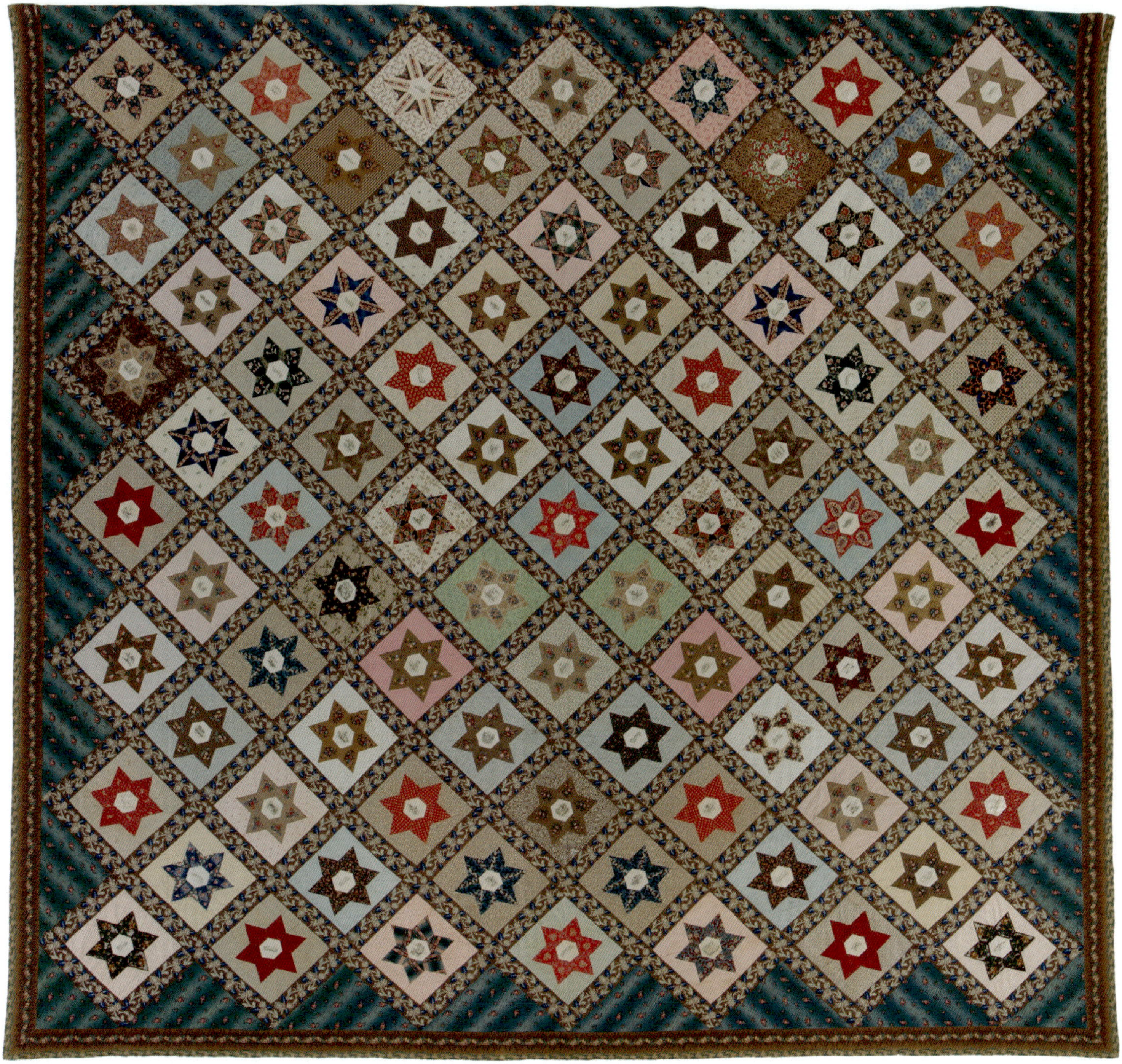

2.14

Stars

Rebecca Savery
Philadelphia, Pennsylvania, 1844
Cotton; hand pieced and quilted
114 x 118.5 in.

Ardis and Robert James Collection, IQM 1997.007.0118

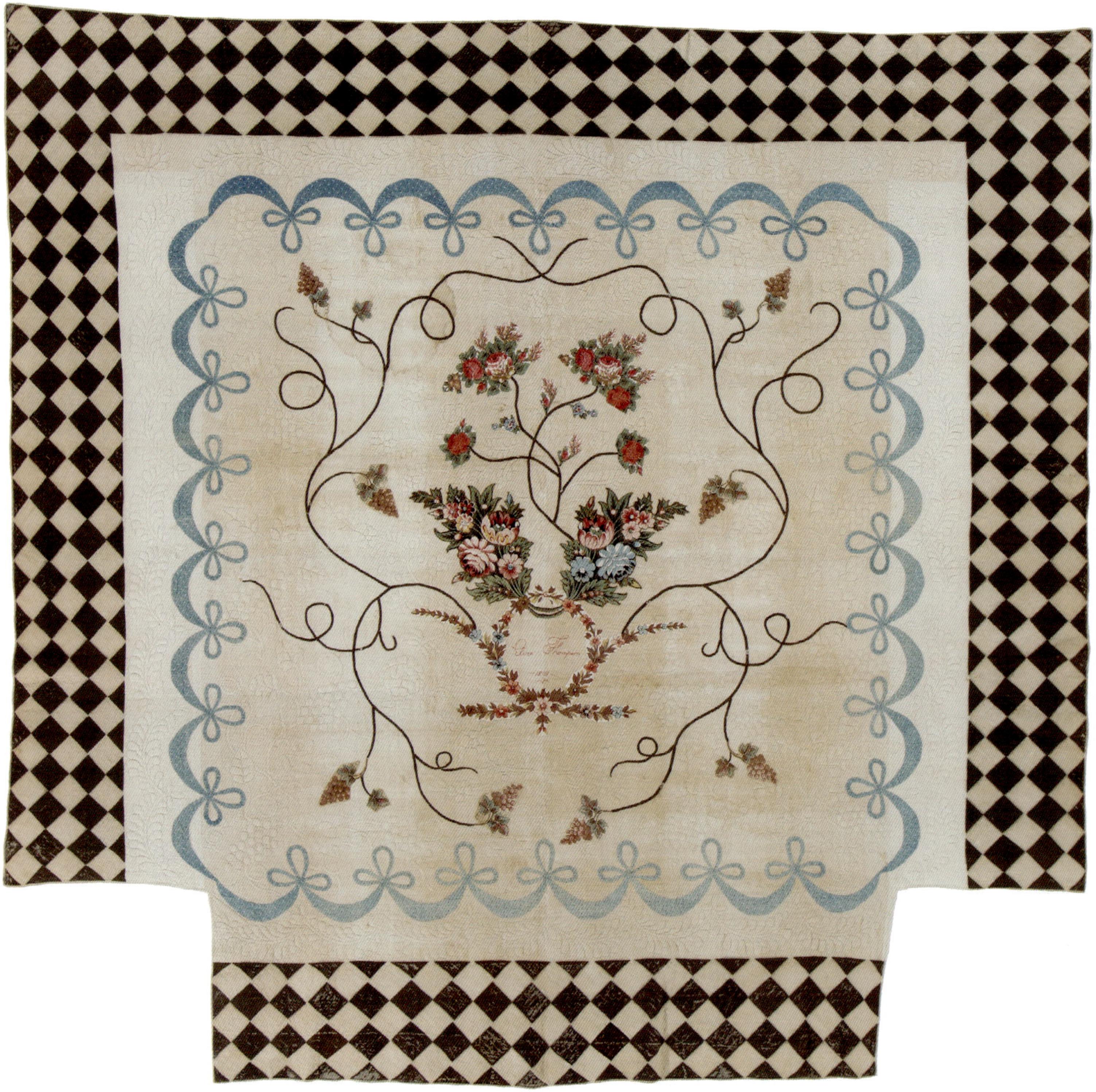

2.15

Medallion

Eliza Thompson
South Carolina or Virginia, 1809
Cotton; hand appliquéd, embroidered, and quilted
101 x 101 in.

Ardis and Robert James Collection, IQM 1997.007.0257

2.16

Album, Queen Victoria

Maker unidentified
Probably made in Shippensburg, Pennsylvania, 1843 and 1844
Cotton; hand appliquéd and quilted
93 x 108.5 in.

Ardis and Robert James Collection, IQM 1997.007.0479

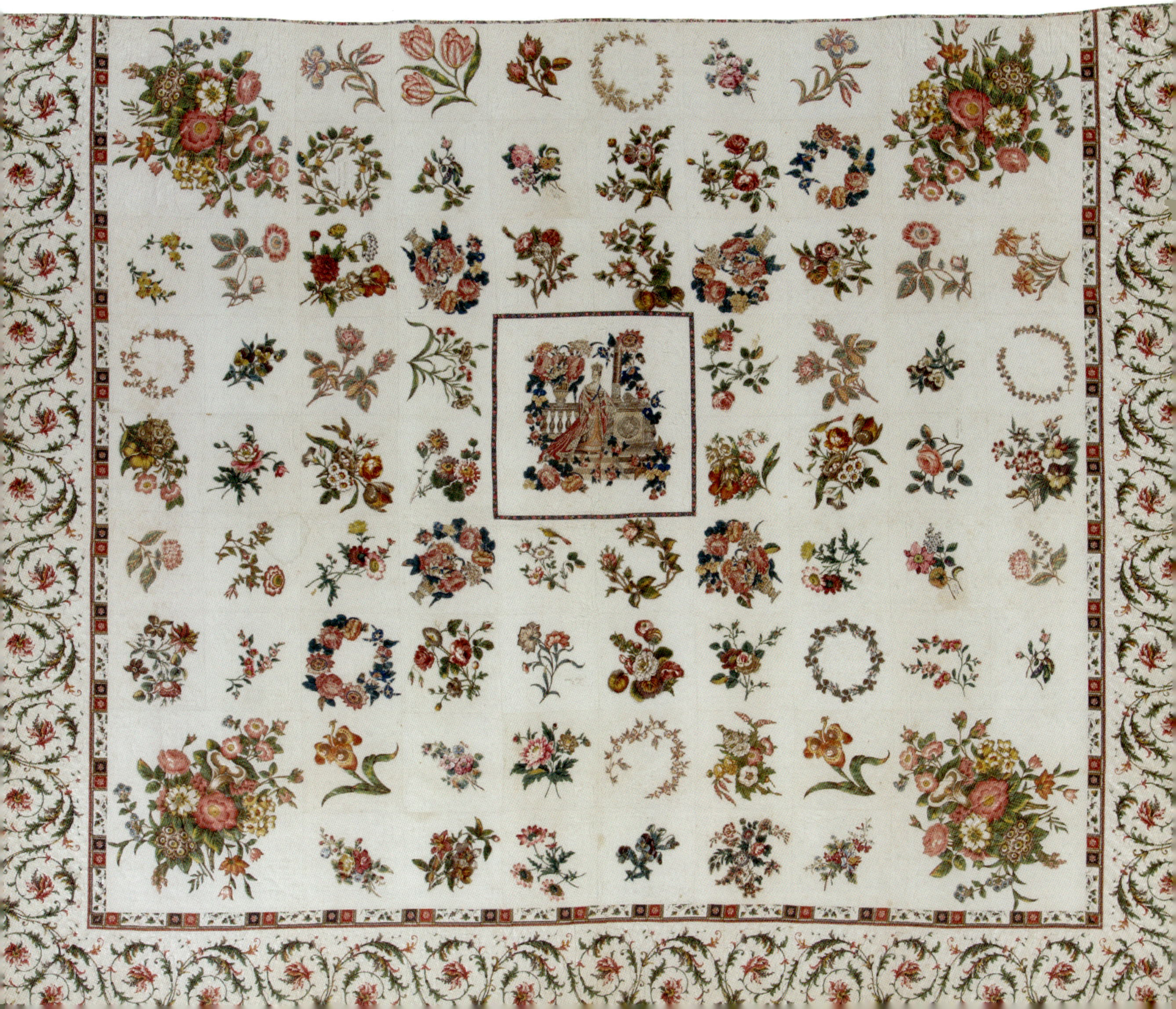

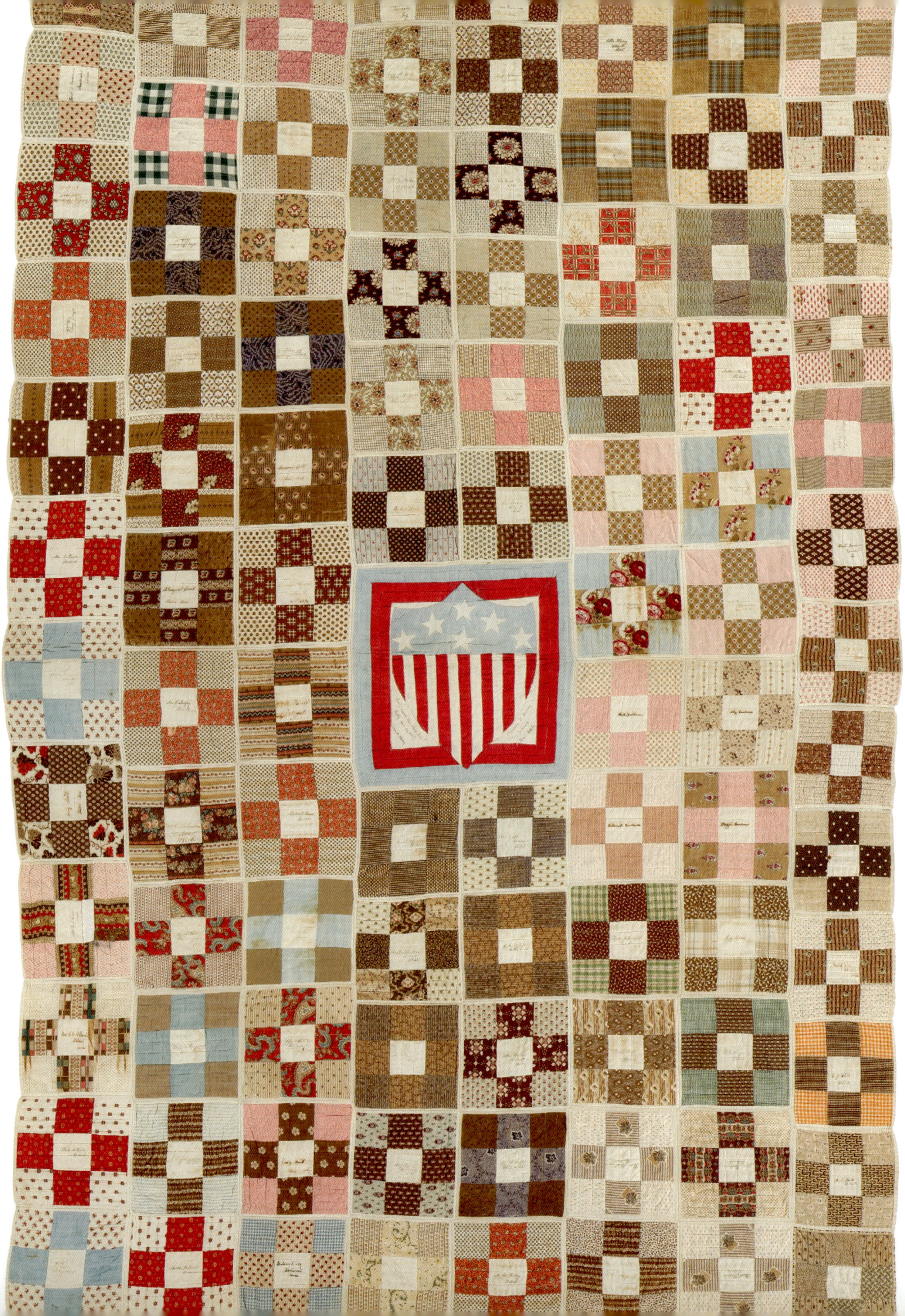

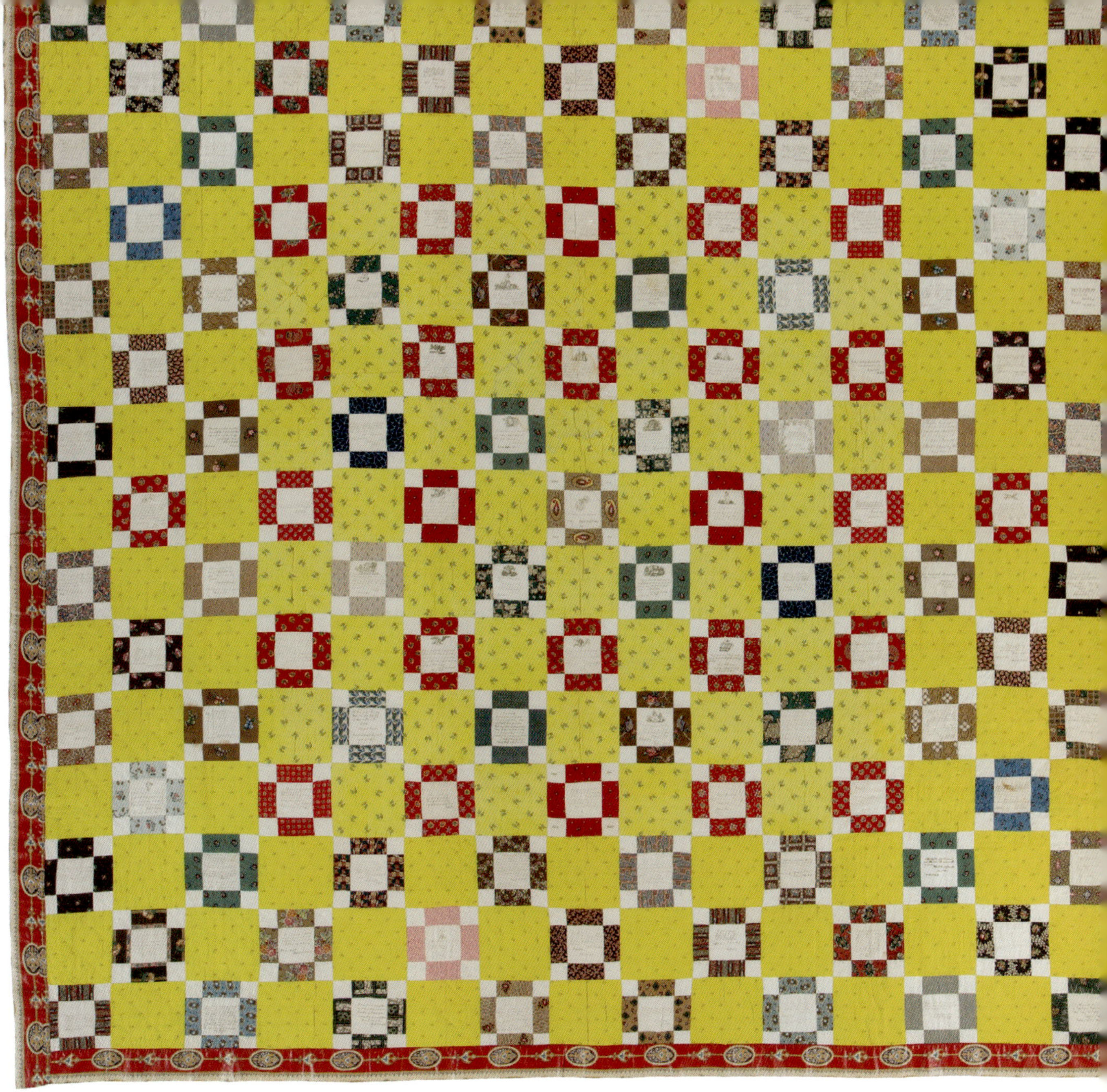

2.18

Nine Patch variation
My Sweet Sister Emma

Martha Knowles and Henrietta Thomas
Darby, Pennsylvania, 1843
Cotton; hand pieced and quilted
107 x 109 in.

Ardis and Robert James Collection, IQM 1997.007.0697

2.17

Nine Patch

Maker unidentified
Probably made in Detroit, Michigan, 1864
Cotton; hand pieced and appliquéd, machine quilted
93 x 58 in.

Ardis and Robert James Collection, IQM 1997.007.0569

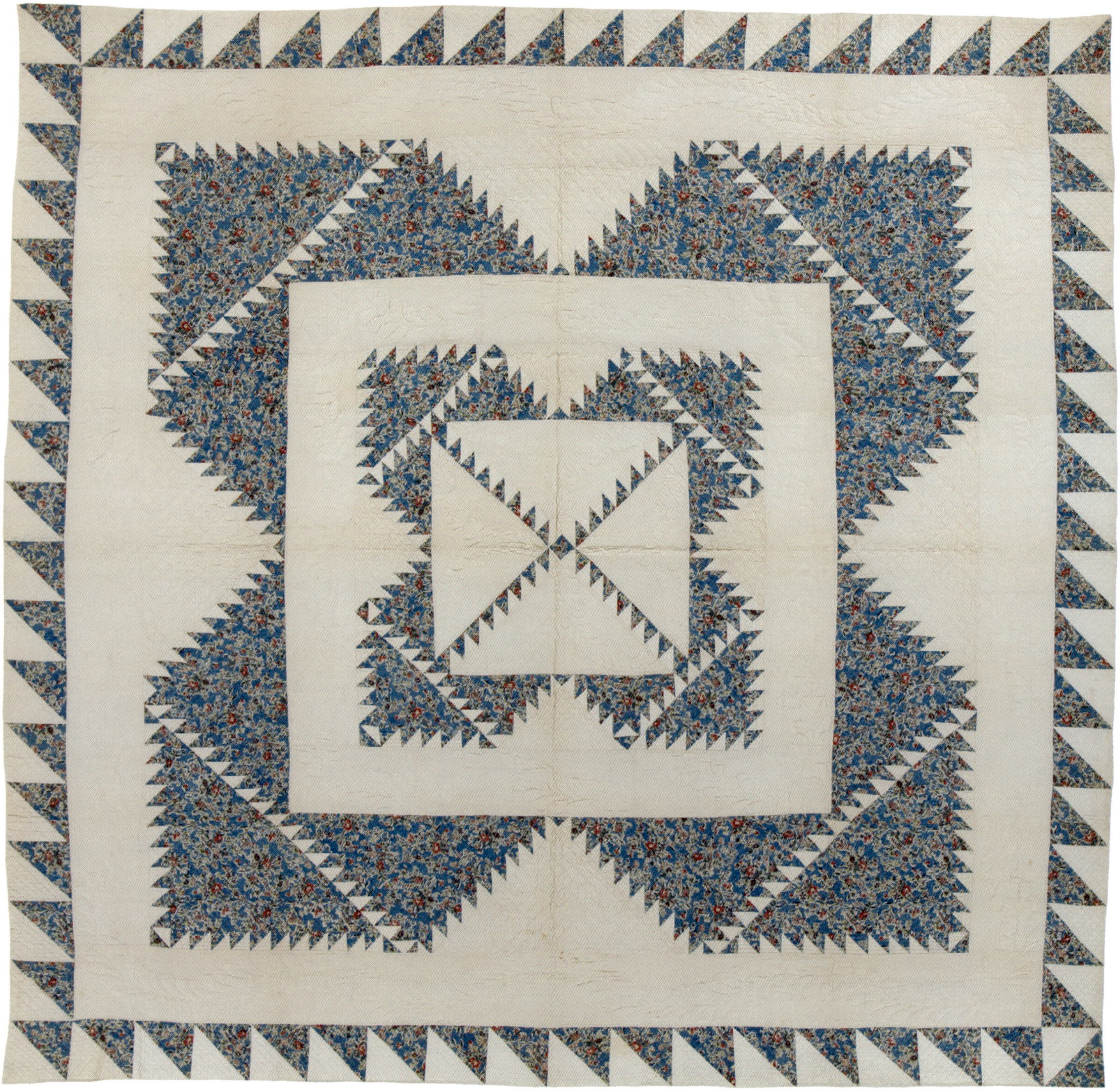

2.19

Delectable Mountains

Maker unidentified
Probably made in Manheim, Pennsylvania, 1820-1830
Cotton; hand pieced and quilted
109 x 106 in.

Ardis and Robert James Collection, IQM 1997.007.0756

2.20

Floral

Maker unidentified
Probably made in Ohio, 1865
Cotton; hand appliquéd and machine appliquéd, hand quilted
80 x 80 in.

Ardis and Robert James Collection, IQM 2006.043.0157

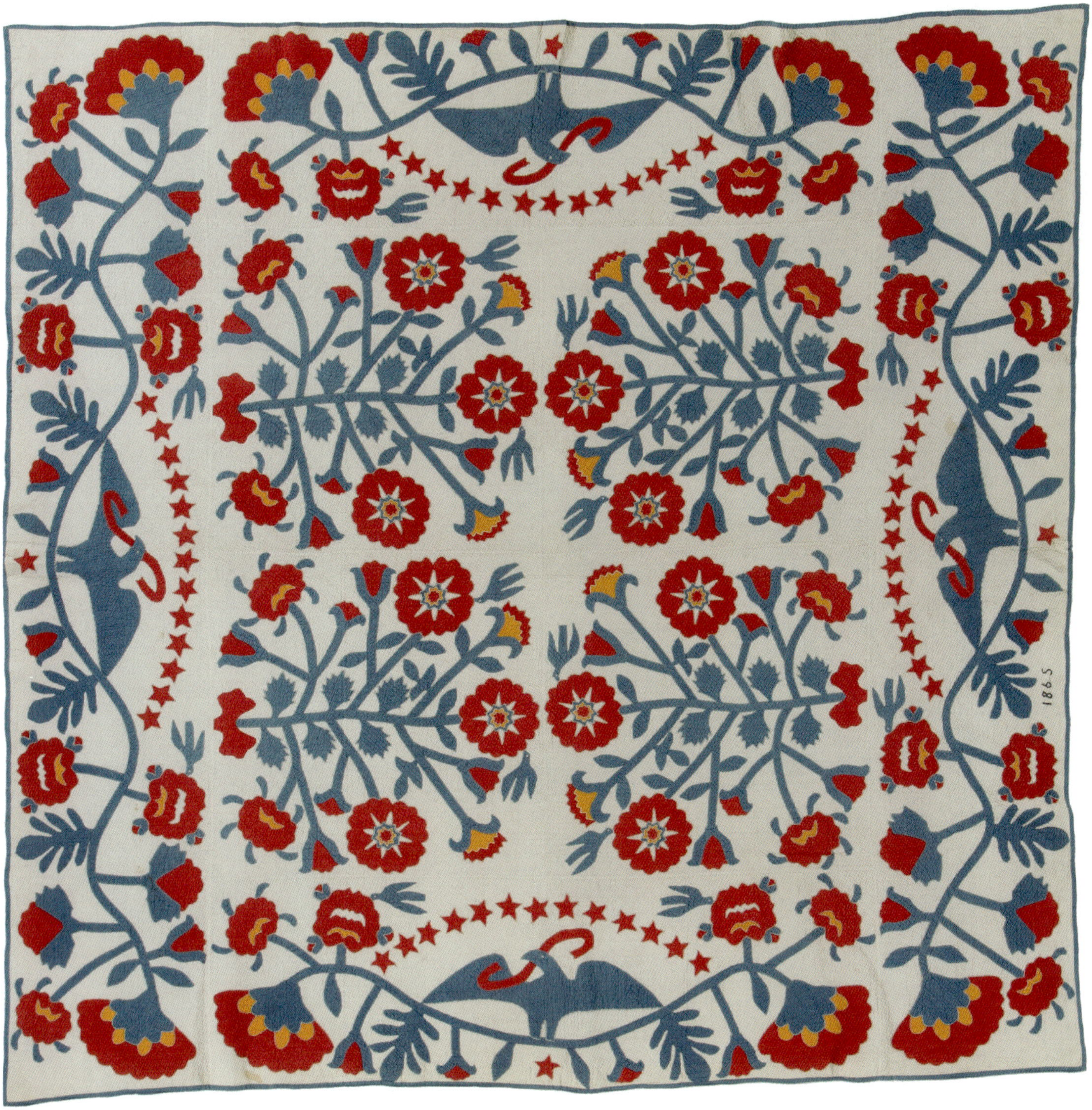

2.21

Album

Salinda Rupp
Lancaster County, Pennsylvania, 1870-1890
Cotton; hand pieced and quilted
88 x 88 in.

Ardis and Robert James Collection, IQM 2006.043.0226

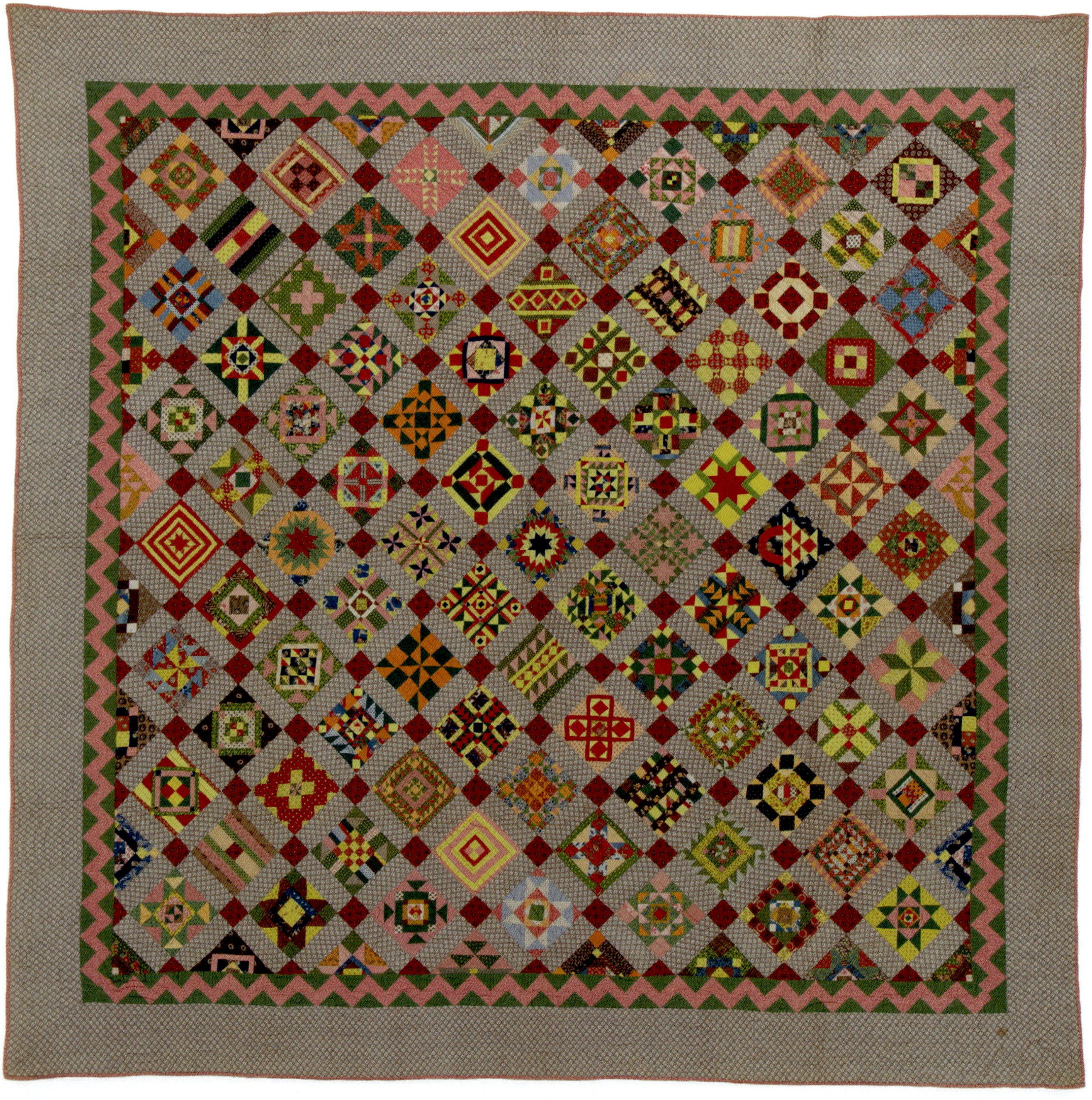

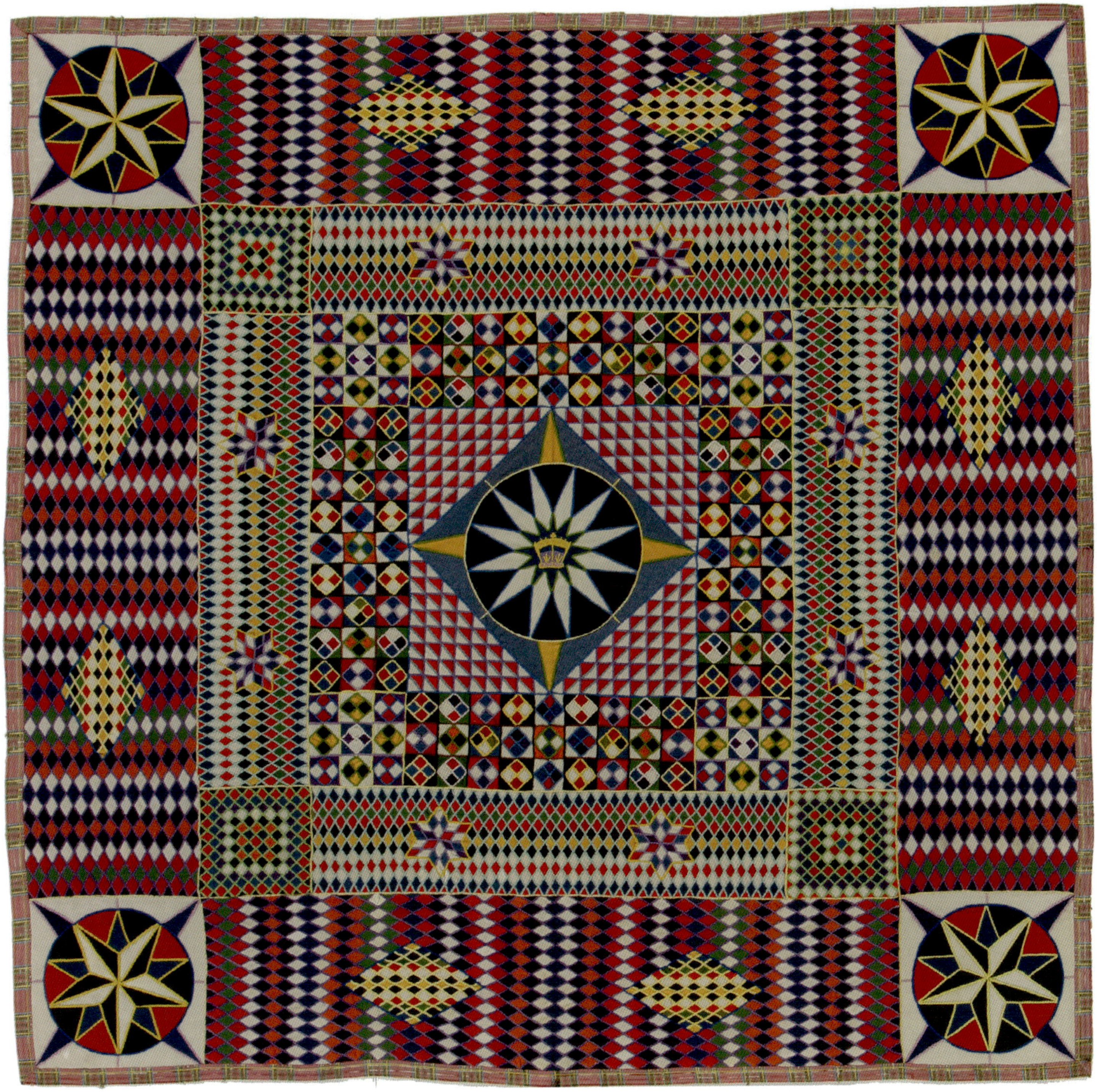

2.22

Mosaic

Maker unidentified
Probably made in the United Kingdom, c. 1880
Wool; hand pieced, no quilting
59 x 59 in.

Ardis and Robert James Collection, IQM 2009.039.0035

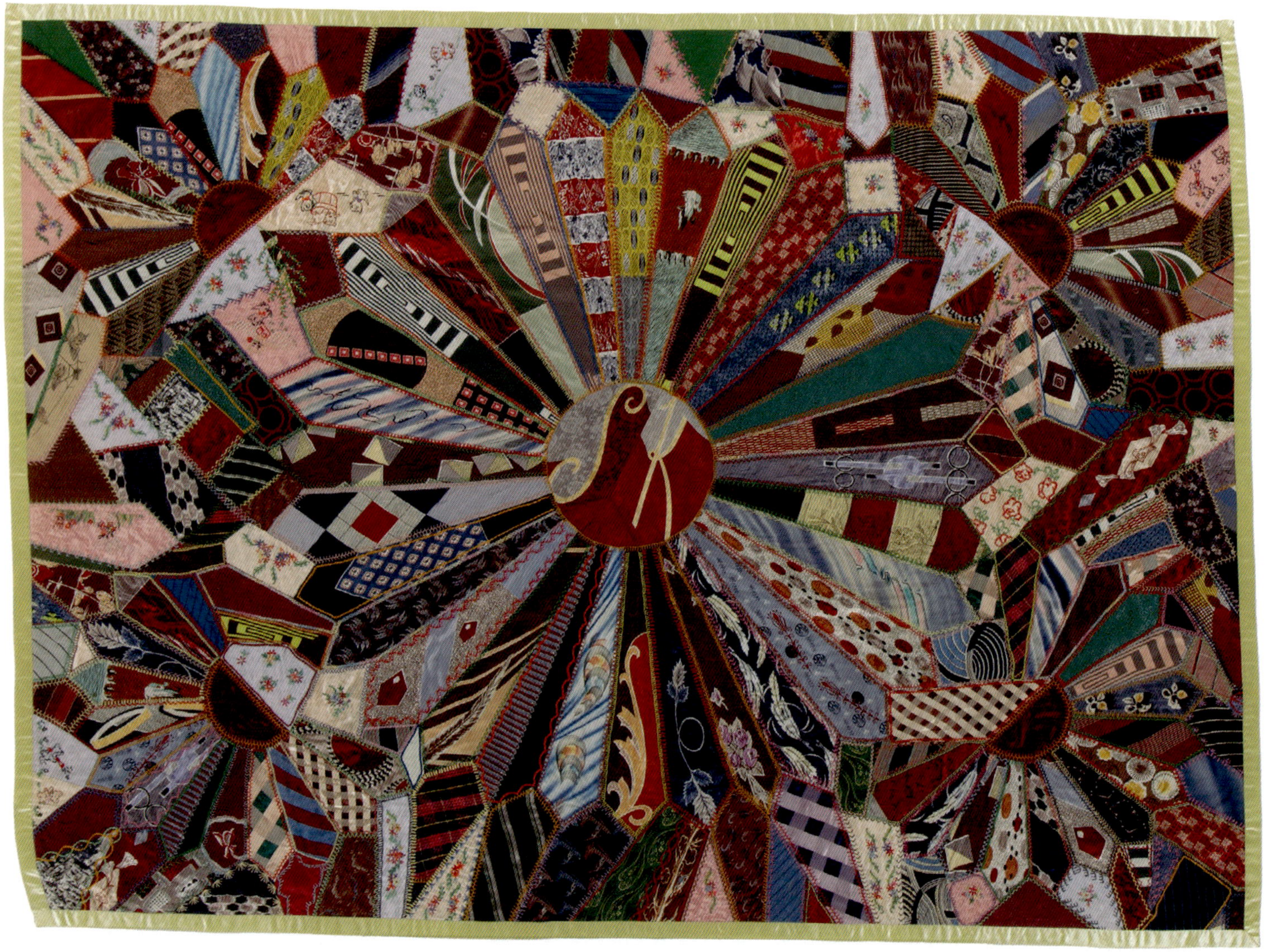

2.23

Crazy

Maker unidentified
Probably made in Anderson, Indiana, c. 1935
Silk; hand pieced (foundation) and embroidered, no quilting
68.5 x 90 in.

Ardis and Robert James Collection, IQM 2009.039.0049

2.24

Crazy Strips

Maker unidentified
United States, 1840-1860
Cotton; hand pieced and quilted
98.5 x 96 in.

Ardis and Robert James Collection, IQM 2009.039.0063

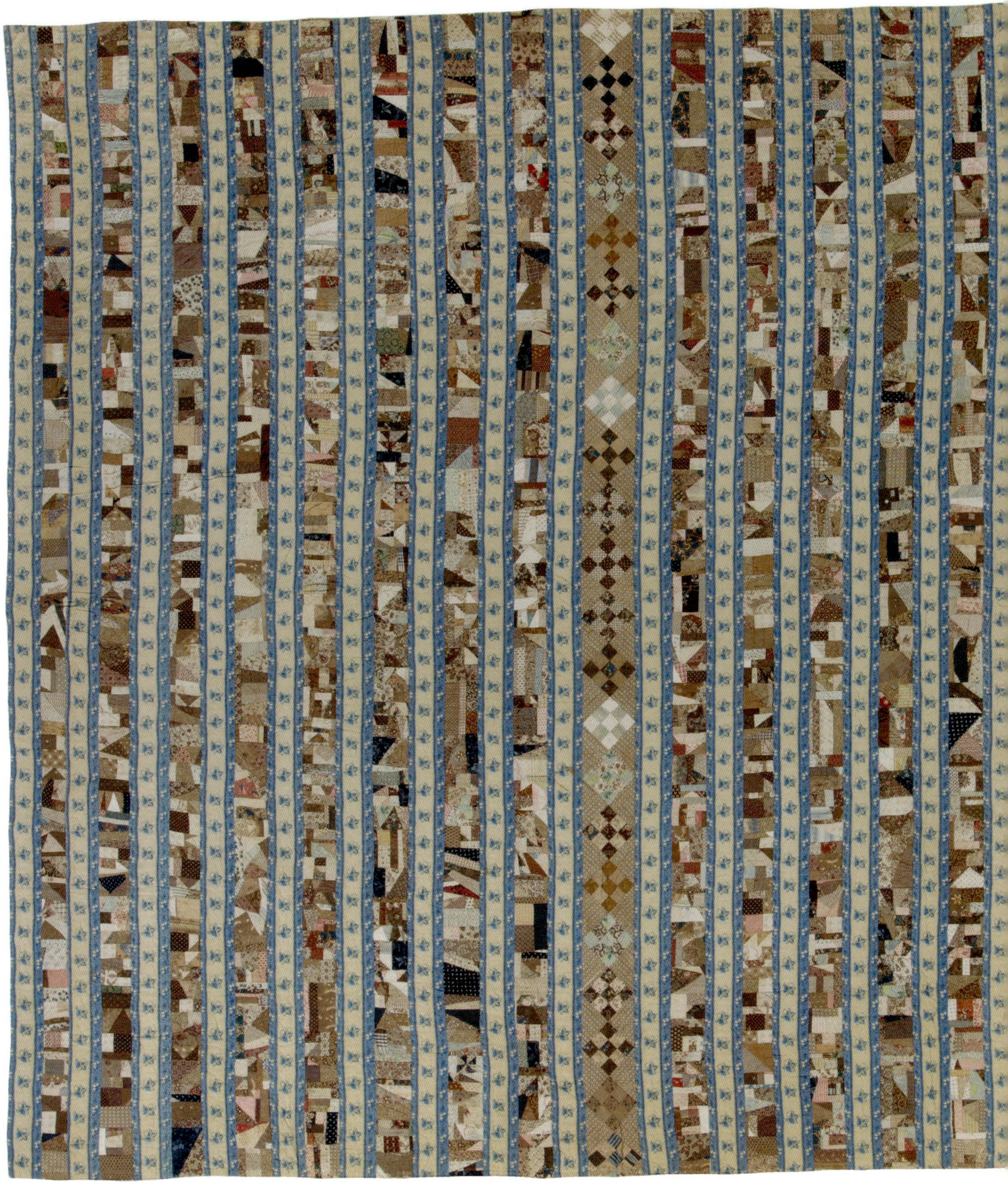

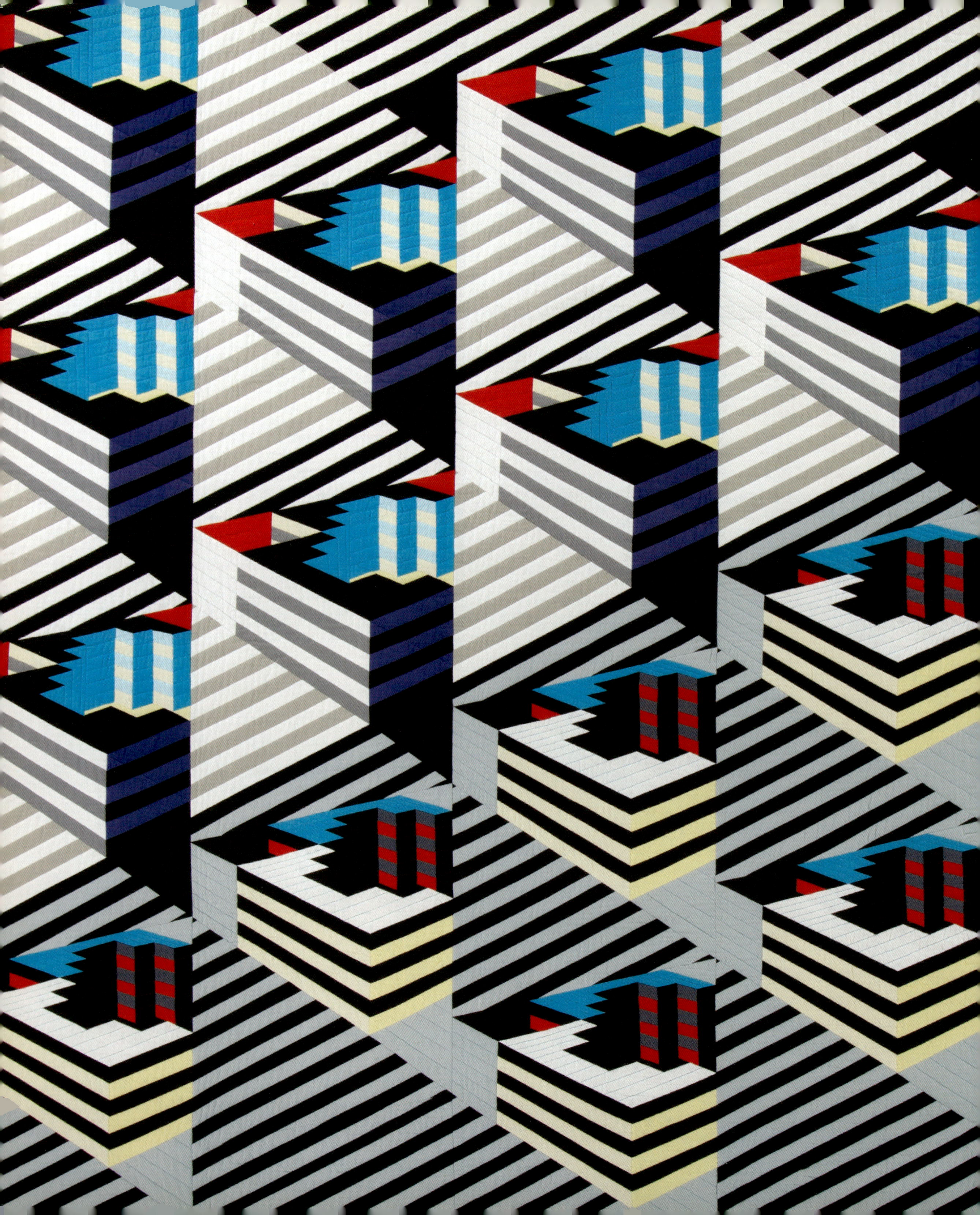

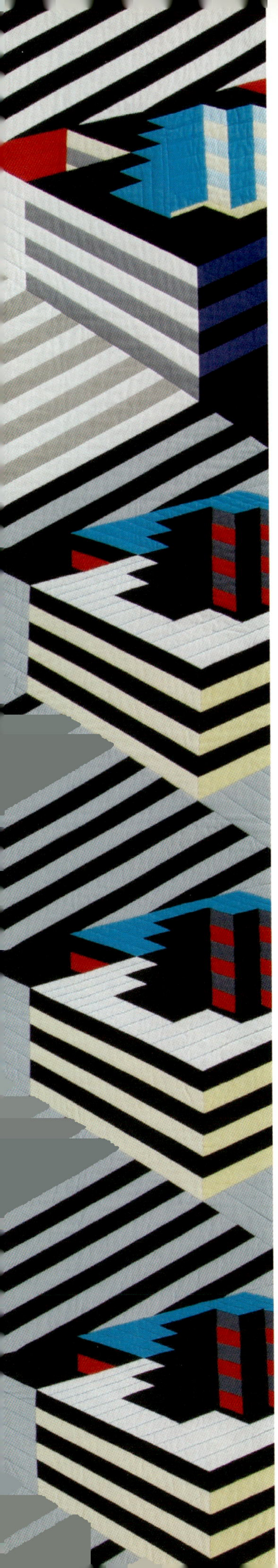

CHAPTER 3

FROM THE STUDIO

Penelope McMorris

Independent curator

THE JAMES COLLECTION: BUILDING A VISION TOGETHER

The James Collection is renowned as the world's largest comprehensive quilt collection. Recognized in 1998 as one of the top 100 treasures in the United States by editors of *Art & Antiques* magazine, the collection contains approximately 1,000 quilts.

Robert and Ardis James aimed to gather together and share an international collection of museum-quality quilts from all time periods in one place. (Bob James would later describe it as doing "the impossible thing ... to have an absolutely comprehensive collection of quilts from all over the world. All types. All genres.") In so doing, they hoped to encourage a reevaluation of a previously underestimated art form.

But the collection didn't start out that way. It started simply—from a desire to share an interest together.

FROM A LOVE OF FABRIC TO THE BEGINNINGS OF A COLLECTION

Their collection grew from Ardis's love of fabric and Robert's joy in encouraging Ardis. Both had some familiarity with quilts—their mothers both quilted. And Ardis had formerly spent nine years as part owner of Threadneedle House, a fabric shop in Chappaqua, New York.

But the seed of collecting wasn't planted until 1979, when Ardis visited her sister-in-law in Troy, Michigan and attended a quilt show. She admired an old Mariner's Compass quilt. She bought it. The next year she returned to the annual show and bought two quilts. The following year she bought four quilts. The collecting bug was biting. She explained that if Bob was happy when she'd purchased one quilt, she'd make him even happier by buying more.

From the start, Bob encouraged her interest. In 1983 he joined her to attend a Tarrytown, New York show. As Ardis later explained, "Bob didn't want to be left out of the fun." Together they bought 13 quilts, proof that they now consciously considered themselves collectors.

Until now they had collected only antique quilts but broadened their scope to include contemporary work in 1983. Ardis had taken a quiltmaking workshop in the late 1970s from the artist Michael James at the Brookfield (CT) Craft Center. Bob, knowing she admired Michael's quilts, wanted to give her one for Christmas. Unable to pick from the six they were offered, Bob bought them all, to cover his bases (Plates 3.14 and 3.15). Ardis later credited Michael's influence, writing: "You can take much of the credit for getting us started on [collecting] contemporary work ... Had I not studied with you and always wanted one of your quilts, we might still be lost in the *Log Cabins*."

What began as an interest quickly grew into a passion. They aimed not only to form the broadest possible collection, but to share their interest with others, encouraging them to appreciate and begin collections of their own. They opened their home to artists, curators, and potential fellow collectors. Rather than hoard sources, they freely shared them.

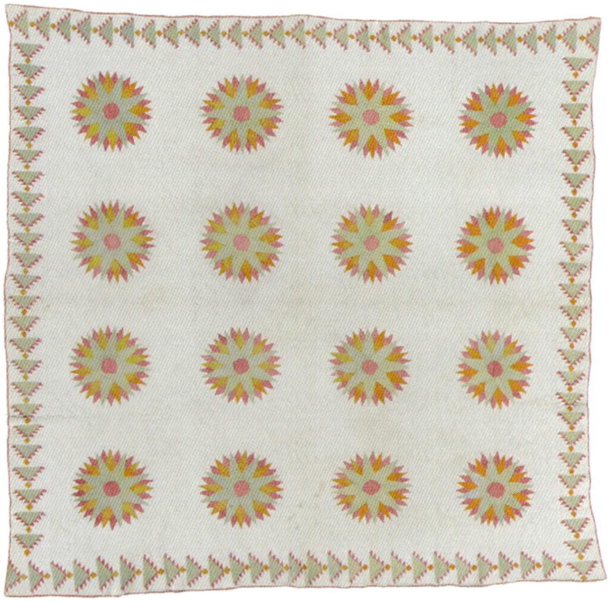

Mariner's Compass, *maker unidentified, United States, 1840-1860, Gift of the Robert and Ardis James Foundation, IQM 1997.007.0100.*

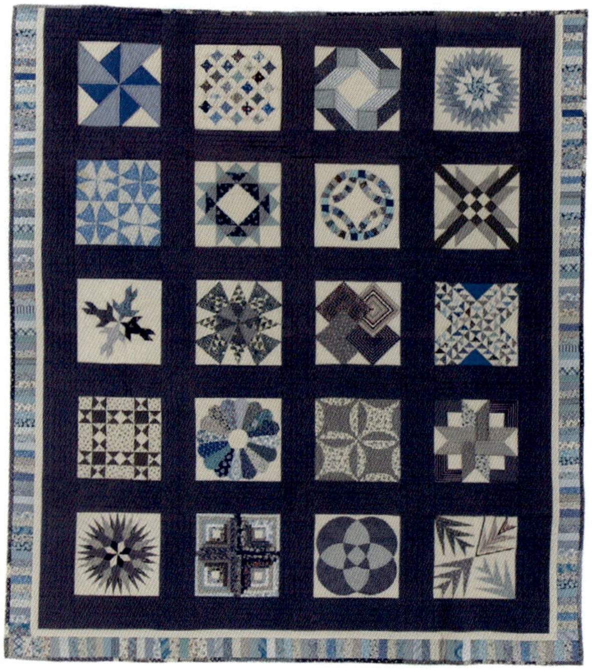

Ardis James's first quilt, Big Blue, *Chappaqua, New York, 1980, Gift of the Robert and Ardis James Foundation, IQM 2009.039.0065.*

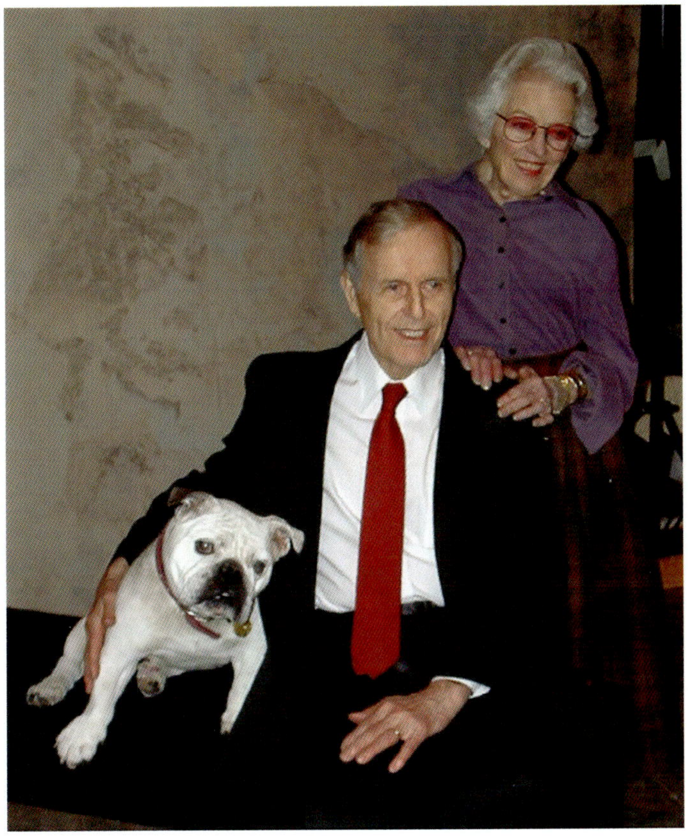

Ardis and Robert James with Beauty, a successor to English bulldog, Hoover, 2006.

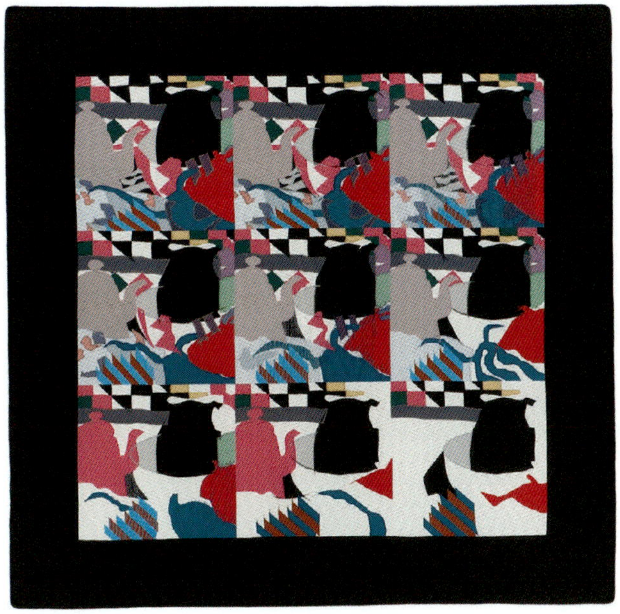

Pink Teapot, *Pauline Burbidge, Nottingham, U.K., 1987, Ardis and Robert James Collection, IQM 1997.007.1081.*

They also began traveling widely on quilt hunts. Artist Pauline Burbidge, then living in Nottingham, England, recalls an early visit from Ardis who—accompanied by her sister-in-law—was searching out contemporary quiltmakers in the U.K. "I was thrilled to have work purchased for their collection! ... I felt so honoured. It boosted my confidence and made me determined to continue to make quiltmaking my profession" (Plate 3.1).

Side Note: Pauline grew to have not only a long-term friendship with and patronage from the Jameses, but she also became the love object of their English bulldog, Hoover. Could he have recognized her as a fellow Brit? We wonder. Each time Pauline visited their home in Chappaqua, New York, where she and Ardis would sit out in the sunporch, Hoover would arduously boost himself up from his cushion by the doorway, waddle over, and snuffingly lavish his complete drooling attention on Pauline, his beloved. Hoover was, in his own way, a canine curator.

CONNECTING WITH CONSULTANTS

Before long the Jameses knew the top quilt dealers and galleries, but often sought advice from consultants who "knew people who knew people." These experts would find quilts before they were snapped up by galleries. Bob and Ardis began working with the late San Francisco quilt dealer, Michael Kile of Kiracofe & Kile, who became an early advisor on antique quilts.

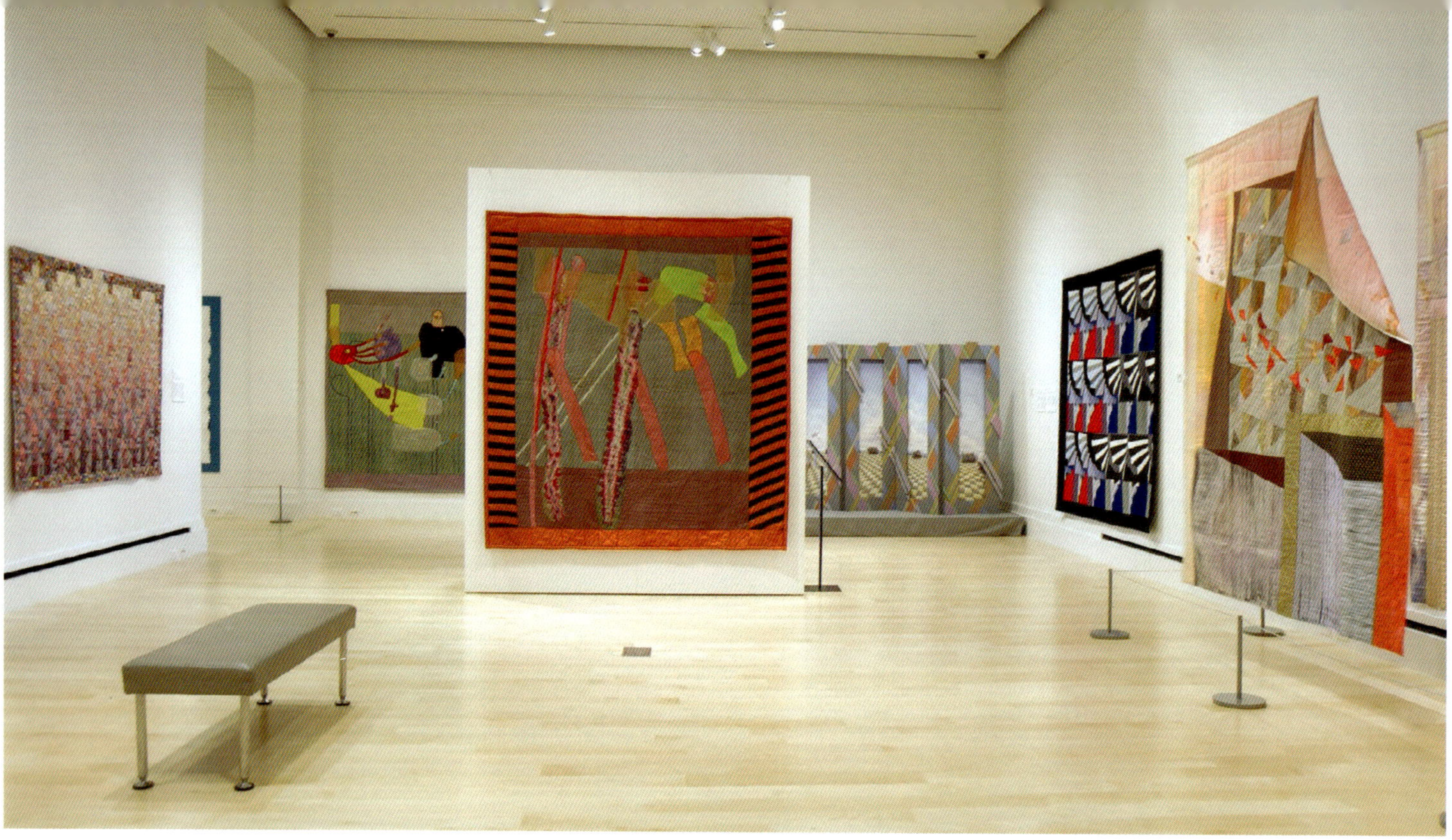

The Art Quilt Revisited, *an IQM reinstallation of nine of the works included in the original exhibition (2010). Photo by Randy Hampton.*

Michael had become newly interested in contemporary work after he and I curated *The Art Quilt*, a traveling museum exhibition of new quilts which opened in 1986. (The James Collection includes these pieces from *The Art Quilt*: Plates 3.2, 3.17, 3.20). Michael always liked putting people together—he was what Malcom Gladwell would call a Connector. He told Bob and Ardis they might like to work with me to build their contemporary collection.

It was, of course, a dream job. I could "acquire" art and lose myself in thinking about what to pursue. And it was a project full of joy. I made both the collectors *and* the artists happy. But I didn't have to actually pay for or care for the works myself (Plate 3.21).

I was then the three-day-a-week corporate art curator for Owens-Corning Corporation in Toledo, Ohio, and as such made regular art-buying trips to New York City. In my free time I would hop on a train heading for Chappaqua, to meet Ardis at the station. We would spend entire afternoons studying slides and catalogs, endlessly discussing various artists and plotting acquisition aims.

Ardis once summed up her collecting goal this way: "I want a collection that's extraordinary, one that attracts people from many different vantage points, for a variety of reasons."

From the start we didn't define collecting categories or themes. Instead, we watched the best quilt artists in the field, and tried to buy their best new work. We also bought some older pieces that artists had intentionally hung onto. Often these quilts were the ones artists considered among their strongest (Plates 3.3, 3.16). We agreed it was fine to buy several pieces by the same artist. We didn't feel it needed to be a "one of these, and one of those" collection.

I also thought it better to buy one wonderful quilt, rather than three less interesting ones available for the same total price. I tried to push them in some directions they may not have understood at the time, but they were very open. Almost always it was "yes." (Four James Collection contemporary quilts made it into the Top 100 Quilts of the Century, as selected by a panel of experts in 1999: Plates 3.4, 3.5, 3.18, 3.22).

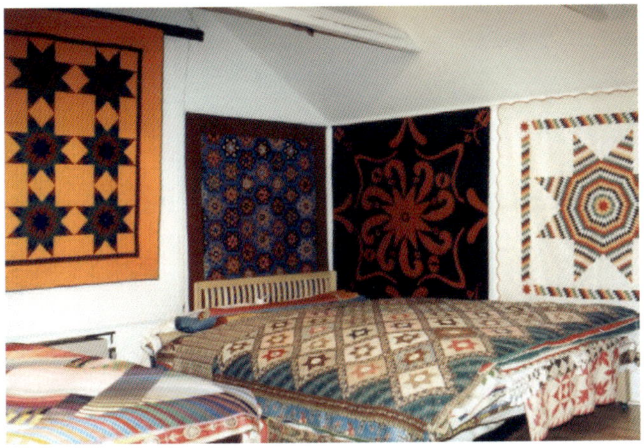

The Jameses' storage area in their home in Chappaqua, New York, 1990s. Bias Cut *by Michael James can be seen lying flat on a bed in the lower left corner of the photograph.*

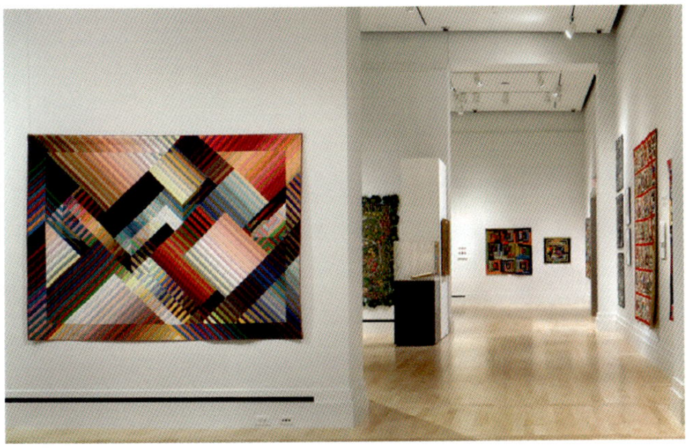

Bias Cut *on display in the 2008 IQM exhibition,* Quilts in Common. *Photo by Aaron Esto.*

Of course, the Jameses weren't just sitting back, waiting for me to bring them leads. They would often suggest artists themselves. And Ardis, (who as anyone who knew her can confirm, was an incredibly prolific and witty correspondent) would reach out to artists, sometimes even visiting their studios. In this way they often formed relationships with quilt artists new to me. Patrick Dorman comes to mind (Plate 3.7).

On our afternoons together on her sunny porch, Ardis would fix us lunch, often a delicious homemade soup, from a recipe clipped from a recent magazine. She read widely, was quite intuitive and thoughtful about her friends' likes and interests, and constantly clipped out cartoons or articles she felt they might like. Seldom was mail from Ardis opened without *New Yorker* cartoons fluttering out.

That kind of observant interest and attention to detail carried right over to the quilts. Ardis noticed everything. She wrote of Wendy Huhn's quilt *The Happy Homemaker* in the catalogue for the 1995 exhibition *Contemporary Quilts from the James Collection* (Plate 3.8):

> When I first saw this quilt, I wished for more contrast in the darker rows so that I could more clearly see the figures against the background. However, closer acquaintance brought a feeling that the dark on dark was the quiltmaker's intention, and that if I need to look more closely, that's exactly what I should be doing.

THE PERFECT COLLECTING TEAM

As collectors, they were a perfect combination. Ardis was in the forefront, taking the lead on acquisition decisions. She kept track of artists and was genuinely interested in their lives. Bob was a natural collector. Once interested in a collecting field, he wanted to know it all, and discover things people weren't already collecting. He saw the big picture: how far the collection could grow, where it could go, and its potential impact.

By 1988 the quilts had overtaken their home. They hung many quilts, storing the rest in stacks laying flat on beds all around, folded in linen closets and even in a painstakingly fabric-lined clothes chute. But as their collection grew, resulting in borrowing requests for this or that show, it became increasingly difficult for Ardis to unearth those specified quilts which might easily rest in the middle or bottom of a pile. Bob's solution? They built a spacious 22 ft. x 30 ft., cathedral-ceilinged gallery and workroom above their garage. ("Bob never does things halfway," Ardis explained.) This added ample wall space for displaying recent acquisitions, even the largest quilts, and plenty of special platforms to hold the quilts flat, avoiding fold lines. I remember how fun it was for them to go up there and enjoy taking fresh looks at quilts they owned. It also made it much easier for Ardis to give quilt tours to their increasing number of interested visitors.

CHAMPIONING CONTEMPORARY QUILTS AND FINDING THEIR COLLECTION A HOME

After collecting a mere 10 years, their collection had become so noted they were invited to mount an exhibit in Japan (complete with a 128-page catalogue—*Quilts: The James Collection*—including a message from the U.S. Ambassador there). The request was for antique quilts. The Jameses insisted 10 contemporary works be included (these included Plates 3.9, 3.10, 3.15, and 3.19).

Their championing of modern quilts made a profound and lasting difference to the artists. Terrie Hancock Mangat, included in the Japanese show, recalls, "The Jameses collecting my early work was of the upmost importance to me. Their patronage verified the value and strength of the work and put it in a collection where it is safe and honored" (Plate 3.23).

Michael James credited Ardis and Bob with support throughout his long artistic career, stating: "Their enthusiasm for and support of my own work made it possible for me to work for two and a half decades as an independent maker and sustain a studio tradition that has evolved and grown."

As they built their collection, they naturally began discussing plans for its future home. They spent years visiting and considering potential institutions. They sought a museum willing to accept the entire collection, not cherry-pick from it. They wanted their quilts exhibited regularly, not held forever captive in storage. Bob's deal-making expertise came into play as they worked out the logistics of donating their collection and confidently settled on the University of Nebraska-Lincoln.

Whenever I think of the James Collection, I remember the joy this joint project brought them. I imagine their fascinating nightly conversations discussing their latest acquisition or artistic discovery. I think of it as sharing their love for one another, each bringing unique strengths and talents to the endeavor. As I wrote in 1995: "the Jameses possess[ed] ...money to buy, eyes educated to recognize quality, time to study the field, boundless energy and love of the hunt."

And now the James Collection is spreading that love, bringing quilt knowledge and wonder to the visitors of the International Quilt Museum from around the world. Ardis's prescient dream of forming an extraordinary collection has come to fruition. And they did it together.

Note: Plates 3.1 – 3.13 appear in the exhibition, **An Evolving Vision: From the Studio.**

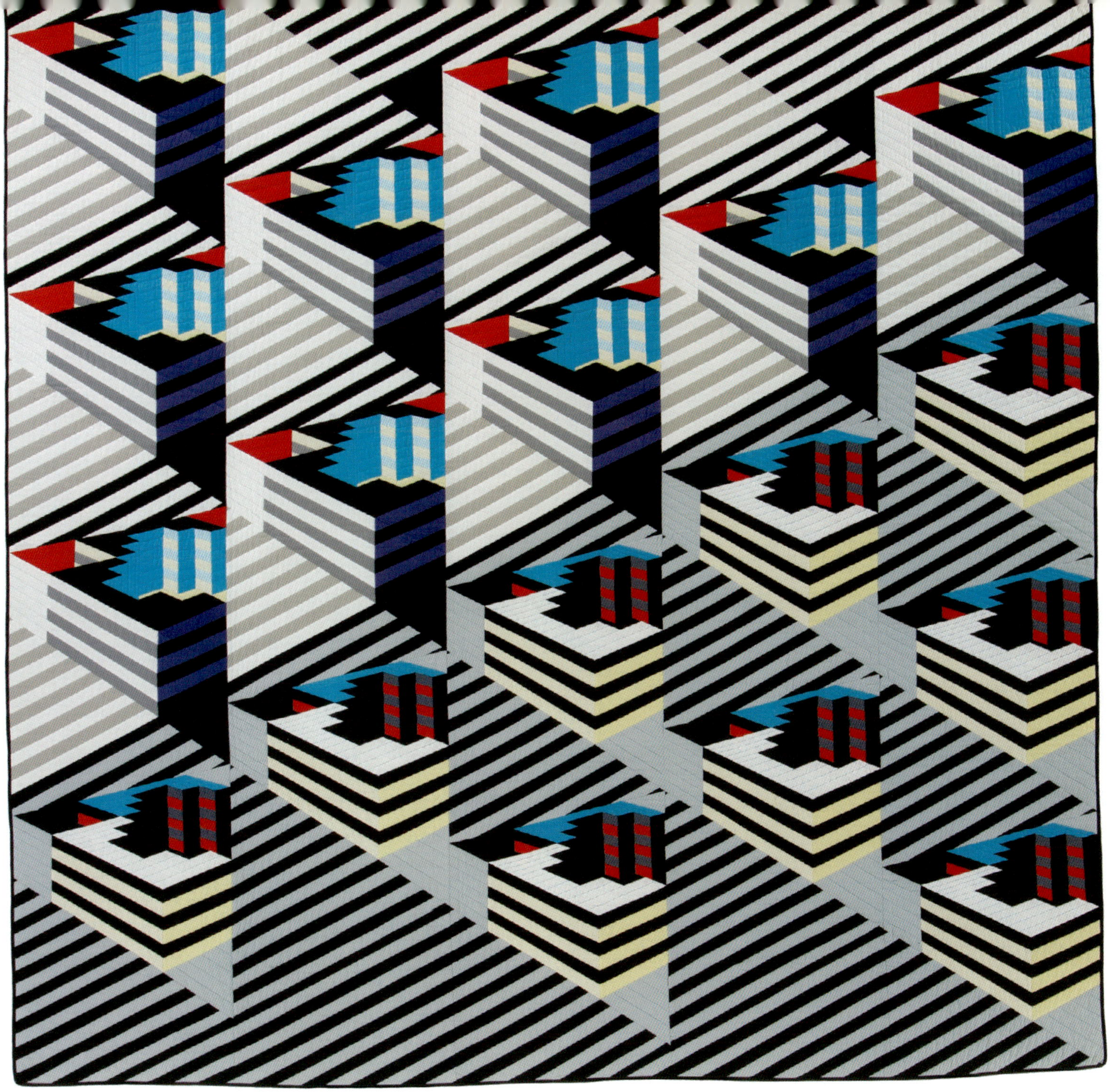

3.1

Finn

Pauline Burbidge
Nottingham, United Kingdom, 1983
Cotton; machine pieced (foundation) and machine quilted
93.5 x 91.5 in.

Ardis and Robert James Collection, IQM 1997.007.1070

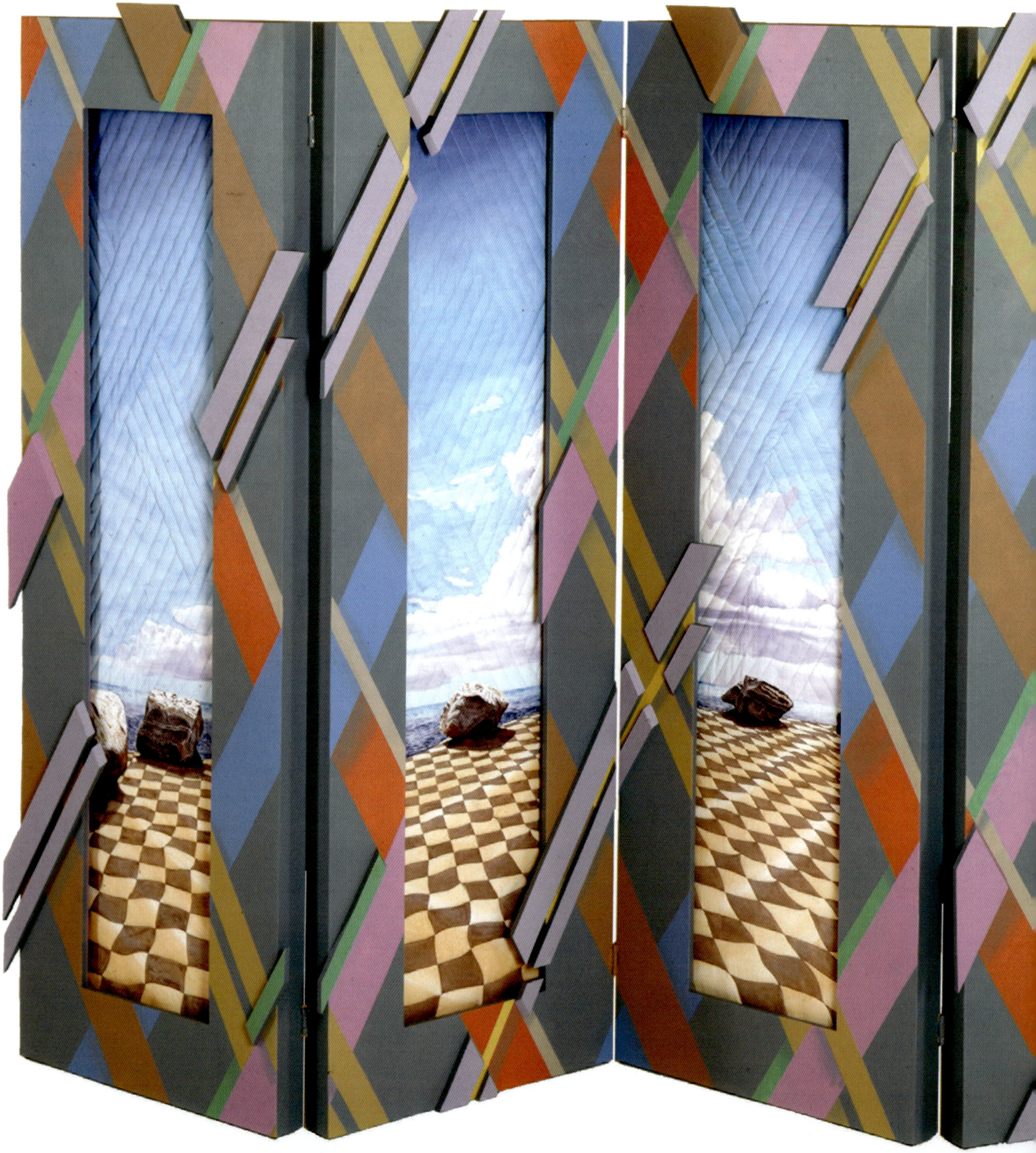

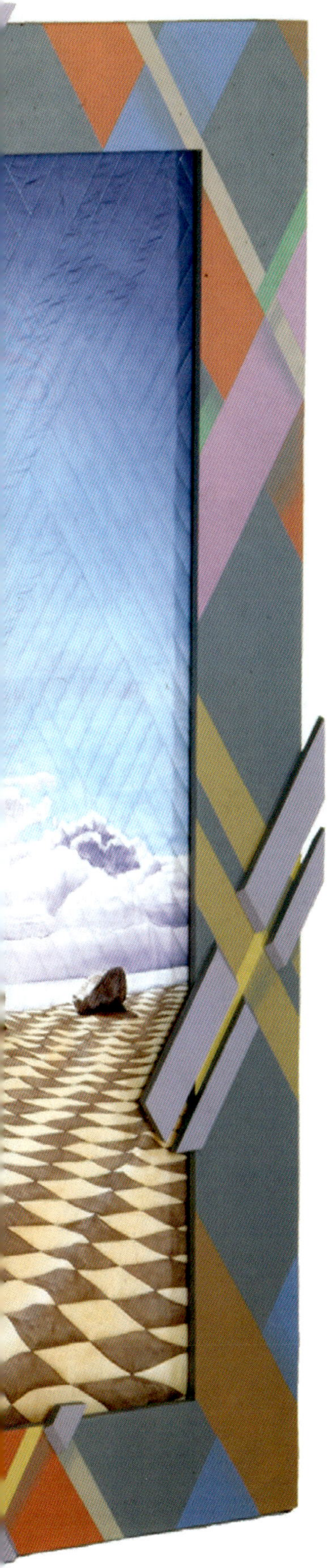

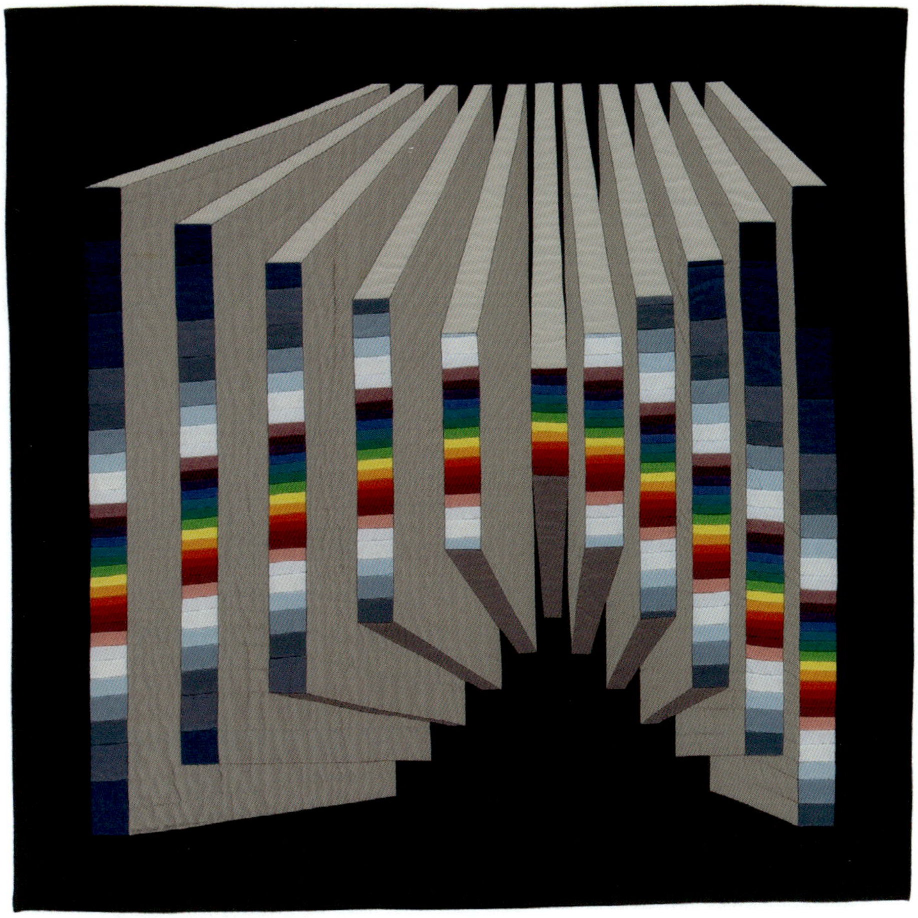

3.3

Night Rainbow 5: The Secondary Bow

Chris Wolf Edmonds
Lawrence, Kansas, 1982
Cotton; machine pieced and machine and hand quilted
48.5 x 48.5 in.

Ardis and Robert James Collection, IQM 1997.007.1002

3.2

Precipice

Gayle Fraas & Duncan Slade
North Edgecomb, Maine, 1985
Cotton, plywood; machine pieced, painted, machine quilted
72 x74 in.

Ardis and Robert James Collection, IQM 1997.007.1076

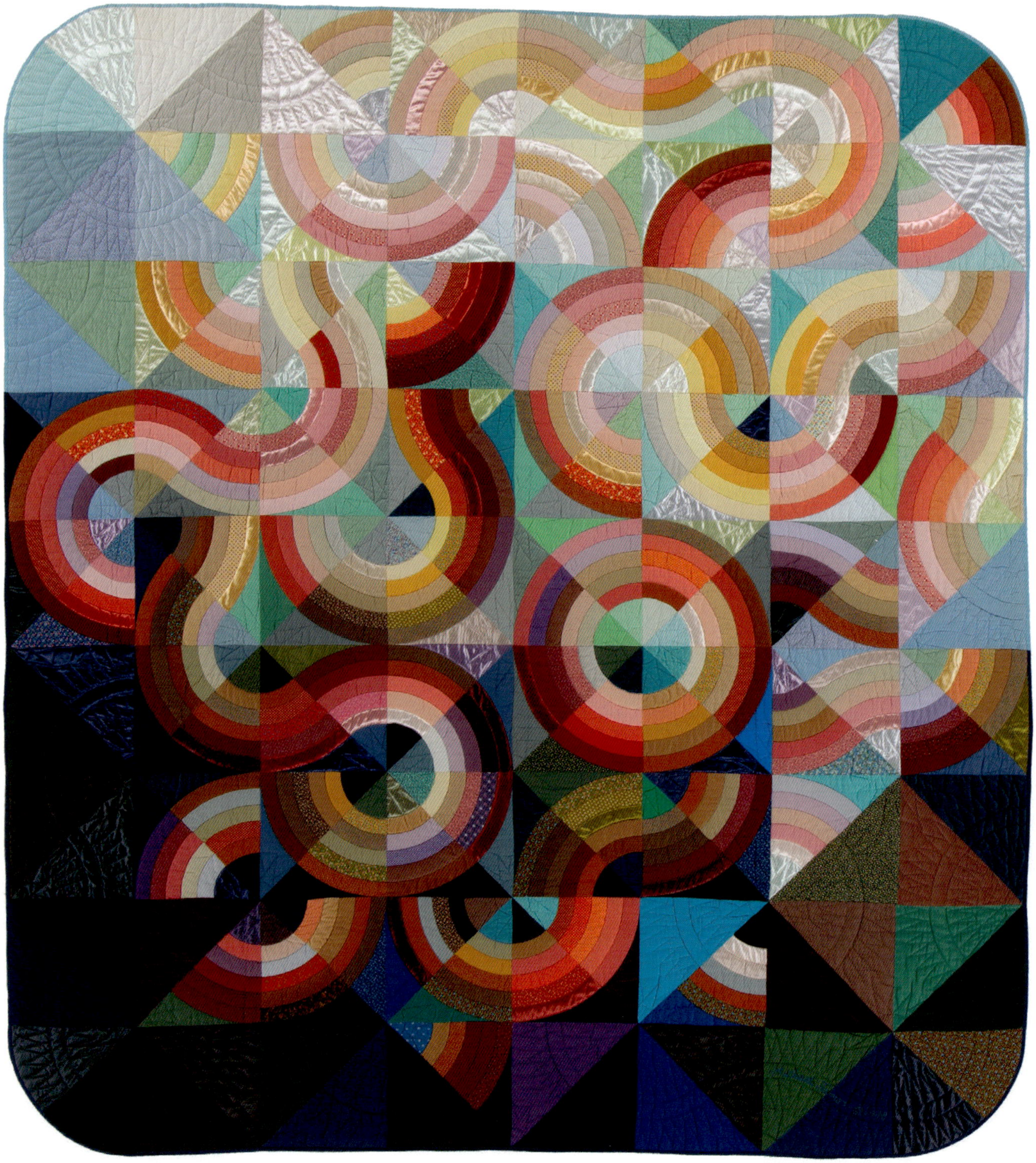

3.4

Aurora

Michael James
Somerset, Massachusetts, 1978
Cotton; hand pieced and quilted
91.5 x 89.5 in.

Ardis and Robert James Collection, IQM 1997.007.1080

3.7

Amur River

Patrick Dorman
Seattle, Washington, 1984
Cotton; hand appliquéd, machine pieced, hand quilted
89.5 x 67.5 in.

Ardis and Robert James Collection, IQM 1997.007.1078

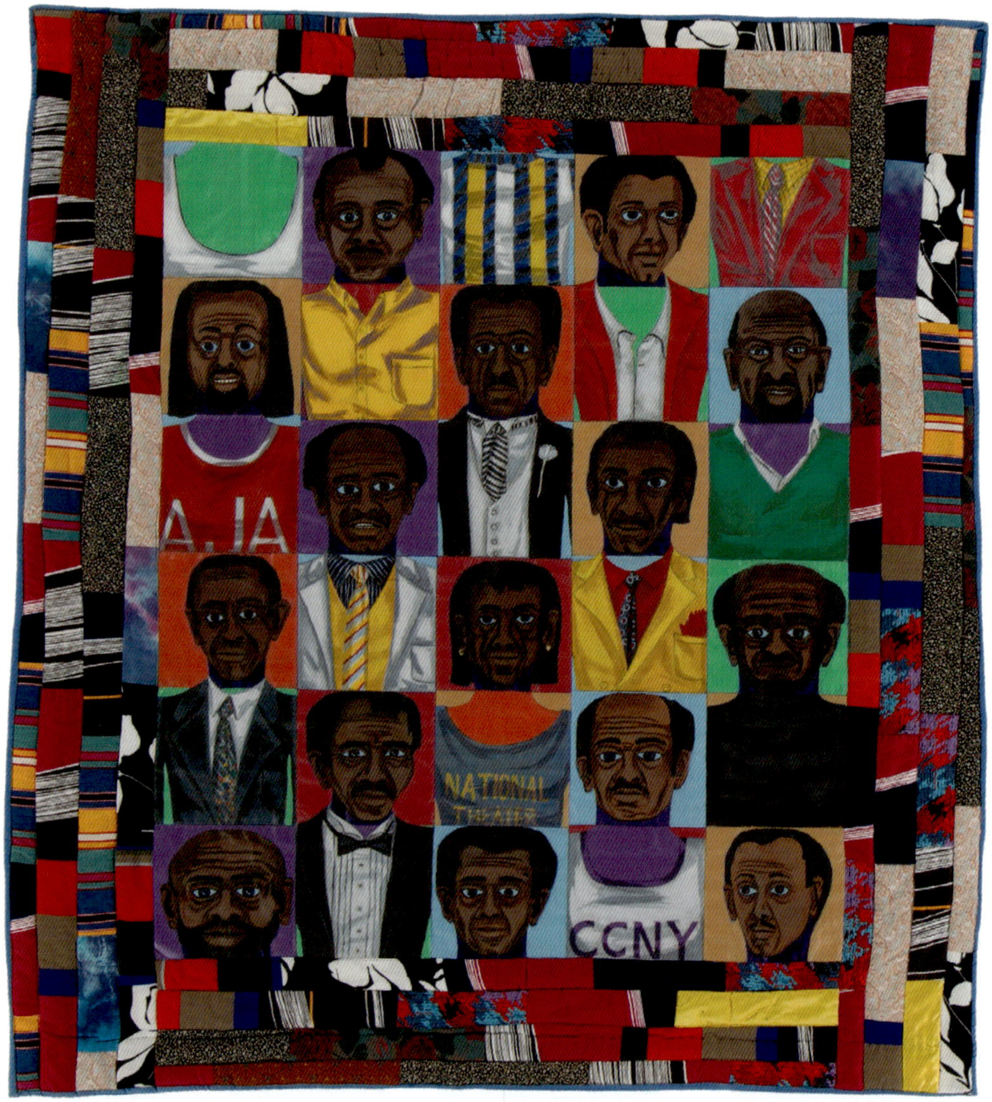

3.5

The Men: Mask Face Quilt #2

Faith Ringgold
New York, New York, 1986
Cotton; machine pieced, painted, machine quilted
69.5 x 62 in.

Ardis and Robert James Collection, IQM 1997.007.1083

3.6

The Women: Mask Face Quilt #1

Faith Ringgold
New York, New York, 1986
Cotton; machine pieced, painted, machine quilted
69 x 61.5 in.

Ardis and Robert James Collection, IQM 1997.007.1082

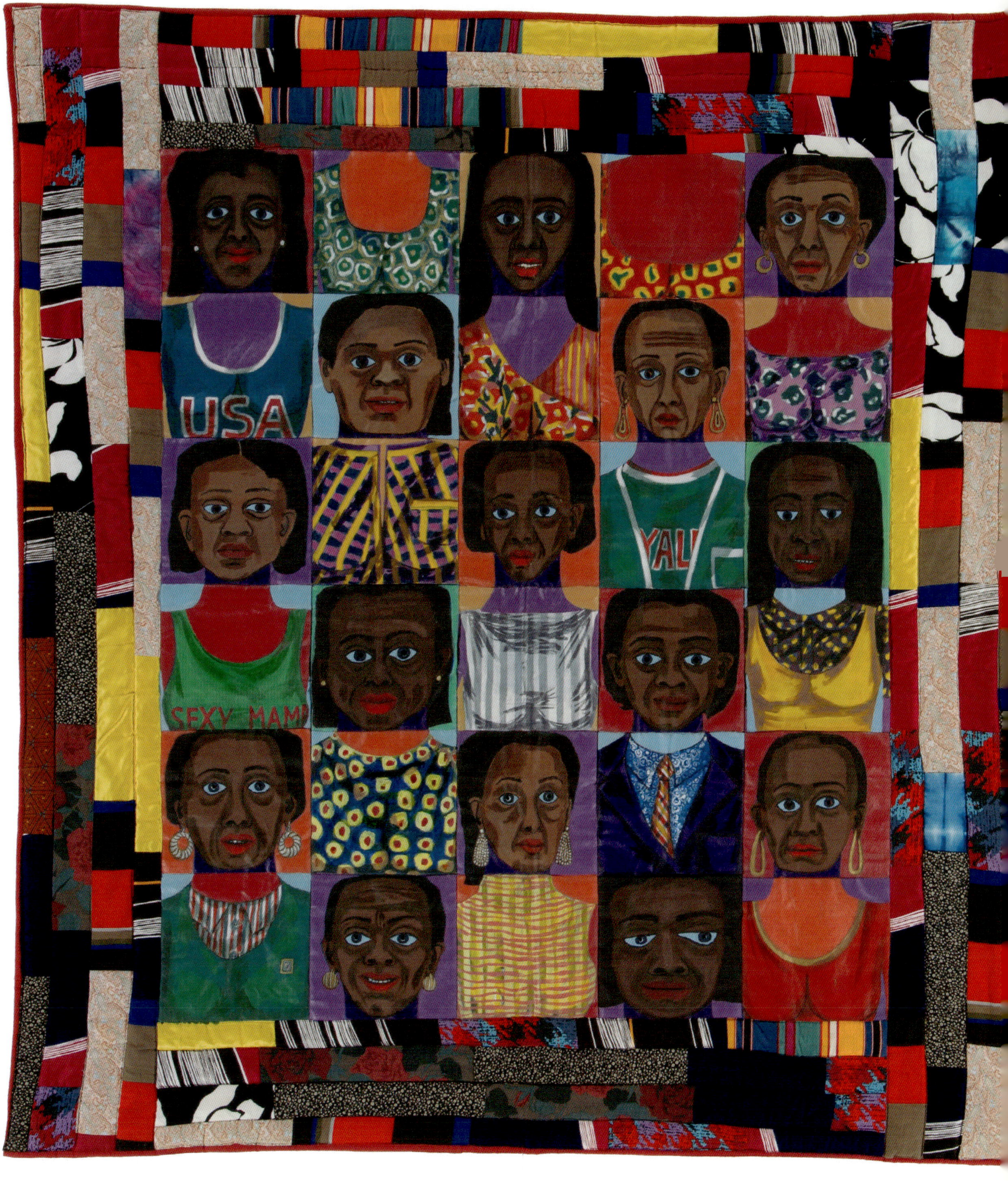
USA
YAL
SEXY MAM

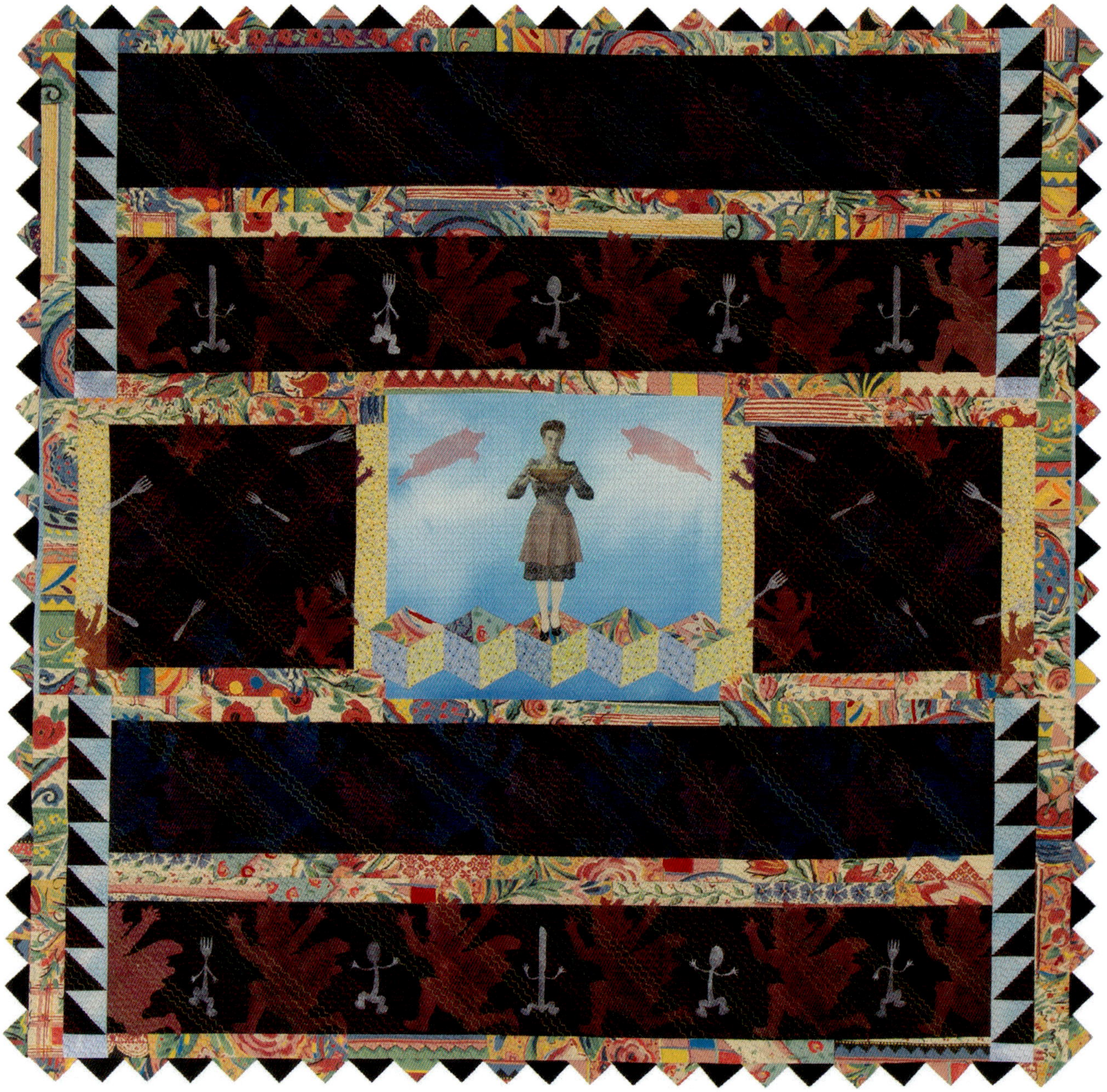

3.8

The Happy Homemaker

Wendy Huhn
Deter, Oregon, 1993
Cotton; machine pieced, screen-printed, machine quilted
73.5 x 74 in.

Ardis and Robert James Collection, IQM 1997.007.1106

3.9

Red and Blue Jar

Judith Larzelere
Newbury, Massachusetts, 1985
Cotton; machine pieced (foundation), no quilting
62.5 x 42 in.

Ardis and Robert James Collection, IQM 1997.007.1038

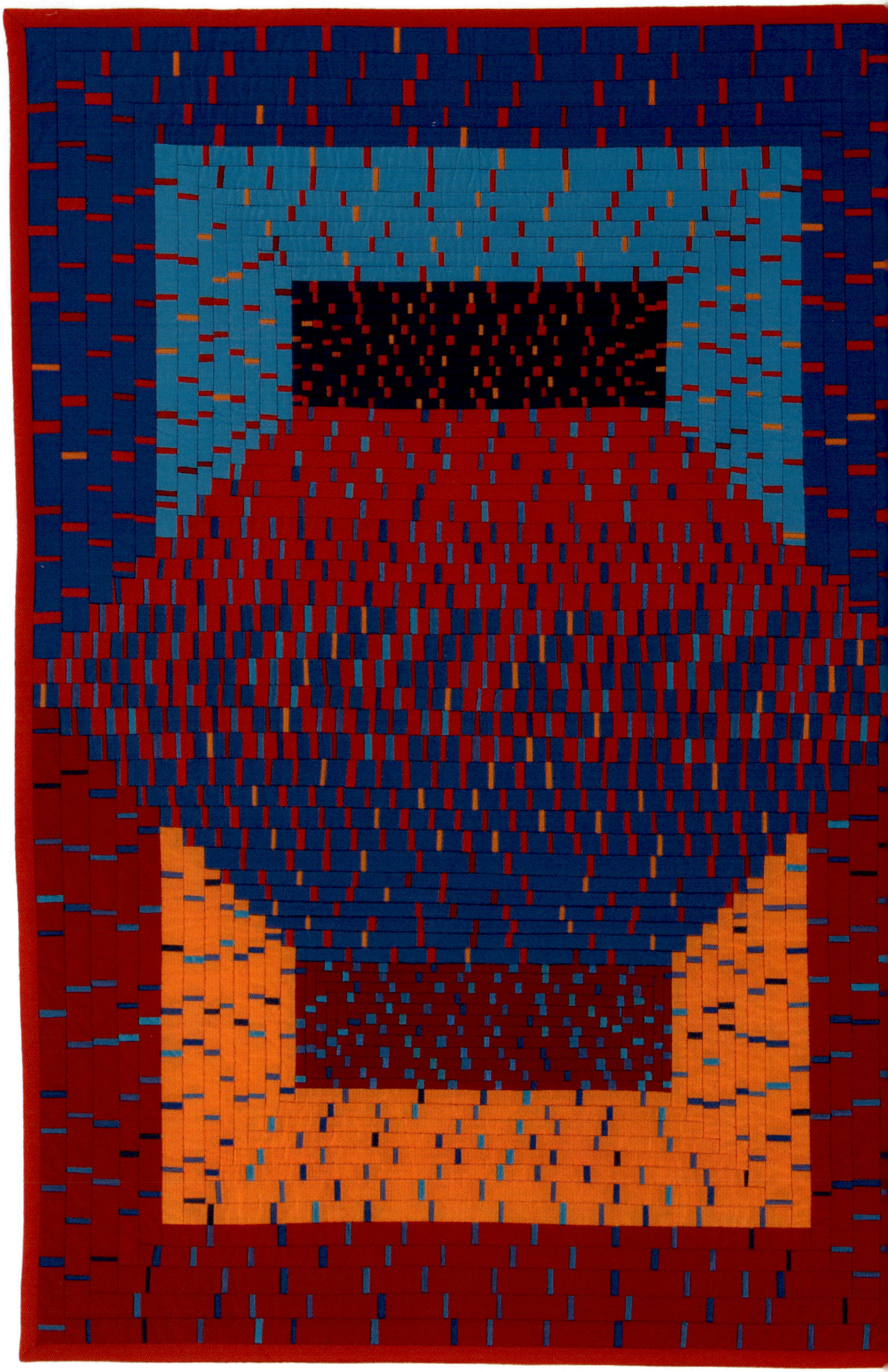

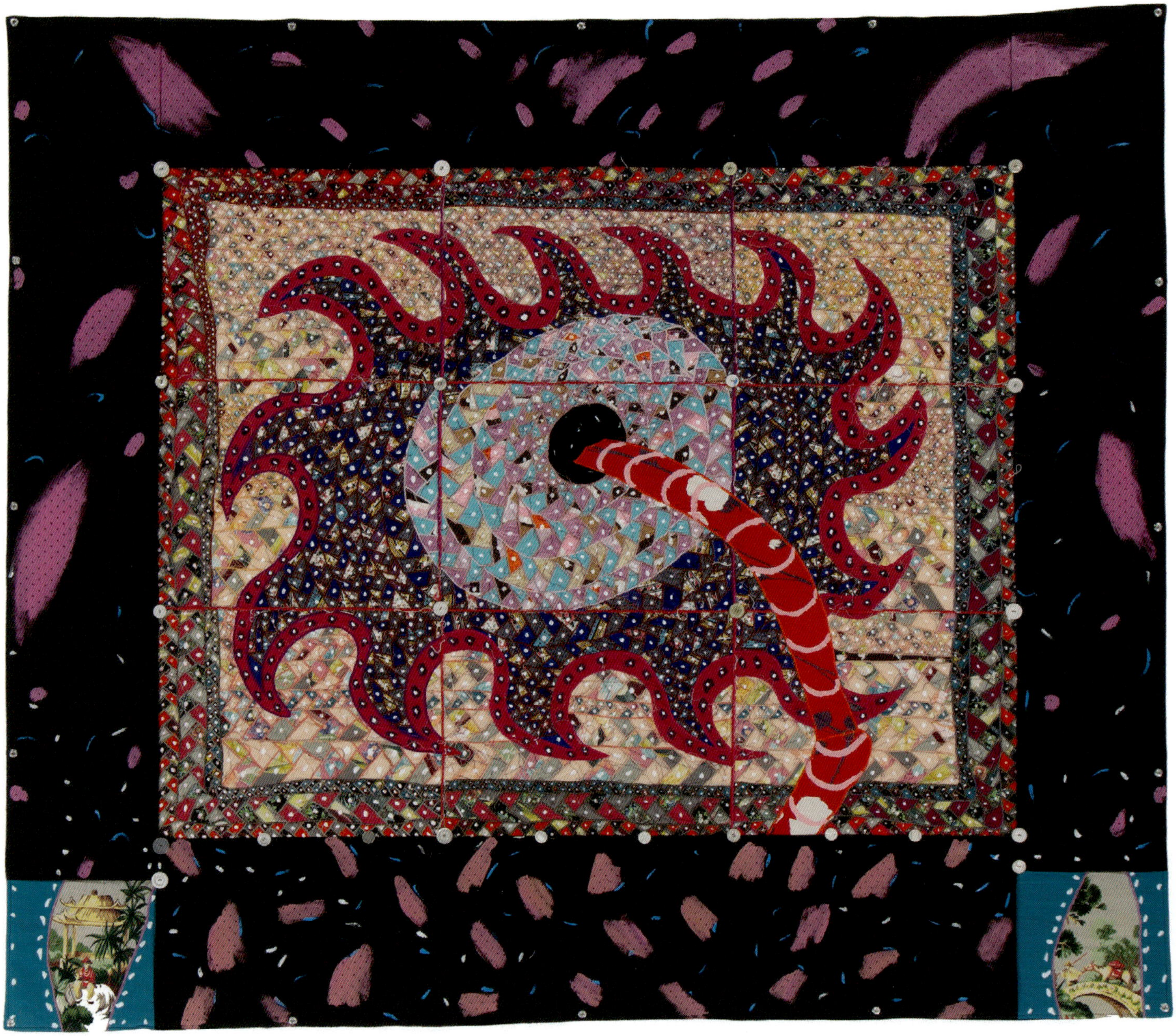

3.10

Sawblade

Therese May
San Jose, California, 1985
Cotton; machine pieced and appliquéd, no quilting
69 x 77 in.

Ardis and Robert James Collection, IQM 1997.007.1079

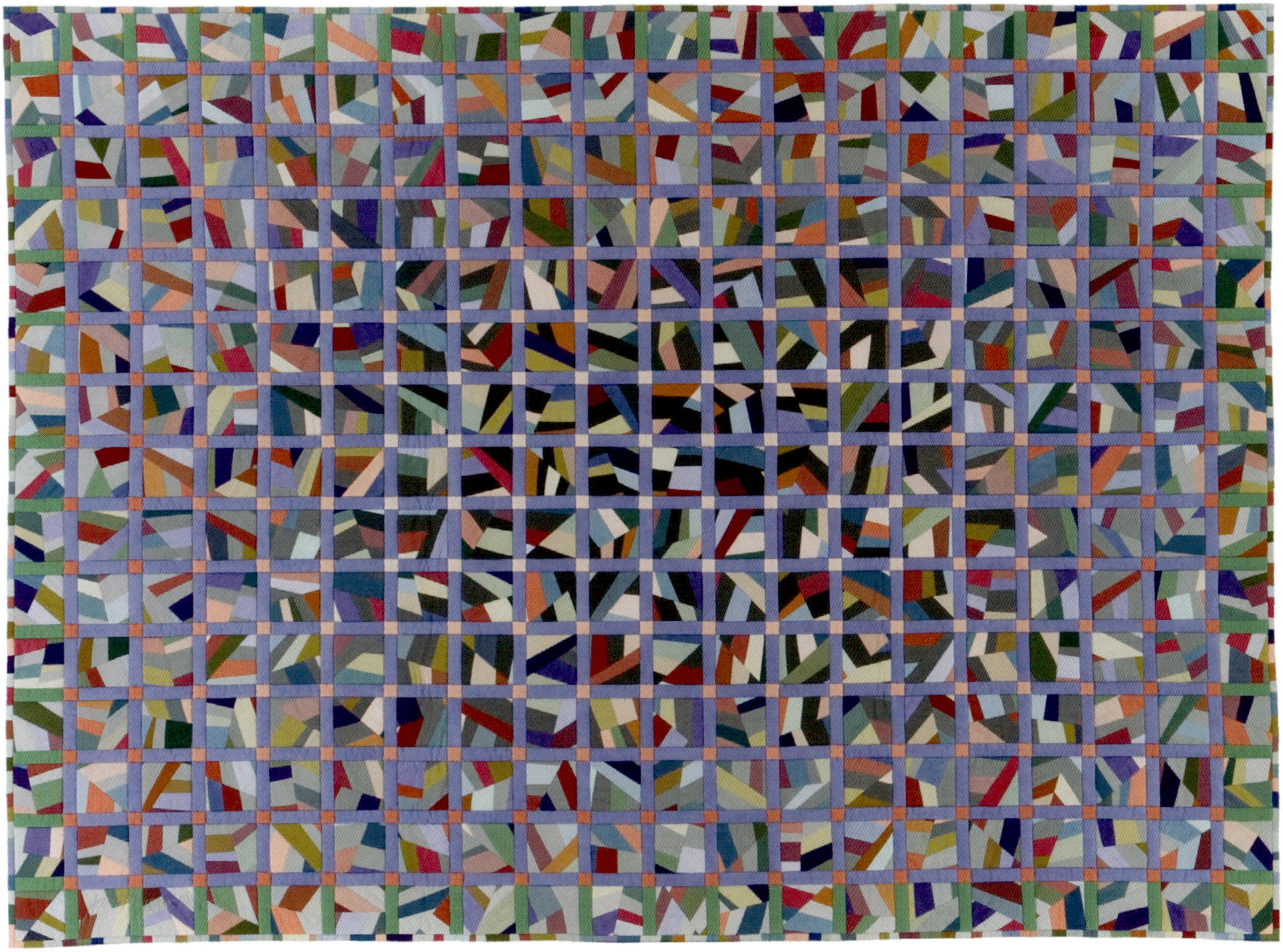

3.11

Morning Glory

Jan Myers (Newbury)
Minneapolis, Minnesota, 1987
Cotton; machine pieced and quilted
50 x 67 in.

Ardis and Robert James Collection, IQM 1997.007.1063

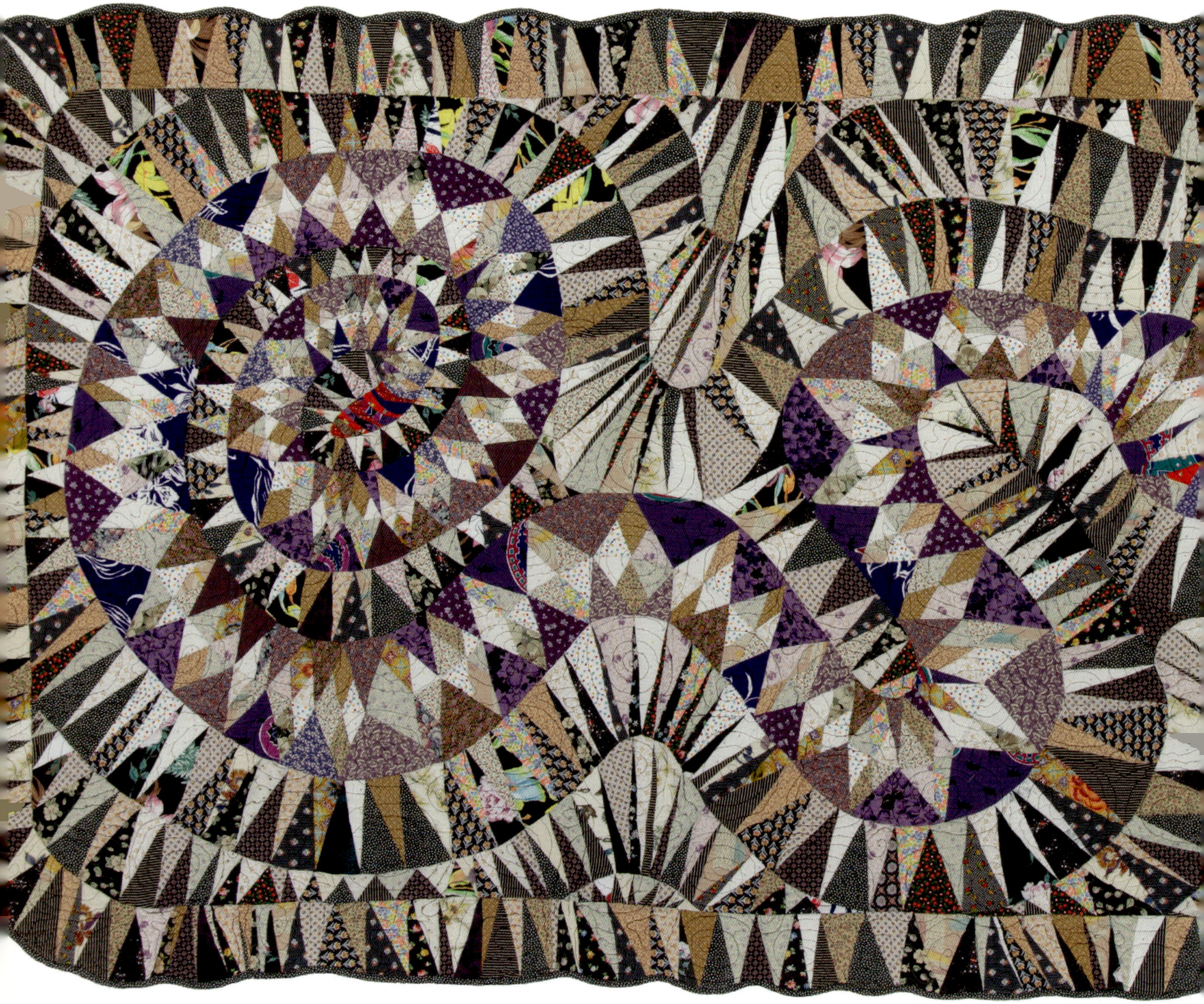

3.12

Snake

Helen Giddens
Mesquite, Texas, 1989
Cotton; machine pieced and quilted
68 x 105 in.

Ardis and Robert James Collection, IQM 1997.007.1090

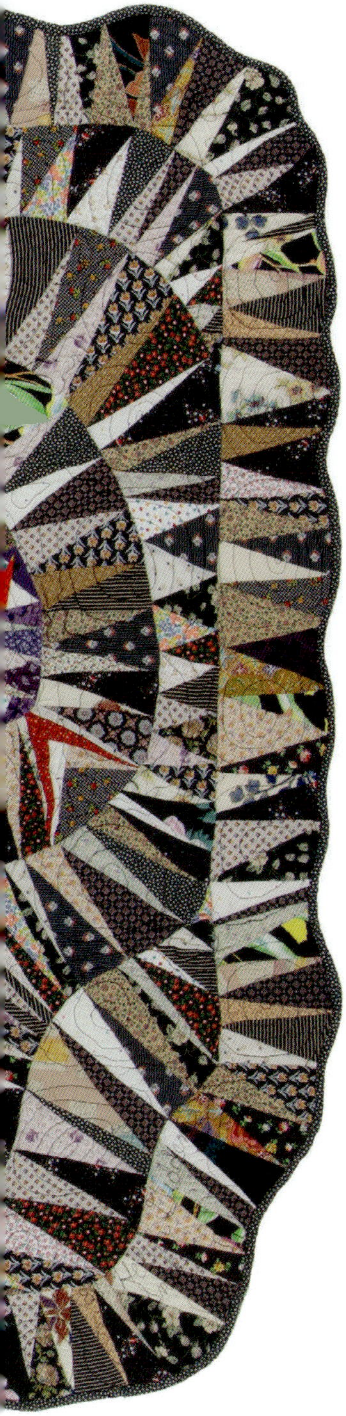

3.13

Gaia

Joan Lintault
Carbondale, Illinois, 1989
Cotton; hand printed, machine quilted
86 x 82.5 in.

Ardis and Robert James Collection, IQM 2009.039.0022

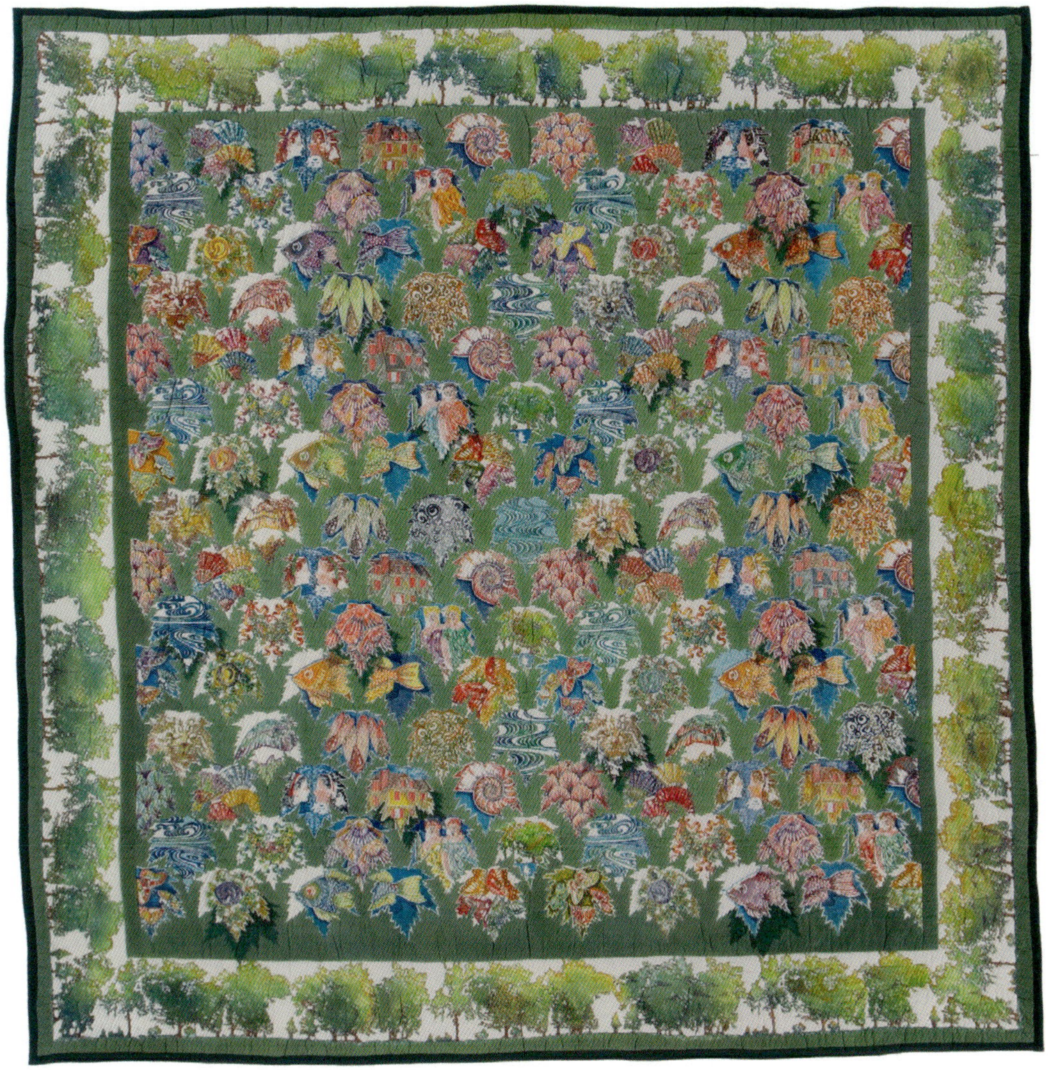

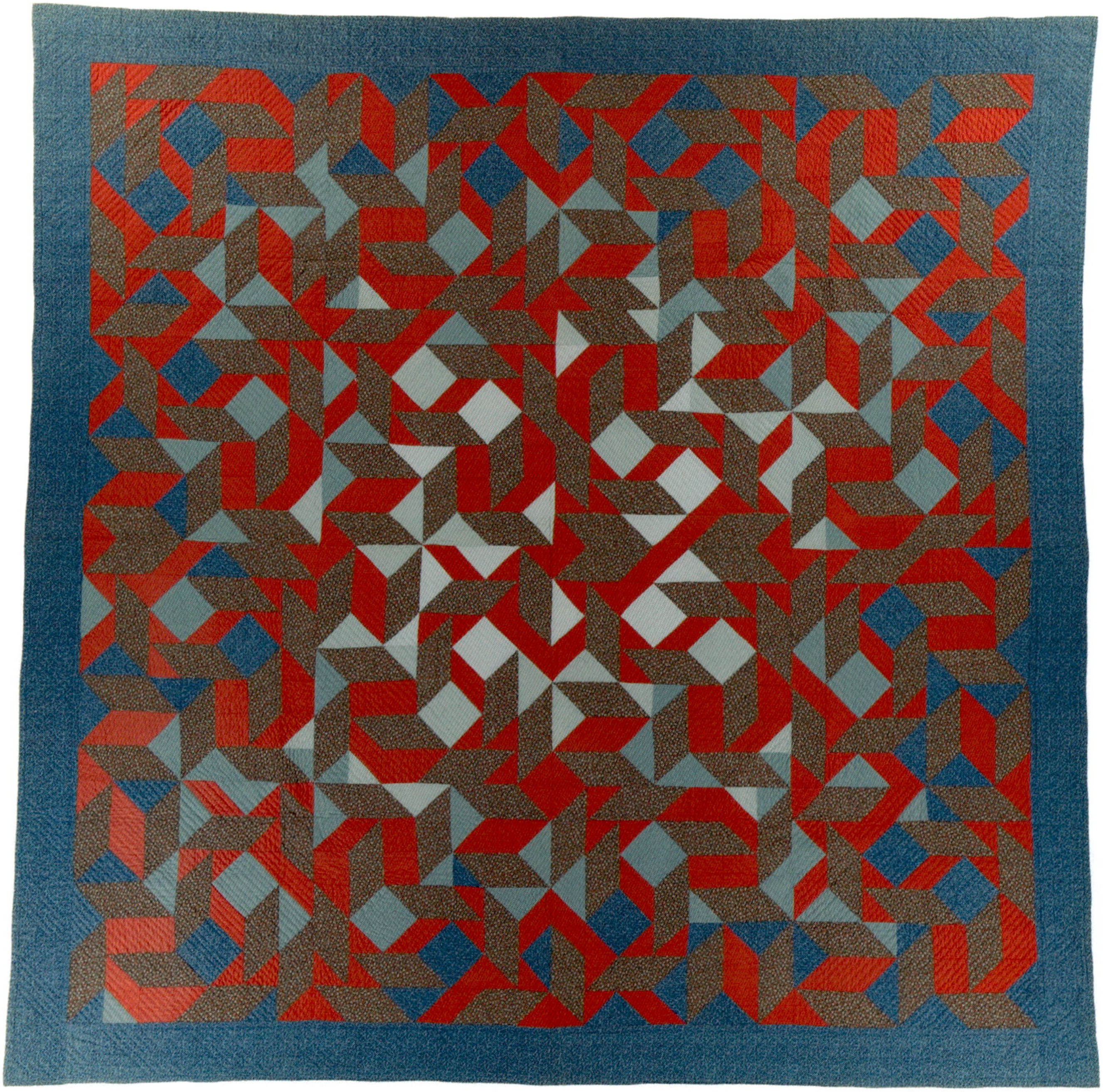

3.14

Elaborated Tangram

Michael James
Somerset, Massachusetts, 1976
Cotton; hand pieced and quilted
91.5 x 89.5 in.

Ardis and Robert James Collection, IQM 1997.007.1012

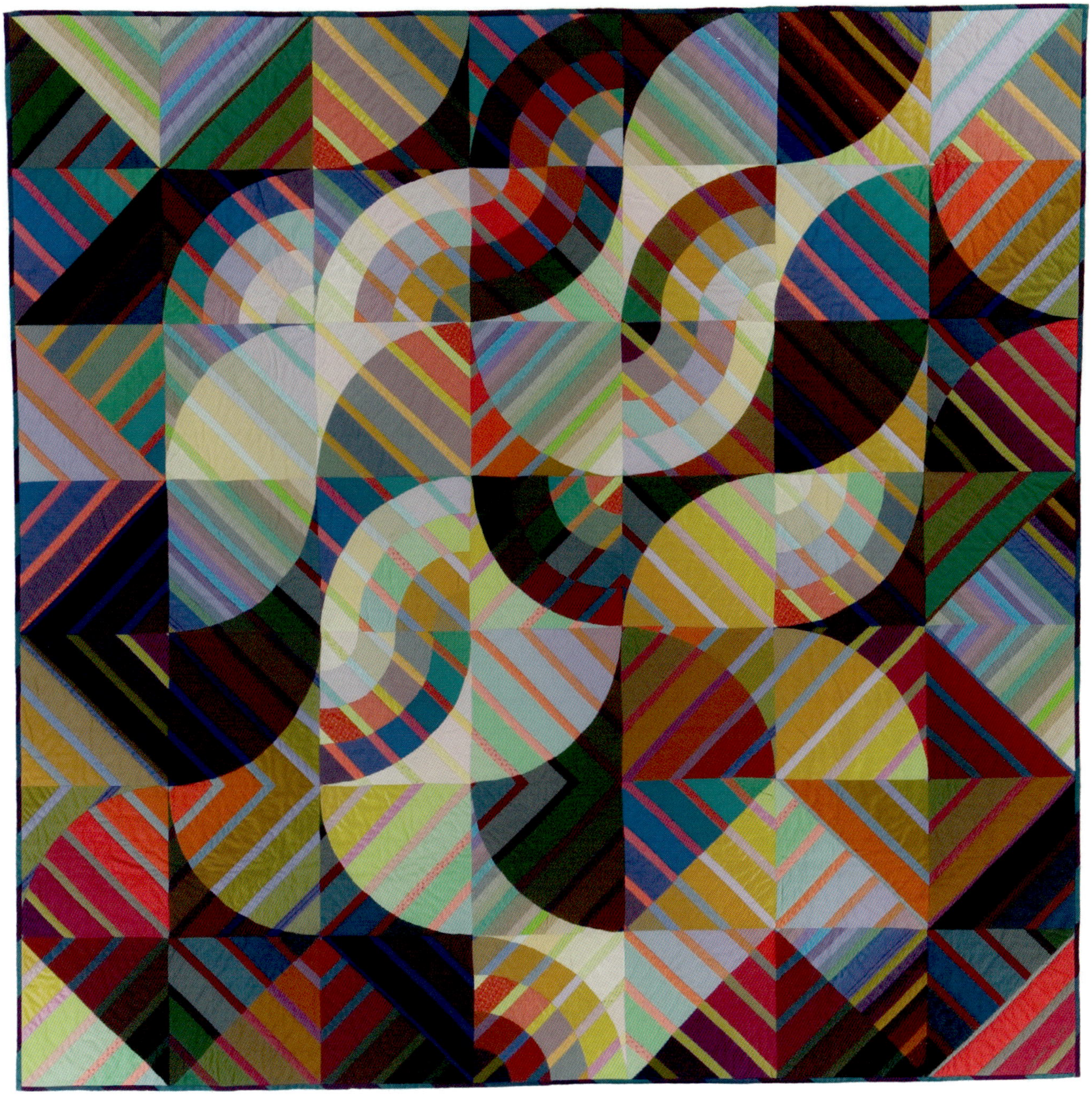

3.15

Blue Undercurrents

Michael James
Somerset, Massachusetts, 1983
Cotton; machine pieced and quilted
70.5 x 69 in.

Ardis and Robert James Collection, IQM 1997.007.1015

3.16

Starfire

Jean Ray Laury
Clovis, California, 1981
Cotton blend; machine pieced, hand quilted
50 x 59 in.

Ardis and Robert James Collection, IQM 1997.007.1031

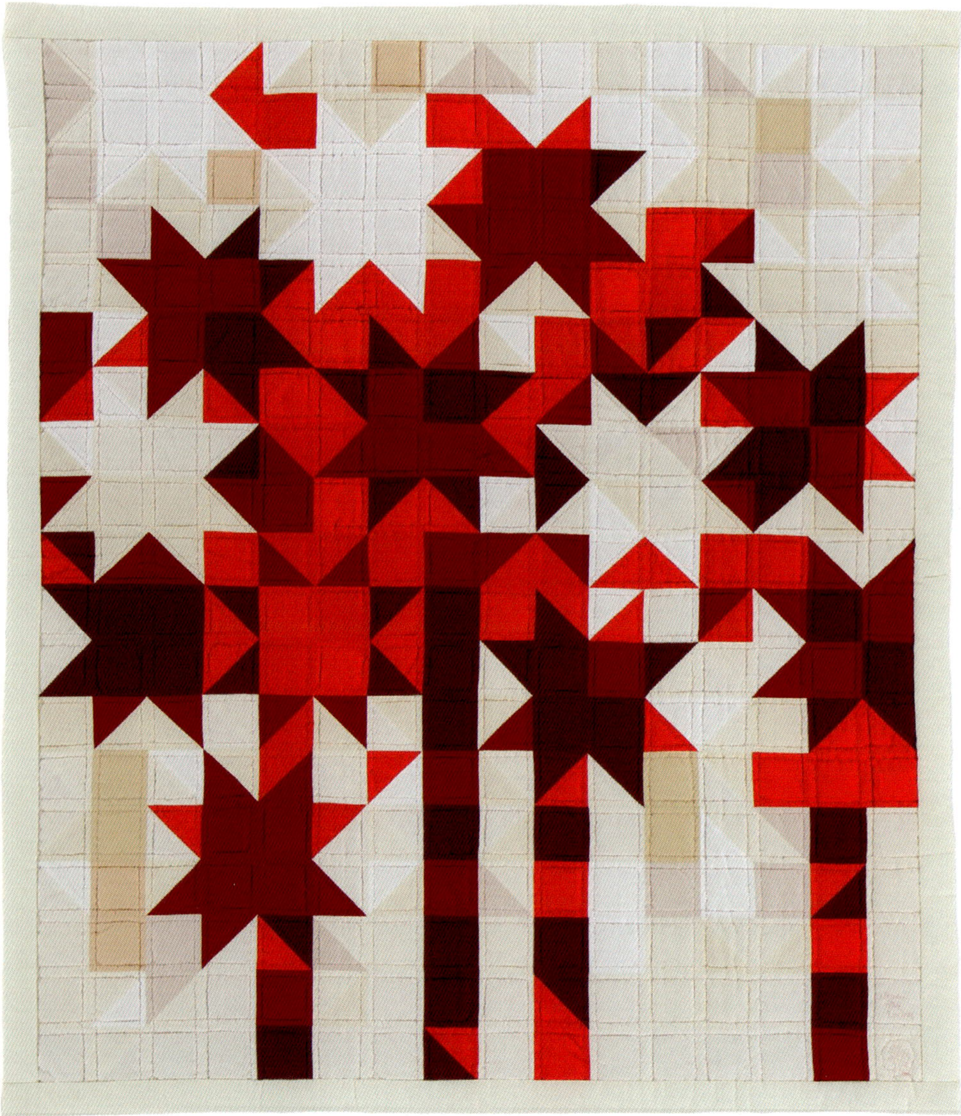

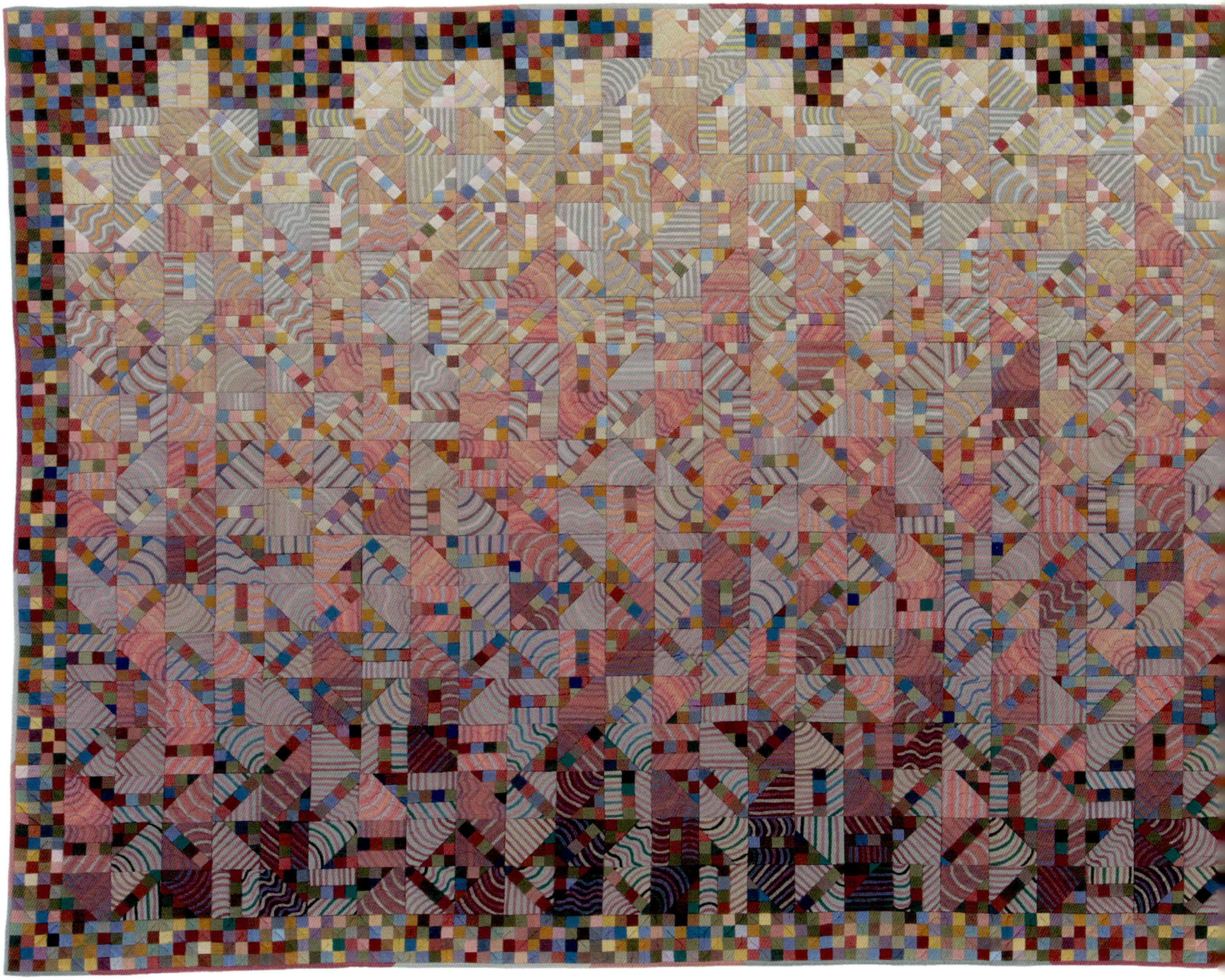

3.17

Number 47

Pamela Studstill
Pipe Creek, Texas, 1985
Cotton blends; machine pieced, painted, hand quilted
60.5 x 85 in.

Ardis and Robert James Collection, IQM 1997.007.1061

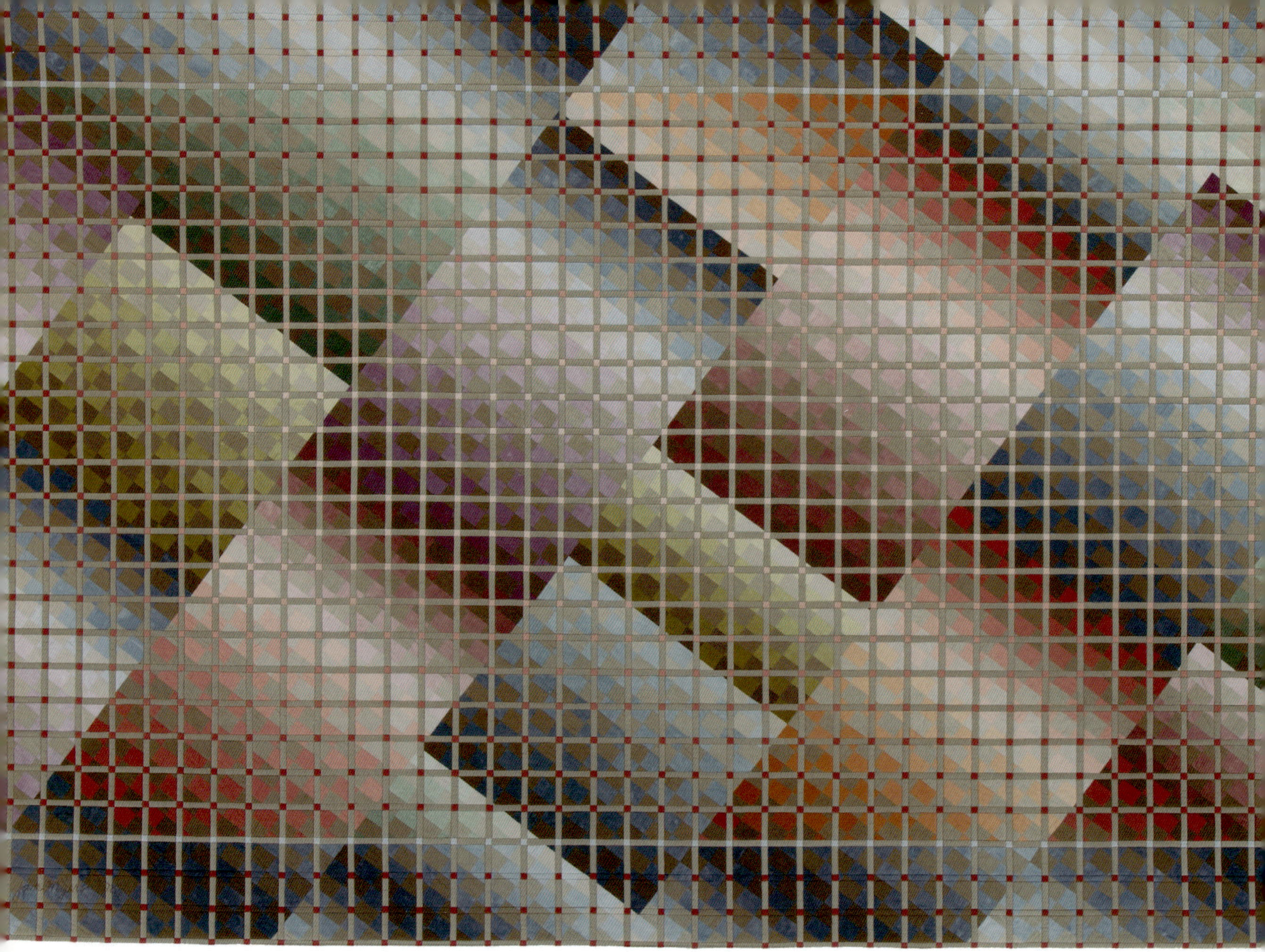

3.18

Depth of Field III: Plane View

Jan Myers (Newbury)
Minneapolis, Minnesota, 1985
Cotton; machine pieced and quilted
85.5 x 132 in.

Ardis and Robert James Collection, IQM 1997.007.1062

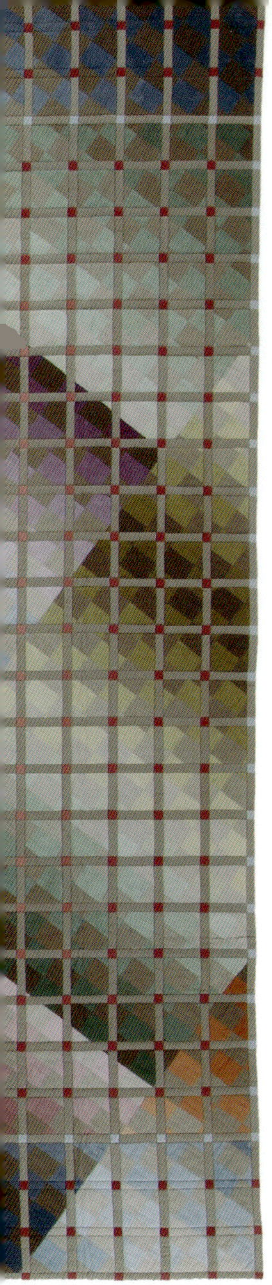

3.19

Number 53

Pamela Studstill
Pipe Creek, Texas, 1985
Cotton; machine pieced, hand quilted
70 x 76.5 in.

Ardis and Robert James Collection, IQM 1997.007.1066

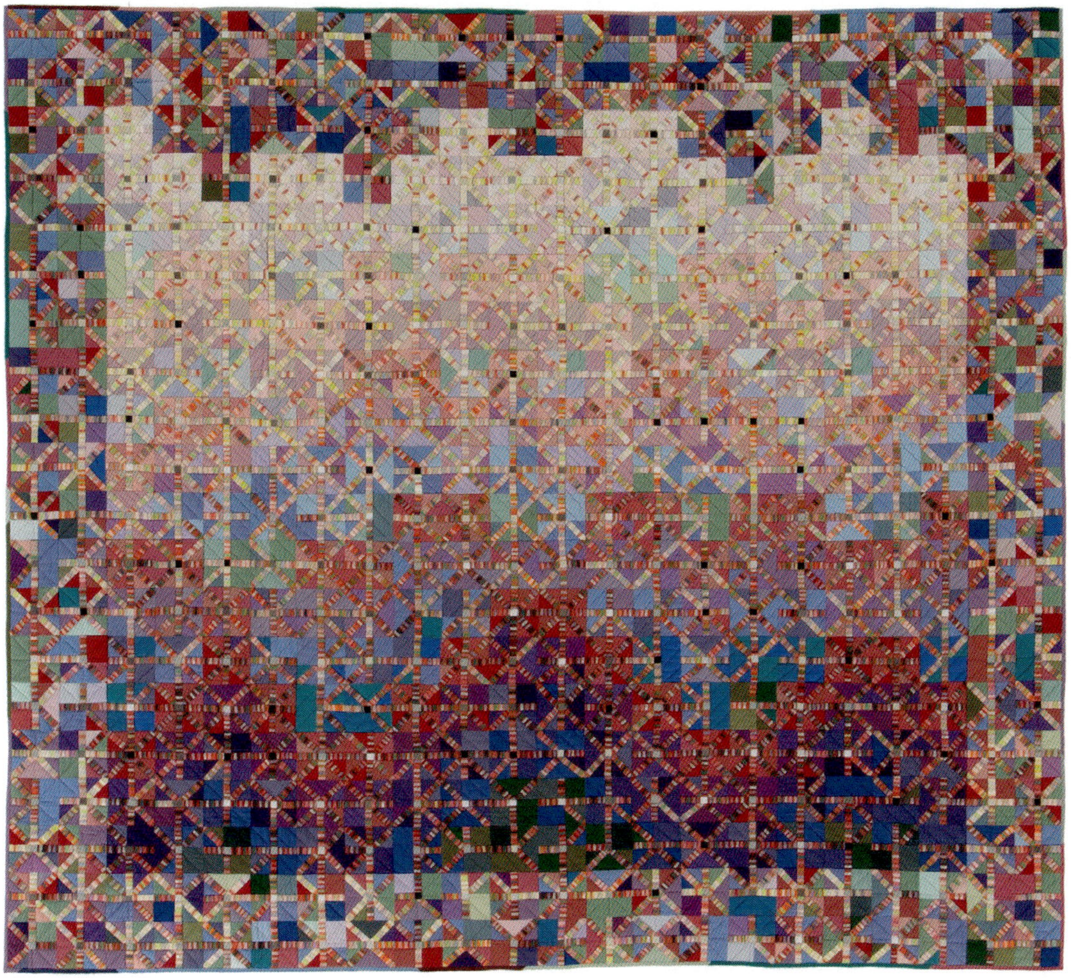

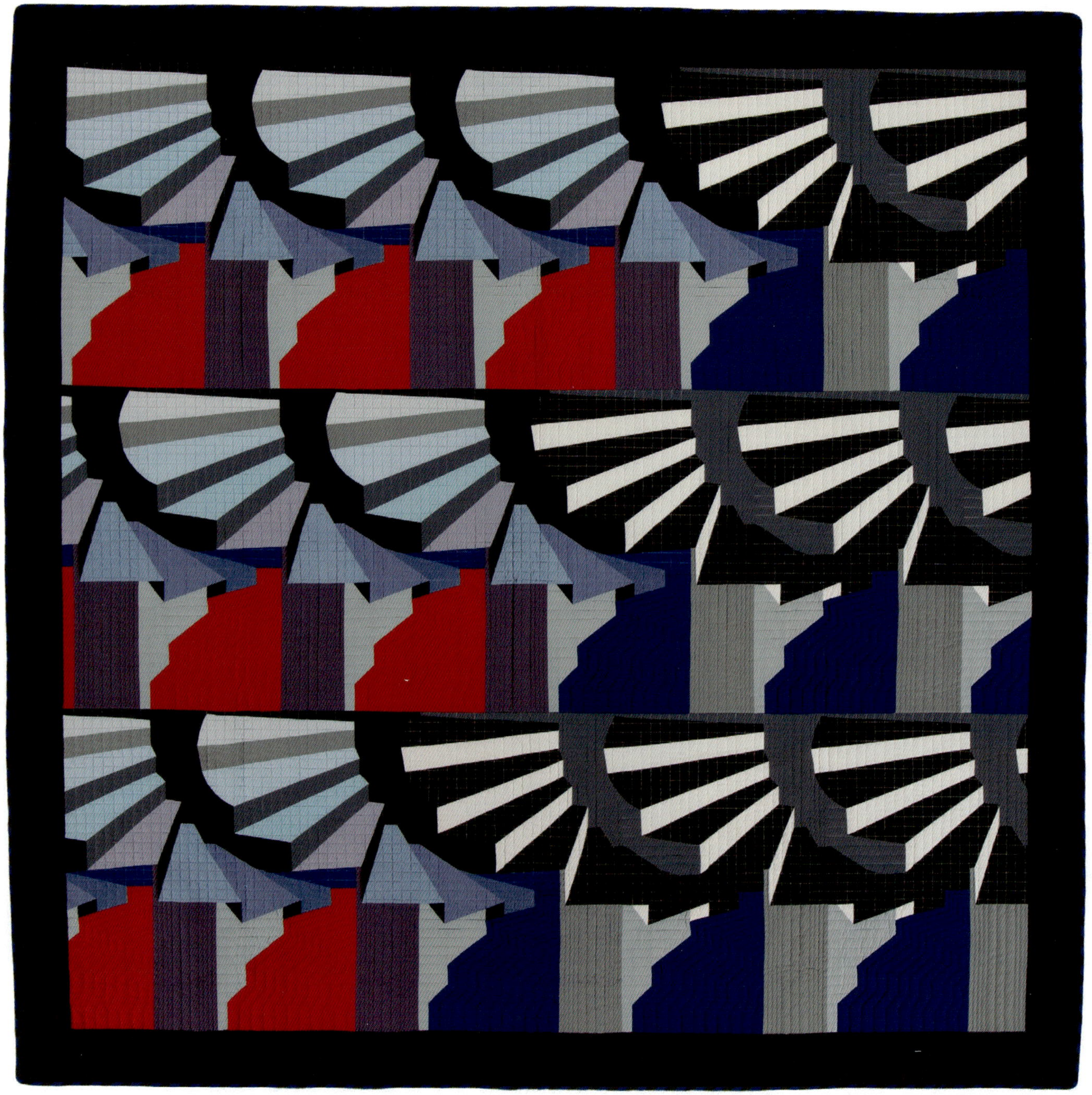

3.20

Spirals I

Pauline Burbidge
Nottingham, United Kingdom, 1985
Cotton; machine pieced and quilted
88.5 x 87 in.

Ardis and Robert James Collection, IQM 1997.007.1071

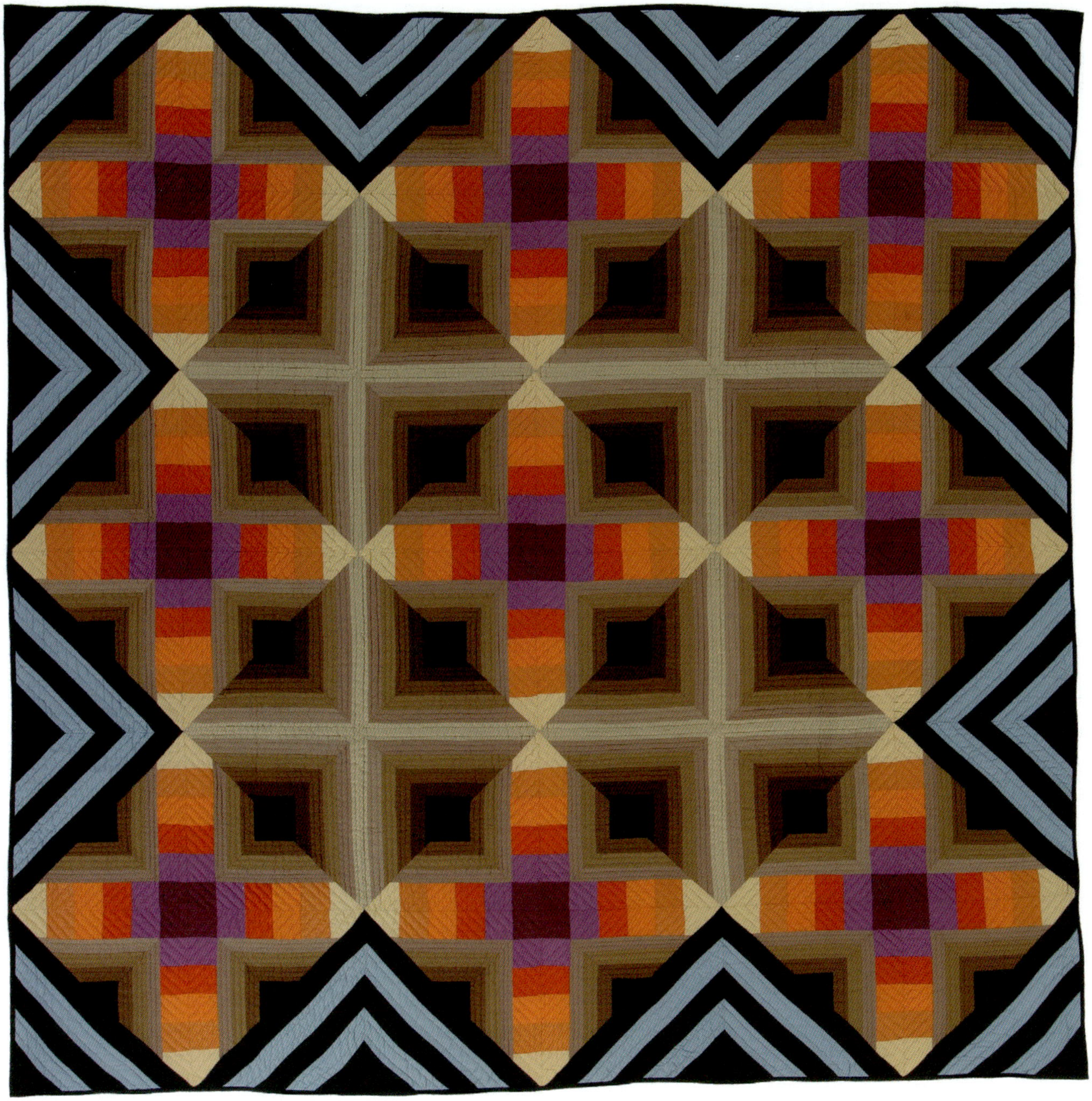

3.21

Crosses

Nancy Crow
Baltimore, Ohio, 1976
Cotton blend; machine pieced, hand quilted
93 x 94 in.

Ardis and Robert James Collection, IQM 1997.007.1088

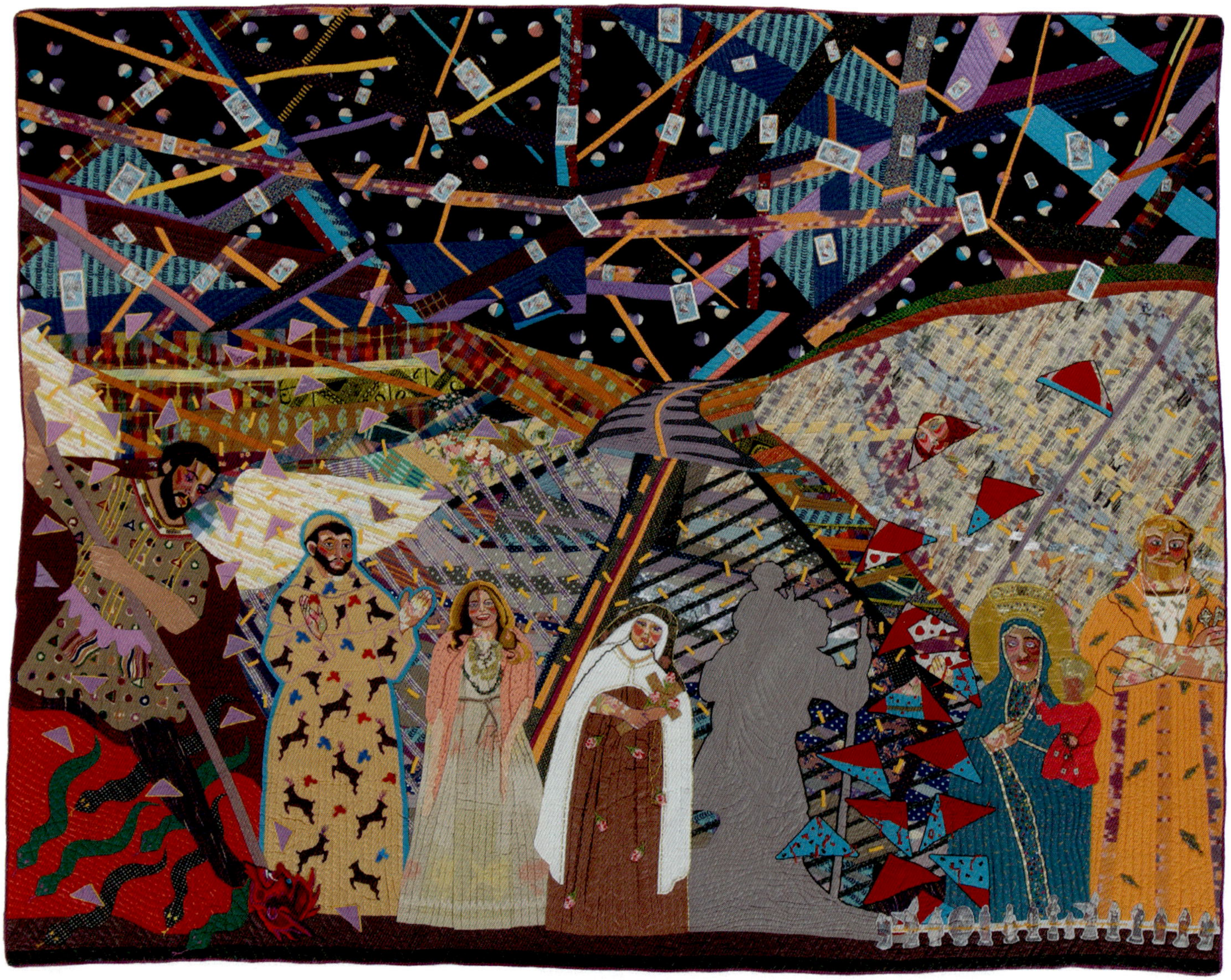

3.22

Dashboard Saints: In Memory of St. Christopher (who lost his magnetism)

Terrie Hancock Mangat
Cincinnati, Ohio, 1985
Cotton; machine pieced, embroidered, hand and machine appliquéd, hand quilted
99 x 124 in.

Ardis and Robert James Collection, IQM 1997.007.1093

3.23

Mexican Graveyard

Terri Hancock Mangat
Cincinnati, Ohio, 1985
Cotton; hand appliquéd, embroidered, and embellished, machine pieced, hand quilted
107.5 x 83 in.

Ardis and Robert James Collection, IQM 2009.039.0054

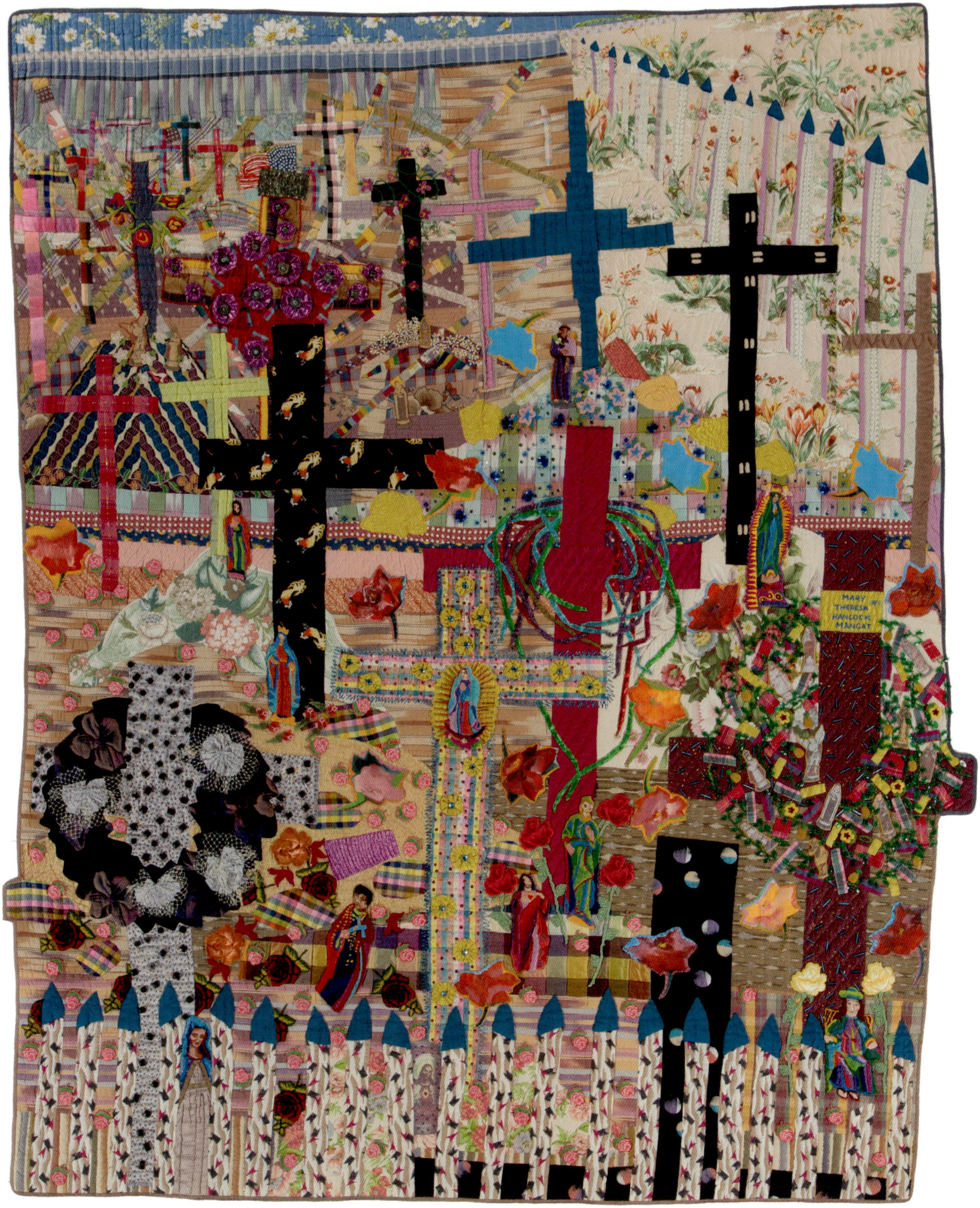
MARY
THERESA
HANCOCK
MANGAT

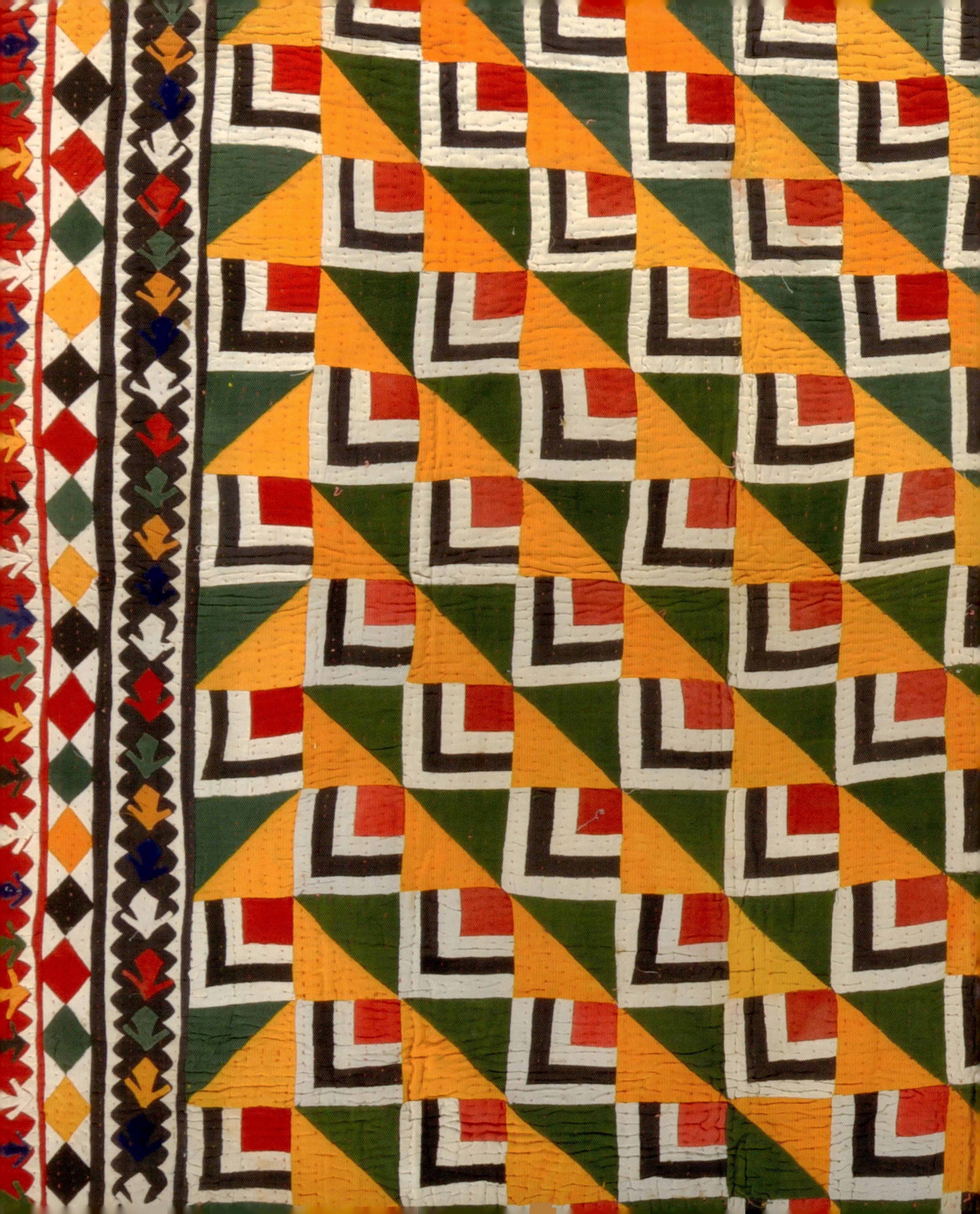

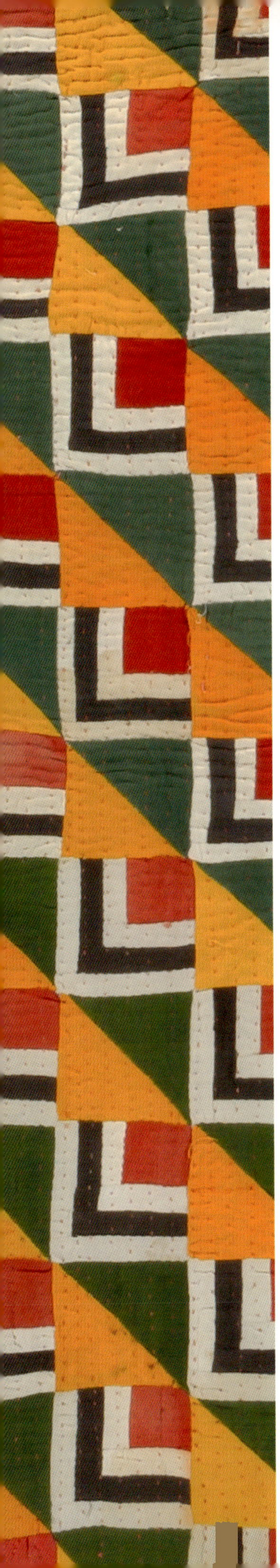

CHAPTER 4

NEW HORIZONS

Marin F. Hanson
Curator of International Collections

The James Collection was already international when it arrived at the University of Nebraska-Lincoln (UNL) in 1997. In addition to the six countries represented by artists in the contemporary quilt section (Canada, England, France, Germany, Japan, and the United States), quilts from nine countries were included in the antique quilt section (Canada, China, England, France, India, Ireland, Japan, the United States, and Wales). At the time that Ardis and Robert James were collecting, studio quilts were becoming a worldwide phenomenon, represented by such James Collection artists as the U.K.'s Pauline Burbidge and Deirdre Amsden, and Germany's Ursula Rauch and Ruth Eissfeldt. And although the Jameses largely collected antique international quilts directly related to American quilts (e.g. antecedent examples from the U.K.), they also acquired a small group of Japanese objects. These patchwork kimonos and ceremonial rice bags indicated that Ardis and Robert James did not view collecting narrowly. In a 2005 interview, Robert James summarized their intentions by saying, "We had the brilliant idea of doing the impossible thing... which is to have an absolutely comprehensive collection of quilts from all over the world."

The 1997 establishment of UNL's International Quilt Study Center (IQSC), now the International Quilt Museum (IQM), via the donation of the James Collection, cemented this global ambition. According to founding director Patricia Crews, two names had been considered: American Quilt Study Center and International Quilt Study Center. The Jameses strongly preferred the latter: "That was the Jameses' vision and it was their determination," Crews recalled. Almost immediately upon the center's opening, a definitive group of 88 quilts was sent to Tokyo, Japan as a centerpiece exhibition in The World Quilt '98 Expo. Organized by Tadanobu Seto, chairman of the craft- and hobby-focused Nihon Vogue Corporation, the Expo built upon the success of previous large-scale quilt events in Japan, and in its four-day run welcomed over 100,000 visitors. (Incidentally, one of those visitors, Nao Nomura, was so inspired by seeing the James Collection quilts that three years later she came to UNL to earn her master's degree, eventually becoming the IQSC's first collections manager). The World Quilt '98's *Masterpieces from the James Collection* was the first of the IQM's many international traveling exhibitions[1] and it set an immediate tone for the museum's global outlook.

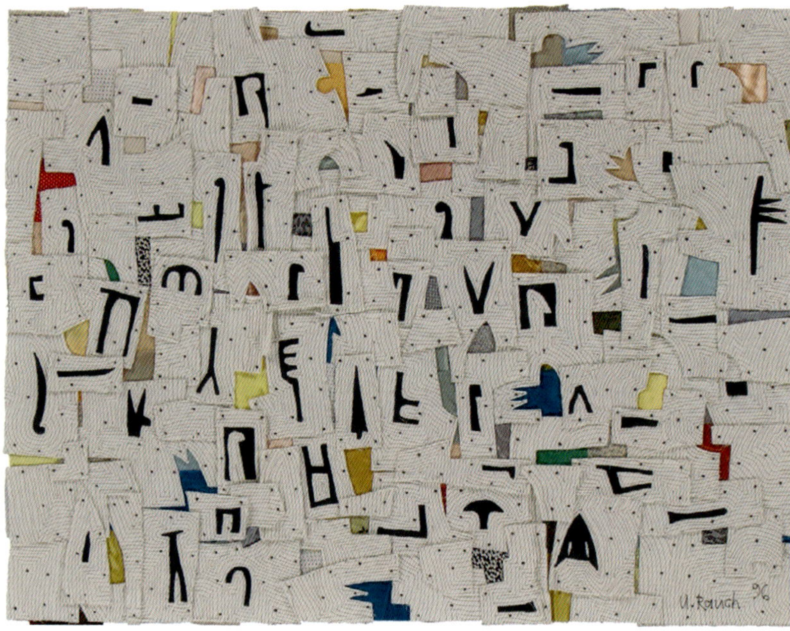

Maze, *Ursula Rauch, Weingarten, Germany, c. 1995, Ardis and Robert James Collection, IQM 2006.043.0013.*

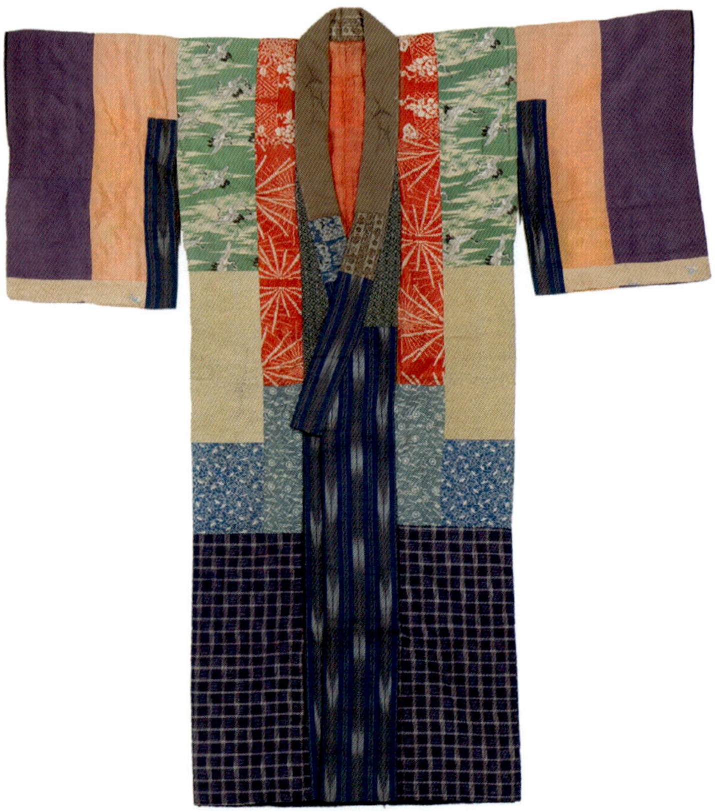

Patchwork Kimono, *maker unidentified, Japan, 1910-1930, Gift of Robert and Ardis James, 1998.003.0002.*

When I came to the University of Nebraska-Lincoln in 1999 as a graduate student in the Textiles, Clothing, and Design (TCD, now Textiles, Merchandising and Fashion Design) and Museum Studies departments, Patricia Crews saw my undergraduate background in Chinese Studies

[1] *IQM exhibitions have traveled all over the U.S. and to China, England, France, Italy, Japan, and South Korea.*

as a resource for expanding the IQSC's research and exhibition offerings. For my TCD master's degree final project, I curated the exhibition *Reflections of the 'Exotic' East in American Quilts* (2001). The exhibition's works illustrated the history of Asian influence on American quilts as well as the ways in which Westerners have interpreted—often inaccurately—Asian culture over the past centuries. This was the first of the more than 25 internationally-focused exhibitions the IQM has produced from its collections in its first 25 years. Some of these exhibitions include: *Quilts in Common* (2008), *South Asian Seams: Quilts from India, Pakistan and Bangladesh* (2010), *Marseille: White Corded Quilting* (2010), *Quilts of Southwest China* (2016), *Blue Echoes: Quilts by Shizuko Kuroha* (2016), *Sacred Scraps: Quilt and Patchwork Traditions of Central Asia* (2017), *From Kente to Kuba: Stitched Textiles from West and Central Africa* (2018), *Old World Quilts* (2019), *Glasnost and Folk Culture: Russian Quilts at the Turn of the 21st Century* (2020), and *Abstract Design in American Quilts at 50: Journey to Japan* (2021).

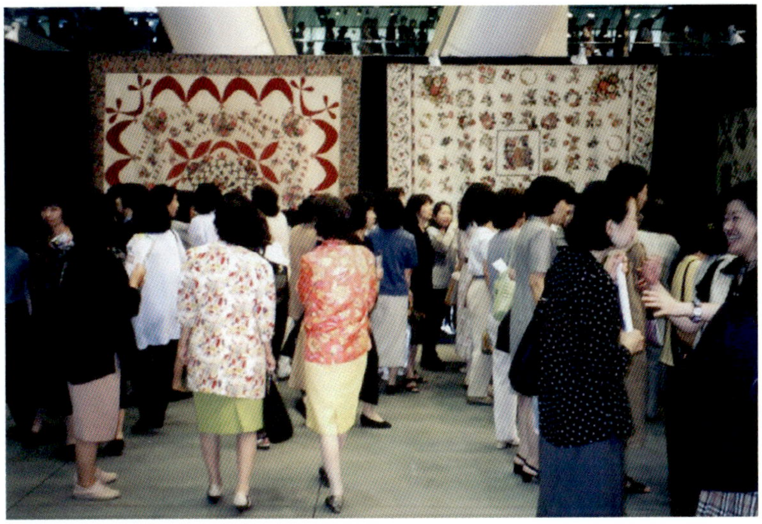

Attendees at The World Quilt '98 Expo in Tokyo, Japan viewing Masterpieces from the James Collection. *The top of the photos shows the long line of visitors waiting to enter the Expo.*

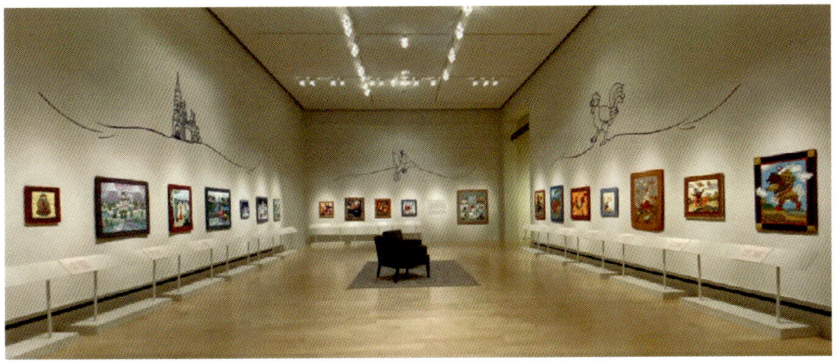

Exhibition: Glasnost and Folk Culture *(August 4, 2020 – February 20, 2021).*

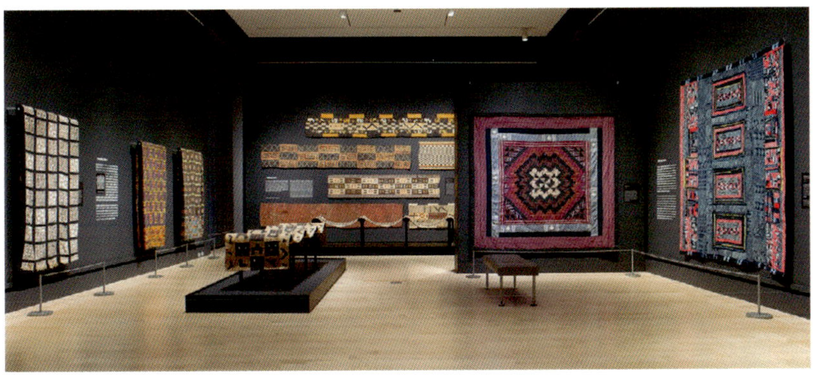

Exhibition: From Kente to Kuba *(December 7, 2018 – May 12, 2019).*

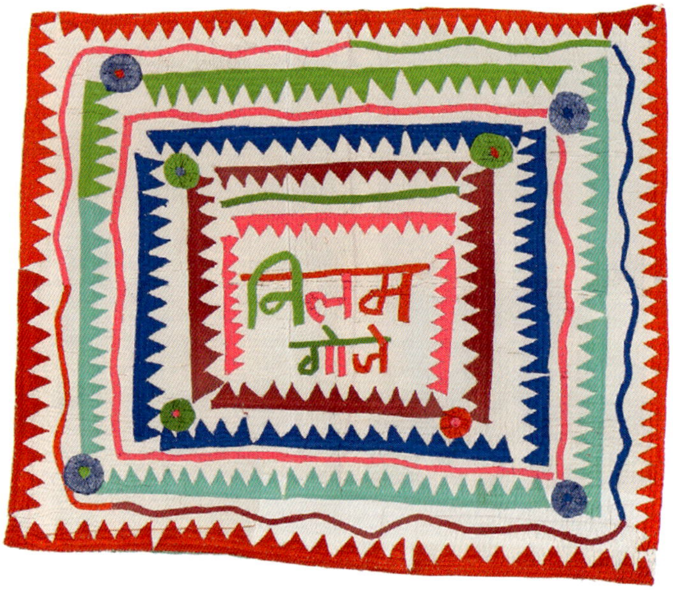

Godhari (quilt), *Sarita Goje, Kunegaon, Lonavala, Maharashtra, India, 1980-2005, Geeta Khandelwal Collection, partial gift of the Robert and Ardis James Foundation, IQM 2015.067.0007.*

Without an expanding international collection, these exhibitions would have been impossible. The original James Collection had fewer than 75 pieces from outside the United States. Today, the IQM international collection numbers nearly 1,800 objects and includes pieces from over 60 countries, from Afghanistan to Zimbabwe. The international collection includes some of our oldest pieces—a pair of circa 1600 silk whole cloth quilts either from southern Europe or Goa, India—to some of our newest works—a group of quilts we commissioned from top Japanese quilt artists in 2020. Our aim is to represent as many quilt-related traditions as we can by collecting examples of quilting, piecing, and appliqué from all over the world. These widely sourced items include quilted petticoats from the south of France, appliquéd and pieced Kuba dance skirts from the Democratic Republic of Congo, appliquéd and pieced quilt covers from various southwest Chinese ethnic minority groups, patchwork tent panels from Central Asia as well as appliquéd tent panels from Egypt, *boro* patchwork from Japan, reverse appliqué *mola* blouse panels from Panama, and quilted prayer rugs from Turkey and Iran. Every year, we are inspired anew by Robert James' goal of building a "comprehensive collection of quilts from all over the world."

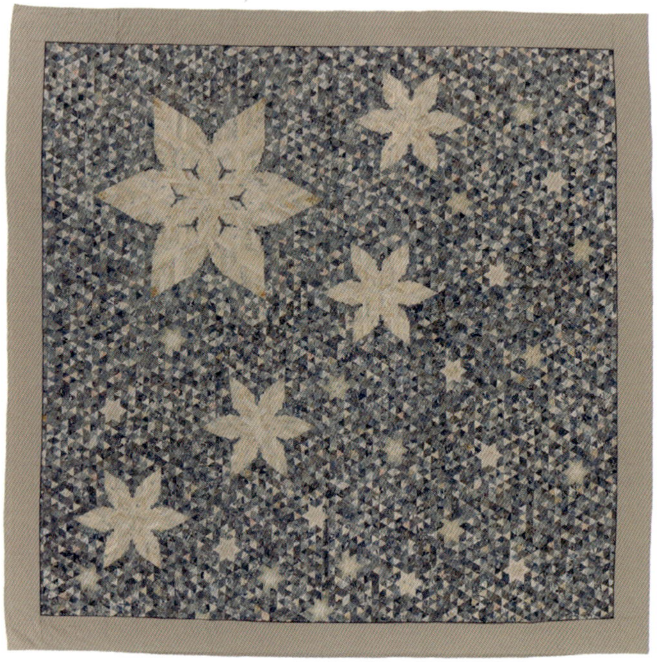

Gift from the Sky, *Shizuko Kuroha, Tokyo, Japan, 2013, Gift of the Robert and Ardis James Foundation, IQM 2020.060.0009.*

While we have received many important pieces via donation, the majority of our international collection has been acquired through partial or outright funding from the Robert and Ardis James Foundation. Two collections acquired through the partial gift/purchase funding process are key components of our South Asian group, which includes over 600 objects from India, Pakistan, Bangladesh, Bhutan, and Sri Lanka. The Patricia Stoddard Collection, consisting of over 200 pieces, is the most significant collection of Pakistani quilts outside of the subcontinent. And acquisition of the Geeta Khandelwal Collection enabled the museum to represent Maharashtra, with over 40 examples from various parts of that Indian state. Thanks to the James Foundation, we were also able to acquire the Kathryn Wilson Berenson Collection of French quilts, West and

Central African textiles from collectors Kay and Lori Triplett, a collection of work by Shizuko Kuroha of Japan, and a group of documented early 20th-century Italian whole cloth quilts discovered by quilt collector, researcher, and author Jonathan Holstein.

Additionally, the Robert and Ardis James Foundation has supported numerous IQM-sponsored international research and collecting trips. Three groups (Patricia Stoddard and Martha Wallace; Patrick Finn; and an IQM curatorial team) have performed research in India, visiting quiltmakers and collectors, performing oral histories, and acquiring objects. IQM research trips have also gone to China, including a trip by Patricia Stoddard and Pamela Najdowski to pursue documentation and acquisitions in numerous Southwest Chinese communities, and one by an IQM team of curators and graduate students to Northwest China to visit with makers and acquire patchwork examples. Multiple research and collecting trips to Central Asia by Christine Martens were also supported by the James Foundation and contributed to the IQM building a comprehensive, 150-plus piece collection representing Afghanistan, Kyrgyzstan, Tajikistan, Turkmenistan, and Uzbekistan. All of these study trips have resulted in or contributed to IQM exhibitions and/or catalogs, a primary way in which we interpret our collection for our global audience.

Beyond exhibitions and catalogs, another way in which we communicate about our international research and collections is through our ongoing project, World Quilts (worldquilts.quiltstudy.org). World Quilts is a series of web modules, each of which takes a "deep dive" into a particular quiltmaking tradition, practice, or global region. Christine Martens' research in Uzbekistan, Kyrgyzstan, and Tajikistan contributed to the creation of World Quilts: The Central Asian Story, and research and documentation conducted by Susan Marks and Jonathan Gregory on U.K. Crazy quilts informed the World Quilts: The Crazy Quilt Story module. Development of World Quilts: The Japanese Story has begun, slowed recently by 2020-2021 COVID-19 pandemic travel restrictions. As with so many of our projects, the James Foundation has funded portions of the World Quilts research and implementation. Quite simply, without James family support—both financial and moral—we could not have built such a comprehensive (and still growing) group of global quilts and related textiles nor would we be able to share them with the world.

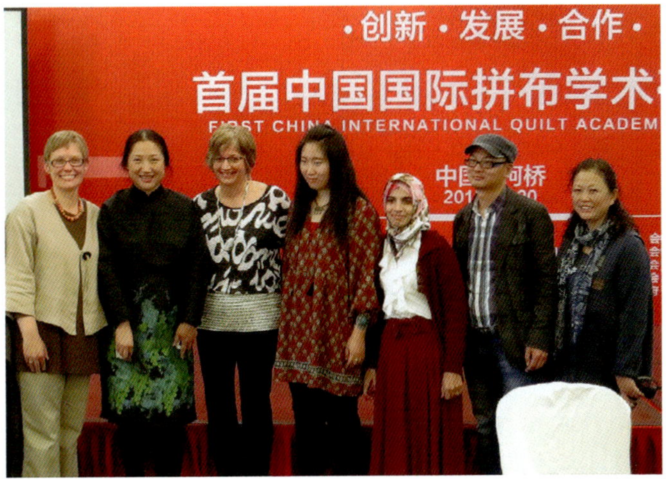

Marin Hanson, IQM Curator of International Collections (far left), with China Academy of Art Professor Qiu Haisuo (second from left) and other speakers at the First China International Quilt Academic Seminar, held in Keqiao District, Shaoxing, China, October 2015.

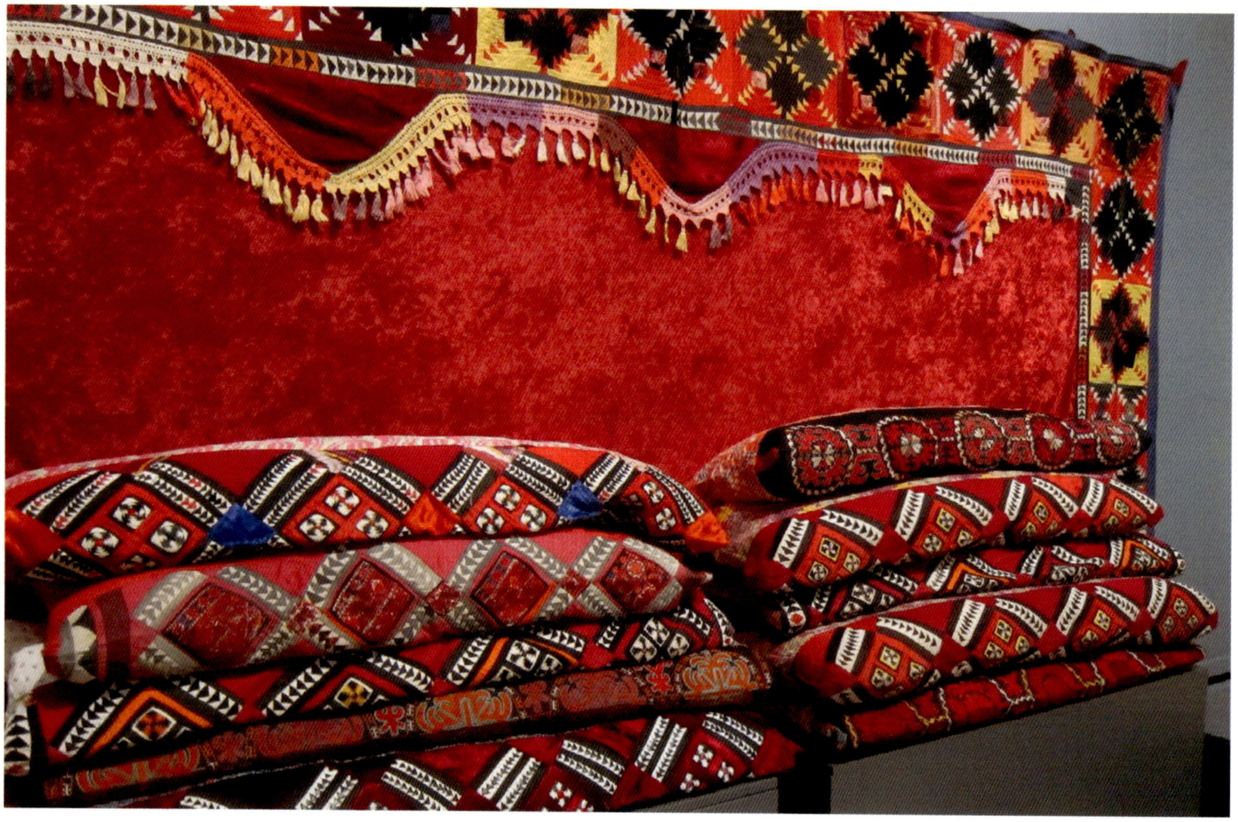

Kyrgyz patchwork pillow covers in the exhibition, Sacred Scraps: Quilt and Patchwork Traditions of Central Asia *(May 12 - December 16, 2017).*

New Horizons showcases the joint efforts thus far of the IQM and the Robert and Ardis James Foundation to represent the world of quilts as fully as possible. For that reason, it is the only exhibition in the *An Evolving Vision* series comprised solely of quilts acquired after 1997. In some ways, those international quilts added to the IQM over the past quarter century can be considered honorary members of the James Collection. Due to space constraints, in this catalog we are limited to featuring the quilts included in the *New Horizons* exhibition, plus a few selected examples that could not be shown in the gallery. The rest of our international collection can always be viewed online, either in our online database or on the web at World Quilts.

New Horizons presents textiles from eighteen countries that were made in three separate centuries (circa 1800 to today). Two quilted Persian textiles are the oldest: a heavily embroidered circa 1800-1820 prayer rug and a mid-19th century quilted cap (Plates 4.1 & 4.2). While the block-printed cap is constructed with regular running stitch quilting, the prayer rug—depicting the form of a *mihrab*, or Islamic prayer niche—features exquisite "false" or "flat" quilting, which is performed with a backstitch and therefore fills in the quilting lines more fully. Another piece from this part of the world is a circa 1900-1920 Kurdish quilt, likely from northwestern Iran (then called Persia), which has a *kilim* (tapestry woven rug) as its center (Plate 4.3).

Another set of quilted items is from the region along the eastern half of the Mediterranean Sea: southern Italy, Albania, Greece, and the Levant (Plates 4.4 – 4.7). A Calabrian silk whole cloth quilt bears imagery reminiscent of a common Christian motif often referred to as "The Pelican in Her Piety": a mother bird feeding her own blood to her chicks to save them, a story with obvious parallels to Christ's sacrifice. Surrounded by the sea, the region of Calabria occupies the "toe" of Italy, a country rich with vineyards and grain fields. Thus, it is not surprising to see seashells, grapes, and wheat sheafs ringing the central scene. From nearby Albania (across the Ionian Sea, an offshoot of the Mediterranean), a boy's handsome quilted jacket is decorated with gold braid and ornate buttons, while a quilted garment from the Levant, possibly Syria, represents a type of robe that was likely sold to pilgrims and tourists on their way to or from the Holy Land in the late 19th and early 20th centuries. A bright yellow whole cloth quilt from Thessaloniki, Greece also went on a journey—with a family who immigrated to the United States in 1951. It was part of the limited luggage this Greek family could bring with them to start their new American lives.

Three other quilted items represent South and East Asia, respectively: a *kantha* from India's Bengal region (Plate 4.8), a pair of southwestern Chinese shoes (Plate 4.9), and a northern Chinese quilted waistcoat (Plate 4.10). A *kantha* is a textile made using layers of recycled sari cloth held together with decorative running stitches that serve as both embroidery and quilting. In this *kantha* there is a delightful range of imagery, including elephants, tigers, fishes, and fearless peacocks performing the job they are famous for in Indian myth and legend: killing snakes. The quilting stitches on the Chinese shoes serve a more utilitarian purpose: to provide layers of protection for the wearer in muddy environments (they also have impressive metal studs on the bottom, which would additionally help with slippery surfaces). A rich black silk forms the base of the late-19th-century Manchu waistcoat and it is quilted with *shou* symbols, which denote longevity. The Manchus were the northeast Asian ethnic group that ruled during the final Chinese dynasty, the Qing, which ruled from 1644-1912. In an interesting brush with fame, this waistcoat was purchased by the assistant costume director for the 1987 Oscar-winning film, "The Last Emperor," apparently as inspiration for costuming.

Another East Asian garment, a Japanese vest (Plate 4.11), is among the oldest of the pieced items in *New Horizons*. Piecing, or patchwork, often holds great symbolic meaning across Asia, either as a protection against malevolent forces, as in Central Asia, or as a symbol of Buddhist asceticism in South and East Asia. The Japanese vest is likely from the Kansai region, where the ancient capital of Kyoto is located. It is composed of many examples of silk *chirimen* (crepe weave) fabrics, some dating from the late 18th century, though the garment was likely constructed later, in the mid-19th century.

All over the world, patchwork textiles have many different functions. In Pakistan (Plate 4.12), quilts serve as a blankets, mattresses, and floor mats, while in Uzbekistan (Plate 4.13), patchwork is a favorite textile for room dividers and decoration in the traditional yurt (tent) homes that some Central Asian people still live in. On the other side of the globe, in North America, patchwork has been used by the Seminole and Miccosukee people since the early 1900s as decoration on clothing (Plate 4.14). The complex patterns the makers piece together have graced garments worn by tribal members as well as items sold to tourists at attractions and shops across South Florida.

Appliqué is the technique most suited to creating cloth pictures, and people from many world cultures have used it to illustrate stories and depict familiar objects. An unknown maker from Rarotonga, one of the Cook Islands in the South Pacific, created a stylized floral motif in her *tivaevae* (Plate 4.15). On many Pacific Islands, including Hawai'i, women have made large-scale "fold and cut" appliqués for generations, often using the local flora as inspiration. Eugenie Tautoonie Kabluitok, an indigenous artist from Canada's Nunavut Territory, used wool felt to create a tableau of Inuit life that includes walruses, sled dogs, bear hunters, and an igloo (Plate 4.16). Below the equator in the southern hemisphere, a Bolivian folk artist illustrated aspects of rural life including cooking, fishing, and tending llamas/alpacas (Plate 4.17). Across the southern Atlantic Ocean, thousands of miles directly east from Bolivia, Zimbabwean quiltmaker Elizabeth Savanhu used appliqué to tell a story of village life filled with daily activities such as fetching firewood, going to the well, and brewing beer (Plate 4.18).

Imagery drawn from beyond daily life also appears in appliquéd textiles. Fantastical creatures can be seen in two examples from very different parts of the world. A quilt cover from the Zhuang people of China's Guangxi Province (Plate 4.19) depicts spiraling dragons in three of its blocks, while an *asafo* (warrior troop) flag from the Fante people of Ghana also features a dragon, depicted with three heads (Plate 4.20)! The Fante people transformed the European flag format into their own art form, which often used the display of threatening creatures as a way to intimidate rival warrior groups. A starkly different African military tradition can be seen in the Sudanese *jibbah*, a tunic worn by officers in the Islamic Mahdist army during the struggle against Egyptian and British presence in the 1880s and '90s (Plate 4.21). The tunic's appliquéd squares not only made an officer more visible on the battlefield, but their simplicity represented the Mahdists' commitment to a strict Islamic lifestyle.

Finally, although they are not included in the *New Horizons* exhibition, I would be remiss if I did not mention the IQM's cross-cultural quilts and research. Connections have always been made across cultures, and quilts sometimes bear evidence of this exchange, whether as the work of an individual artist or the products of groups of makers. Examples include: the quilts of Ai Kijima (Plate 4.22), a Japanese artist whose work examines and juxtaposes the visual and popular culture of Japan and the U.S.; the "song quilts" of Eliza Hardy Jones, in particular those in which she visually transcribes Russian folk songs in quilt form (Plate 4.23); the work of British artist Lynn Setterington, who collaborates with immigrant groups in her home city of Manchester and whose quilts deftly combine Western themes and South Asian techniques (Plate 4.24); and 21st-century community quilts made by American families to welcome their adopted Chinese daughters to their new homes. My own doctoral research focused on these aptly named "One Hundred Good Wishes Quilts" and was supported by the Robert and Ardis James Foundation, for which I am deeply grateful.

From the beginning, the International Quilt Museum has endeavored to live up to its international moniker. I am honored to have been part of working towards Robert and Ardis James's goal of building a global quilt collection to be shared with a worldwide audience. Onward!

Note: Plates 4.1 – 4.21 appear in the exhibition, **An Evolving Vision: New Horizons.**

4.1

Prayer Rug

Maker unidentified
Probably made in Persia, 1800-1820
Cotton and silk; hand embroidered and quilted
46 x 31 in.

Gift of the Robert and Ardis James Foundation, IQM 2019.043.0008

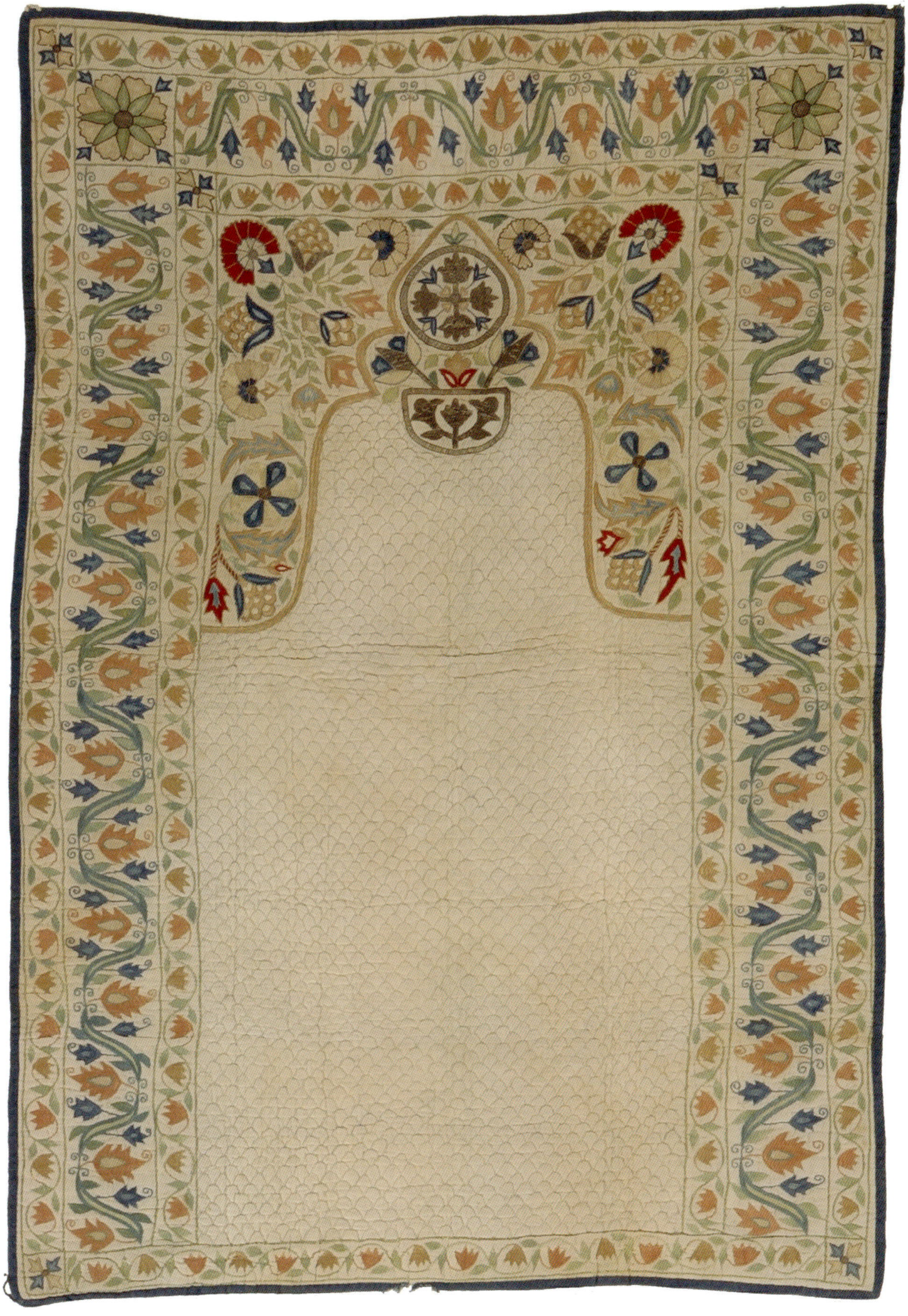

4.3

Quilt with Kilim Center

Maker unidentified
Probably made in Persia, 1900-1920
Cotton; hand pieced and quilted
75 x 59.5 in.

Gift of the Robert and Ardis James Foundation, IQM 2010.045.0015

4.2

Cap

Maker unidentified
Probably made in Persia, 1840-1860
Cotton; hand quilted
9 x 10.5 in.

Gift of the Robert and Ardis James Foundation, IQM 2021.038.0001

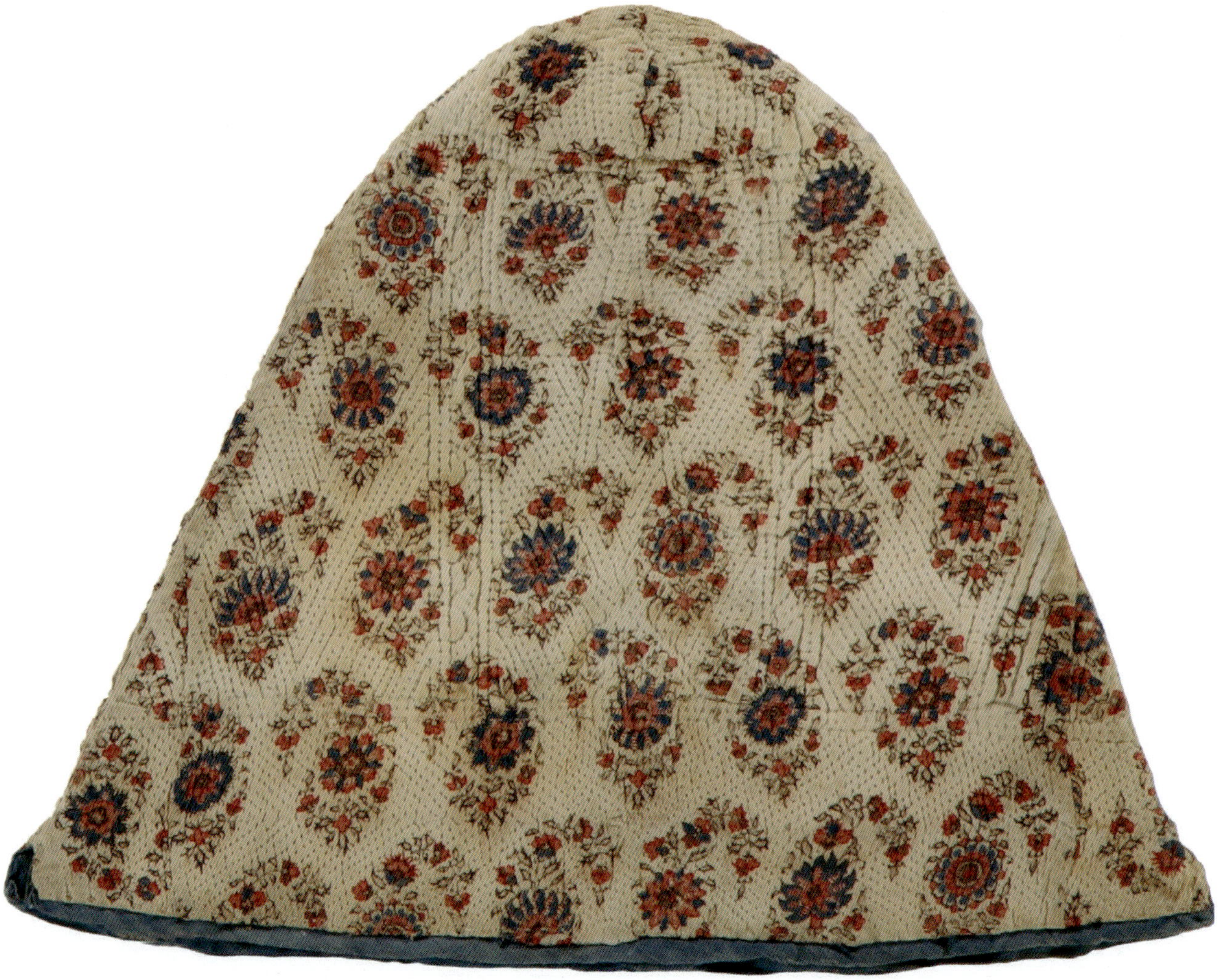

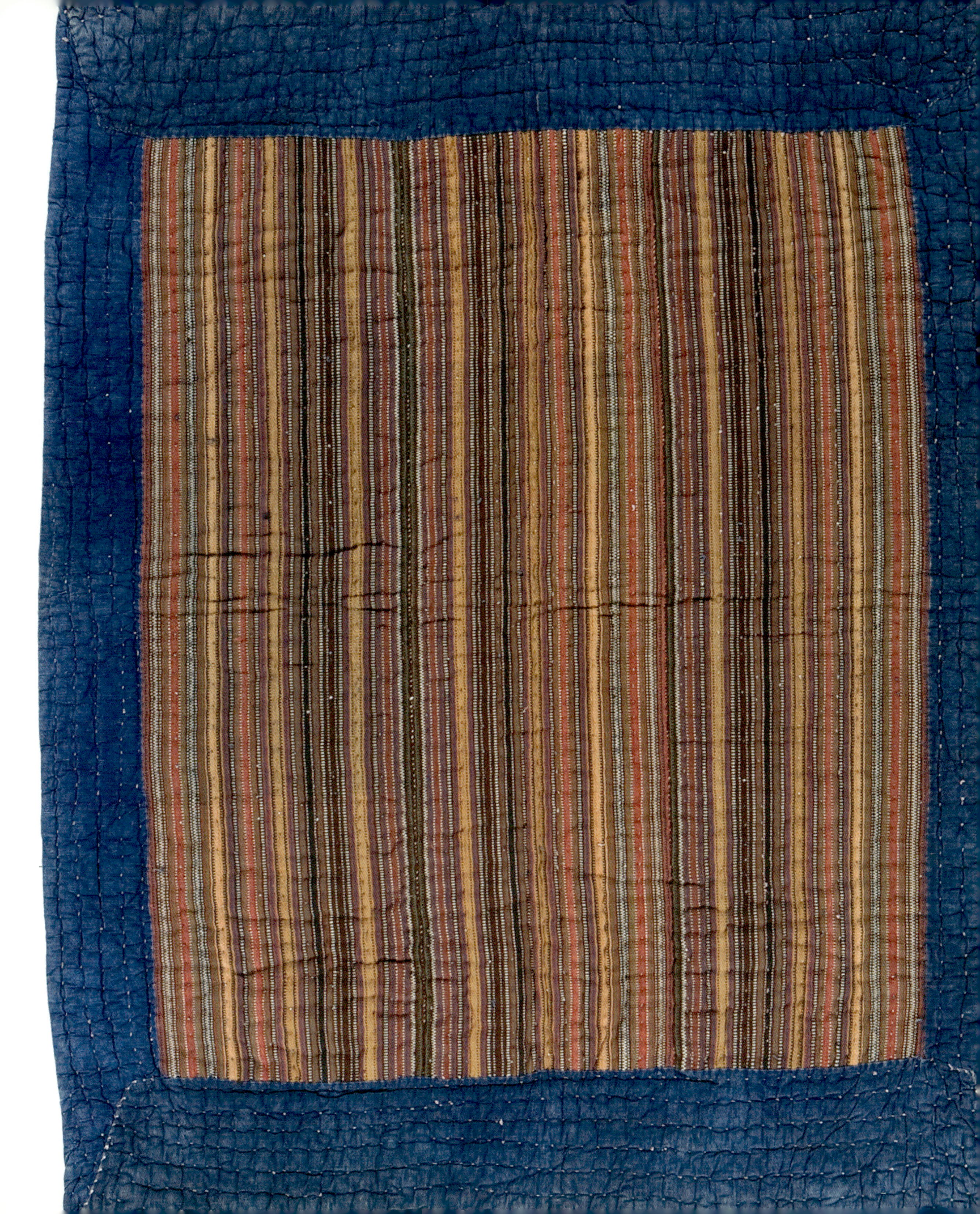

4.4

Whole Cloth Quilt

Probably made by Fortunata Cimato
Probably made in Calabria, Italy, 1900-1920
Silk; hand quilted
99 x 105 in.

Gift of the Robert and Ardis James Foundation, IQM 2019.001.0001

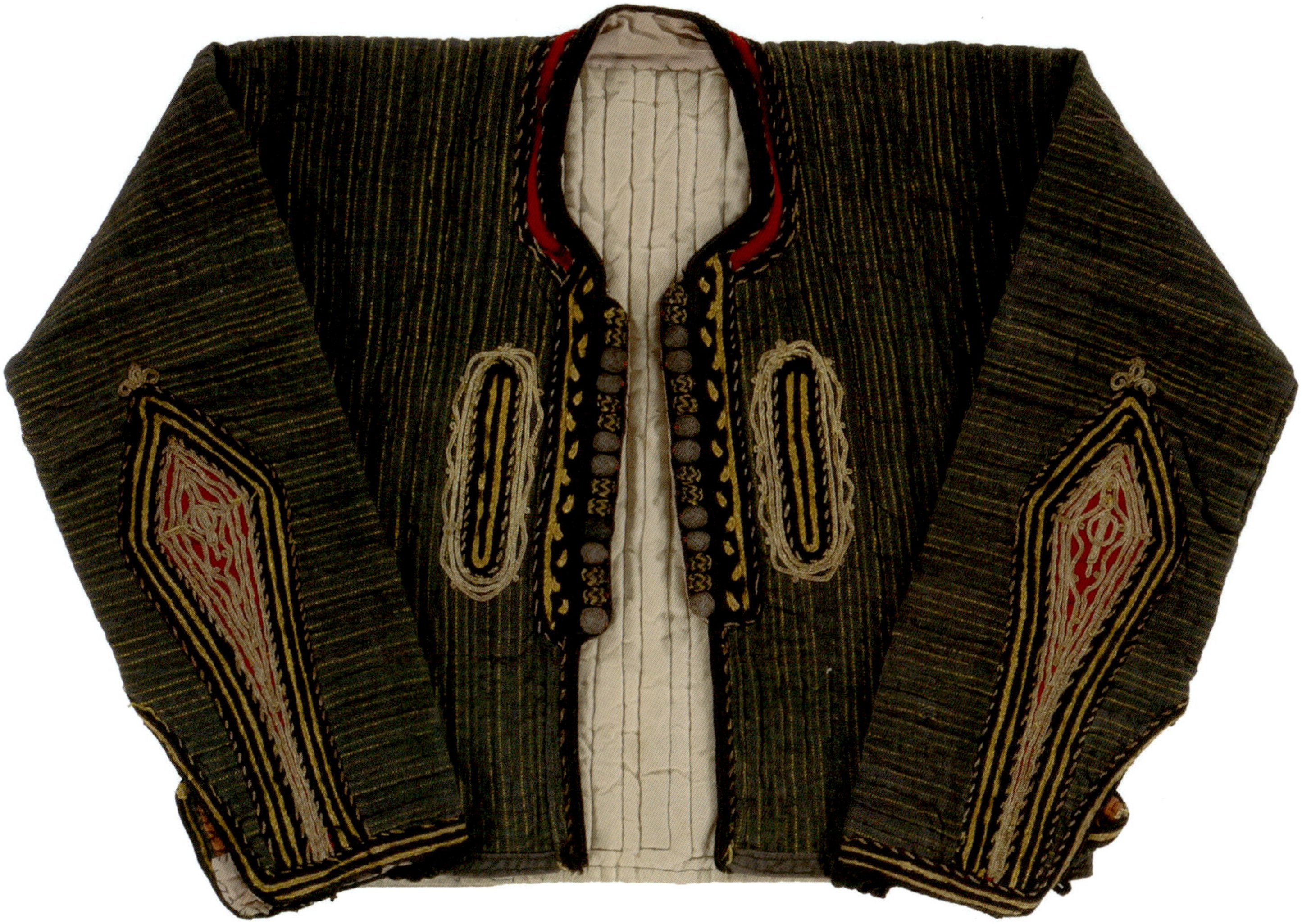

4.5

Child's Jacket

Maker unidentified
Made in Albania, 1910-1930
Cotton; hand embroidered and quilted
19 x 56 in.

Gift of the Robert and Ardis James Foundation, IQM 2019.073.0004

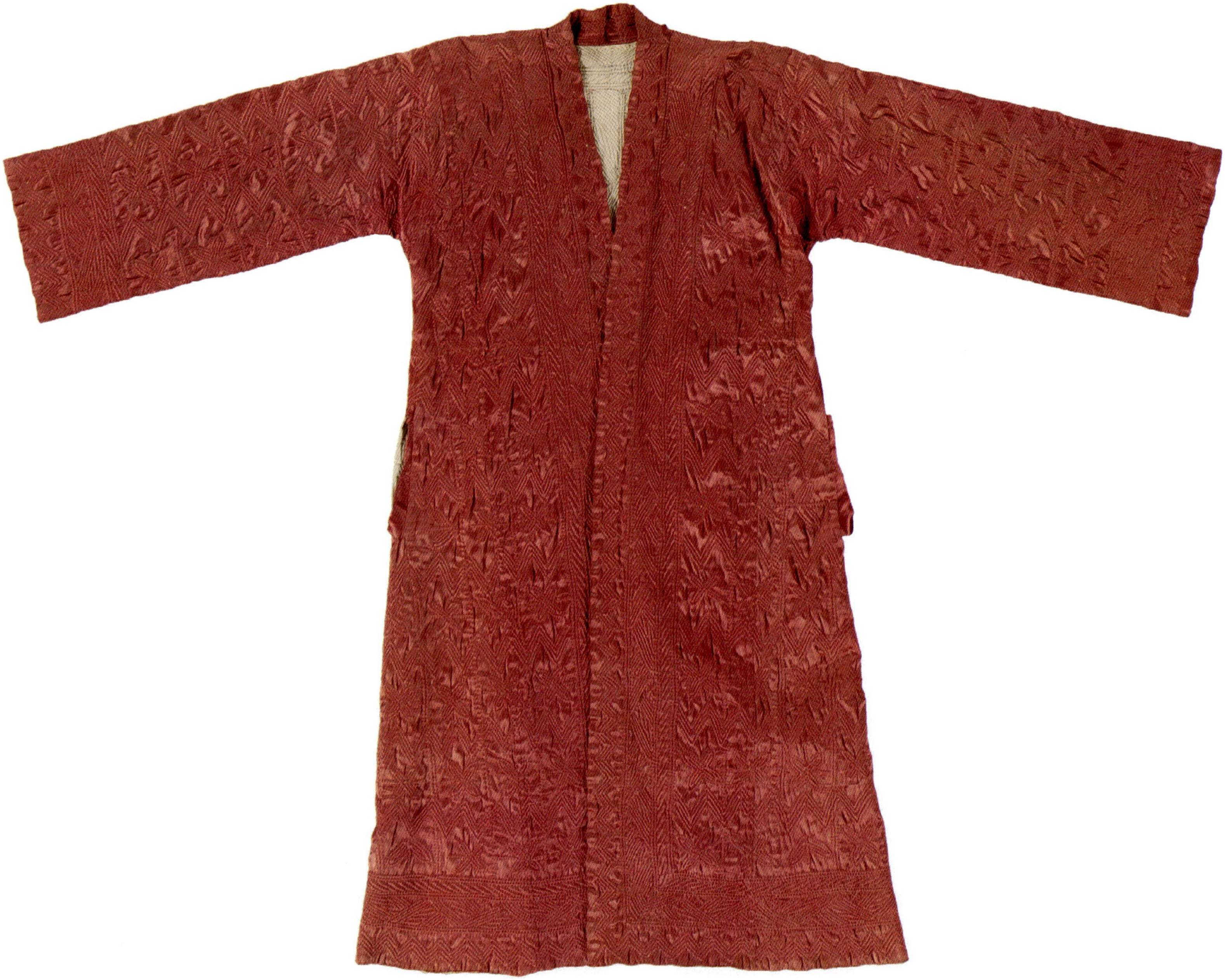

4.6

Robe

Maker unidentified
Possibly made in Syria, 1890-1910
Cotton; hand quilted
34.5 x 16.5 in.

Gift of the Robert and Ardis James Foundation, IQM 2011.001.0002

4.7

Whole Cloth Quilt

Maker unidentified
Probably made in Thessaloniki, Greece, 1930-1950
Cotton; hand quilted
80 x 68.5 in.

Gift of the Robert and Ardis James Foundation, IQM 2014.052.0001

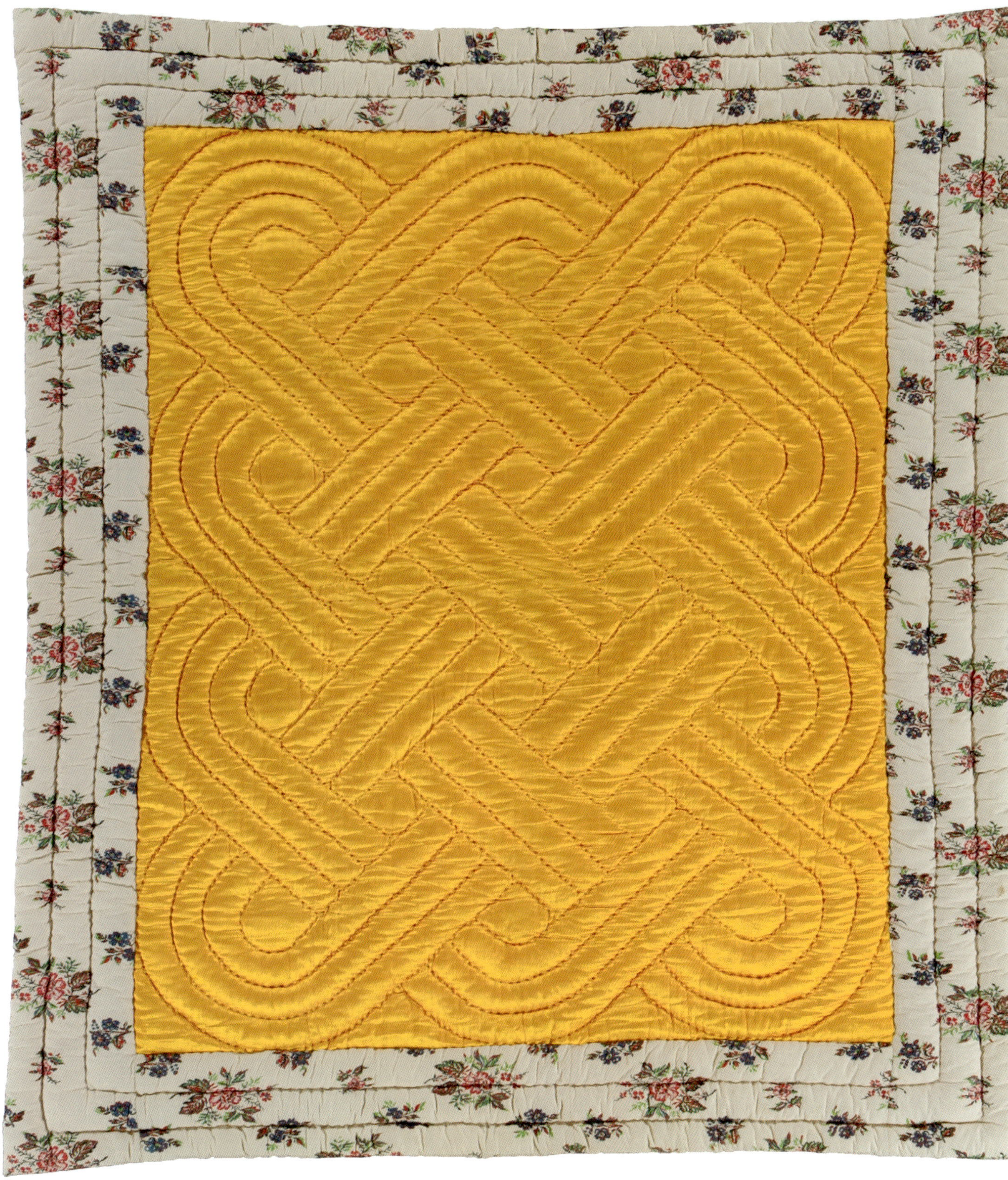

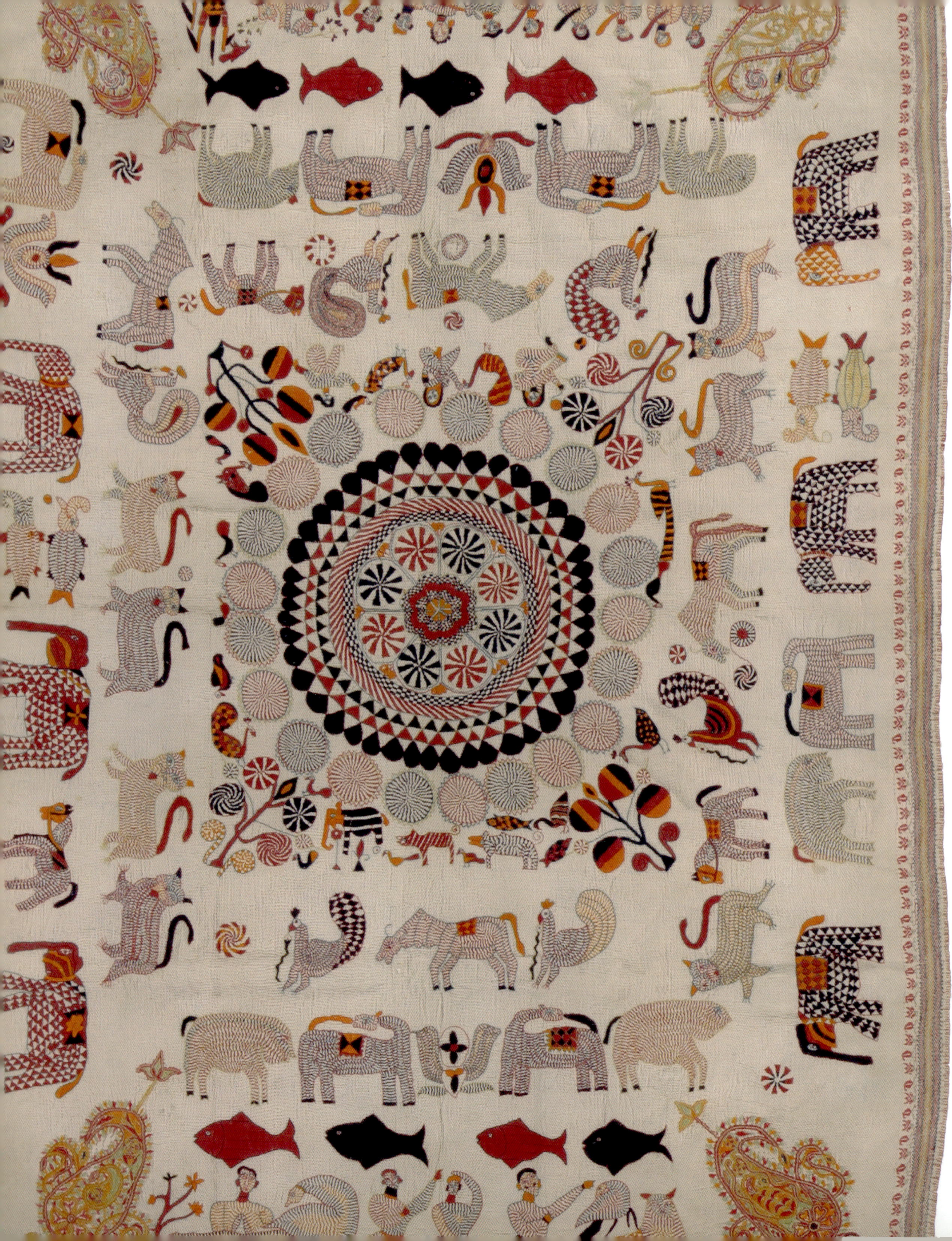

4.8

Kantha

Maker unidentified
Made in Bengal, India, 1910-1930
Cotton; hand embroidered and quilted
68 x 44.5 in.

Gift of the Robert and Ardis James Foundation, IQM 2019.073.0002

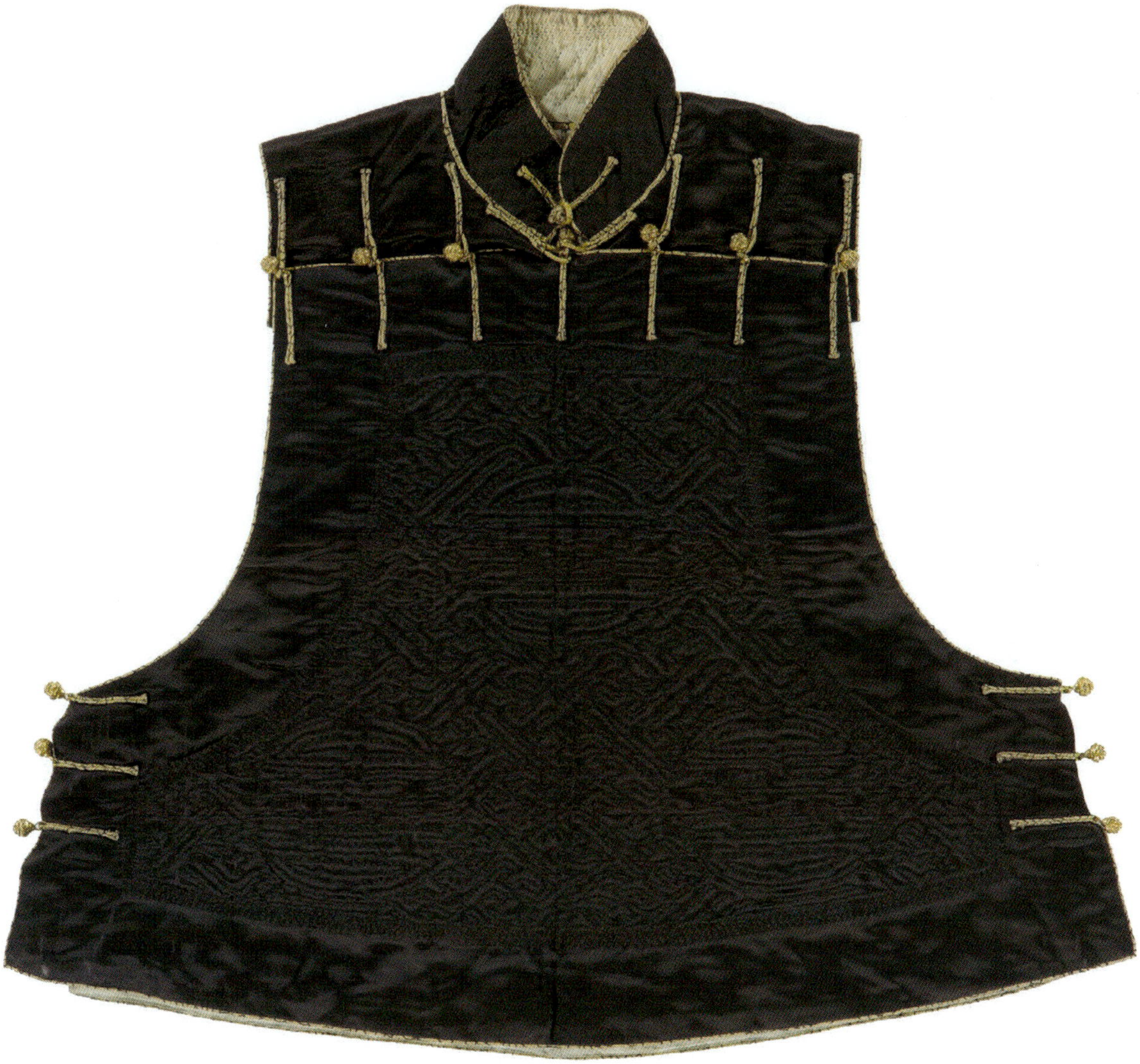

4.9

Waistcoat

Maker unidentified
Made in northern China, 1880-1900
Silk; hand quilted
26.5 x 27.5 in.

Gift of the Robert and Ardis James Foundation, IQM 2011.020.0001

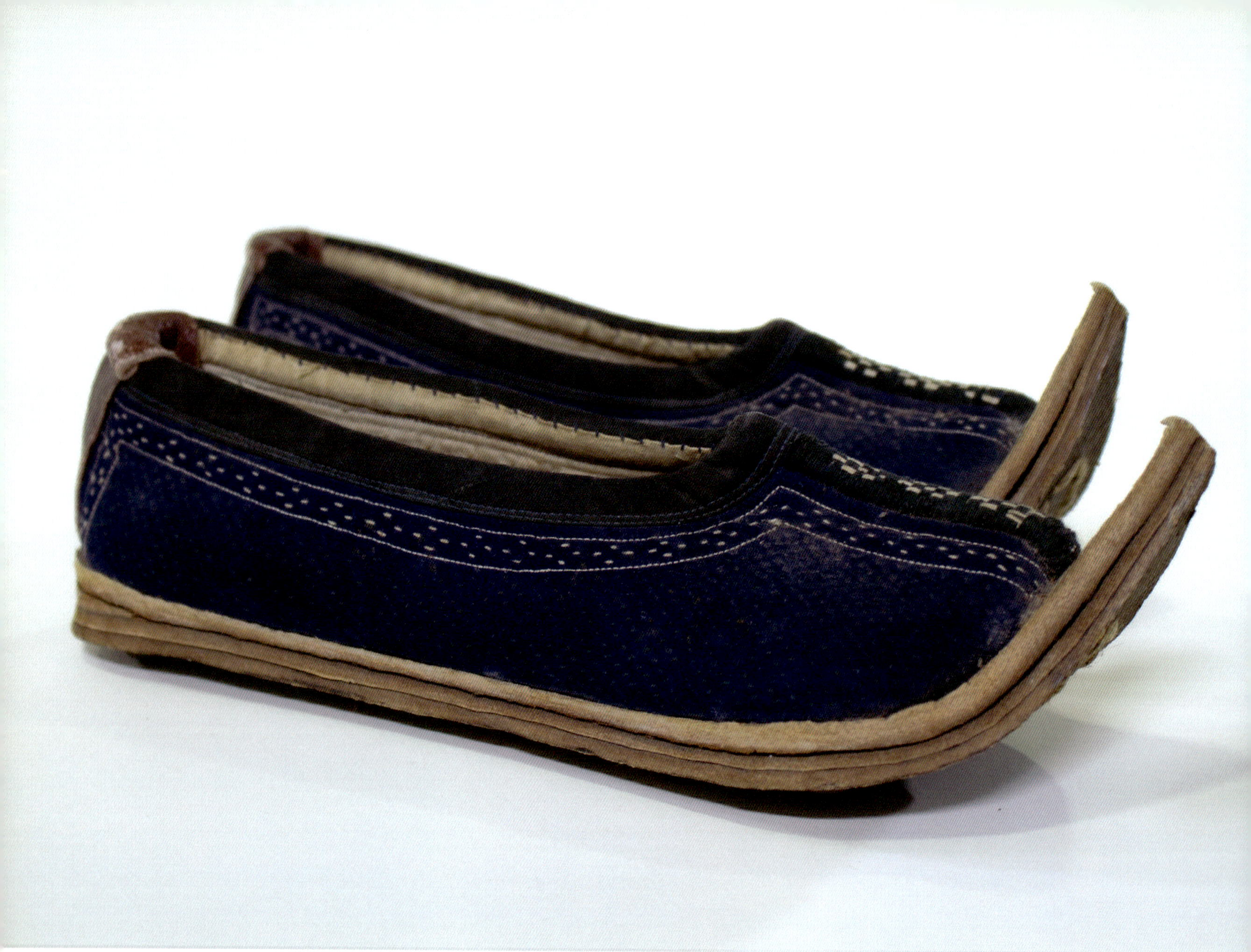

4.10

Mud Shoes

Maker unidentified
Made in southern China, 1920-1950
Cotton, leather, metal studs; hand quilted
10.5 x 4 in. each

Gift of the Robert and Ardis James Foundation, IQM 2020.069.0001

4.11

Vest

Maker unidentified
Made in Japan, 1850-1870
Silk; hand pieced
25.5 x 19 in.

Gift of the Robert and Ardis James Foundation, IQM 2021.048.0001

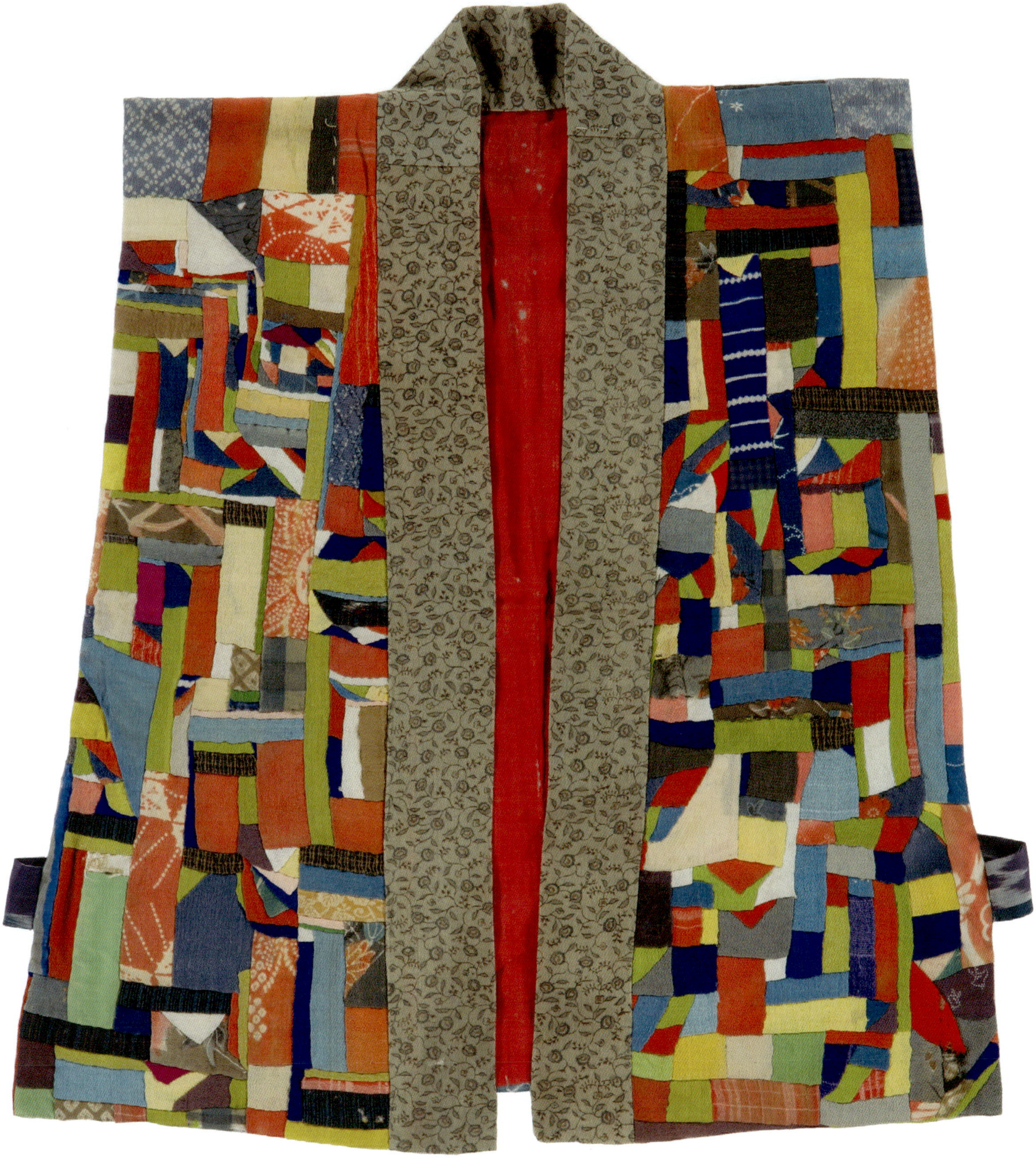

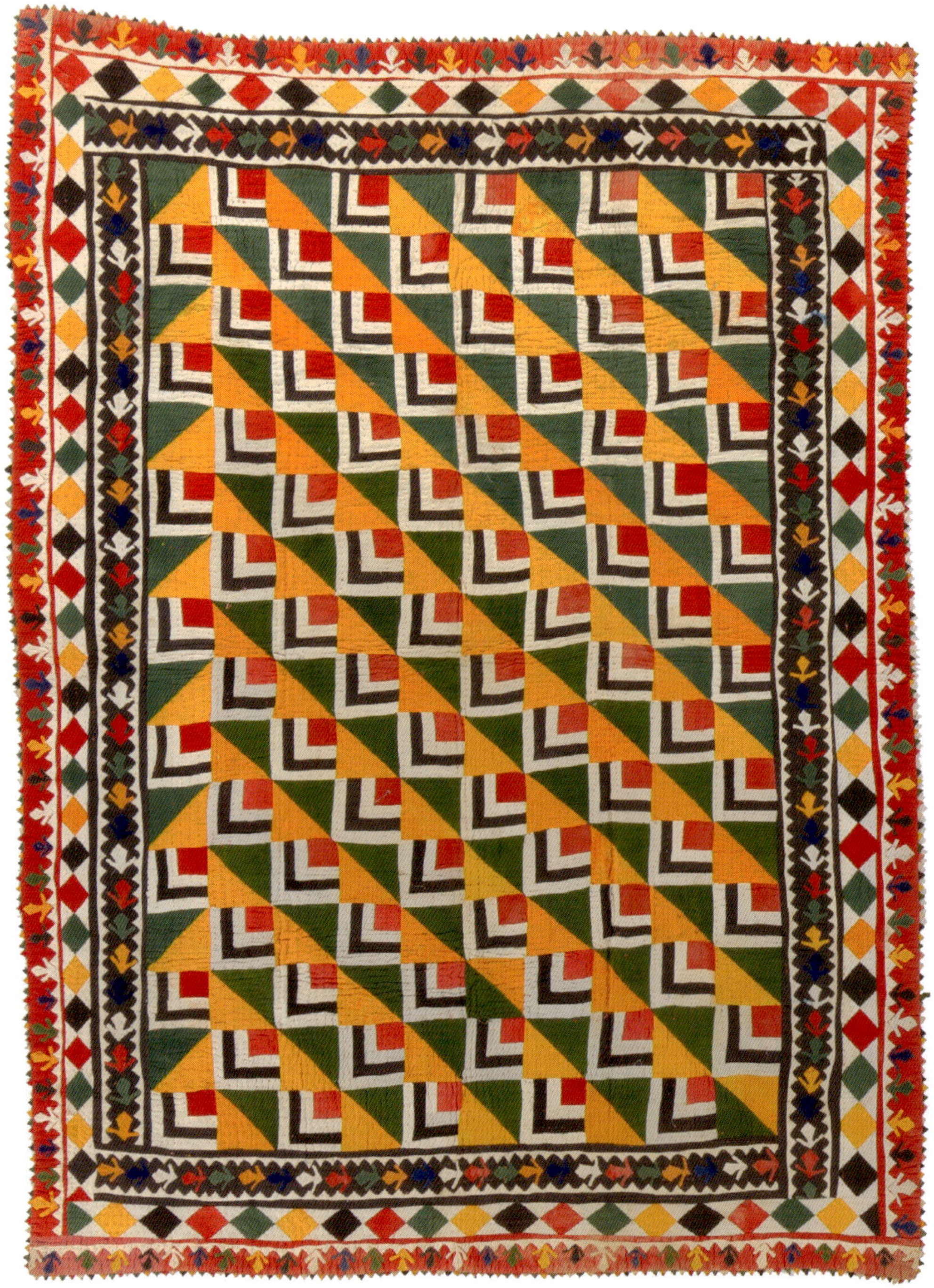

4.12

Ralli in a Biso Bulo ("Nose Jewel and Nose Ring") Pattern

Made by Haleema
Made in Phuleli Village, Middle Sindh, Pakistan, circa 1994
Cotton; hand pieced, appliquéd, and quilted
84 x 59.5 in.

Patricia Stoddard Collection, Partial gift of the Robert and Ardis James Foundation, IQM 2016.012.0077

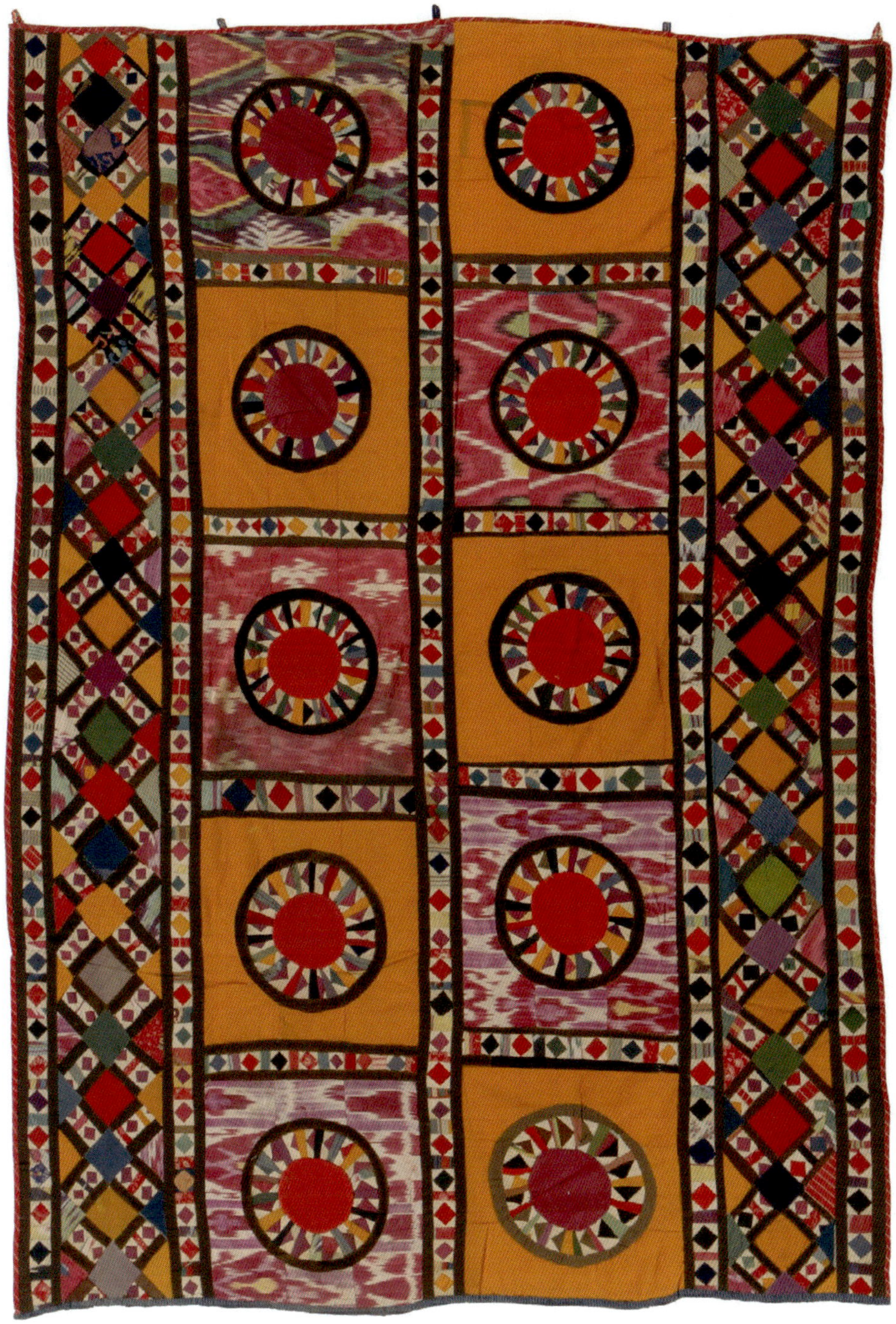

4.13

Hanging

Maker unidentified
Probably made in Uzbekistan, 1900-1920
Cotton; hand pieced
67 x 46.5 in.

Gift of the Robert and Ardis James Foundation, IQM 2019.043.0001

4.14

Seminole Patchwork Skirt

Unidentified Seminole or Miccosukee maker
Probably made in Florida, United States, 1985-1995
Cotton; hand pieced
23 x 45 in.

Gift of the Robert and Ardis James Foundation, IQM 2001.014.0002

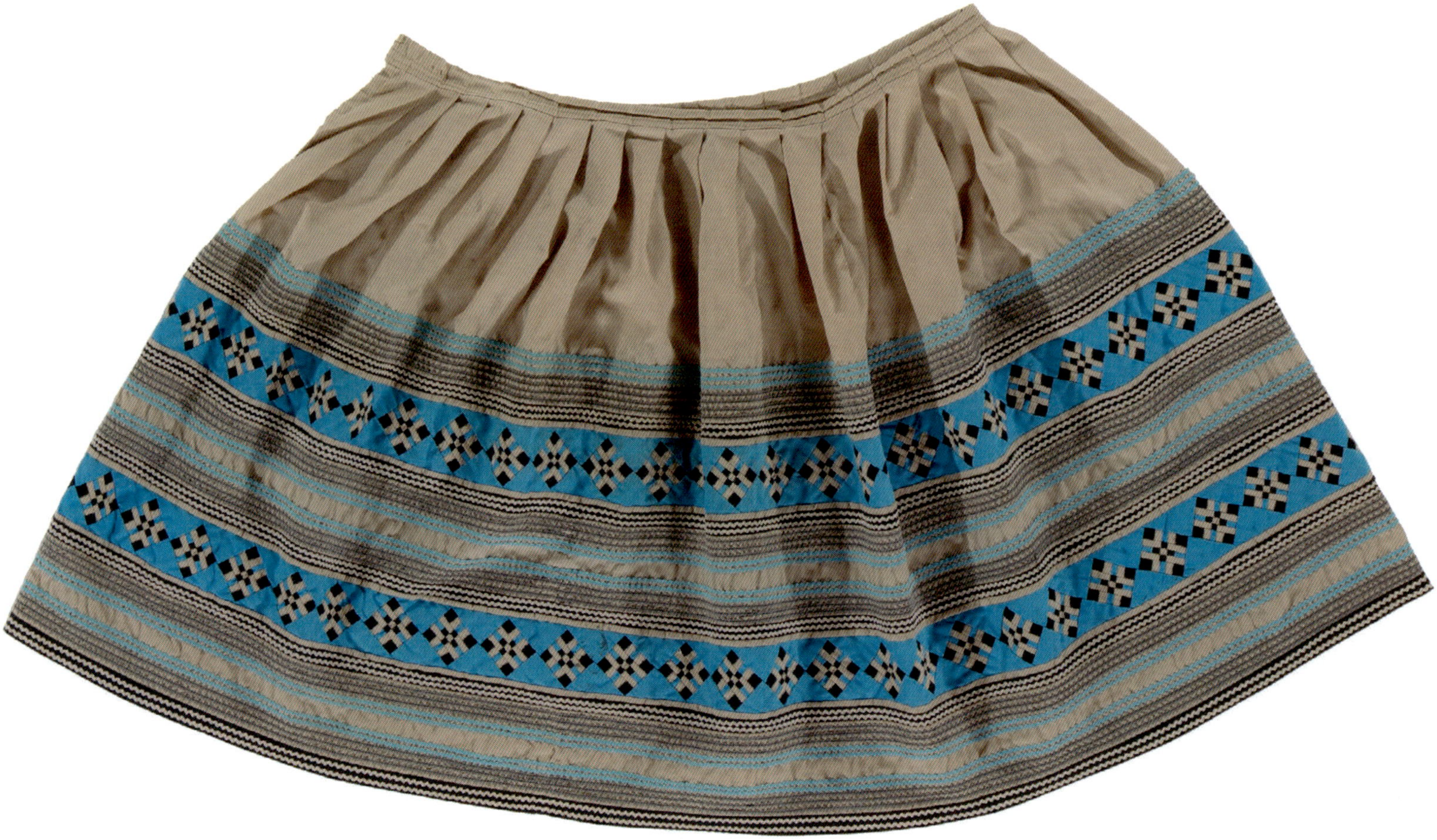

4.15

Tivaevae Bed Cover

Maker unidentified
Made in Cook Islands, 1990-2000
Cotton; hand appliquéd and reverse appliquéd
98.5 x 98 in.

Gift of the Robert and Ardis James Foundation, IQM 2021.041.0001

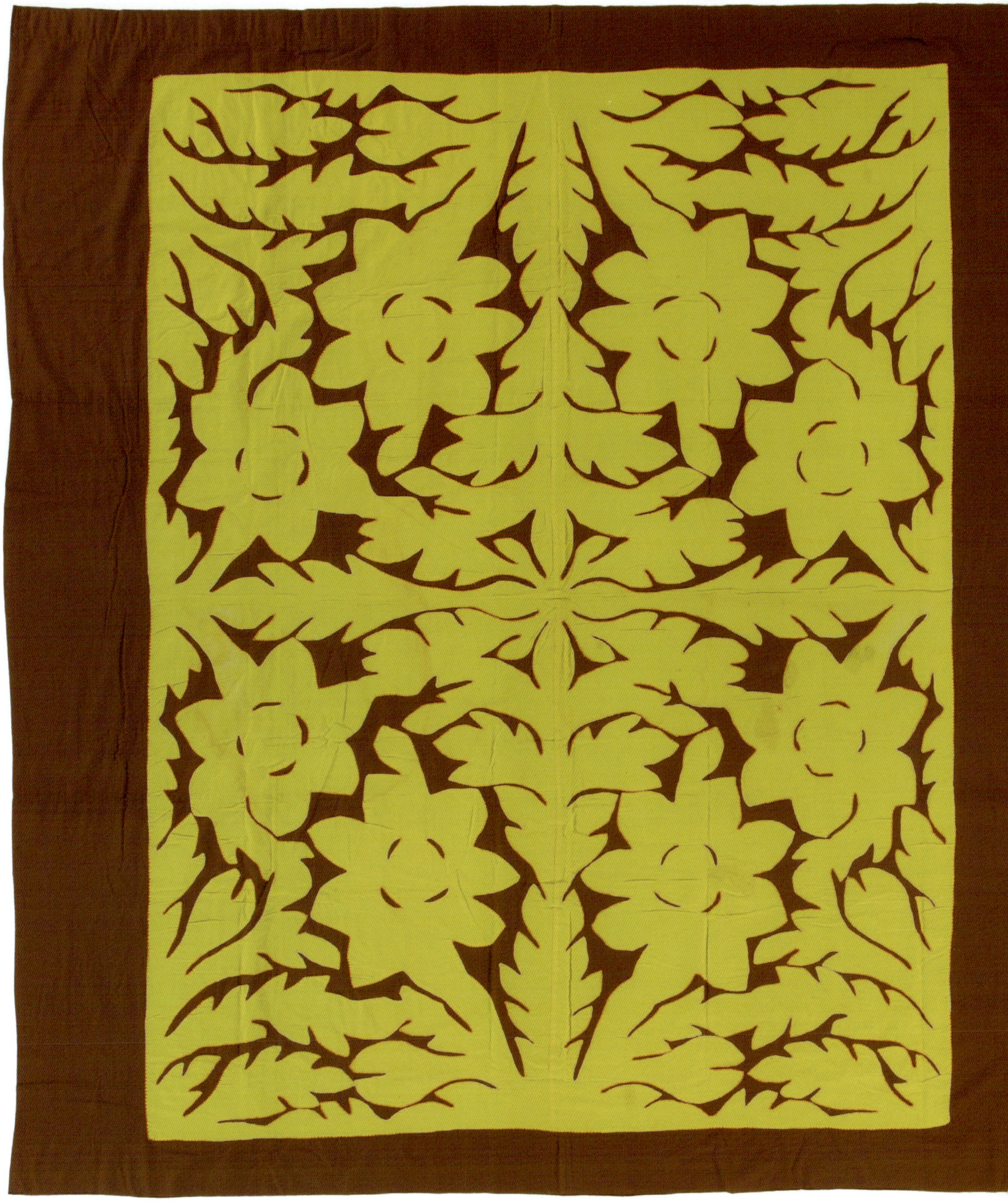

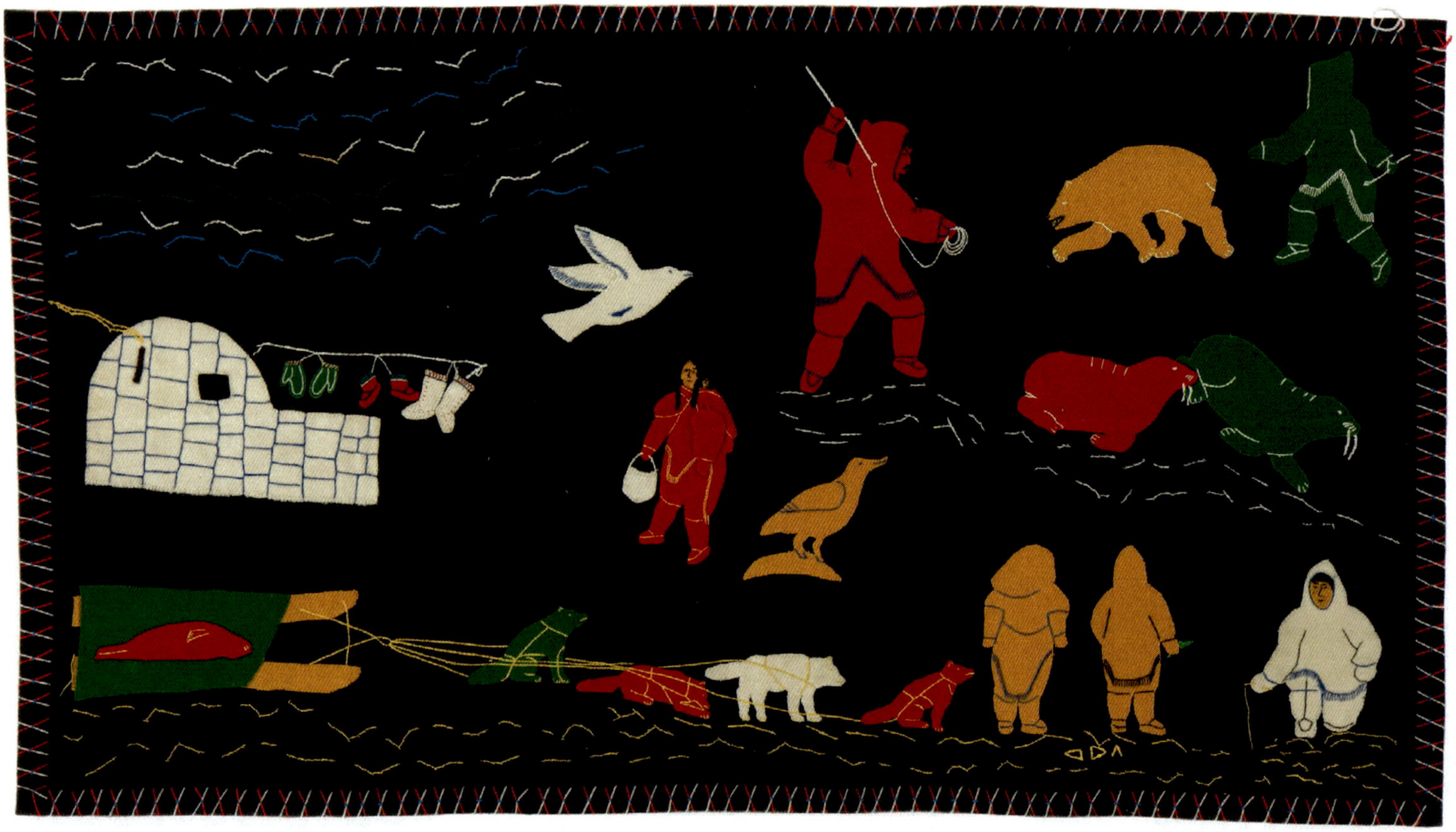

4.16

Hanging

Made by Eugenie Tautoonie Kabluitok (1914-1986)
Made in Kangiqliniq (Rankin Inlet), Nunavut, Canada, 1950-1970
Wool; hand appliquéd
32 x 56 in.

Gift of the Robert and Ardis James Foundation, IQM 2021.032.0001

4.17

Hanging

Maker unidentified
Probably made in Bolivia, 1950-1970
Cotton; hand appliquéd
90 x 60.5 in.

Gift of the Robert and Ardis James Foundation, IQM 2021.059.0001

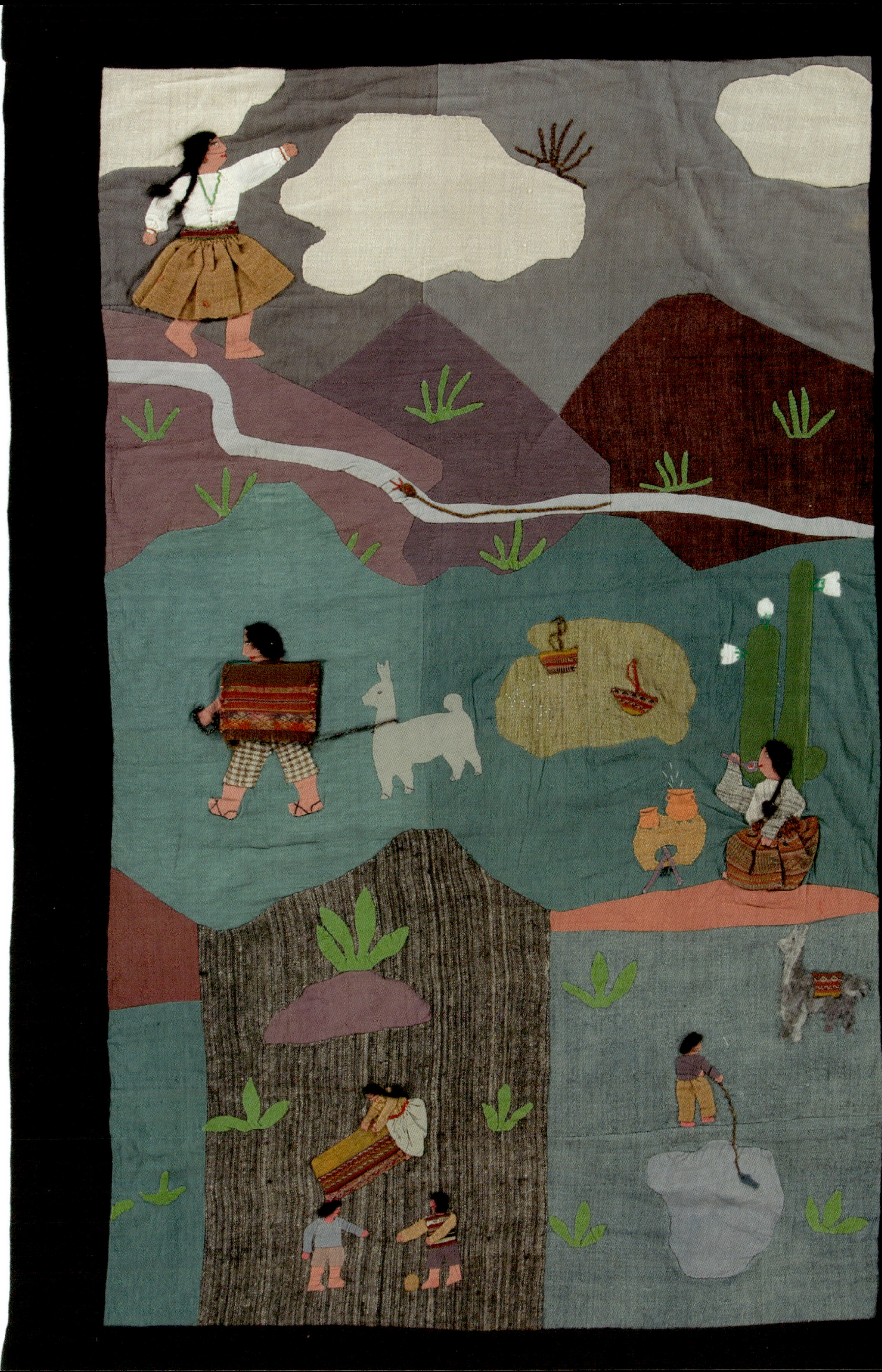

4.18

Hanging

Made by Elizabeth Savanhu
Made in Zimbabwe, circa 2006
Cotton; hand appliquéd
56 x 59.5 in.

Gift of the Robert and Ardis James Foundation, IQM 2006.040.0002

4.19

Quilt Cover

Unidentified maker from the Zhuang ethnic group
Made in Tian'e County, Guangxi, China, 1910-1930
Wool and cotton; hand appliquéd
55.5 x 41 in.

Gift of the Robert and Ardis James Foundation, IQM 2014.027.0001

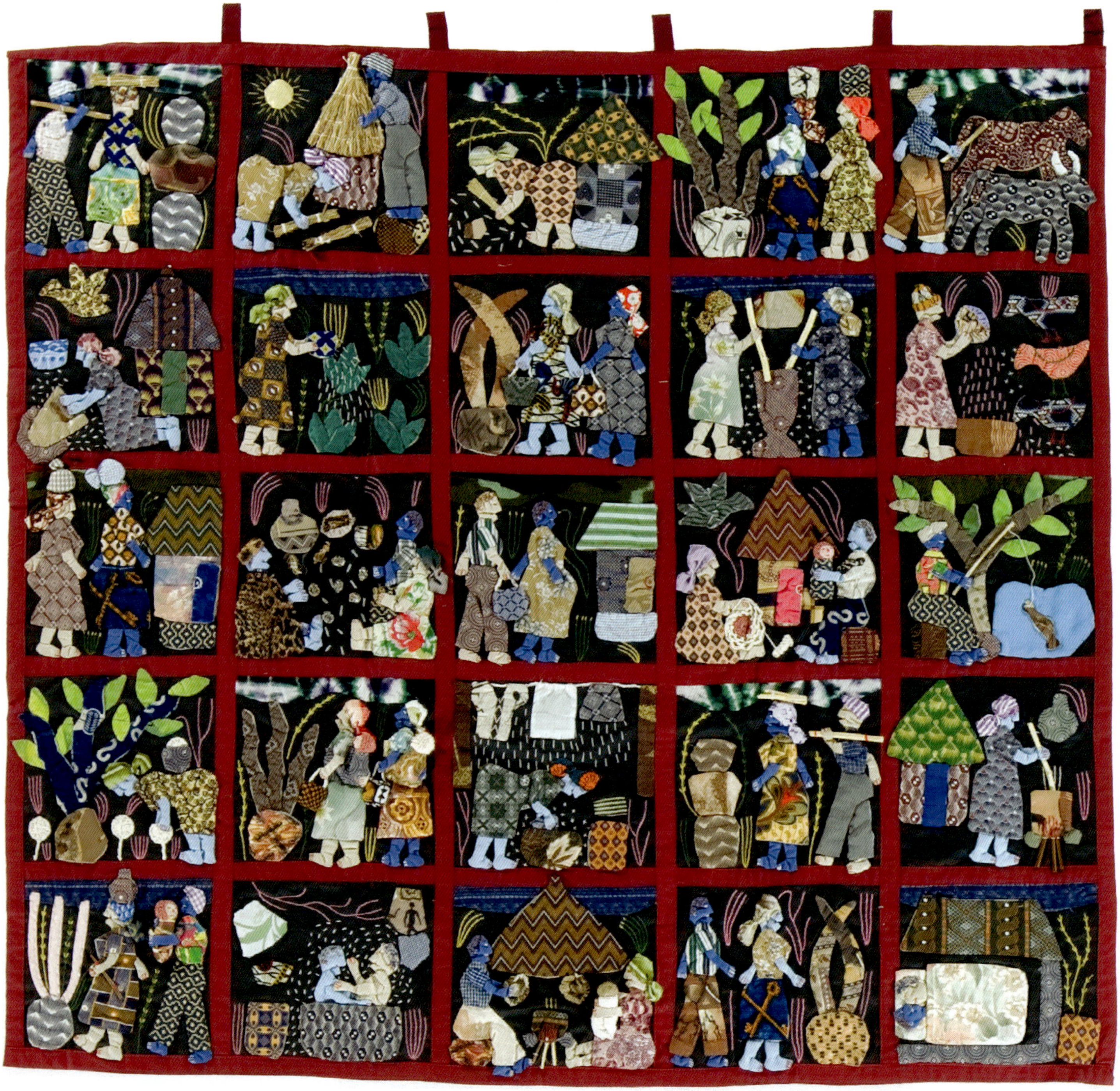

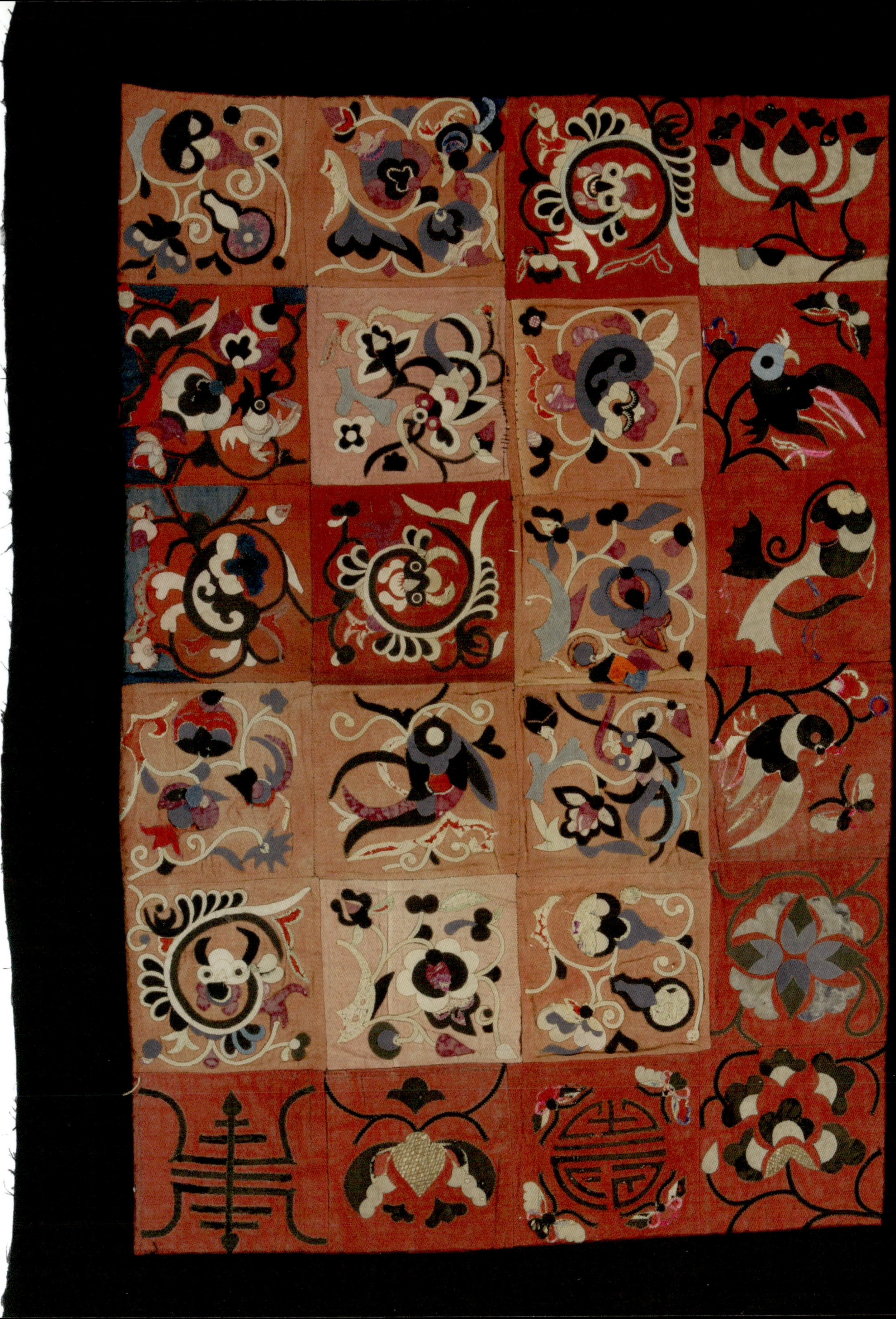

4.20

Asafo Flag

Unidentified maker from the Fante ethnic group
Made in Ghana, 1920-1940
Cotton; hand appliquéd, pieced, and embroidered, machine pieced
34.5 x 56 in.

Gift of the Robert and Ardis James Foundation, IQM 2020.067.0001

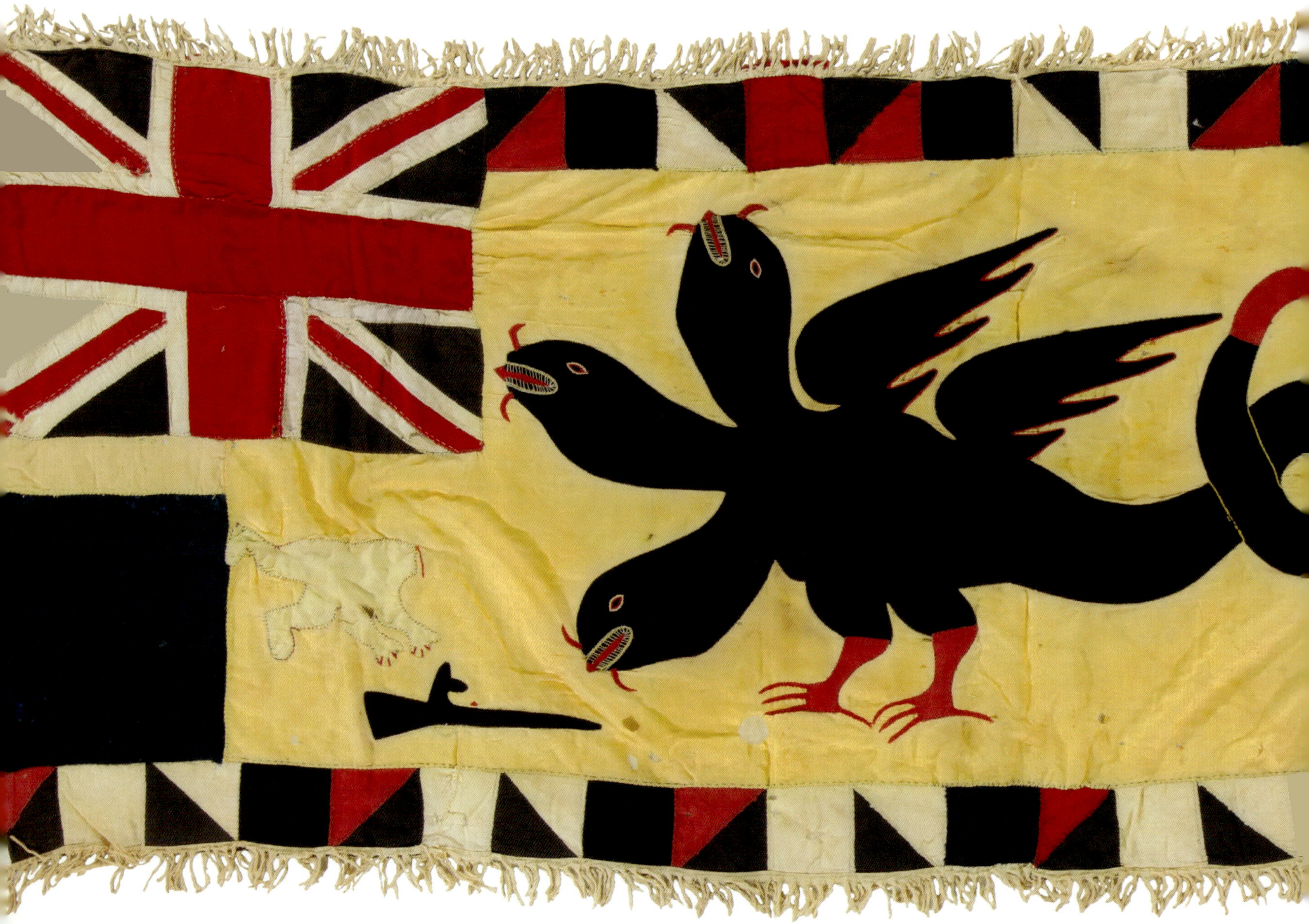

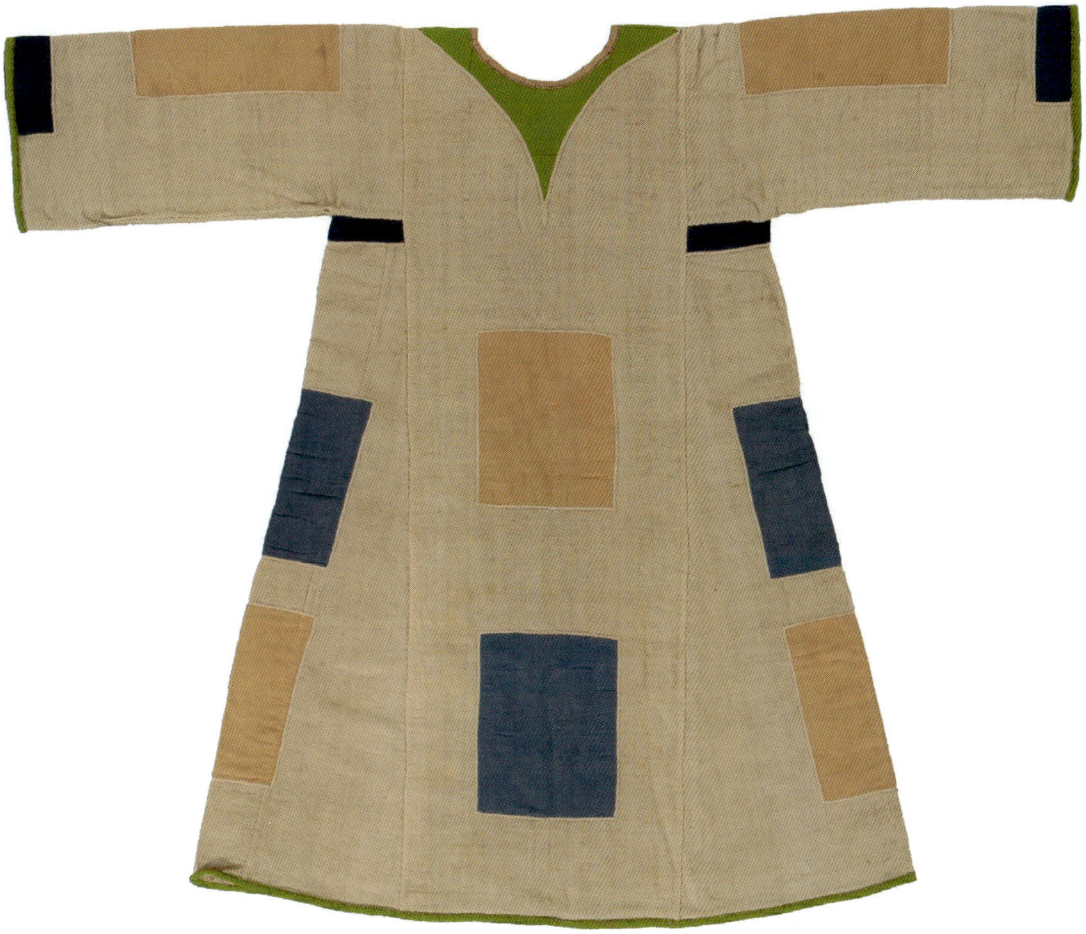

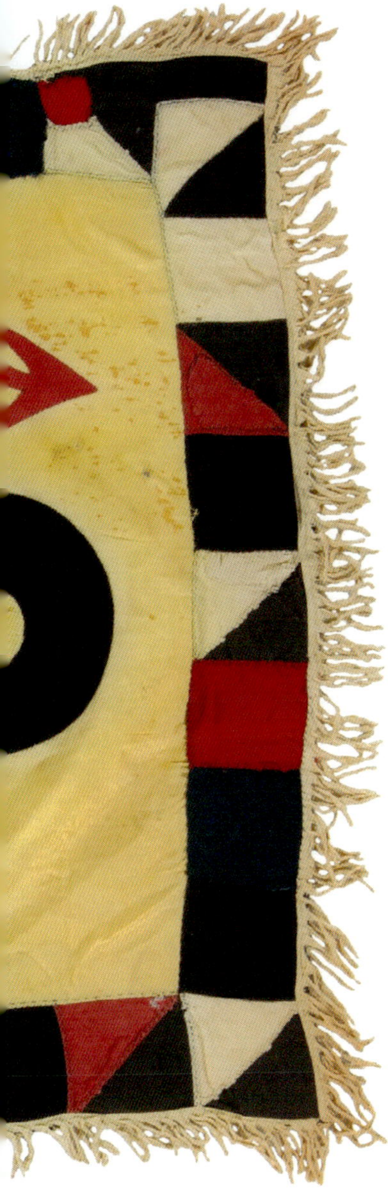

4.21

Jibbah

Maker unidentified
Made in Sudan, 1880-1890
Cotton; hand appliquéd
43 x 51.5 in.

Gift of the Robert and Ardis James Foundation, IQM 2019.059.0001

4.22

Sun Kissed Summer

Ai Kijima
Brooklyn, New York, U.S., 2012
Cotton; machine appliquéd and quilted
53 x 88 in.

Gift of the Robert and Ardis James Foundation, IQM 2021.052.0002

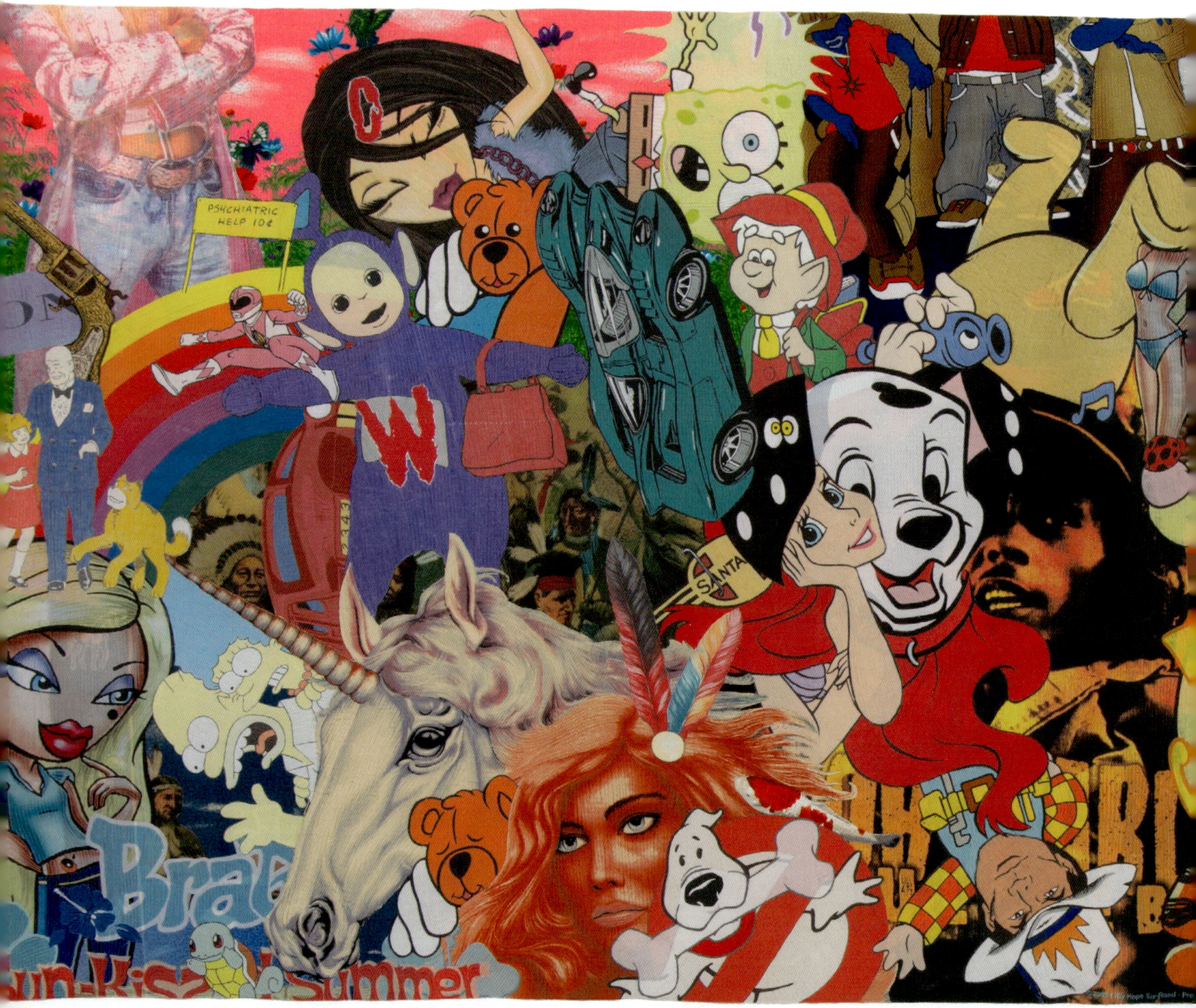

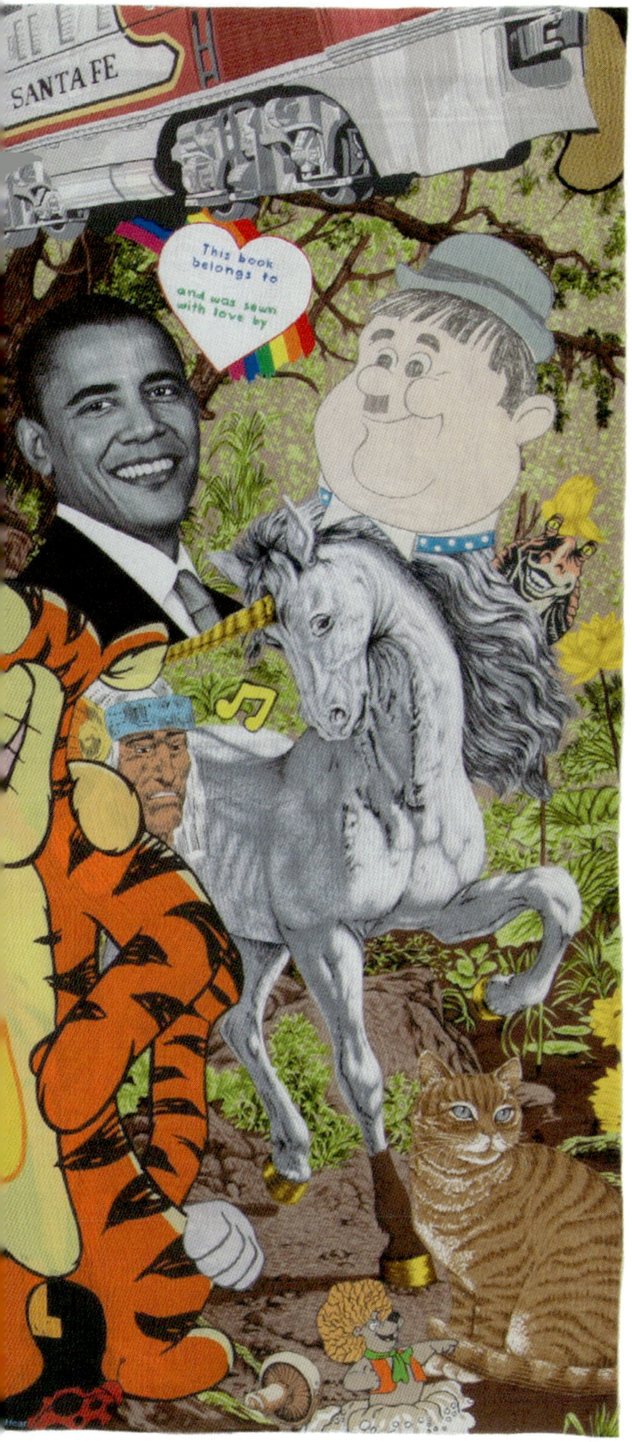

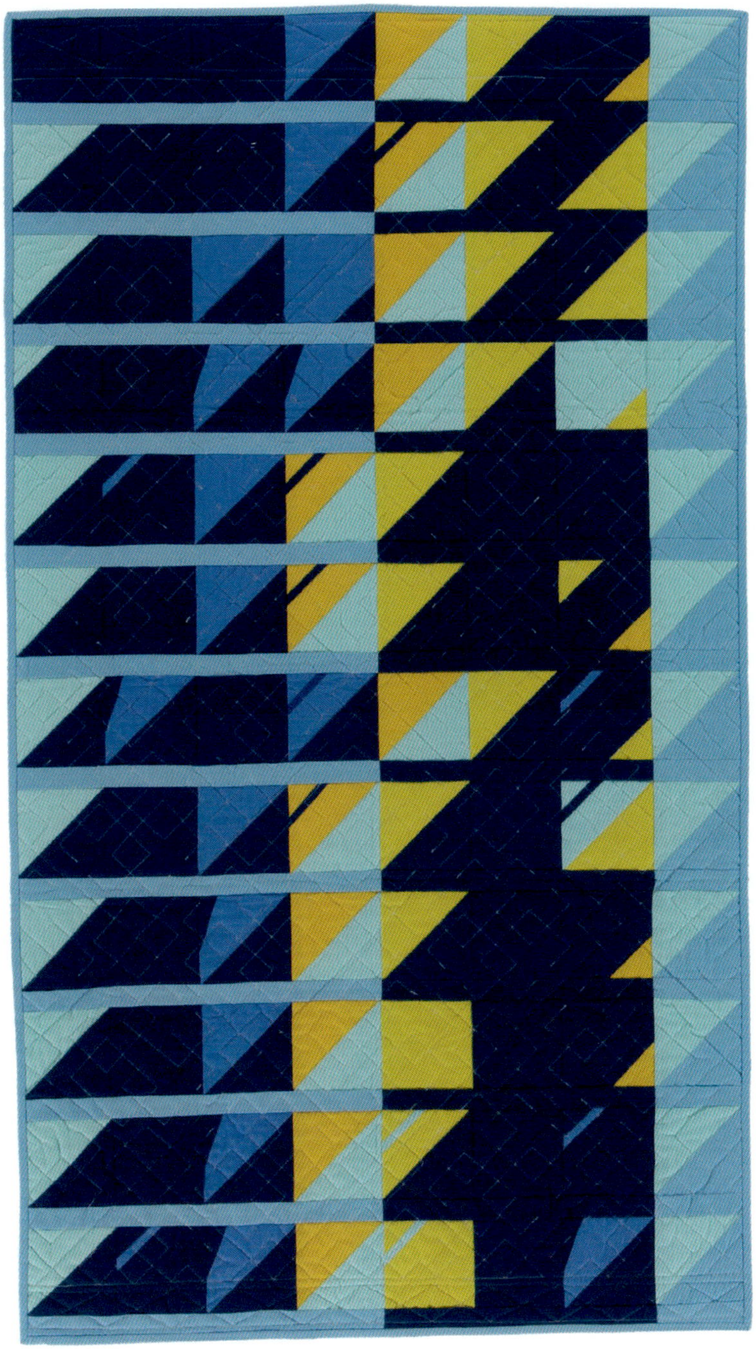

4.23

Vdol Po Travke (Walking in the Grass)

Eliza Hardy Jones
Philadelphia, Pennsylvania, U.S., 2018
Cotton; machine pieced and quilted
57 x 31.5 in.

Gift of the Robert and Ardis James Foundation, IQM 2021.020.0004

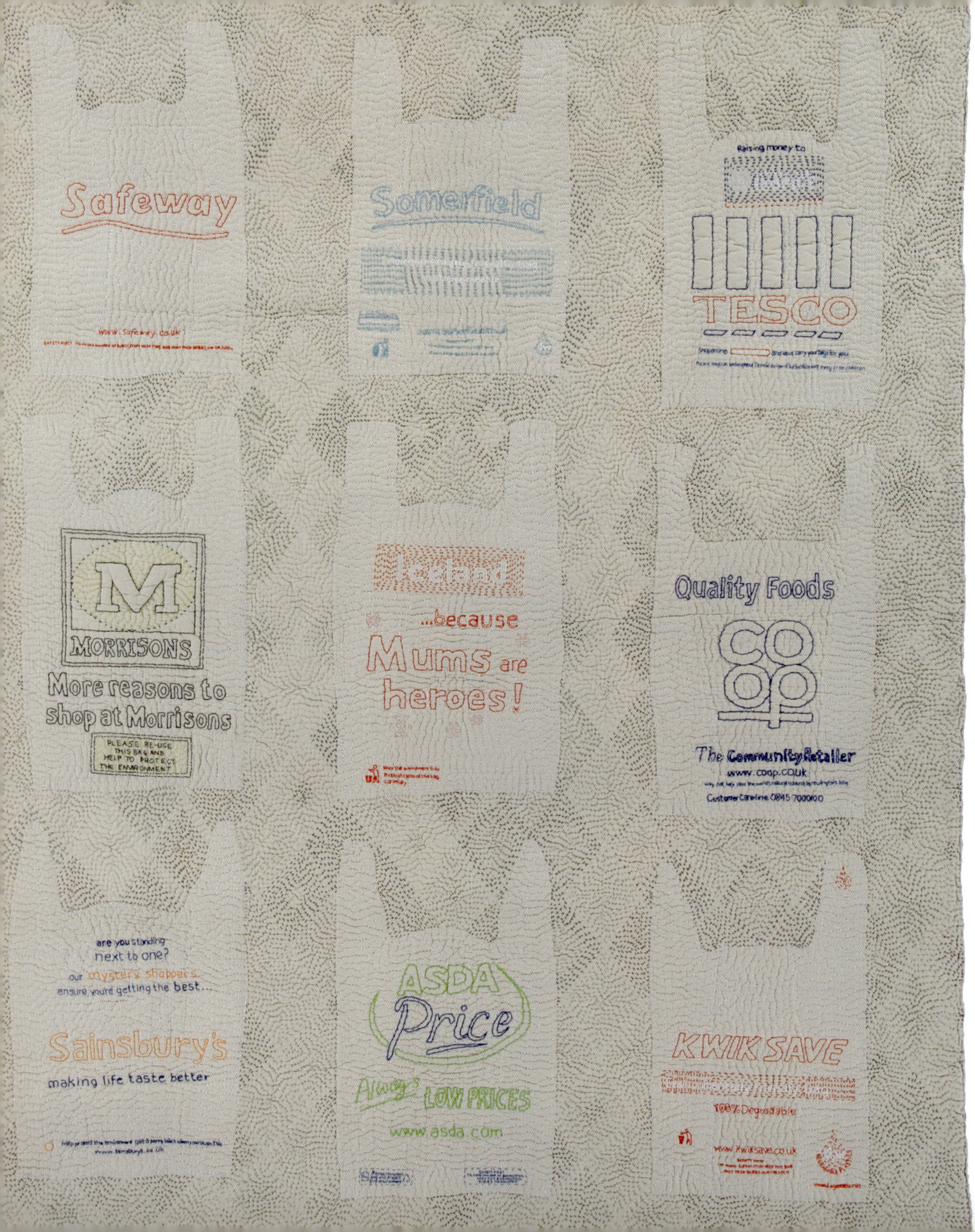

Safeway
www.safeway.co.uk
Somerfield
Raising money to
TESCO
Quality Foods
MORRISONS
More reasons to
shop at Morrisons
PLEASE RE-USE
THIS BAG AND
HELP TO PROTECT
THE ENVIRONMENT
Iceland
...because
Mums are
heroes!
co
op
The CommunityRetailer
www.coop.co.uk
Customer Careline 0845 7000000
are you standing
next to one?
our mystery shoppers
ensure you're getting the best...
Sainsbury's
making life taste better
ASDA
Price
Always LOW PRICES
www.asda.com
KWIK SAVE
100% Degradable
www.kwiksave.co.uk

4.24

Mums are Heroes

Lynn Setterington
Manchester, U.K., 2005
Cotton; Hand quilted
67.5 x 53 in.

Gift of the Robert and Ardis James Foundation, IQM 2006.015.0001

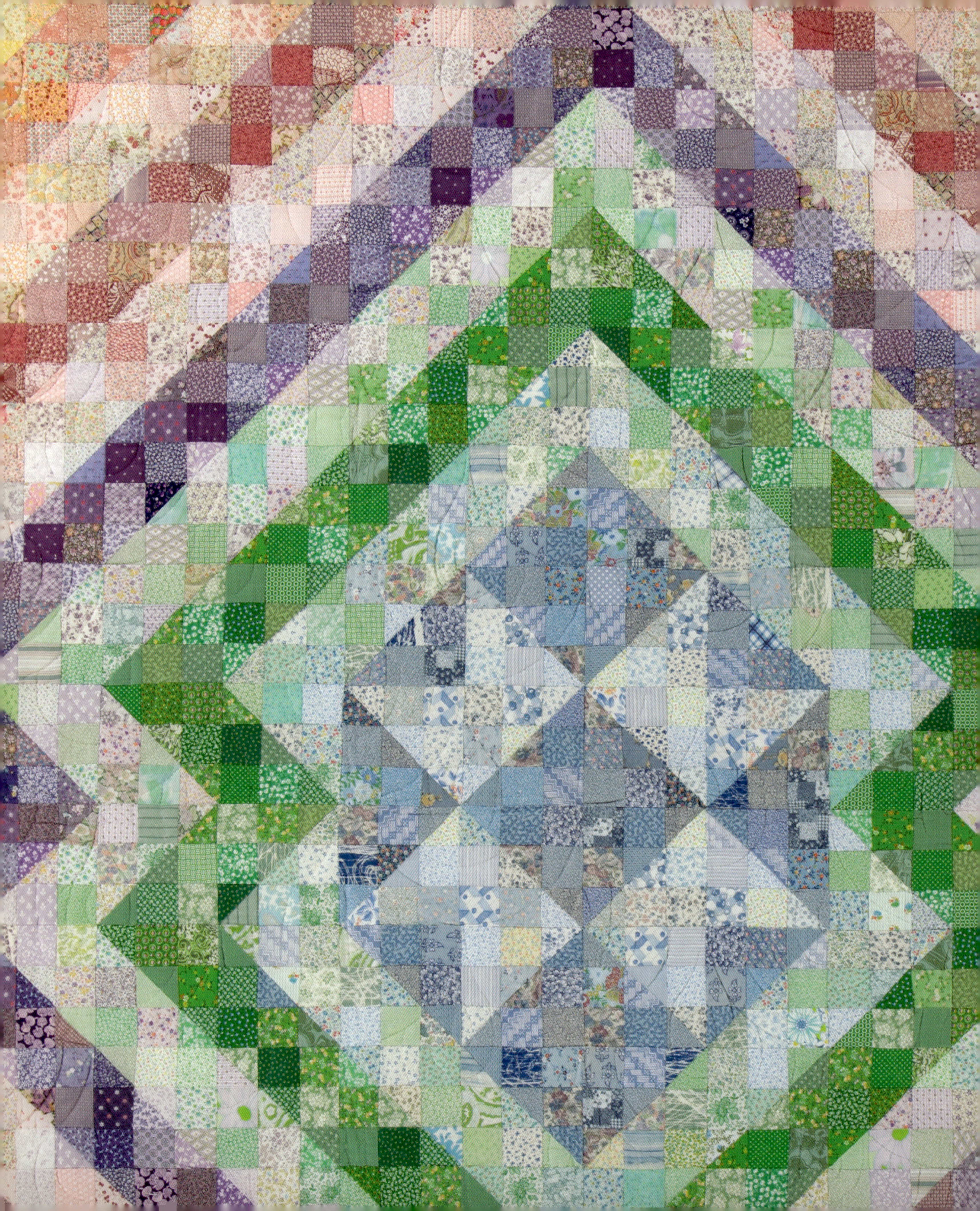

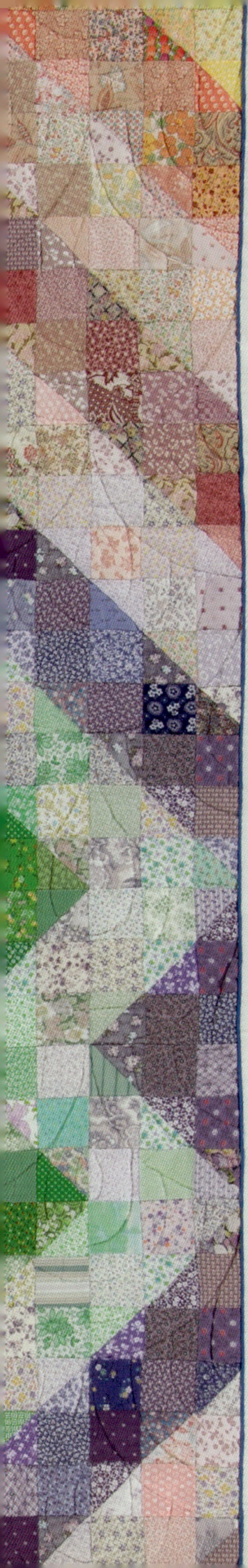

THE JAMES COLLECTION

The Ardis and Robert James Collection consists of the main body of quilts that arrived at the University of Nebraska-Lincoln in 1997 as well as several other smaller groups that the Jameses kept in their personal collection, eventually donating them to the International Quilt Museum in 2006 and 2009.

The James Collection quilts are presented here in object number order, which is based on the year they were donated and the order in which the Jameses kept track of them, which roughly follows their date of acquisition. For condition-related and other reasons, some quilts from the James Collection have been moved to the IQM Education Collection or deaccessioned, which explains why certain object numbers are skipped. Additionally, quilts that were featured earlier as full Plates are not included in this section.

Nine Patch Log Cabin, *Ardis James, Chappaqua, New York, 1982, Ardis and Robert James Collection, IQM 1997.007.1058*

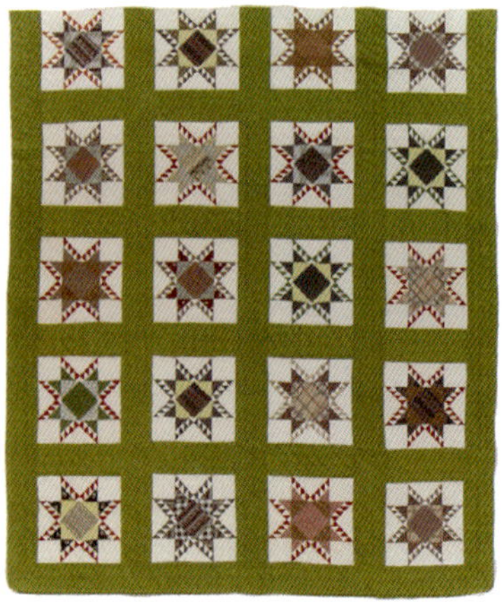

Feathered Star

Maker unidentified
Made in United States
1880 - 1900
77 x 65.5 in.

IQM 1997.007.0001

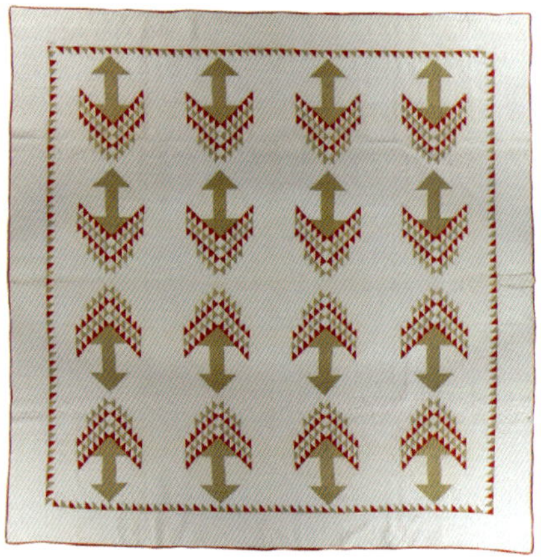

Pine Tree

Maker unidentified
Made in United States
1865 - 1885
81 x 79 in.

IQM 1997.007.0003

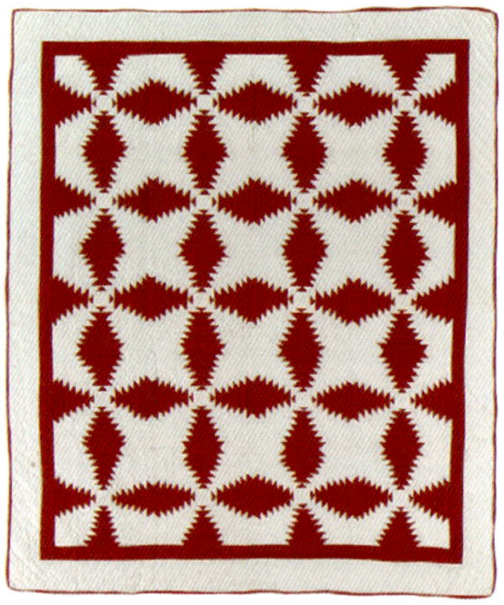

Log Cabin

Maker unidentified
Made in United States
1900 - 1920
67 x 53.5 in.

IQM 1997.007.0004

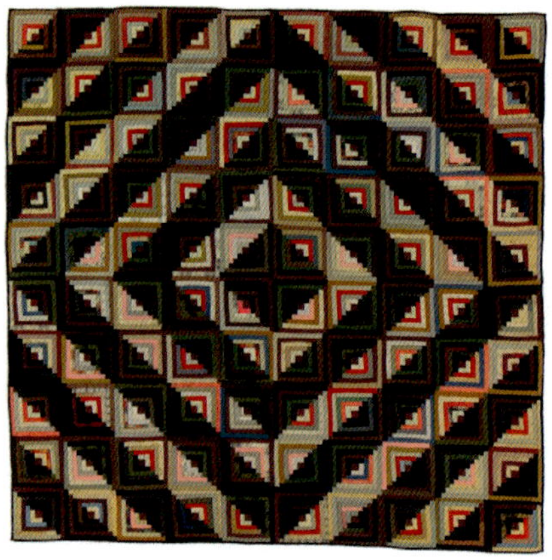

Log Cabin

Maker unidentified
Possibly made in Berks County, Pennsylvania
1880 - 1900
75 x 75 in.

IQM 1997.007.0005

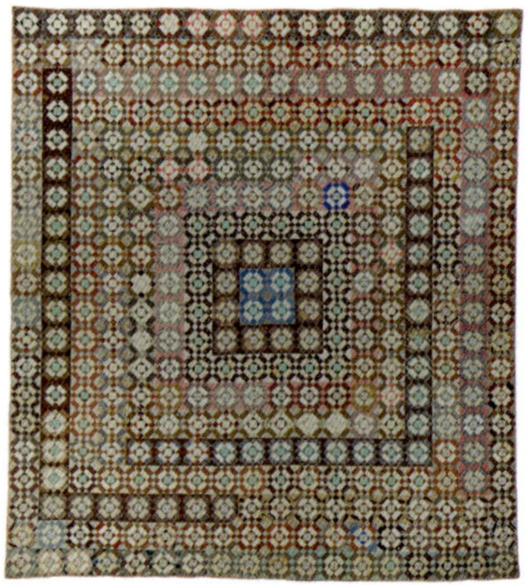

Nine Patch variation

Maker unidentified
Probably made in New England
1860 - 1880
93.5 x 85.5 in.

IQM 1997.007.0006

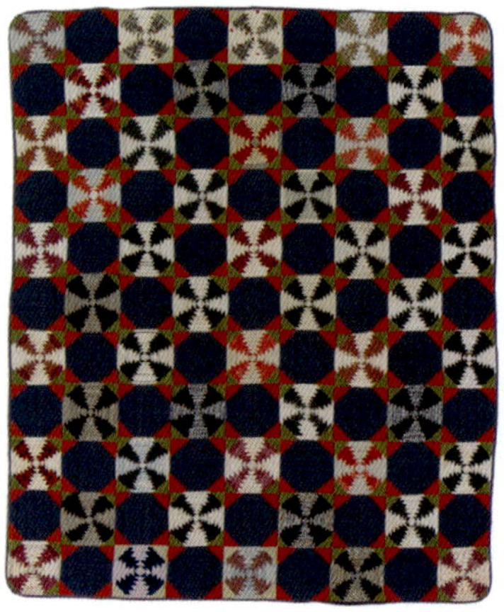

Log Cabin

Maker unidentified
Possibly made in Ohio
1900 - 1920
80 x 63.5 in.

IQM 1997.007.0010

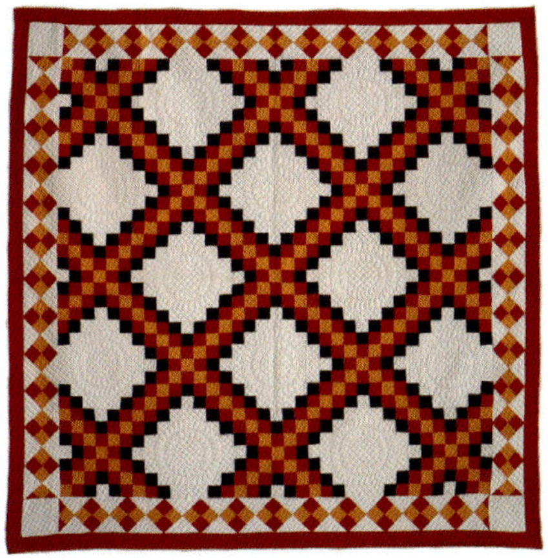

Triple Irish Chain

Maker unidentified
Possibly made in northeastern Ohio
1880 - 1900
75 x 72.5 in.
IQM 1997.007.0012

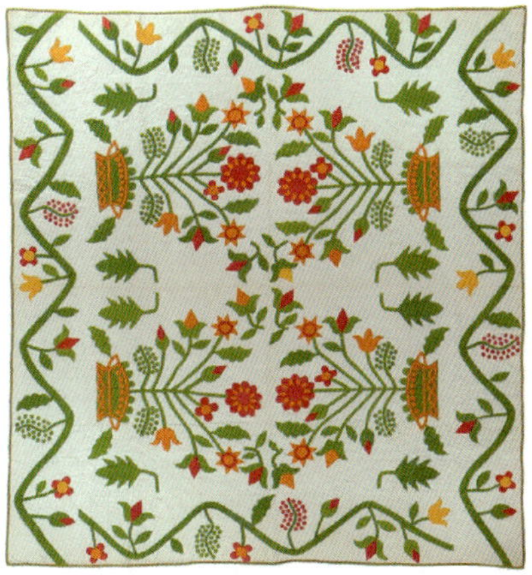

Basket of Flowers

Maker unidentified
Possibly made in Indiana, Ohio or Pennsylvania
1850 - 1870
80 x 86 in.
IQM 1997.007.0013

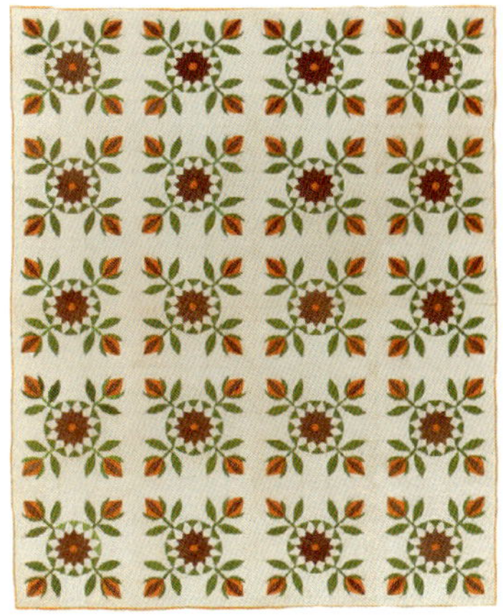

Texas Star variation with Tulips

Maker unidentified
Possibly made in southern United States
1860 - 1880
86.5 x 69.5 in.
IQM 1997.007.0014

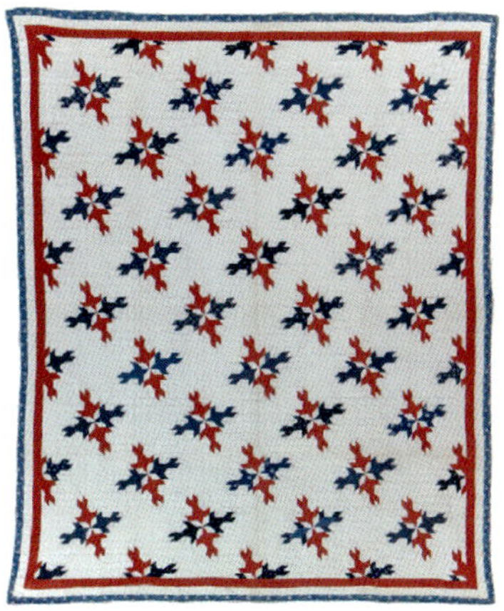

Four Swallows

Maker unidentified
Possibly made in Illinois
Circa 1925
76.5 x 62.5 in.
IQM 1997.007.0015

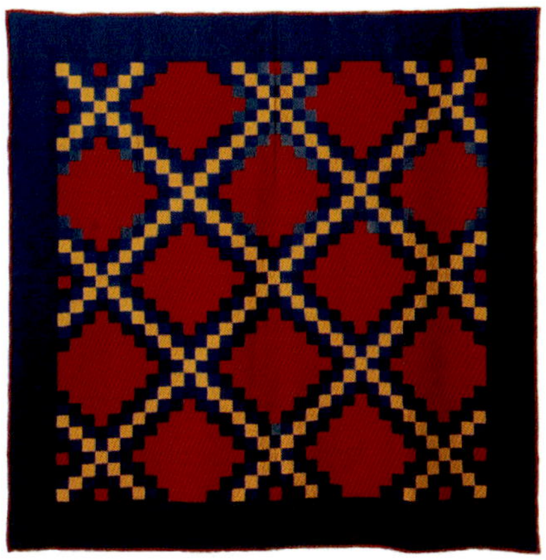

Double Irish Chain

Maker unidentified
Possibly made in Mifflin County, Pennsylvania
1860 - 1880
83 x 82.5 in.
IQM 1997.007.0018

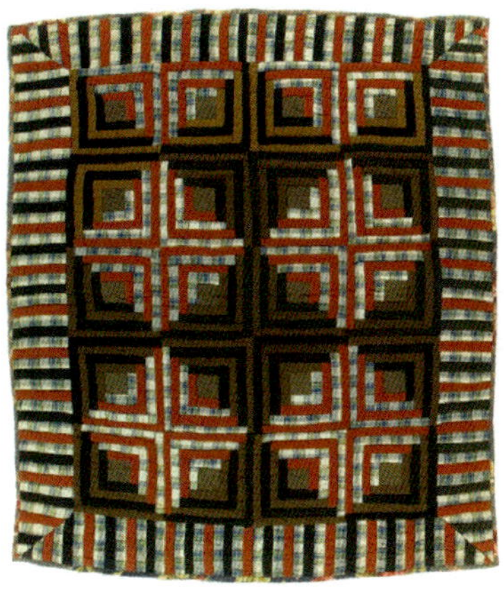

Log Cabin

Maker unidentified
Possibly made in Montgomery County, Ohio
1870 - 1890
35 x 32 in.
IQM 1997.007.0019

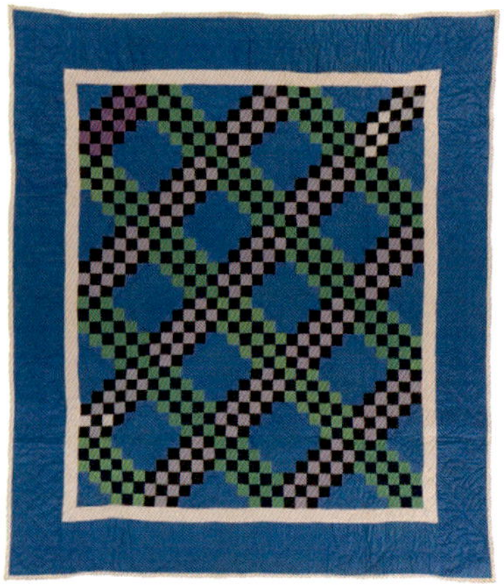

Triple Irish Chain

Maker unidentified
Possibly made in midwestern United States
1930 - 1940
82 x 71 in.
IQM 1997.007.0024

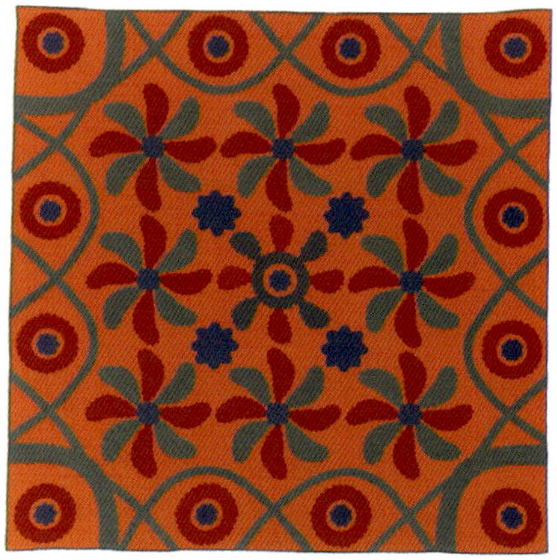

Princess Feather

Maker unidentified
Possibly made in York County, Pennsylvania
1880 - 1900
84.5 x 83.5 in.
IQM 1997.007.0026

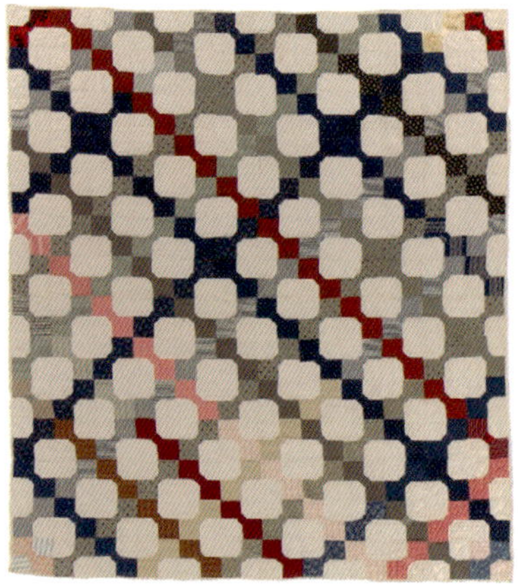

Bow Tie

Maker unidentified
Possibly made in southern Indiana
1890 - 1910
76 x 88 in.
IQM 1997.007.0029

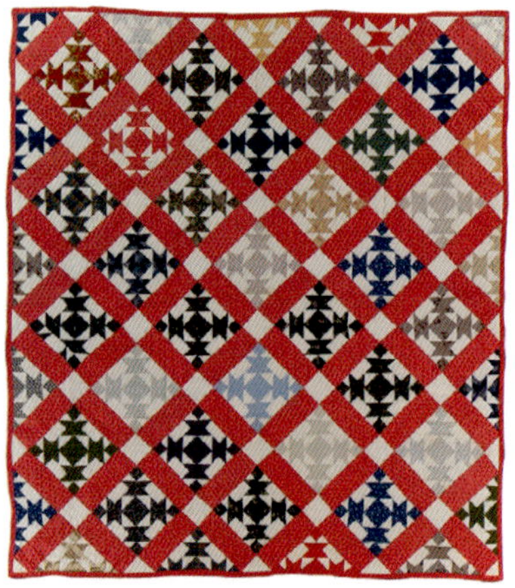

Broken Dishes

Maker unidentified
Possibly made in New York
1880 - 1900
71.5 x 82 in.
IQM 1997.007.0030

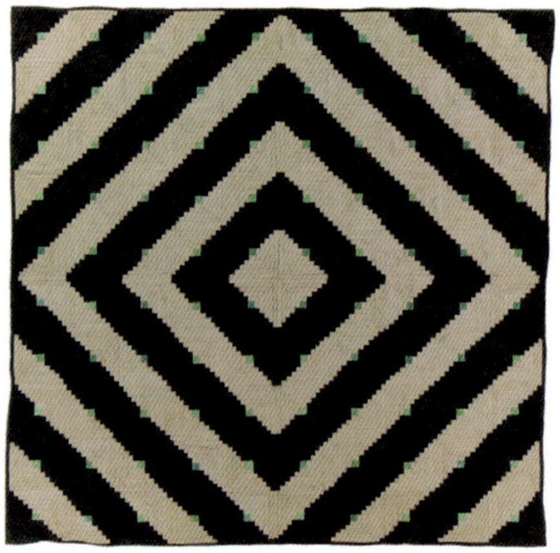

Log Cabin

Maker unidentified
Possibly made in Hastings, New York
1870 - 1890
81 x 80.5 in.
IQM 1997.007.0031

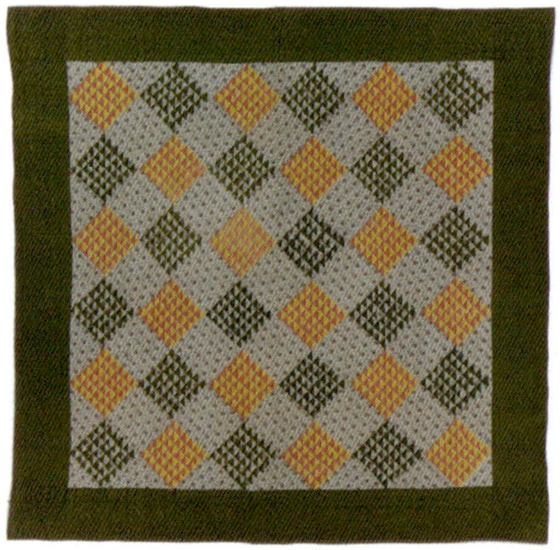

Birds in Air

Maker unidentified
Possibly made in Lancaster County, Pennsylvania
1880 - 1900
73.5 x 73 in.
IQM 1997.007.0034

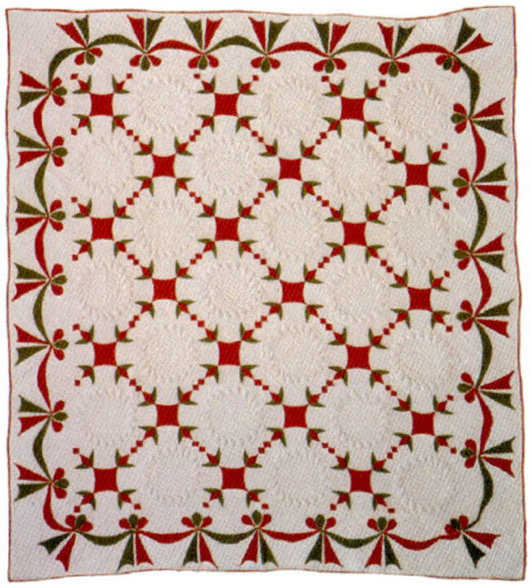

Turkey Tracks

Probably made by E. E. McNary
Probably made in Randolph County, Indiana
1850 - 1870
81 x 72 in.

IQM 1997.007.0035

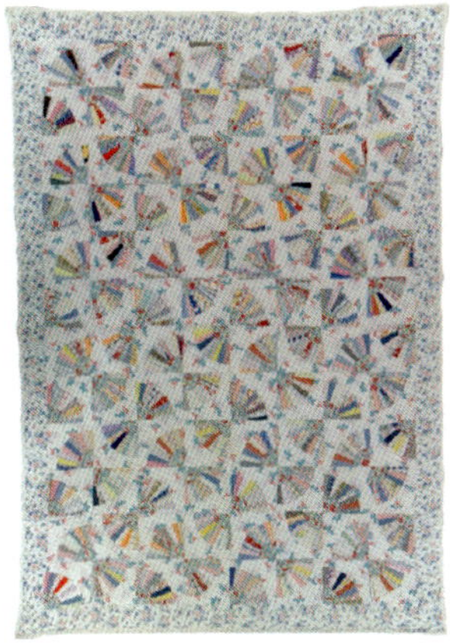

Grandmother's Fan

Maker unidentified
Possibly made in midwestern United States
1920 - 1940
93 x 63.5 in.

IQM 1997.007.0036

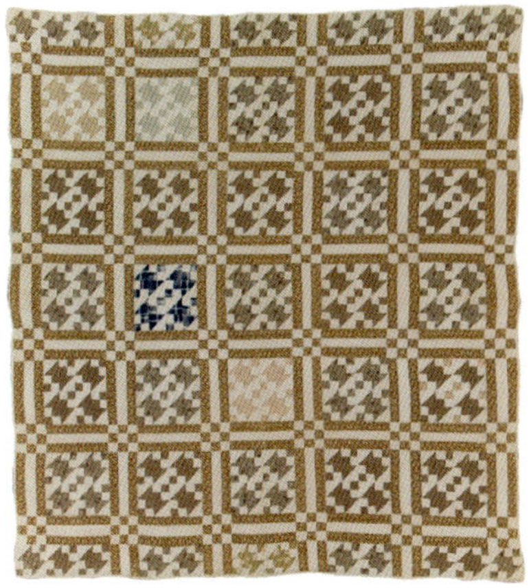

Jacob's Ladder

Maker unidentified
Made in United States
1870 - 1890
74.5 x 67.5 in.

IQM 1997.007.0037

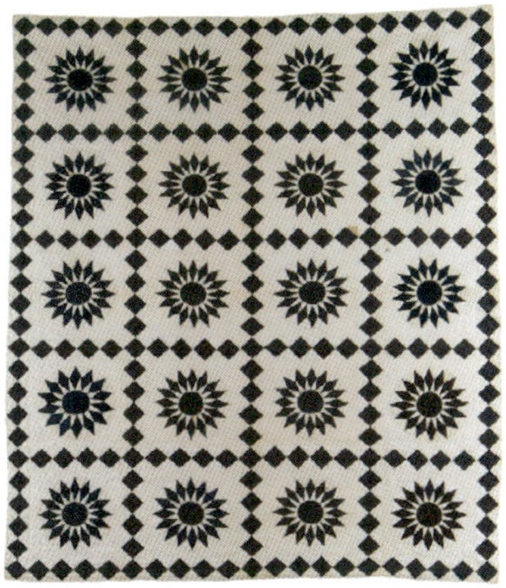

Rising Sun

Maker unidentified
Possibly made in Van Buren County, Michigan
1860 - 1880
86 x 72 in.

IQM 1997.007.0038

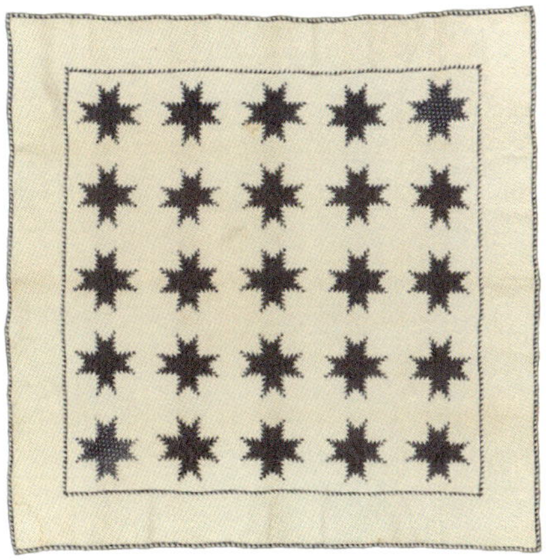

Feathered Star

Probably made by Margaret Story
Possibly made in London, Carroll County, Ohio
Dated 1847
90 x 85.5 in.

IQM 1997.007.0039

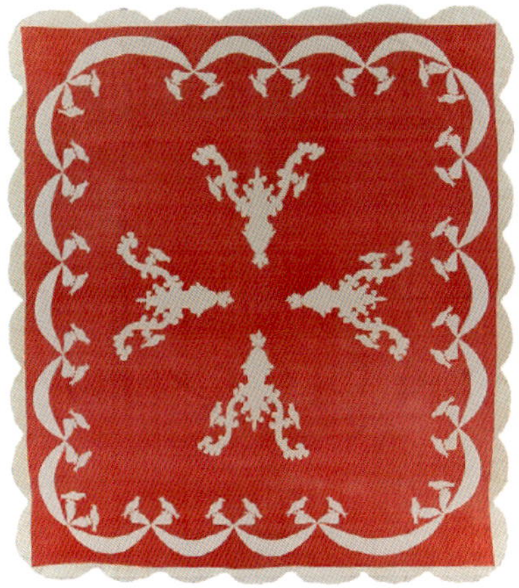

Original

Maker unidentified
Made in United States
1880 - 1900
88 x 72.5 in.

IQM 1997.007.0040

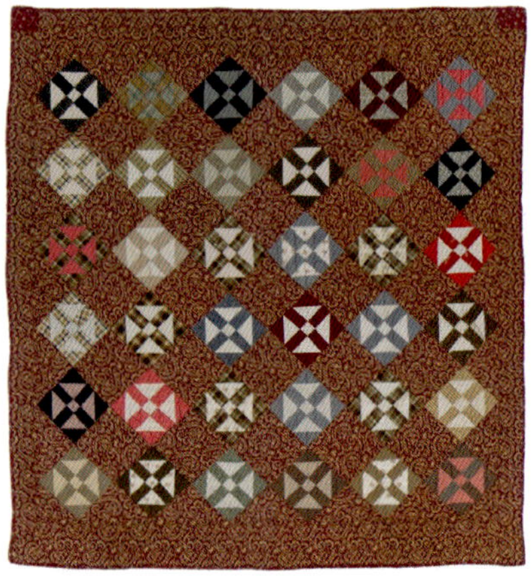

Shoo Fly variation

Maker unidentified
Possibly made in Portland, Michigan
1900 - 1920
80 x 72.5 in.
IQM 1997.007.0041

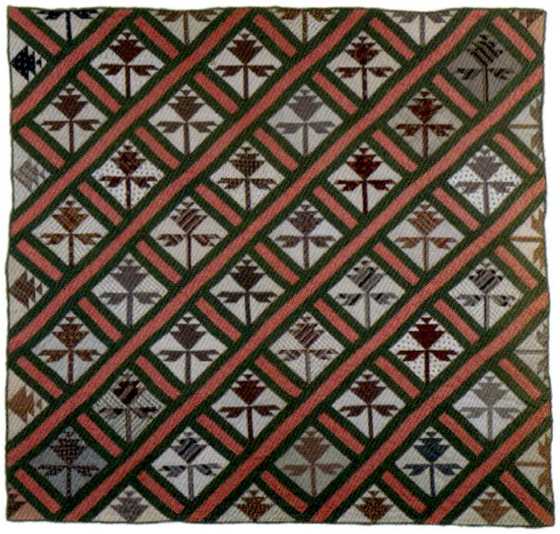

Lily

Maker unidentified
Possibly made in Indiana County, Pennsylvania
1880 - 1900
82 x 80 in.
IQM 1997.007.0042

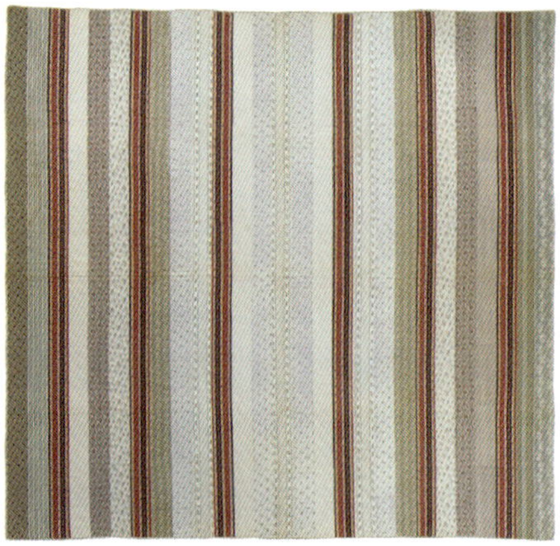

Bars

Maker unidentified
Made in United States
1860 - 1880
88 x 85 in.
IQM 1997.007.0044

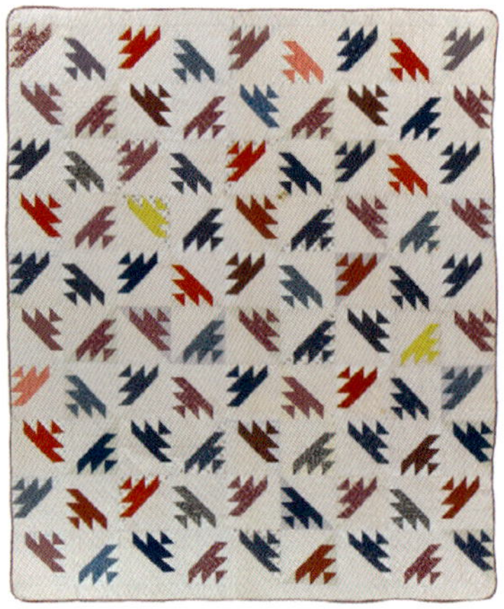

Sailboat

Maker unidentified
Possibly made in Indiana
1890 - 1910
88.5 x 72.5 in.
IQM 1997.007.0045

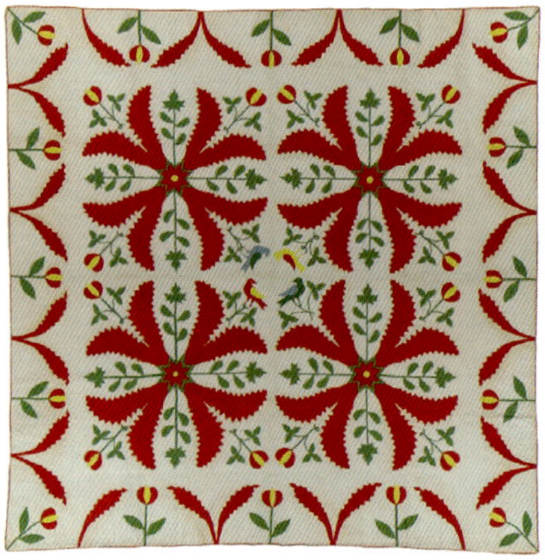

Jester's Plume

Maker unidentified
Possibly made in Germantown, Ohio
1860 - 1880
93 x 91 in.
IQM 1997.007.0047

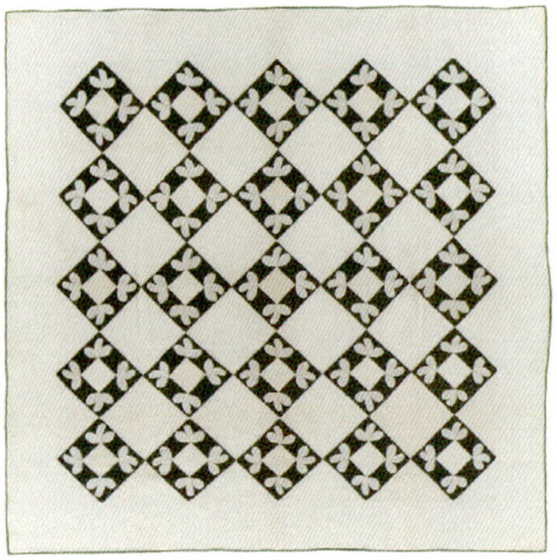

Turkey Tracks

Maker unidentified
Made in United States
1850 - 1870
86 x 84 in.
IQM 1997.007.0048

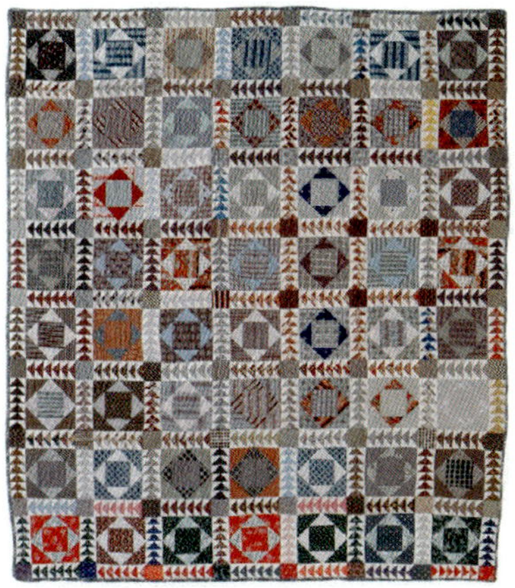

Square in a Square

Maker unidentified
Made in United States
1860 - 1910
80.5 x 68 in.

IQM 1997.007.0051

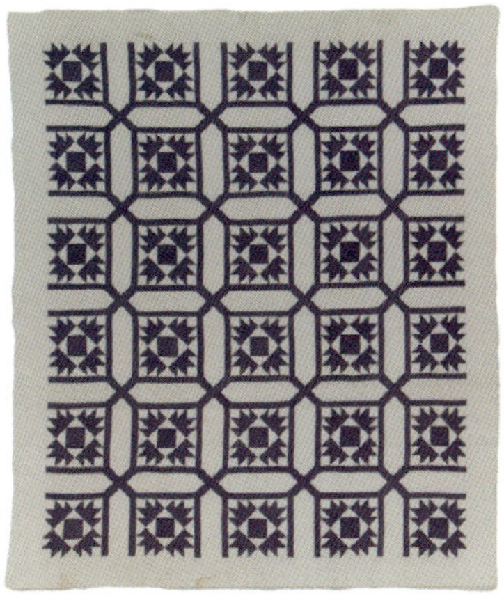

Union Square

Maker unidentified
Possibly made in Cass County, Michigan
1875 - 1895
77.5 x 63.5 in.

IQM 1997.007.0053

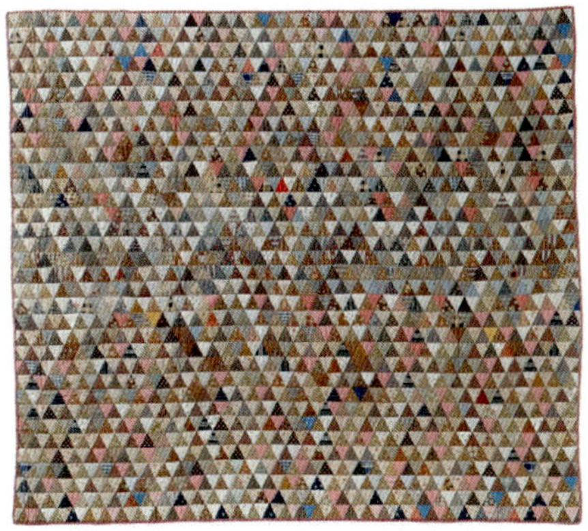

Thousand Pyramids

Maker unidentified
Possibly made in Pennsylvania
1870 - 1890
75 x 80.5 in.

IQM 1997.007.0055

Pots of Flowers

Maker unidentified
Possibly made in Muskingum County, Ohio
1850 - 1870
87 x 76 in.

IQM 1997.007.0056

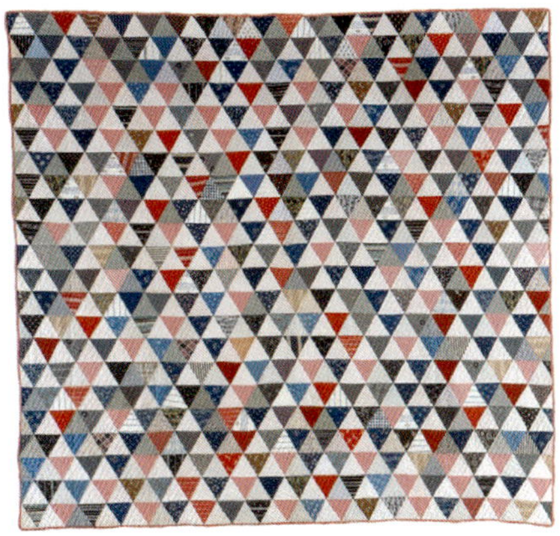

Thousand Pyramids

Maker unidentified
Possibly made in Posey County, Indiana
1890 - 1910
79.5 x 83 in.

IQM 1997.007.0058

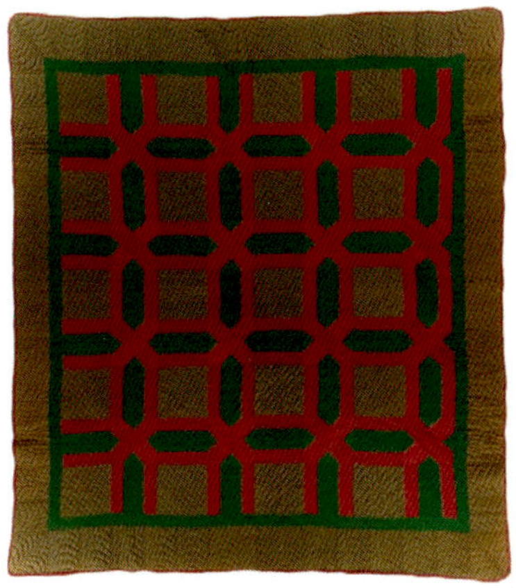

Garden Maze

Maker unidentified
Possibly made in Wells or Adams County, Indiana
1880 - 1900
85 x 74 in.

IQM 1997.007.0062

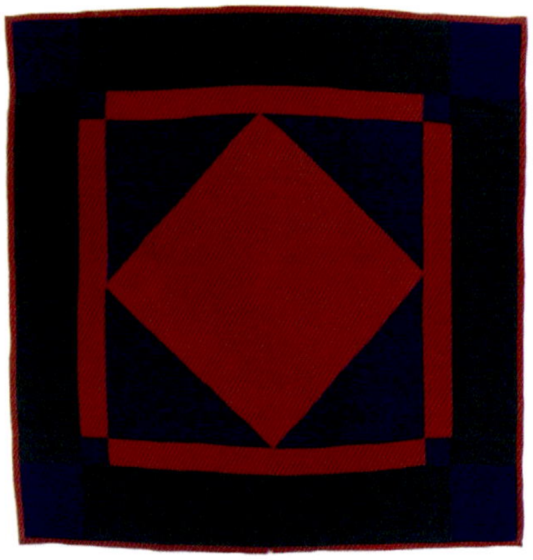

Center Diamond

Possibly made by Melinda King
Probably made in Lancaster County, Pennsylvania
1910 - 1930
72.5 x 69.5 in.

IQM 1997.007.0063

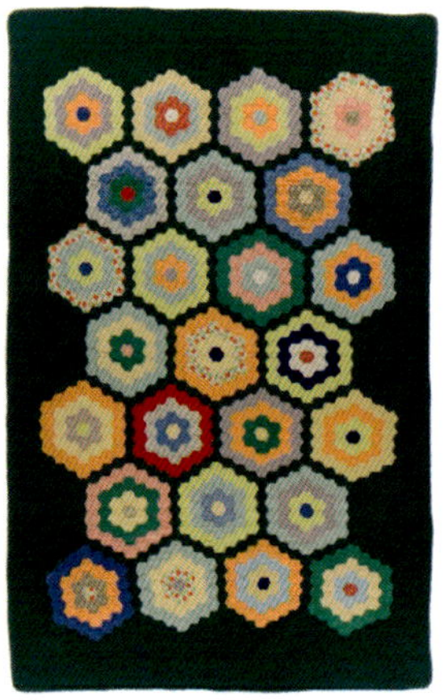

Grandmother's Flower Garden

Maker unidentified
Possibly made in Davies County, Indiana
Dated 1932
82 x 52 in.

IQM 1997.007.0064

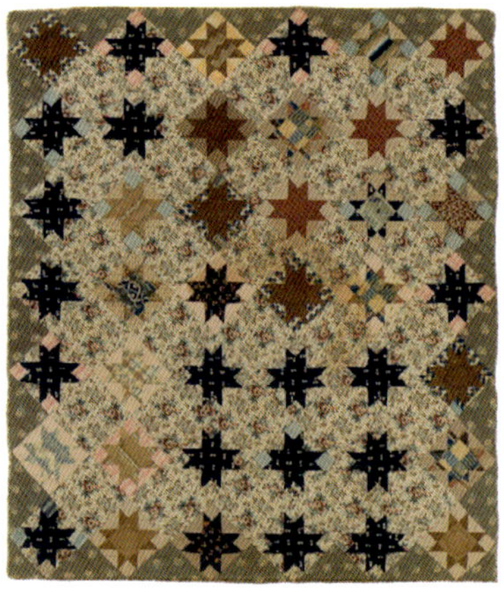

Sawtooth Star

Maker unidentified
Possibly made in Cullman County, Alabama
1830 - 1850
79 x 67.5 in.

IQM 1997.007.0065

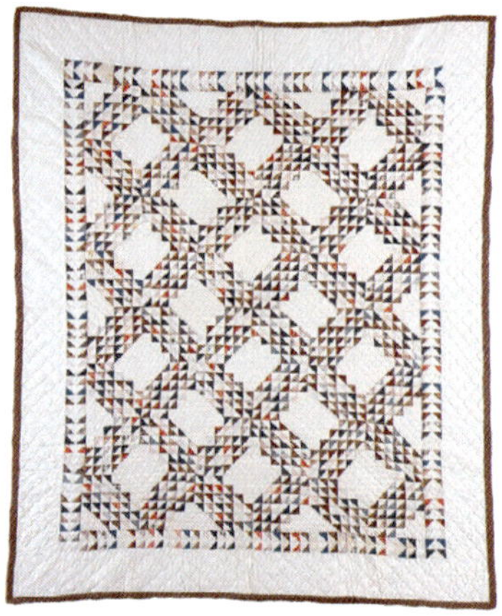

Ocean Waves

Maker unidentified
Possibly made in Henry County, Indiana
1870 - 1890
79.5 x 64 in.

IQM 1997.007.0070

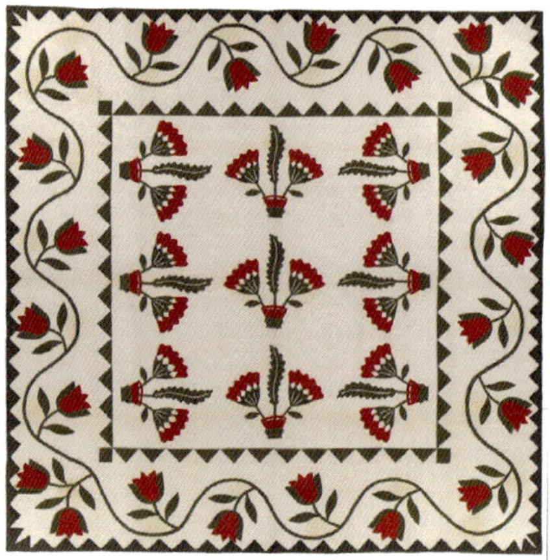

Coxcomb

Maker unidentified
Possibly made in Cumberland, Ohio
1850 - 1860
95 x 94 in.

IQM 1997.007.0075

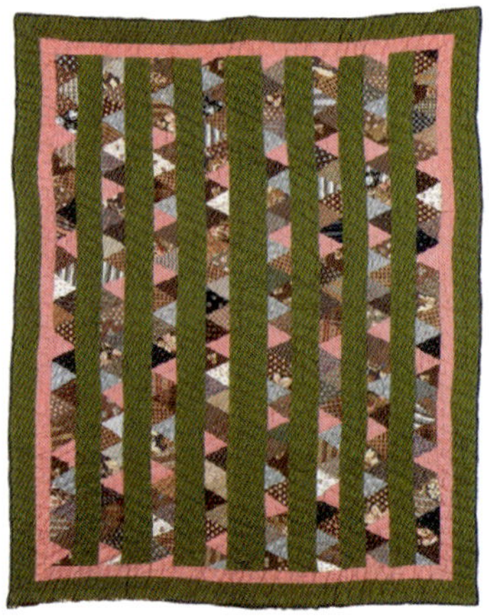

Thousand Pyramids variation

Maker unidentified
Possibly made in Michigan
1880 - 1900
84 x 64 in.

IQM 1997.007.0079

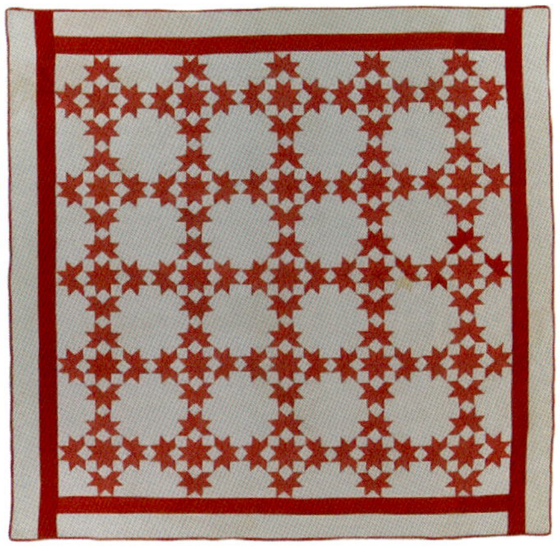

All Hands Around

Maker unidentified
Possibly made in eastern Ohio
1875 - 1920
80 x 79.5 in.

IQM 1997.007.0080

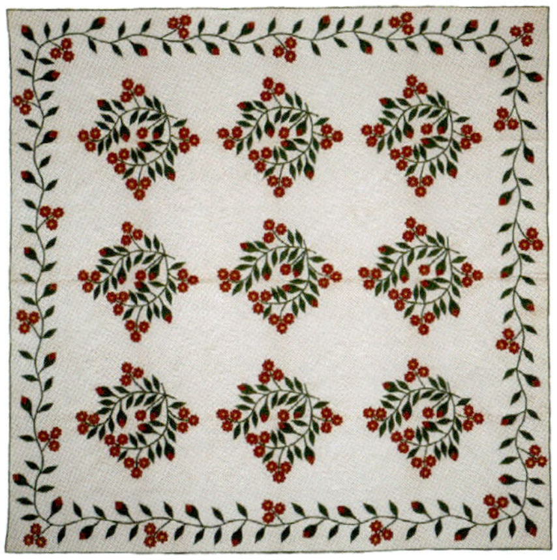

Wreath

Maker unidentified
Made in United States
1850 - 1860
85.5 x 84.5 in.

IQM 1997.007.0085

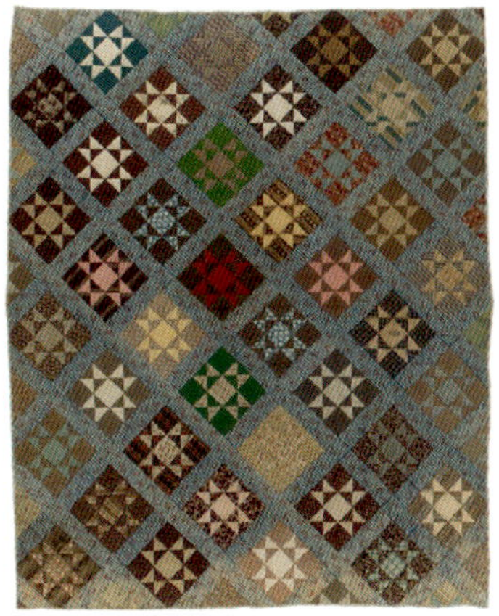

Variable Star

Maker unidentified
Possibly made in Pennsylvania
1860 - 1880
91 x 71 in.

IQM 1997.007.0087

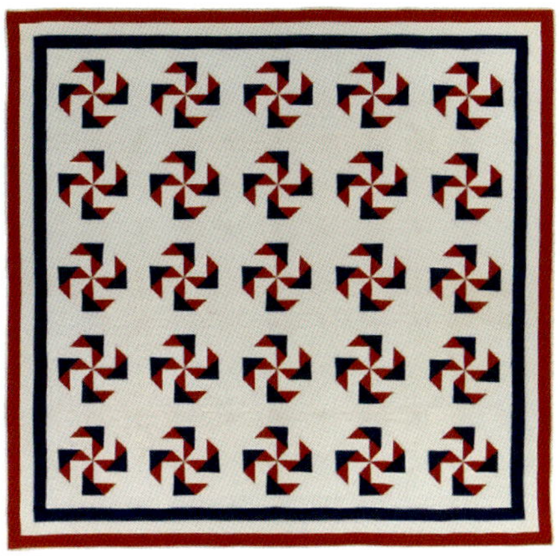

Crazy Ann variation

Maker unidentified
Made in United States
Dated 1920
77.5 x 77.5 in.

IQM 1997.007.0088

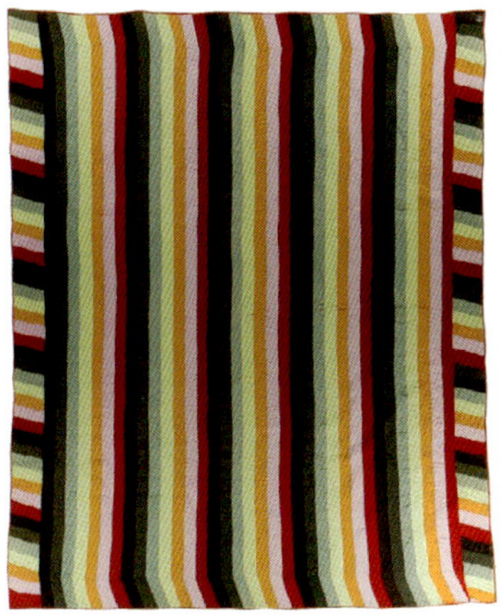

Joseph's Coat

Maker unidentified
Possibly made in Pennsylvania
1890 - 1910
91 x 73.5 in.

IQM 1997.007.0089

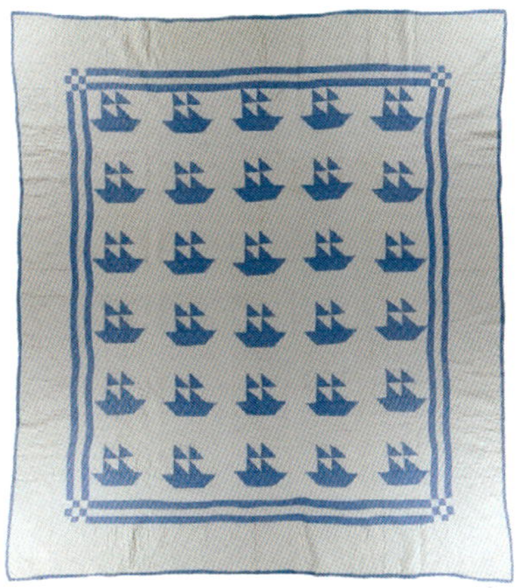

Sailboat

Maker unidentified
Possibly made in Middlefield, Ohio
1930 - 1950
87 x 78.5 in.

IQM 1997.007.0090

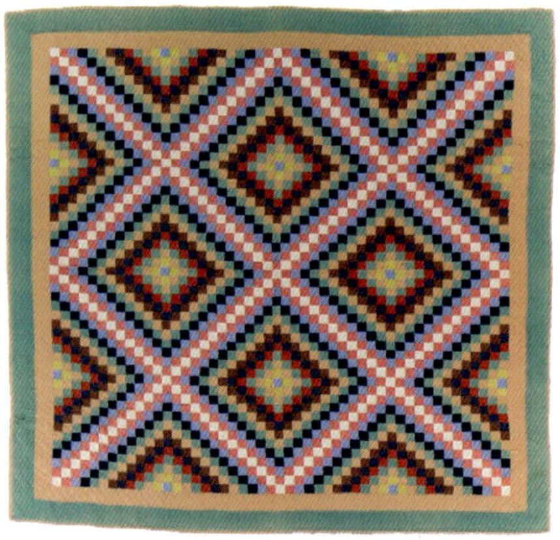

Philadelphia Pavement

Maker unidentified
Possibly made in eastern Pennsylvania
1910 - 1930
83 x 80 in.

IQM 1997.007.0091

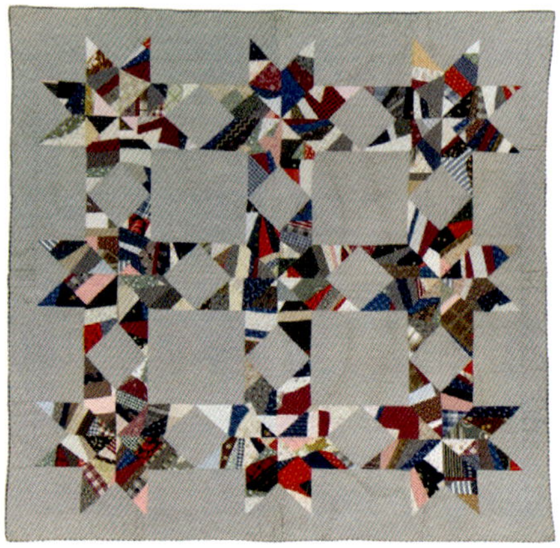

String Star

Maker unidentified
Possibly made in Ohio
1890 - 1910
77.5 x 76 in.

IQM 1997.007.0093

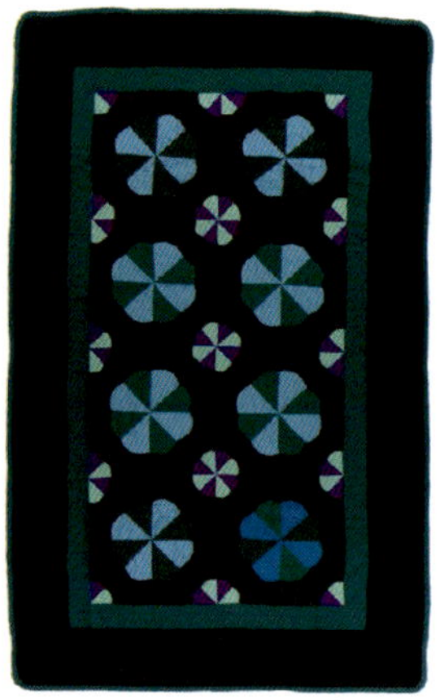

Hearts and Gizzards

Maker unidentified
Possibly made in Holmes County, Ohio
1920 - 1940
80.5 x 48.5 in.

IQM 1997.007.0096

French Wreath

Maker unidentified
Possibly made in Michigan
Circa 1932
92.5 x 77.5 in.

IQM 1997.007.0097

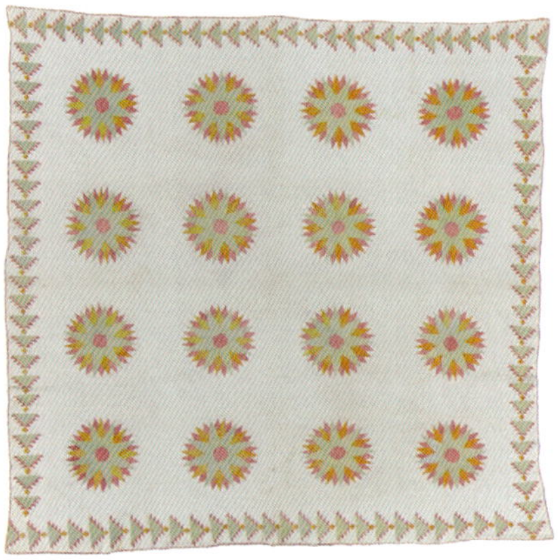

Mariner's Compass

Maker unidentified
Made in United States
1840 - 1860
96 x 98 in.

IQM 1997.007.0100

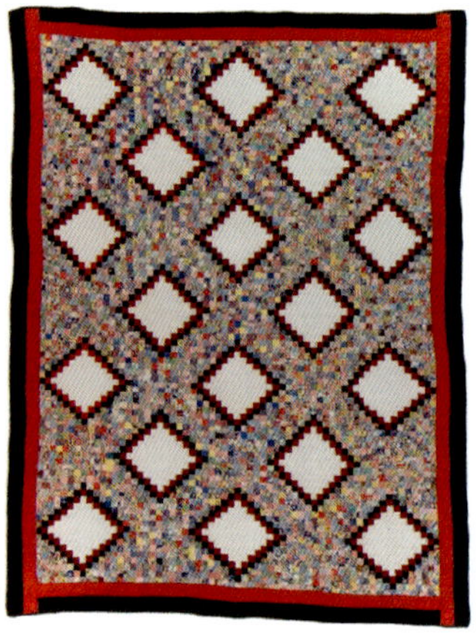

Rainbow Around the World

Maker unidentified
Made in United States
Circa 1934
89.5 x 66.5 in.

IQM 1997.007.0103

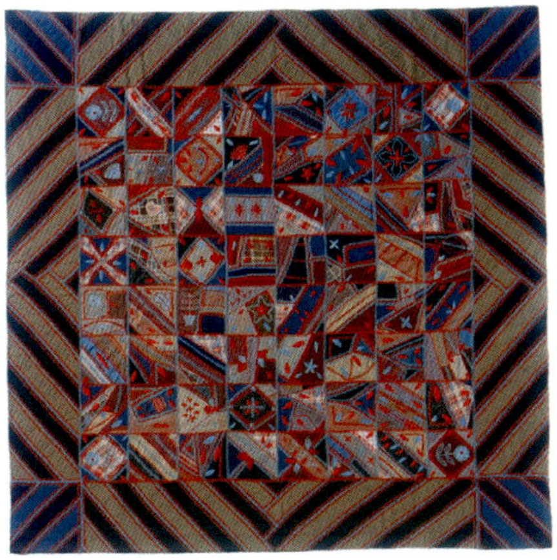

Crazy

Maker unidentified
Probably made in Lancaster County, Pennsylvania
Dated 1891
82.5 x 64 in.

IQM 1997.007.0107

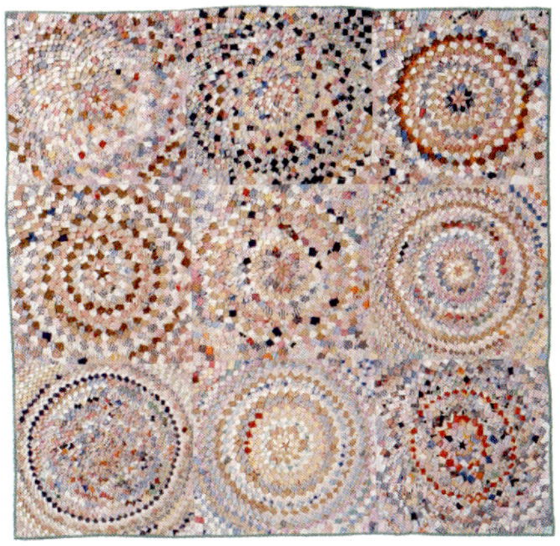

Target

Maker unidentified
Probably made in midwestern United States
1930 - 1950
70 x 69 in.

IQM 1997.007.0108

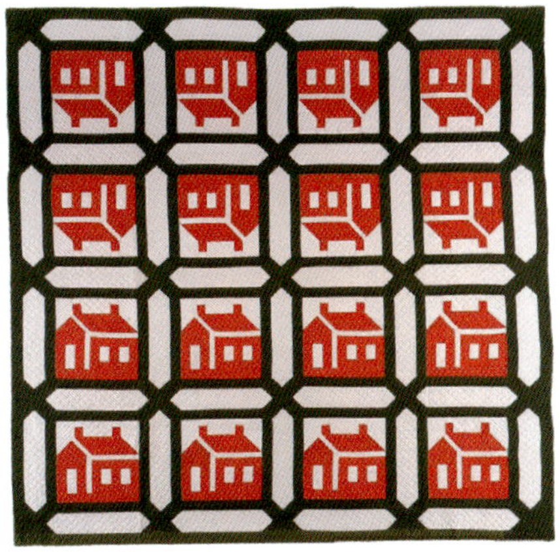

Schoolhouse

Maker unidentified
Possibly made in Wayne County, Indiana
1875 - 1895
82.5 x 82.5 in.

IQM 1997.007.0109

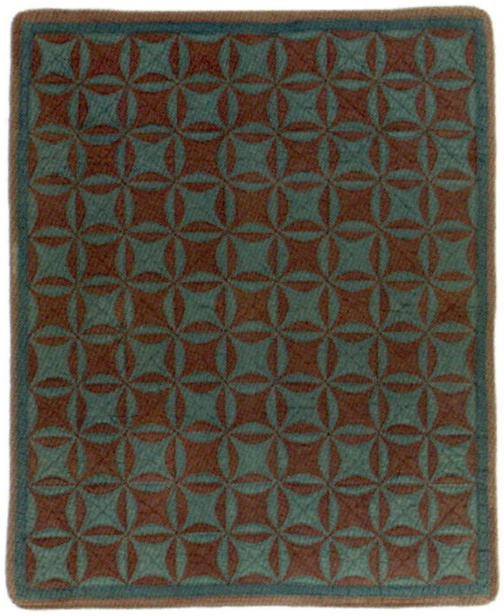

Rob Peter to Pay Paul

Maker unidentified
Possibly made in LaGrange County, Indiana
1880 - 1900
82.5 x 66 in.

IQM 1997.007.0110

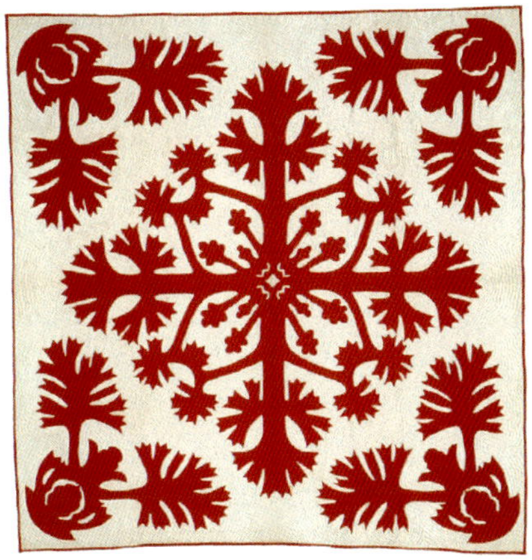

Hawaiian Appliqué

Maker unidentified
Probably made in Hawaii
1930 - 1950
85 x 81 in.

IQM 1997.007.0111

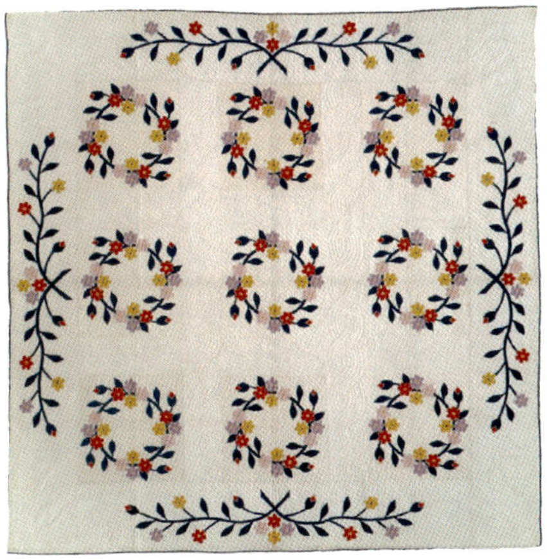

Wreath of Roses

Maker unidentified
Possibly made in Coshocton County, Ohio
1935 - 1945
77 x 75 in.

IQM 1997.007.0112

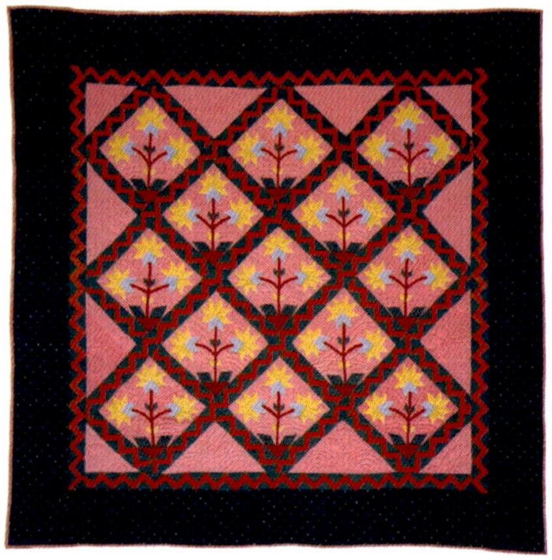

Lily

Maker unidentified
Possibly made in Lancaster County, Pennsylvania
1875 - 1895
93.5 x 91.5 in.

IQM 1997.007.0113

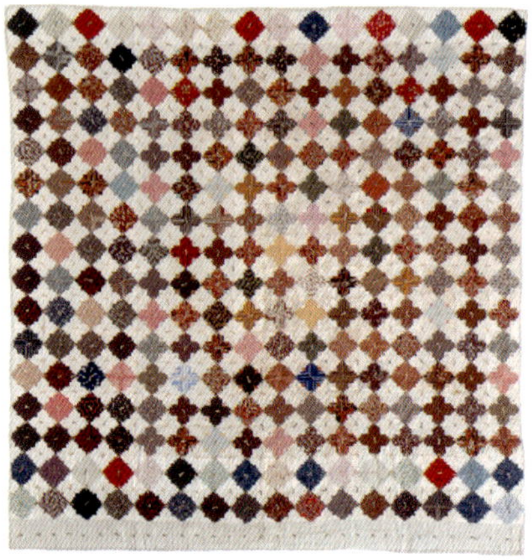

Log Cabin

Maker unidentified
Probably made in New England
1890 - 1910
74.5 x 70.5 in.

IQM 1997.007.0114

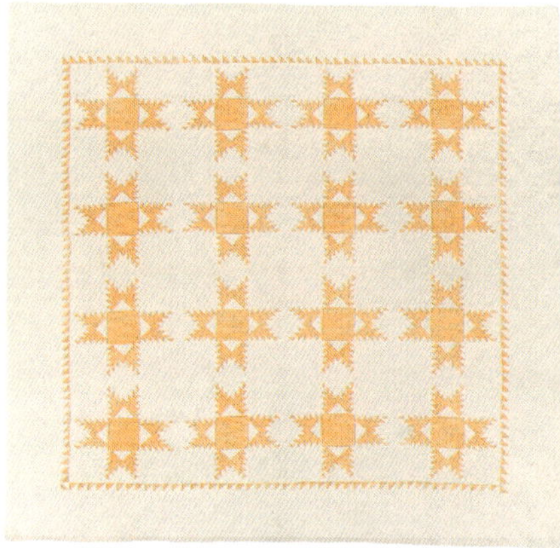

Ohio Star

M. Jane Brown
Probably made in Loudon, Franklin County, Pennsylvania
1850 - 1860
91.5 x 89 in.

IQM 1997.007.0115

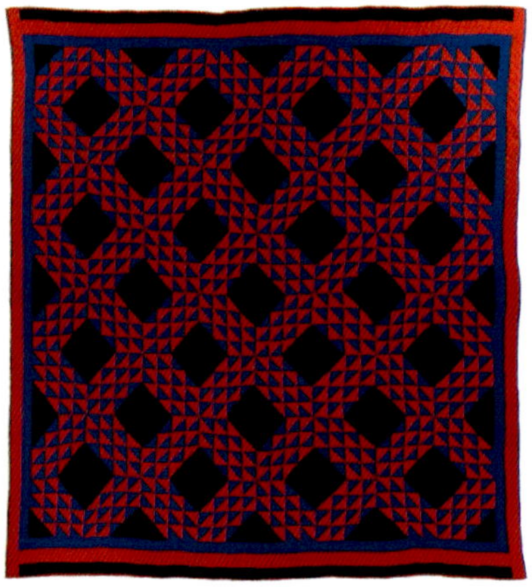

Ocean Waves

Maker unidentified
Possibly made in West Virginia
1875 - 1895
79 x 74 in.

IQM 1997.007.0119

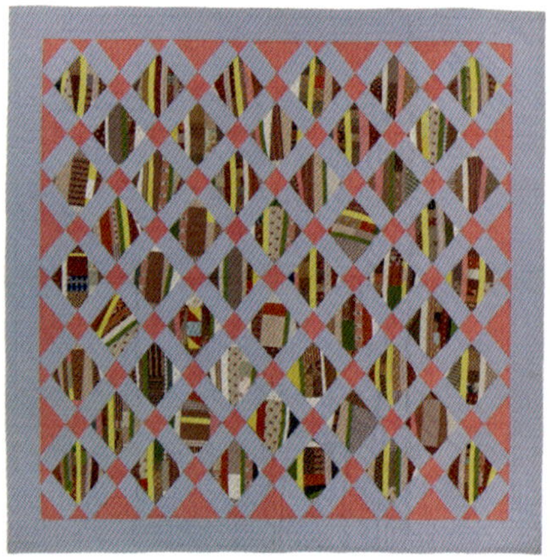

Crazy

Maker unidentified
Possibly made in Pennsylvania
1870 - 1890
81.5 x 80 in.

IQM 1997.007.0120

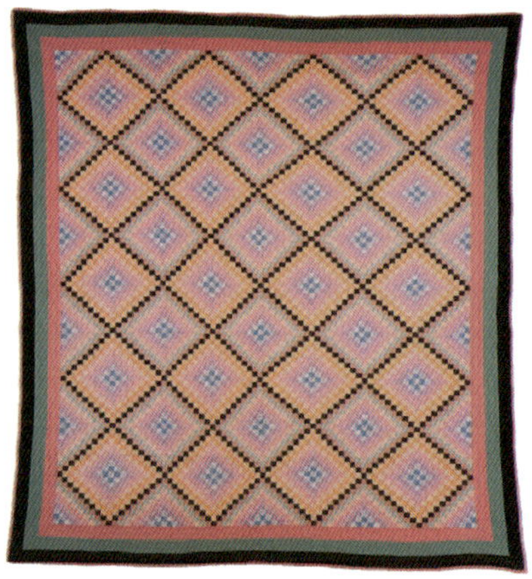

Trip Around the World variation

Maker unidentified
Made in United States
1925 - 1945
81 x 73.5 in.

IQM 1997.007.0122

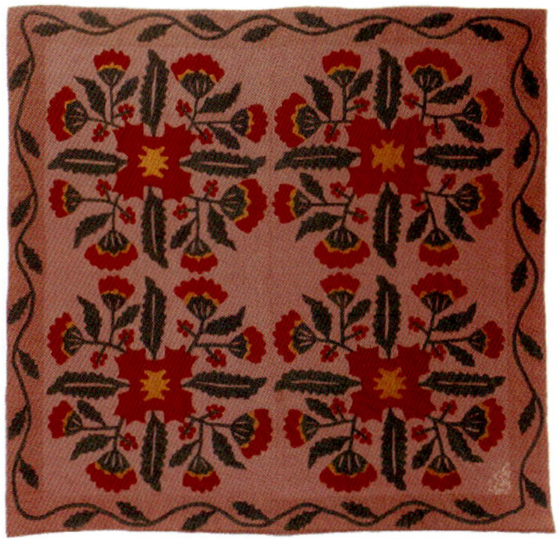

Coxcomb

Maker unidentified
Probably made in Pennsylvania
1880 - 1900
76.5 x 76 in.

IQM 1997.007.0123

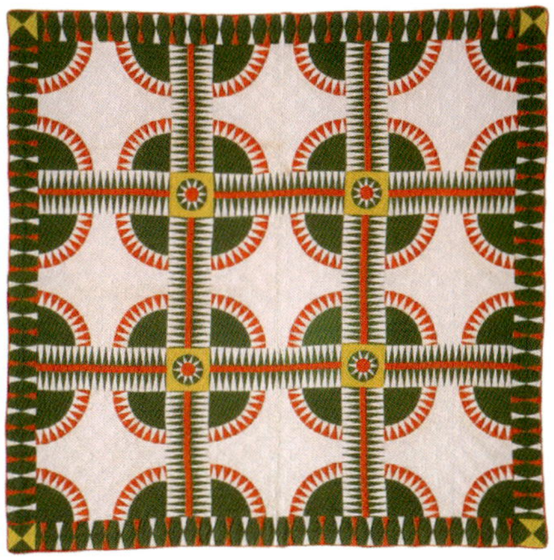

New York Beauty

Maker unidentified
Probably made in Missouri
1850 - 1870
79.5 x 80.5 in.

IQM 1997.007.0124

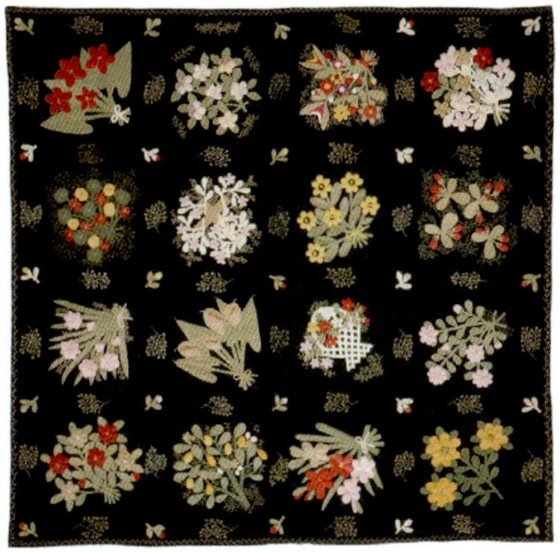

Album

Maker unidentified
Possibly made in Philadelphia, Pennsylvania
1920 - 1930
87 x 87 in.

IQM 1997.007.0125

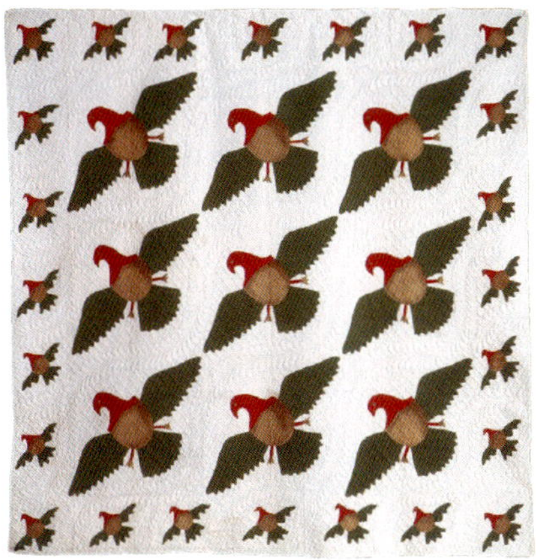

Eagle

Maker unidentified
Possibly made in Cherrytree County, Pennsylvania
1870 - 1890
77 x 73.5 in.

IQM 1997.007.0126

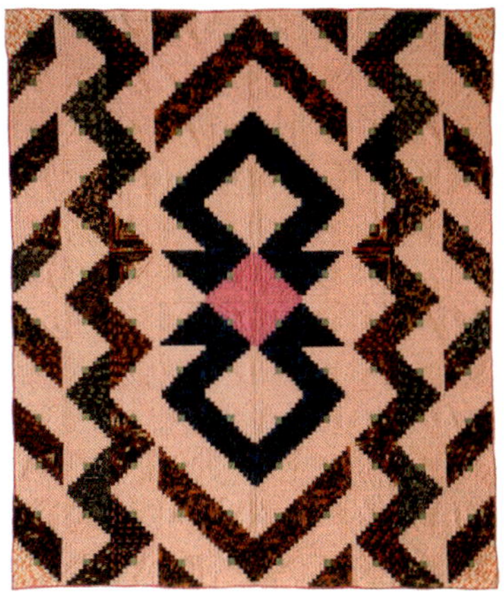

Log Cabin

Maker unidentified
Possibly made in York County, Pennsylvania
1870 - 1890
90 x 75.5 in.

IQM 1997.007.0127

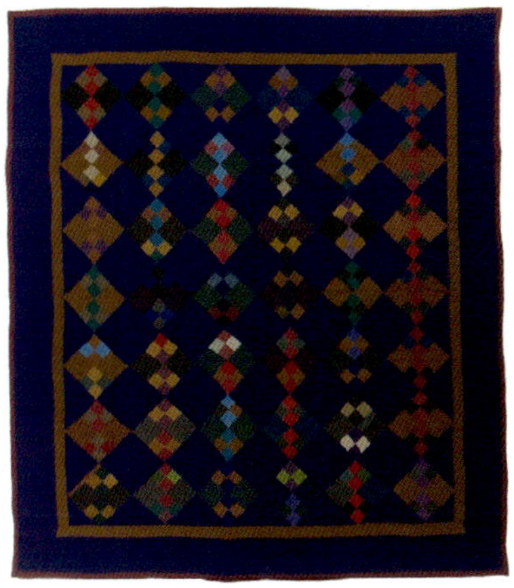

Double Four Patch

Lydia Schmucker
Probably made in Elkhart County, Indiana
Dated 1913
82.5 x 71.5 in.

IQM 1997.007.0128

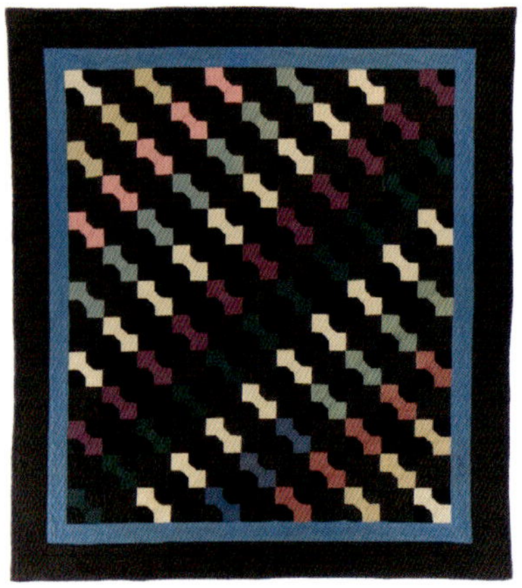

Bow Tie

Possibly made by Ervin Hochstetler
Probably made in LaGrange County, Indiana
Dated 1947
81.5 x 70.5 in.
IQM 1997.007.0129

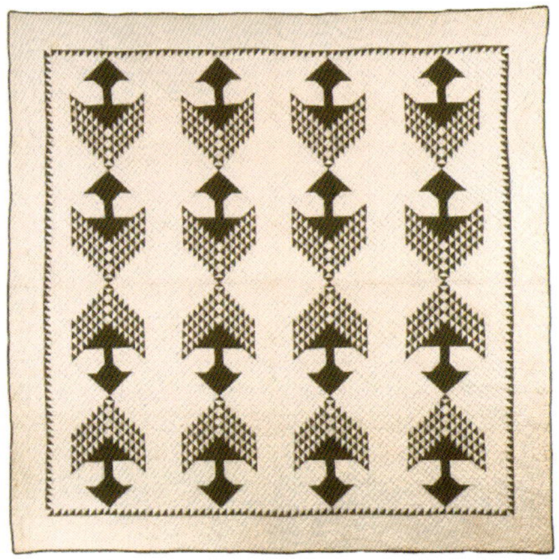

Pine Tree

Maker unidentified
Possibly made in Ohio
1880 - 1900
80 x 81 in.
IQM 1997.007.0130

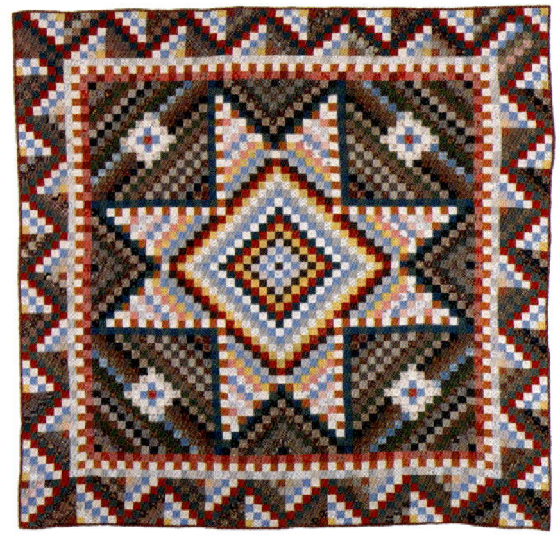

Postage Stamp Star

Maker unidentified
Probably made in Bowmansville, Lancaster County, Pennsylvania
1880 - 1900
79 x 78 in.
IQM 1997.007.0133

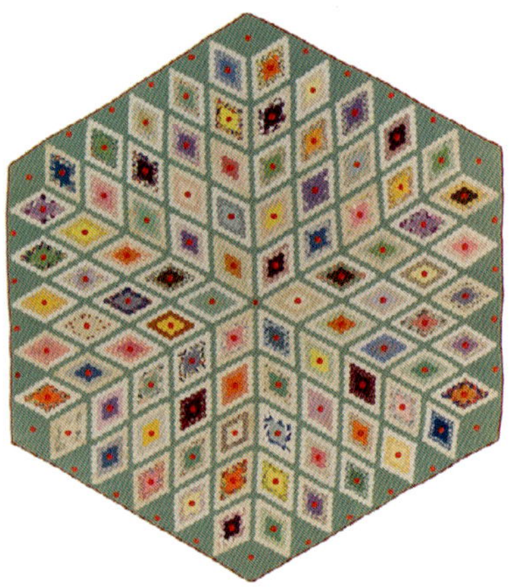

Diamond Field

Maker unidentified
Possibly made in Iowa City, Iowa
1930 - 1940
107 x 104 in.
IQM 1997.007.0139.1

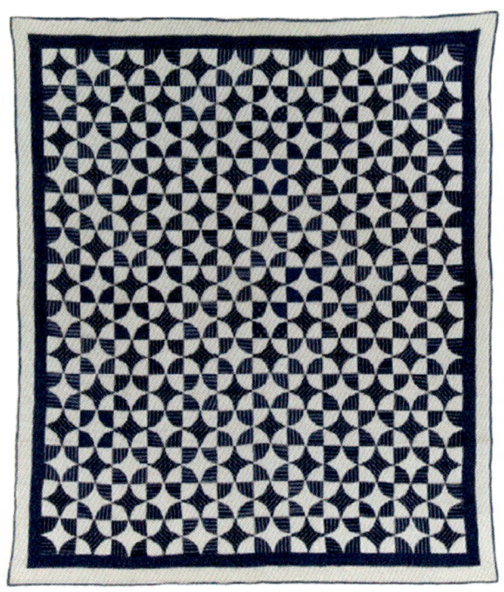

Mill Wheel

Maker unidentified
Possibly made in southern Indiana
1875 - 1895
81 x 67.5 in.
IQM 1997.007.0141

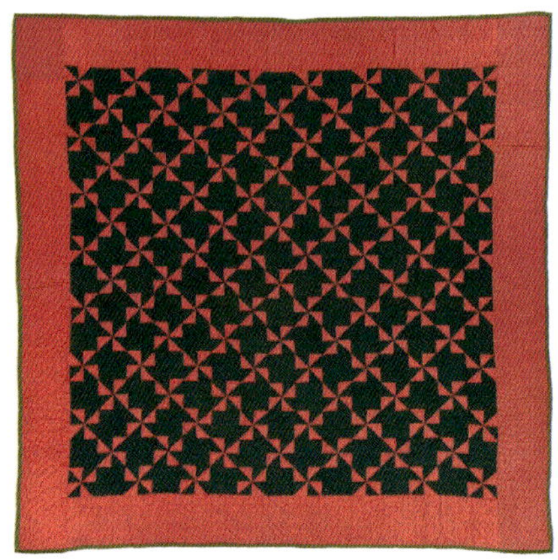

Pinwheel

Maker unidentified
Possibly made in Pennsylvania
1880 - 1900
78.5 x 74.5 in.
IQM 1997.007.0142

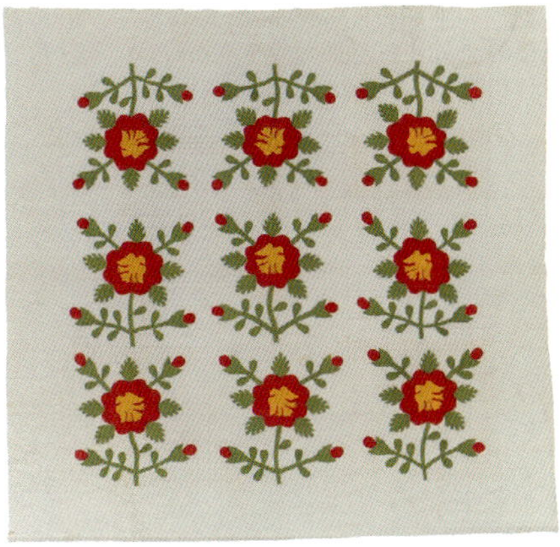

Rose

Maker unidentified
Possibly made in Pennsylvania
1860 - 1880
79 x 78 in.

IQM 1997.007.0144

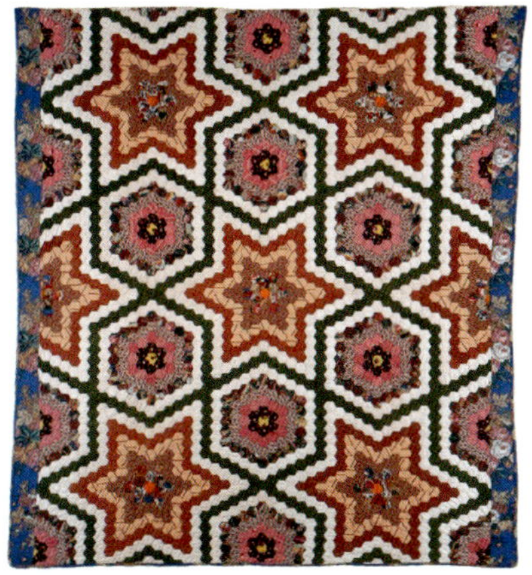

Hexagon

Maker unidentified
Possibly made in Pennsylvania
1870 - 1890
94 x 83 in.

IQM 1997.007.0145

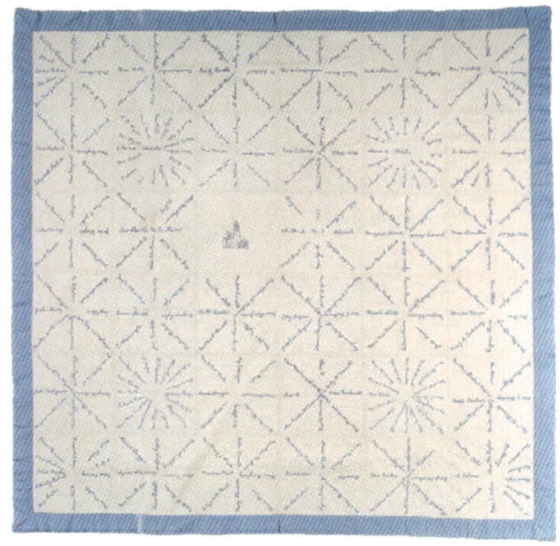

Original

Maker unidentified
Made in New York City, New York
Dated 1927
69 x 69.5 in.

IQM 1997.007.0148

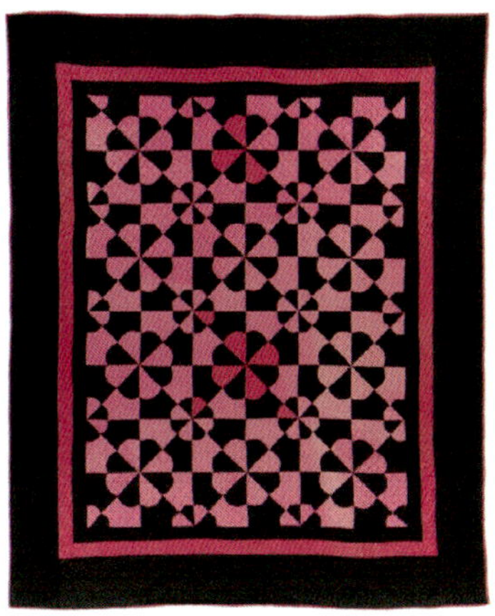

Hearts and Gizzards

Maker unidentified
Possibly made in Holmes County, Ohio
1920 - 1940
93 x 75 in.

IQM 1997.007.0150

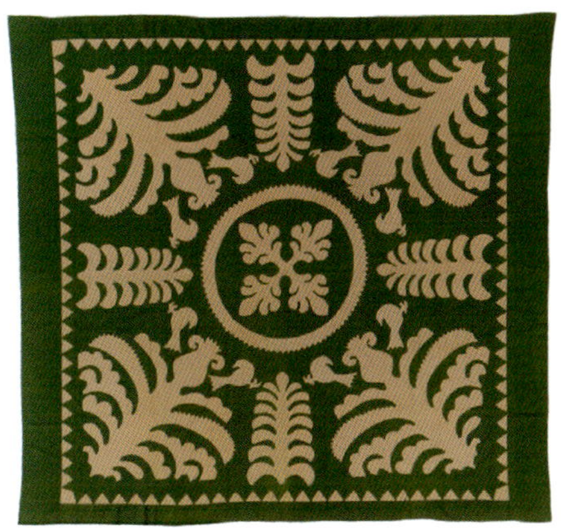

Original

Maker unidentified
Possibly made in Pennsylvania
1850 - 1870
86 x 82.5 in.

IQM 1997.007.0151

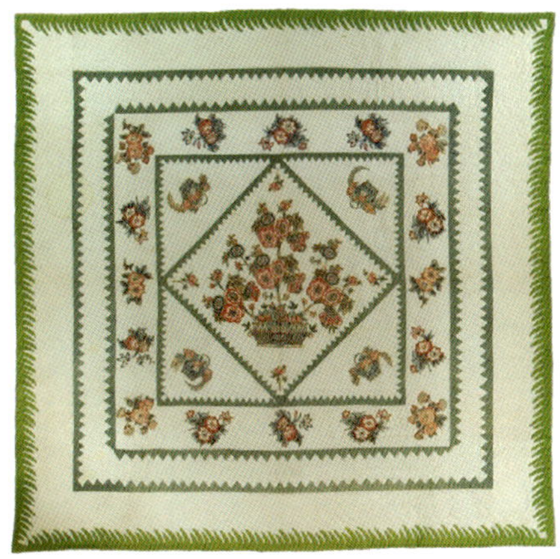

Medallion

Maker unidentified
Possibly made in Virginia
1820 - 1840
100.5 x 102 in.

IQM 1997.007.0152

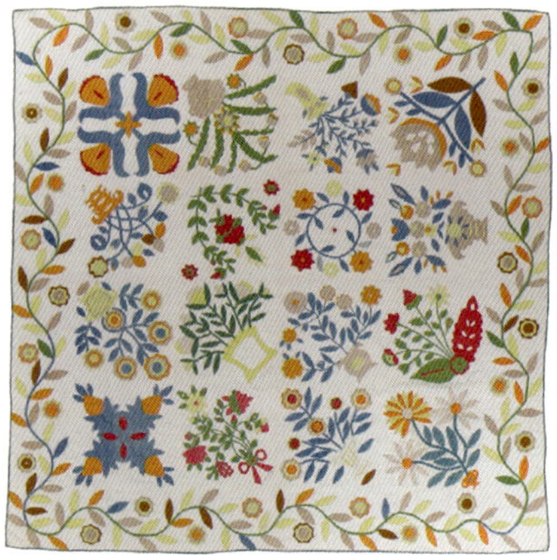

Album

Maker unidentified
Probably made in Auburn, Illinois
1860 - 1870
85 x 84.5 in.
IQM 1997.007.0153

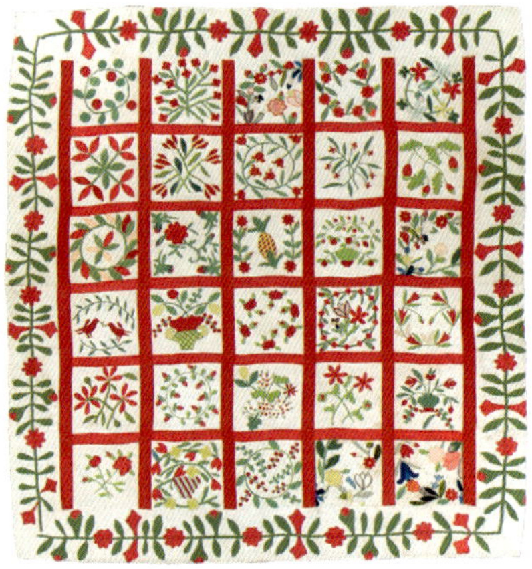

Album

Maker unidentified
Possibly made in Maryland
1850 - 1870
83 x 77.5 in.
IQM 1997.007.0154

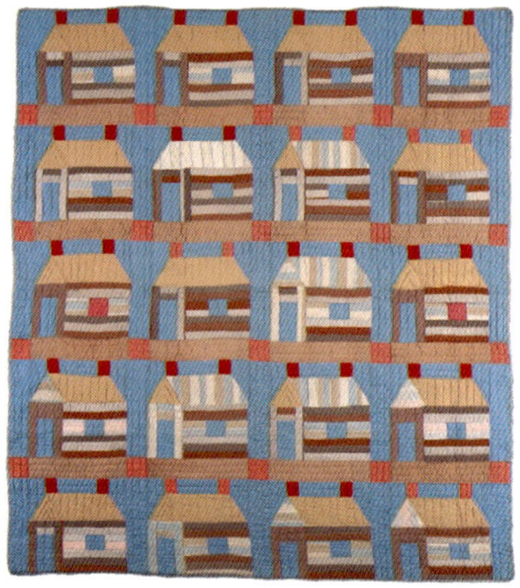

Schoolhouse

Maker unidentified
Possibly made in Tennessee
1925 - 1945
84.5 x 73 in.
IQM 1997.007.0156

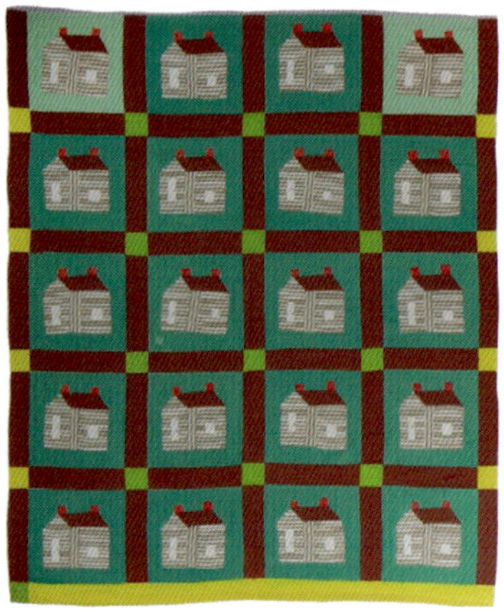

Schoolhouse

Maker unidentified
Possibly made in Lake Geneva, Wisconsin
1960 - 1980
79 x 65.5 in.
IQM 1997.007.0157

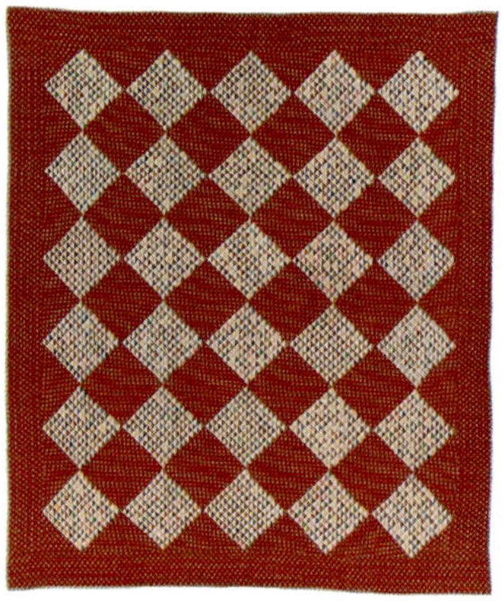

Birds in Air

Maker unidentified
Possibly made in Blair County, Pennsylvania
1870 - 1890
78.5 x 66 in.
IQM 1997.007.0158

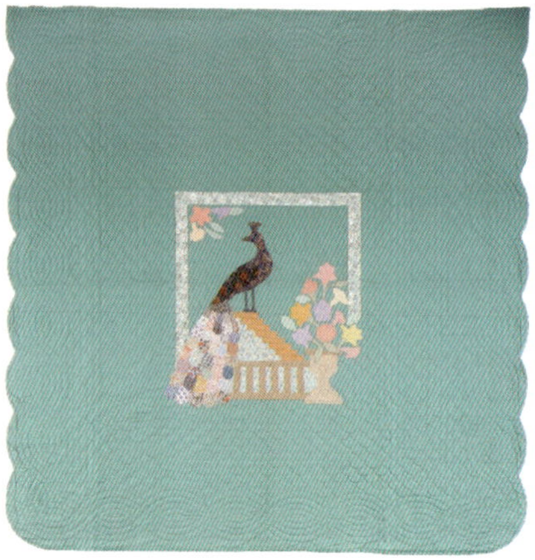

Peacock

Maker unidentified
Possibly made in St. Louis, Missouri
Circa 1933
85.5 x 81 in.
IQM 1997.007.0159

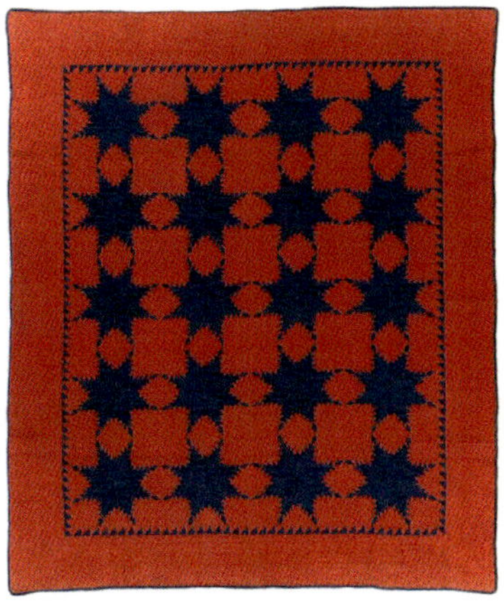

Feathered Star

Maker unidentified
Possibly made in Ohio
1850 - 1870
79 x 66 in.

IQM 1997.007.0161

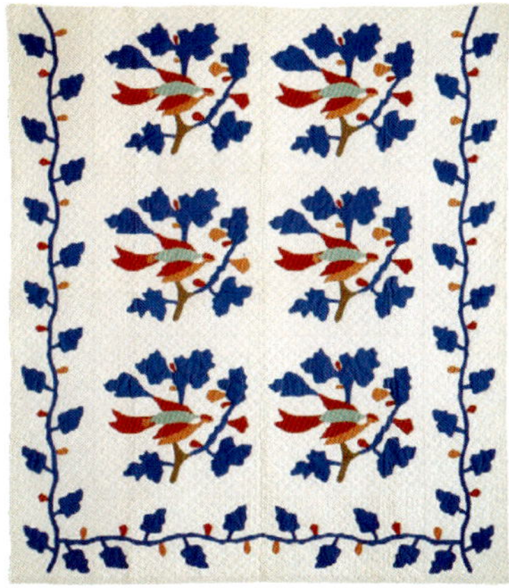

Bird of Paradise

Maker unidentified
Possibly made in Maryland
1940 - 1950
78.5 x 66.25 in.

IQM 1997.007.0162

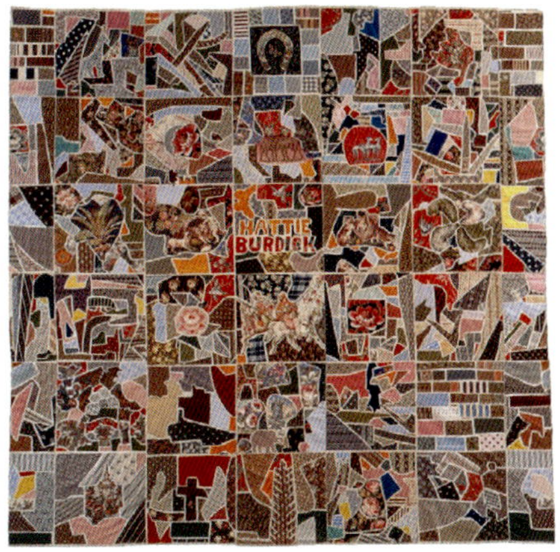

Tile Quilt

Burdick family members
Probably made in
Massachusetts
1884 - 1887
81 x 80 in.

IQM 1997.007.0163

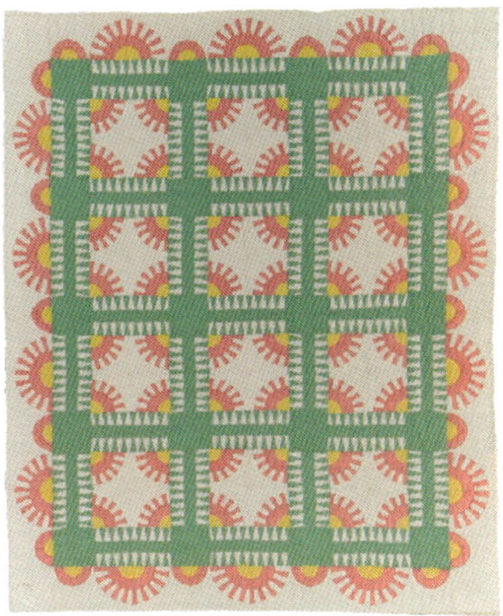

Springtime in the Rockies

Maker unidentified
Possibly made in Maryland
Circa 1935
91 x 73 in.

IQM 1997.007.0165

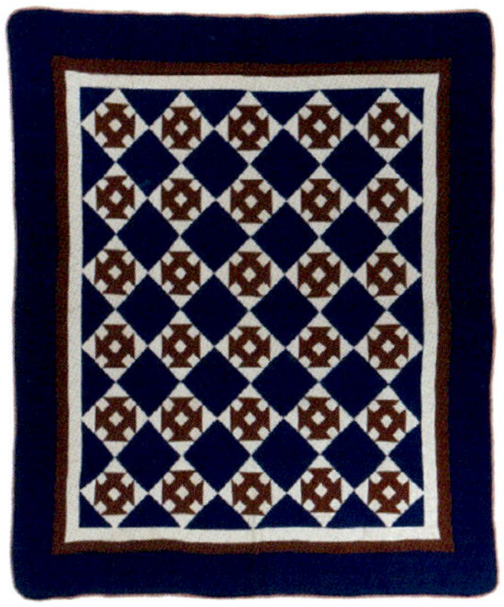

Hole in the Barn Door

Maker unidentified
Possibly made in Ohio
1875 - 1895
77 x 66.5 in.

IQM 1997.007.0166

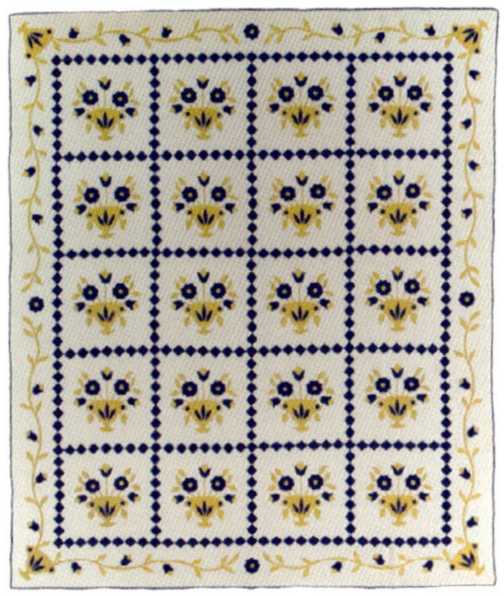

Pots of Flowers

Maker unidentified
Possibly made in Ohio or
Pennsylvania
1935 - 1945
94.5 x 79 in.

IQM 1997.007.0167

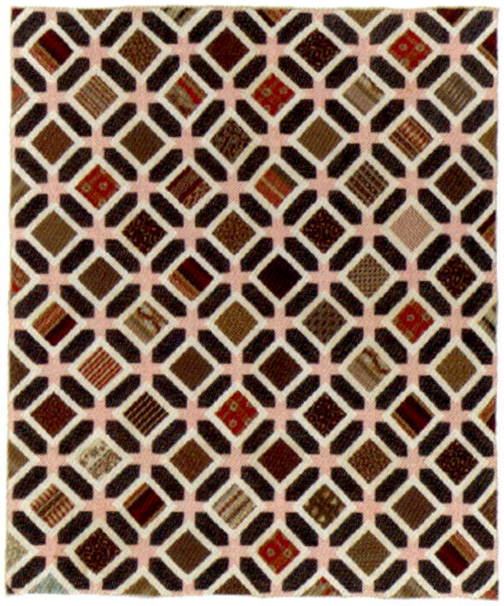

Garden Maze

Maker unidentified
Possibly made in Ohio
1860 - 1880
86.5 x 70.5 in.

IQM 1997.007.0170

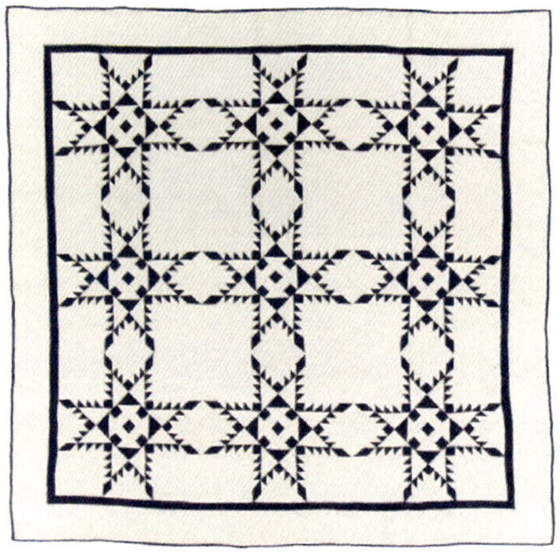

Feathered Star

Mary Caroline Robinson Olds
Made in DeKalb County, Indiana
Circa 1895
78 x 78 in.

IQM 1997.007.0172

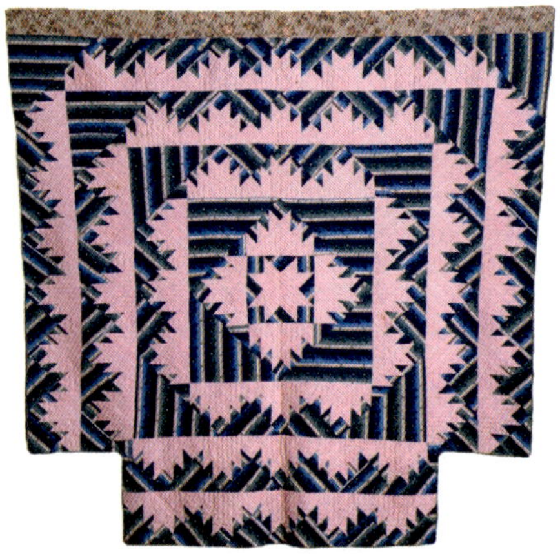

Delectable Mountains

Maker unidentified
Possibly made in New England
1830 - 1850
93 x 94.25 in.

IQM 1997.007.0173.1

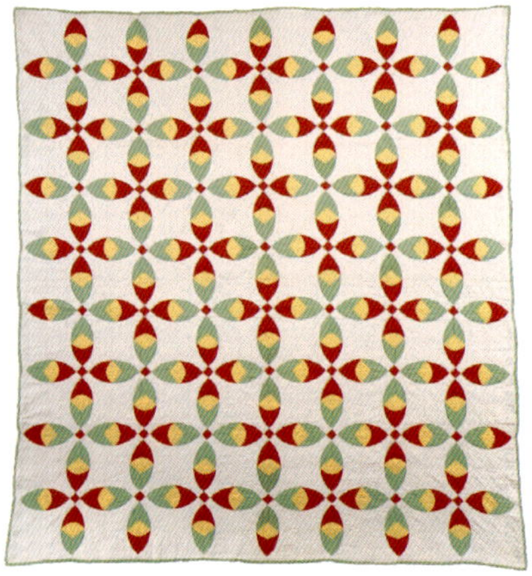

Orange Peel

Maker unidentified
Possibly made in Indiana or Pennsylvania
1910 - 1930
84 x 76 in.

IQM 1997.007.0174

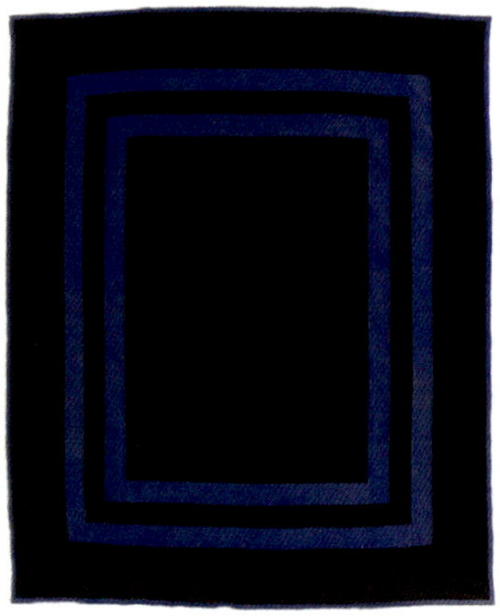

Plain Quilt

Maker unidentified
Possibly made in Holmes County, Ohio
Dated 1948
78 x 64.5 in.

IQM 1997.007.0175

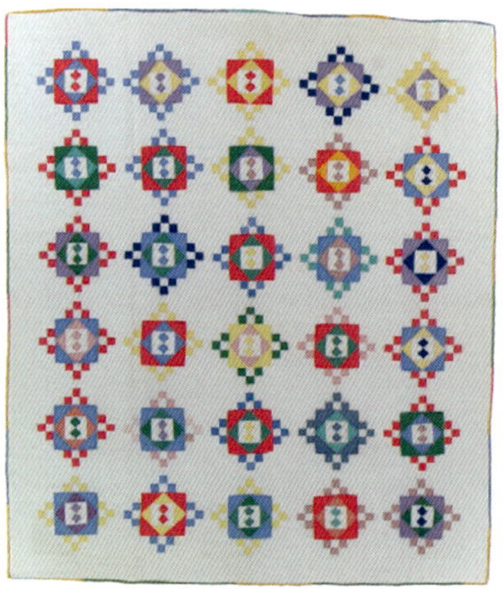

Four Patch variation

Maker unidentified
Possibly made in West Virginia
1920 - 1940
83 x 70.5 in.

IQM 1997.007.0176

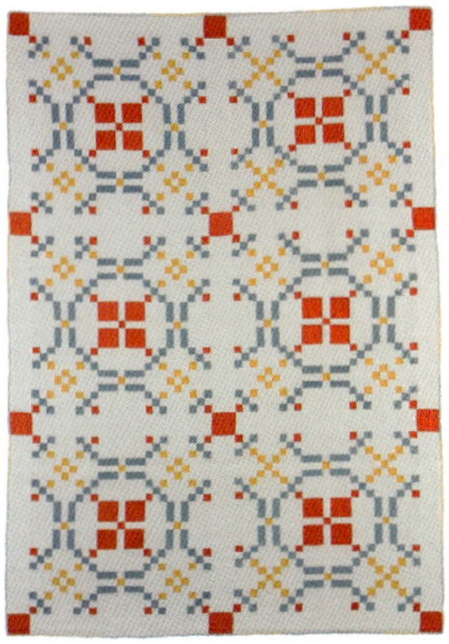

Burgoyne Surrounded

Maker unidentified
Possibly made in West Virginia
1935 - 1945
84 x 58 in.

IQM 1997.007.0177

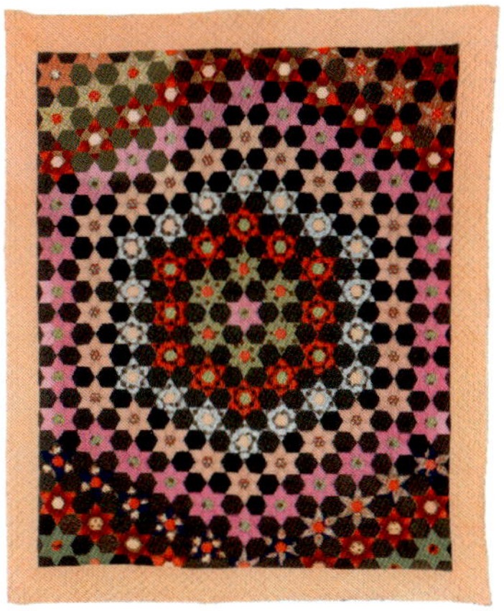

Hexagon Star

Maker unidentified
Possibly made in Kentucky
1860 - 1880
81 x 66 in.

IQM 1997.007.0178

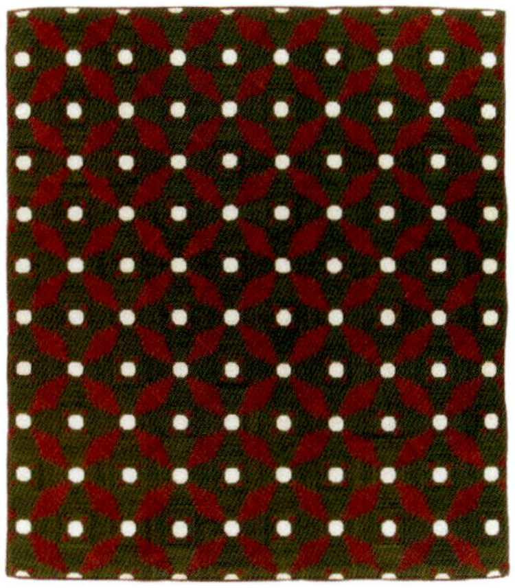

Log Cabin

Maker unidentified
Possibly made in Ohio
1865 - 1885
79 x 70 in.

IQM 1997.007.0179

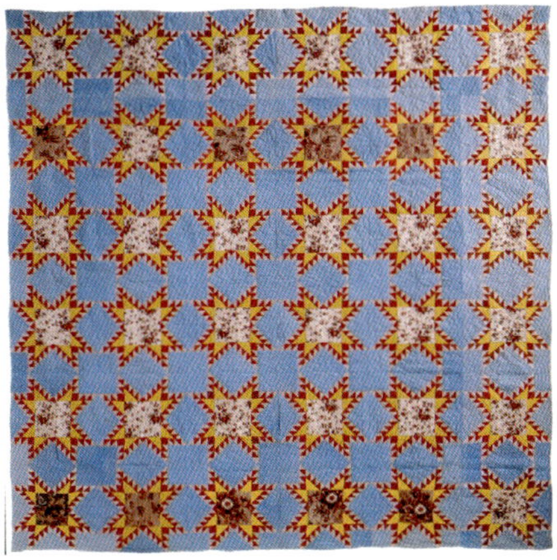

Feathered Star

Maker unidentified
Possibly made in Lancaster County, Pennsylvania
1840 - 1860
112.5 x 110 in.

IQM 1997.007.0180

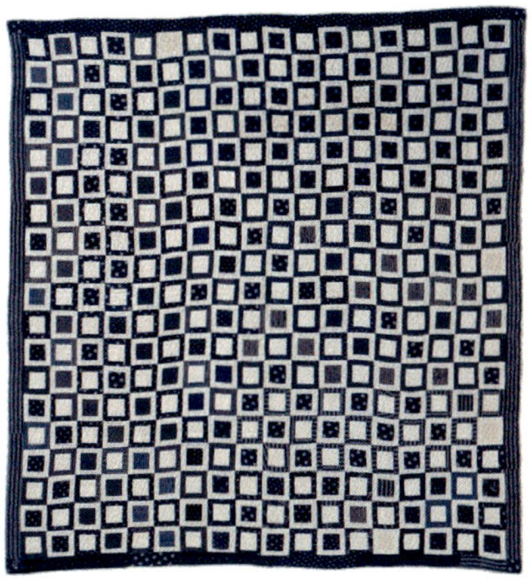

Square in a Square

Maker unidentified
Possibly made in Illinois
1900 - 1920
74 x 70 in.

IQM 1997.007.0181

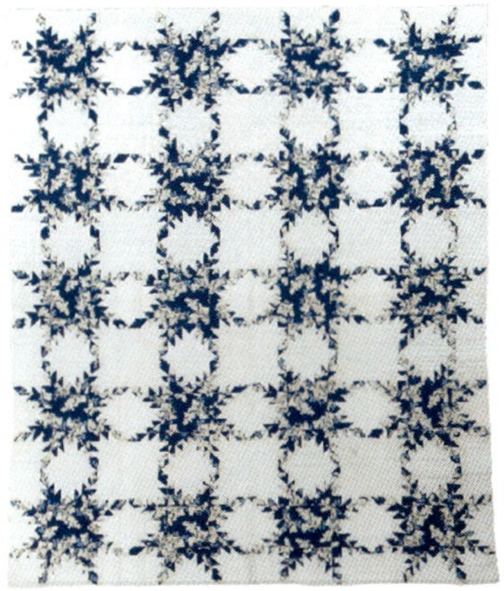

Feathered Star

Maker unidentified
Possibly made in Illinois
Dated 1846 - 1898
81 x 68 in.

IQM 1997.007.0182

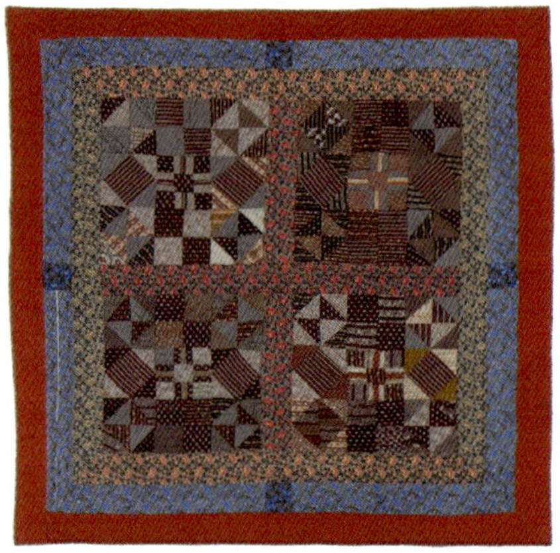

Nine Patch variation

Maker unidentified
Possibly made in Ohio
1880 - 1900
42 x 42.5 in.

IQM 1997.007.0183

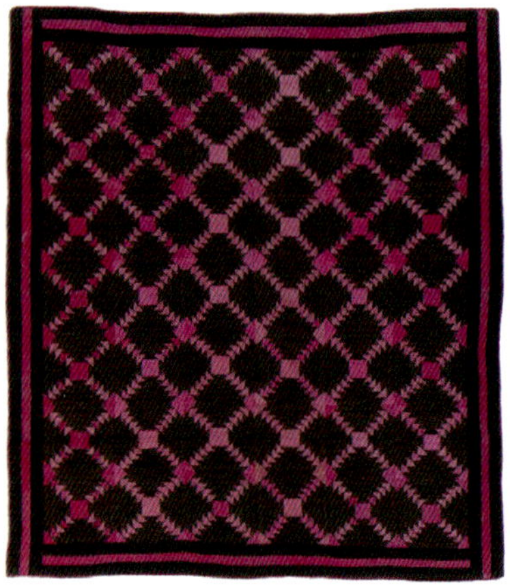

Log Cabin

Maker unidentified
Possibly made in Ohio
or Pennsylvania
1870 - 1890
76.5 x 66 in.

IQM 1997.007.0184

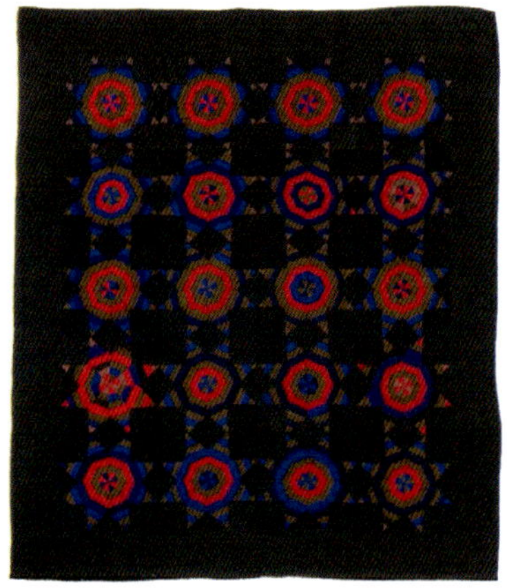

String Star

Maker unidentified
Possibly made in Waterloo
County, Ontario, Canada
1940 - 1960
79 x 67 in.

IQM 1997.007.0191

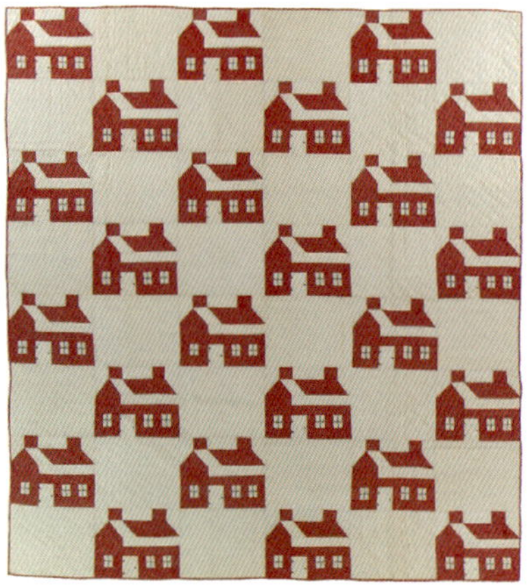

Schoolhouse

Maker unidentified
Made in United States
Dated 1931
86 x 77 in.

IQM 1997.007.0192

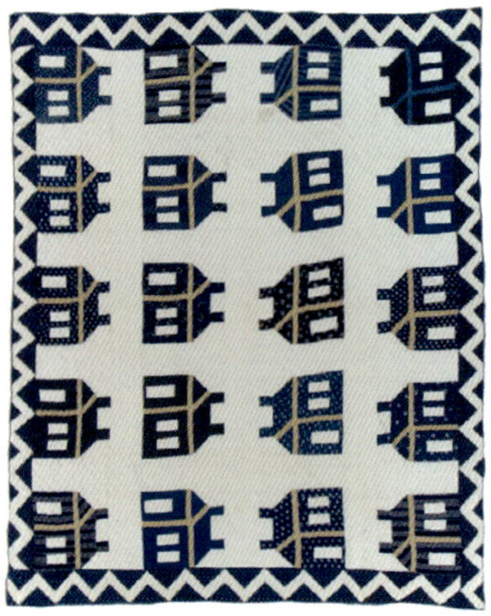

Schoolhouse

Maker unidentified
Possibly made in Pennsylvania
1890 - 1910
70 x 86.5 in.

IQM 1997.007.0193

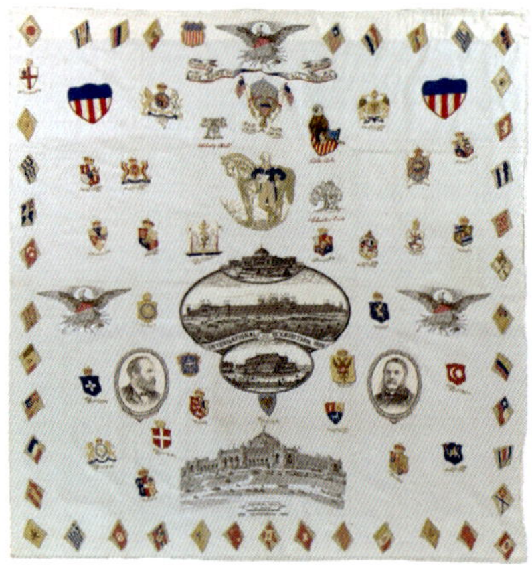

Centennial Commemorative

Maker unidentified
Possibly made in Ohio
1878 - 1890
60 x 55.5 in.

IQM 1997.007.0194

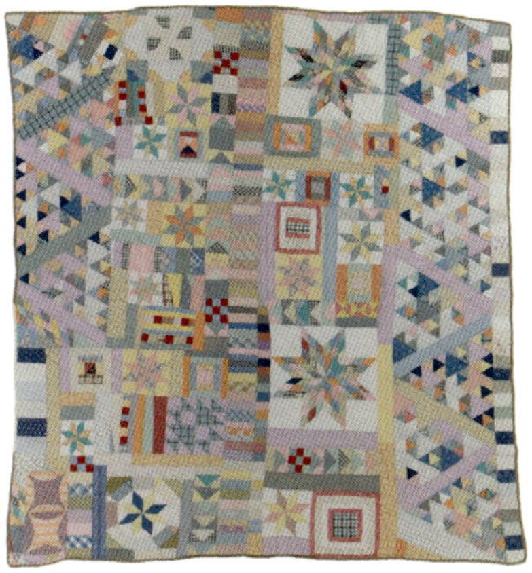

Album

Maker unidentified
Made in United States
1920 - 1940
77.5 x 70.5 in.

IQM 1997.007.0196

Original

Maker unidentified
Possibly made in Ohio
1850 - 1870
79.5 x 68.5 in.

IQM 1997.007.0197

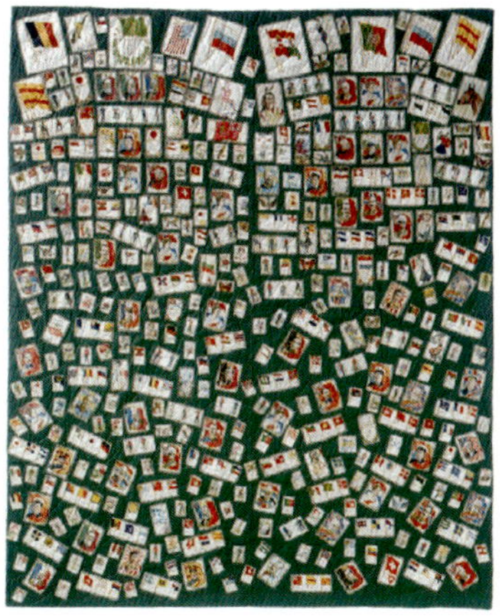

Tobacco Premium

Maker unidentified
Probably made in Michigan
1915 - 1925
86.5 x 69.5 in.

IQM 1997.007.0198

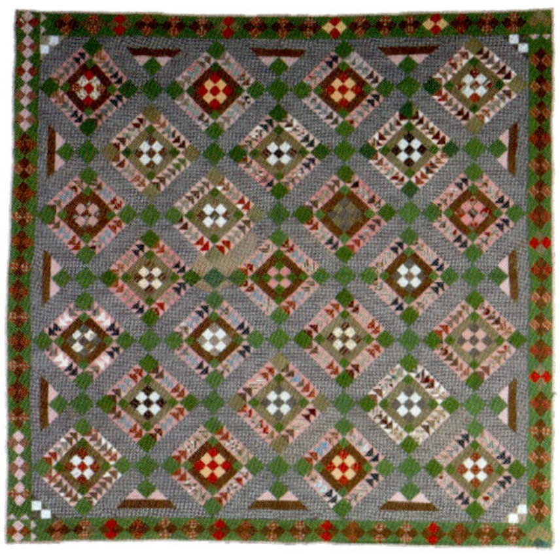

Nine Patch variation

Maker unidentified
Possibly made in Vermont
1875 - 1900
86 x 84 in.

IQM 1997.007.0199

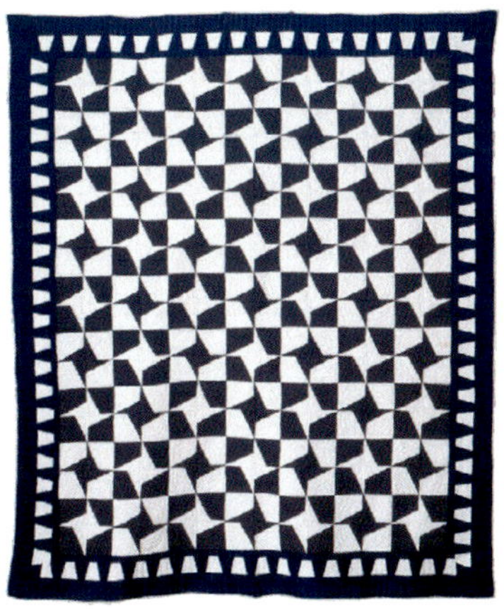

Shooting Star

Maker unidentified
Possibly made in Indiana or Ohio
1870 - 1890
89 x 72 in.

IQM 1997.007.0200

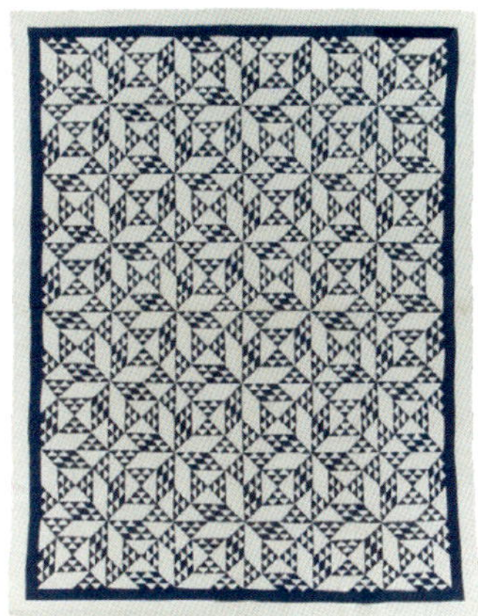

Triangles

Maker unidentified
Possibly made in midwestern United States
1870 - 1890
86 x 66 in.

IQM 1997.007.0202

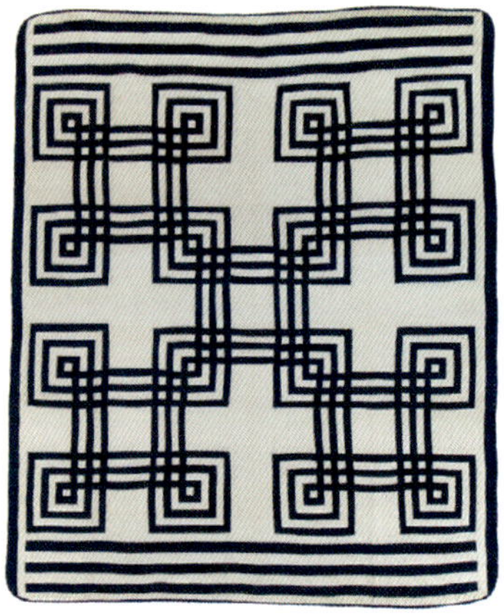

Carpenter's Square

Maker unidentified
Possibly made in Indiana
1880 - 1900
77 x 63.5 in.

IQM 1997.007.0203

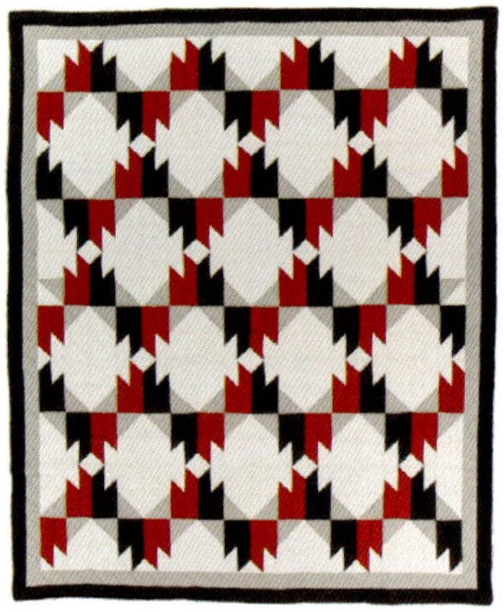

The Chief

Maker unidentified
Made in United States
Circa 1944
91 x 73.5 in.

IQM 1997.007.0208

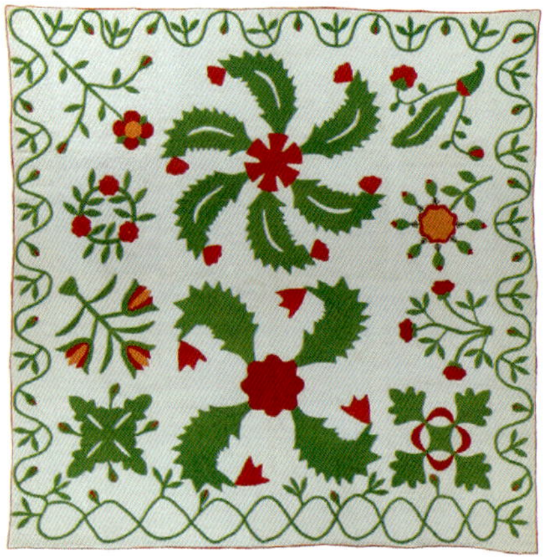

Album

Maker unidentified
Made in United States
1850 - 1870
80.5 x 78 in.

IQM 1997.007.0211

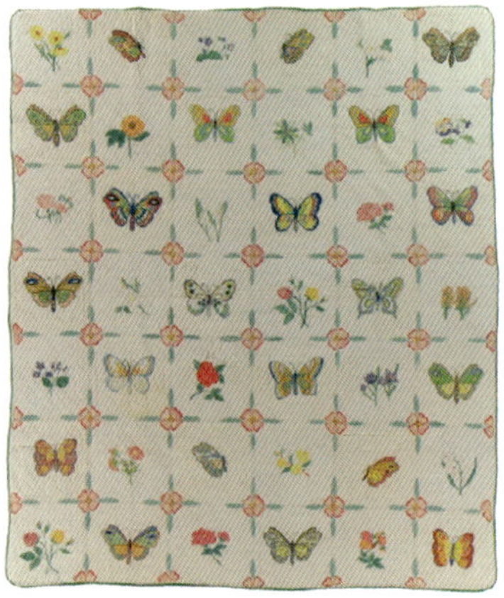

Butterfly

Maker unidentified
Possibly made in Tennessee
1920 - 1940
82 x 67 in.

IQM 1997.007.0213

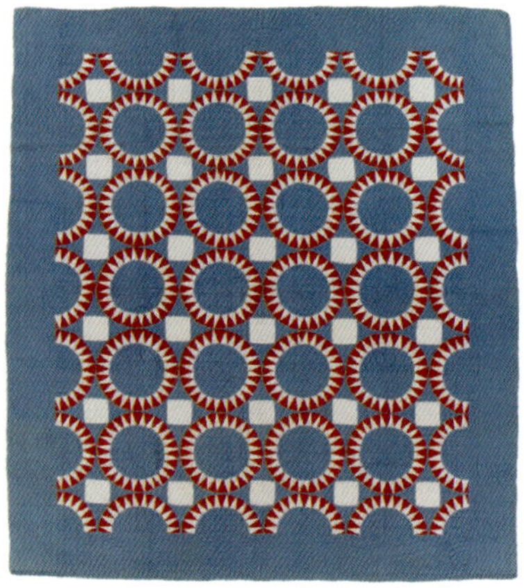

Sunburst

Maker unidentified
Probably made in Hamilton County, Ohio
1900 - 1920
78 x 68 in.

IQM 1997.007.0215

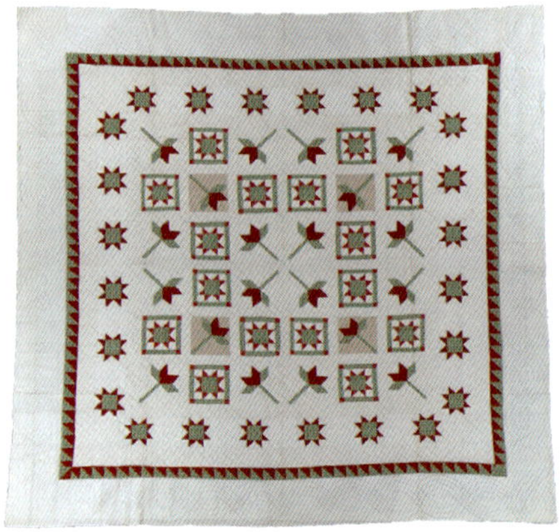

Lily

Maker unidentified
Possibly made in Reading, Pennsylvania
1850 - 1870
83 x 83 in.

IQM 1997.007.0216

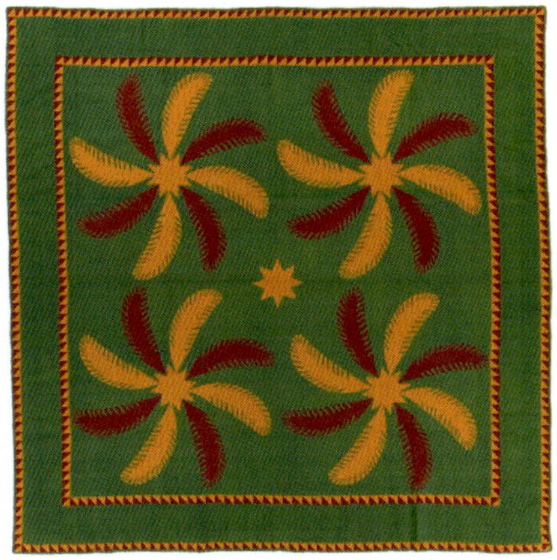

Princess Feather

Maker unidentified
Possibly made in Pennsylvania
1870 - 1890
94 x 96 in.

IQM 1997.007.0217

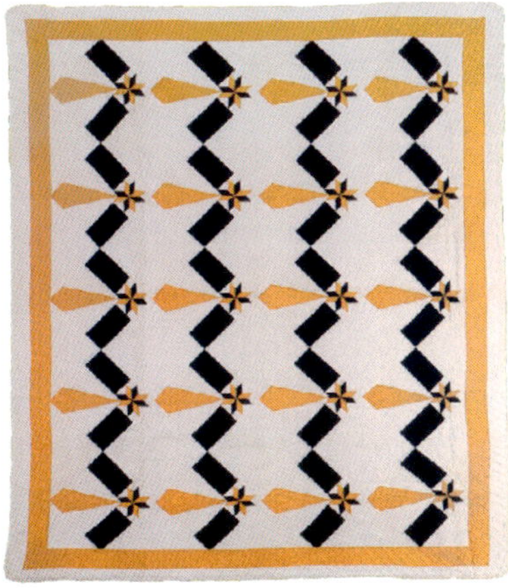

Shooting Star

Maker unidentified
Possibly made in Indiana
1920 - 1940
72 x 85.5 in.

IQM 1997.007.0218

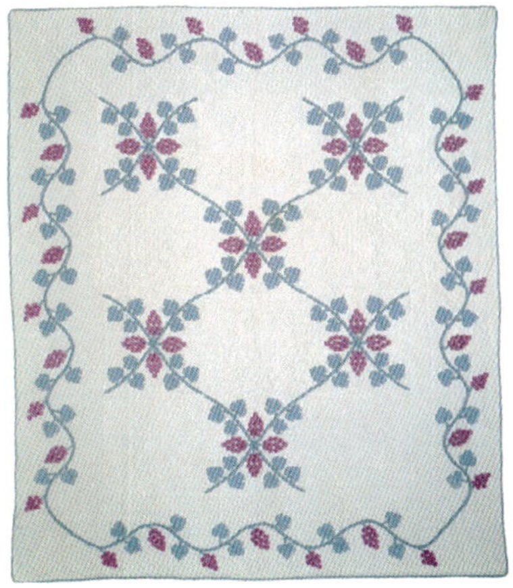

Martha's Vineyard

Maker unidentified
Possibly made in Ohio
Circa 1931
92 x 78 in.

IQM 1997.007.0219

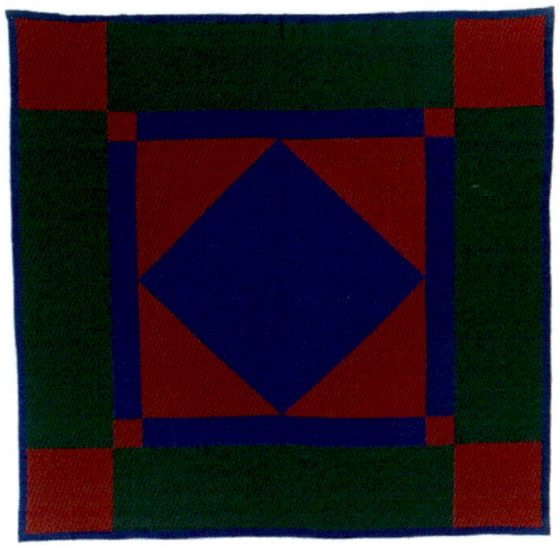

Center Diamond

Possibly made by Mattie King Stoltzfus
Probably made in Lancaster County, Pennsylvania
1915 - 1935
77 x 76 in.

IQM 1997.007.0220

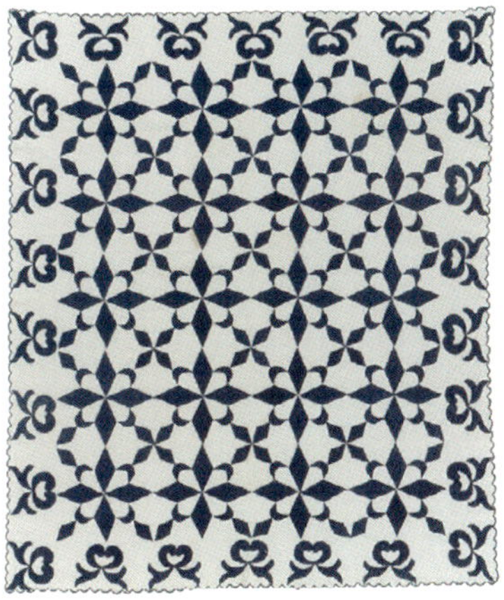

Star and Crescent

Maker unidentified
Possibly made in New York
1850 - 1870
92 x 75 in.

IQM 1997.007.0221

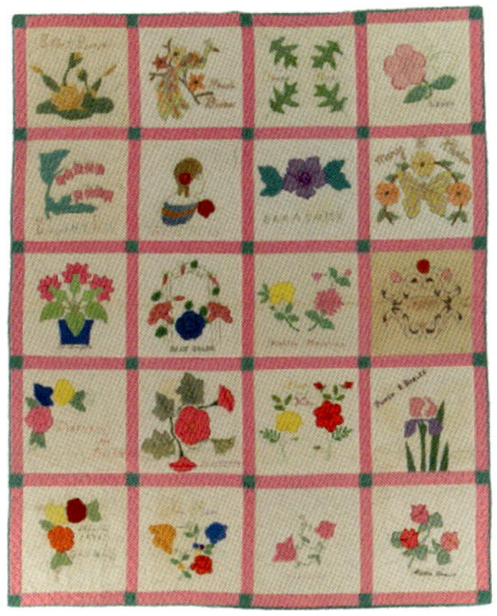

Album

Maker unidentified
Probably made in Graves County, Kentucky
Dated 1933
85 x 68.5 in.

IQM 1997.007.0223

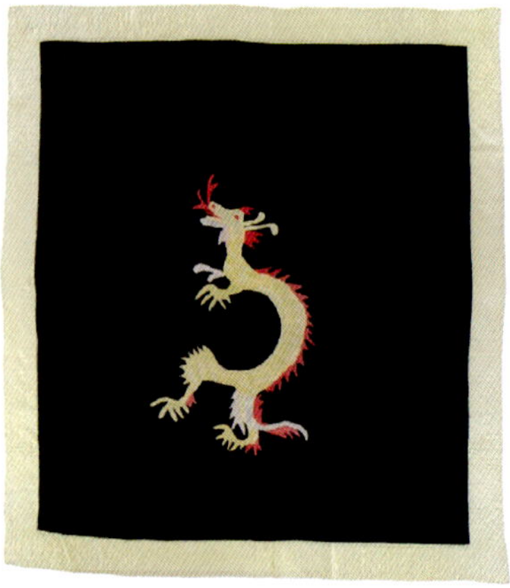

Dragon

Maker unidentified
Made in United States
1930 - 1940
90.5 x 80 in.
IQM 1997.007.0225

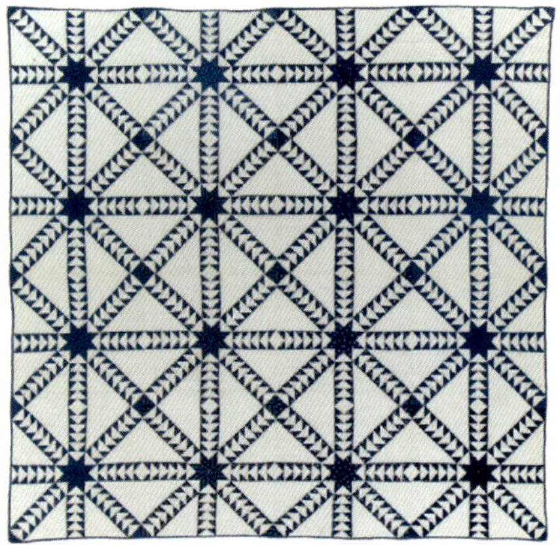

Flying Geese

Maker unidentified
Possibly made in Ohio
1880 - 1900
74 x 75 in.
IQM 1997.007.0227

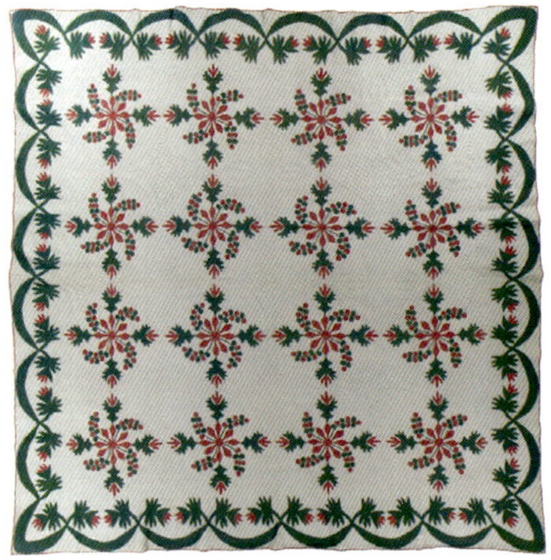

Flowers and Buds

Maker unidentified
Possibly made in Tennessee
1850 - 1870
111 x 104.5 in.
IQM 1997.007.0228

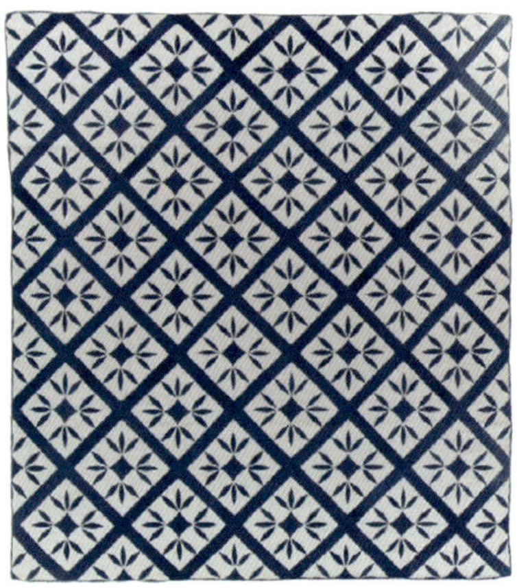

Turkey Tracks

Maker unidentified
Made in United States
1875 - 1895
86.5 x 70.5 in.
IQM 1997.007.0229

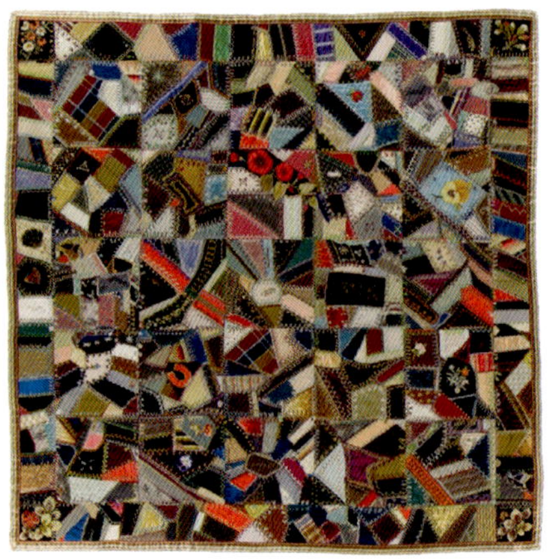

Crazy

Probably made by Dorothy Tompkins
Probably made in Yonkers, New York
1880 - 1890
65.25 x 65 in.
IQM 1997.007.0230.1

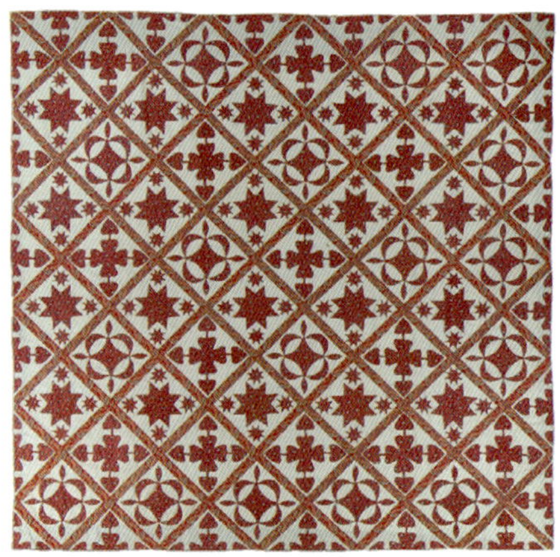

Oak Reel

Maker unidentified
Possibly made in Montgomery County, Pennsylvania
1850 - 1870
92 x 91.5 in.
IQM 1997.007.0231

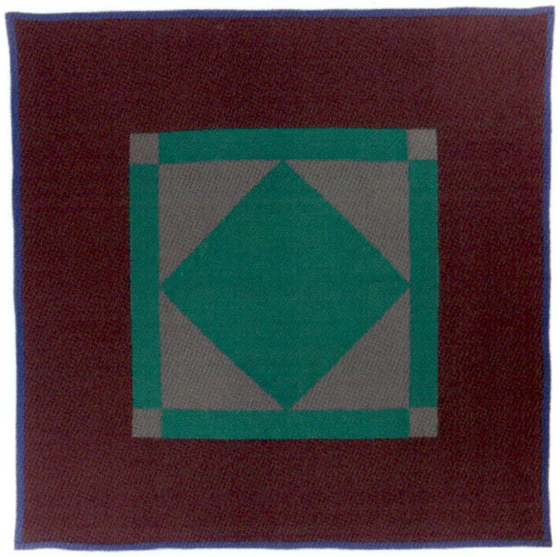

Center Diamond

Possibly made by Sarah Smoker
Probably made in Lancaster County, Pennsylvania
1915 - 1935
78 x 78.5 in.

IQM 1997.007.0232

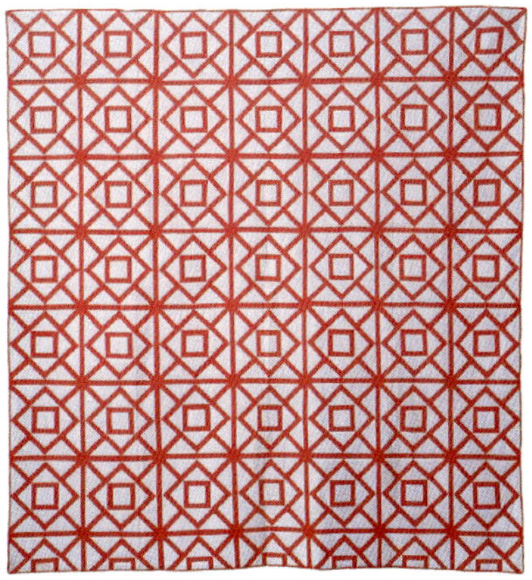

Garden Maze

Maker unidentified
Possibly made in Pennsylvania
1880 - 1900
87 x 79 in.

IQM 1997.007.0233

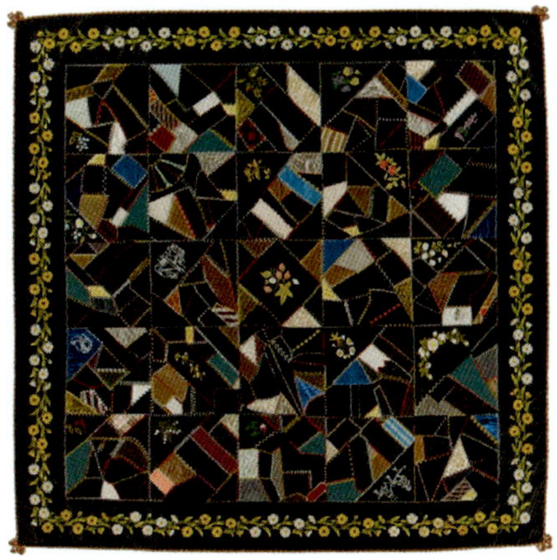

Crazy

Maker unidentified
Possibly made in Indiana
1880 - 1890
71 x 70 in.

IQM 1997.007.0234

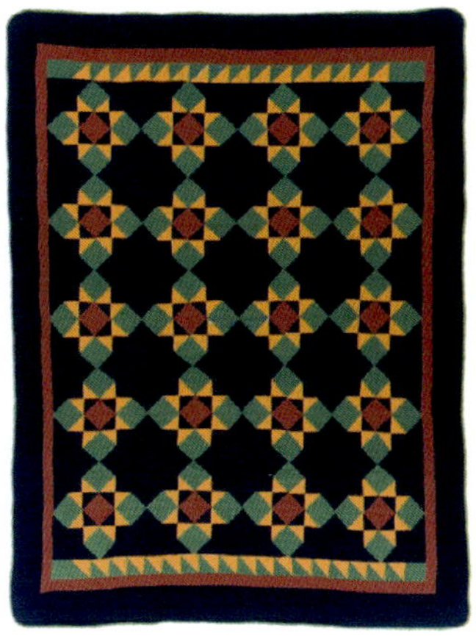

Variable Star

Maker unidentified
Possibly made in Holmes County, Ohio
1880 - 1900
86 x 62.5 in.

IQM 1997.007.0235

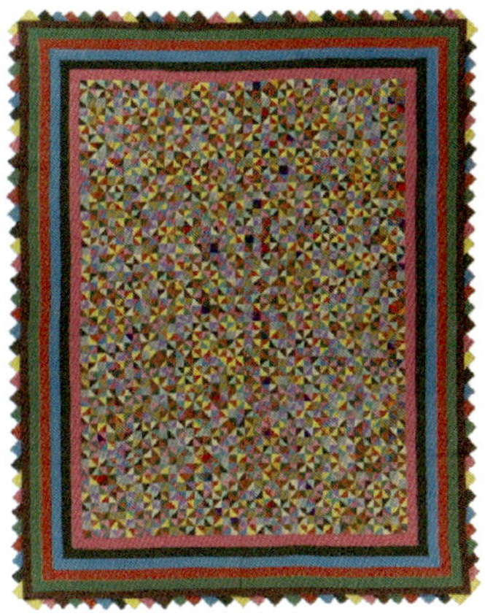

Broken Dishes

Maker unidentified
Made in United States
1940 - 1960
83 x 63.75 in.

IQM 1997.007.0236

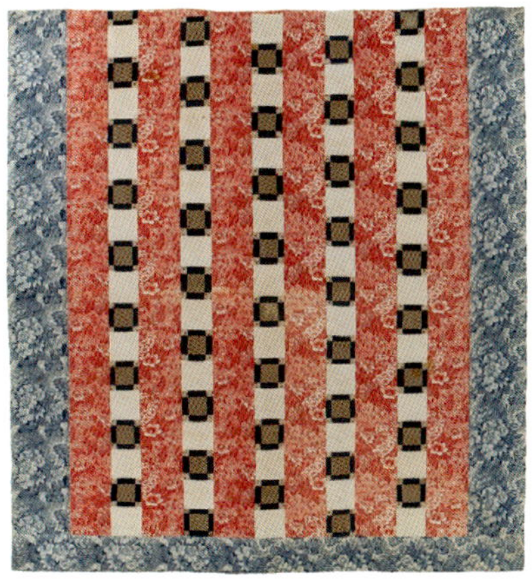

Modified Nine Patch Bars

Maker unidentified
Possibly made in Pennsylvania
1820 - 1840
105 x 97.5 in.

IQM 1997.007.0237

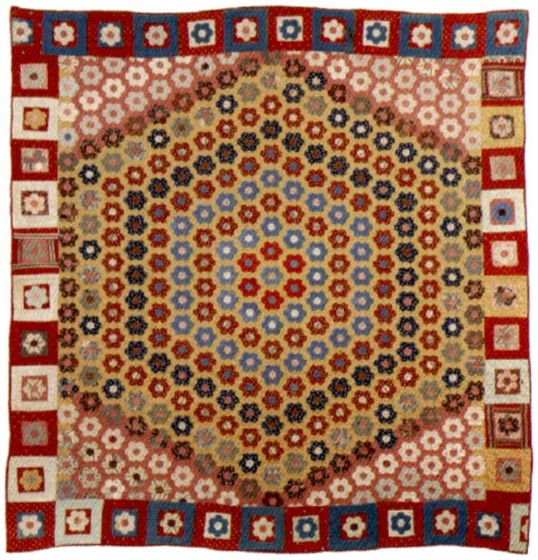

Hexagon

Maker unidentified
Possibly made in New England
1870 - 1890
84.5 x 79.5 in.
IQM 1997.007.0238

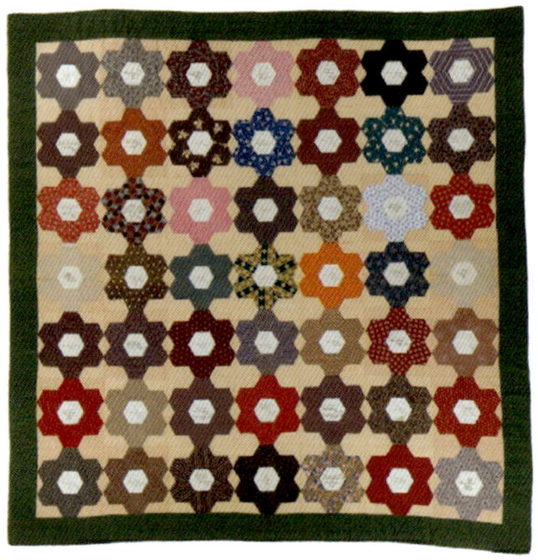

Hexagon

Maker unidentified
Possibly made in Cheshire, Massachusetts
Dated 1862
89.5 x 86.5 in.
IQM 1997.007.0240

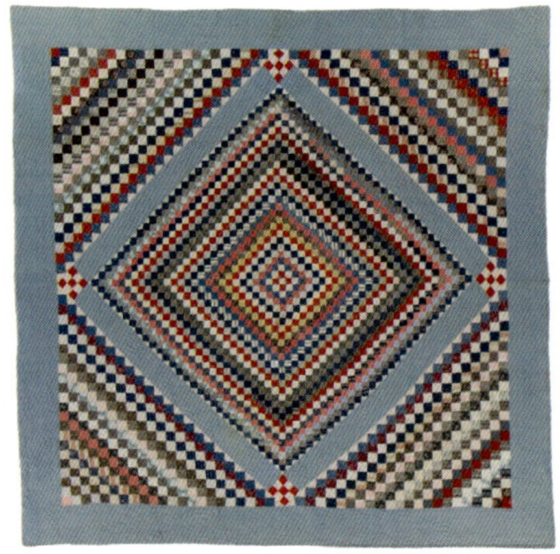

Trip around the World

Maker unidentified
Possibly made in Pennsylvania
1890 - 1910
76.5 x 75 in.
IQM 1997.007.0242

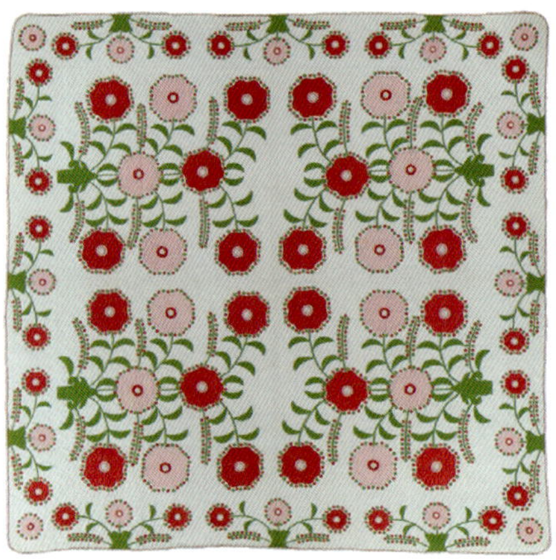

Pots of Flowers

Maker unidentified
Probably made in Ohio
1850 - 1870
82 x 80.5 in.
IQM 1997.007.0243

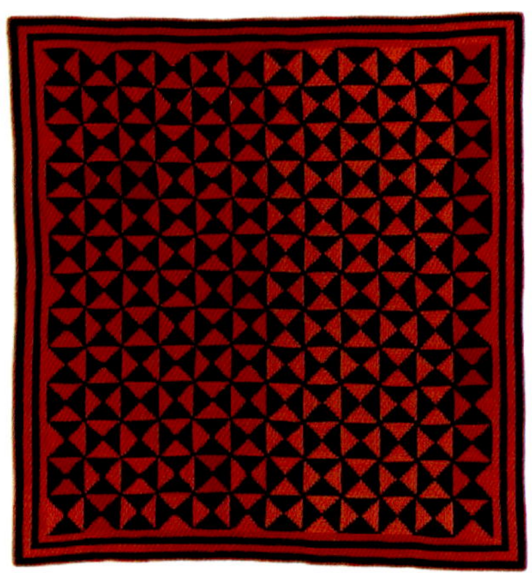

Log Cabin

Maker unidentified
Possibly made in Ohio
1870 - 1890
75.5 x 69 in.
IQM 1997.007.0245

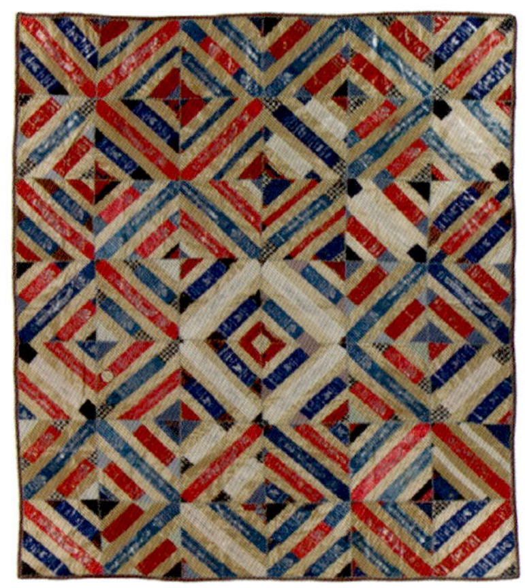

Chicken Ribbons

Maker unidentified
Possibly made in Sikeston, Missouri
Circa 1914
79 x 65 in.
IQM 1997.007.0246

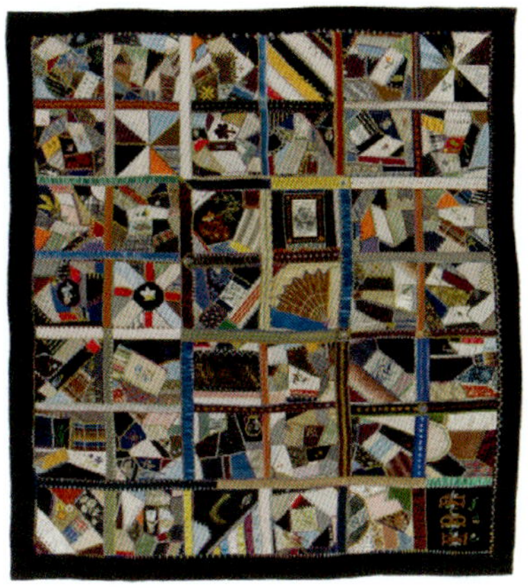

Crazy

Maker unidentified
Possibly made in St. Louis,
Missouri
Dated 1886
66.5 x 59 in.

IQM 1997.007.0247

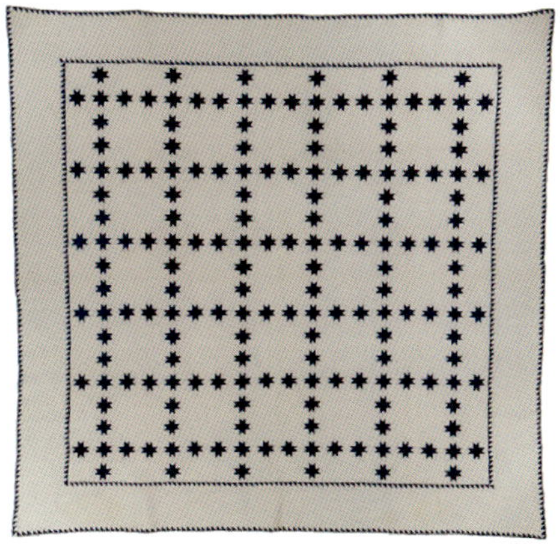

Sawtooth Star

Maker unidentified
Possibly made in Ohio
1840 - 1860
89 x 87 in.

IQM 1997.007.0248

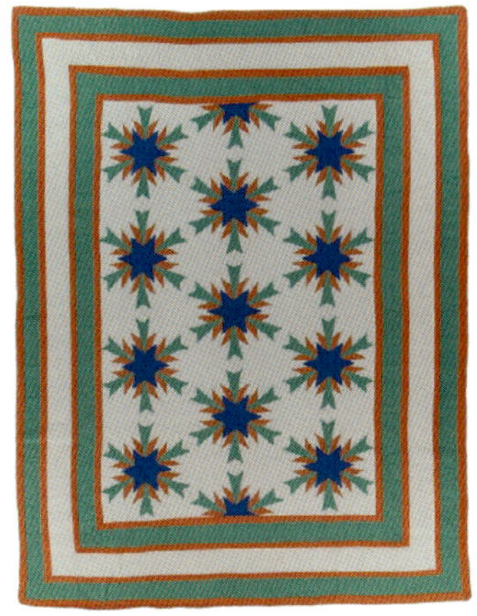

Star

Maker unidentified
Possibly made in Moline,
Illinois
1930 - 1950
106.5 x 79.5 in.

IQM 1997.007.0250

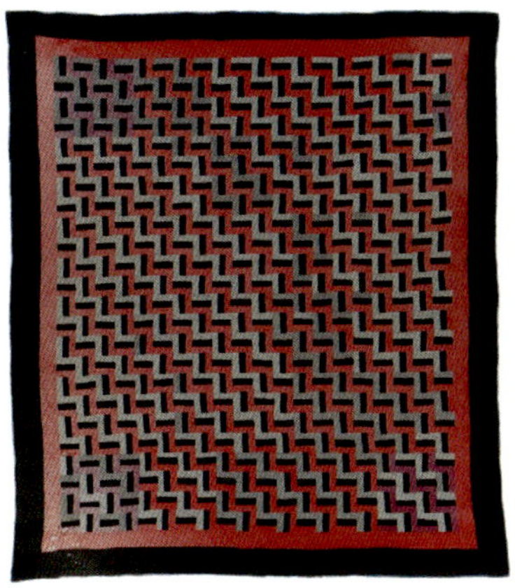

Rail Fence

Maker unidentified
Possibly made in LaGrange
County, Indiana
1910 - 1930
81.5 x 70 in.

IQM 1997.007.0251.1

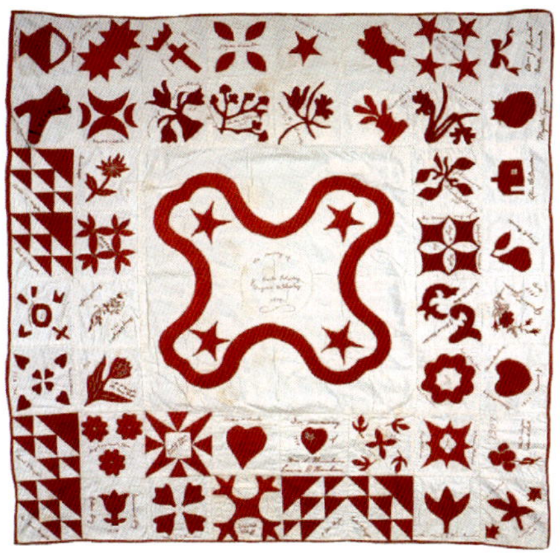

Album

Maker unidentified
Made in Monmouth County,
New Jersey
Dated 1908 - 1915
65.5 x 63.5 in.

IQM 1997.007.0252

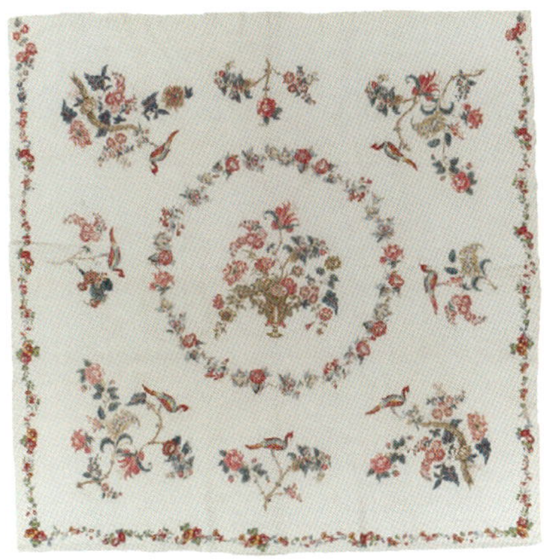

Medallion

Maker unidentified
Possibly made in Ohio
1820 - 1840
93.5 x 89.5 in.

IQM 1997.007.0253

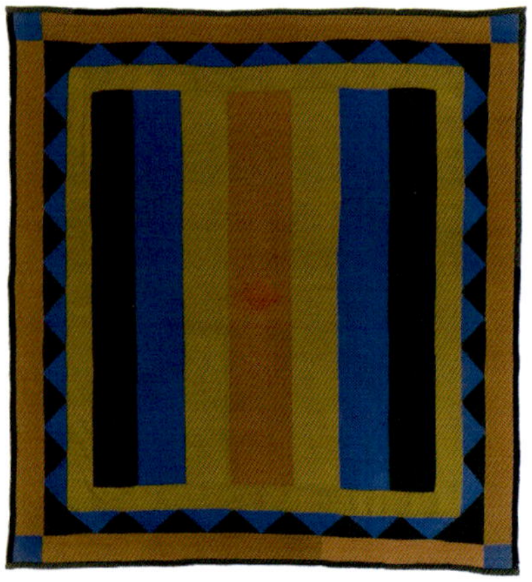

Bars

Maker unidentified
Possibly made in Ontario, Canada
1910 - 1930
72.5 x 65.5 in.
IQM 1997.007.0254

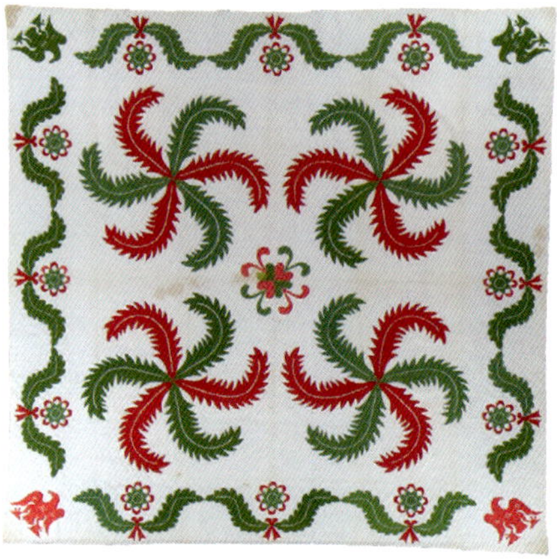

Princess Feather

Maker unidentified
Made in United States
1860 - 1880
94 x 92.5 in.
IQM 1997.007.0255

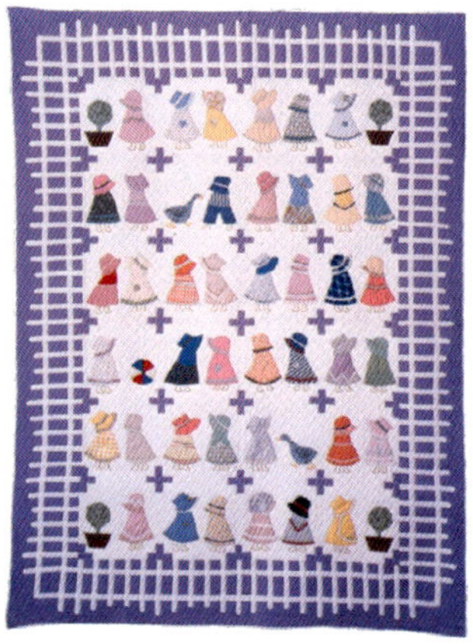

Sunbonnet Sue

Maker unidentified
Made in United States
1920 - 1940
84 x 60 in.
IQM 1997.007.0256

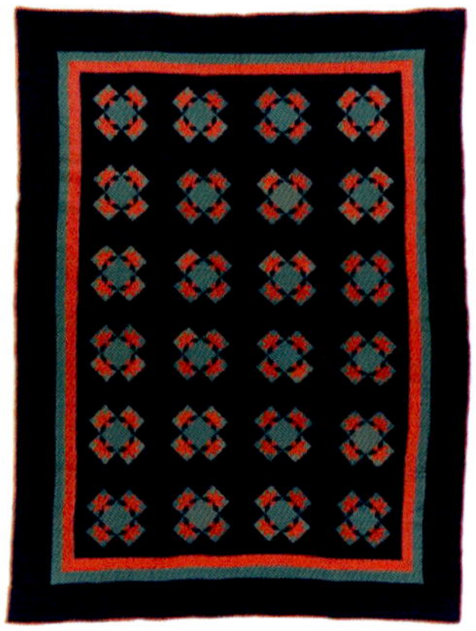

Peony Cross

Maker unidentified
Possibly made in Ohio
1930 - 1950
85 x 65.5 in.
IQM 1997.007.0258

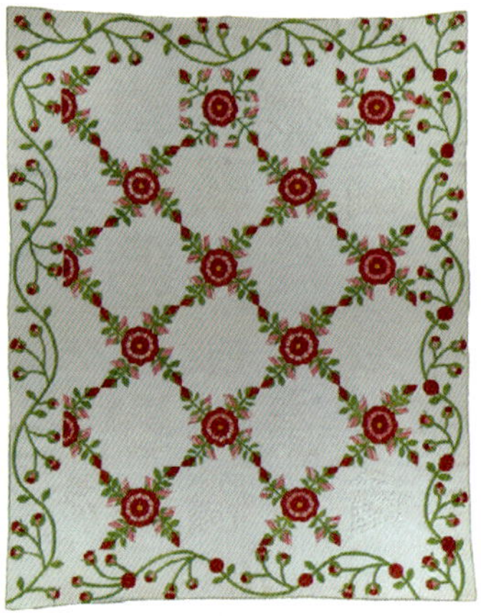

Whig Rose variation

Maker unidentified
Possibly made in Ohio
1850 - 1870
98.5 x 77 in.
IQM 1997.007.0259

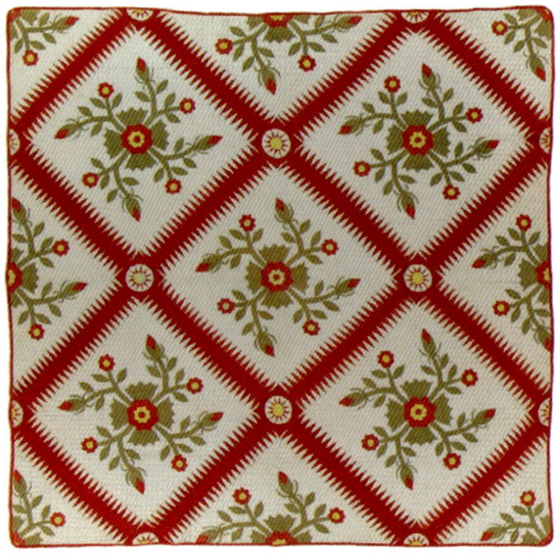

Whig Rose

Probably made by Dell Patterson
Probably made in Fayetteville, Tennessee
1895 - 1905
83.5 x 85 in.
IQM 1997.007.0261

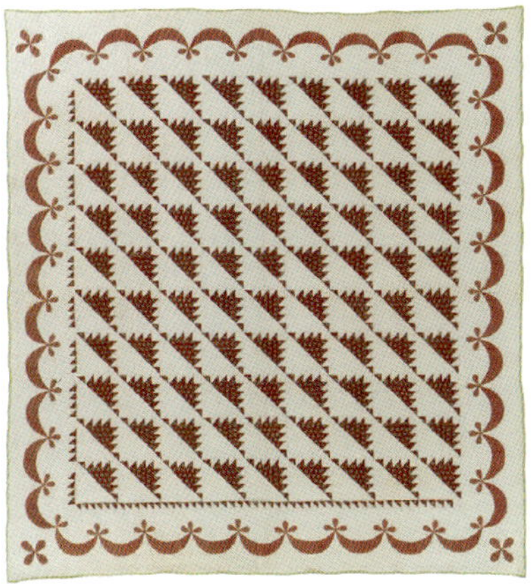

Delectable Mountains

Maker unidentified
Made in United States
1850 - 1870
95 x 85 in.

IQM 1997.007.0262

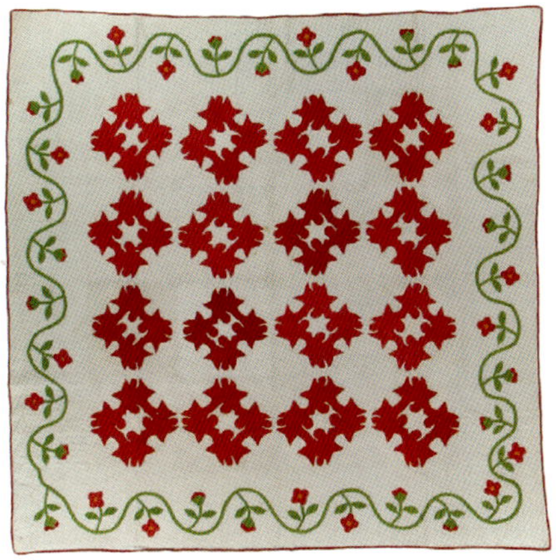

Snowflake

Maker unidentified
Possibly made in Ohio
1880 - 1900
82.5 x 81 in.

IQM 1997.007.0263.1

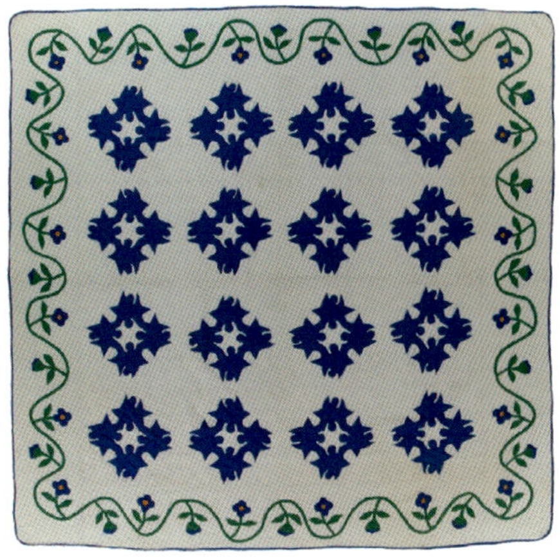

Snowflake

Maker unidentified
Possibly made in Ohio
1930 - 1950
84 x 82 in.

IQM 1997.007.0263.2

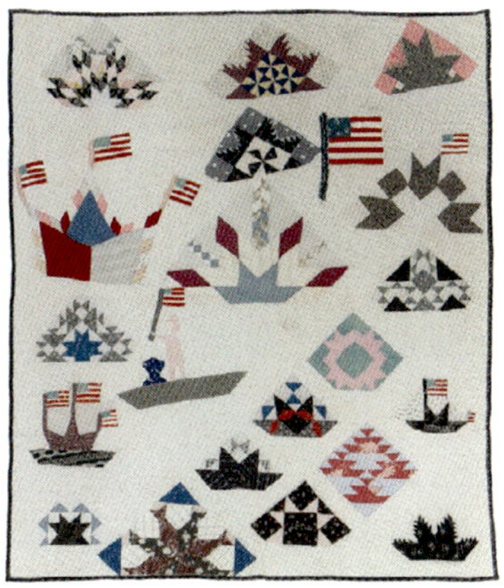

Original - Ship of State

Probably made by Peet sisters (Cordelia Peet, Jane Hull, Helen Lind, and Lois Sage)
Probably made in Kent County, Michigan
1908 - 1909
67 x 55.5 in.

IQM 1997.007.0265

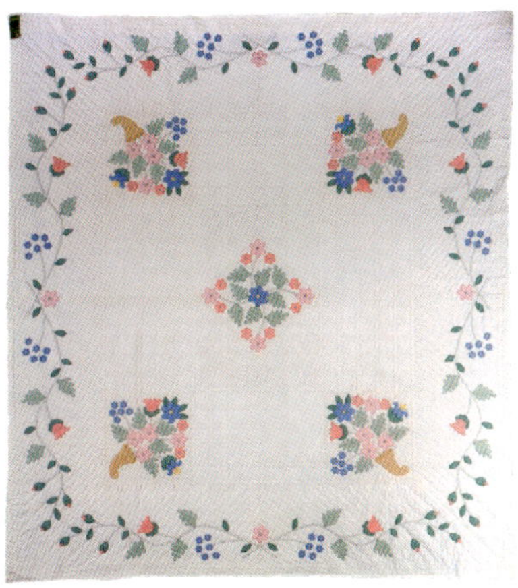

Cornucopia

Marie Mueller
Made in Garnavillo, Iowa
Dated 1933
95 x 85 in.

IQM 1997.007.0266

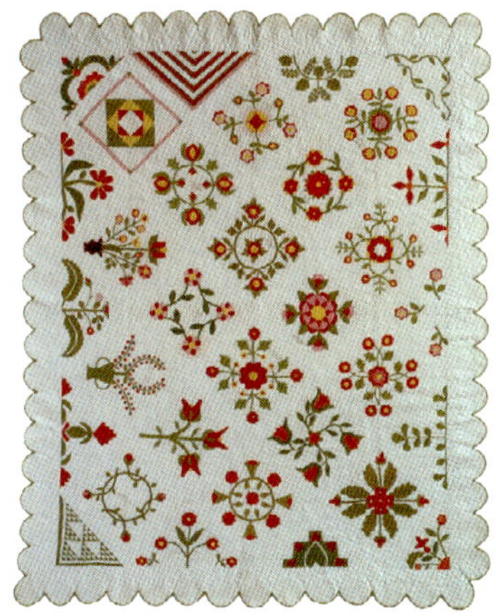

Album

Friends and Relatives of Margaret Morton
Made in Preble County, Ohio
Dated 1853 - 1856
100 x 80.5 in.

IQM 1997.007.0267

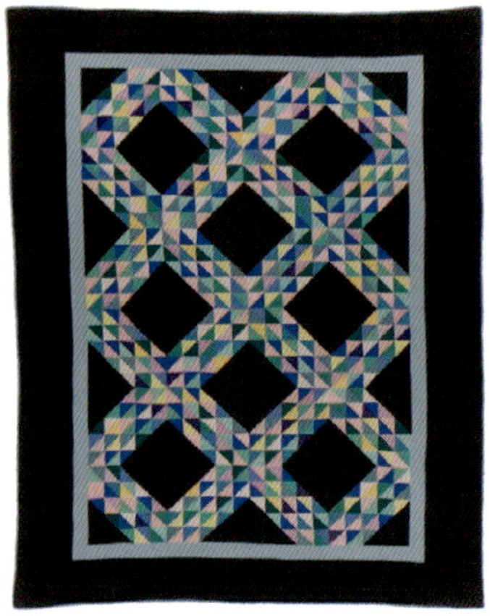

Ocean Waves

Maker unidentified
Possibly made in Holmes County, Ohio
1920 - 1940
83.5 x 66 in.

IQM 1997.007.0268

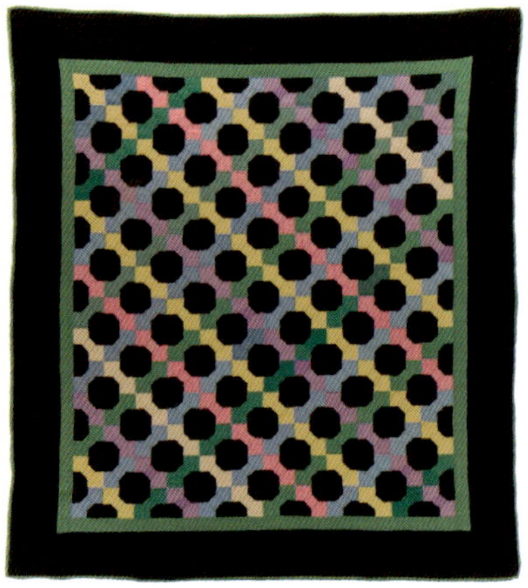

Bow Tie

Maker unidentified
Possibly made in Holmes County, Ohio
1920 - 1940
87 x 78 in.

IQM 1997.007.0269

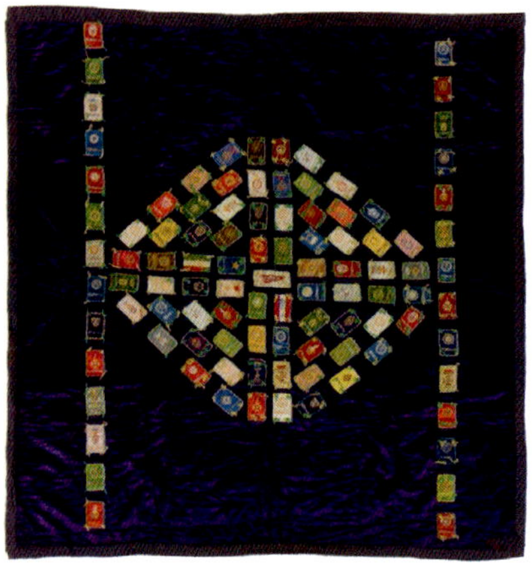

Tobacco Premium

Maker unidentified
Made in United States
1900 - 1920
56.25 x 52.75 in.

IQM 1997.007.0271

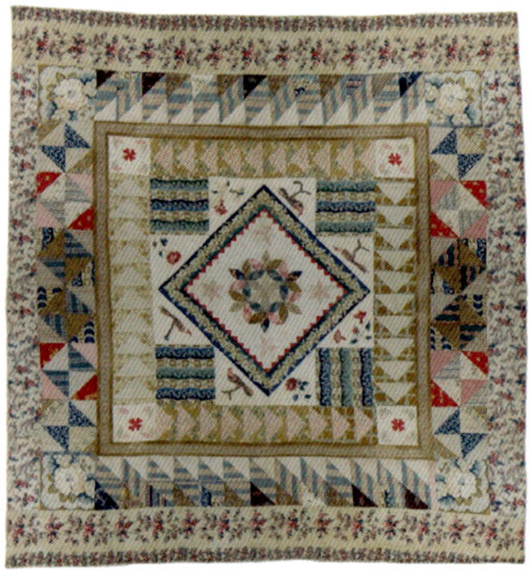

Medallion

Maker unidentified
Possibly made in United Kingdom
1820 - 1840
108 x 97 in.

IQM 1997.007.0272

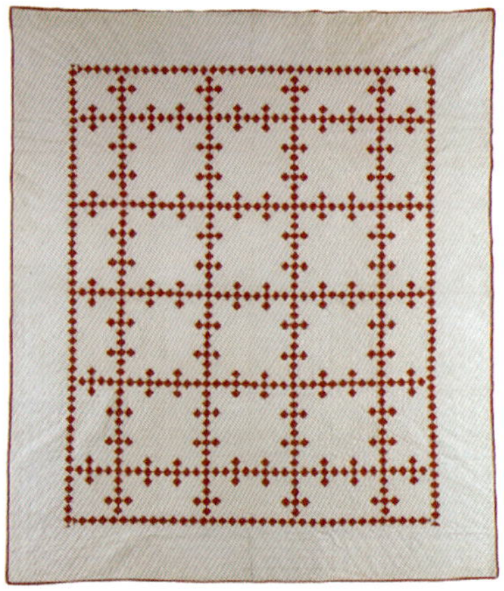

Double Nine Patch

Maker unidentified
Possibly made in Ohio
Dated 1907
89 x 75 in.

IQM 1997.007.0273

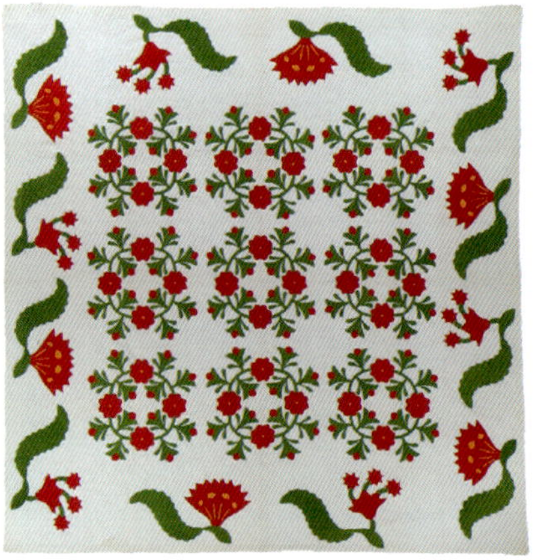

Martha Washington Wreath

Maker unidentified
Possibly made in Pennsylvania
1850 - 1860
87.5 x 82 in.

IQM 1997.007.0275

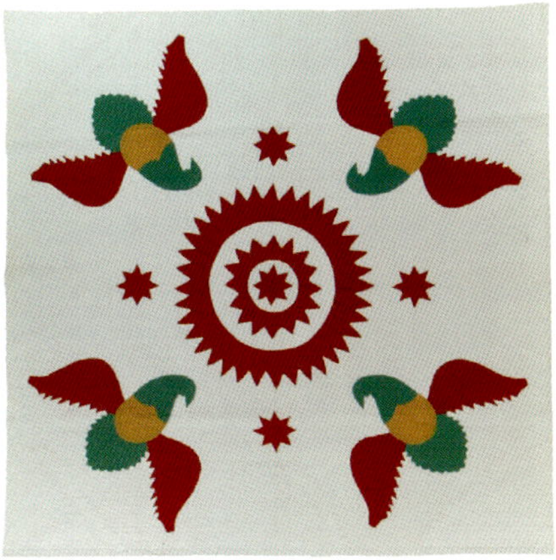

Eagle

Maker unidentified
Possibly made in Pennsylvania
1910 - 1930
76.5 x 76.5 in.

IQM 1997.007.0278

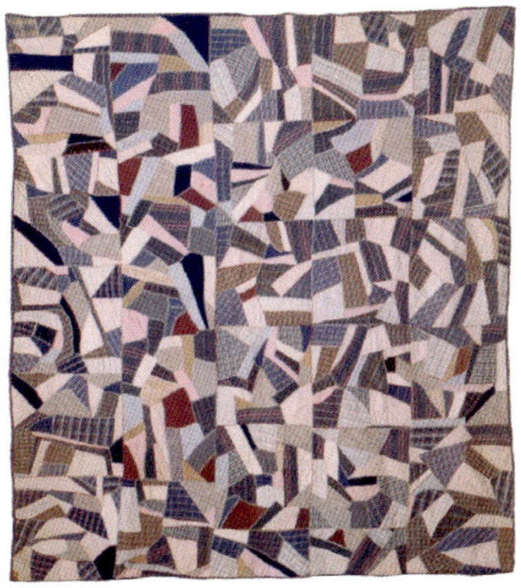

Crazy

Maker unidentified
Possibly made in Minnesota
1900 - 1920
84 x 76 in.

IQM 1997.007.0279

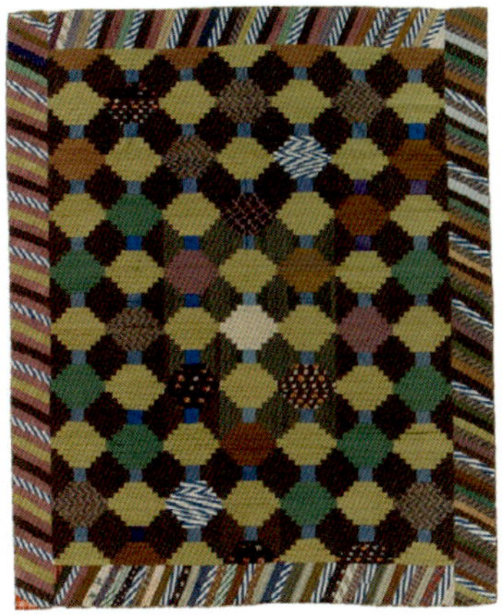

Log Cabin

Maker unidentified
Possibly made in Ohio
1870 - 1890
77 x 62.5 in.

IQM 1997.007.0280

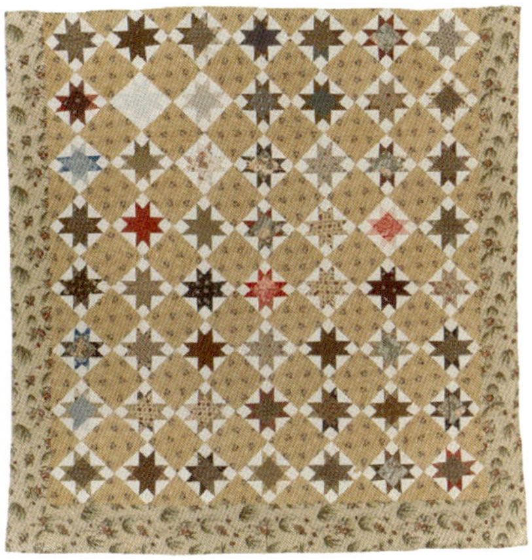

Sawtooth Star

Maker unidentified
Probably made in Pennsylvania
1830 - 1850
90 x 84 in.

IQM 1997.007.0281

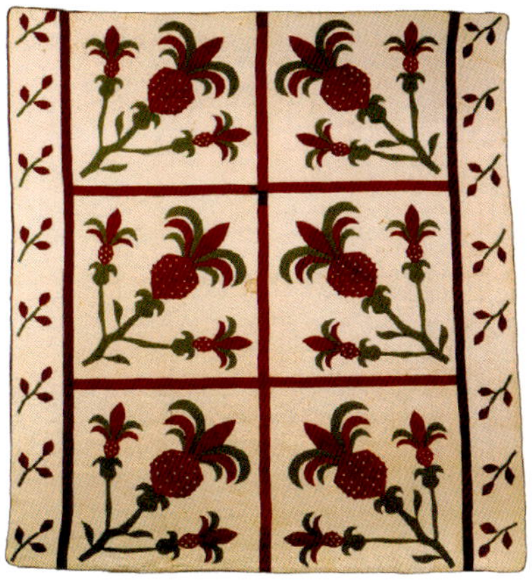

Pineapple

Maker unidentified
Possibly made in Kentucky
1860 - 1880
86 x 79 in.

IQM 1997.007.0282

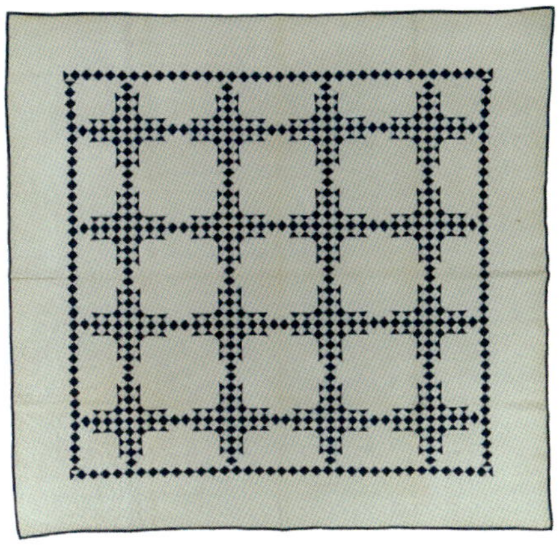

Reverse Irish Chain

Maker unidentified
Possibly made in Cincinnati, Ohio
1860 - 1880
79.5 x 77.5 in.

IQM 1997.007.0283

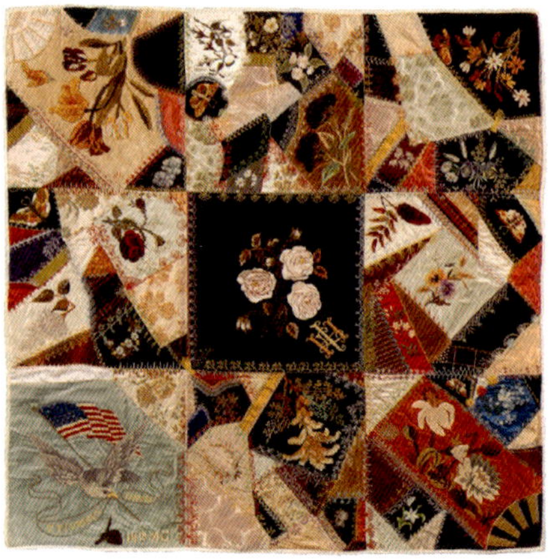

Crazy

Maker unidentified
Possibly made in Indiana
1880 - 1900
53 x 52.5 in.

IQM 1997.007.0284

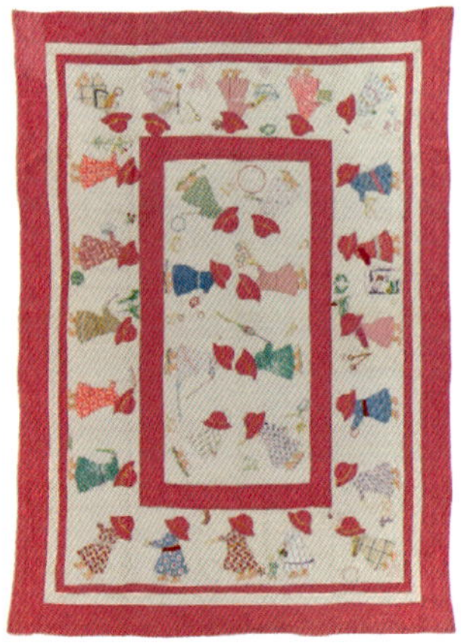

Sunbonnet Sue

Maker unidentified
Possibly made in Indiana
1920 - 1940
72.5 x 50 in.

IQM 1997.007.0285

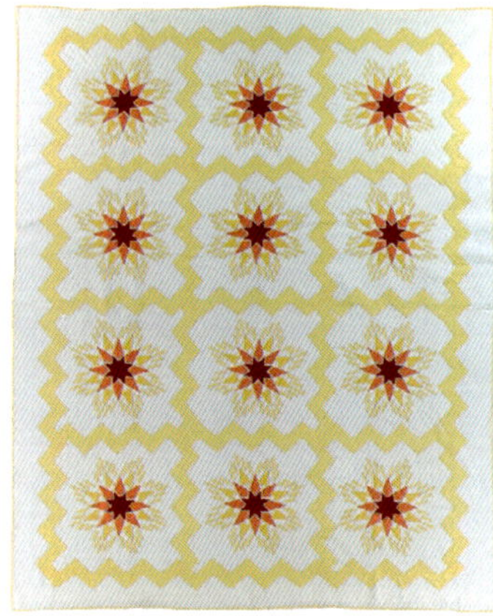

Mountain Star

Maker unidentified
Possibly made in Ohio
Circa 1932
92 x 72.75 in.

IQM 1997.007.0286

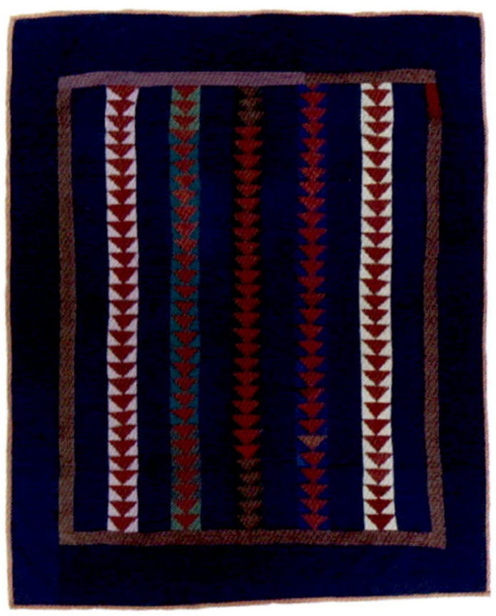

Wild Goose Chase

Maker unidentified
Possibly made in Holmes County, Ohio
1920 - 1940
85 x 69.5 in.

IQM 1997.007.0287

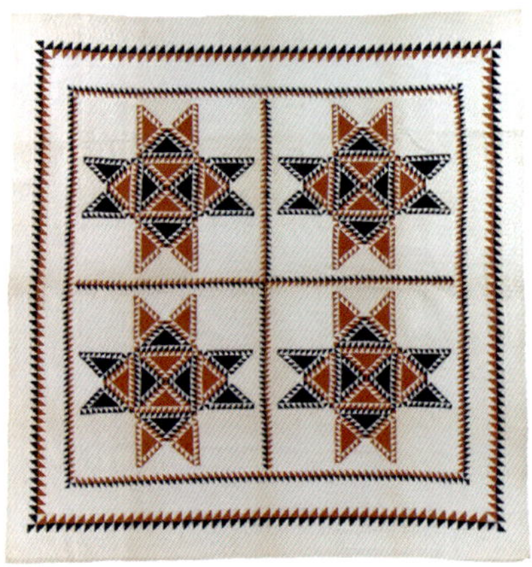

Feathered Star

Maker unidentified
Made in United States
1890 - 1910
72.5 x 67 in.

IQM 1997.007.0288

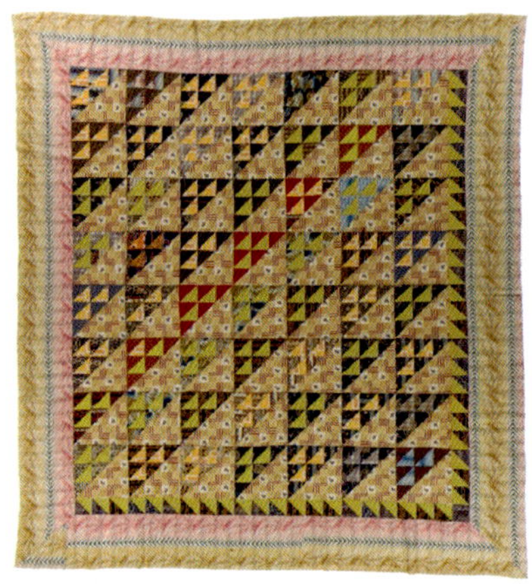

Birds in Air

Maker unidentified
Possibly made in Massachusetts
1850 - 1870
87 x 79 in.

IQM 1997.007.0289

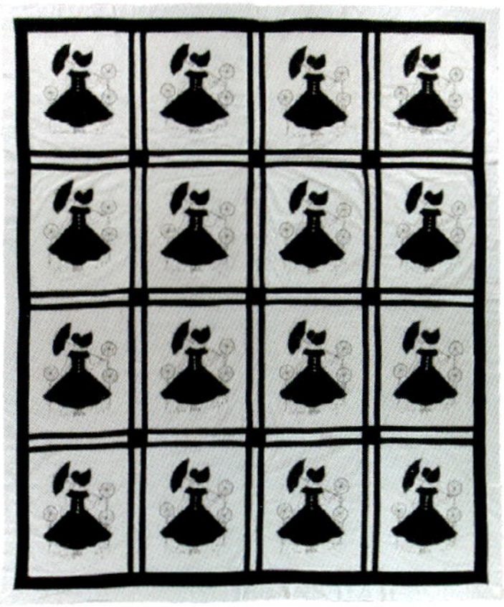

Colonial Lady

Maker unidentified
Possibly made in Ohio
1925 - 1945
103 x 87.5 in.

IQM 1997.007.0290

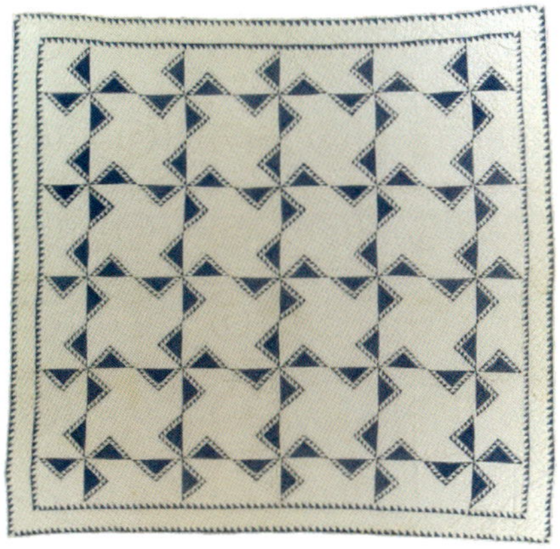

Pinwheel

Maker unidentified
Made in United States
1900 - 1920
71 x 69 in.

IQM 1997.007.0291

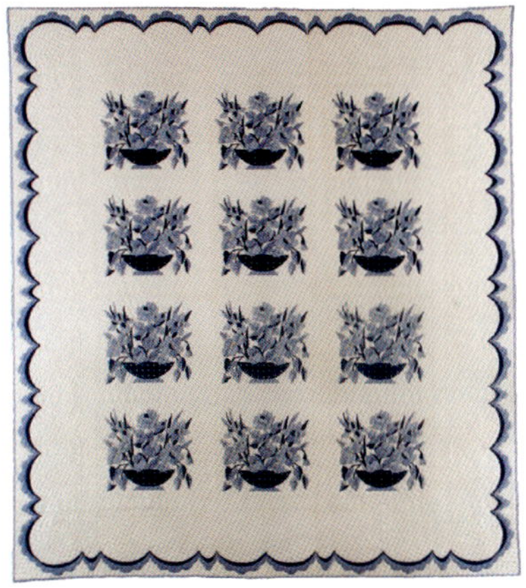

Blue Basket

Maker unidentified
Possibly made in Pennsylvania
Circa 1950
98.5 x 85.5 in.

IQM 1997.007.0292

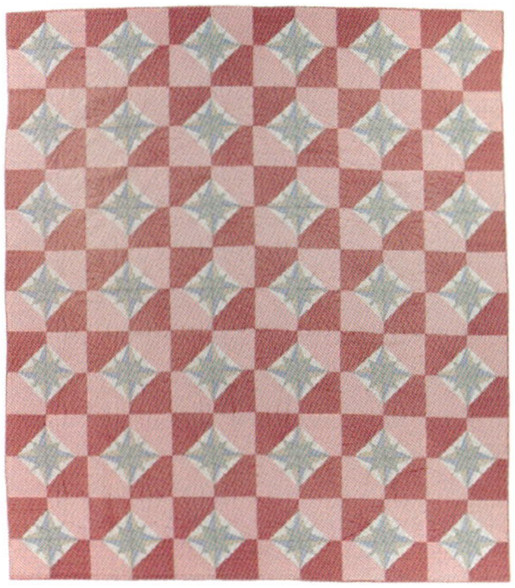

Morning Star

Maker unidentified
Possibly made in Ohio
1920 - 1940
91.5 x 78 in.

IQM 1997.007.0293

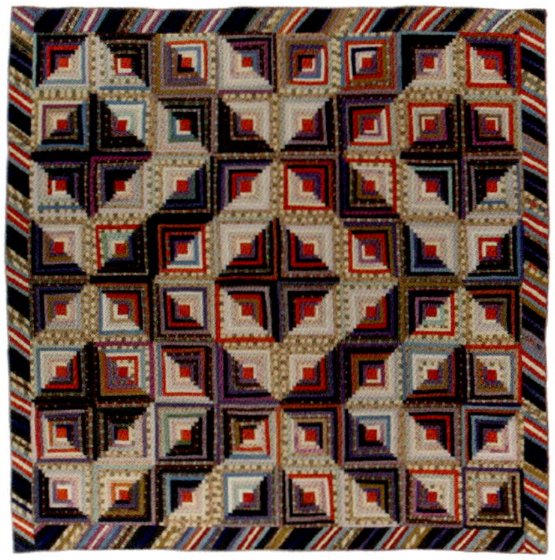

Log Cabin

Maker unidentified
Possibly made in Pennsylvania
1870 - 1890
82 x 85 in.

IQM 1997.007.0294

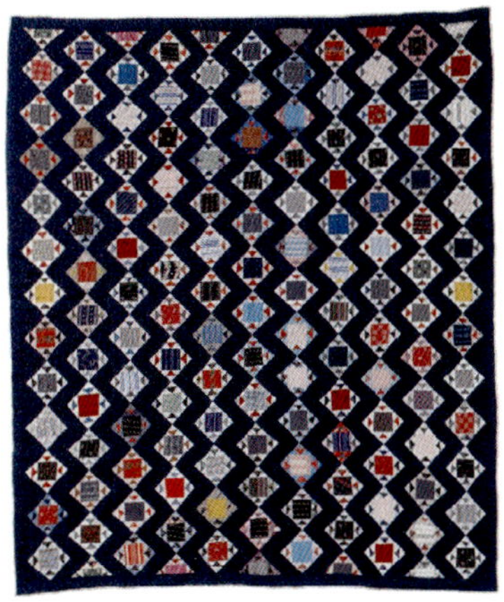

Jack in the Pulpit variation

Maker unidentified
Probably made in Indiana
1890 - 1910
91 x 74 in.

IQM 1997.007.0295

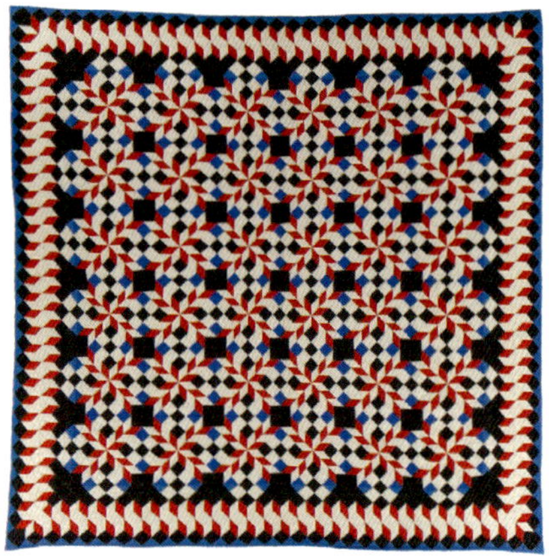

Nine Patch variation

Maker unidentified
Possibly made in Holmes County, Ohio
1915 - 1935
79 x 77 in.

IQM 1997.007.0296

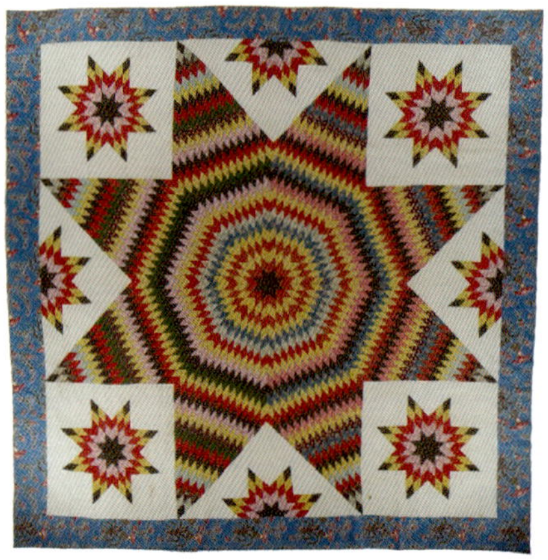

Star of Bethlehem

Walker Family
Probably made in Maryland
1830 - 1850
128.5 x 124.8 in.

IQM 1997.007.0297

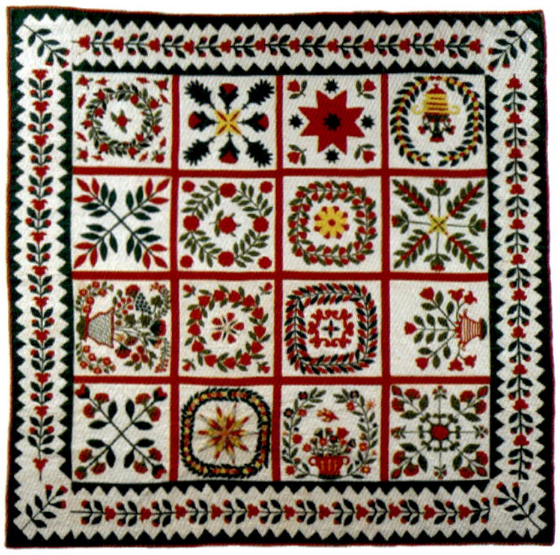

Album

Maker unidentified
Possibly made in Baltimore, Maryland
1845 - 1855
96 x 96 in.

IQM 1997.007.0300

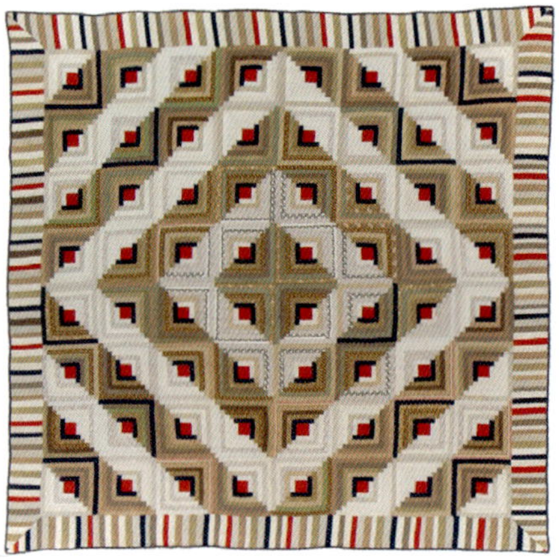

Log Cabin

Maker unidentified
Possibly made in midwestern United States
1880 - 1900
81 x 78.5 in.

IQM 1997.007.0305

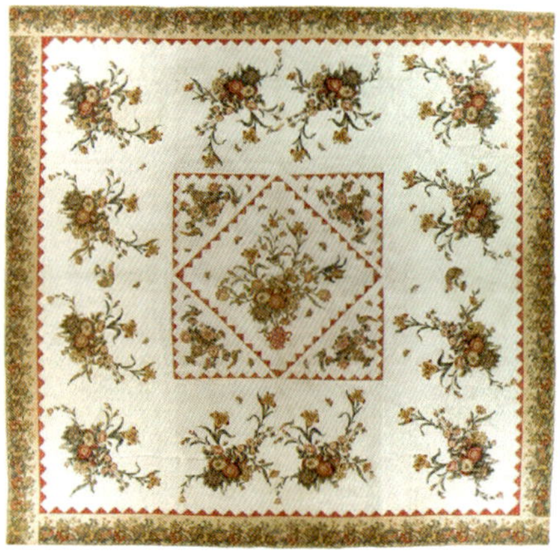

Medallion

Maker unidentified
Possibly made in Baltimore, Maryland
1830 - 1850
130 x 133 in.

IQM 1997.007.0306

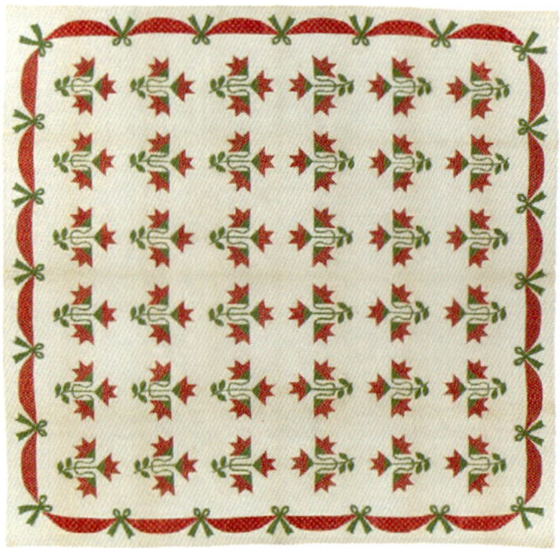

Lily

Maker unidentified
Made in United States
1850 - 1870
86 x 87 in.

IQM 1997.007.0307

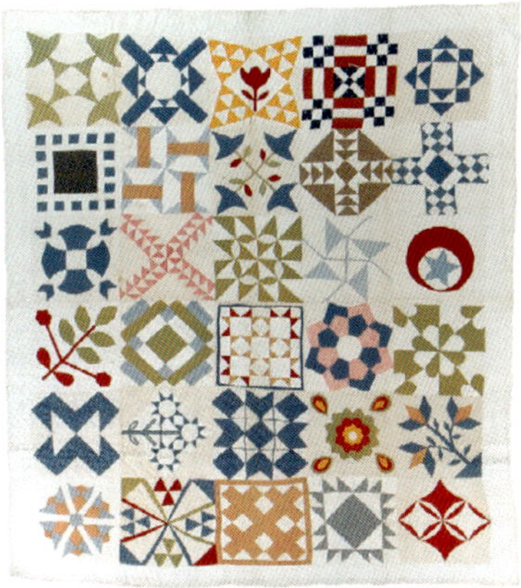

Album

Maker unidentified
Possibly made in Battle Creek, Michigan
1900 - 1920
89 x 77 in.
IQM 1997.007.0308

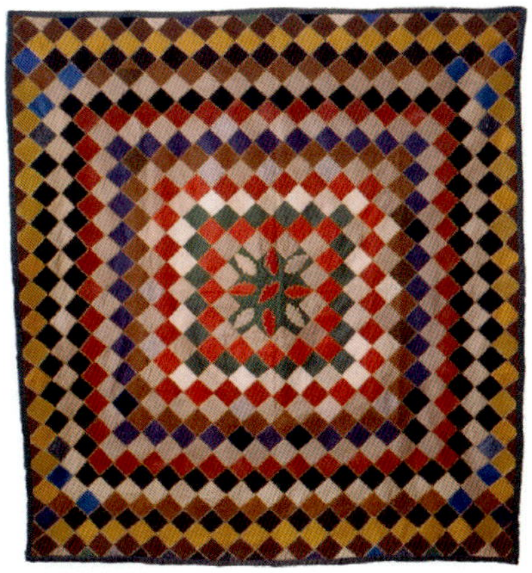

One Patch

Maker unidentified
Possibly made in Ontario, Canada
Dated 1914
73 x 65 in.
IQM 1997.007.0311

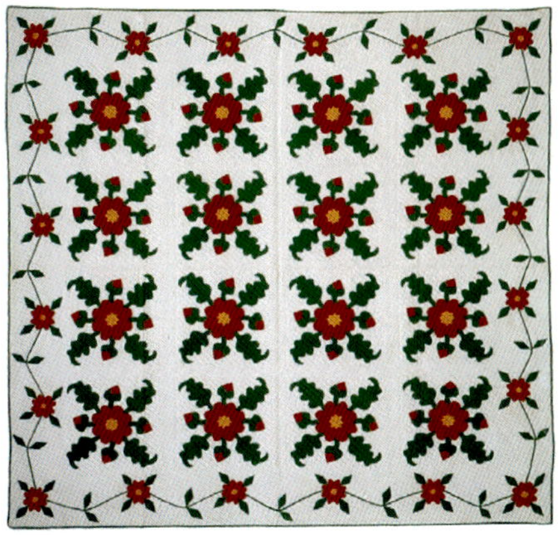

Oak Leaves and Acorns

Maker unidentified
Made in United States
1860 - 1880
83 x 79.5 in.
IQM 1997.007.0312

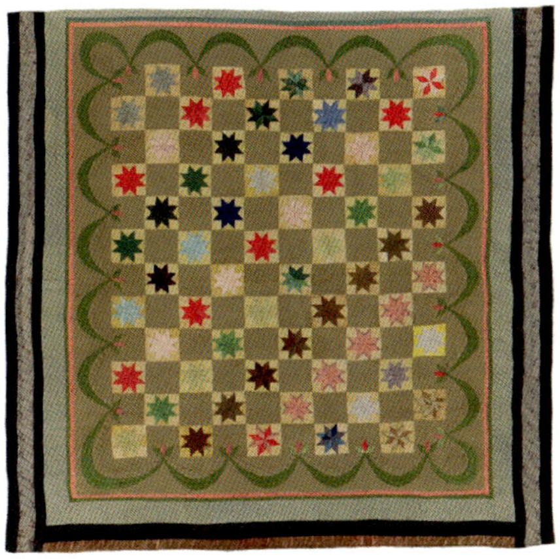

Eight Pointed Star

Maker unidentified
Made in United States
1850 - 1870
68.5 x 68.5 in.
IQM 1997.007.0313

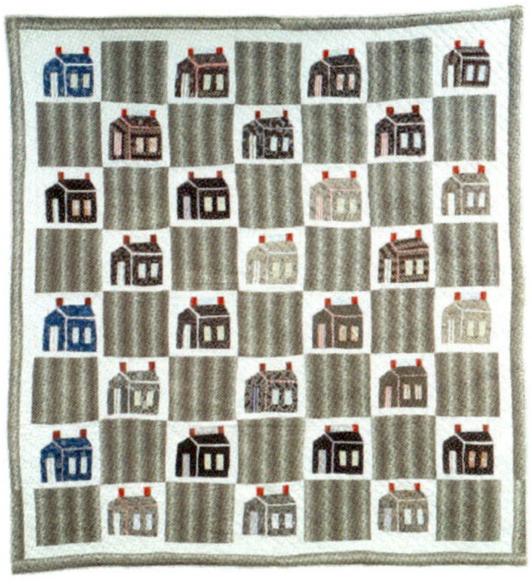

Schoolhouse

Maker unidentified
Probably made in Oklahoma
1890 - 1910
78 x 72 in.
IQM 1997.007.0314

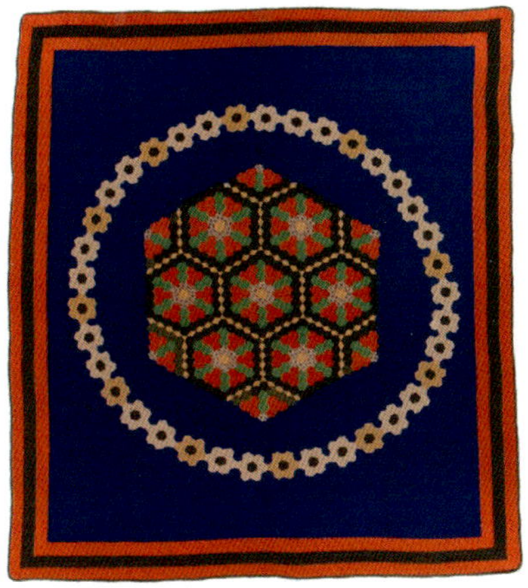

Hexagon

Maker unidentified
Possibly made in Virginia
1870 - 1890
87 x 75.5 in.
IQM 1997.007.0315

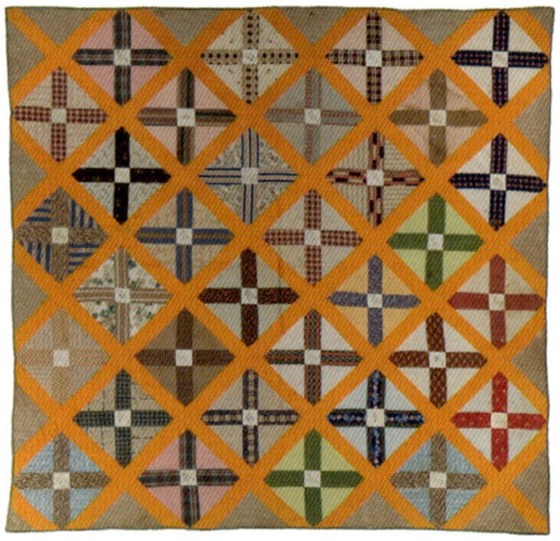

Crosses

Amwell First English Presbyterian Church members
Made in Hunterdon County, New Jersey
Dated 1844
86 x 85 in.

IQM 1997.007.0317

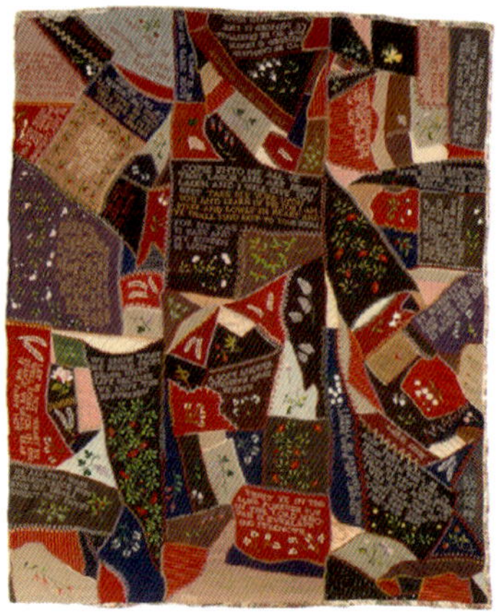

Crazy

Mary T. H. Willard
Made in Evanston, Illinois
Circa 1889
92.25 x 75.5 in.

IQM 1997.007.0318

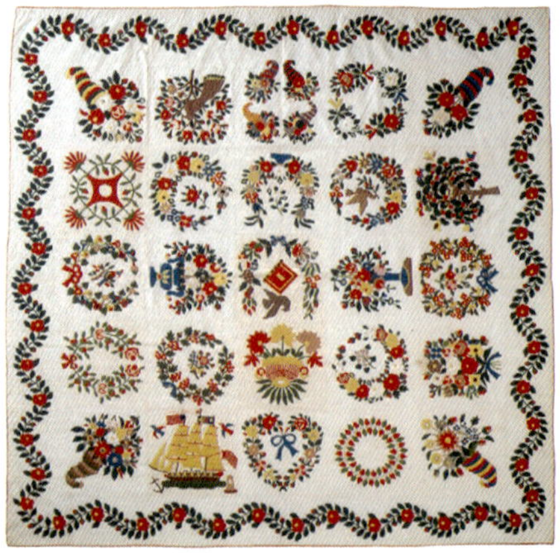

Album

Maker unidentified
Probably made in Baltimore, Maryland
1845 - 1855
106 x 105 in.

IQM 1997.007.0320

Log Cabin

Maker unidentified
Possibly made in York County, Pennsylvania
1865 - 1885
71.5 x 69 in.

IQM 1997.007.0321

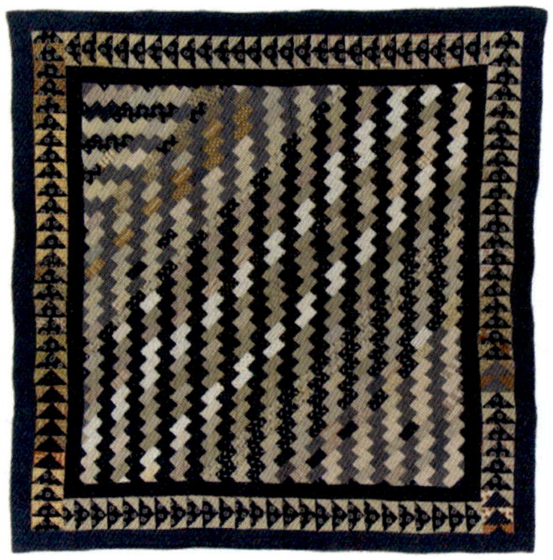

Brick Wall

Maker unidentified
Possibly made in Wabash County, Indiana
1880 - 1900
75 x 74.5 in.

IQM 1997.007.0323

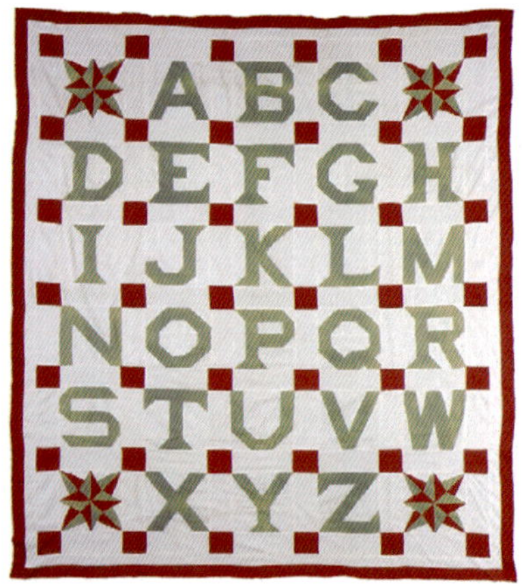

Alphabet

Maker unidentified
Possibly made in Cook County, Illinois
Circa 1910
91.5 x 77.5 in.

IQM 1997.007.0324

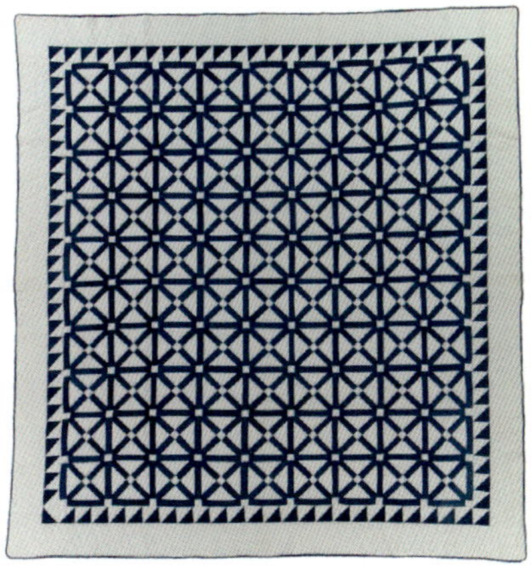

Crosses

Probably made by Nancy Miller
Probably made in Vistula, Indiana
Dated 1888
79.5 x 73 in.
IQM 1997.007.0327

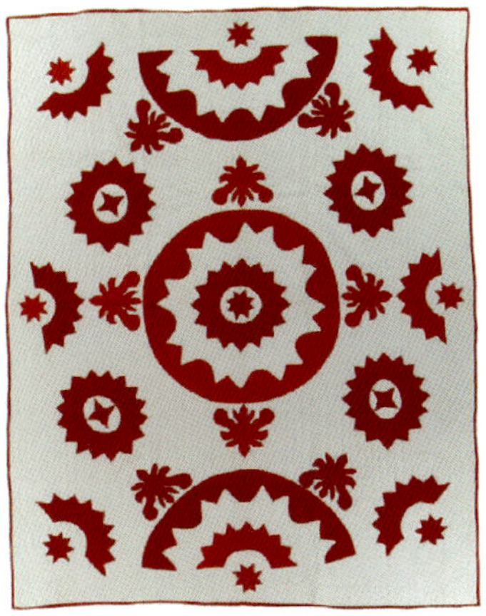

Original

Maker unidentified
Possibly made in Grant County, Indiana
1910 - 1930
86 x 68 in.
IQM 1997.007.0328

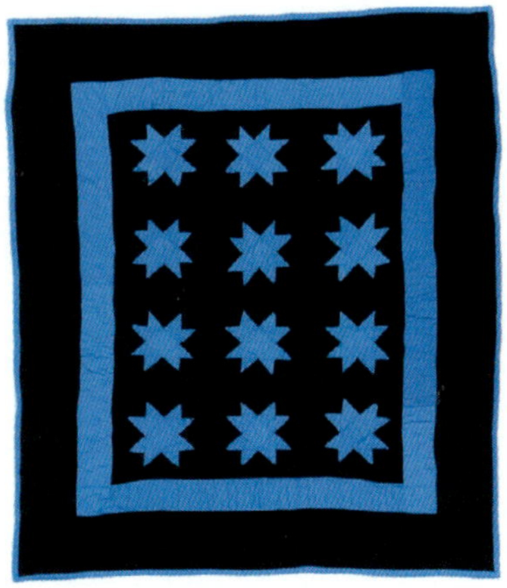

Sawtooth Star

Maker unidentified
Possibly made in Ohio
1915 - 1935
47 x 39.5 in.
IQM 1997.007.0329

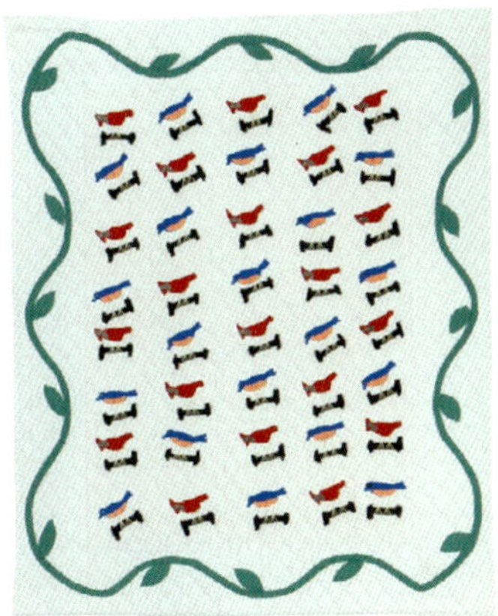

Original

Maker unidentified
Possibly made in Whitley County, Indiana
1960 - 1970
44 x 35 in.
IQM 1997.007.0330

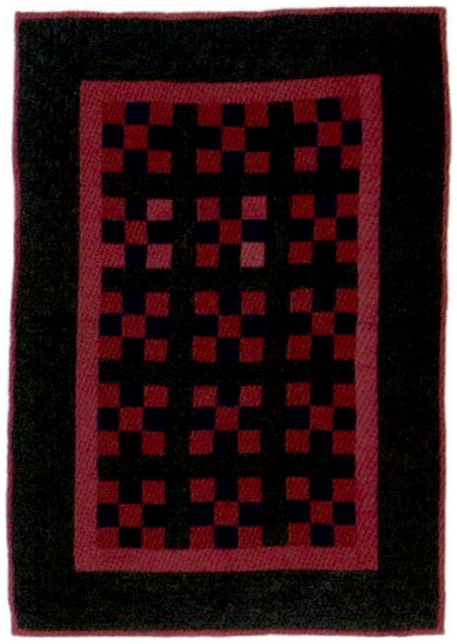

Nine Patch

Maker unidentified
Possibly made in LaGrange County, Indiana
1915 - 1935
52 x 36 in.
IQM 1997.007.0331

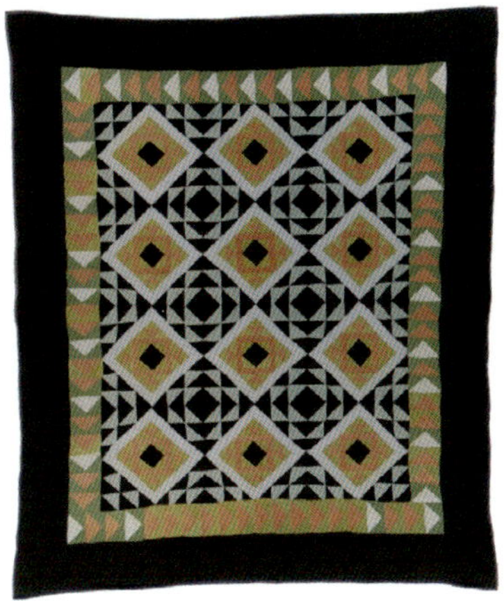

Jack in the Pulpit

Maker unidentified
Possibly made in LaGrange County, Indiana
1920 - 1940
79 x 66.5 in.
IQM 1997.007.0334

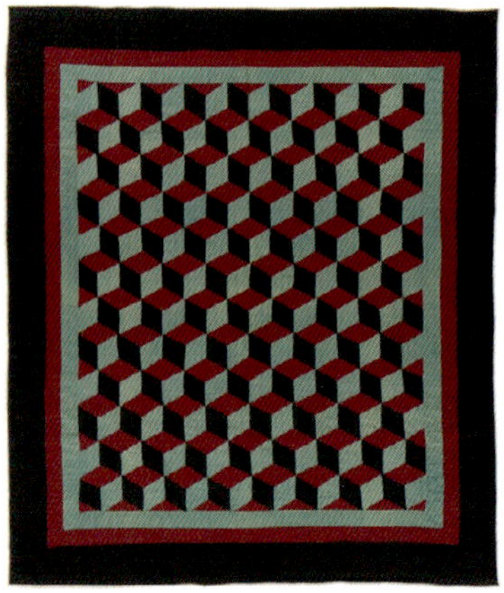

Tumbling Blocks

Maker unidentified
Possibly made in Geauga County, Ohio
1900 - 1920
83 x 85 in.
IQM 1997.007.0337

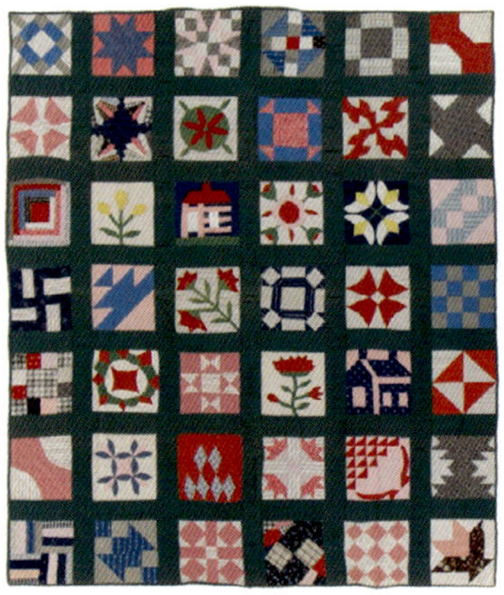

Album

Maker unidentified
Possibly made in Pennsylvania
1900 - 1920
80 x 68 in.
IQM 1997.007.0338

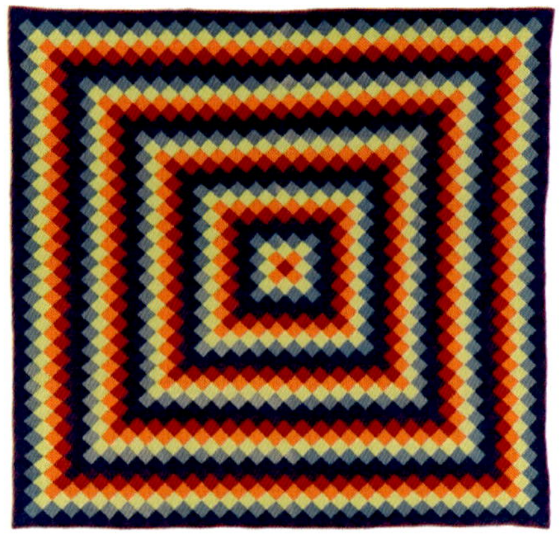

Trip Around the World

Maker unidentified
Possibly made in Lancaster County, Pennsylvania
1875 - 1895
73 x 71 in.
IQM 1997.007.0339

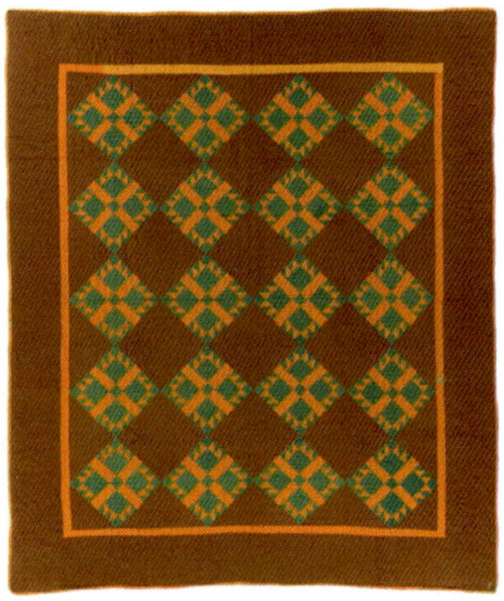

Bear's Paw

Possibly made by Clara Bontrager
Probably made in Holmes County, Ohio
Dated 1874
81 x 68 in.
IQM 1997.007.0340

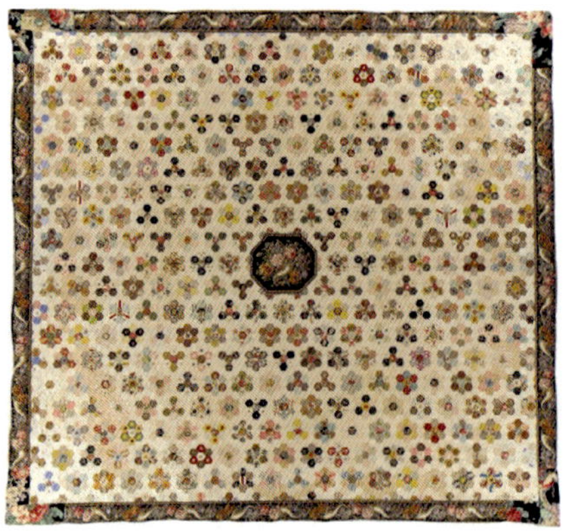

Hexagon Mosaic

Maker unidentified
Possibly made in United Kingdom
1820 - 1840
98 x 93 in.
IQM 1997.007.0341

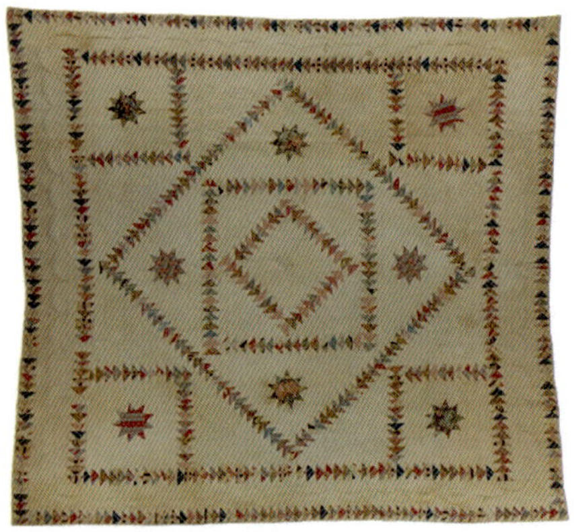

Center Diamond

Probably made by Rebecca Turner
Made in United States
Dated 1824
88.5 x 83 in.
IQM 1997.007.0342

Whole Cloth

Maker unidentified
Possibly made in Holmes County, Ohio
1880 - 1900
86 x 77.5 in.
IQM 1997.007.0345

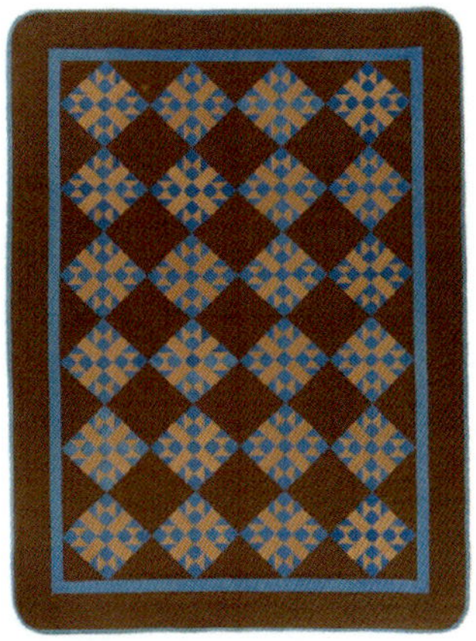

Crosses & Losses

Maker unidentified
Possibly made in Holmes County, Ohio
1880 - 1900
90 x 64 in.
IQM 1997.007.0346

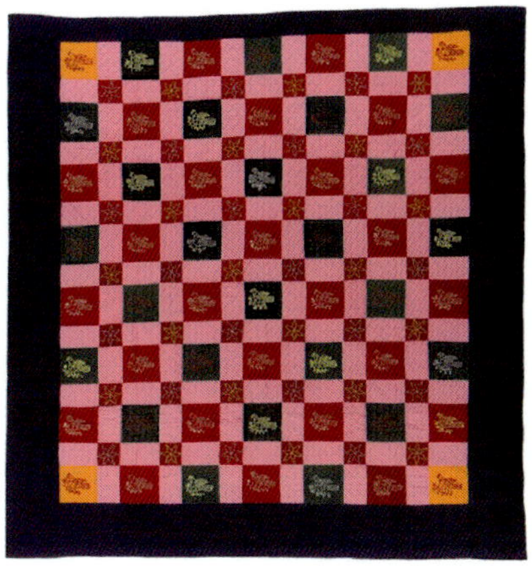

Birds

Maker unidentified
Possibly made in Lancaster County, Pennsylvania
1870 - 1890
75.5 x 70.5 in.
IQM 1997.007.0347

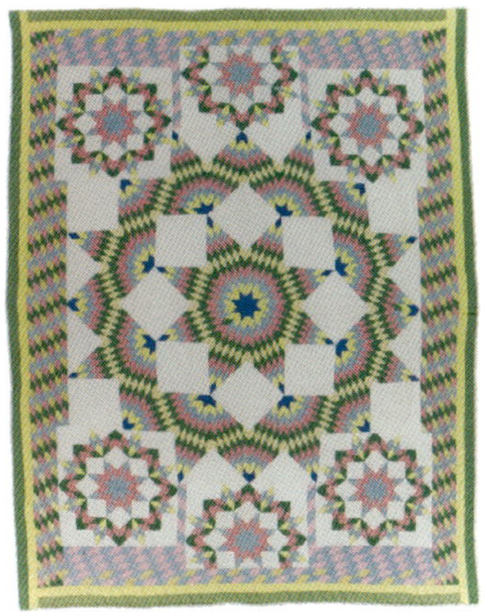

Broken Star

Maker unidentified
Possibly made in Montgomery County, Ohio
1930 - 1940
79.5 x 62 in.
IQM 1997.007.0348

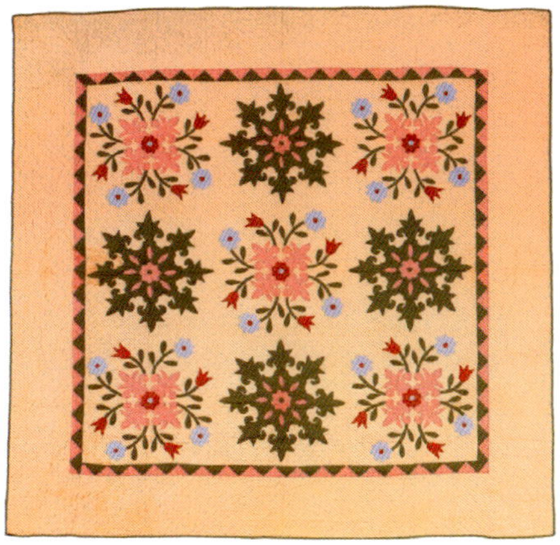

Fleur de Lis

Maker unidentified
Possibly made in Lancaster County, Pennsylvania
1870 - 1890
91 x 89.5 in.
IQM 1997.007.0349

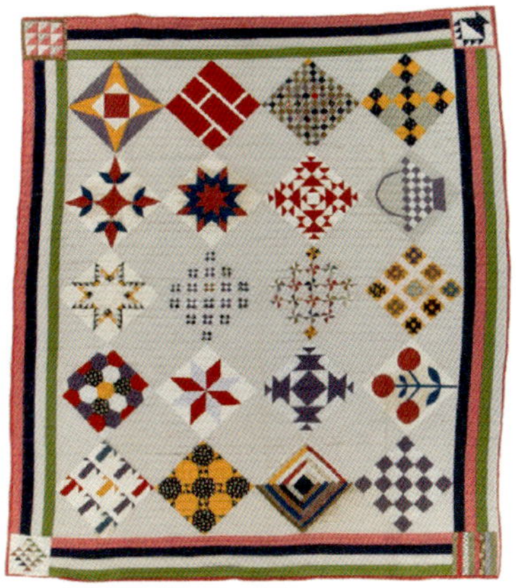

Album

Maker unidentified
Possibly made in Logansport, Indiana
1890 - 1910
82.5 x 69 in.
IQM 1997.007.0352

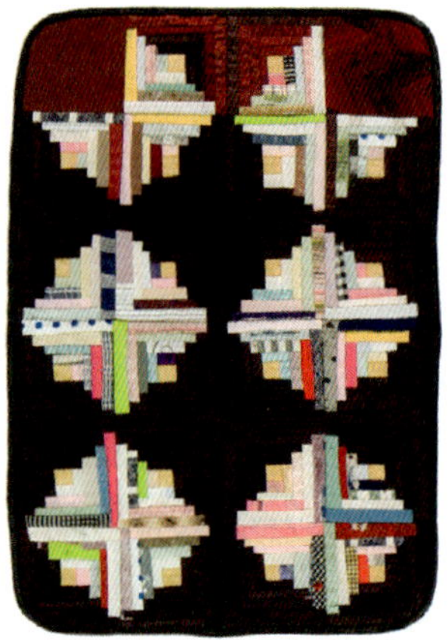

Log Cabin

Maker unidentified
Possibly made in Elkhart County, Indiana
Dated 1919
21 x 14 in.

IQM 1997.007.0354

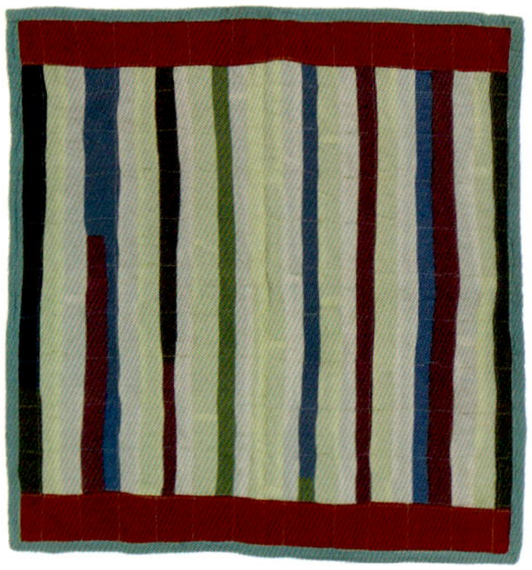

Bars

Possibly made by Mary Plank
Possibly made in Arthur, Illinois
1935 - 1955
26 x 24 in.

IQM 1997.007.0356

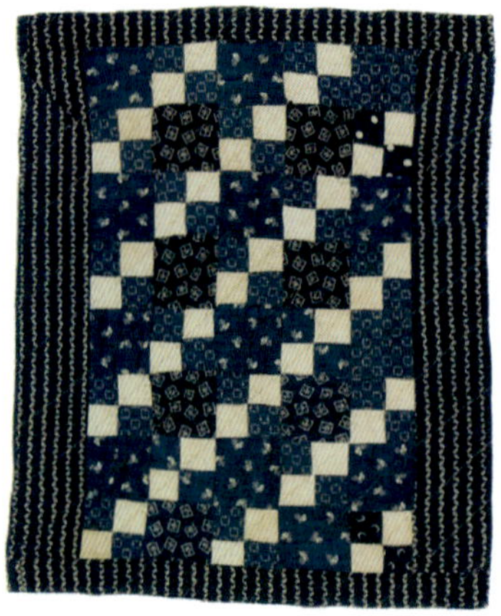

Four Patch

Maker unidentified
Possibly made in Indiana
1870 - 1890
24.5 x 20 in.

IQM 1997.007.0357

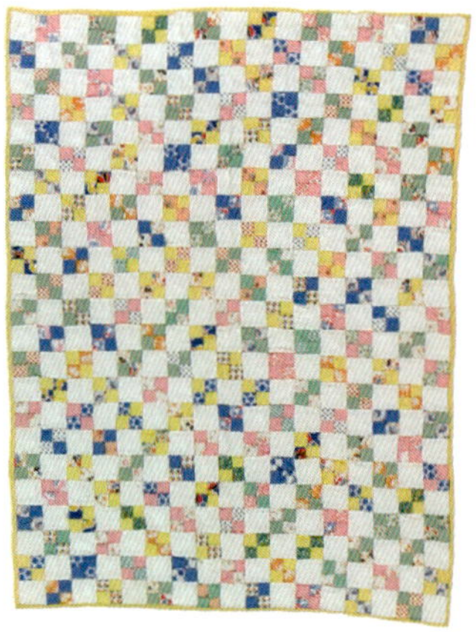

Four Patch

Maker unidentified
Made in United States
Circa 1955
22 x 16 in.

IQM 1997.007.0358

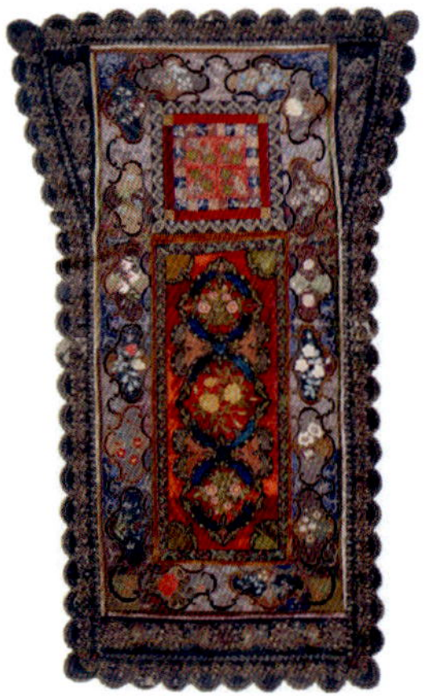

Crazy

Maker unidentified
Probably made in Florida
1880 - 1900
101 x 61 in.

IQM 1997.007.0360

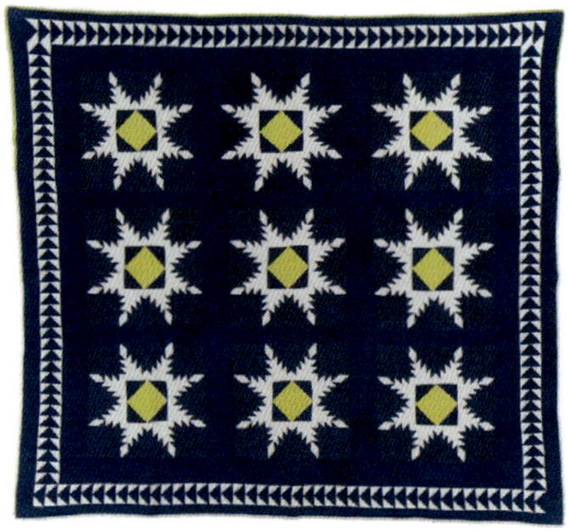

Feathered Star

Maker unidentified
Possibly made in Ohio
1860 - 1880
73.75 x 75 in.

IQM 1997.007.0361

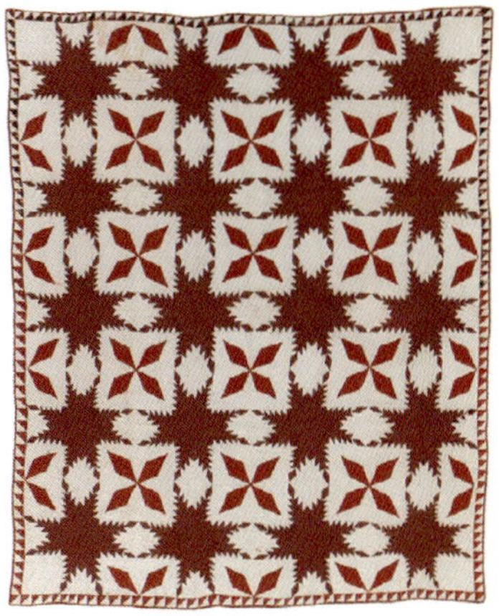

Feathered Star

Maker unidentified
Possibly made in Pennsylvania
1860 - 1880
88 x 72.5 in.

IQM 1997.007.0362

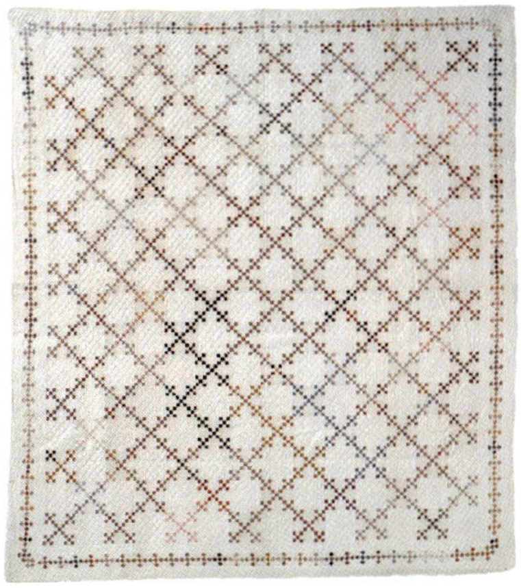

Double Nine Patch

Maker unidentified
Probably made in Pittsburgh, Pennsylvania
1880 - 1900
83.5 x 73.5 in.

IQM 1997.007.0363

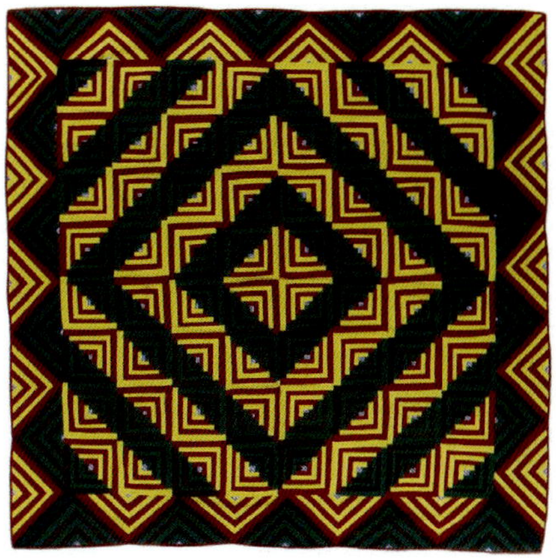

Log Cabin

Maker unidentified
Possibly made in Pennsylvania
1870 - 1890
73 x 76 in.

IQM 1997.007.0364

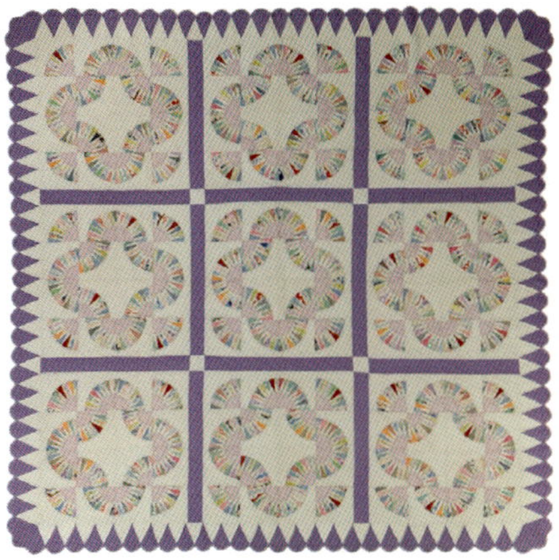

Chinese Fan

Maker unidentified
Possibly made in Cass County, Illinois
1930 - 1945
81 x 81 in.

IQM 1997.007.0366

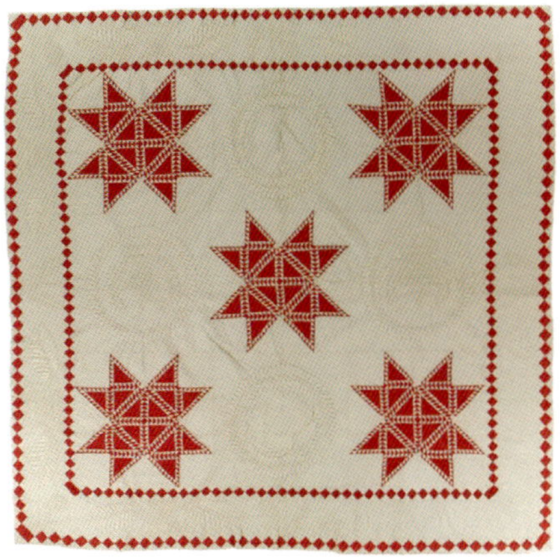

Feathered Star

Maker unidentified
Possibly made in Ohio
1930 - 1940
94.5 x 93.5 in.

IQM 1997.007.0367

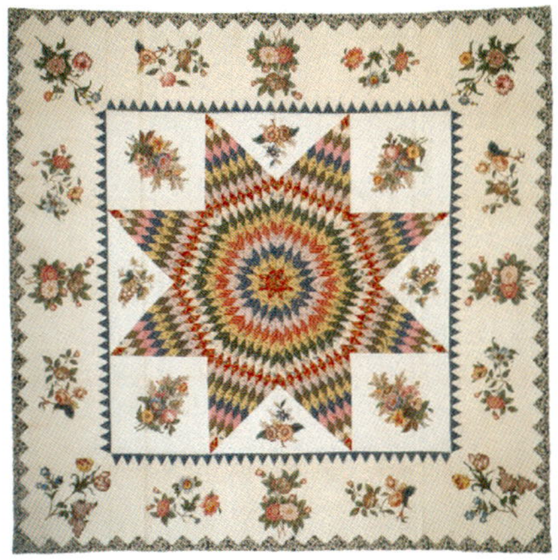

Star of Bethlehem

Maker unidentified
Probably made in southeastern United States
1830 - 1850
102 x 103 in.

IQM 1997.007.0369

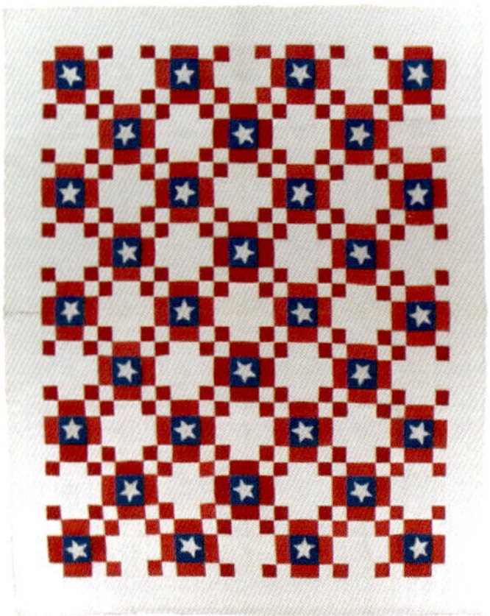

Nine Patch variation

Maker unidentified
Possibly made in Holmes County, Ohio
1935 - 1945
94 x 73 in.
IQM 1997.007.0370

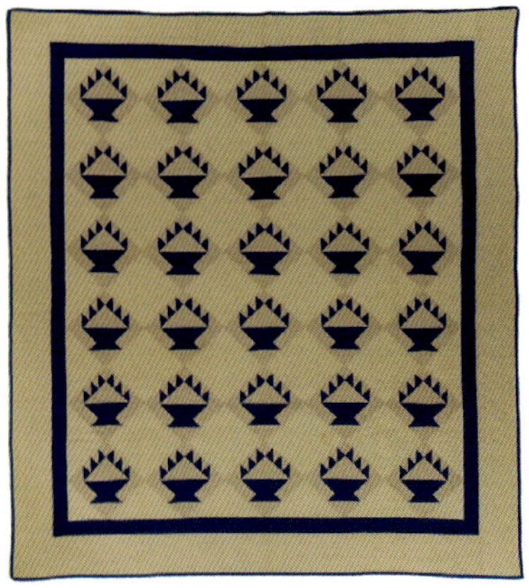

Basket

Possibly made by Mary Yoder
Probably made in Holmes County, Ohio
1910 - 1930
88.5 x 77.5 in.
IQM 1997.007.0371

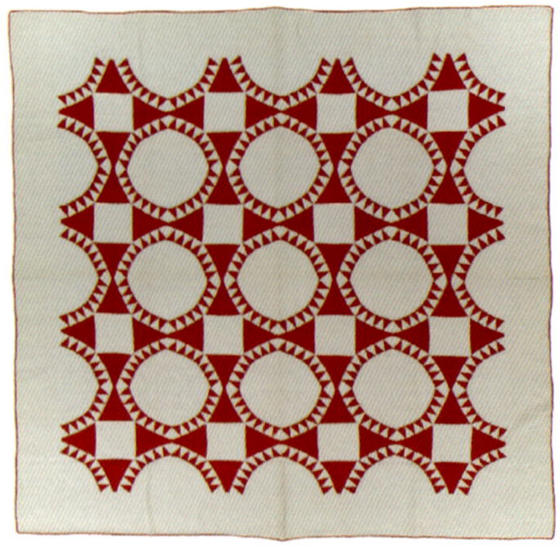

Sunburst

Maker unidentified
Possibly made in Union County, Pennsylvania
1875 - 1895
84.5 x 83.5 in.
IQM 1997.007.0372

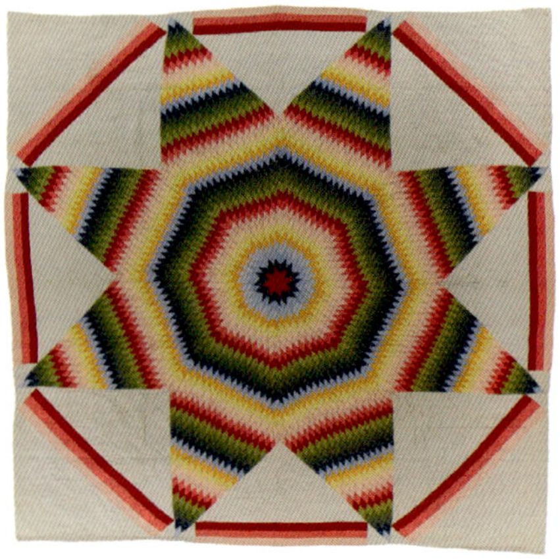

Star of Bethlehem

Maker unidentified
Possibly made in Pennsylvania
1900 - 1920
85 x 85.5 in.
IQM 1997.007.0374

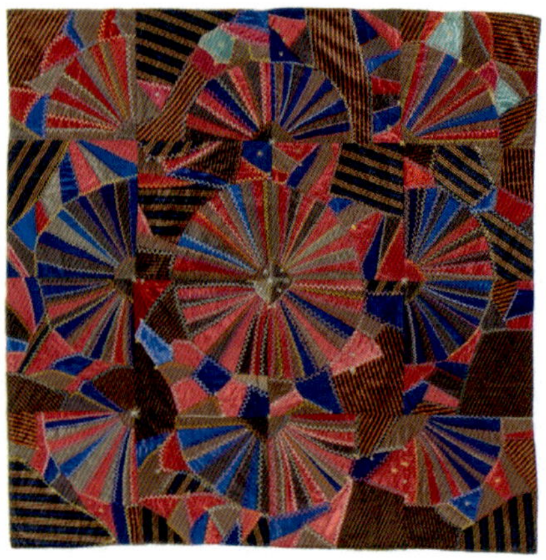

Crazy

Maker unidentified
Possibly made in Massachusetts
1890 - 1910
58.25 x 57 in.
IQM 1997.007.0375

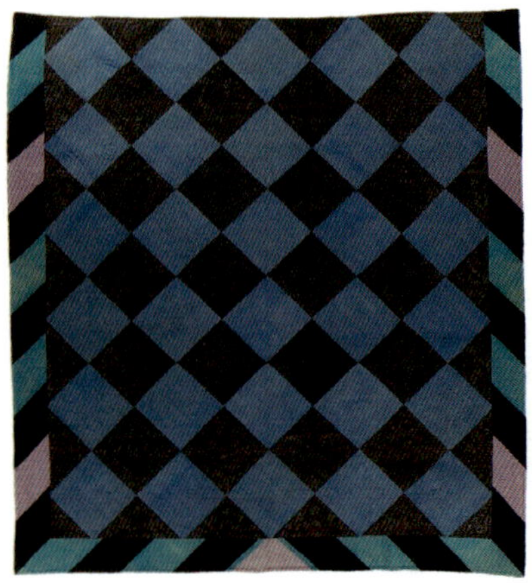

Checkerboard

Maker unidentified
Made in northeastern United States
1800 - 1820
92 x 83 in.
IQM 1997.007.0376

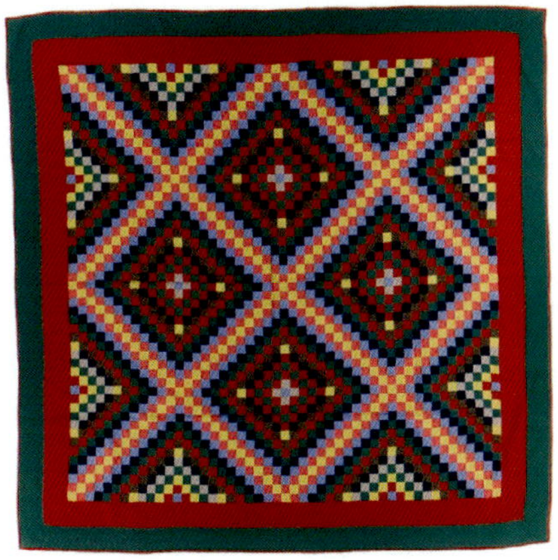

Philadelphia Pavement

Maker unidentified
Possibly made in Lancaster County, Pennsylvania
1875 - 1895
83 x 83 in.
IQM 1997.007.0377

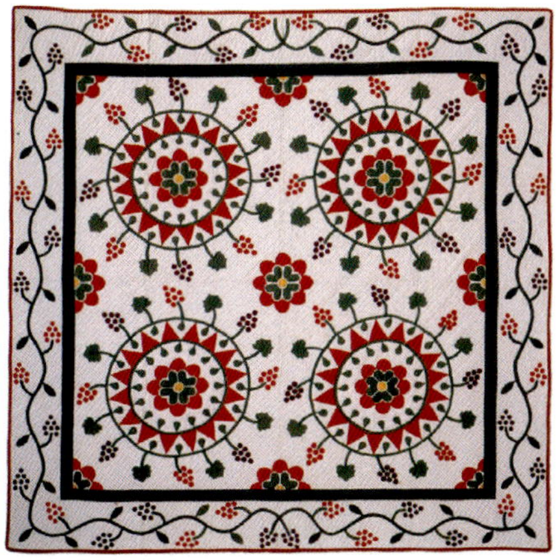

Flowers and Grapes

Maker unidentified
Possibly made in Pennsylvania
1860 - 1880
82.5 x 82.25 in.
IQM 1997.007.0378

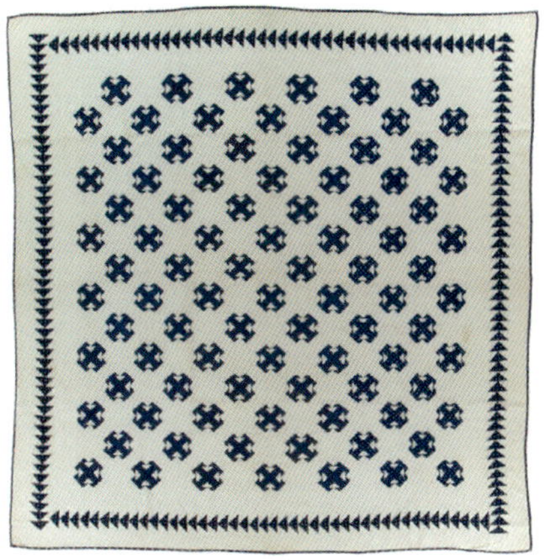

Crossed Ts

Maker unidentified
Possibly made in western Pennsylvania
1880 - 1900
84 x 82.5 in.
IQM 1997.007.0379

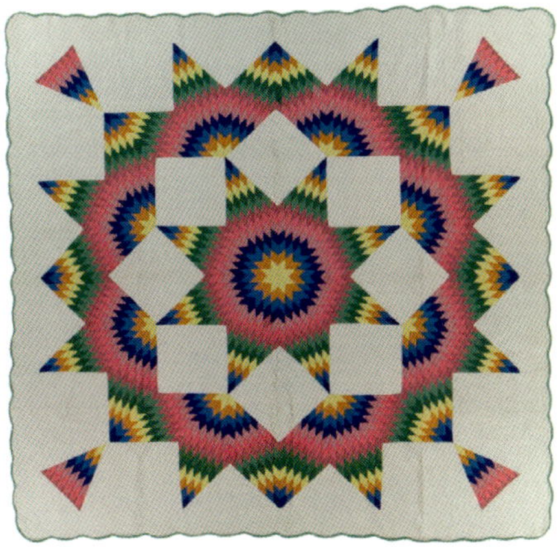

Broken Star

Maker unidentified
Possibly made in central Ohio
1920 - 1940
87.5 x 85 in.
IQM 1997.007.0380

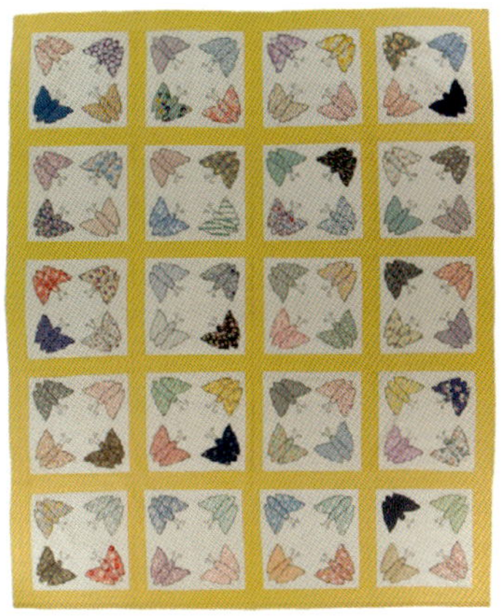

Butterfly

Maker unidentified
Possibly made in Pennsylvania
1920 - 1940
105 x 83 in.
IQM 1997.007.0383

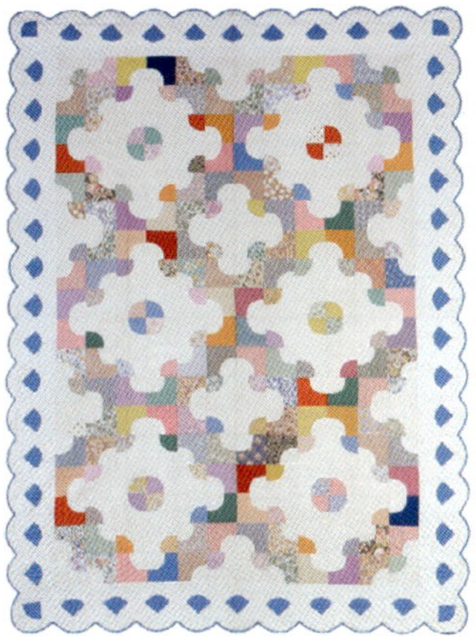

Around the World

Maker unidentified
Possibly made in Ohio
1930 - 1940
94 x 68 in.
IQM 1997.007.0384

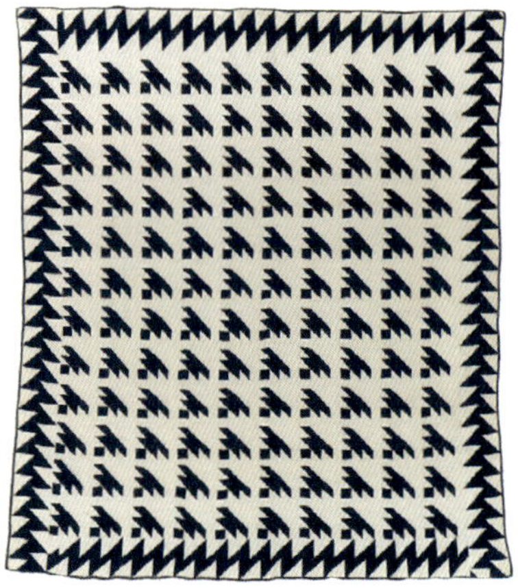

Ships of Maine

Maker unidentified
Possibly made in Pennsylvania
1850 - 1870
92 x 82 in.

IQM 1997.007.0386

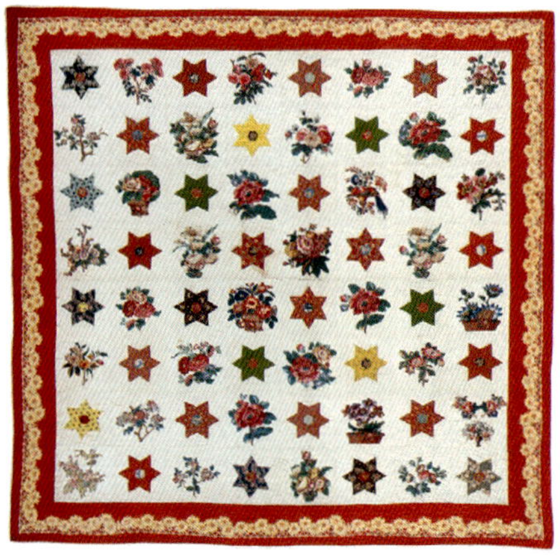

Cut-out Chintz

Maker unidentified
Possibly made in Pennsylvania
1935 - 1955
84.5 x 82 in.

IQM 1997.007.0387

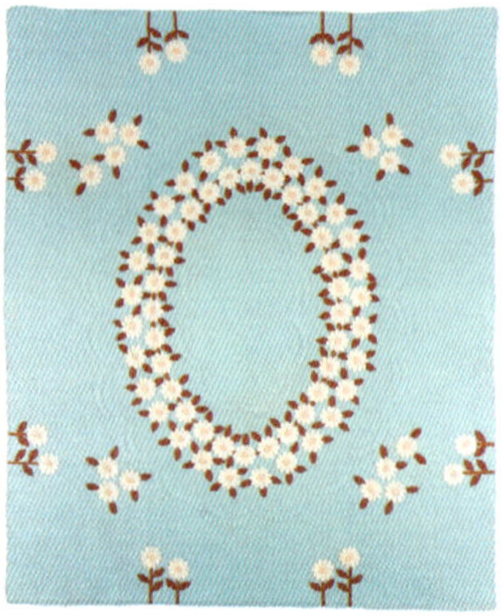

Daisy Chain

Ruth Augustyn
Possibly made in Wisconsin
Dated 1938
91 x 73.5 in.

IQM 1997.007.0389

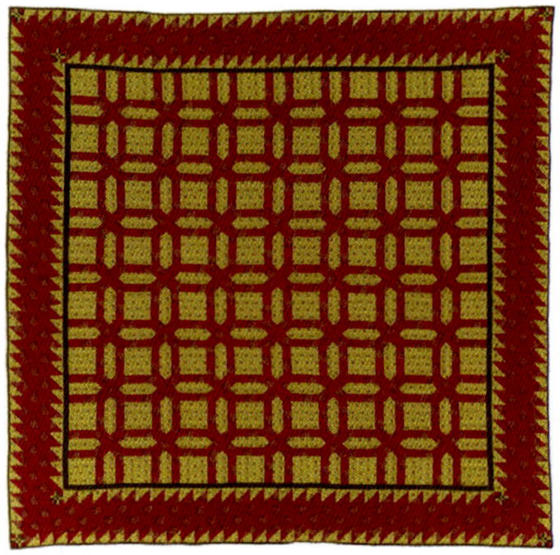

Garden Maze

Maker unidentified
Possibly made in Lancaster County, Pennsylvania
1830 - 1850
97 x 97 in.

IQM 1997.007.0390

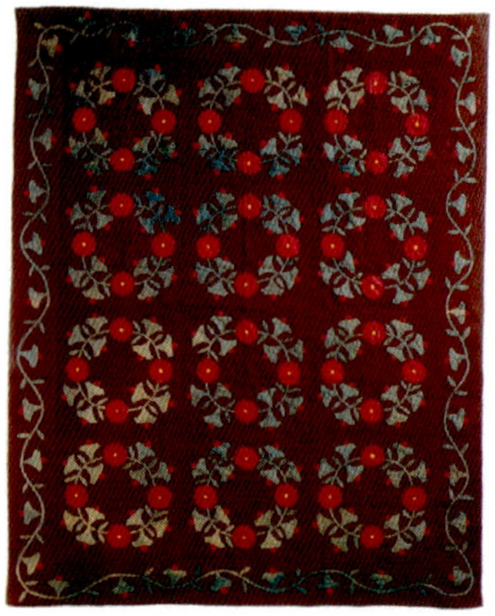

President's Wreath

Maker unidentified
Probably made in Pennsylvania
1890 - 1910
103.5 x 83 in.

IQM 1997.007.0391

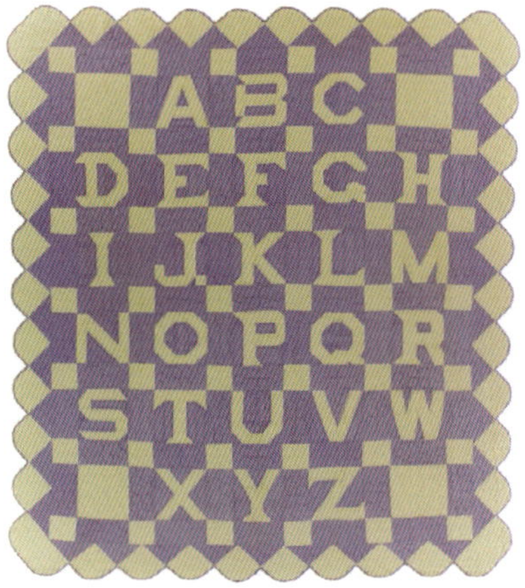

Alphabet

Maker unidentified
Possibly made in Ohio
1930 - 1940
89 x 78.5 in.

IQM 1997.007.0392

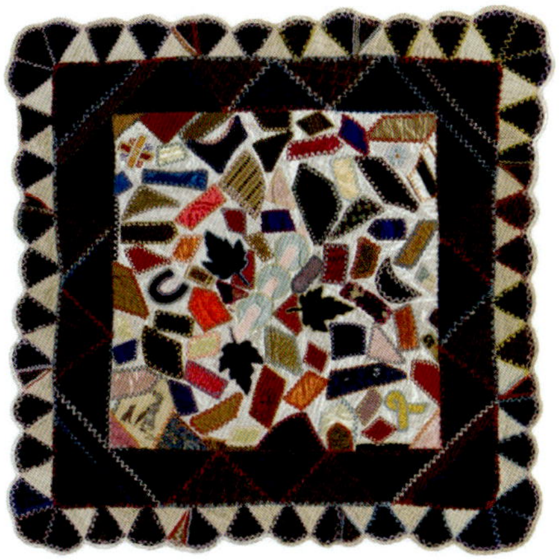

Crazy

Maker unidentified
Possibly made in Indianapolis, Indiana
1880 - 1900
37.5 x 36.5 in.

IQM 1997.007.0393

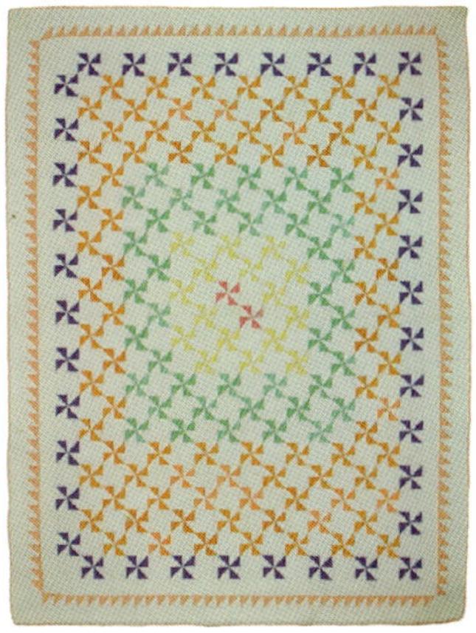

Pinwheel

Maker unidentified
Possibly made in Findlay, Ohio
1920 - 1940
59 x 43 in.

IQM 1997.007.0394

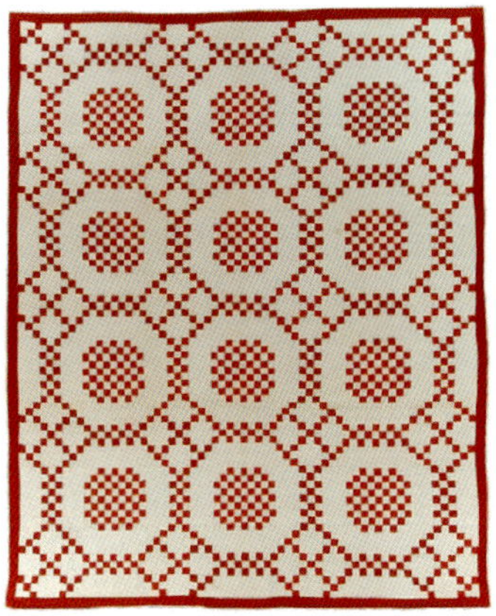

Burgoyne Surrounded

Maker unidentified
Made in United States
1900 - 1920
86 x 69 in.

IQM 1997.007.0395

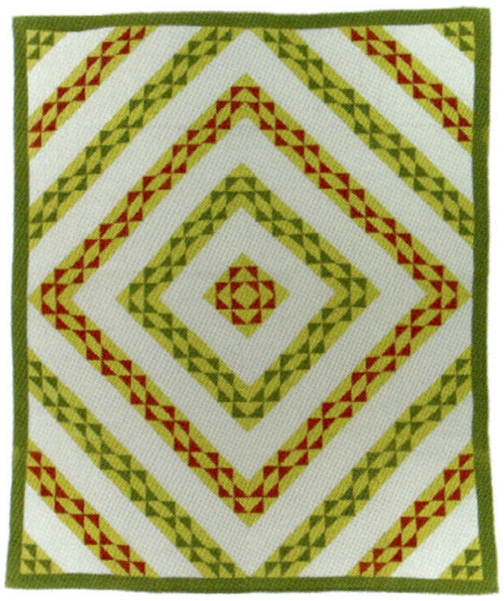

Ocean Waves variation

Maker unidentified
Possibly made in Pennsylvania
Dated 1872 - 1897
85.5 x 70 in.

IQM 1997.007.0396

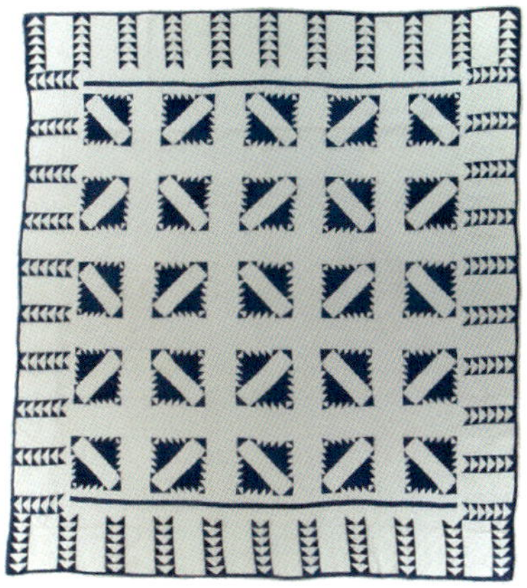

Delectable Squares

Maker unidentified
Possibly made in Ohio
1860 - 1880
88 x 77 in.

IQM 1997.007.0397

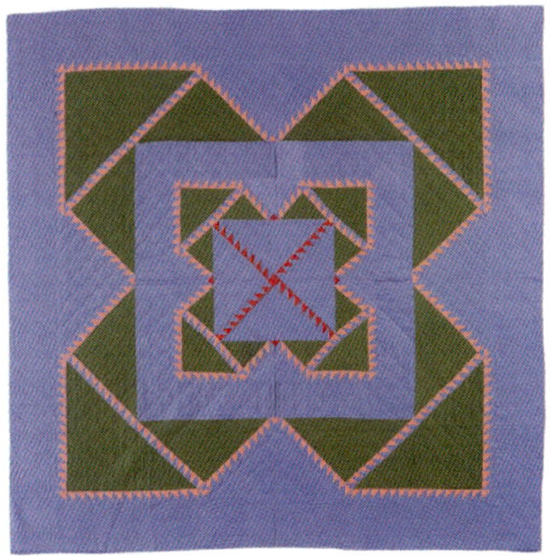

Delectable Mountains variation

Maker unidentified
Probably made in Lancaster County, Pennsylvania
1865 - 1885
76 x 75 in.

IQM 1997.007.0398

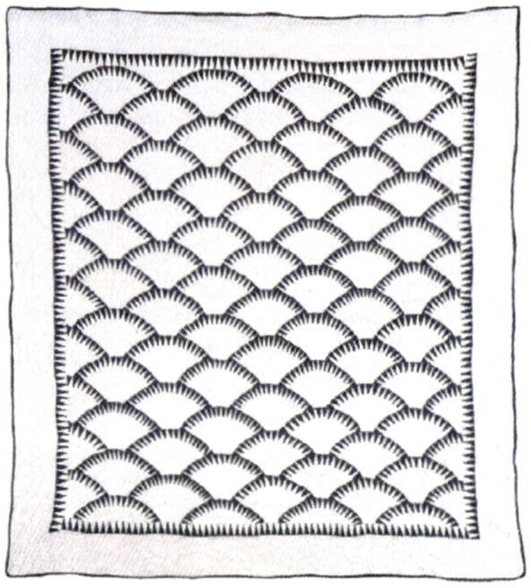

Sunrise

Maker unidentified
Possibly made in Ohio
1880 - 1900
83.5 x 74.5 in.

IQM 1997.007.0399

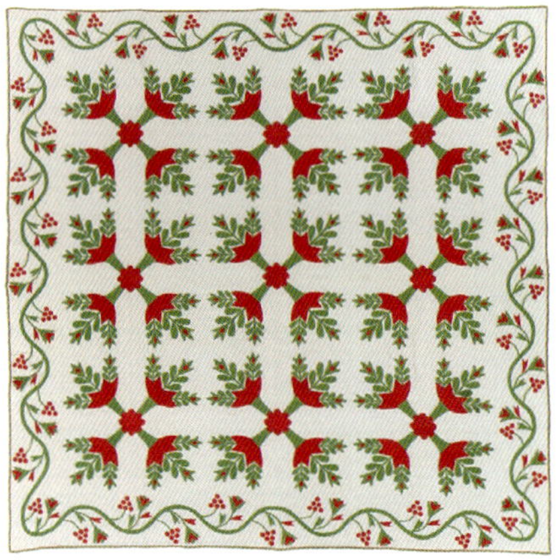

Peony variation

Maker unidentified
Possibly made in Blairsville, Pennsylvania
1860 - 1880
90.5 x 91 in.

IQM 1997.007.0403

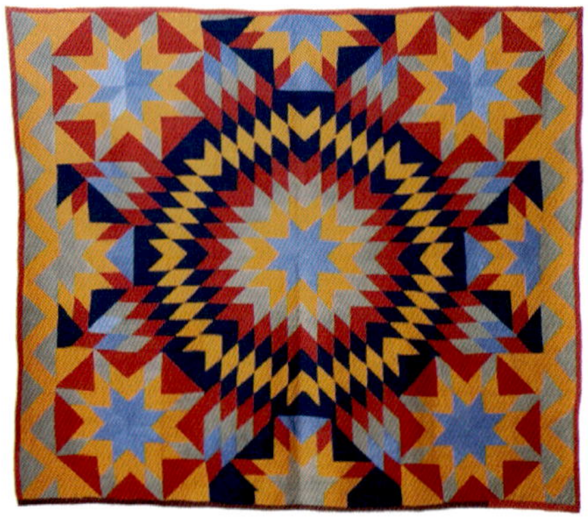

Blazing Star

Maker unidentified
Probably made in Nashville, Illinois
1880 - 1900
91 x 82 in.

IQM 1997.007.0405

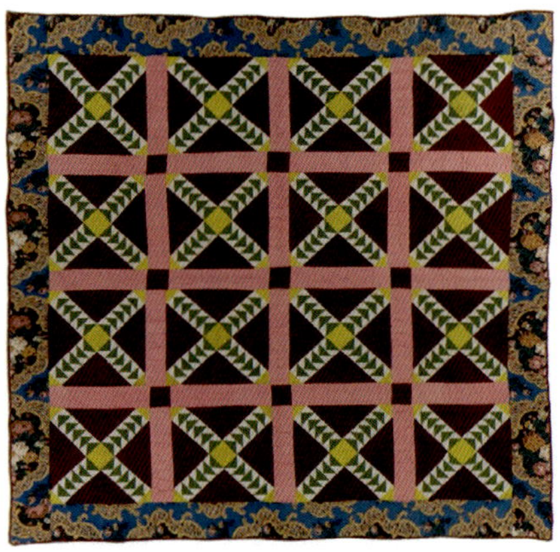

Wild Goose Chase

Maker unidentified
Possibly made in New York
1850 - 1870
78 x 80 in.

IQM 1997.007.0406

Magpie Rose

Euphemia Medora Anderson Mounts
Made in Carlinville, Illinois
Circa 1933
85 x 75 in.

IQM 1997.007.0407

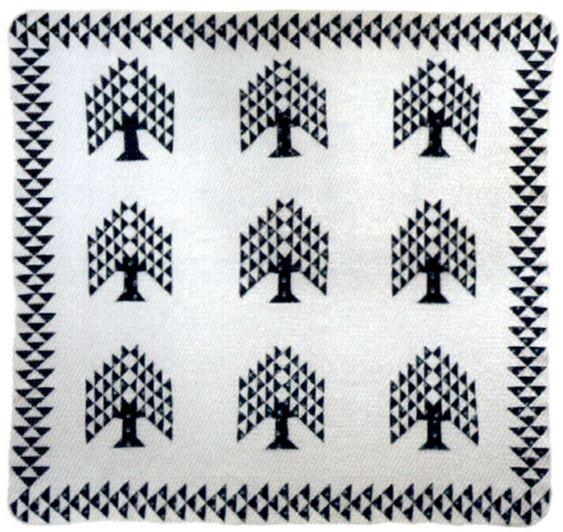

Pine Tree

Maker unidentified
Probably made in Indiana, Pennsylvania
1890 - 1910
67.5 x 70 in.

IQM 1997.007.0408

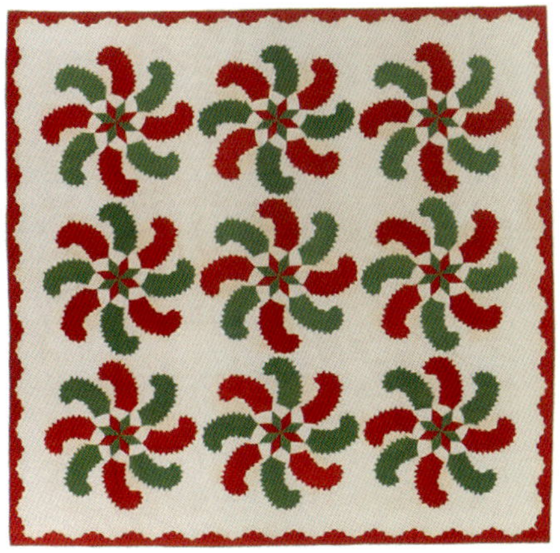

Princess Feather

Maker unidentified
Made in United States
1850 - 1870
103.5 x 103 in.

IQM 1997.007.0410

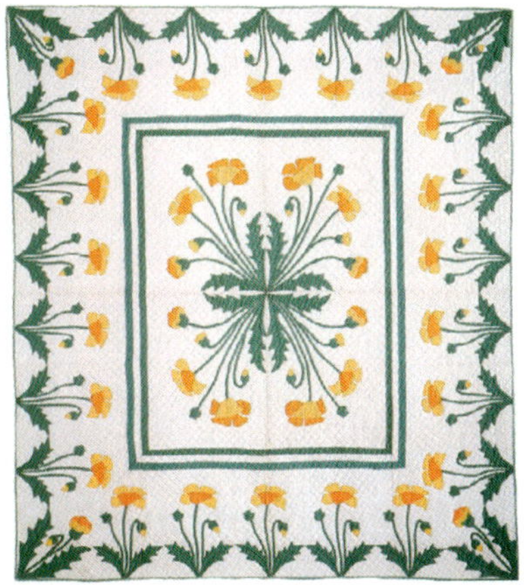

Poppy

Maker unidentified
Made in United States
1920 - 1940
88 x 76 in.

IQM 1997.007.0411.1

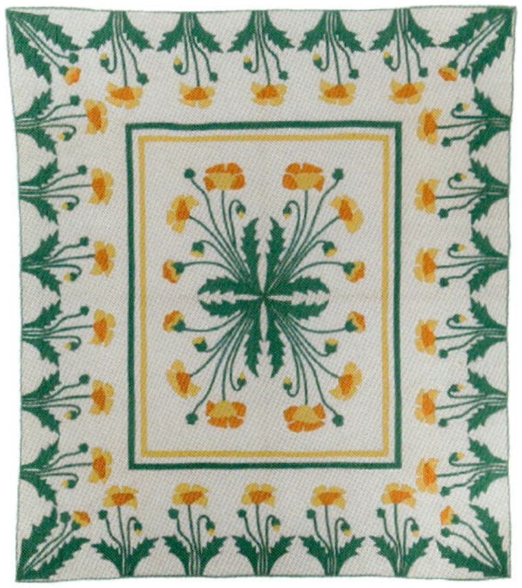

Poppy

Maker unidentified
Made in United States
1920 - 1940
89 x 77 in.

IQM 1997.007.0411.2

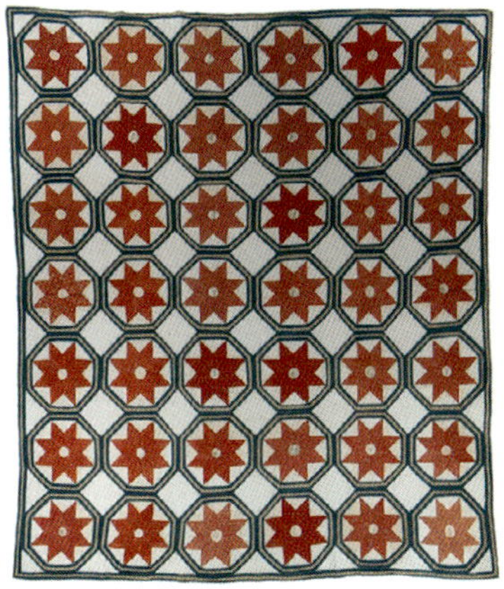

Eight Pointed Star

Friends and Relatives of the William Wright Family
Made in Burlington County, New Jersey
Dated 1843 - 1844
106 x 91 in.

IQM 1997.007.0412

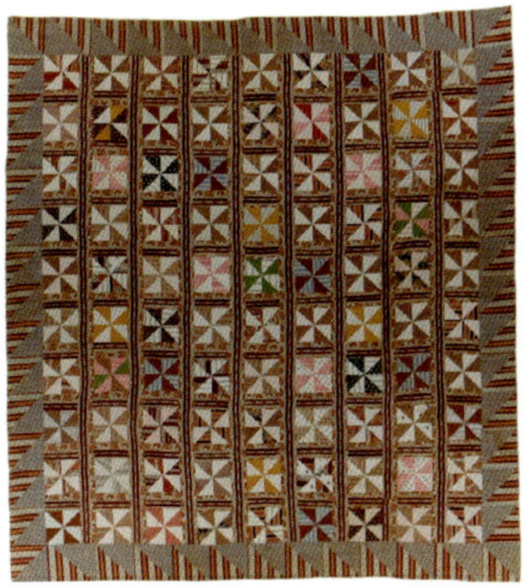

Pinwheel

Maker unidentified
Possibly made in Maryland
1860 - 1880
97 x 85 in.

IQM 1997.007.0413

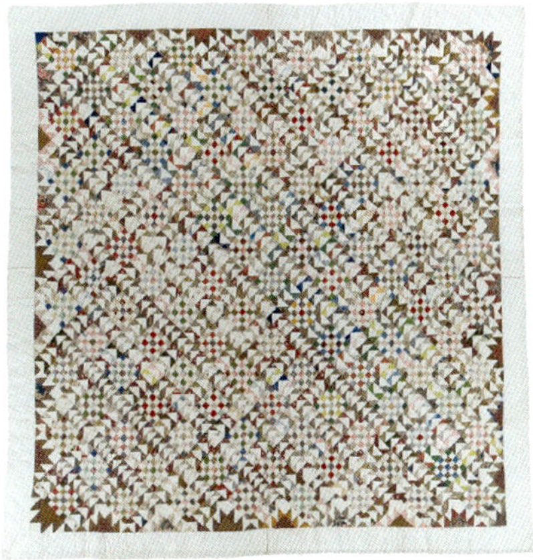

Wild Goose Chase

Maker unidentified
Possibly made in Lebanon, Pennsylvania
1850 - 1870
99.5 x 94.5 in.

IQM 1997.007.0414

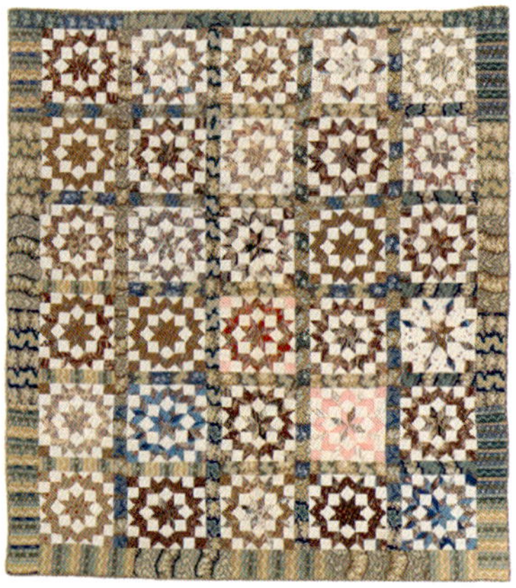

Carpenter's Wheel

Maker unidentified
Possibly made in New England
1830 - 1850
77 x 69 in.

IQM 1997.007.0415

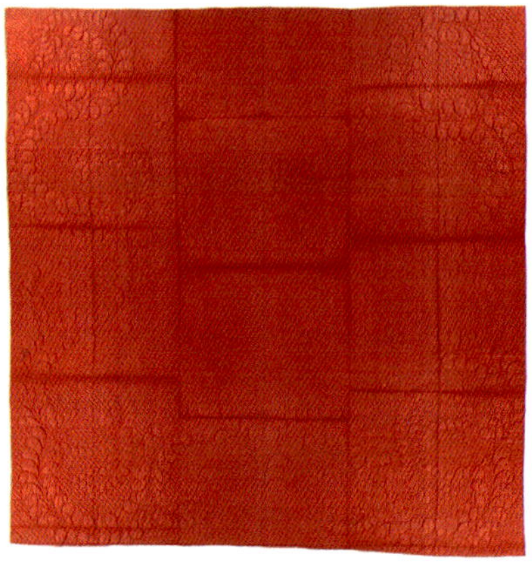

Whole Cloth

Maker unidentified
Possibly made in Vermont
1790 - 1830
99.5 x 95 in.

IQM 1997.007.0416

Whole Cloth

Possibly made by Eliza G. Clark
Possibly made in Wayne County, Iowa
Dated 1868
94.5 x 85 in.

IQM 1997.007.0417

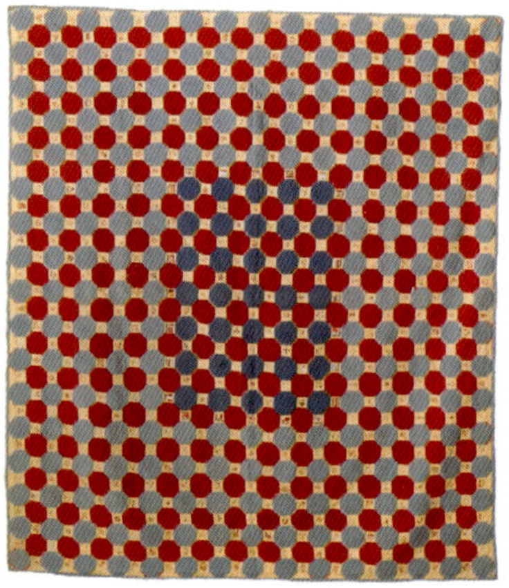

Snowball variation

Maker unidentified
Possibly made in Indiana
1880 - 1900
66 x 57 in.

IQM 1997.007.0418

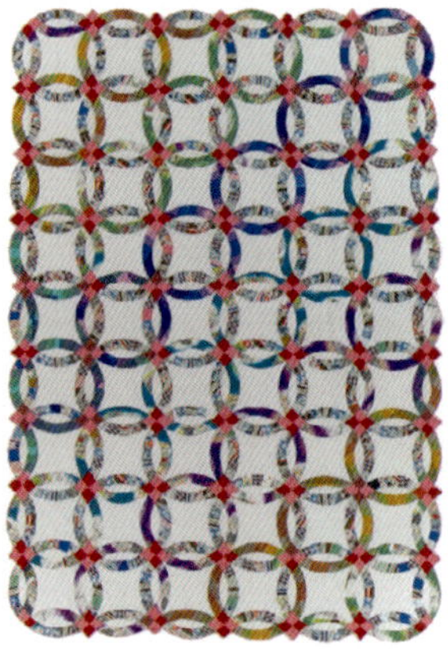

Double Wedding Ring

Maker unidentified
Possibly made in Pennsylvania
1940 - 1960
89.5 x 60.5 in.

IQM 1997.007.0420

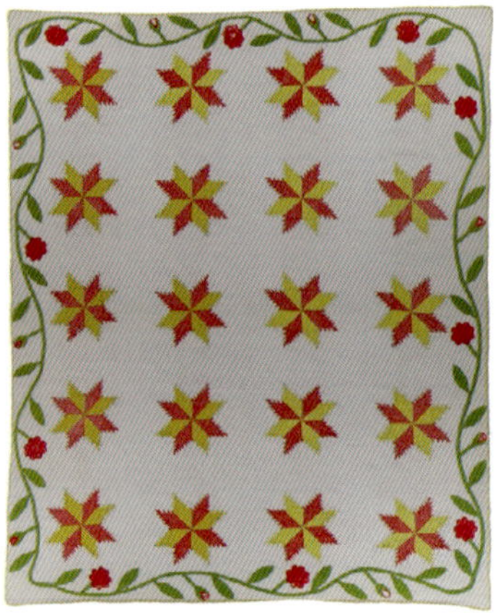

Feathered Star

Elizabeth, Maria, and Emily Dobson
Made in Huntsville, Madison County, Indiana
1840 - 1865
100 x 80.5 in.

IQM 1997.007.0421

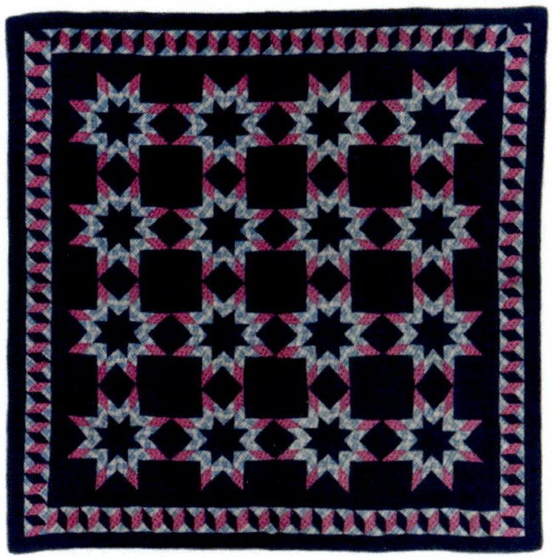

Touching Stars

Probably made by Anna Swickard
Possibly made in Pennsylvania
1850 - 1870
78.5 x 78 in.
IQM 1997.007.0422

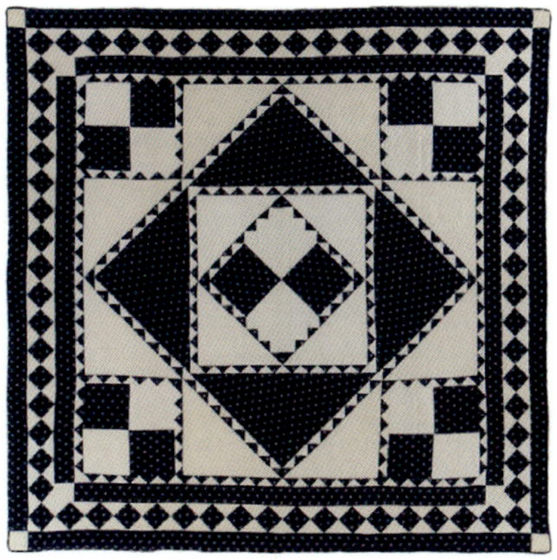

Center Diamond

Maker unidentified
Possibly made in Pennsylvania
1890 - 1910
83 x 82 in.
IQM 1997.007.0423

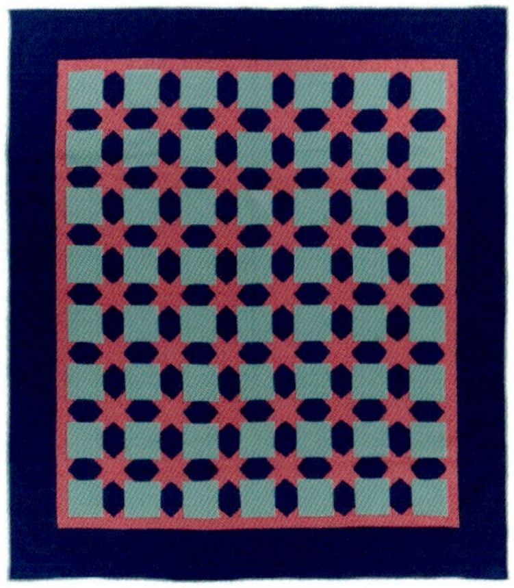

Star

Possibly made by Mary Troyer
Probably made in Charm, Holmes County, Ohio
1930 - 1950
84.5 x 75 in.
IQM 1997.007.0424

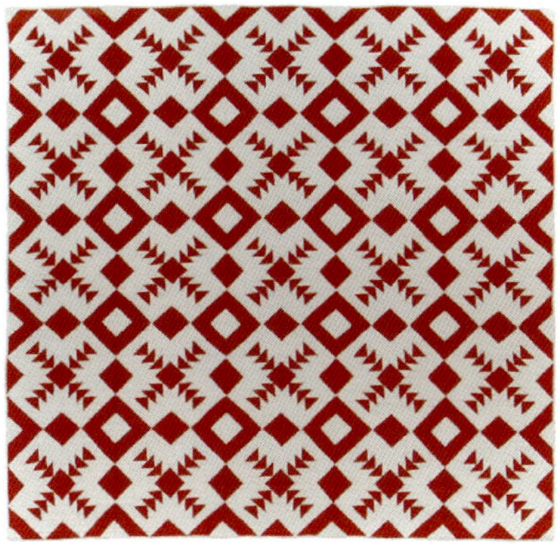

Wild Goose Chase

Maker unidentified
Possibly made in western Pennsylvania
1880 - 1900
78.5 x 77.5 in.
IQM 1997.007.0425

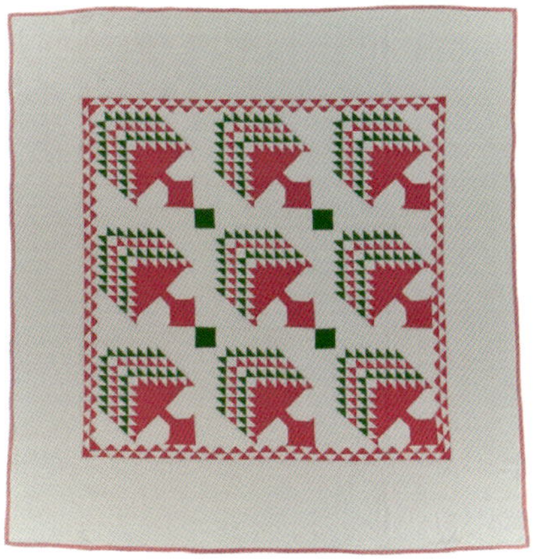

Pine Tree

Maker unidentified
Possibly made in western Pennsylvania
1940 - 1950
81 x 77 in.
IQM 1997.007.0426

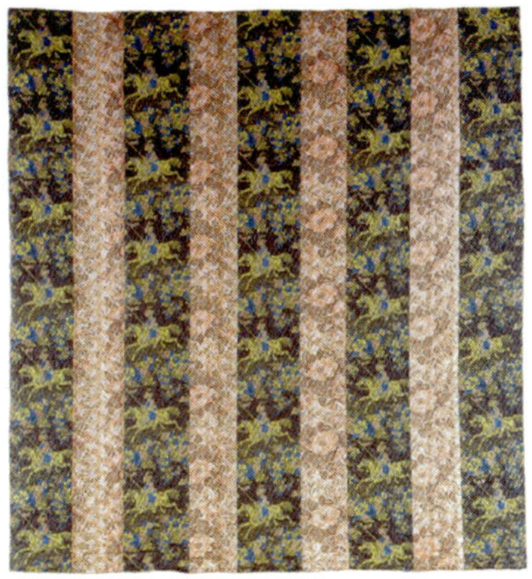

Bars

Maker unidentified
Possibly made in Pennsylvania
1830 - 1850
97 x 86 in.
IQM 1997.007.0427

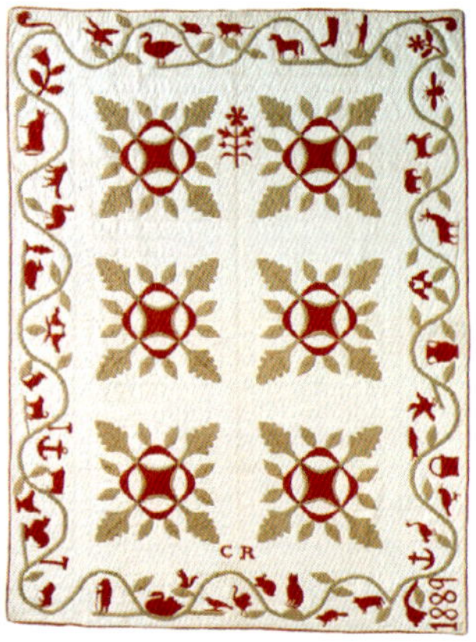

Oak Reel

Caroline Ruth
Made in Marion County, Ohio
Dated 1889
91 x 68 in.

IQM 1997.007.0429

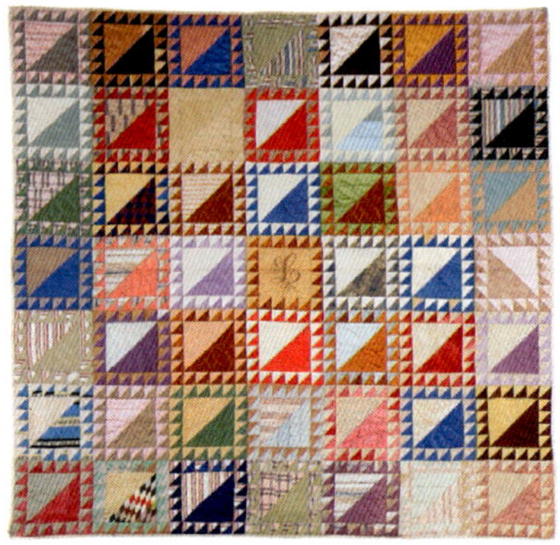

Squares, Sawtooth

Maker unidentified
Made in United States
1880 - 1900
73 x 73 in.

IQM 1997.007.0430

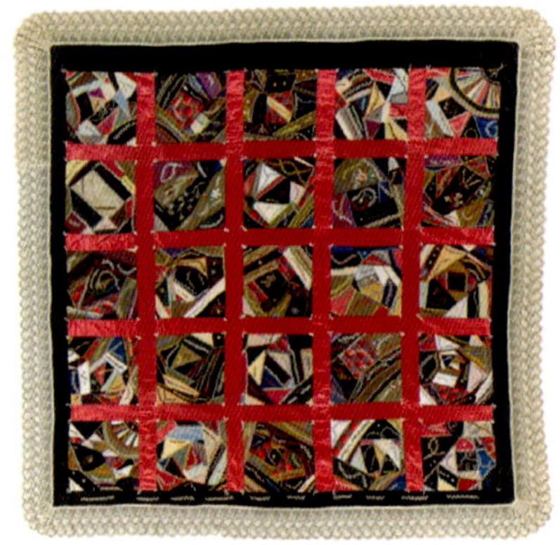

Crazy

Maker unidentified
Made in United States
Dated 1888
74 x 74 in.

IQM 1997.007.0431

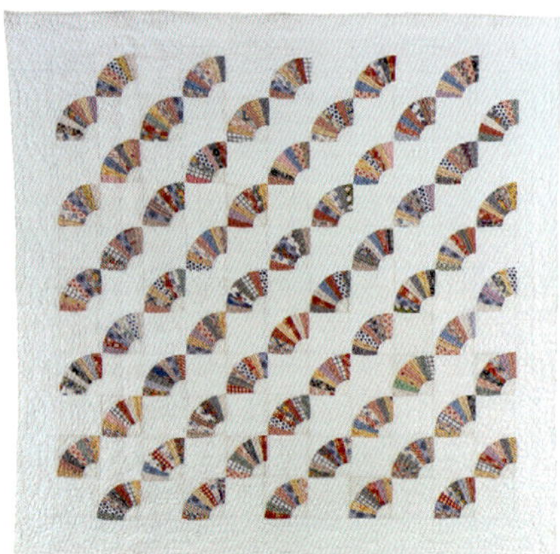

Grandmother's Fan

Maker unidentified
Probably made in midwestern United States
1930 - 1940
80 x 81.5 in.

IQM 1997.007.0432

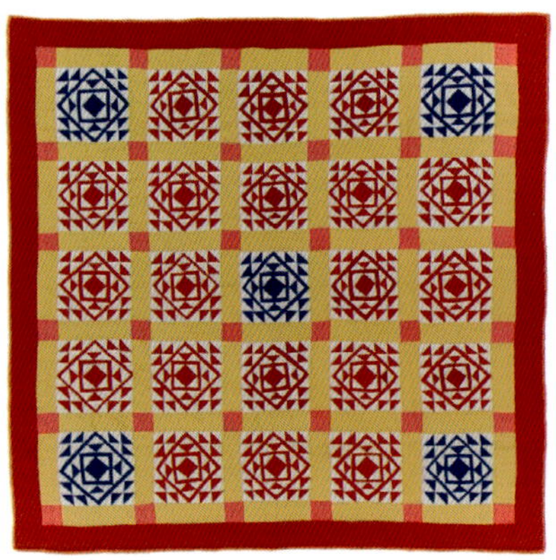

County Fair

Maker unidentified
Possibly made in York County, Pennsylvania
1930 - 1950
71.5 x 71.5 in.

IQM 1997.007.0435

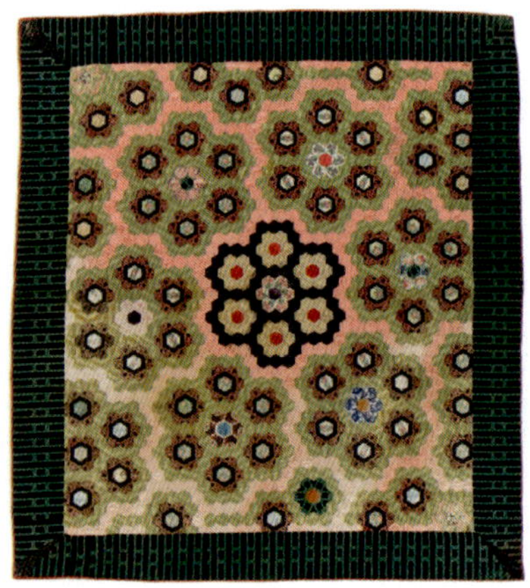

Hexagon

Maker unidentified
Possibly made in Ohio
1860 - 1880
81 x 71 in.

IQM 1997.007.0437

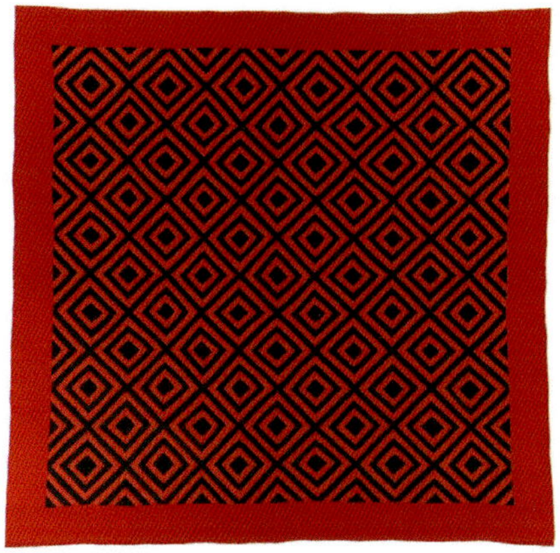

Diamonds

Maker unidentified
Made in United States
1875 - 1895
72 x 72 in.

IQM 1997.007.0438

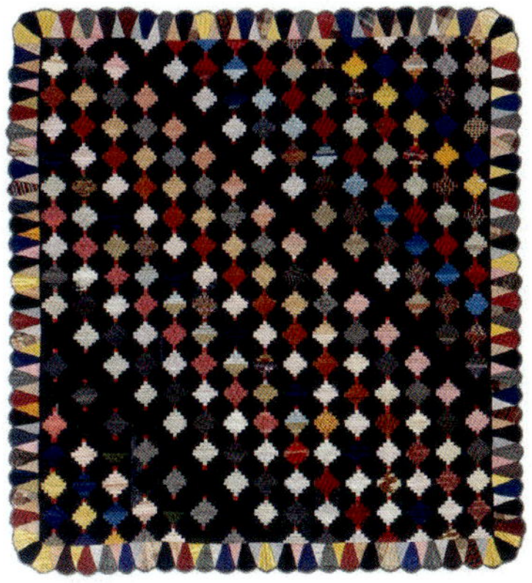

Log Cabin

Maker unidentified
Probably made in southeastern Ohio
1870 - 1890
65 x 59 in.

IQM 1997.007.0439

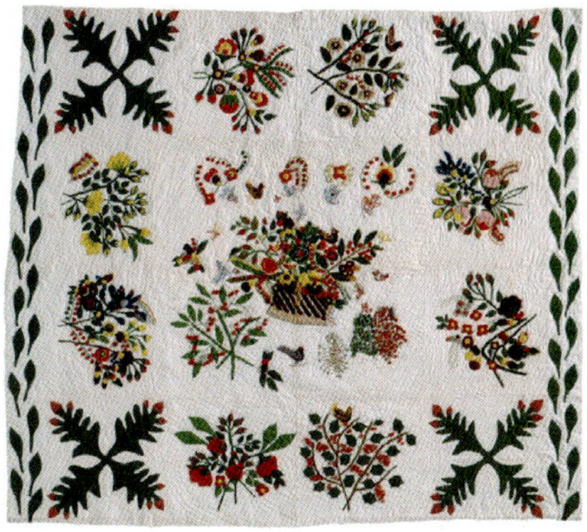

Album

Maker unidentified
Probably made in Harrisburg, Pennsylvania
1870 - 1890
68.5 x 76 in.

IQM 1997.007.0440

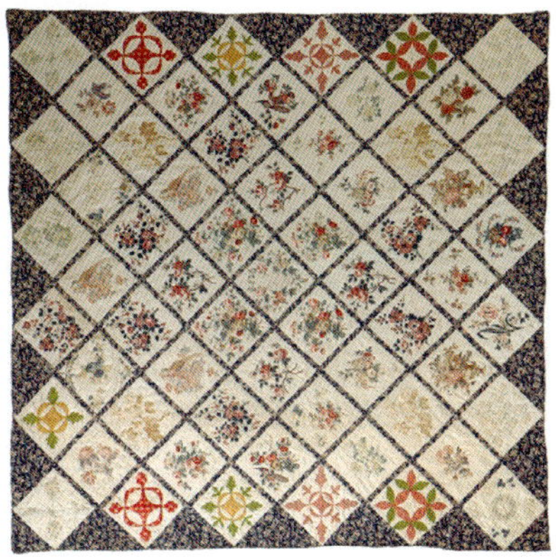

Album

Freehold Baptist Church members
Made in Upper Freehold Township, Monmouth County, New Jersey
Dated 1852
103.5 x 107 in.

IQM 1997.007.0441

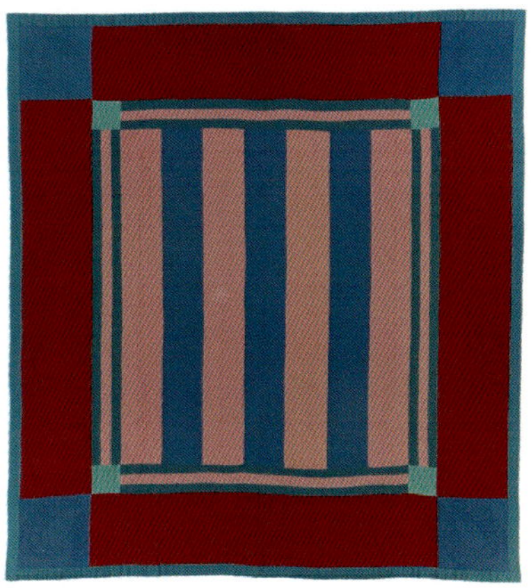

Bars

Maker unidentified
Possibly made in Lancaster County, Pennsylvania
1920 - 1940
81 x 72 in.

IQM 1997.007.0442

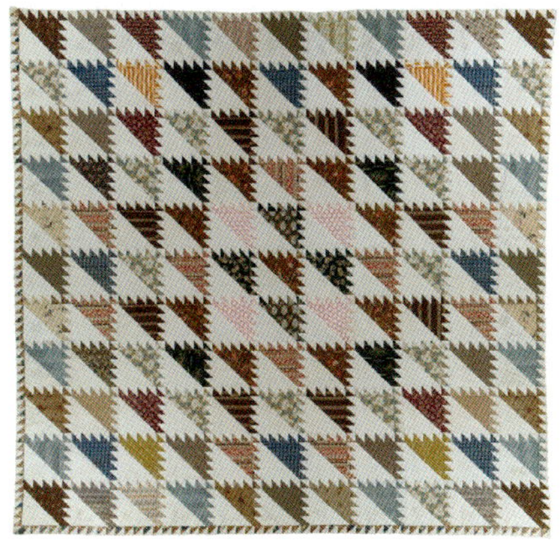

Sawtooth

Agnes S. Burtis
Probably made in Burlington County, New Jersey
Dated 1846
96 x 94.5 in.

IQM 1997.007.0444

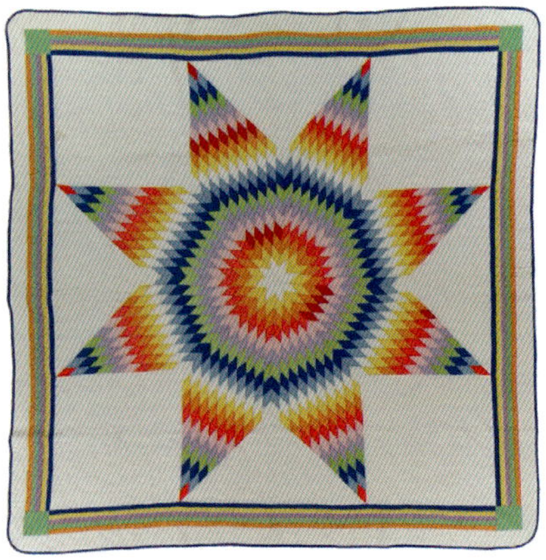

Star of Bethlehem

Maker unidentified
Possibly made in Akron, Ohio
1930 - 1950
83 x 83 in.

IQM 1997.007.0445

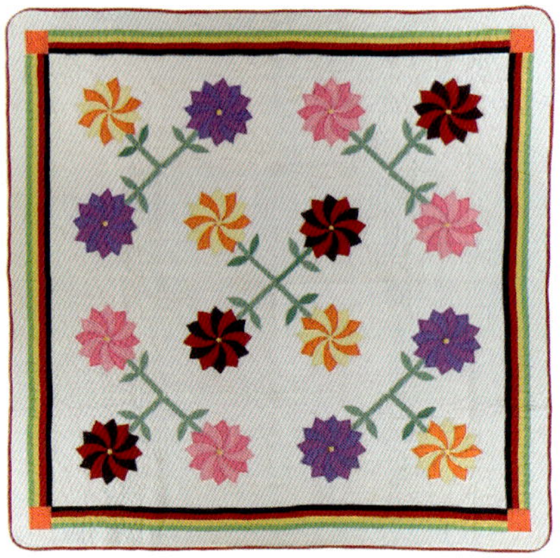

Dahlia

Maker unidentified
Possibly made in Akron, Ohio
1940 - 1960
79.5 x 79 in.

IQM 1997.007.0446

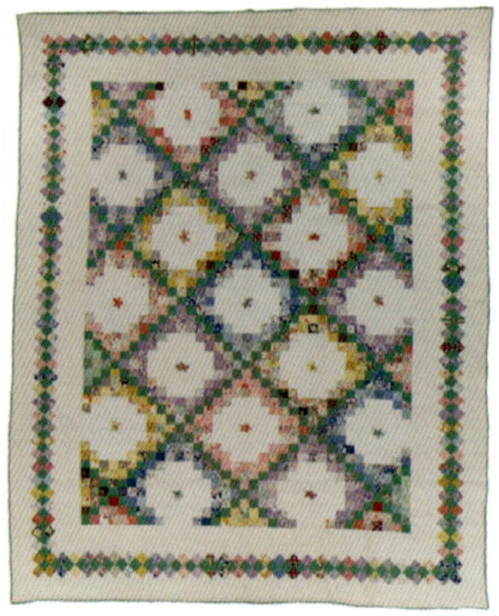

Double Irish Chain

Maker unidentified
Possibly made in western Pennsylvania
Dated 1939
104.5 x 83 in.

IQM 1997.007.0447

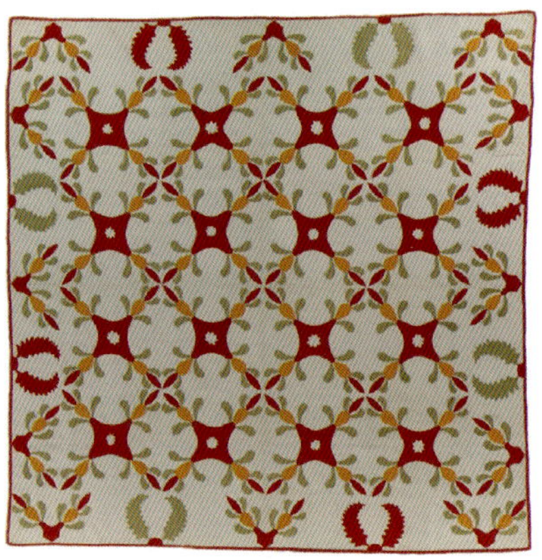

Original

Possibly made by Elizabeth Heldman Walther
Possibly made in Bethel Township, Allegheny County, Pennsylvania
1880 - 1900
81.5 x 79 in.

IQM 1997.007.0448

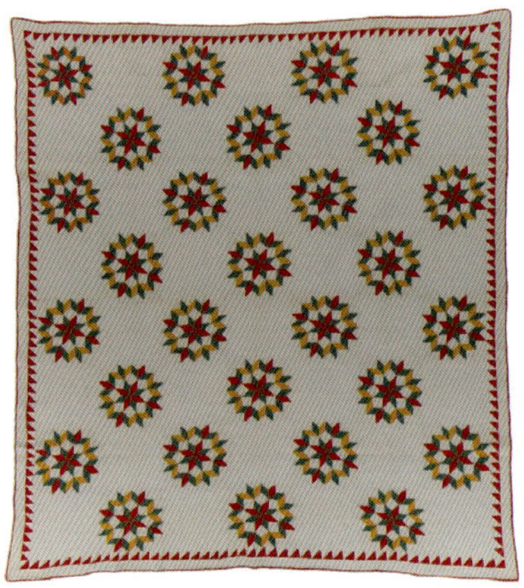

Carpenter's Wheel

Maker unidentified
Possibly made in York County, Pennsylvania
1850 - 1870
85.5 x 74.5 in.

IQM 1997.007.0449

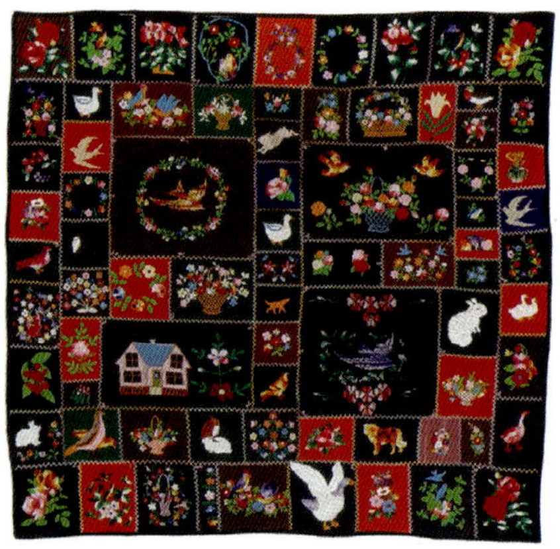

Album

Maker unidentified
Made in United States
1910 - 1930
64.5 x 64.5 in.

IQM 1997.007.0450

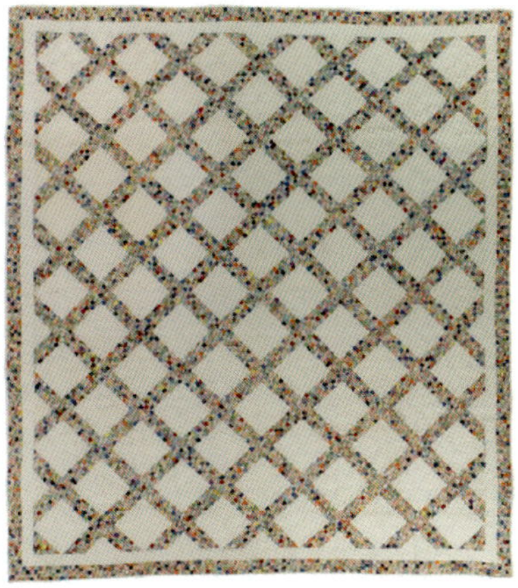

Squares

Maker unidentified
Made in United States
1925 - 1945
84 x 73.5 in.

IQM 1997.007.0451

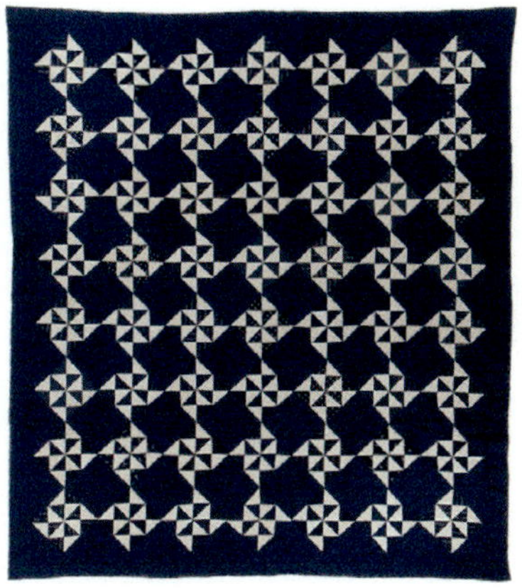

Pinwheel

Maker unidentified
Made in United States
1890 - 1910
89.5 x 79 in.

IQM 1997.007.0452

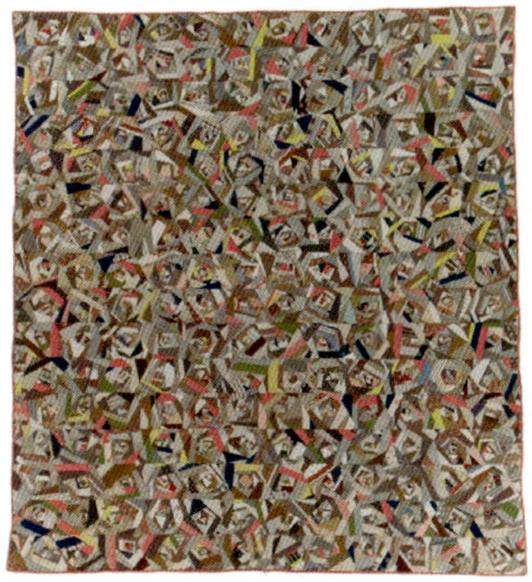

Crazy

Maker unidentified
Made in United States
1880 - 1900
83.5 x 74 in.

IQM 1997.007.0453

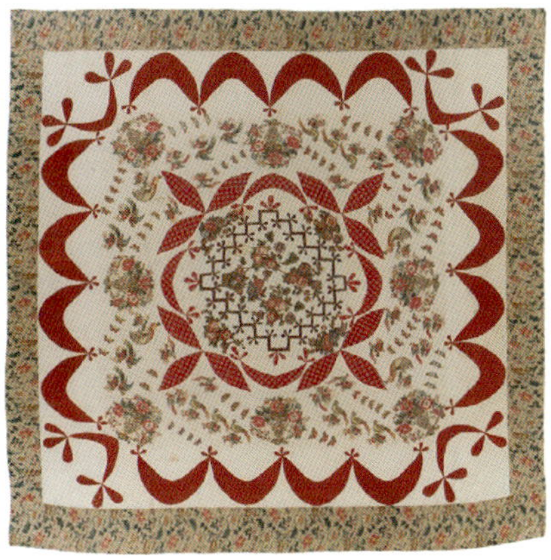

Medallion

Maker unidentified
Probably made in United States
1830 - 1850
110.5 x 112.5 in.

IQM 1997.007.0454

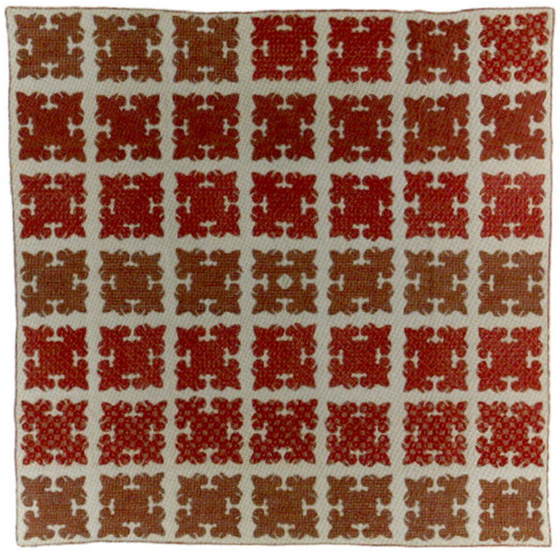

Papercut Appliqué

Emily Anna Carter
Possibly made in Philadelphia, Pennsylvania
1840 - 1860
83.5 x 85 in.

IQM 1997.007.0455

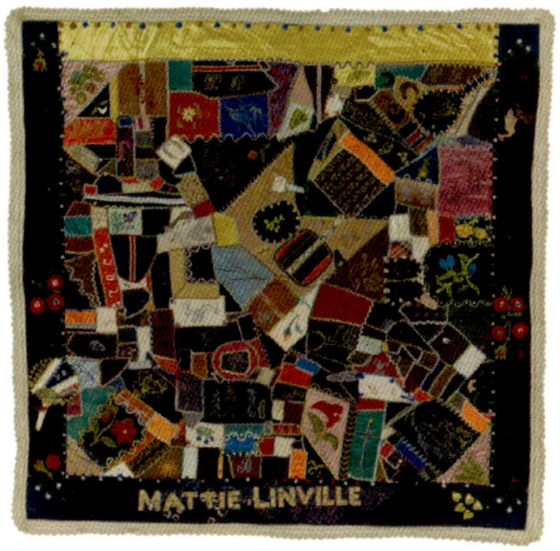

Crazy

Probably made by Mattie Linville
Possibly made in Ohio
1880 - 1890
54 x 55 in.

IQM 1997.007.0456

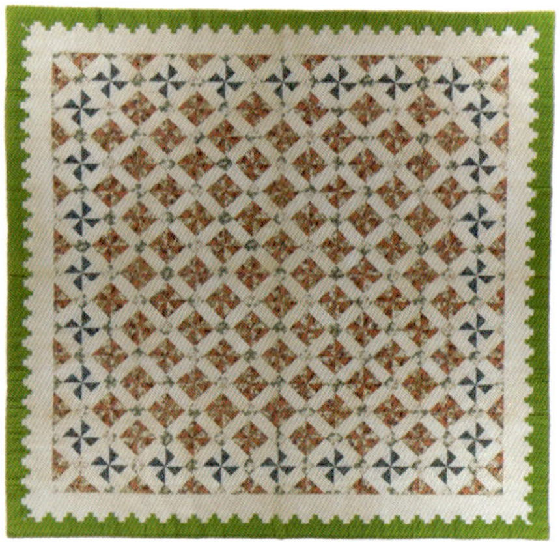

Pinwheel

Possibly made by Emeline Rounds Adams
Possibly made in Maryland
1830 - 1850
100.5 x 99.5 in.
IQM 1997.007.0457

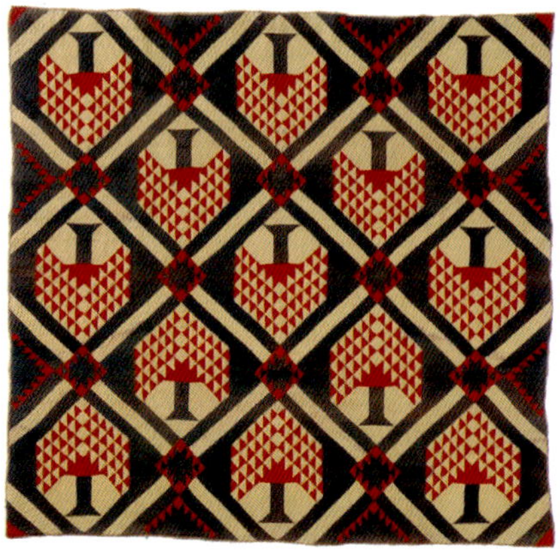

Pine Tree

Maker unidentified
Made in United States
1880 - 1900
75.5 x 75.5 in.
IQM 1997.007.0458

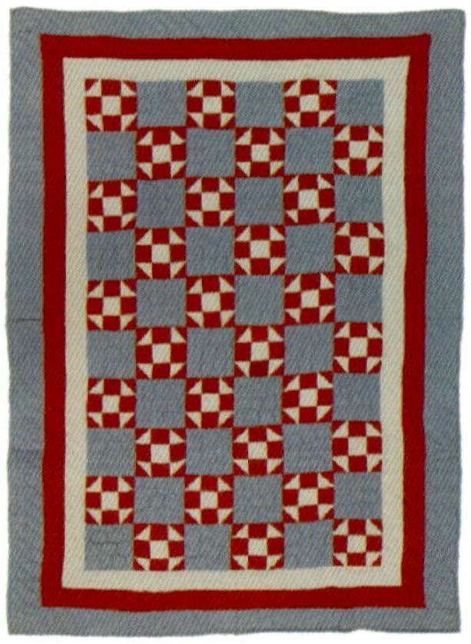

Shoo Fly

Maker unidentified
Possibly made in Pennsylvania
1890 - 1910
44 x 31.5 in.
IQM 1997.007.0459

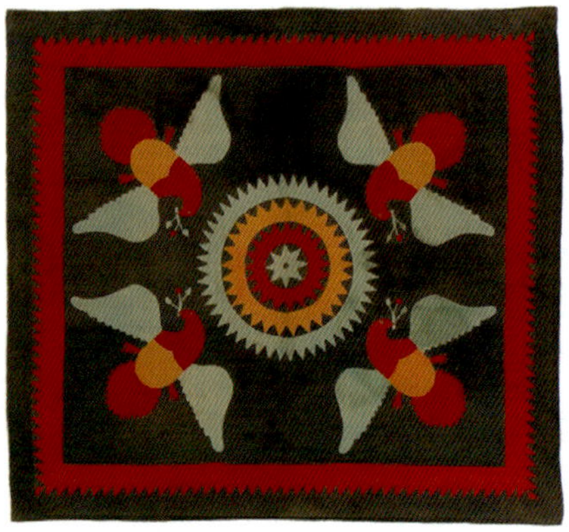

Eagle

Maker unidentified
Probably made in Pennsylvania
1870 - 1890
80.5 x 86 in.
IQM 1997.007.0460

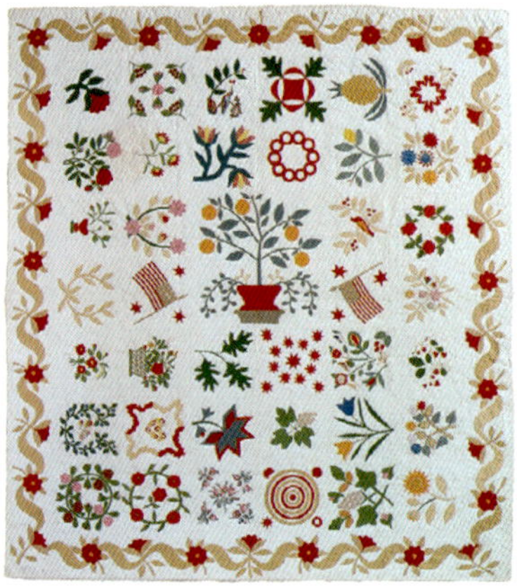

Album

Maker unidentified
Possibly made in Maryland
1870 - 1890
94.5 x 82.5 in.
IQM 1997.007.0462

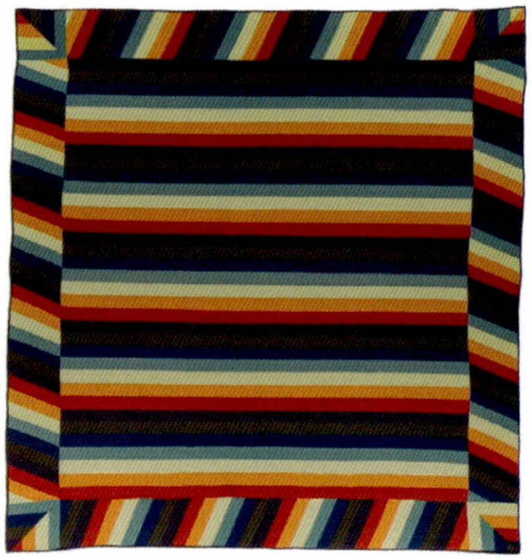

Joseph's Coat

Maker unidentified
Possibly made in Lancaster County, Pennsylvania
1870 - 1890
87.5 x 82.5 in.
IQM 1997.007.0463

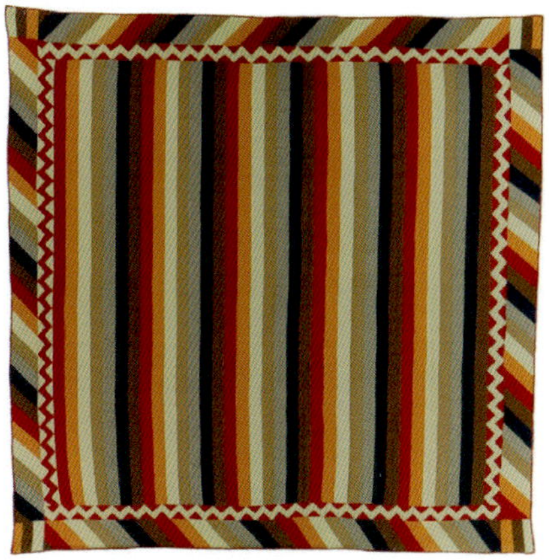

Joseph's Coat

Maker unidentified
Possibly made in Pennsylvania
1905 - 1925
84.5 x 82.5 in.

IQM 1997.007.0464

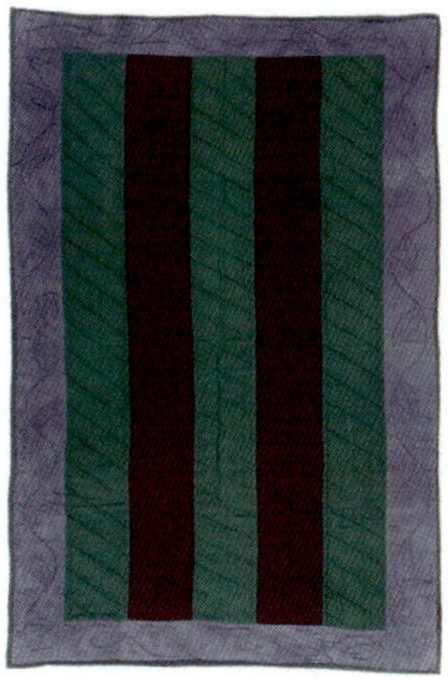

Bars

Maker unidentified
Possibly made in Mifflin County, Pennsylvania
1900 - 1920
49.5 x 32 in.

IQM 1997.007.0466

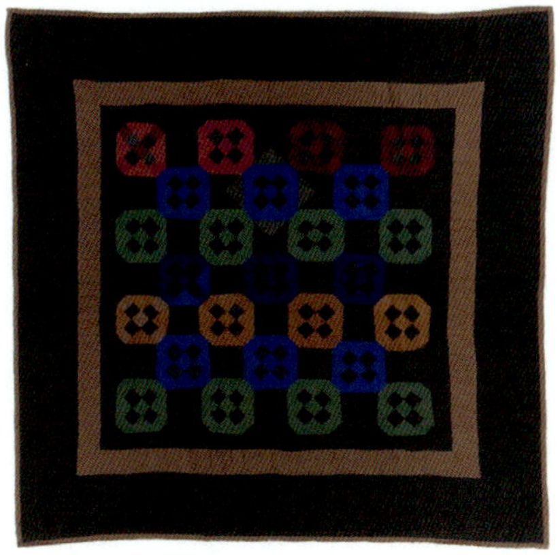

Four Patch

Maker unidentified
Possibly made in Holmes County, Ohio
1930 - 1950
67.5 x 67.5 in.

IQM 1997.007.0468

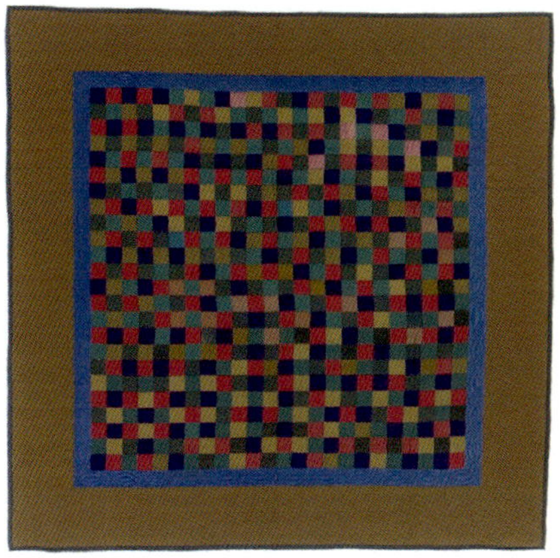

One Patch

Maker unidentified
Made in United States
1900 - 1920
67.5 x 67.5 in.

IQM 1997.007.0469

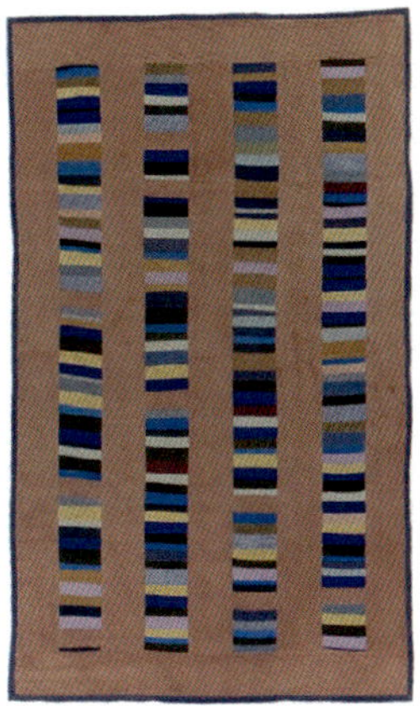

Chinese Coins

Maker unidentified
Possibly made in Holmes County, Ohio
1930 - 1950
72.5 x 43 in.

IQM 1997.007.0470

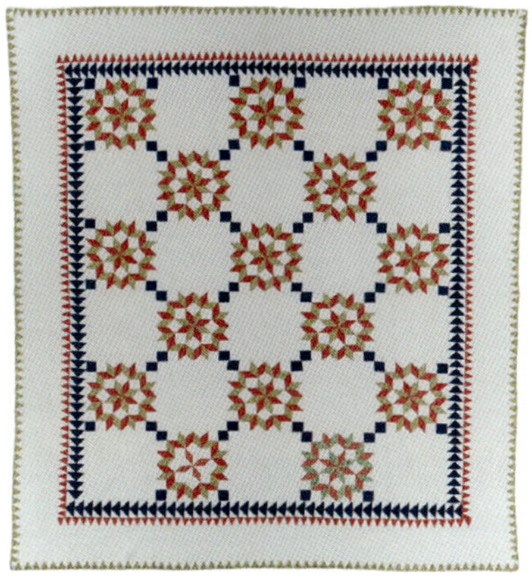

Carpenter's Wheel

Possibly made by Dillman family member
Possibly made in Pennsylvania
1840 - 1860
88.5 x 80.5 in.

IQM 1997.007.0471

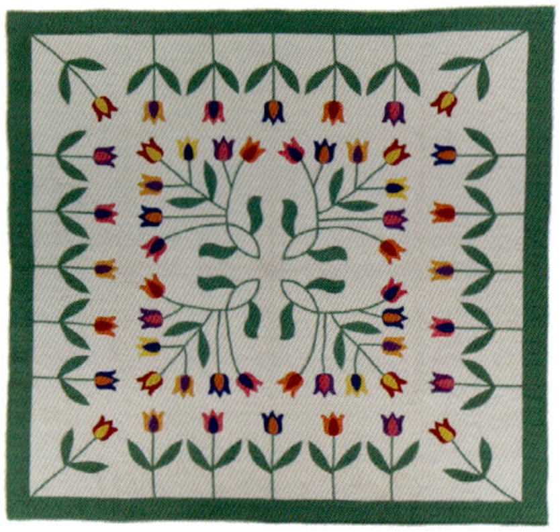

Tulip

Maker unidentified
Possibly made in western Pennsylvania
1920 - 1940
78 x 82.5 in.
IQM 1997.007.0472

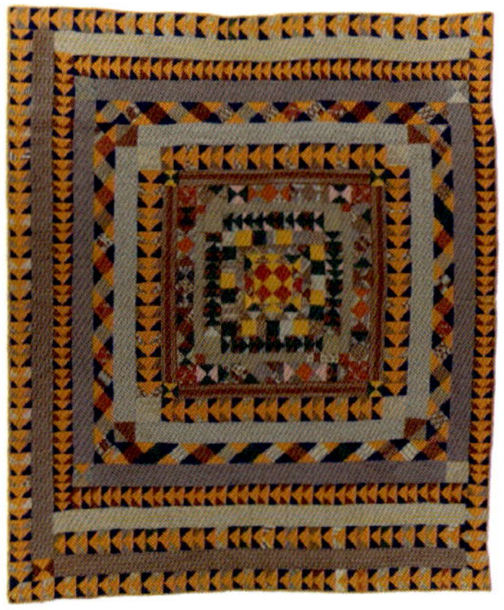

Medallion

Maker unidentified
Possibly made in York County, Pennsylvania
1850 - 1870
78 x 64.5 in.
IQM 1997.007.0473

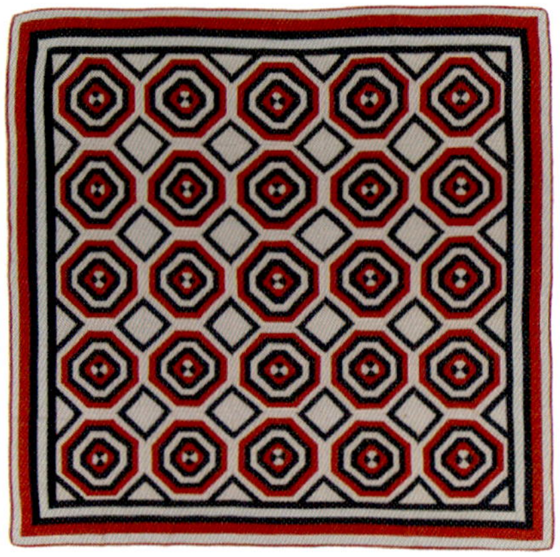

Spider Web

Maker unidentified
Possibly made in Michigan or Ohio
1890 - 1910
71 x 70.5 in.
IQM 1997.007.0475

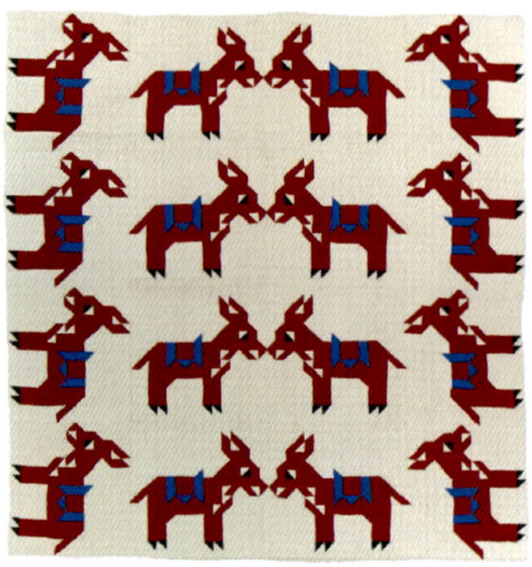

Donkeys

Maker unidentified
Possibly made in Illinois
1940 - 1950
86.5 x 80.5 in.
IQM 1997.007.0476

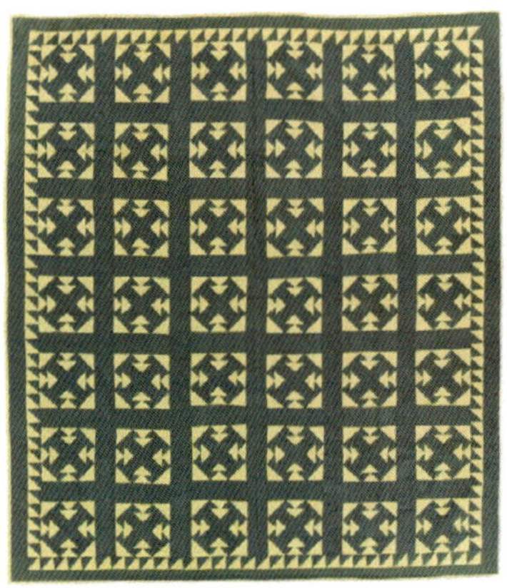

Crossed Ts

Maker unidentified
Possibly made in Pennsylvania
1880 - 1900
88 x 77 in.
IQM 1997.007.0477

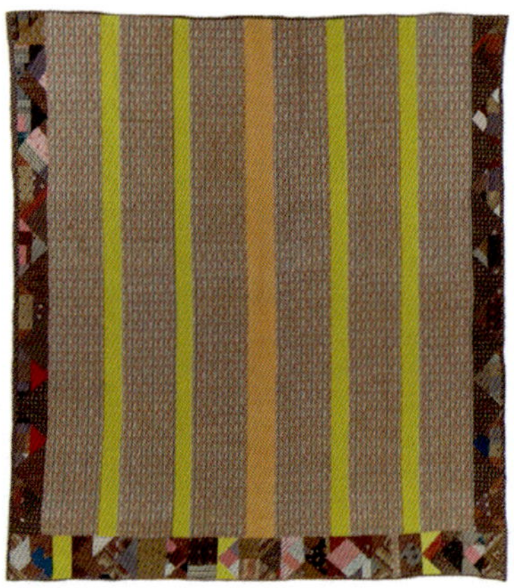

Bars

Maker unidentified
Possibly made in New England
1830 - 1850
88 x 75.5 in.
IQM 1997.007.0480

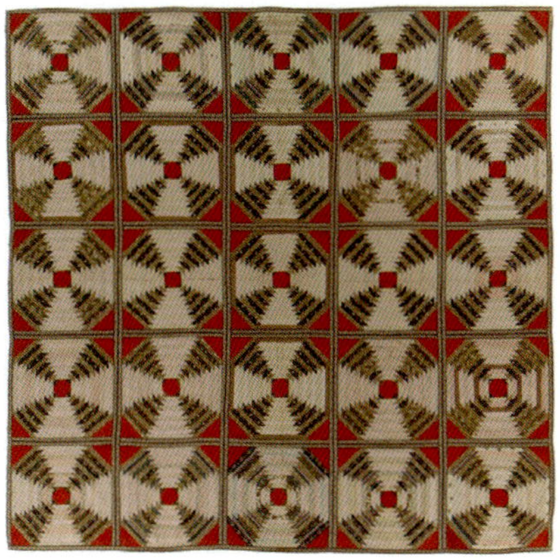

Log Cabin

Possibly made by Jennie M. Bryant
Possibly made in Greenwood, Massachusetts
1870 - 1890
74.5 x 74 in.
IQM 1997.007.0483

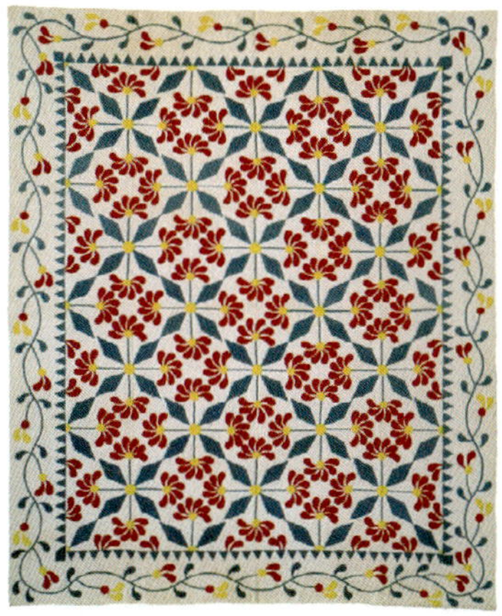

Mexican Rose

Maker unidentified
Possibly made in Kansas
1840 - 1860
93.5 x 75 in.
IQM 1997.007.0484

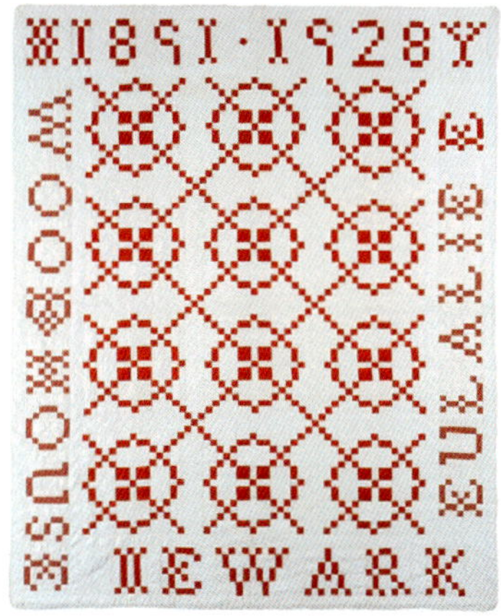

Burgoyne Surrounded

Probably made by Addie Fish Woodhouse
Probably made in Newark, New York
Circa 1928
88.5 x 72 in.
IQM 1997.007.0485

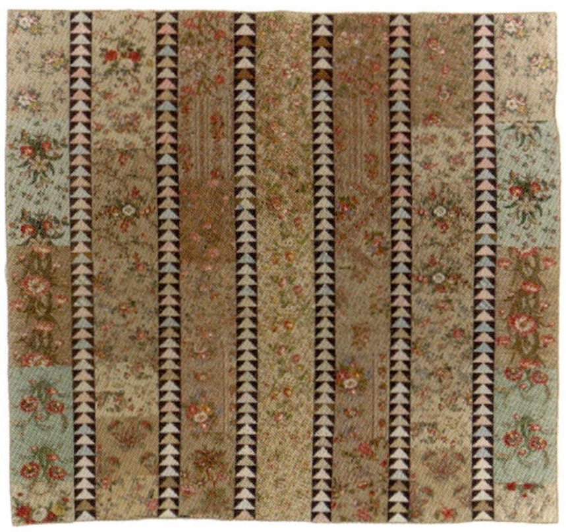

Wild Goose Chase

Maker unidentified
Probably made in New England
1830 - 1850
106 x 111 in.
IQM 1997.007.0486

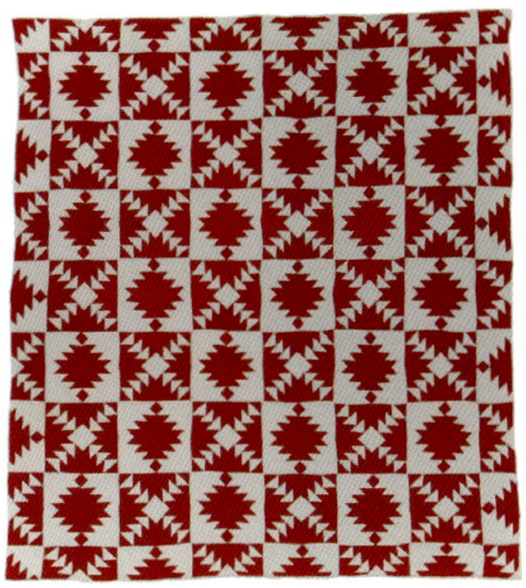

Flying Geese

Maker unidentified
Possibly made in Ohio
1900 - 1920
79.5 x 70 in.
IQM 1997.007.0487

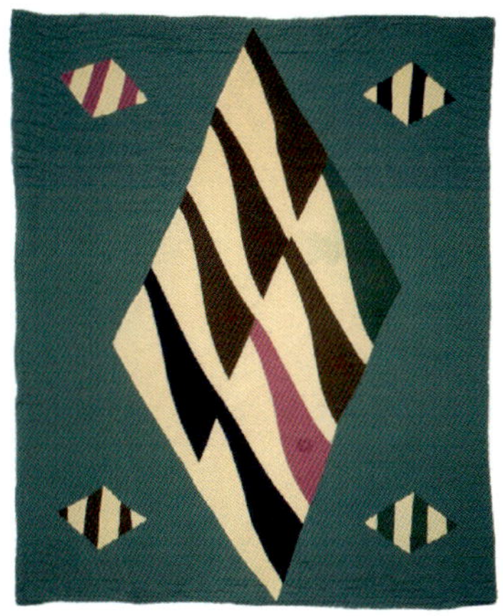

Original - Landon/Knox Quilt

Maker unidentified
Possibly made in Kansas
Circa 1936
83 x 67 in.
IQM 1997.007.0488

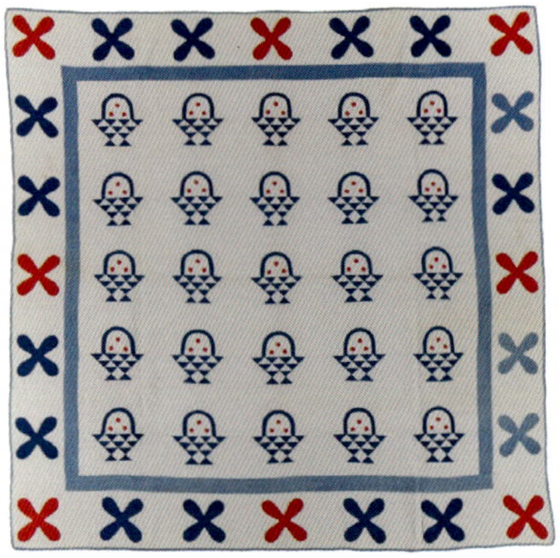

Basket

Maker unidentified
Probably made in Ohio
1900 - 1920
79.5 x 79 in.
IQM 1997.007.0489

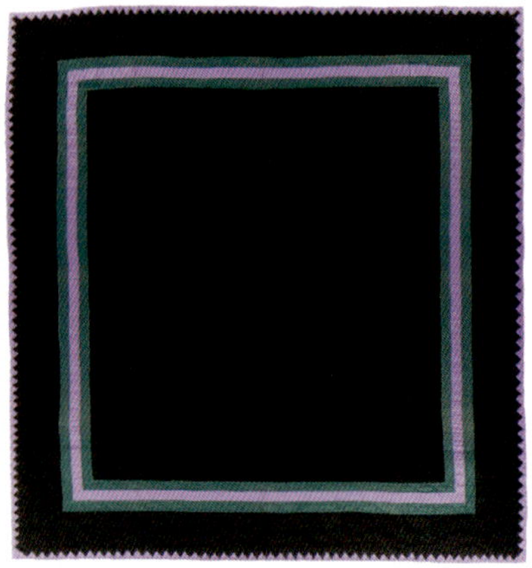

Plain Quilt

Maker unidentified
Possibly made in Holmes County, Ohio
1925 - 1945
80.5 x 75 in.
IQM 1997.007.0490

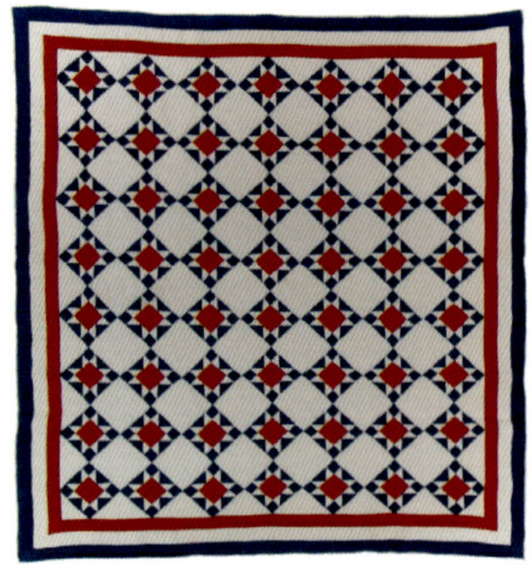

Sawtooth Star

Maker unidentified
Made in United States
1900 - 1920
77.5 x 70 in.
IQM 1997.007.0491

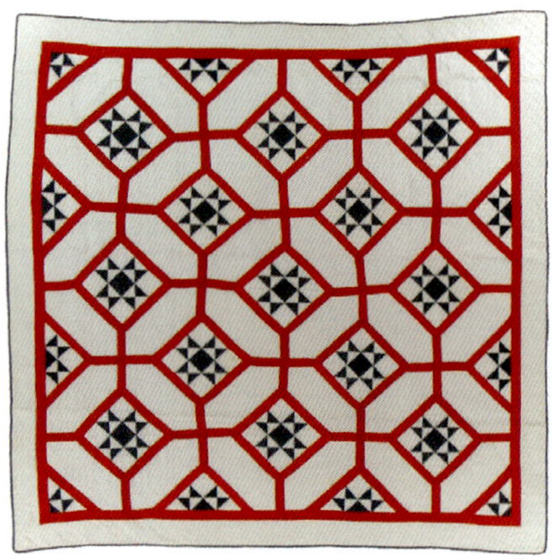

Garden Maze Star

Maker unidentified
Possibly made in Ohio
1875 - 1895
72 x 70.5 in.
IQM 1997.007.0493

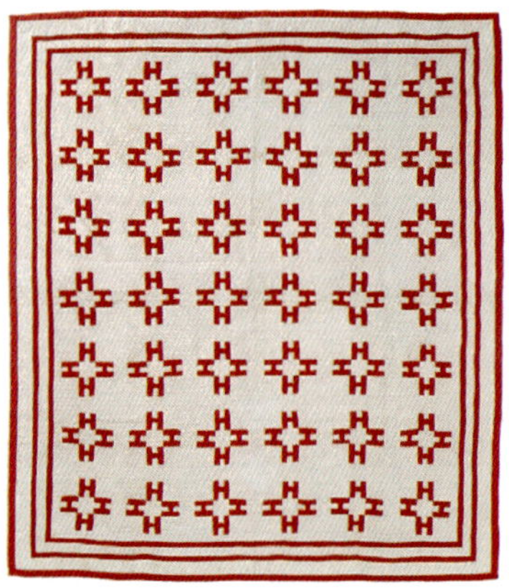

Four H

Maker unidentified
Probably made in Ohio
1900 - 1920
74 x 63.5 in.
IQM 1997.007.0494

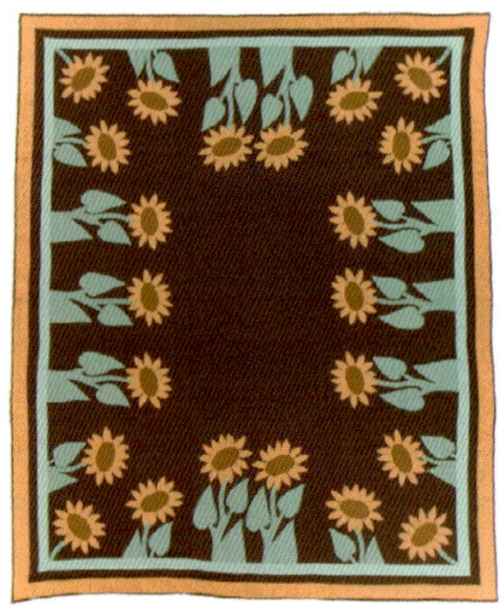

Sunflower

Maker unidentified
Possibly made in Ohio
Dated 1943
90 x 71.5 in.
IQM 1997.007.0496

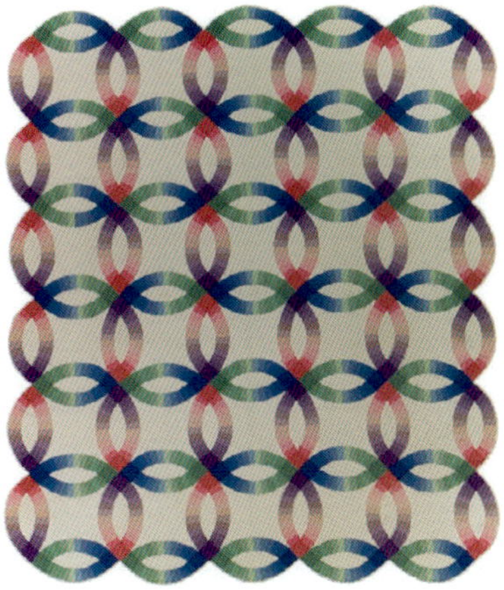

Double Wedding Ring

Maker unidentified
Possibly made in Kentucky
1930 - 1940
98 x 84.5 in.

IQM 1997.007.0497

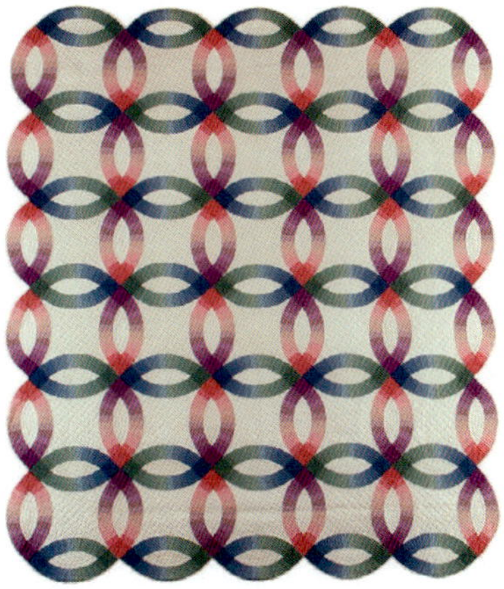

Double Wedding Ring

Maker unidentified
Possibly made in Kentucky
1930 - 1940
97 x 79.5 in.

IQM 1997.007.0498

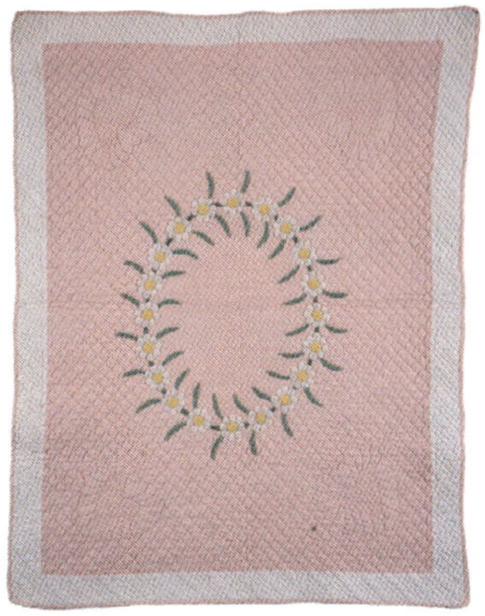

Painted Daisy

Maker unidentified
Possibly made in Indiana
Circa 1936
36.5 x 27.5 in.

IQM 1997.007.0499

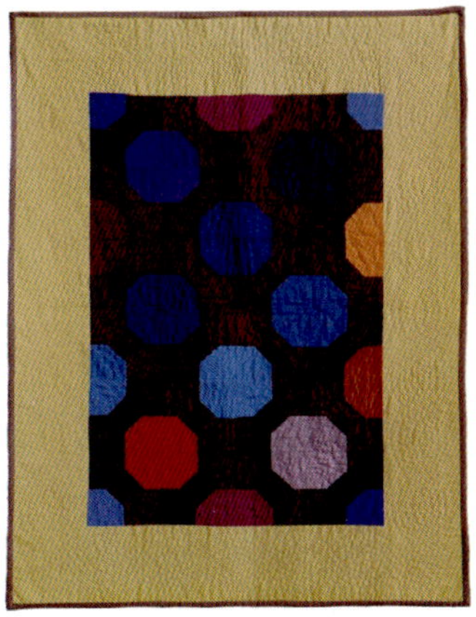

Bow Tie

Probably made by Lydia Miller
Probably made in Wayne County, Ohio
Circa 1975
39.5 x 30.5 in.

IQM 1997.007.0506

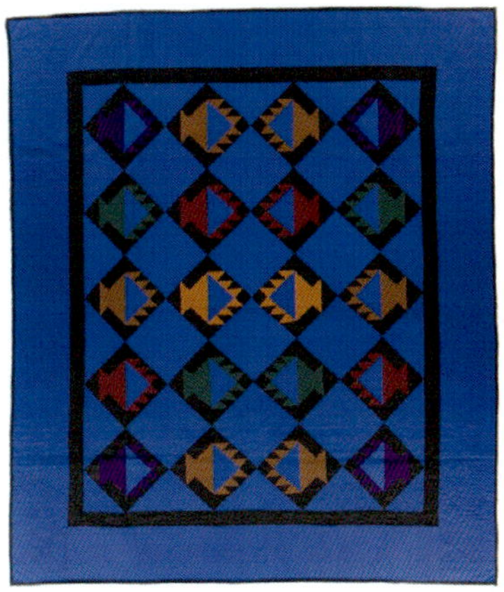

Basket

Amanda Hostetler and Anna Miller
Holmes County, Ohio
Dated 1982
82 x 69.5 in.

IQM 1997.007.0510

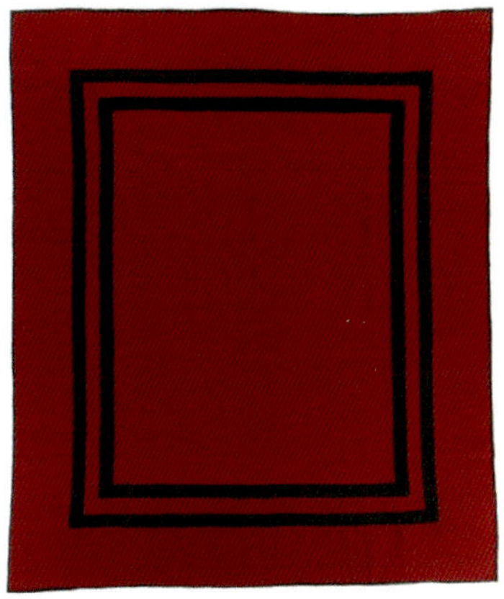

Plain Quilt

Probably made by L. Miller
Probably made in Holmes County, Ohio
Circa 1975
80 x 67 in.

IQM 1997.007.0511

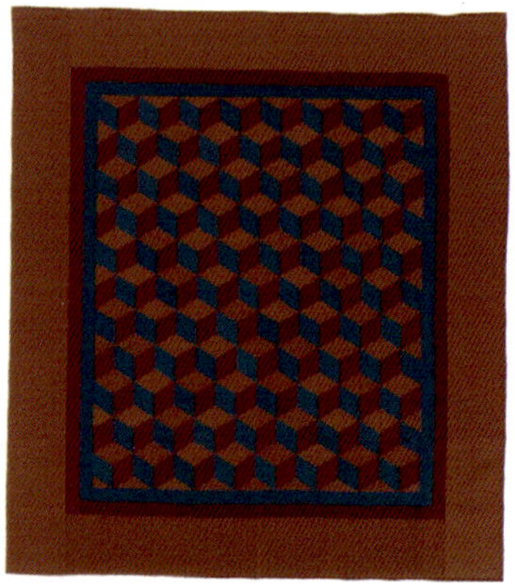

Tumbling Blocks

Probably made by L. Miller
Probably made in Wayne County, Ohio
Circa 1975
81.5 x 70 in.

IQM 1997.007.0512

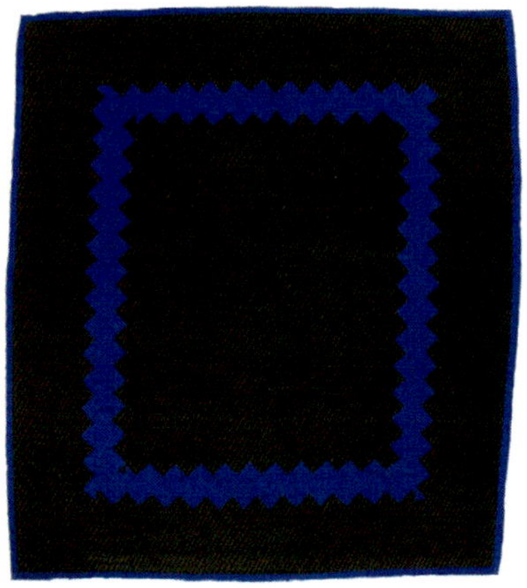

Plain Quilt

Probably made by L. Miller
Probably made in Wayne County, Ohio
Circa 1975
36 x 31.5 in.

IQM 1997.007.0513

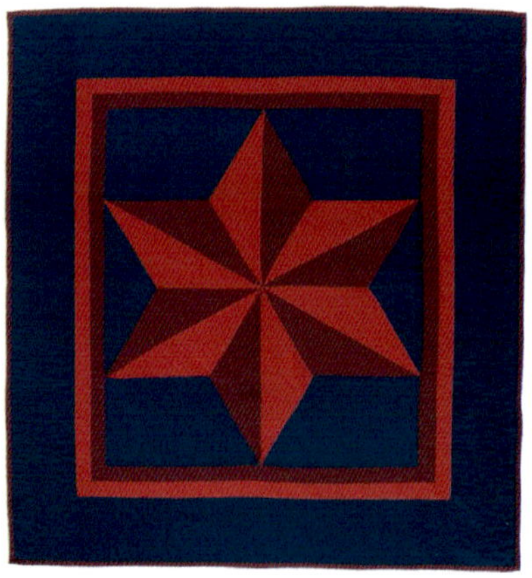

Six Pointed Star

Probably made by L. Miller
Probably made in Wayne County, Ohio
Circa 1978
51 x 47 in.

IQM 1997.007.0515

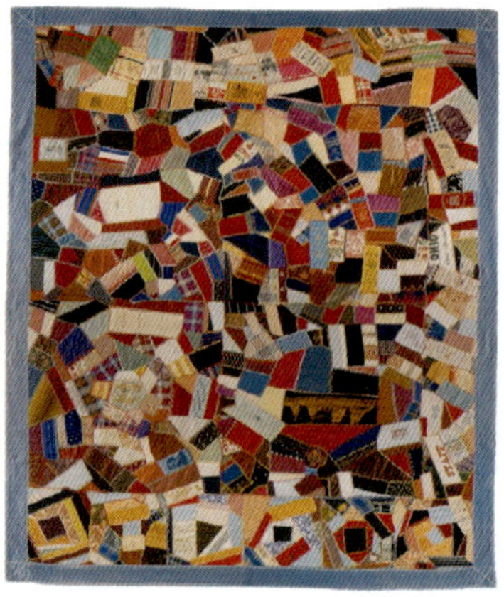

Crazy

Maker unidentified
Possibly made in Ohio
1915 - 1925
77.5 x 64 in.

IQM 1997.007.0516

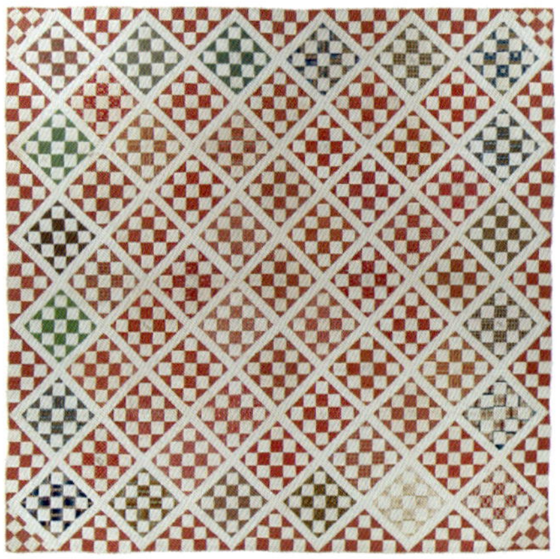

Nine Patch Checkerboard

Maker unidentified
Probably made in Bucks County, Pennsylvania
1847 - 1850
101 x 101 in.

IQM 1997.007.0520

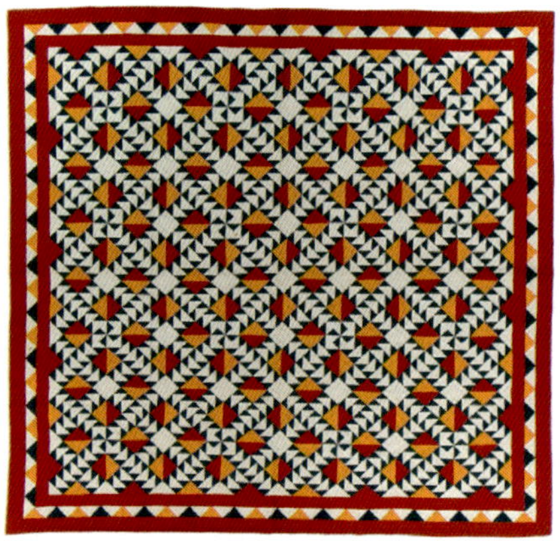

Wild Goose Chase

Maker unidentified
Possibly made in Pennsylvania
Dated 1902
89.5 x 88.5 in.

IQM 1997.007.0521

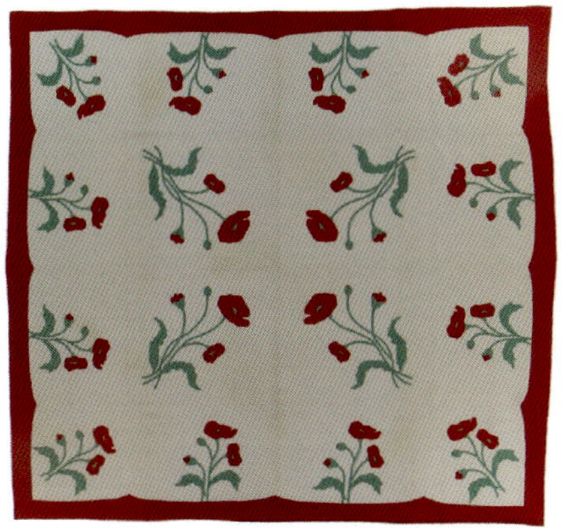

Poppy

Maker unidentified

Possibly made in Ohio
1925 - 1935
84.5 x 82 in.

IQM 1997.007.0522

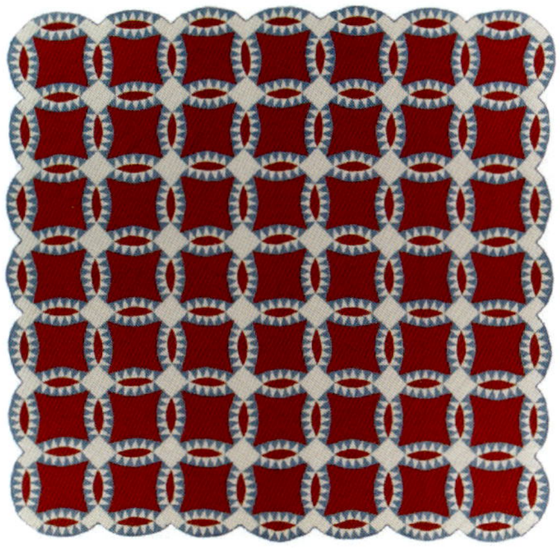

Pickle Dish

Maker unidentified
Possibly made in Ohio
1930 - 1950
79.5 x 81 in.

IQM 1997.007.0524

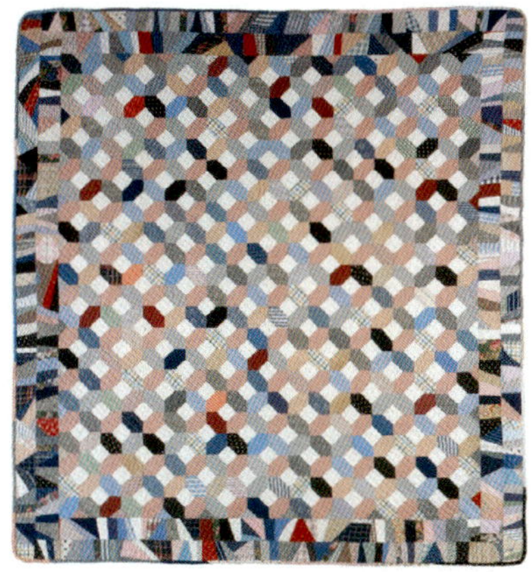

Lattice

Maker unidentified
Possibly made in southern Indiana
1910 - 1930
75 x 68 in.

IQM 1997.007.0525

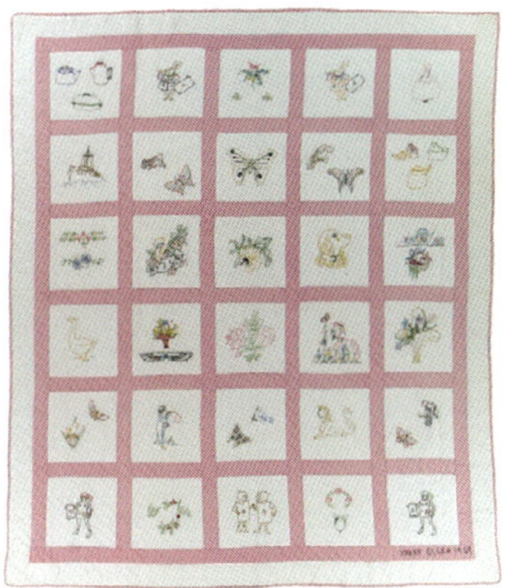

Album

Maker unidentified
Possibly made in Peru, Indiana
Dated 1929
86.5 x 72.5 in.

IQM 1997.007.0526

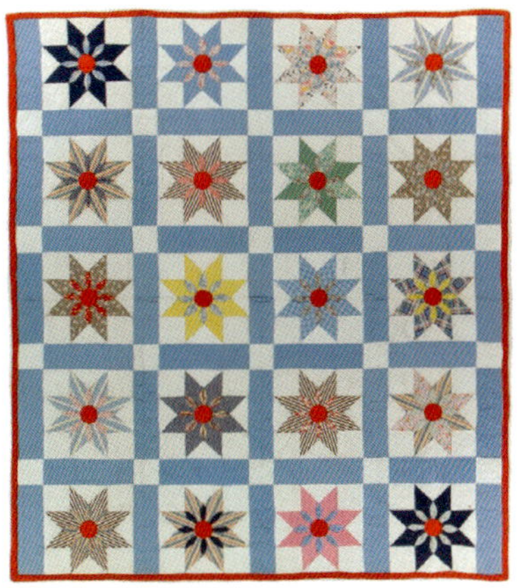

Missouri Daisy

Hattie Broadbent Vermillion
Made in Madison County, Indiana
Dated 1938
86 x 76.5 in.

IQM 1997.007.0527

Whole Cloth

Maker unidentified
Possibly made in Ohio
1830 - 1860
92 x 73 in.

IQM 1997.007.0528

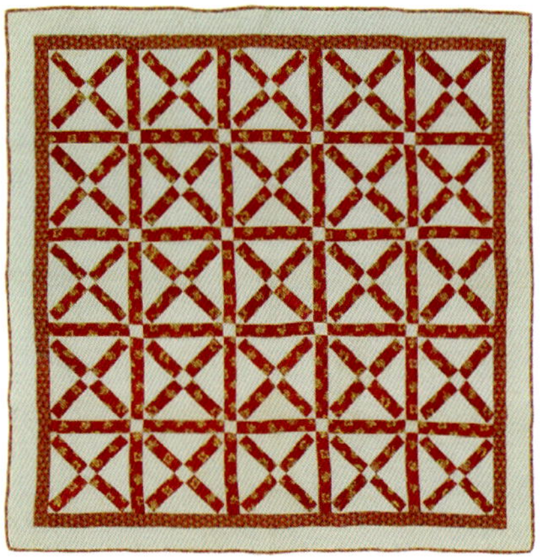

Crosses

Maker unidentified
Possibly made in Pennsylvania
1830 - 1850
37 x 36 in.
IQM 1997.007.0529

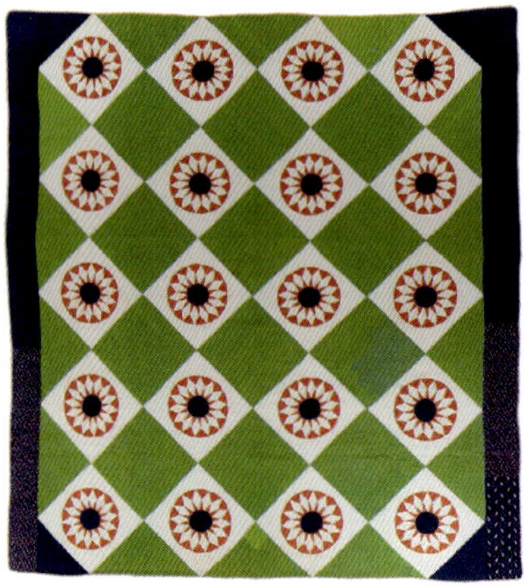

Rising Sun

Elizabeth Hostetter
Possibly made in Ohio or Pennsylvania
1850 - 1870
91 x 83 in.
IQM 1997.007.0530

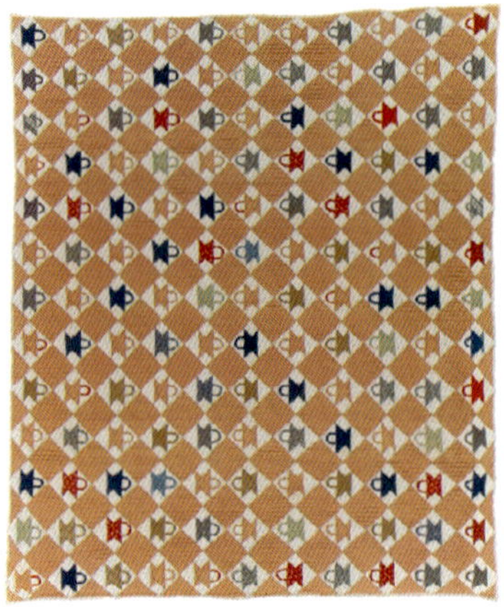

Basket

Maker unidentified
Possibly made in southern Indiana
1890 - 1910
78 x 64 in.
IQM 1997.007.0532

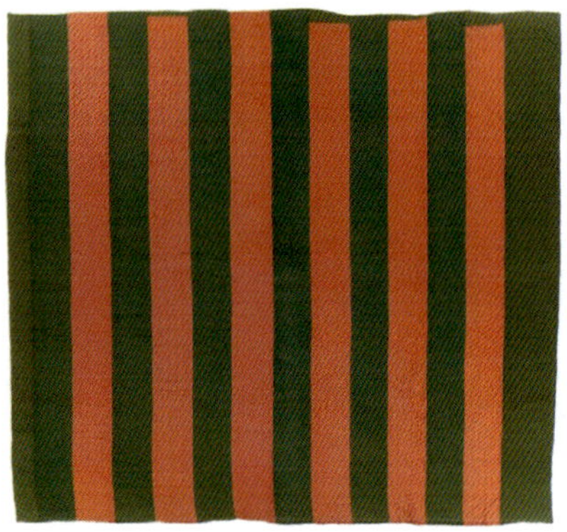

Bars

Maker unidentified
Possibly made in New Hampshire
1800 - 1820
85 x 93.5 in.
IQM 1997.007.0533

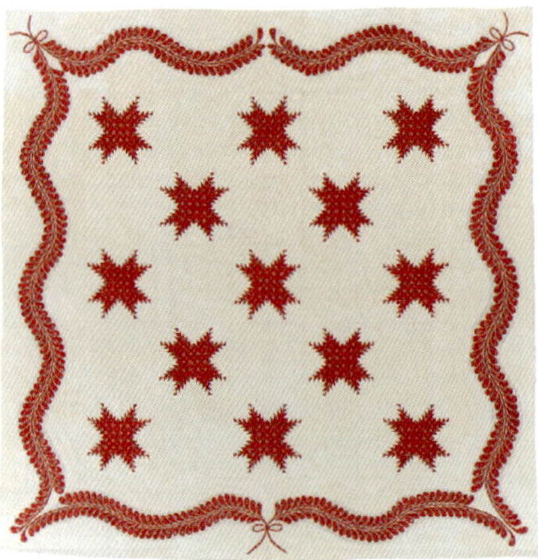

Feathered Star

Maker unidentified
Possibly made in Maryland or Pennsylvania
1845 - 1855
96 x 93 in.
IQM 1997.007.0534

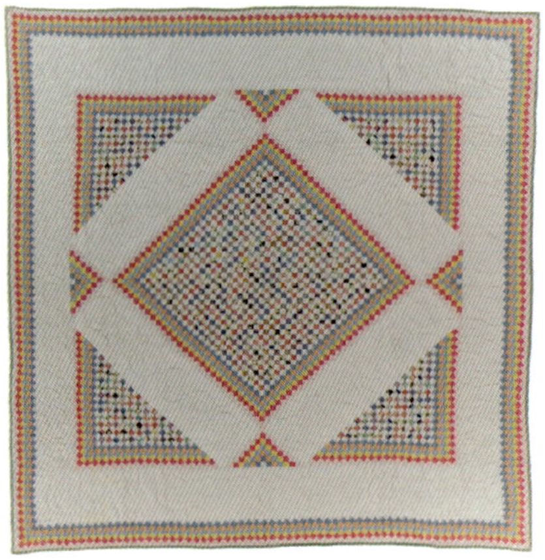

Center Diamond

Maker unidentified
Possibly made in Indiana or Pennsylvania
1930 - 1950
75.5 x 71.5 in.
IQM 1997.007.0535

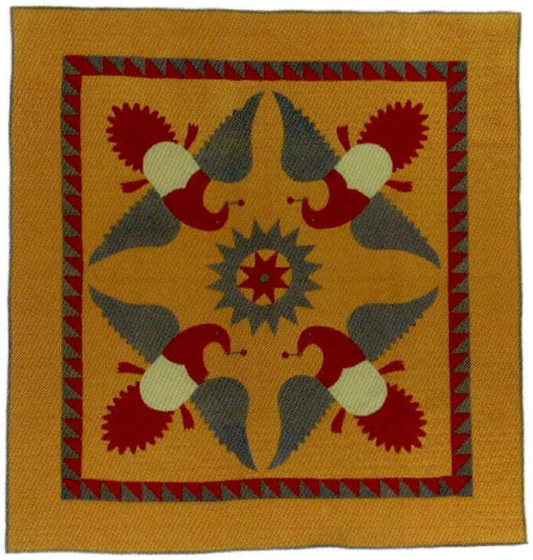

Eagle

Maker unidentified
Possibly made in York or Lancaster County, Pennsylvania
1880 - 1900
79 x 75 in.
IQM 1997.007.0536

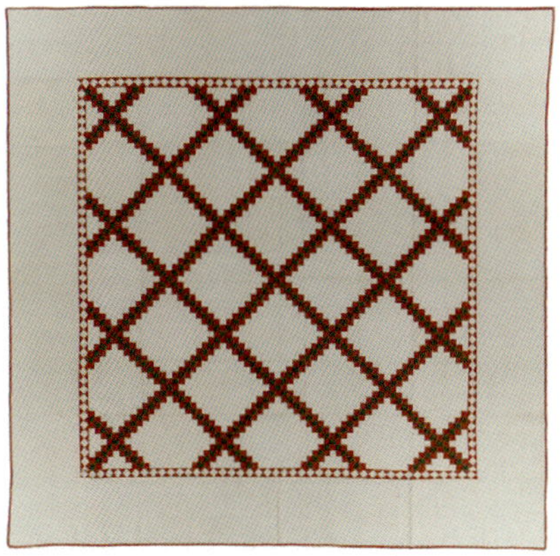

Irish Chain

Maker unidentified
Possibly made in Pennsylvania
1840 - 1860
82 x 81 in.
IQM 1997.007.0537

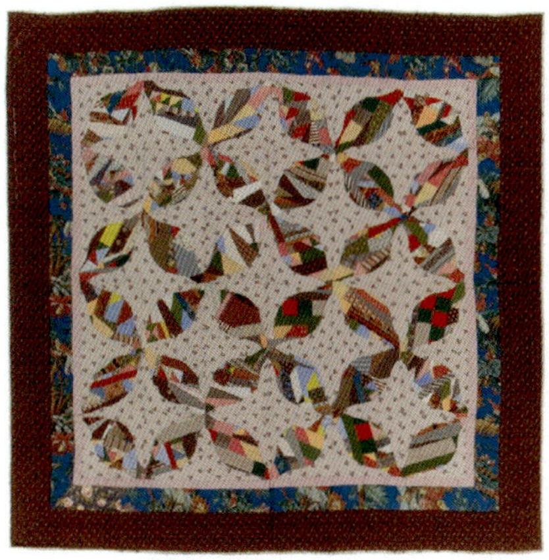

Chinese Lantern

Maker unidentified
Possibly made in Pennsylvania
1880 - 1900
67 x 67 in.
IQM 1997.007.0538

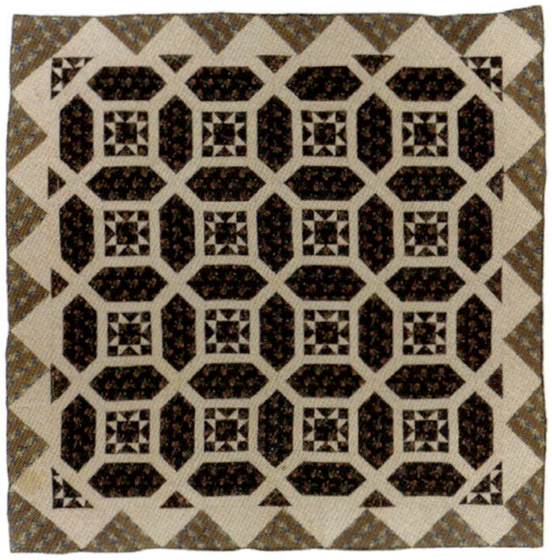

Garden Maze Star

Grandmother Hurlbert
Possibly made in Montgomery County, Pennsylvania
1820 - 1840
90 x 91.5 in.
IQM 1997.007.0540

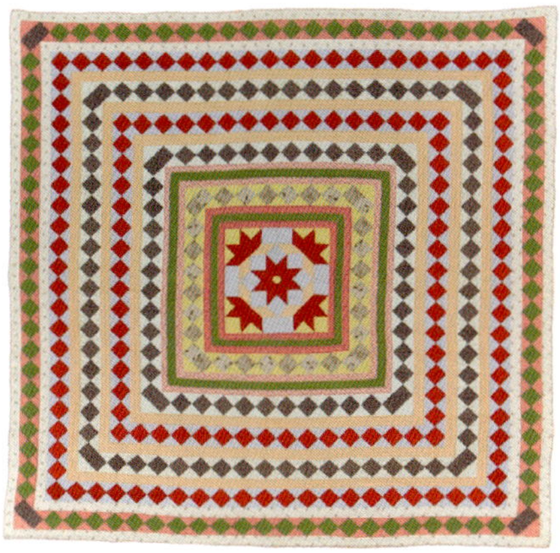

Medallion

Maker unidentified
Possibly made in Pennsylvania
1870 - 1890
75 x 72 in.
IQM 1997.007.0542

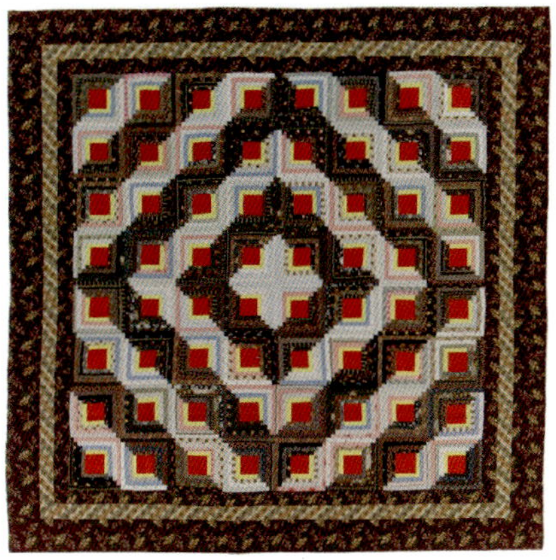

Log Cabin

Maker unidentified
Possibly made in Pennsylvania
1880 - 1900
78 x 78 in.
IQM 1997.007.0543

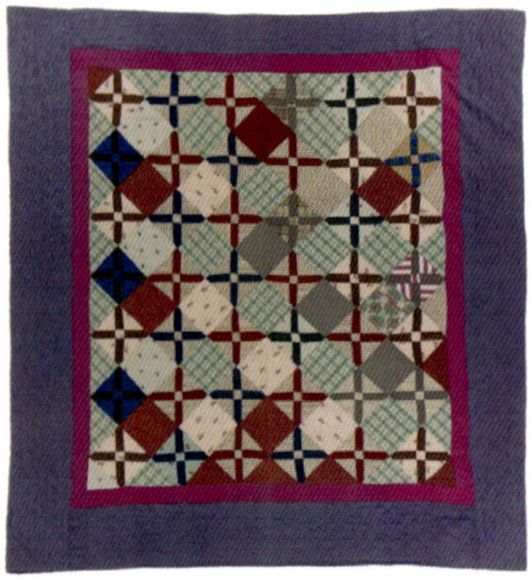

Cross and Block

Maker unidentified
Possibly made in Kentucky
1870 - 1890
90 x 84 in.

IQM 1997.007.0545

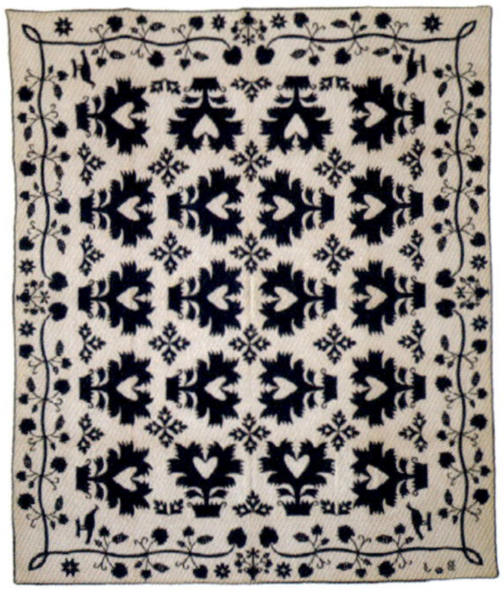

Hearts & Trees

Maker unidentified
Made in United States
1850 - 1870
97 x 80.5 in.

IQM 1997.007.0547

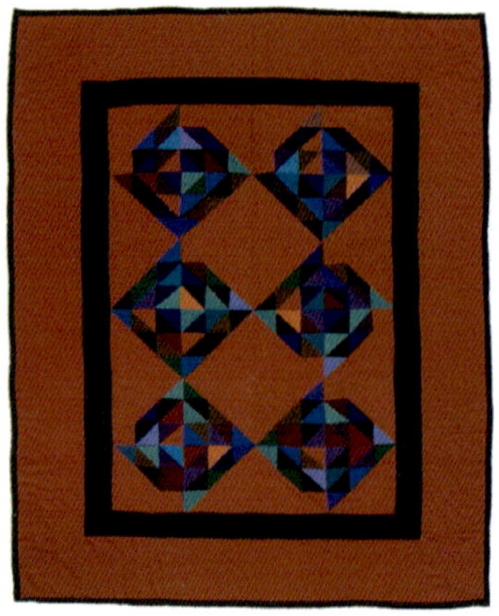

Triangles

Probably made by Miller sisters
Probably made in Delagrange, Ohio
Circa 1975
41.5 x 33 in.

IQM 1997.007.0548

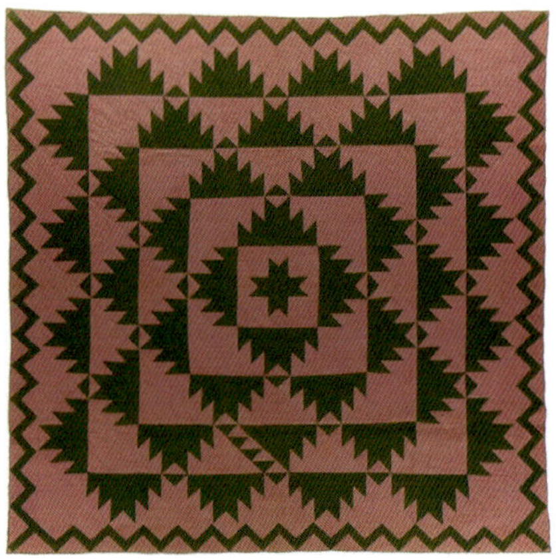

Delectable Mountains

Maker unidentified
Possibly made in Lancaster County, Pennsylvania
1850 - 1870
84 x 84 in.

IQM 1997.007.0549

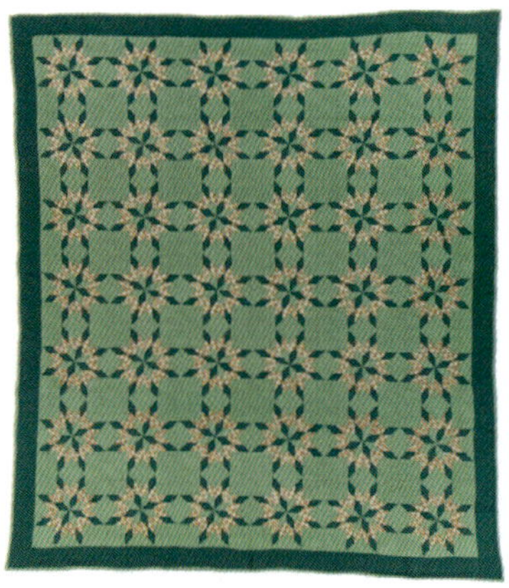

Star of the Bluegrass

Maker unidentified
Possibly made in Florida
1948 - 1955
91.5 x 76 in.

IQM 1997.007.0550

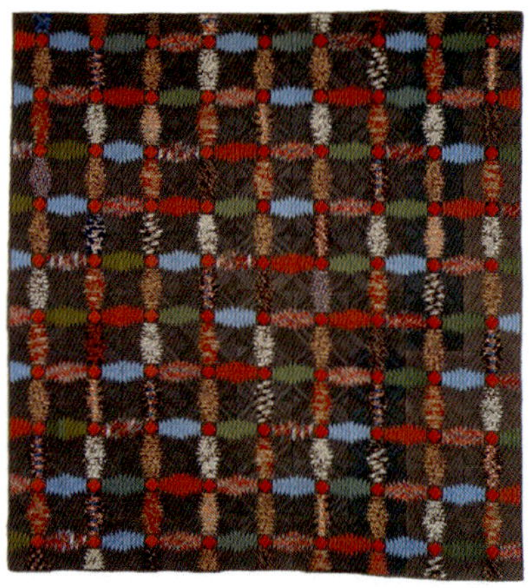

Log Cabin

Maker unidentified
Possibly made in Ohio
1865 - 1885
77 x 68 in.

IQM 1997.007.0551

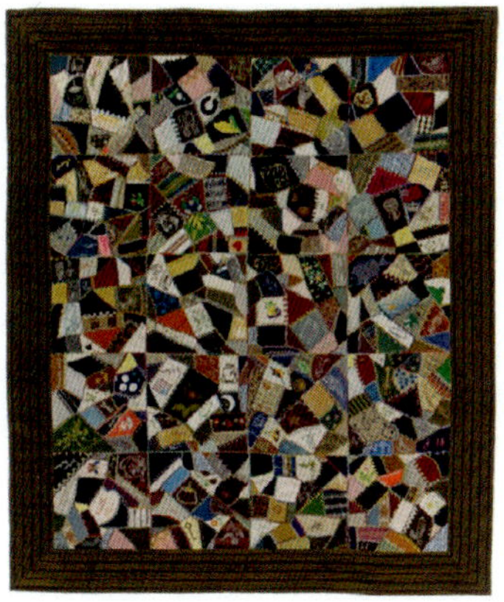

Crazy

Maker unidentified
Possibly made in Mt. Clemens, Michigan
Dated 1884
76 x 63 in.

IQM 1997.007.0552

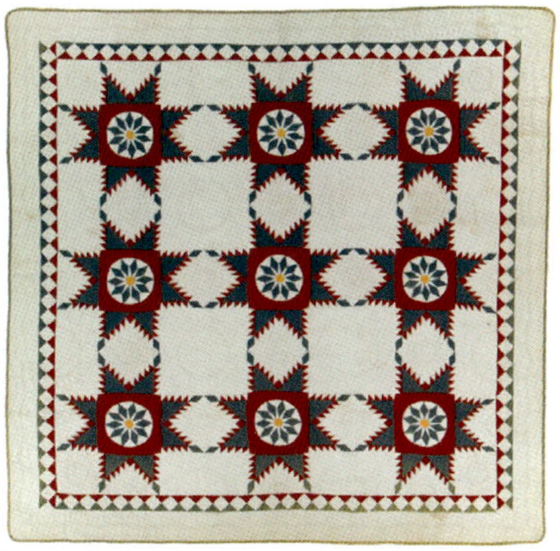

Feathered Star

Maker unidentified
Possibly made in Indiana
1890 - 1910
83 x 82.5 in.

IQM 1997.007.0554

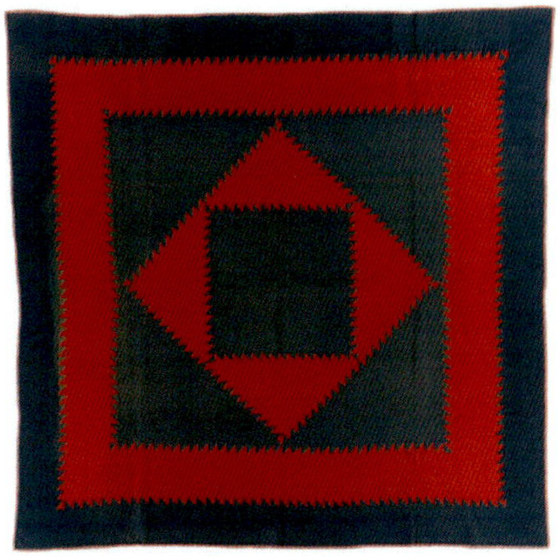

Center Diamond

Maker unidentified
Possibly made in Lancaster County, Pennsylvania
Circa 1875
76 x 76 in.

IQM 1997.007.0555

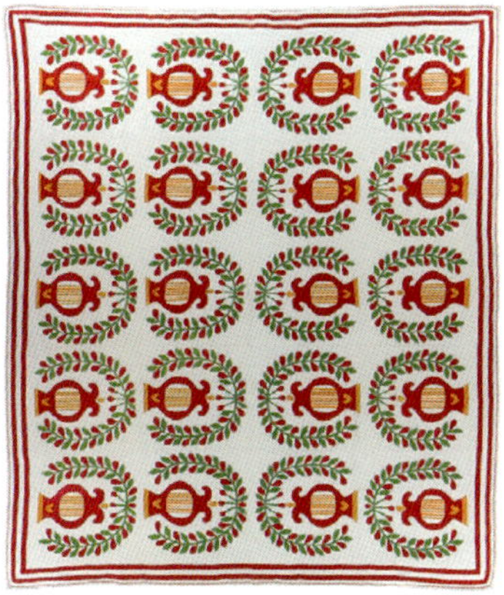

Lyre and Wreath

Maker unidentified
Possibly made in Pennsylvania
1850 - 1870
92 x 76 in.

IQM 1997.007.0556

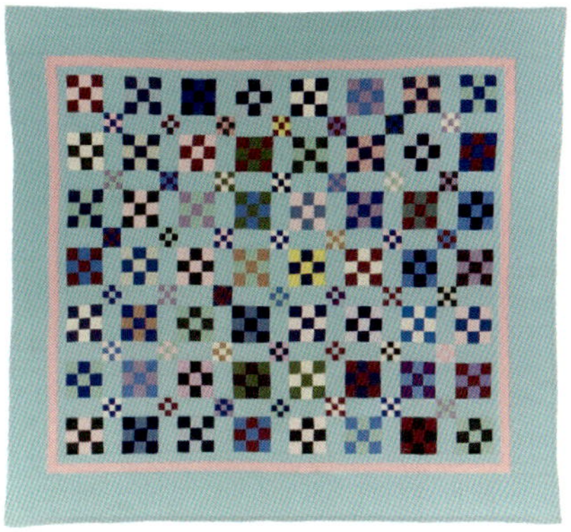

Nine Patch

Maker unidentified
Possibly made in Holmes County, Ohio
1925 - 1945
73.5 x 69.25 in.

IQM 1997.007.0557

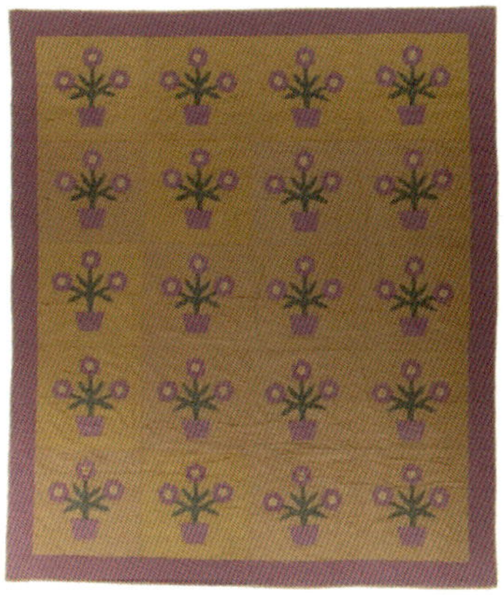

Pots of Flowers

Maker unidentified
Possibly made in Holmes County, Ohio
1915 - 1935
85.25 x 72 in.

IQM 1997.007.0558

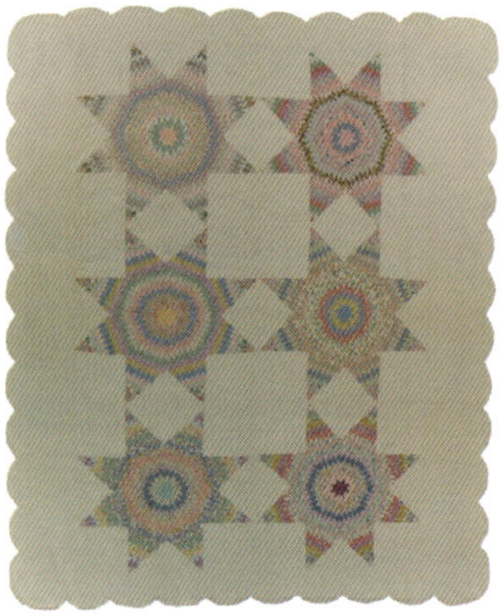

Touching Stars

Possibly made by Mr. & Mrs. Stutzman
Possibly made in Elkhart, Indiana
1930 - 1940
92 x 64.5 in.
IQM 1997.007.0559

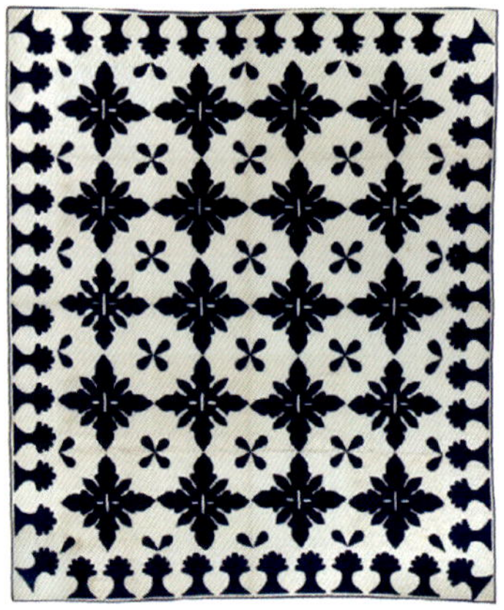

Papercut Appliqué

Maker unidentified
Made in Dutchess County, New York
Dated 1856
99 x 82 in.
IQM 1997.007.0560

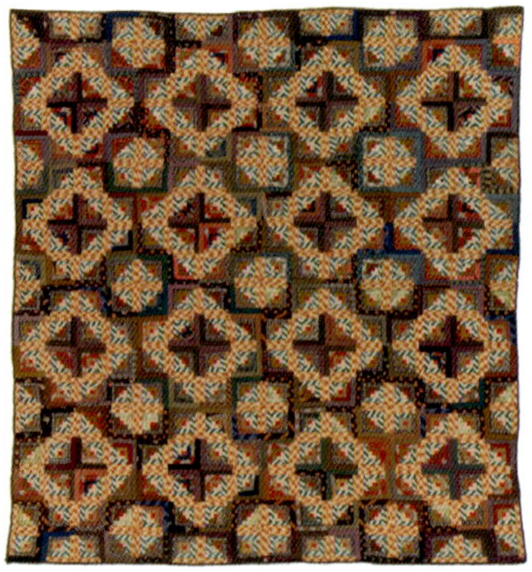

Log Cabin

Maker unidentified
Probably made in Ohio
1880 - 1900
74 x 68 in.
IQM 1997.007.0561

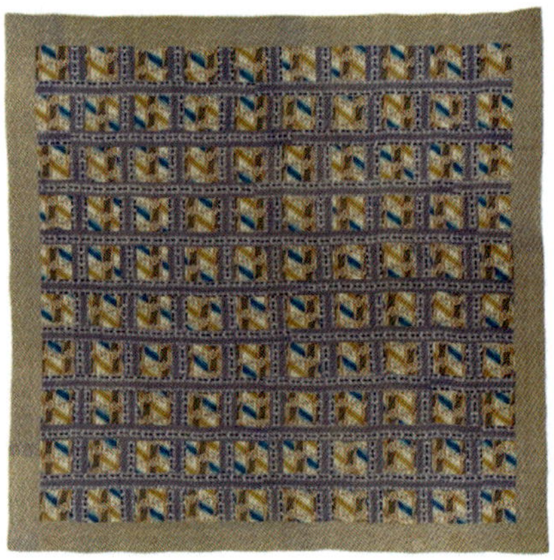

Squares

Maker unidentified
Possibly made in Pennsylvania
1840 - 1860
98.5 x 101.5 in.
IQM 1997.007.0562

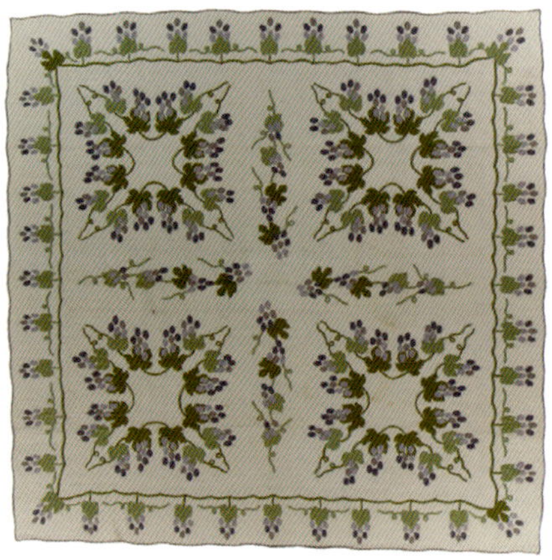

Grapes & Vines

Maker unidentified
Possibly made in Indiana
Circa 1914
82.5 x 82 in.
IQM 1997.007.0563

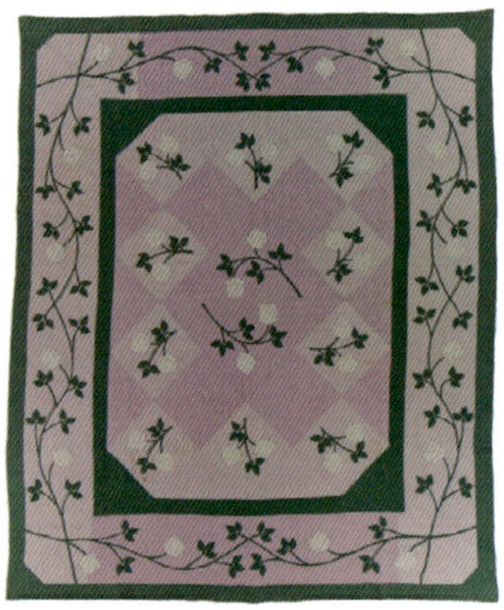

Rose

Maker unidentified
Possibly made in Ohio
1920 - 1940
90 x 72 in.
IQM 1997.007.0565

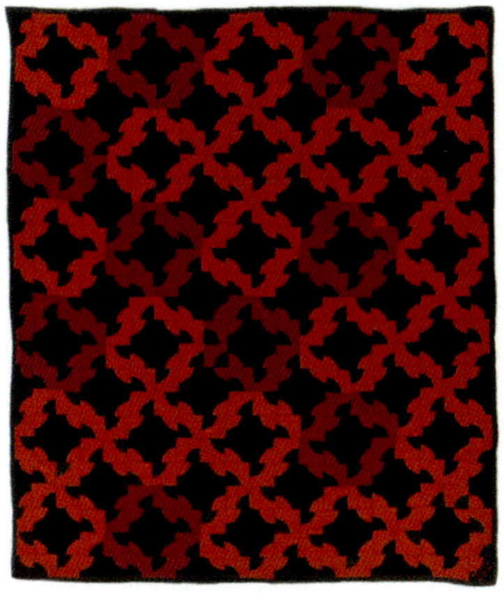

Drunkard's Path

Possibly made by E. & B. Mitchell
Possibly made in Bowling Green, Kentucky
1890 - 1930
83 x 68 in.

IQM 1997.007.0566

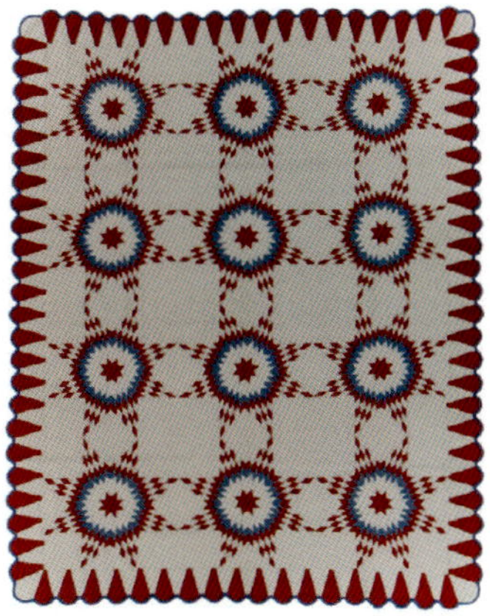

Touching Stars

Maker unidentified
Possibly made in Ohio
1935 - 1945
90.25 x 69.75 in.

IQM 1997.007.0567

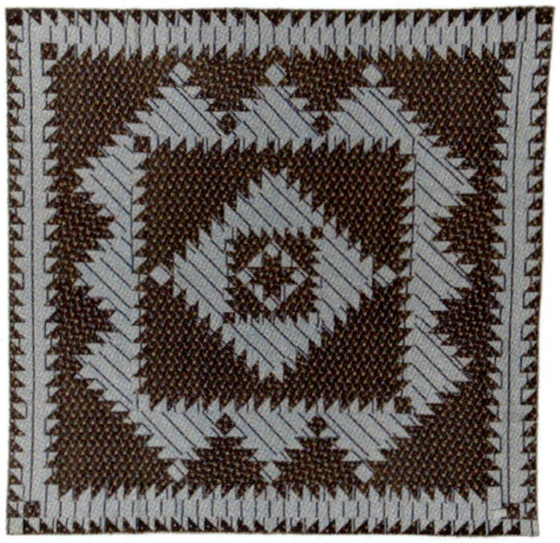

Delectable Mountains

Maker unidentified
Possibly made in Pennsylvania
1830 - 1850
93 x 94.5 in.

IQM 1997.007.0568

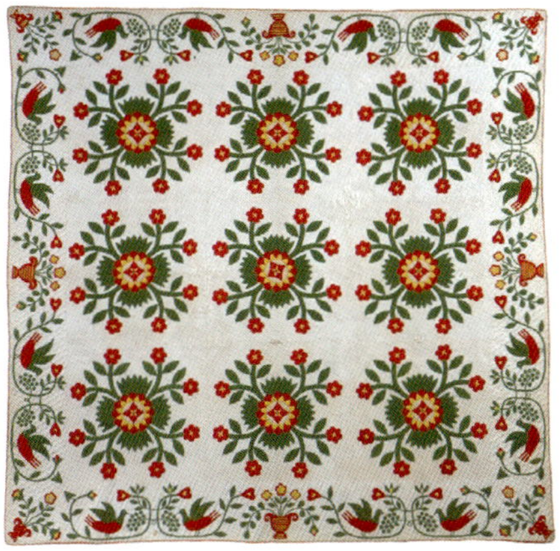

Whig Rose variation

Maker unidentified
Possibly made in Ohio
Dated 1853
87.5 x 88 in.

IQM 1997.007.0570

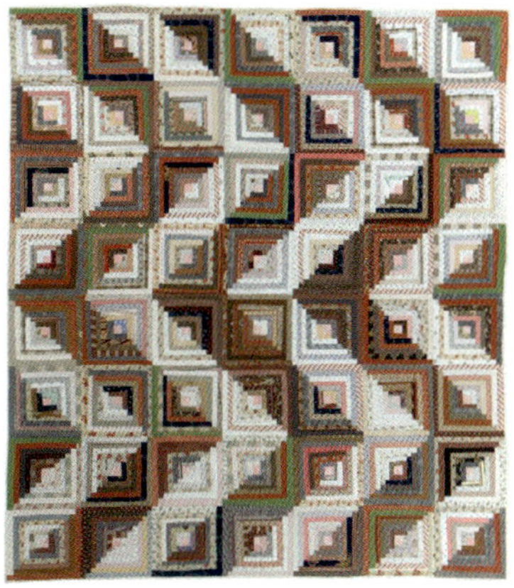

Log Cabin

Probably made by Mary Schultz
Possibly made in Jackson County, Missouri
1880 - 1900
76 x 66.25 in.

IQM 1997.007.0572

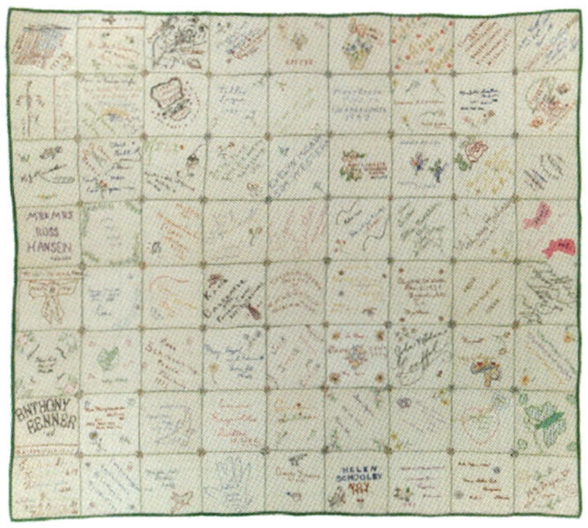

Original

Maker unidentified
Probably made in Peoria, Illinois
Dated 1939 - 1941
79.5 x 93.75 in.

IQM 1997.007.0574

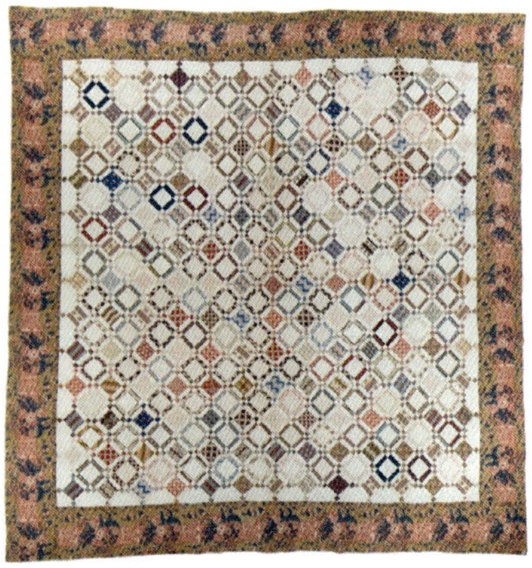

Nine Patch variation

Possibly made by Jane Gibb
Possibly made in Quincy, Illinois
1840 - 1860
103 x 97 in.
IQM 1997.007.0575

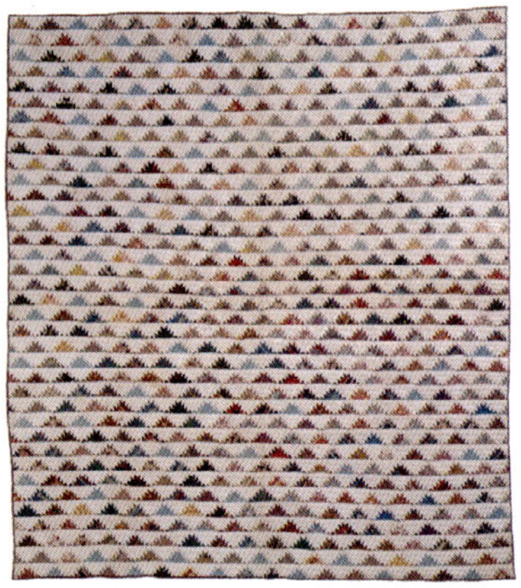

Delectable Mountains variation

Possibly made by Jane Gibb
Possibly made in Quincy, Illinois
1830 - 1850
95.5 x 82.5 in.
IQM 1997.007.0576

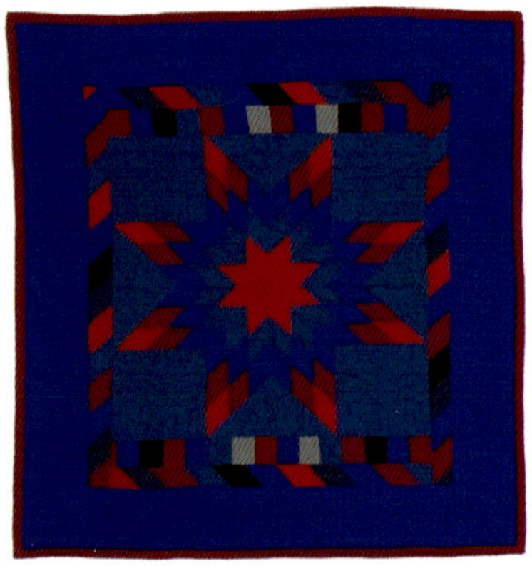

Star of Bethlehem

Maker unidentified
Possibly made in Ohio
Circa 1985
37.5 x 35 in.
IQM 1997.007.0582

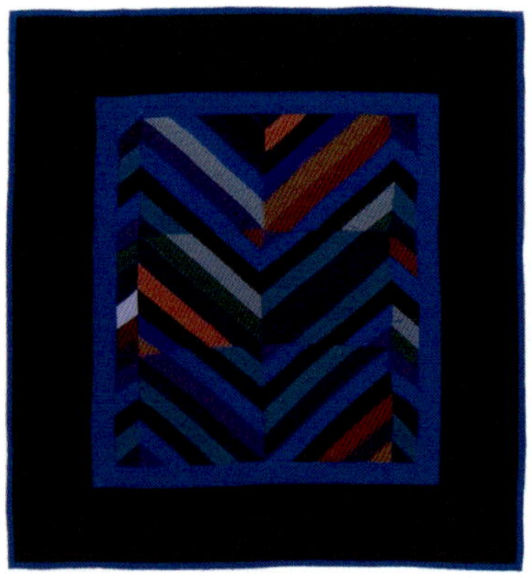

Stripes

Probably made by Miller sisters
Probably made in Holmes County, Ohio
Circa 1985
35.5 x 33 in.
IQM 1997.007.0583

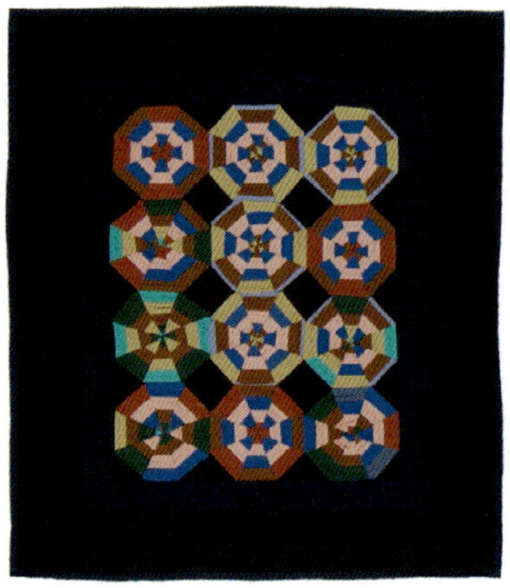

Spiderweb

Probably made by Miller sisters
Probably made in Holmes County, Ohio
Circa 1985
32 x 27.5 in.
IQM 1997.007.0584

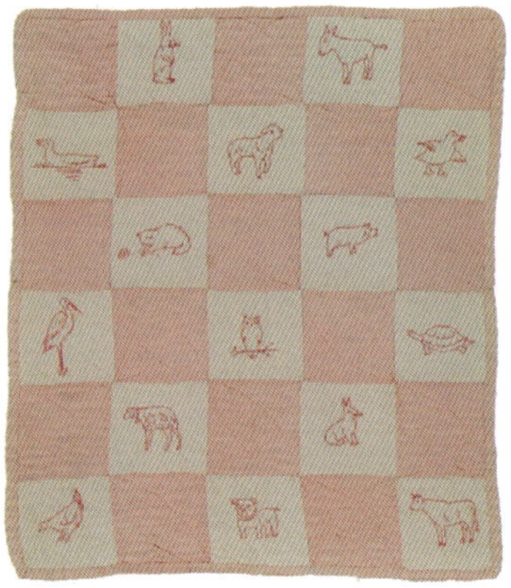

Animals

Maker unidentified
Made in United States
Circa 1930
23 x 19 in.
IQM 1997.007.0585

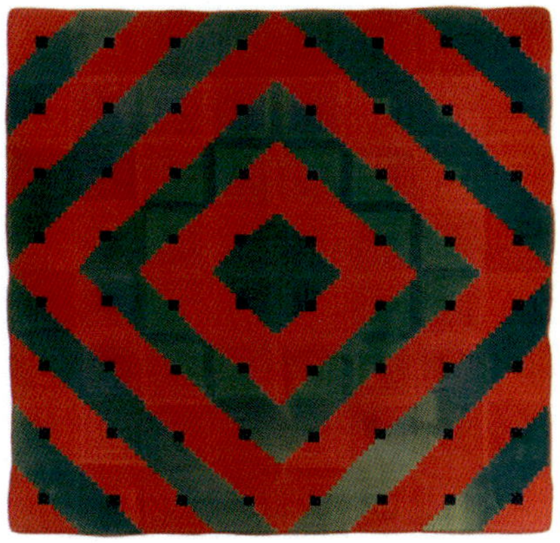

Log Cabin

Maker unidentified
Possibly made in Lancaster County, Pennsylvania
1875 - 1895
82.5 x 85 in.
IQM 1997.007.0586

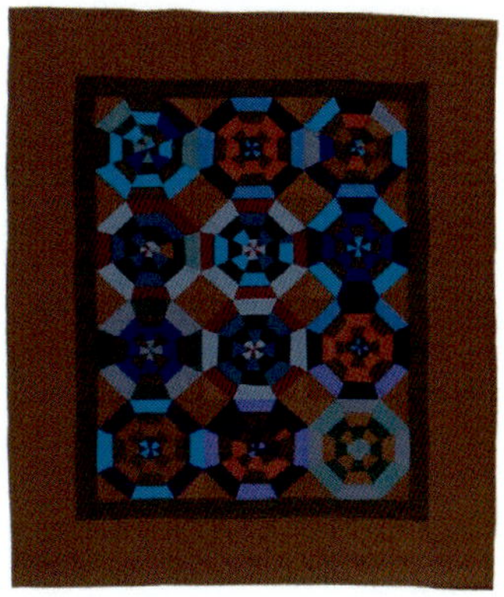

Spiderweb

Probably made by Miller sisters
Probably made in Holmes County, Ohio
Circa 1985
38.5 x 32.5 in.
IQM 1997.007.0587

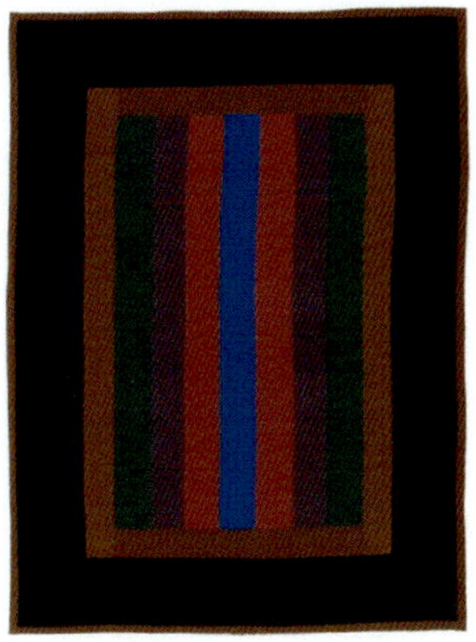

Bars

Probably made by Miller sisters
Probably made in Holmes County, Ohio
Circa 1985
38 x 28 in.
IQM 1997.007.0590

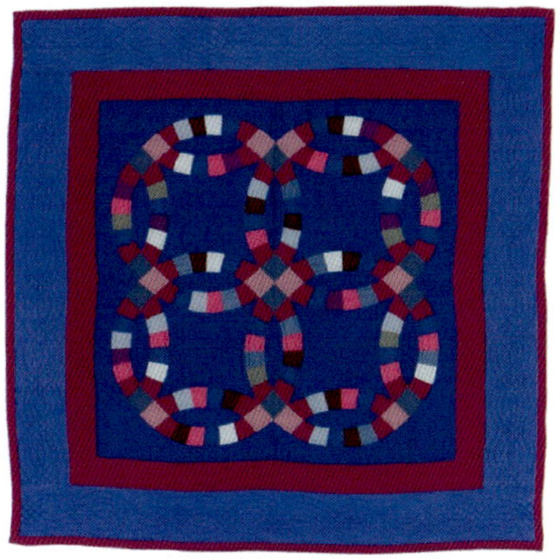

Double Wedding Ring

Maker unidentified
Possibly made in Ohio
Circa 1985
42.5 x 43.5 in.
IQM 1997.007.0591

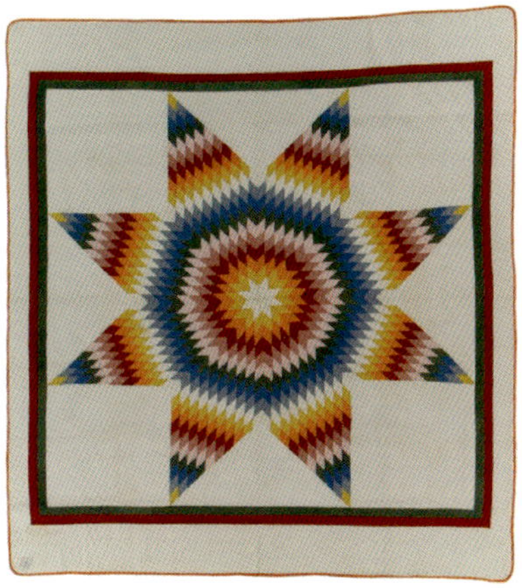

Star of Bethlehem

Maker unidentified
Possibly made in Ohio
1920 - 1940
68 x 67 in.
IQM 1997.007.0592

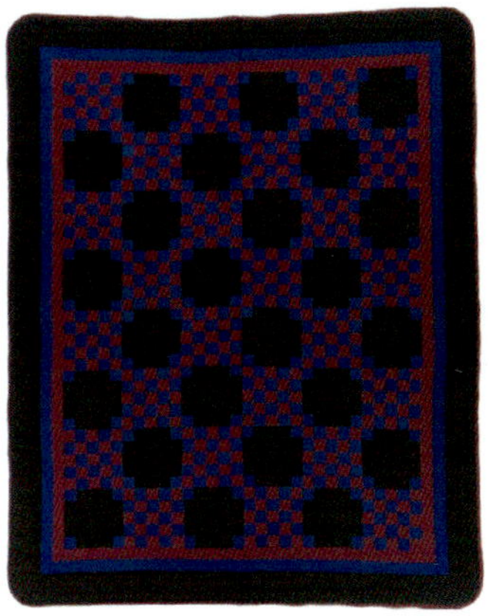

Double Irish Chain

Probably made by Hersberger family
Possibly made in Holmes County, Ohio
1900 - 1920
87 x 67 in.
IQM 1997.007.0593

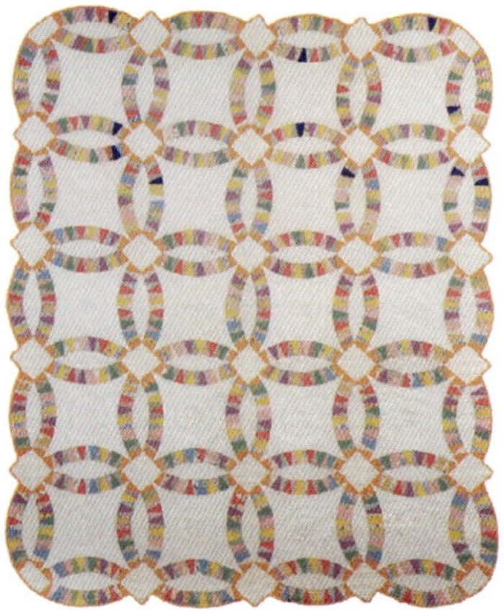

Pickle Dish

Maker unidentified
Possibly made in Cleveland, Ohio
1930 - 1940
85 x 67.5 in.

IQM 1997.007.0594

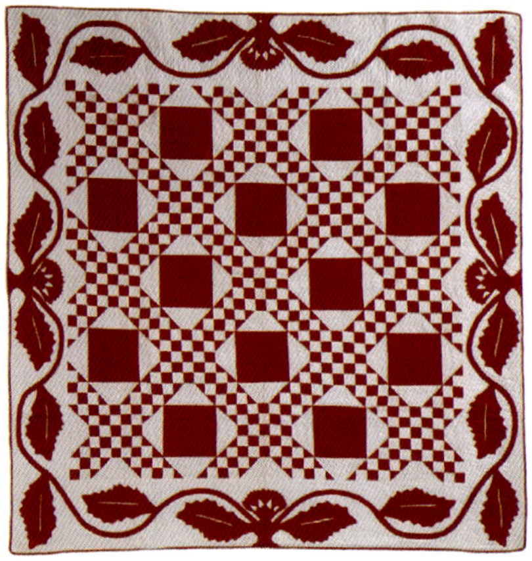

Chain & Block

Maker unidentified
Possibly made in Columbus, Ohio
1860 - 1880
76.5 x 80.5 in.

IQM 1997.007.0595

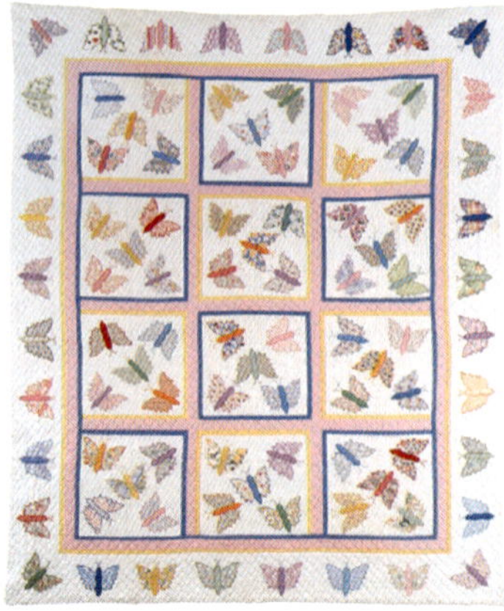

Butterfly

Maker unidentified
Possibly made in Ohio
1920 - 1940
92 x 74 in.

IQM 1997.007.0596

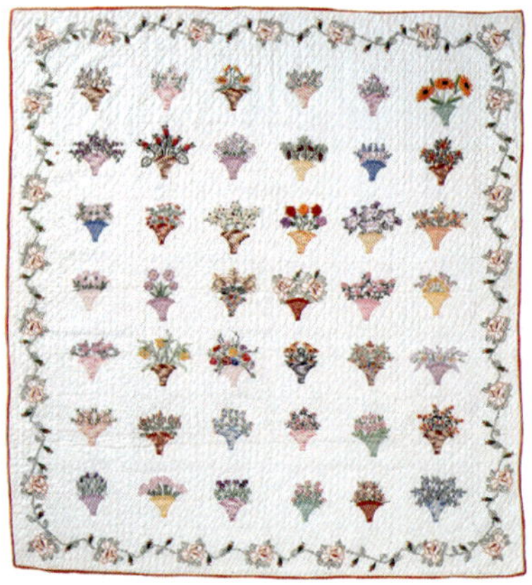

Basket of Flowers

Maker unidentified
Probably made in Zanesville, Ohio
1920 - 1940
86 x 78 in.

IQM 1997.007.0597

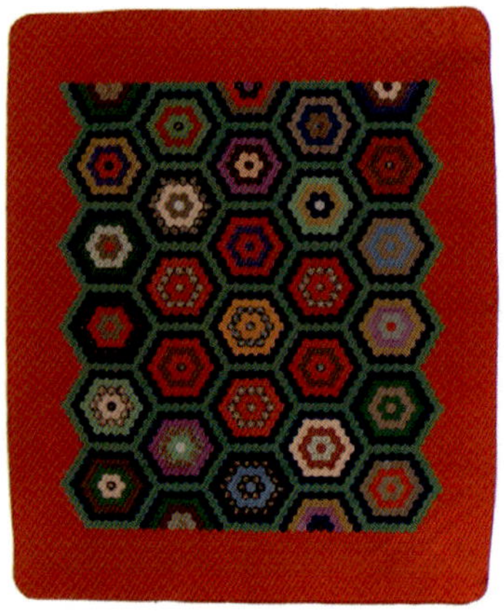

Hexagon

Maker unidentified
Possibly made in Kentucky
1860 - 1880
80.5 x 66 in.

IQM 1997.007.0598

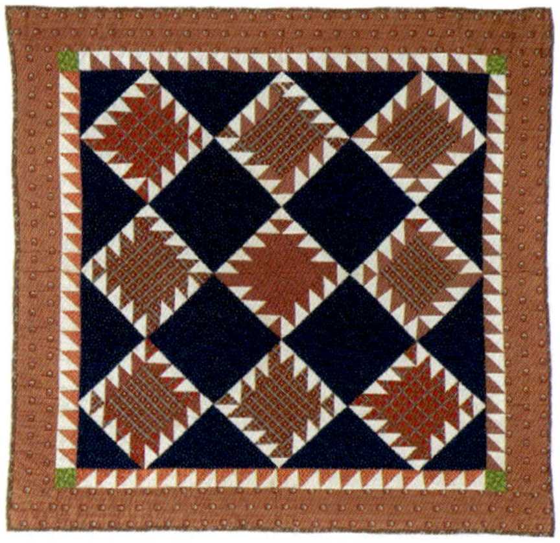

Delectable Mountains variation

Maker unidentified
Probably made in Pennsylvania
1850 - 1870
47 x 46 in.

IQM 1997.007.0599

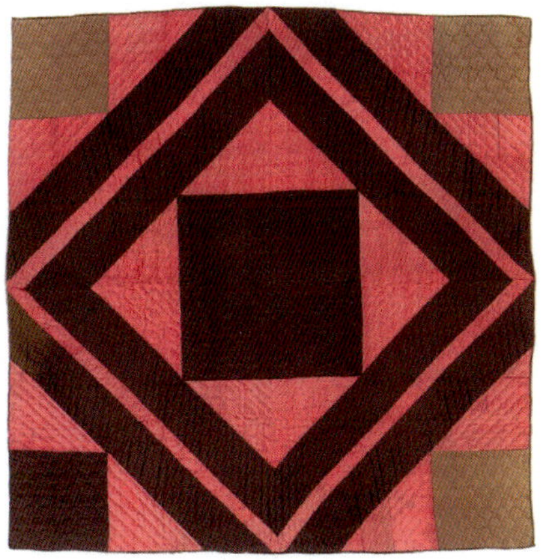

Center Diamond

Maker unidentified
Possibly made in New York
1820 - 1860
76 x 76 in.

IQM 1997.007.0601

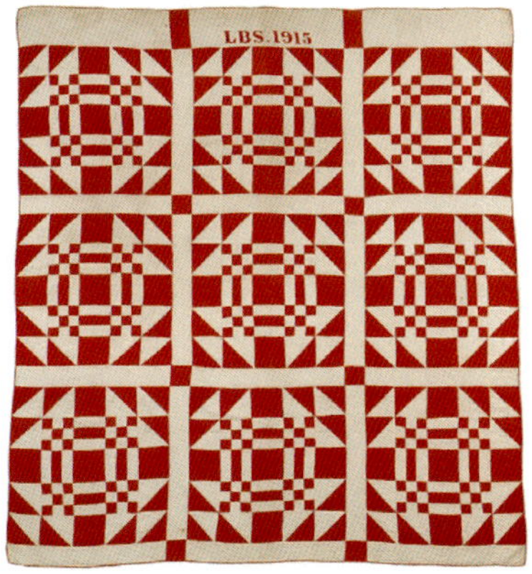

Goose in the Pond

Maker unidentified
Possibly made in Amsterdam, New York
Dated 1915
78.5 x 71 in.

IQM 1997.007.0602

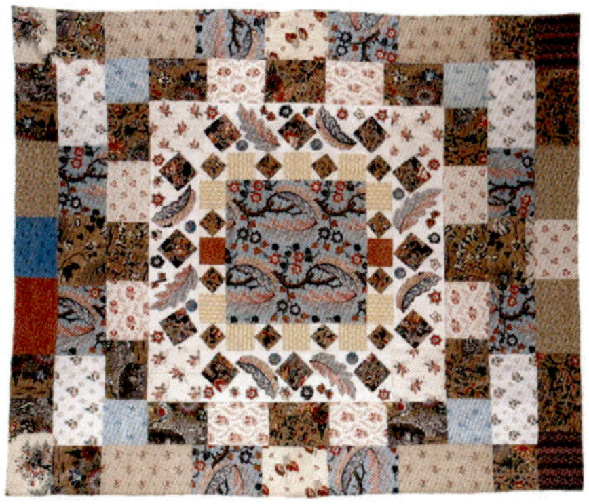

Medallion

Maker unidentified
Possibly made in United Kingdom
1800 - 1840
96.5 x 83 in.

IQM 1997.007.0604

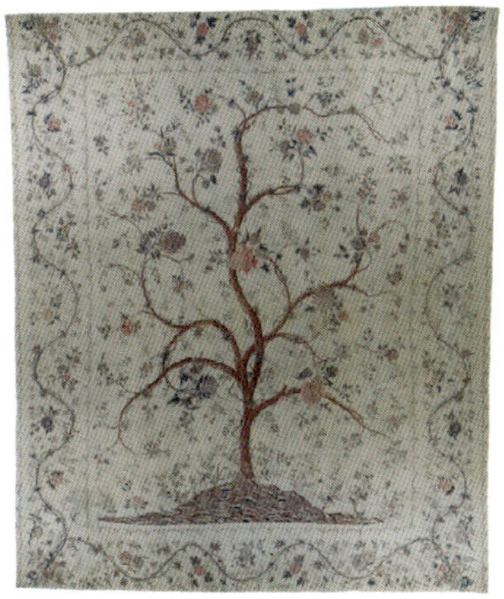

Palampore

Maker unidentified
Possibly made in France
1875 - 1900
128.5 x 107.5 in.

IQM 1997.007.0606

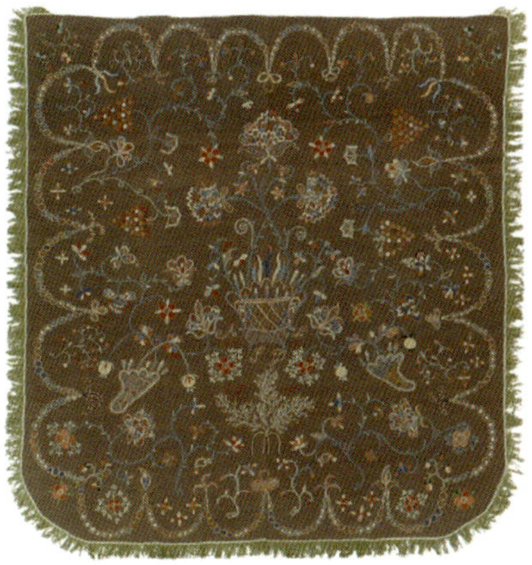

Medallion

Maker unidentified
Possibly made in New Hampshire
Dated 1816
87.5 x 79 in.

IQM 1997.007.0607

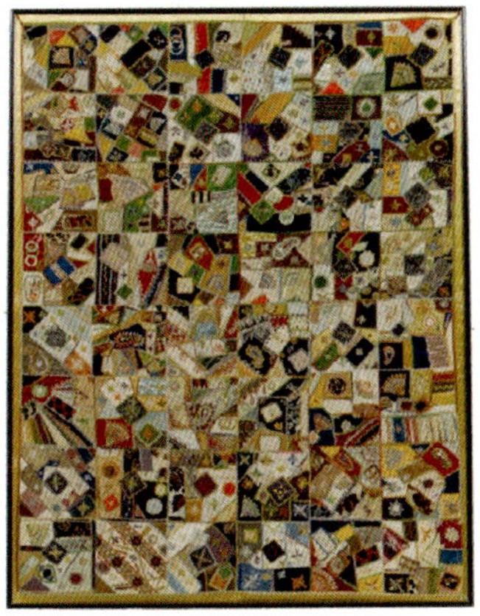

Crazy

Maker unidentified
Made in United States
1880 - 1900
55 x 41.5 in.

IQM 1997.007.0608

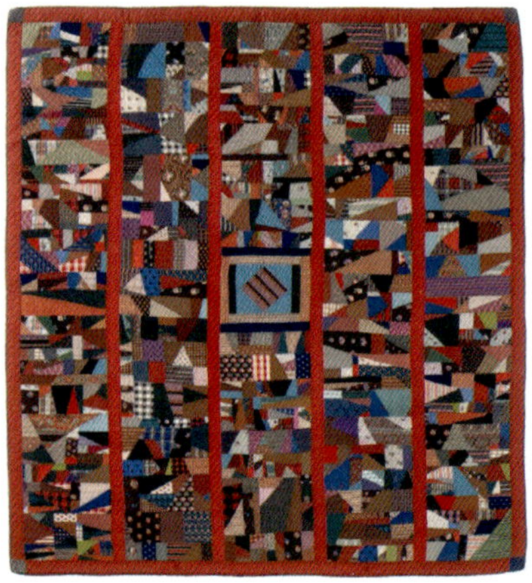

Crazy

Maker unidentified
Probably made in Pennsylvania
1870 - 1890
82 x 73 in.

IQM 1997.007.0610

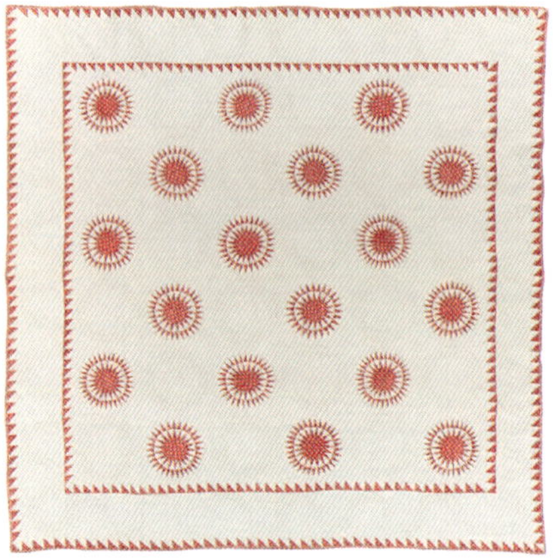

Rising Sun

Maker unidentified
Made in United States
1840 - 1860
90 x 87 in.

IQM 1997.007.0611

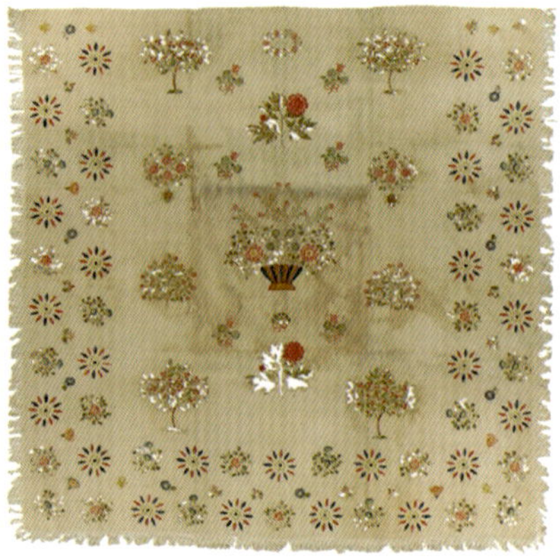

Stenciled Coverlet

Maker unidentified
Possibly made in New England
1820 - 1840
94 x 92 in.

IQM 1997.007.0612

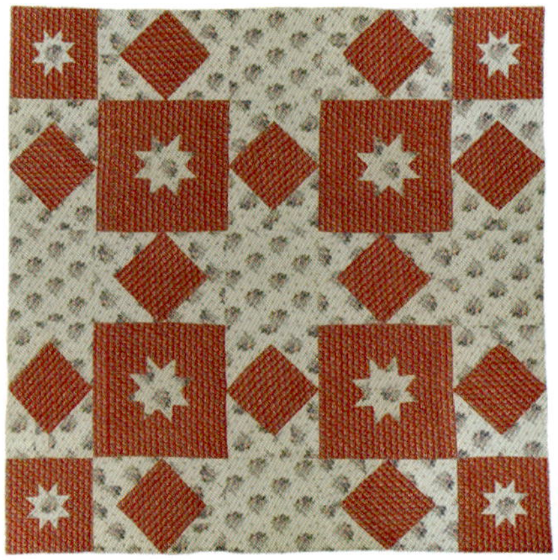

Star variation

Maker unidentified
Possibly made in eastern Pennsylvania
1830 - 1850
100.5 x 100.5 in.

IQM 1997.007.0613

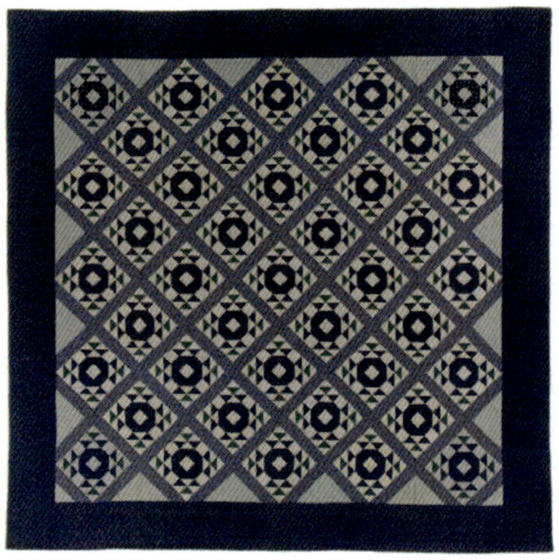

Crown of Thorns

Maker unidentified
Possibly made in eastern Pennsylvania
1890 - 1910
85 x 86 in.

IQM 1997.007.0614

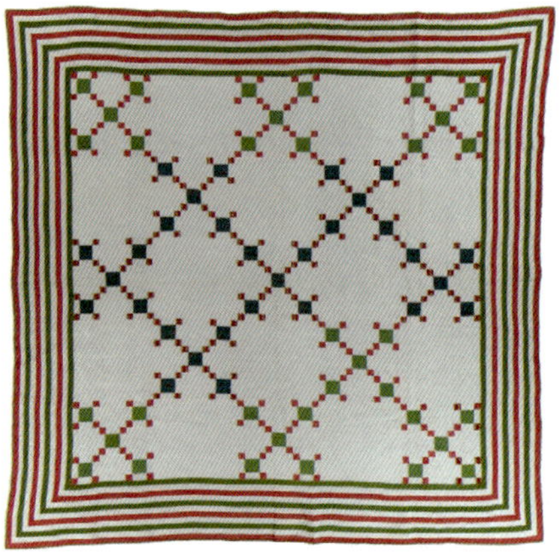

Double Nine Patch

Maker unidentified
Possibly made in Ohio
1850 - 1870
82.5 x 81.5 in.

IQM 1997.007.0615

Whole Cloth

Maker unidentified
Made in United States
1810 - 1840
100 x 92.5 in.

IQM 1997.007.0617

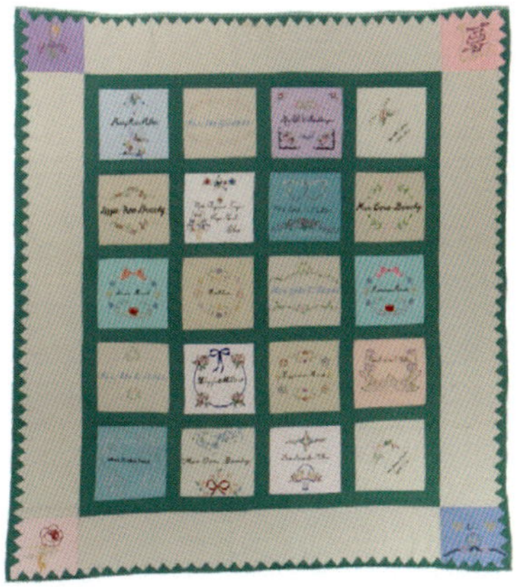

Album

Maker unidentified
Probably made in Sugar Creek, Ohio
Dated 1943
87.5 x 76 in.

IQM 1997.007.0618

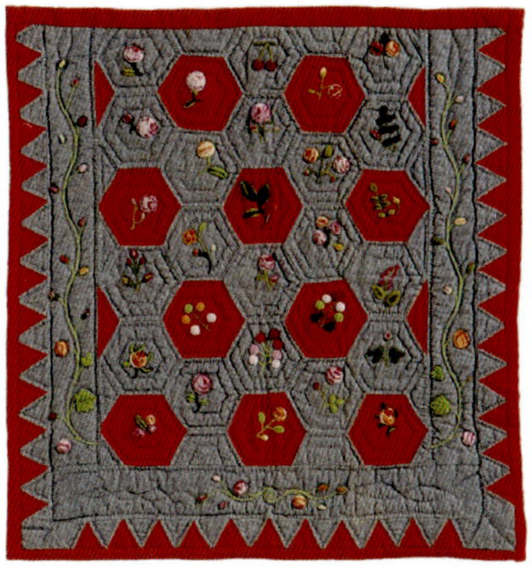

Hexagon

Maker unidentified
Probably made in Pennsylvania
Circa 1890
36.5 x 34.5 in.

IQM 1997.007.0619

Whole Cloth

Maker unidentified
Possibly made in Provence, France
Dated 1815
100.5 x 91 in.

IQM 1997.007.0620

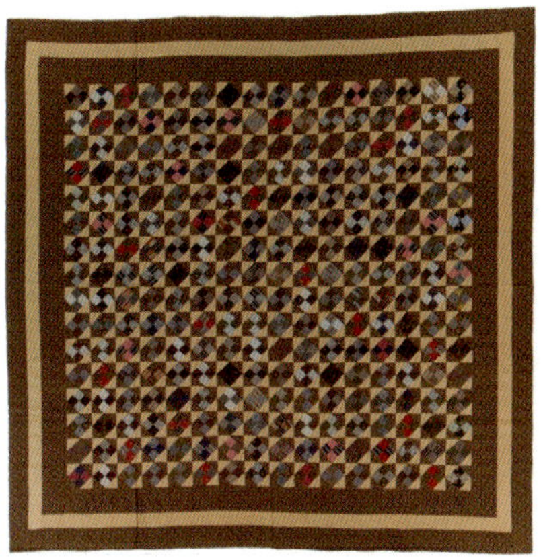

Four Patch variation

Maker unidentified
Possibly made in Lancaster County, Pennsylvania
1870 - 1890
83 x 80.5 in.

IQM 1997.007.0622

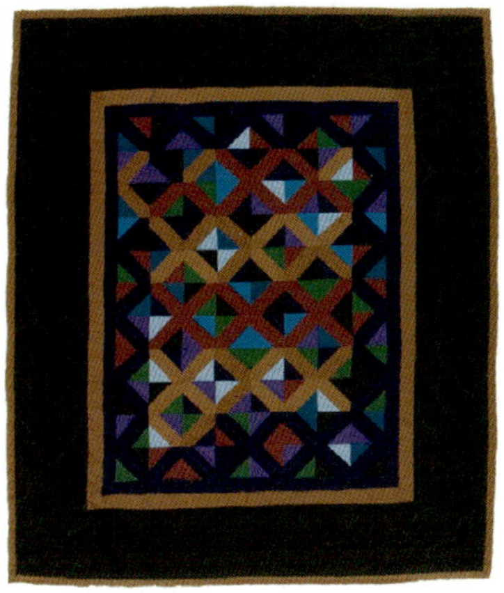

Four Patch

Probably made by Miller sisters
Probably made in Holmes County, Ohio
Circa 1991
36.5 x 31.5 in.

IQM 1997.007.0624

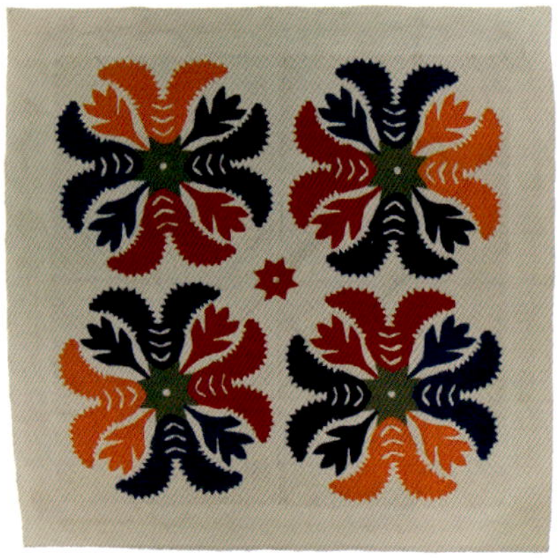

Jester's Plume

Maker unidentified
Possibly made in Lancaster County, Pennsylvania
1890 - 1910
89 x 88.5 in.
IQM 1997.007.0625

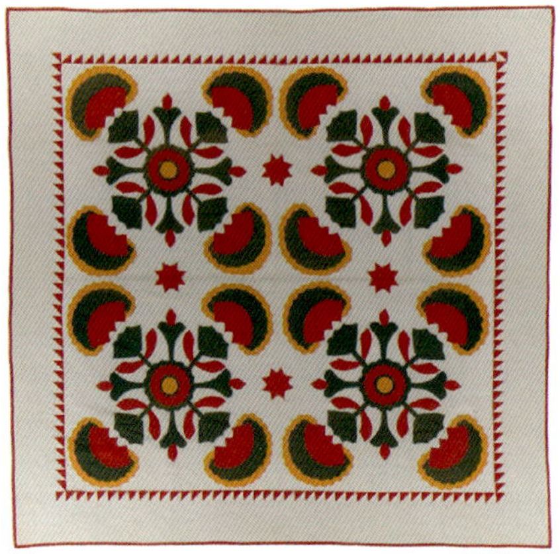

Coxcomb

Maker unidentified
Possibly made in Ohio
1860 - 1880
86.5 x 86.5 in.
IQM 1997.007.0626

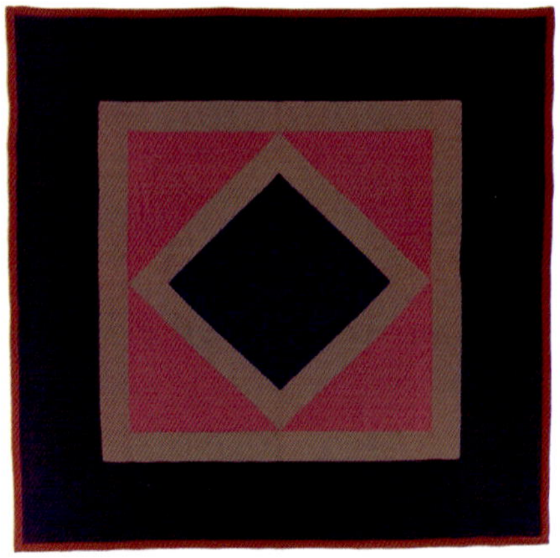

Center Diamond

Maker unidentified
Probably made in Lancaster County, Pennsylvania
1925 - 1945
81.5 x 80.5 in.
IQM 1997.007.0627

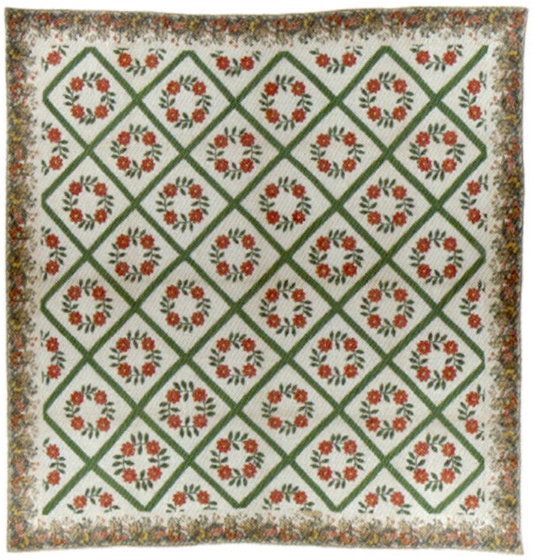

President's Wreath

Maker unidentified
Possibly made in New Jersey
1840 - 1860
114 x 110 in.
IQM 1997.007.0628

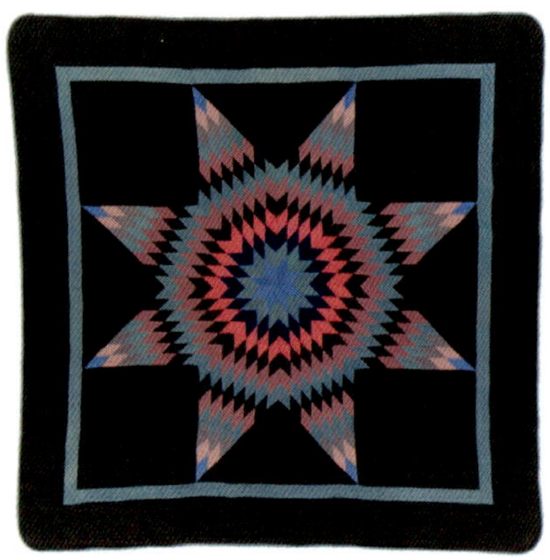

Star of Bethlehem

Probably made by Susan Hochstetler
Probably made in LaGrange County, Indiana
Dated 1934
82 x 81.5 in.
IQM 1997.007.0630

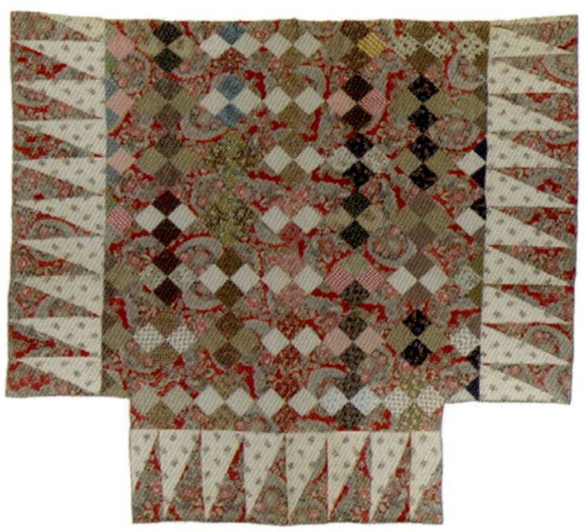

Four Patch

Maker unidentified
Possibly made in New England
1850 - 1860
96 x 108 in.
IQM 1997.007.0632

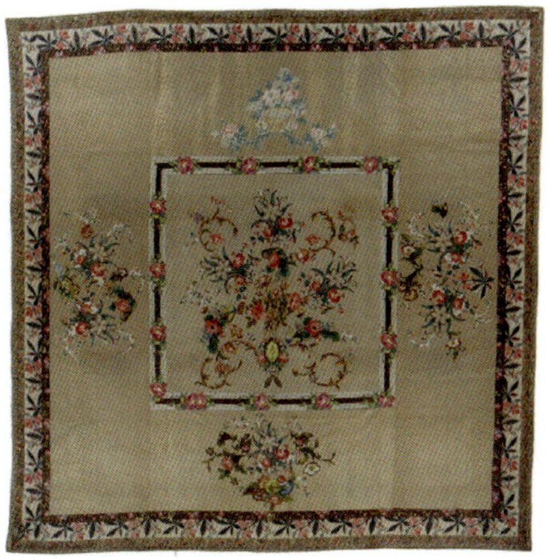

Medallion

Maker unidentified
Possibly made in New Jersey
1830 - 1850
109 x 106 in.

IQM 1997.007.0633

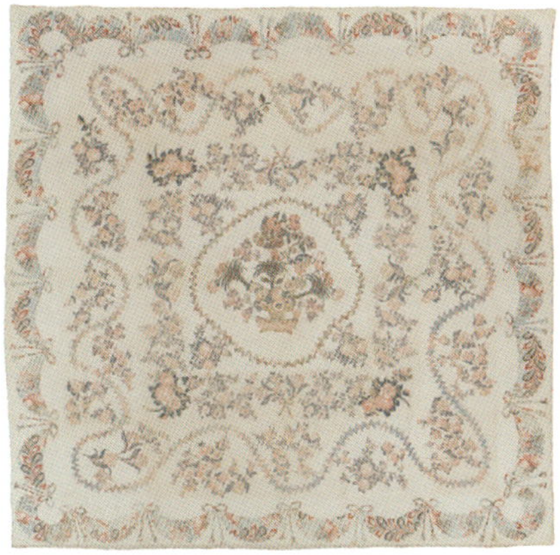

Medallion

Maker unidentified
Possibly made in Maryland
1810 - 1830
112 x 112 in.

IQM 1997.007.0634

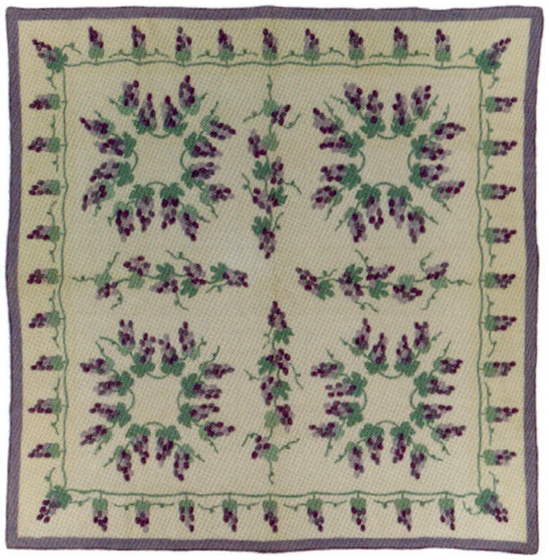

Grapes & Vines

Probably made by Josephine Justus
Probably made in Trenton, Missouri
Circa 1914
85 x 85 in.

IQM 1997.007.0635

Whole Cloth

Maker unidentified
Made in United States
1780 - 1800
78 x 74 in.

IQM 1997.007.0636

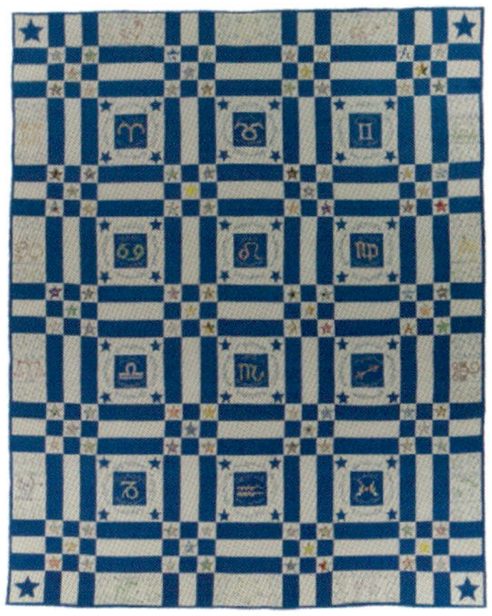

Old Almanac

Maker unidentified
Possibly made in Pittsburgh, Pennsylvania
Circa 1933
103.5 x 82 in.

IQM 1997.007.0637

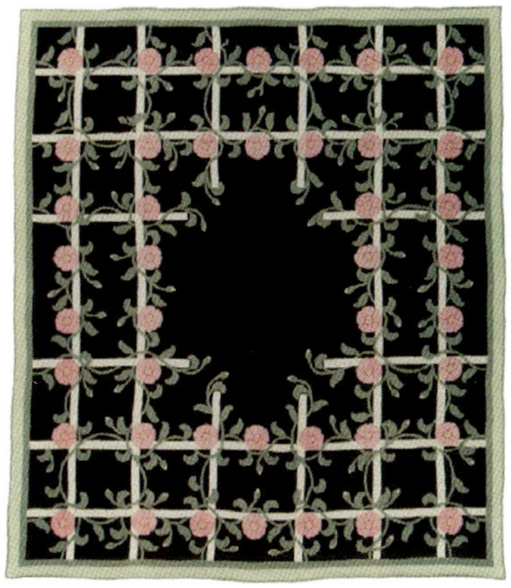

Rose Bower

Probably made by Rose Modjeska
Probably made in Downer's Grove, Illinois
Circa 1935
85 x 72 in.

IQM 1997.007.0638

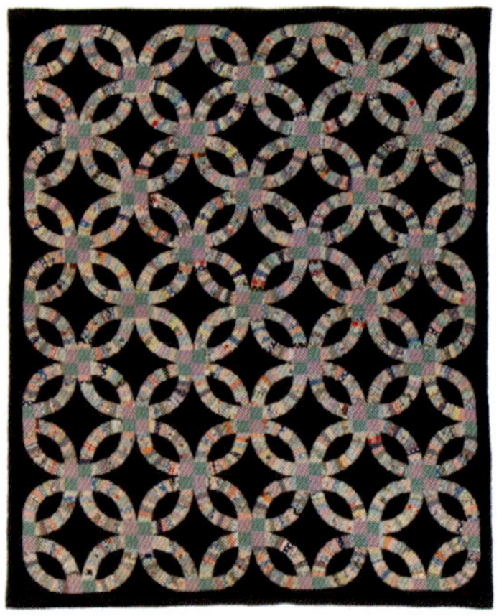

Double Wedding Ring

Maker unidentified
Possibly made in Missouri
1930 - 1940
83 x 65.5 in.

IQM 1997.007.0639

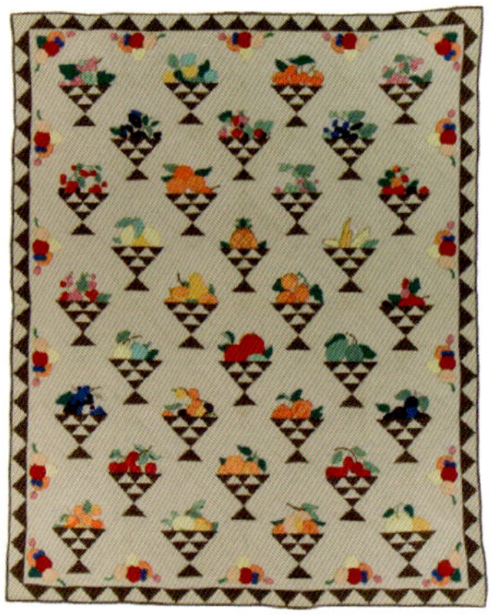

Fruit Basket

Maker unidentified
Possibly made in Pennsylvania
Dated 1921
86.25 x 68.5 in.

IQM 1997.007.0640

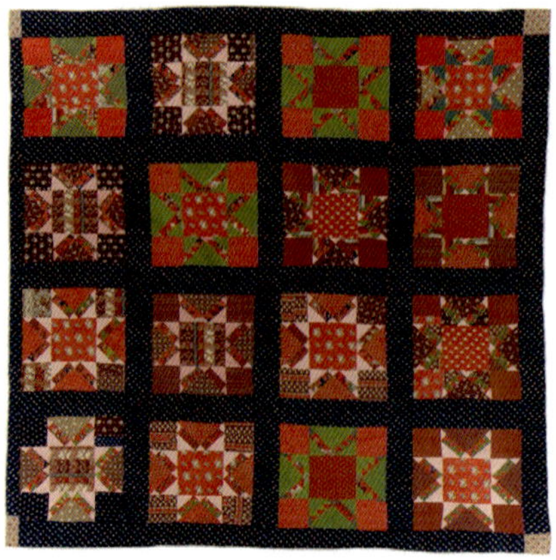

Feathered Star

Maker unidentified
Possibly made in Pennsylvania
1860 - 1880
87.5 x 85 in.

IQM 1997.007.0641

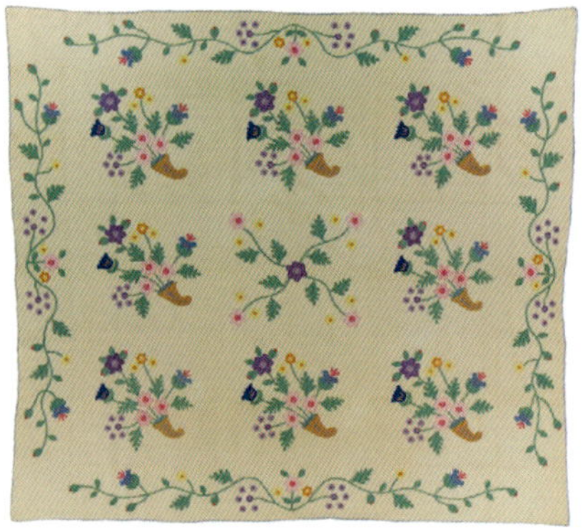

Horn of Plenty

Probably made by Josephine Justus
Probably made in Trenton, Missouri
1920 - 1935
91 x 81.5 in.

IQM 1997.007.0642

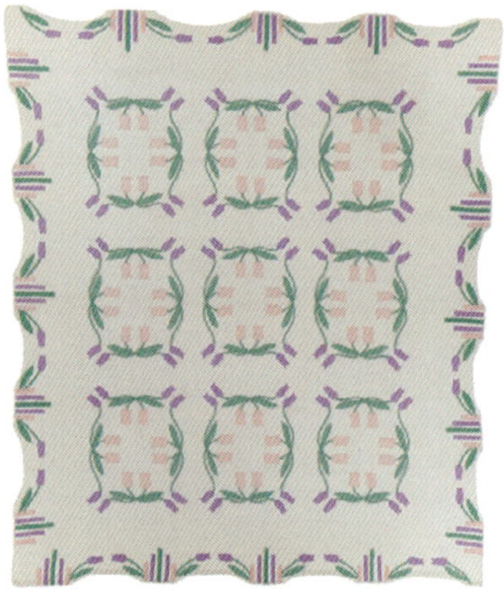

May Tulips

Maker unidentified
Possibly made in Ohio
Circa 1925
91 x 76 in.

IQM 1997.007.0643

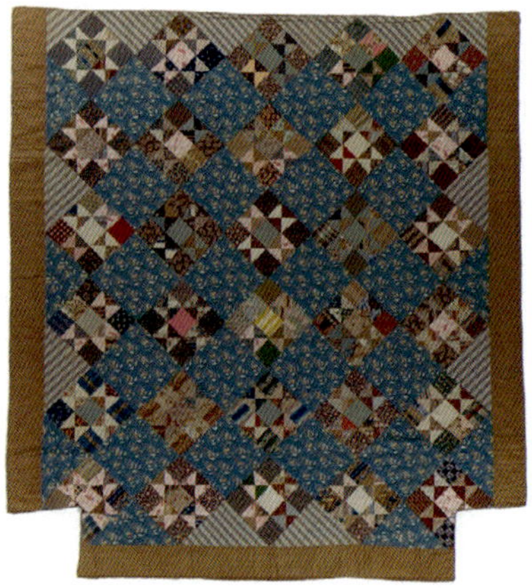

Variable Star

Maker unidentified
Possibly made in New England
1830 - 1850
86 x 76 in.

IQM 1997.007.0644

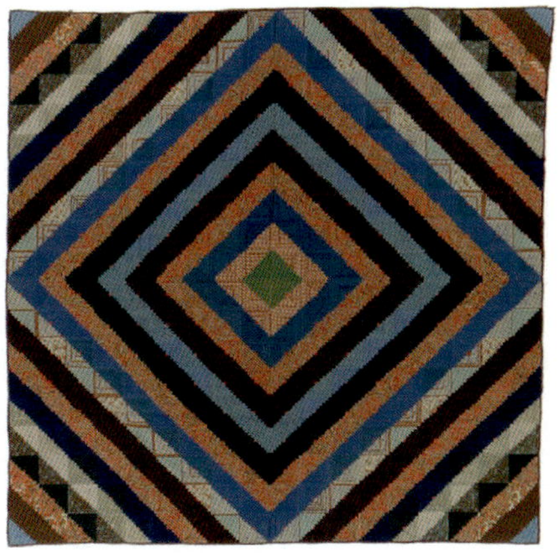

Log Cabin

Maker unidentified
Possibly made in Lancaster County, Pennsylvania
Circa 1879
82 x 81.5 in.

IQM 1997.007.0645

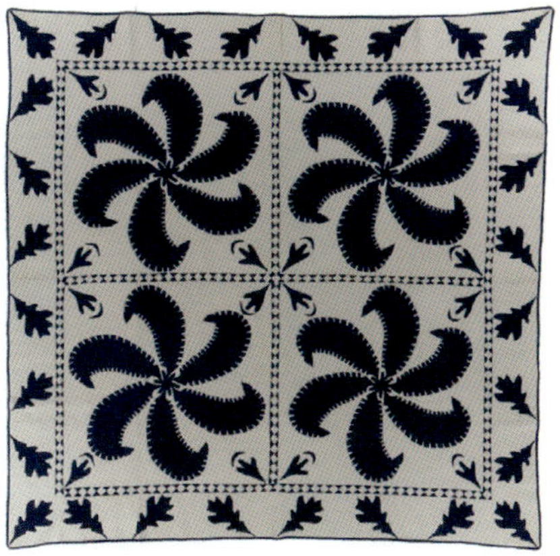

Princess Feather

Maker unidentified
Possibly made in Anneville, Pennsylvania
1860 - 1880
85.75 x 84.5 in.

IQM 1997.007.0646

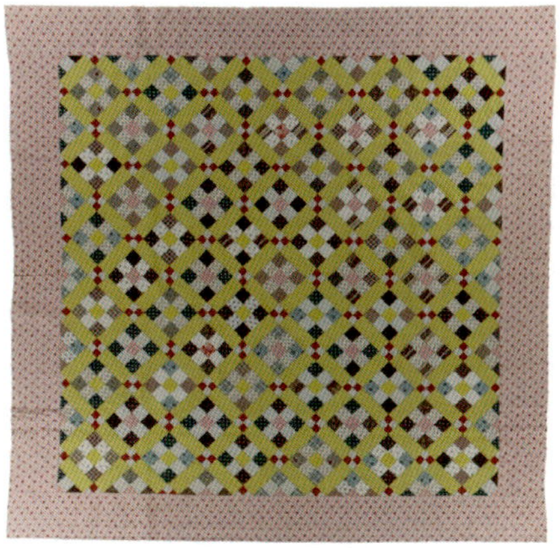

Nine Patch

Anna B. Eshleman
Probably made in Lancaster County, Pennsylvania
1860 - 1870
92 x 90 in.

IQM 1997.007.0647

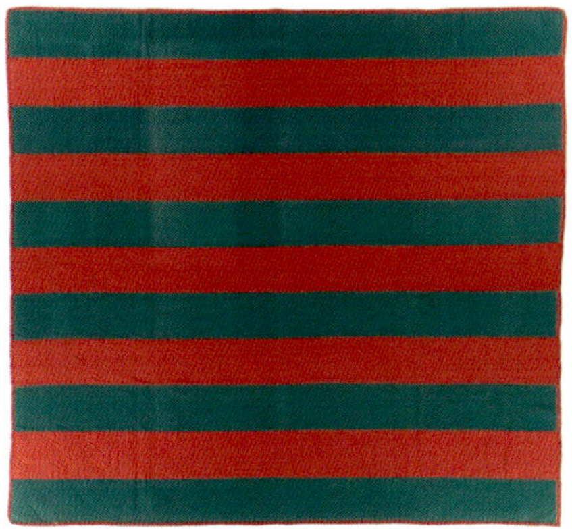

Bars

Maker unidentified
Possibly made in Berks County, Pennsylvania
1875 - 1895
88.5 x 84 in.

IQM 1997.007.0648

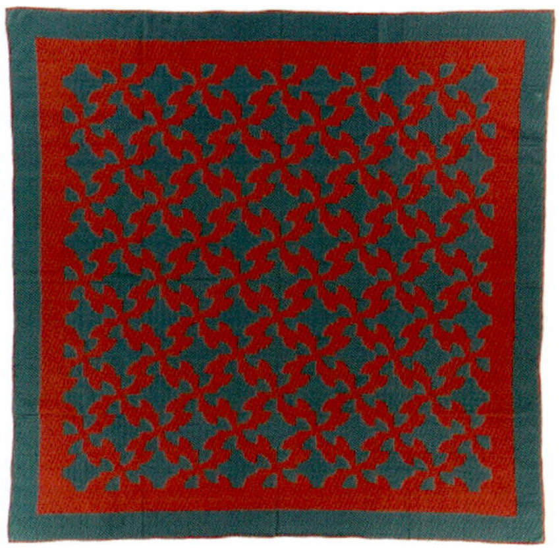

Drunkard's Path

Possibly made by Hosler family
Possibly made in Pennsylvania
1875 - 1895
81.5 x 81 in.

IQM 1997.007.0649

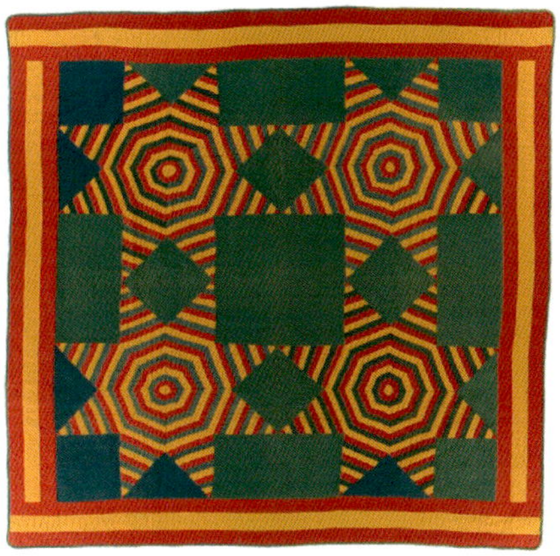

String Star

Maker unidentified
Possibly made in Pennsylvania
Circa 1885
82 x 82 in.

IQM 1997.007.0650

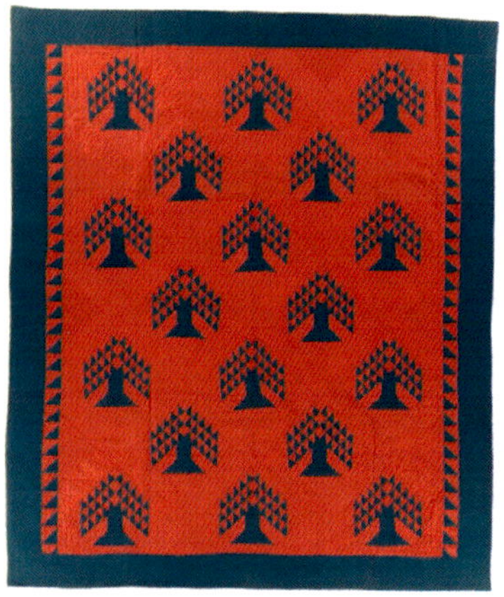

Pine Tree

Maker unidentified
Possibly made in Lititz, Pennsylvania
1875 - 1895
89 x 75 in.

IQM 1997.007.0651

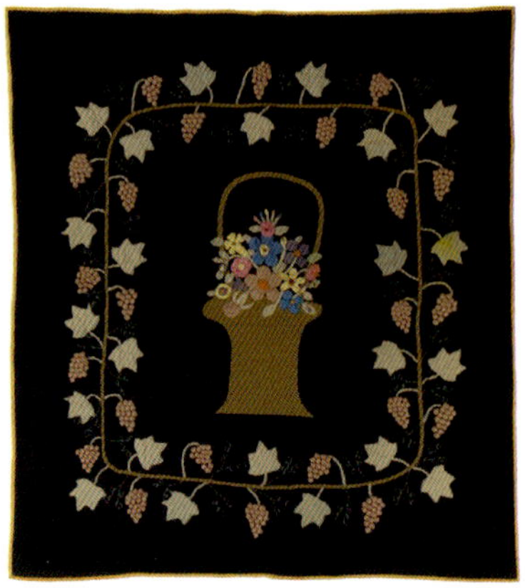

Basket of Flowers

Maker unidentified
Possibly made in Berks County, Pennsylvania
1920 - 1940
77.5 x 69 in.

IQM 1997.007.0652

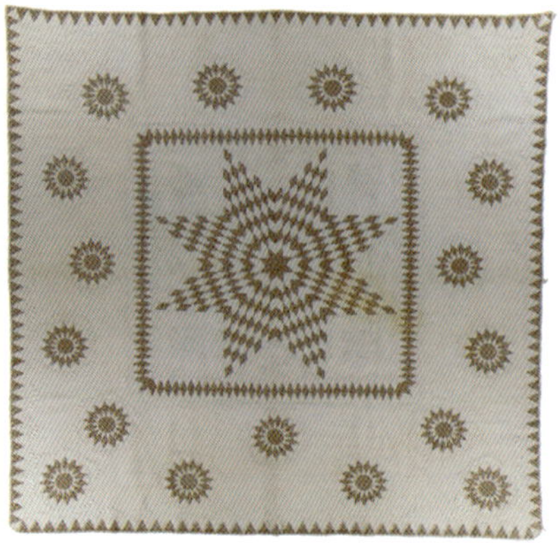

Star of Bethlehem

Maker unidentified
Probably made in Connecticut
1830 - 1850
95 x 93 in.

IQM 1997.007.0653

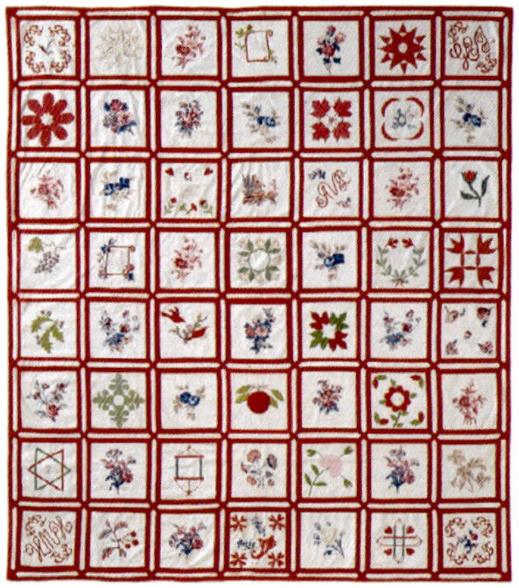

Album

Maker unidentified
Probably made in New York
Dated 1849 - 1854
95.5 x 84 in.

IQM 1997.007.0654

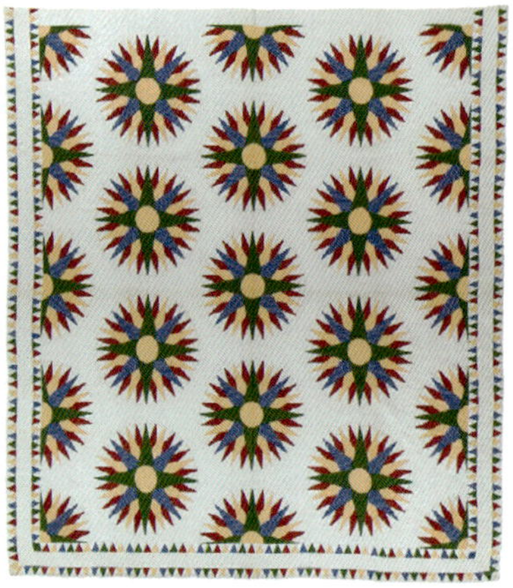

Mariner's Compass

Maker unidentified
Made in United States
1840 - 1860
93.5 x 82 in.

IQM 1997.007.0655

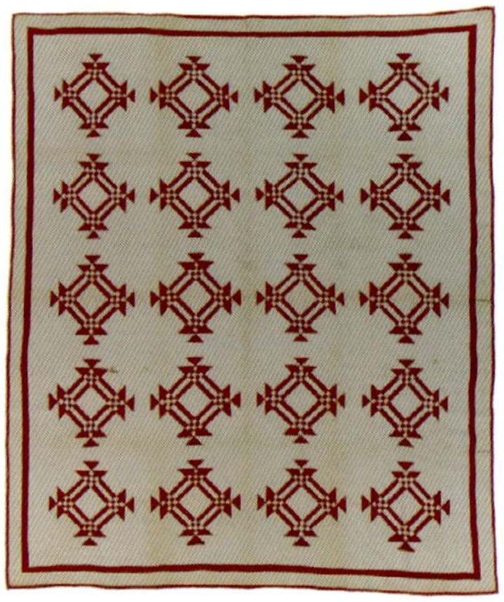

Goose in the Pond

Maker unidentified
Possibly made in Ohio
1900 - 1920
89.5 x 74.5 in.

IQM 1997.007.0656

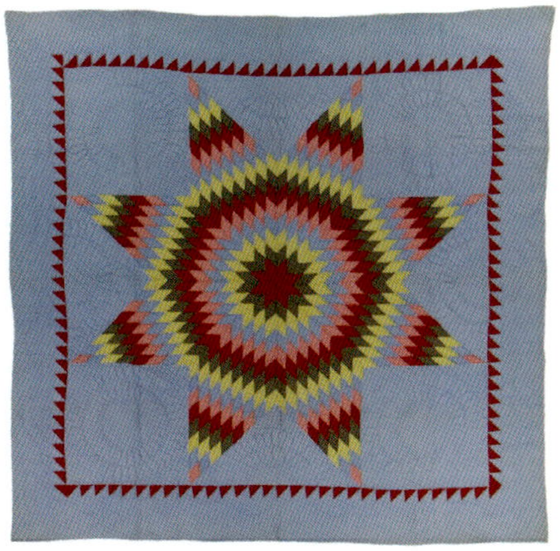

Star of Bethlehem

Maker unidentified
Made in United States
1890 - 1910
80 x 78.5 in.

IQM 1997.007.0657

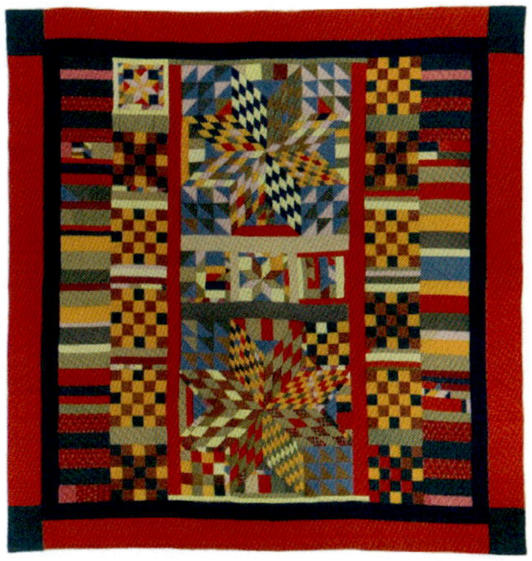

Crazy Stars

Amy Bucher
Made in Lebanon County, Pennsylvania
1890 - 1910
84 x 80.5 in.

IQM 1997.007.0658

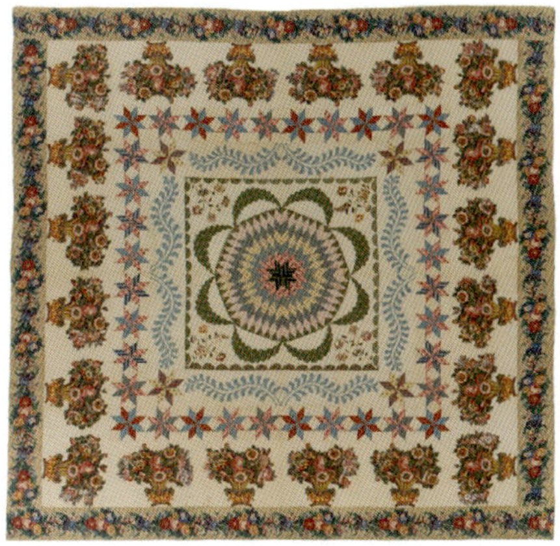

Medallion

Maker unidentified
Probably made in United States
1830 - 1850
108.5 x 107.5 in.

IQM 1997.007.0659

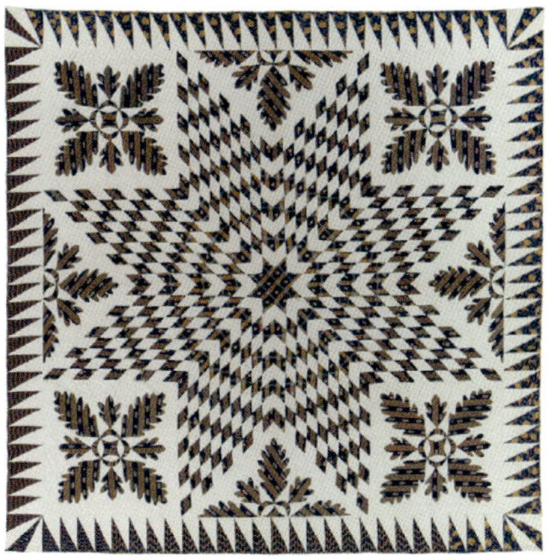

Star of Bethlehem

Maker unidentified
Possibly made in Pennsylvania
1840 - 1860
93.5 x 93.5 in.

IQM 1997.007.0660

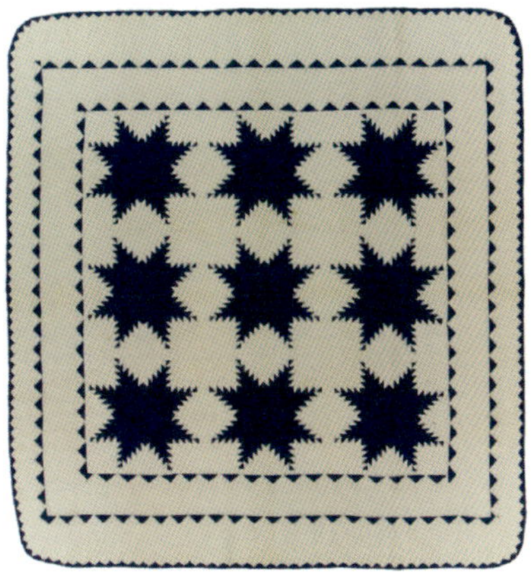

Feathered Star

Possibly made by Matilda B. Houk
Possibly made in New England
1900 - 1920
80.5 x 74 in.

IQM 1997.007.0661

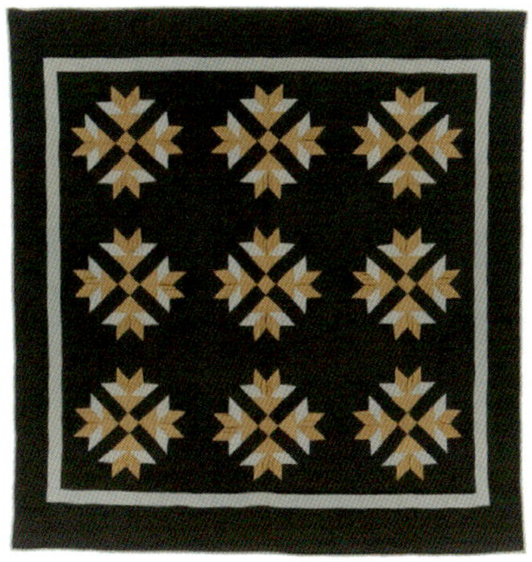

Goose Tracks

Maker unidentified
Possibly made in western Pennsylvania
1875 - 1895
75.25 x 71 in.

IQM 1997.007.0662

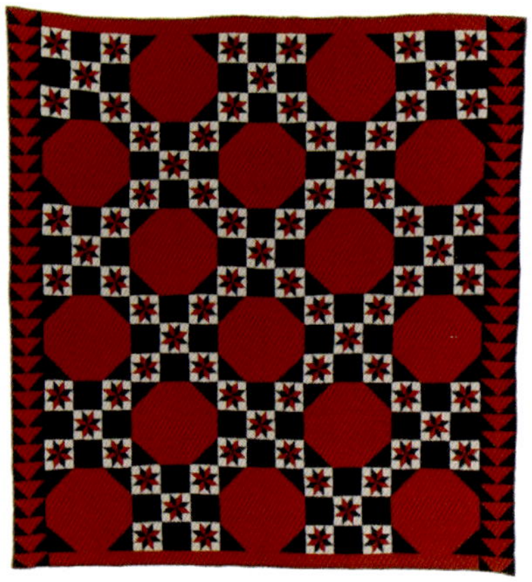

LeMoyne Star

Maker unidentified
Possibly made in Ohio
1900 - 1920
78 x 71 in.

IQM 1997.007.0663

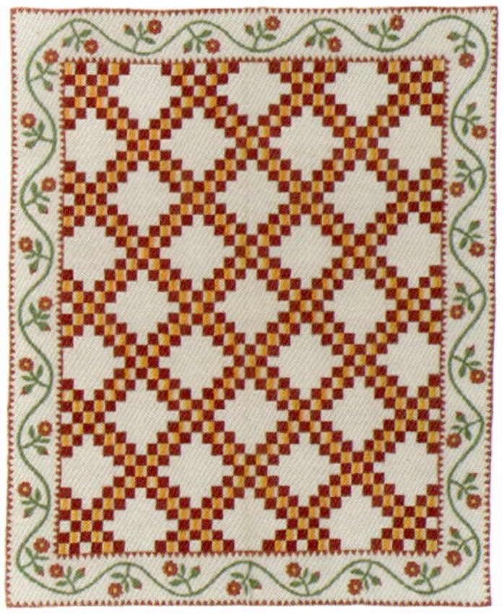

Double Irish Chain

Rhoda E. Smith Nutt
Made in Benton, New York
Dated 1853
102 x 82 in.

IQM 1997.007.0665.1

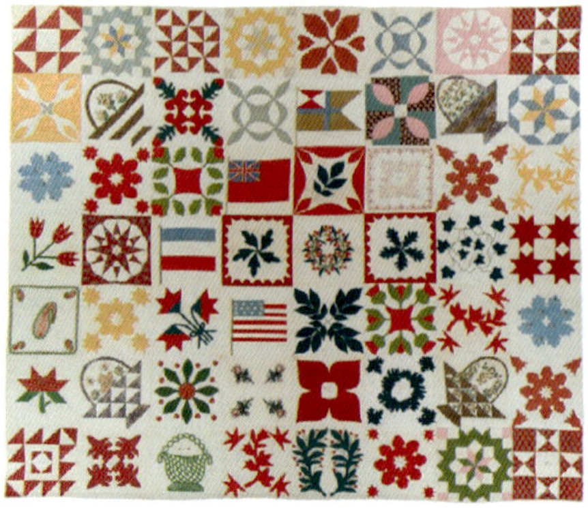

Album

Maker unidentified
Made in New Jersey or Pennsylvania
Dated 1851 - 1852
96 x 109 in.

IQM 1997.007.0666

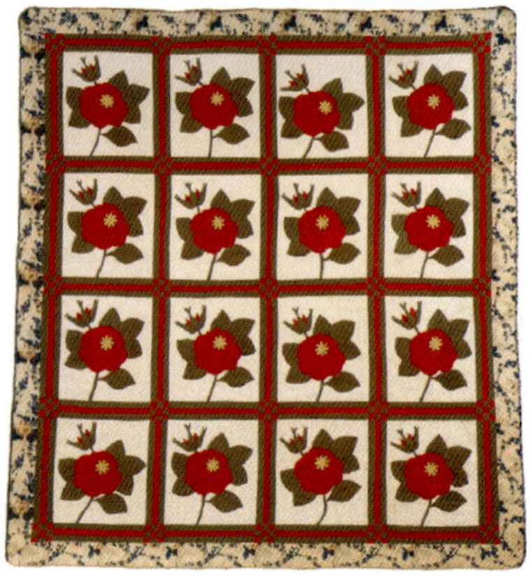

Rose

Maker unidentified
Possibly made in Pennsylvania
1890 - 1910
96 x 86.5 in.

IQM 1997.007.0667

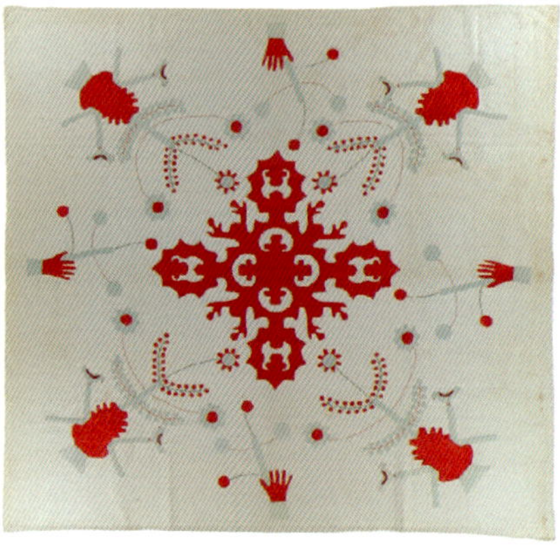

Appliqué

Maker unidentified
Made in United States
1880 - 1900
78 x 75 in.

IQM 1997.007.0668

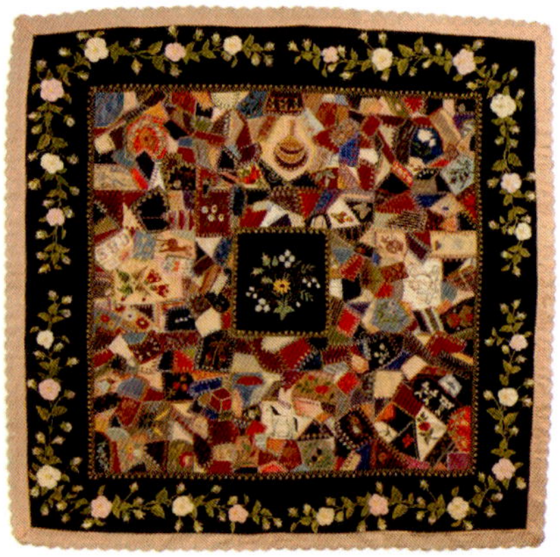

Crazy

Maker unidentified
Possibly made in Ohio
1880 - 1890
66 x 62.5 in.

IQM 1997.007.0670

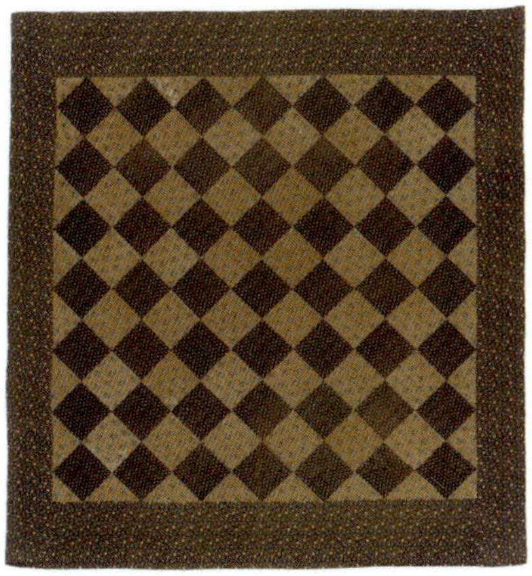

Squares

Maker unidentified
Made in United States
1810 - 1830
97.5 x 89 in.

IQM 1997.007.0671

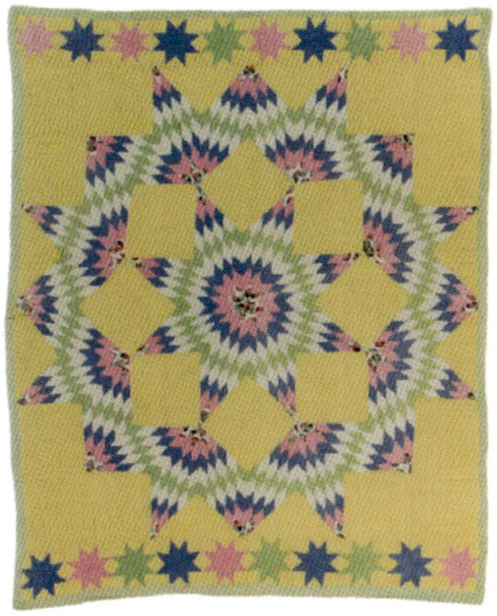

Broken Star

Maker unidentified
Possibly made in Arkansas
1930 - 1950
69.5 x 54.5 in.

IQM 1997.007.0672

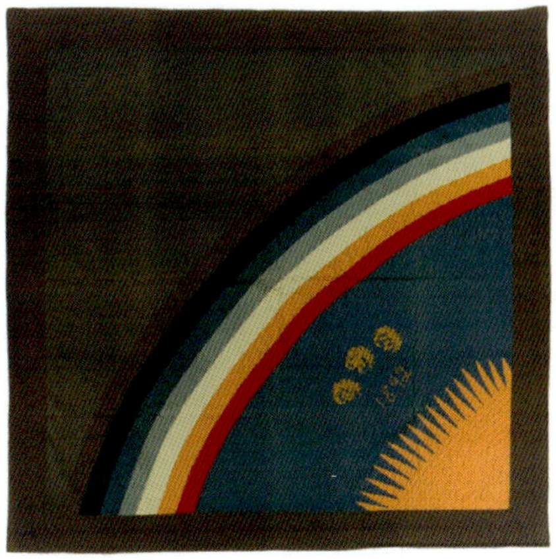

Rainbow Quilt

S.F. Schenck Habecker
Probably made in Pennsylvania
Dated 1892
78.5 x 79.5 in.

IQM 1997.007.0673

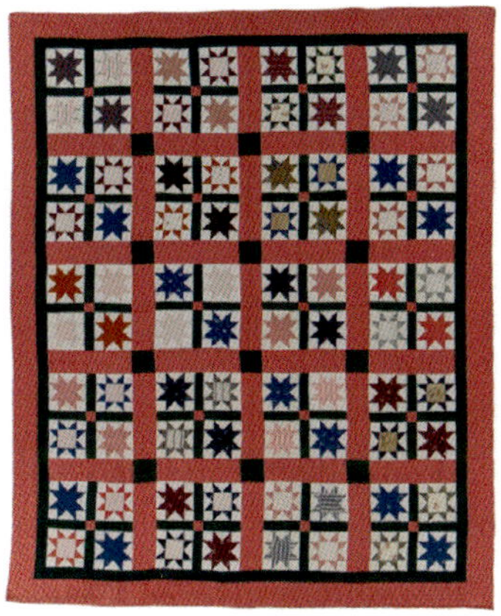

Sawtooth Star

Maker unidentified
Possibly made in Ohio
1890 - 1910
81 x 63.5 in.

IQM 1997.007.0674

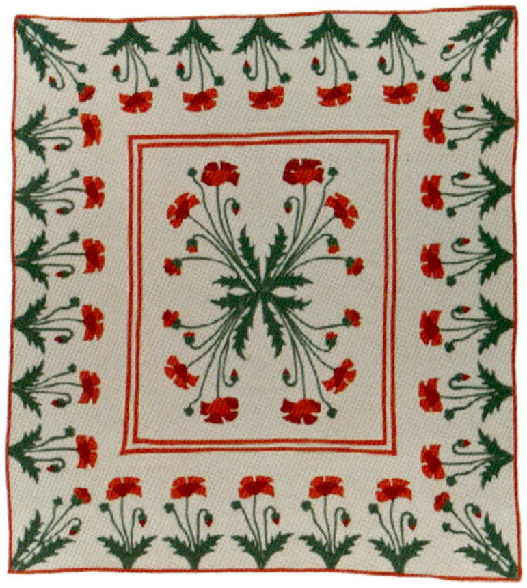

Poppy

Maker unidentified
Possibly made in Indiana
1930 - 1940
89.5 x 80.5 in.

IQM 1997.007.0675

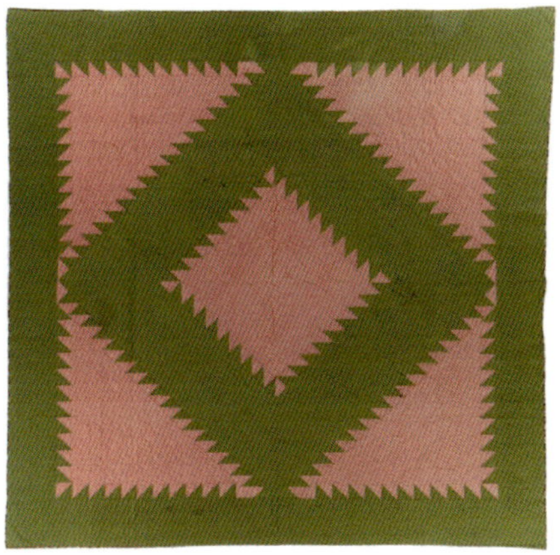

Center Diamond

Maker unidentified
Possibly made in Pennsylvania
1860 - 1880
85.25 x 84.25 in.

IQM 1997.007.0676

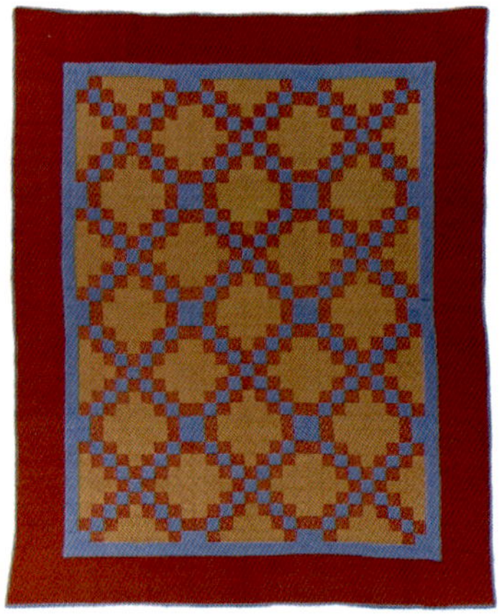

Double Irish Chain variation

Maker unidentified
Possibly made in Pennsylvania
1880 - 1900
91.5 x 72.5 in.

IQM 1997.007.0677

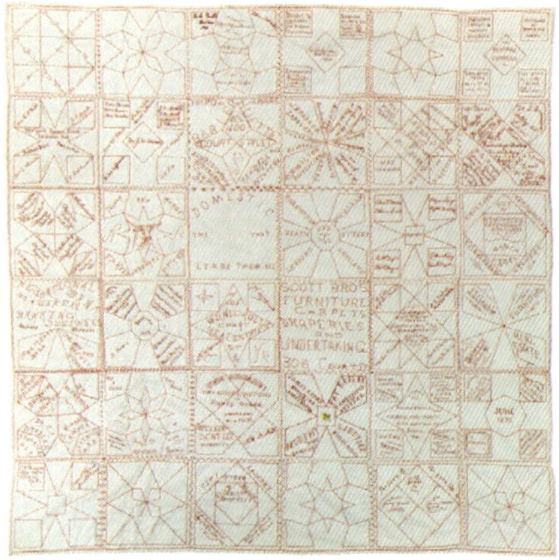

Original

Maker unidentified
Made in Beatrice, Nebraska
Dated 1890
69 x 69 in.

IQM 1997.007.0678

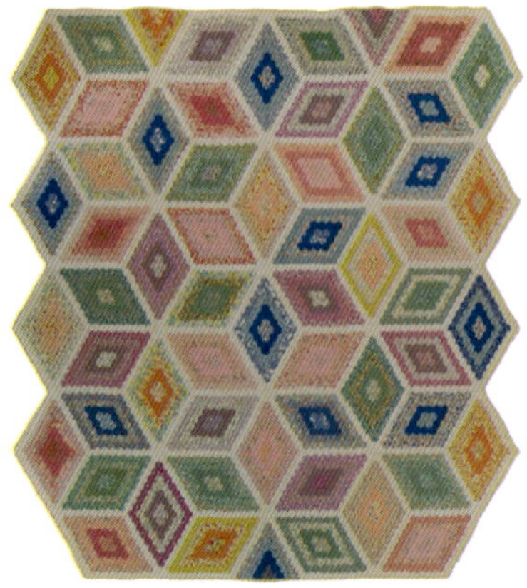

Diamond Flower Garden

Maker unidentified
Made in United States
1930 - 1940
87 x 77 in.

IQM 1997.007.0679

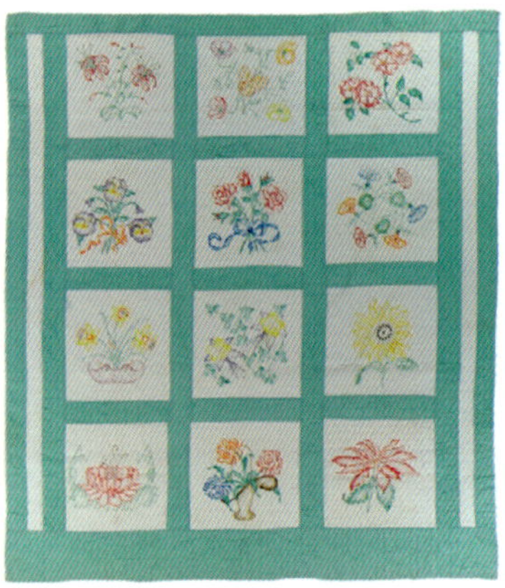

Album

Maker unidentified
Possibly made in Iowa
1935 - 1945
83 x 70.5 in.

IQM 1997.007.0680

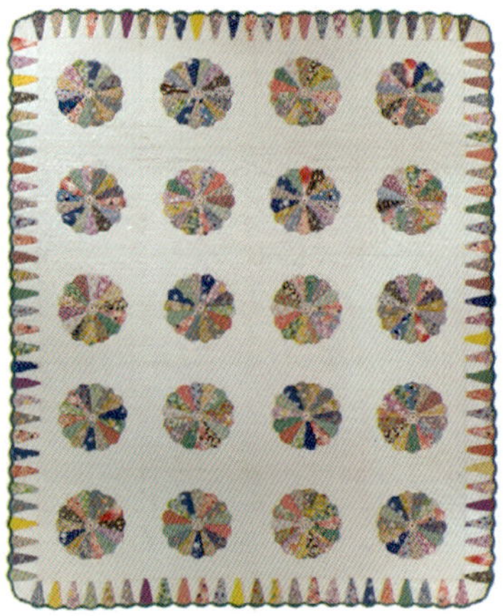

Dresden Plate

Probably made by Louise Thonstad
Probably made in Deadwood, South Dakota
1930 - 1940
97 x 76.5 in.

IQM 1997.007.0681

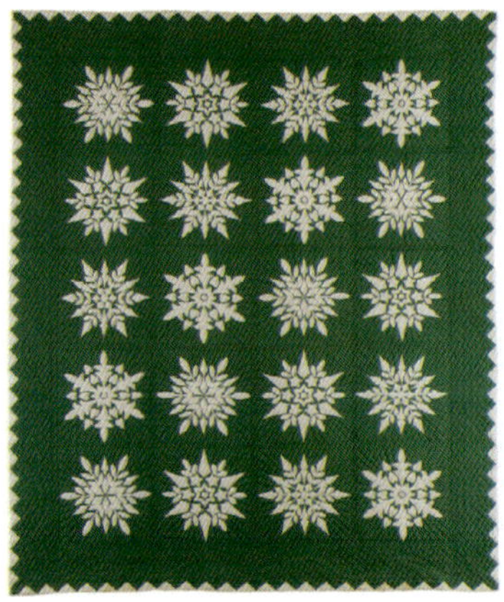

Snowflake

Maker unidentified
Made in United States
Circa 1963
92 x 76.5 in.

IQM 1997.007.0682

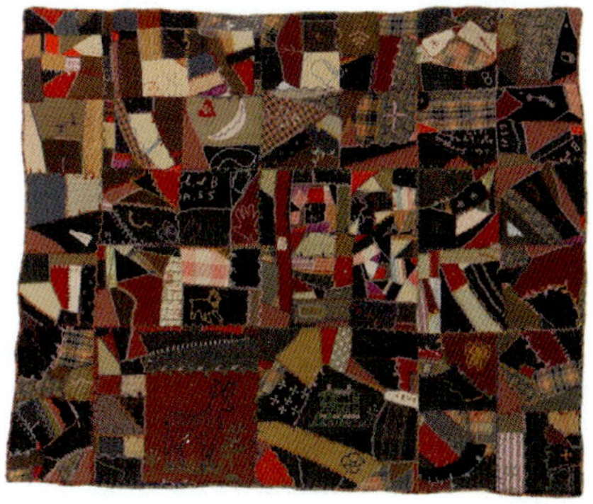

Crazy

Maker unidentified
Possibly made in Michigan
Dated 1897
86 x 64 in.

IQM 1997.007.0683

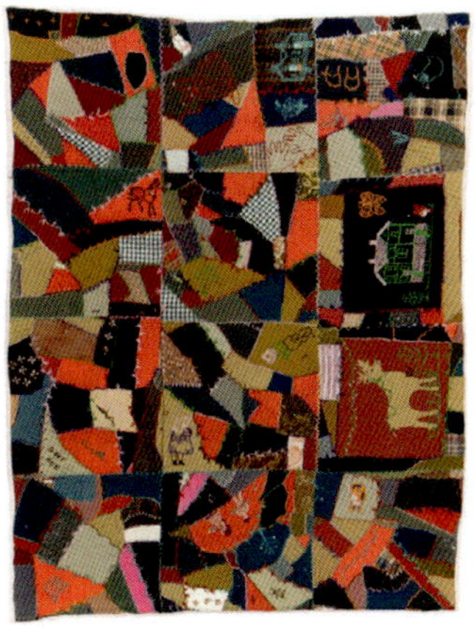

Crazy

Maker unidentified
Possibly made in Michigan
Dated 1897
80 x 69.75 in.

IQM 1997.007.0684

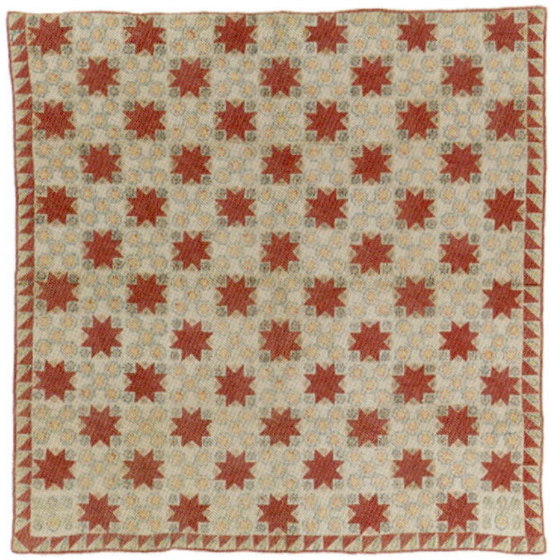

Eight Pointed Star

Maker unidentified
Possibly made in Pennsylvania
1850 - 1870
81 x 78 in.

IQM 1997.007.0685

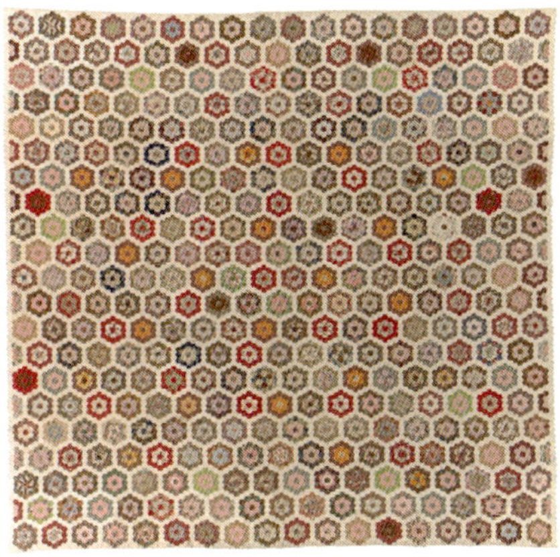

Hexagon

Maker unidentified
Possibly made in Baltimore, Maryland
1830 - 1850
100 x 99.5 in.

IQM 1997.007.0687

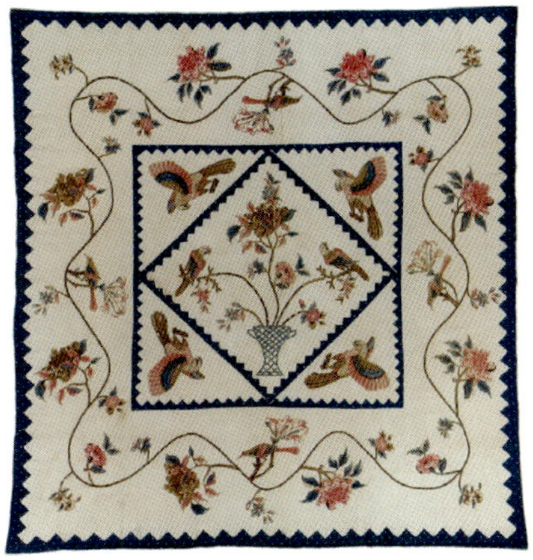

Medallion

Maker unidentified
Possibly made in Baltimore, Maryland
1800 - 1820
100.5 x 93 in.

IQM 1997.007.0688

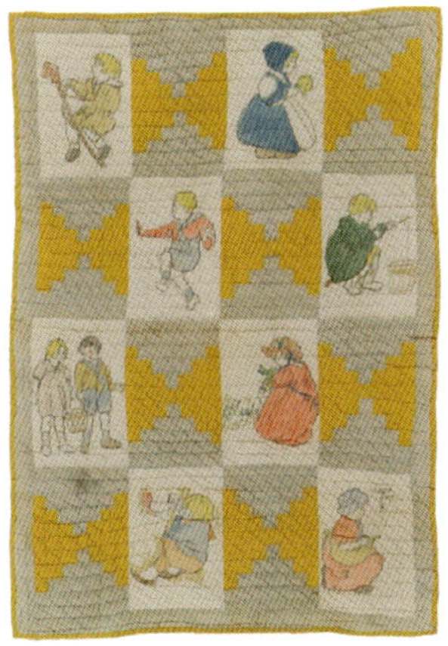

Log Cabin

Maker unidentified
Possibly made in Northville, Michigan
1900 - 1920
52 x 34 in.

IQM 1997.007.0689

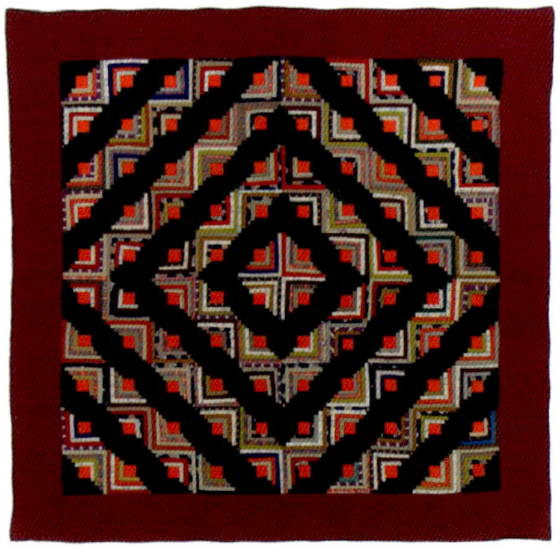

Log Cabin

Maker unidentified
Possibly made in Lebanon, Pennsylvania
Circa 1885
83.5 x 84.5 in.
IQM 1997.007.0690

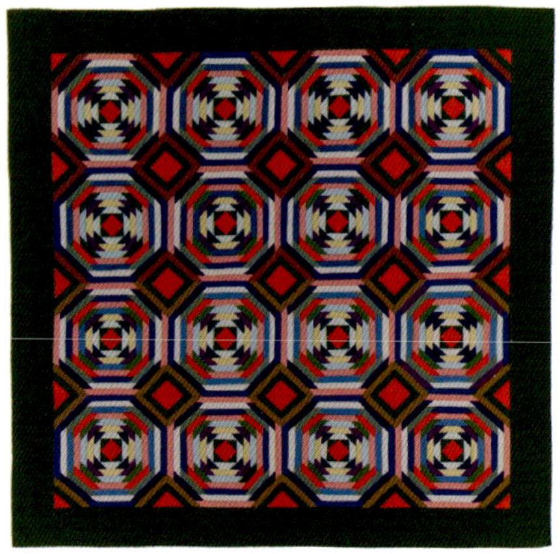

Log Cabin

Maker unidentified
Possibly made in Lancaster County, Pennsylvania
1880 - 1900
82 x 82 in.
IQM 1997.007.0691

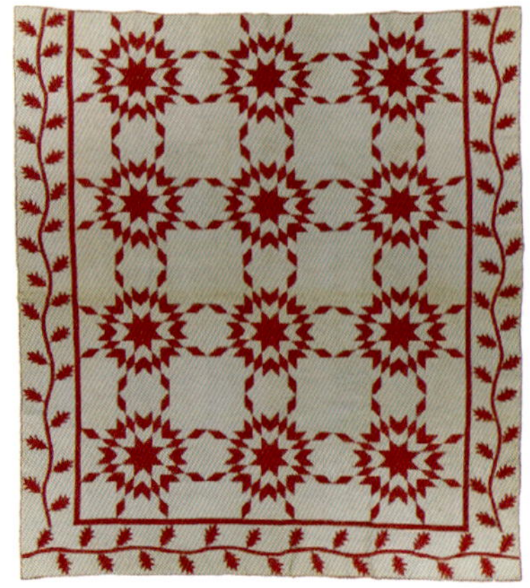

Touching Stars

Maker unidentified
Possibly made in Connecticut
1850 - 1870
96 x 84 in.
IQM 1997.007.0692

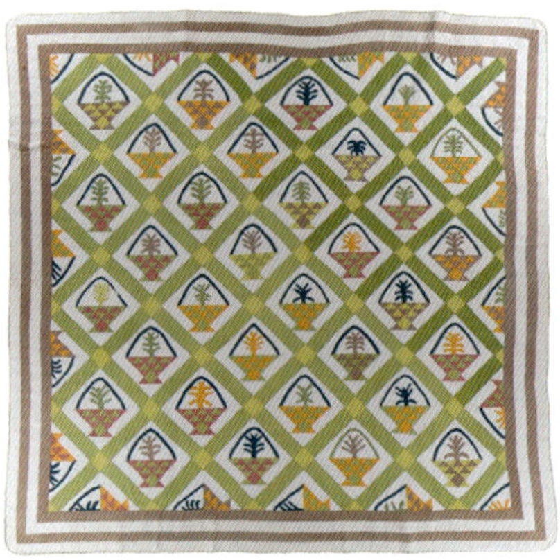

Basket

Maker unidentified
Possibly made in Somerset County, Maryland
1840 - 1860
95 x 95 in.
IQM 1997.007.0693

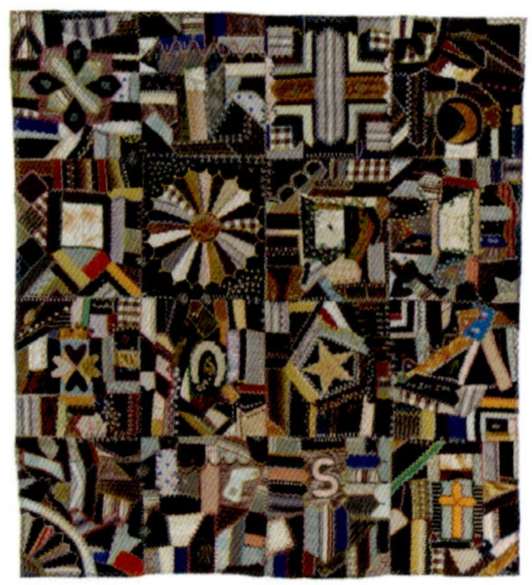

Crazy

Sarah C. Schooley
Made in Noble County, Ohio
Dated 1890
74.5 x 67 in.
IQM 1997.007.0695

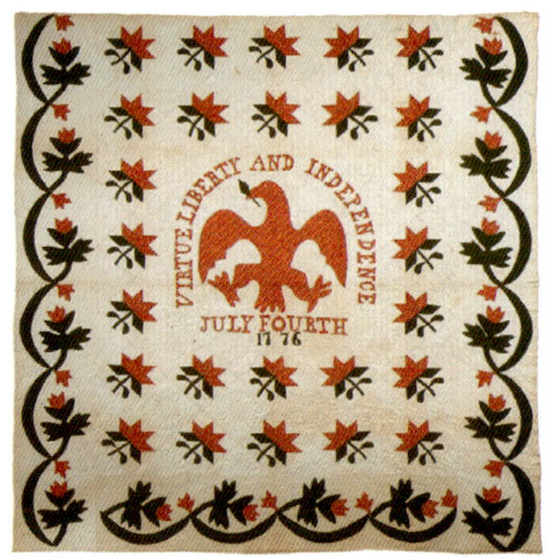

Eagle

Maker unidentified
Made in United States
Circa 1876
90.5 x 83 in.
IQM 1997.007.0696

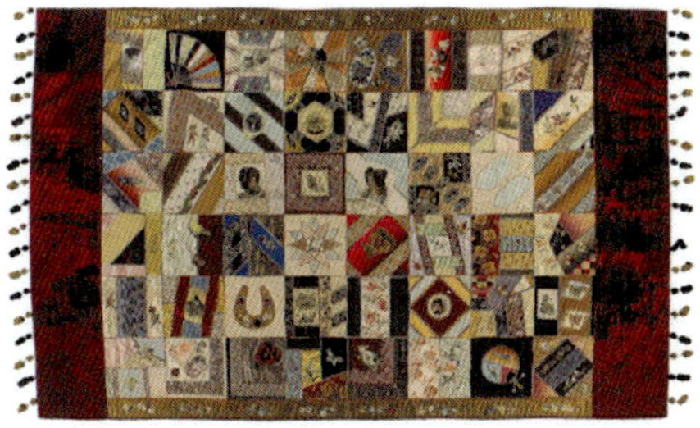

Crazy

Maker unidentified
Made in United States
1885 - 1900
60 x 91 in.

IQM 1997.007.0698

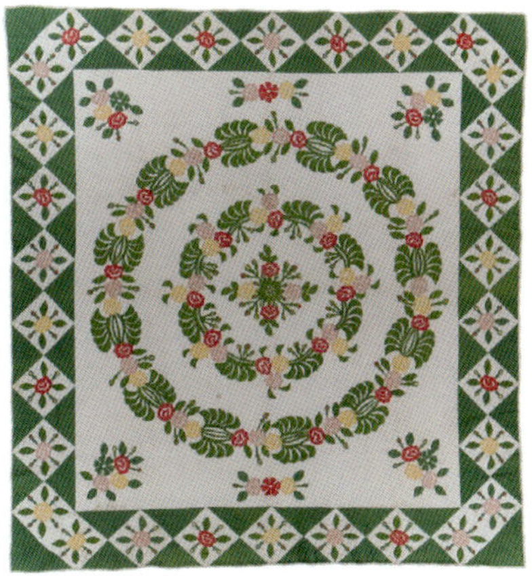

Wreath

Maker unidentified
Possibly made in South Carolina
1850 - 1860
93.5 x 86 in.

IQM 1997.007.0699

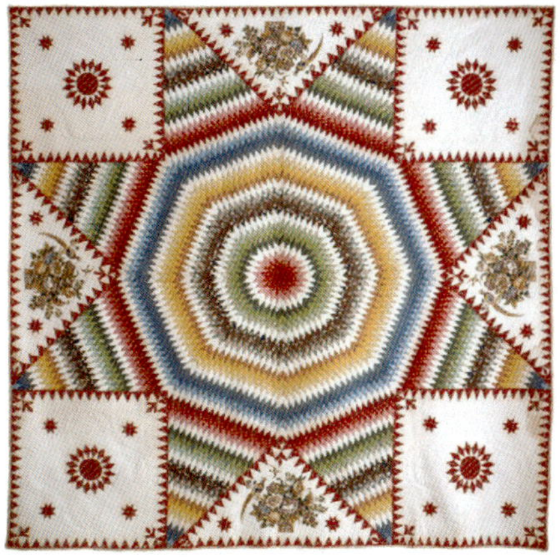

Star of Bethlehem

Probably made by Anna Chambers Deacon
Possibly made in Springfield, New Jersey
Circa 1850
107 x 107.5 in.

IQM 1997.007.0701

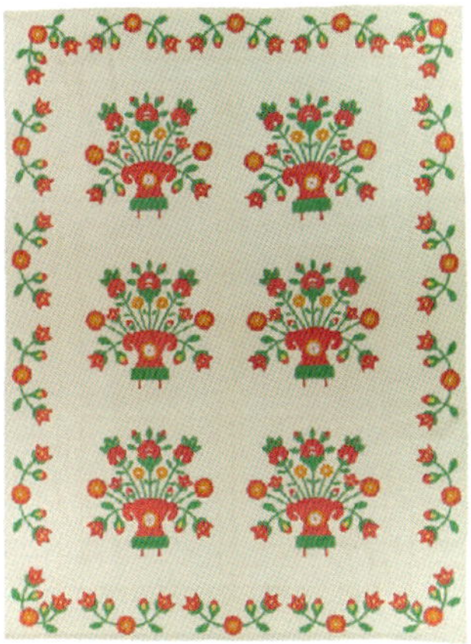

Pots of Flowers

Maker unidentified
Possibly made in Pennsylvania
1930 - 1950
105 x 74.5 in.

IQM 1997.007.0702

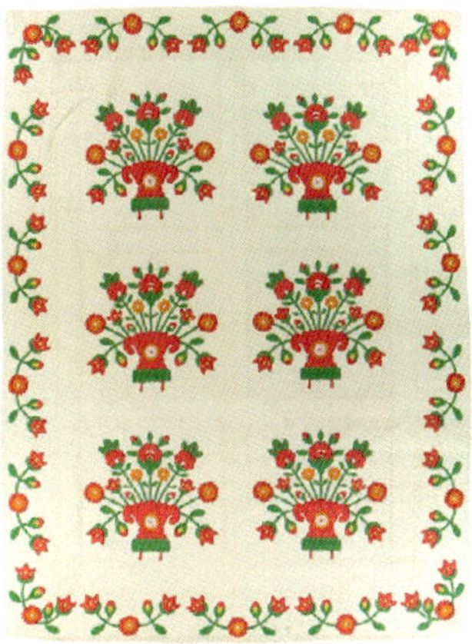

Pots of Flowers

Maker unidentified
Possibly made in Pennsylvania
1930 - 1950
105.5 x 76.5 in.

IQM 1997.007.0703

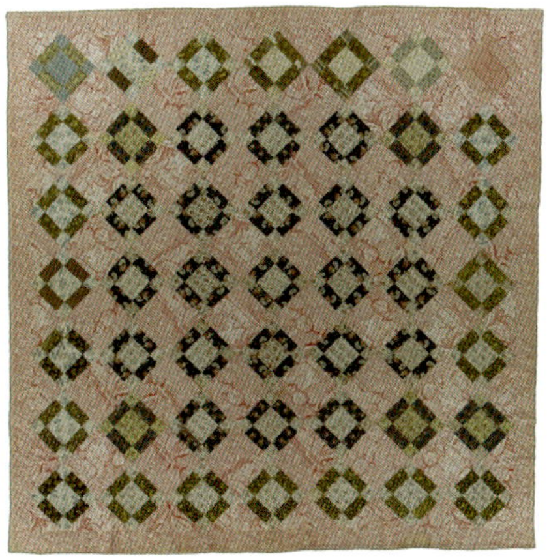

Modified Nine Patch

Maker unidentified
Probably made in eastern United States
1830 - 1850
99 x 97 in.

IQM 1997.007.0704

Concentric Squares

Maker unidentified
Made in United States
1890 - 1910
42 x 41.5 in.

IQM 1997.007.0705

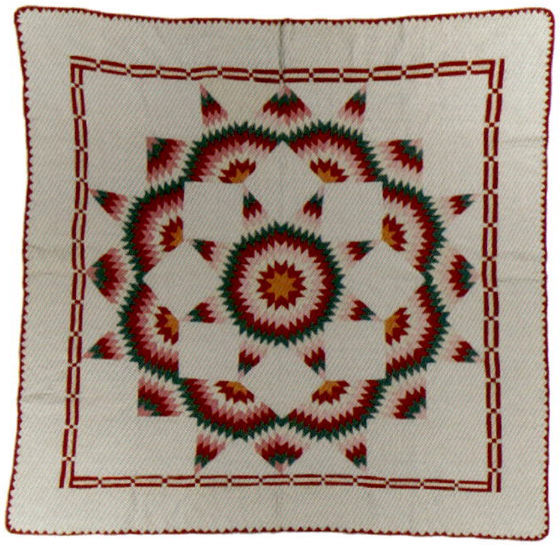

Broken Star

Maker unidentified
Possibly made in Canton, Ohio
1920 - 1940
83.5 x 81 in.

IQM 1997.007.0710

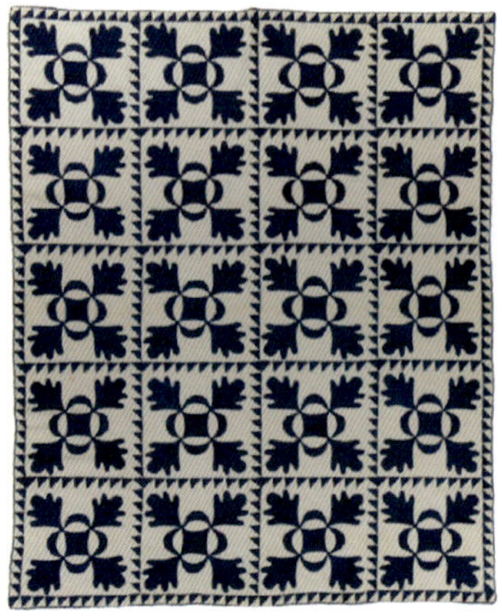

Oak Leaf

Maker unidentified
Possibly made in New York
1840 - 1850
91 x 73.5 in.

IQM 1997.007.0711

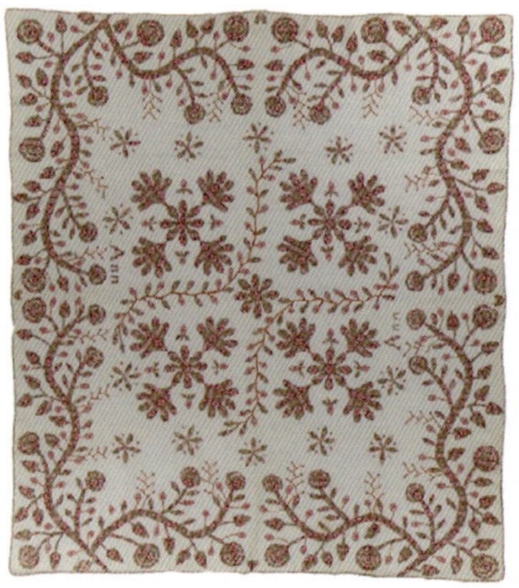

Original

Maker unidentified
Possibly made in New York
1840 - 1860
89 x 78.5 in.

IQM 1997.007.0712

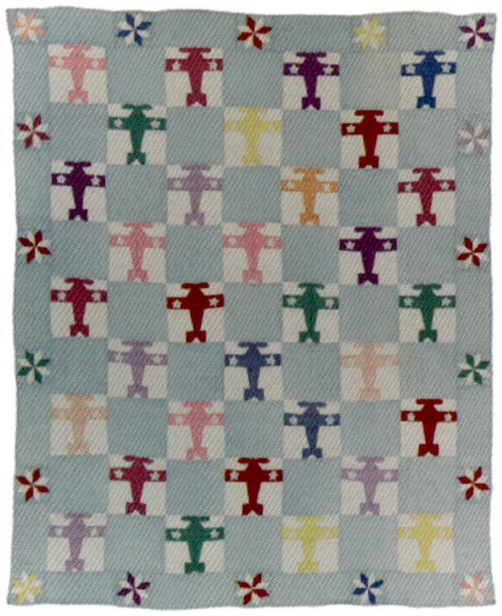

Airplane

Maker unidentified
Possibly made in Ohio
1930 - 1940
90 x 72.5 in.

IQM 1997.007.0713

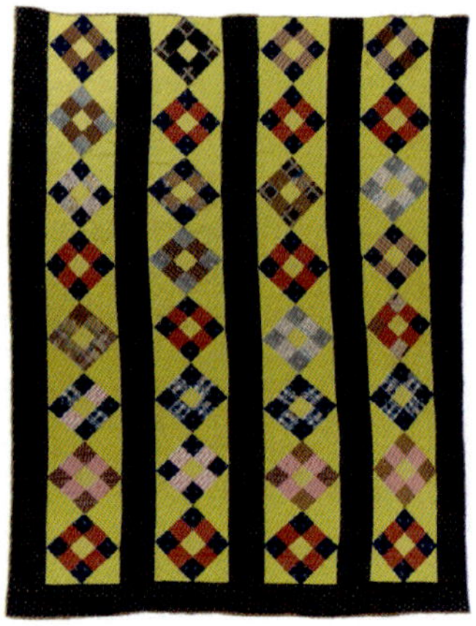

Nine Patch Bars

Maker unidentified
Possibly made in Lancaster County, Pennsylvania
1840 - 1860
97 x 71.5 in.

IQM 1997.007.0714

Whole Cloth

Maker unidentified
Possibly made in New England
1800 - 1830
92 x 78.25 in.

IQM 1997.007.0715

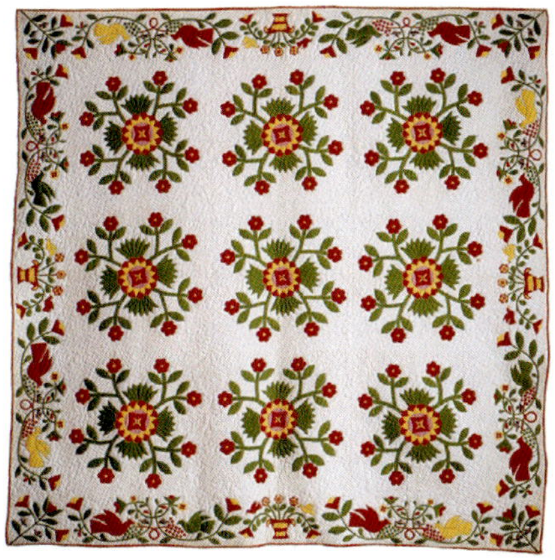

Whig Rose

Maker unidentified
Possibly made in Indiana
1850 - 1860
92 x 92 in.

IQM 1997.007.0718

Whole Cloth

Maker unidentified
Possibly made in Washington County, Pennsylvania
1810 - 1830
111 x 109 in.

IQM 1997.007.0719

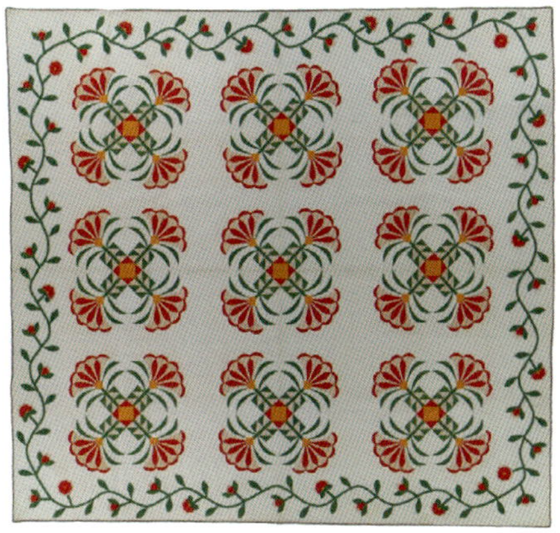

Coxcomb

Sarah Margaret Franklin Hart
Probably made in Clark County, Kentucky
Dated 1858
97.5 x 101.5 in.

IQM 1997.007.0720

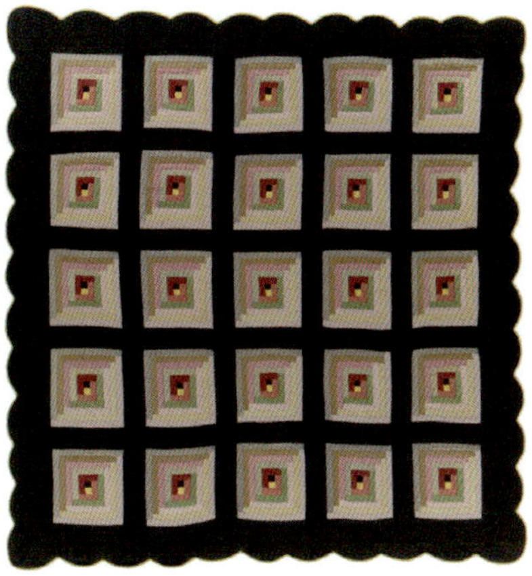

Log Cabin

Maker unidentified
Possibly made in Holmes County, Ohio
1925 - 1945
85 x 80 in.

IQM 1997.007.0721

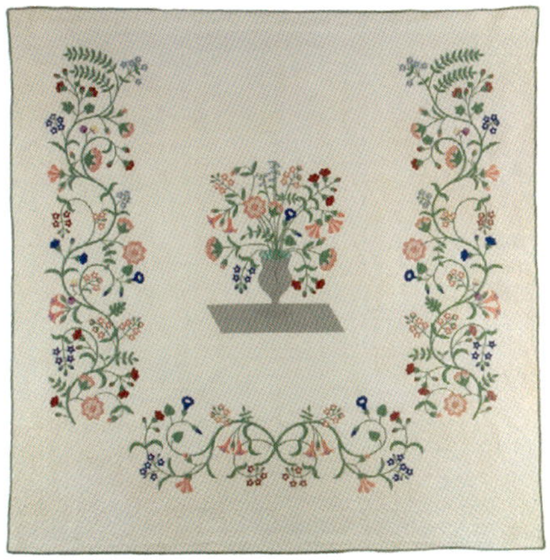

Vase of Flowers

Maker unidentified
Possibly made in Michigan
1935 - 1950
90.5 x 86.5 in.

IQM 1997.007.0722

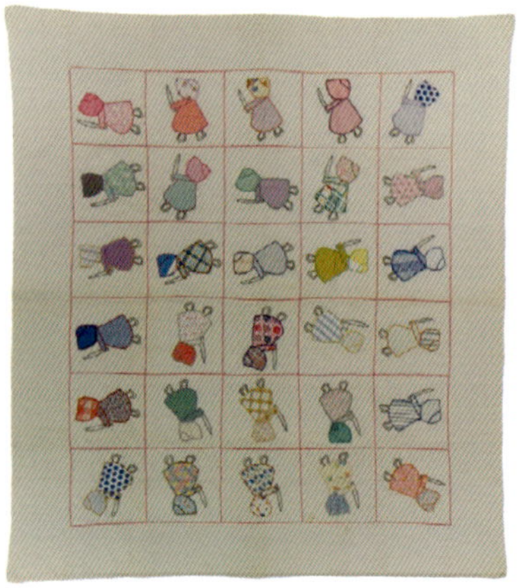

Sunbonnet Sue variation

Maker unidentified
Made in United States
1930 - 1940
82.5 x 71 in.

IQM 1997.007.0723

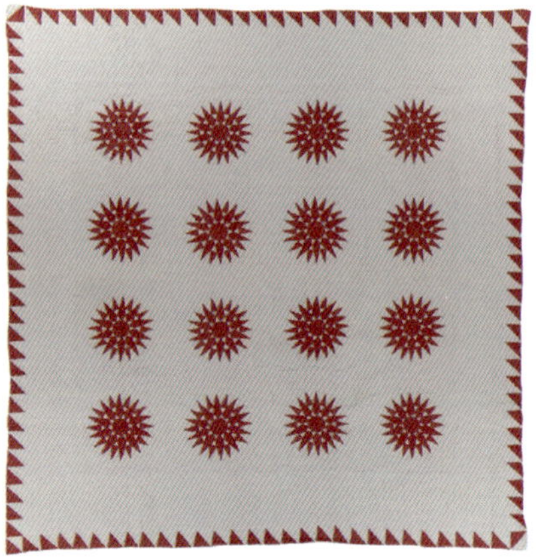

Sunburst (reproduction)

Maker unidentified
Made in China
Dated 1992
83 x 81 in.

IQM 1997.007.0724

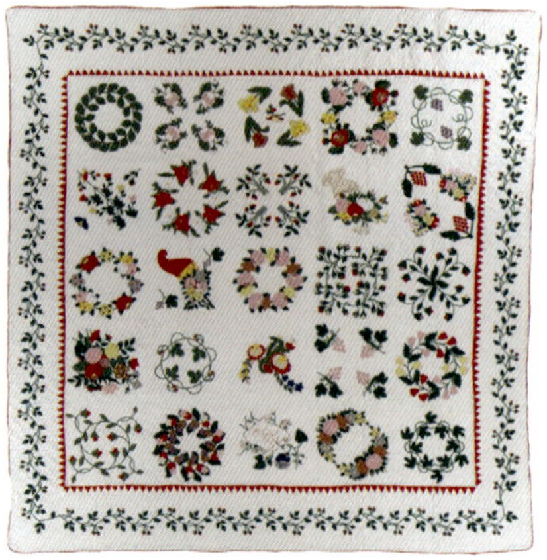

Album (reproduction)

Maker unidentified
Made in China
Dated 1992
88.5 x 86 in.

IQM 1997.007.0725

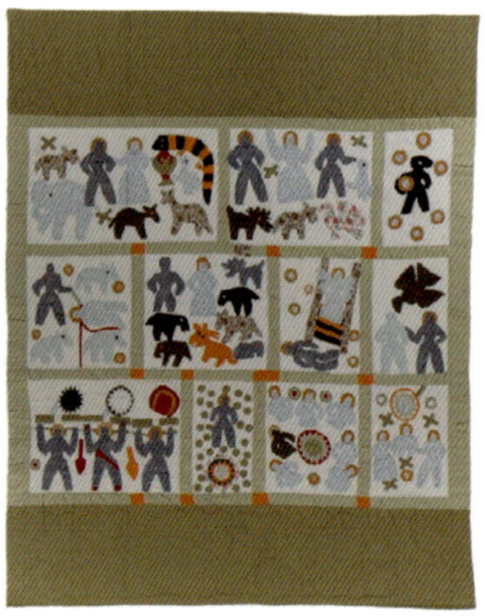

Bible Quilt (reproduction)

Maker unidentified
Made in China
Dated 1992
85 x 67 in.

IQM 1997.007.0726

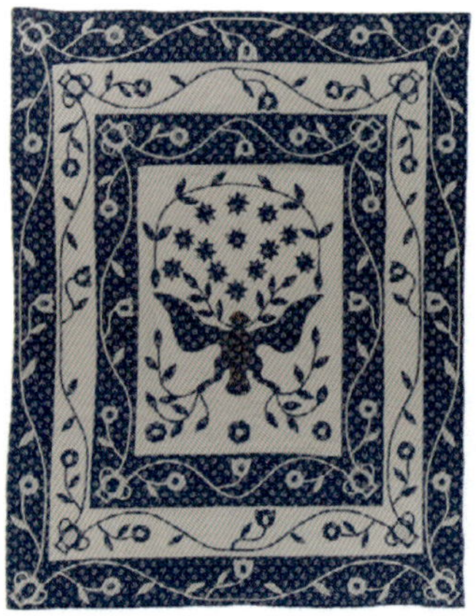

Great Seal Quilt (reproduction)

Maker unidentified
Made in China
Dated 1992
84 x 64 in.

IQM 1997.007.0727

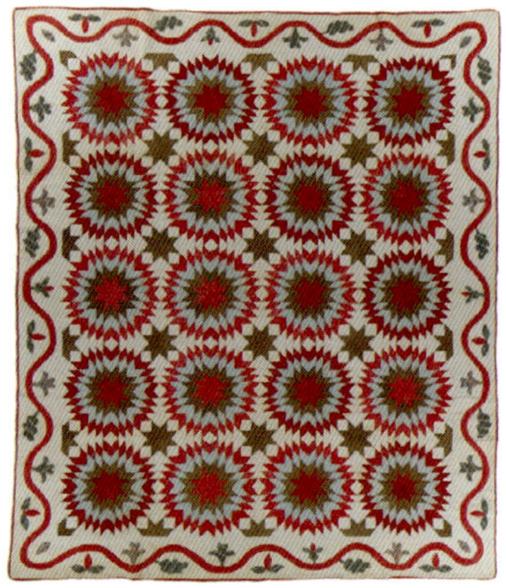

Sunburst Variation

Maker unidentified
Made in United States
1840 - 1860
96.5 x 82.5 in.

IQM 1997.007.0729

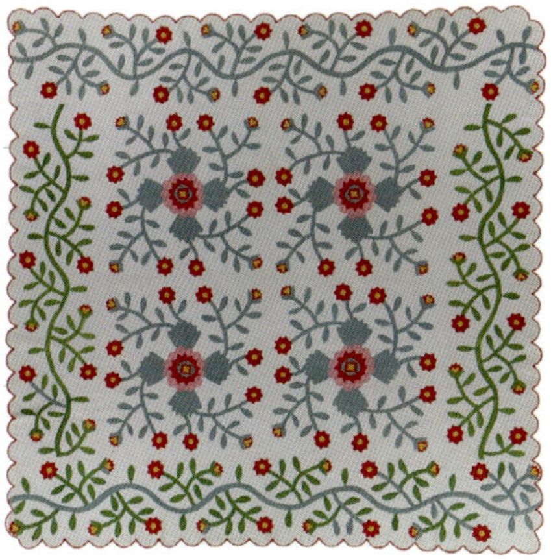

Whig Rose

P. M. Sleght
Probably made in Ontario, Canada
Dated 1858
92 x 94 in.

IQM 1997.007.0730

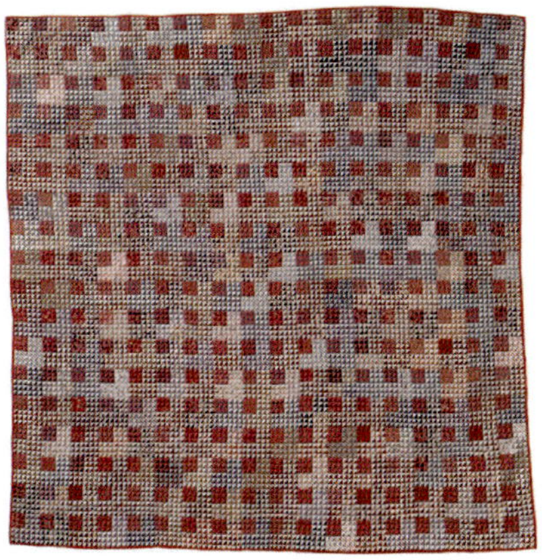

Birds in Air

Possibly made by Mary Linderburger
Possibly made in New Jersey
1880 - 1900
86 x 83 in.

IQM 1997.007.0731

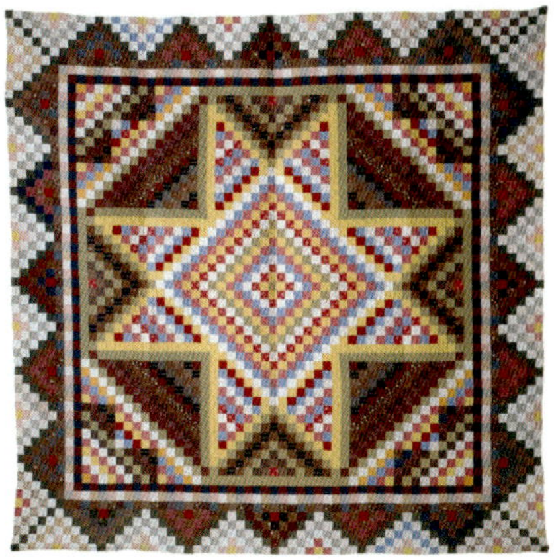

Postage Stamp Star

Maker unidentified
Probably made in Bowmansville, Lancaster County, Pennsylvania
1880 - 1900
82.5 x 80 in.

IQM 1997.007.0733

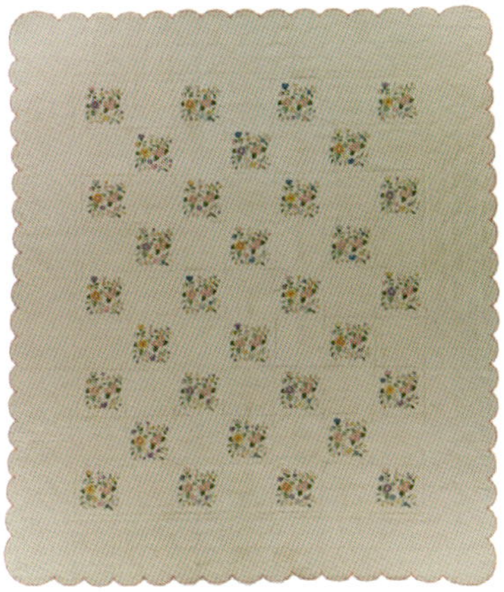

Original

Maker unidentified
Possibly made in China
1910 - 1930
94 x 78 in.

IQM 1997.007.0734

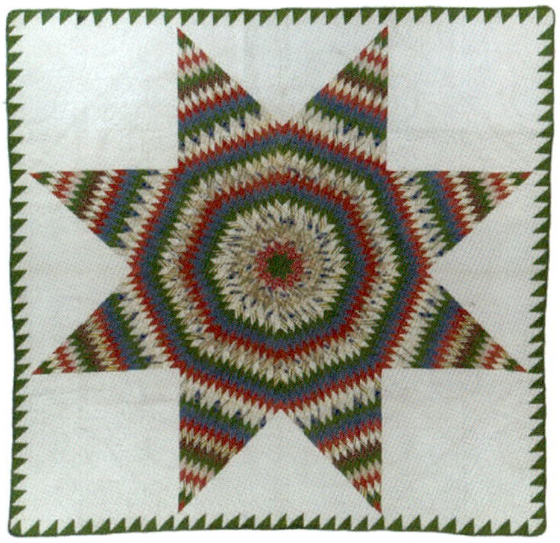

Star of Bethlehem

Maker unidentified
Possibly made in Maryland
1840 - 1860
102 x 102 in.

IQM 1997.007.0736

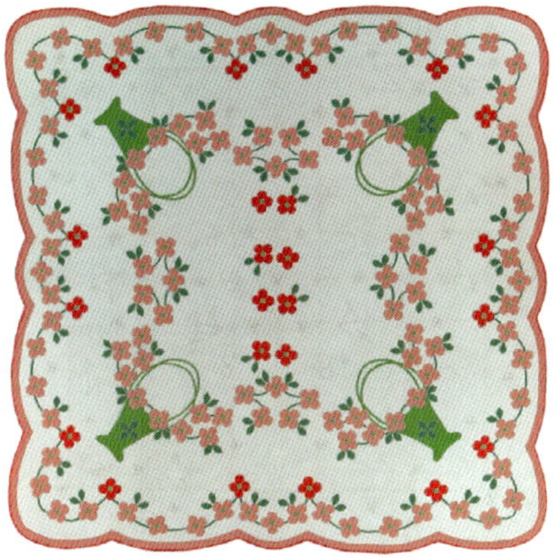

Pink Dogwood

Probably made by Sarah Laughlin
Probably made in Guernsey County, Ohio
Circa 1927
76 x 76 in.

IQM 1997.007.0737

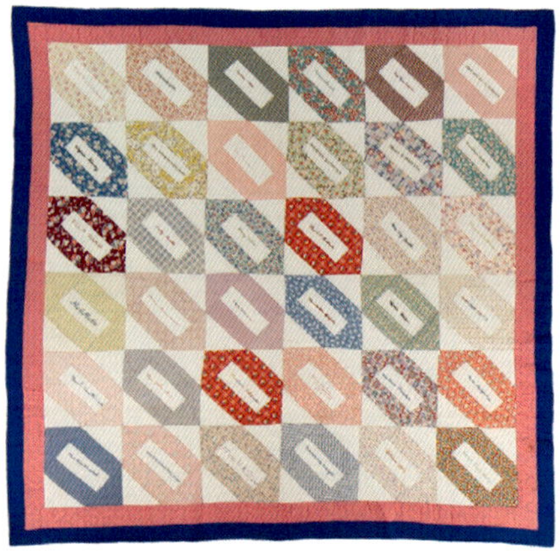

Album

Maker unidentified
Made in St. Louis, Missouri
Circa 1932
85 x 83 in.
IQM 1997.007.0738

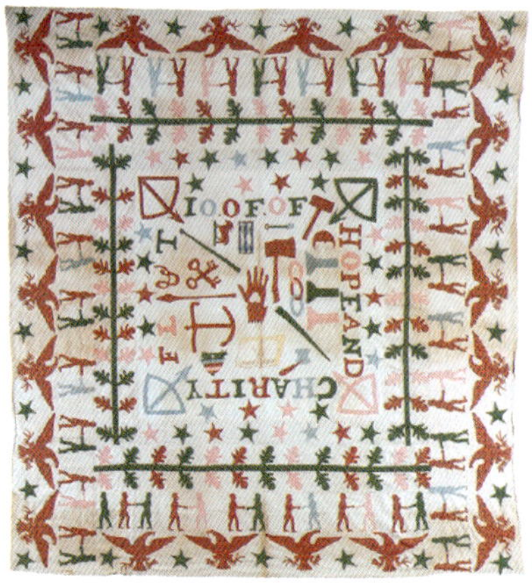

Original - Oddfellows Quilt

Charlotte Gardner
Probably made in New Jersey or New York
1885 - 1890
97 x 92 in.
IQM 1997.007.0739

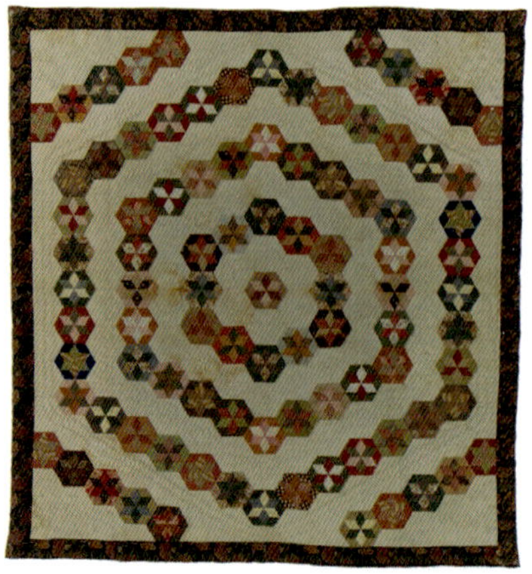

Hexagon Star

Maker unidentified
Possibly made in Maryland
1820 - 1840
105 x 95.5 in.
IQM 1997.007.0741

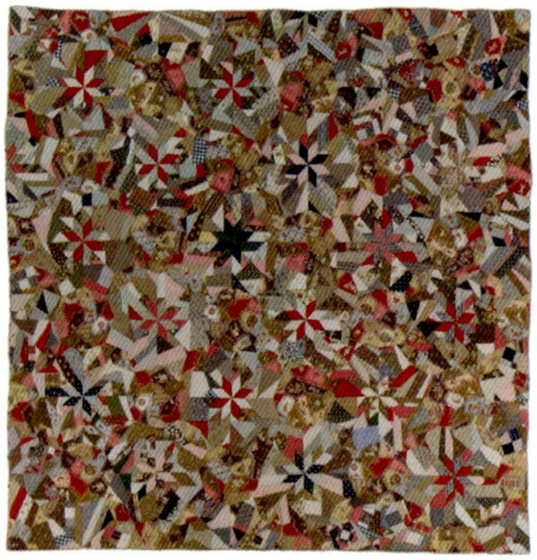

Crazy Stars

Maker unidentified
Made in United States
1890 - 1900
86 x 82.5 in.
IQM 1997.007.0742

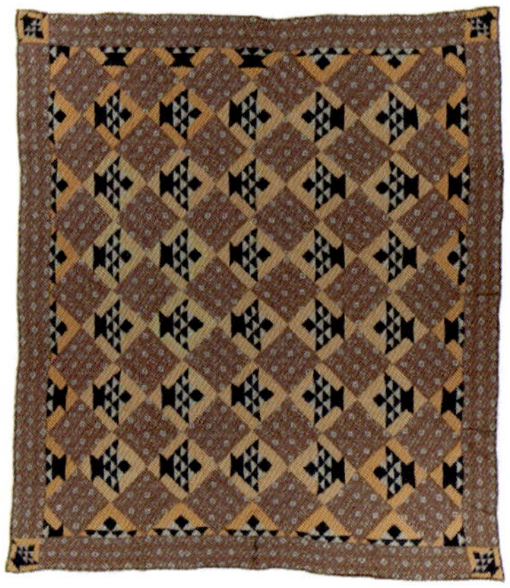

Basket

Maker unidentified
Possibly made in Pennsylvania
1850 - 1870
83 x 73 in.
IQM 1997.007.0743

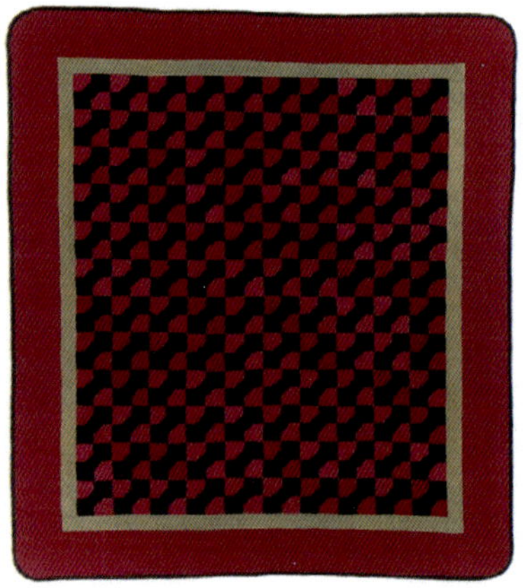

Bow Tie

Maker unidentified
Possibly made in Holmes County, Ohio
1900 - 1920
78 x 68 in.
IQM 1997.007.0744

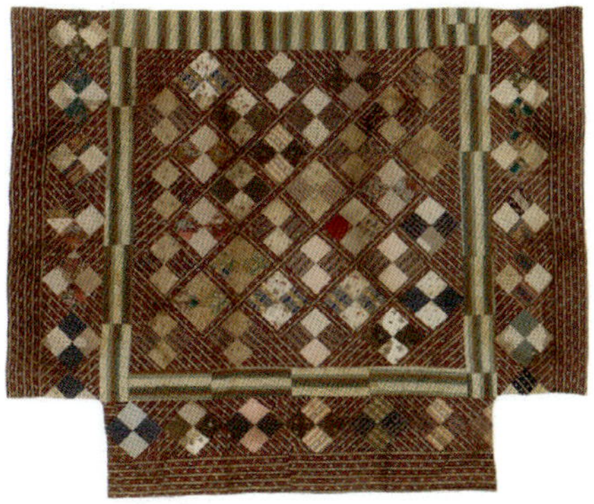

Four Patch

Maker unidentified
Possibly made in Pennsylvania
1800 - 1820
84 x 100 in.

IQM 1997.007.0745

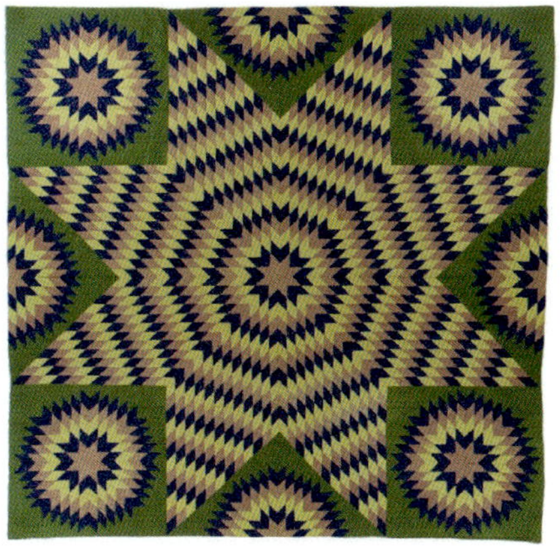

Star of Bethlehem

Maker unidentified
Possibly made in Pennsylvania
1850 - 1870
113 x 113 in.

IQM 1997.007.0746

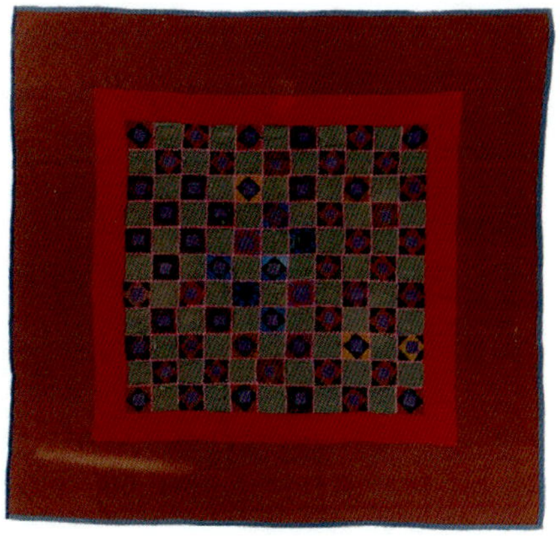

Square on Square

Kanagy family member
Made in Mifflin County, Pennsylvania
Dated 1897
73 x 71.5 in.

IQM 1997.007.0748

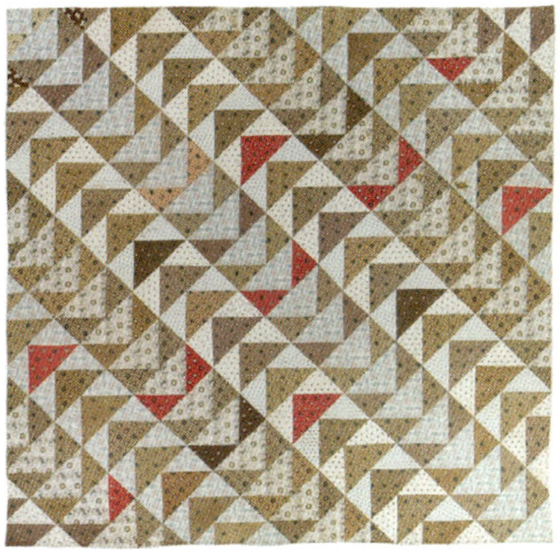

Flying Geese

Sarah K. Headly
Made in Falls Township, Bucks County, Pennsylvania
Dated 1838
96 x 98 in.

IQM 1997.007.0749

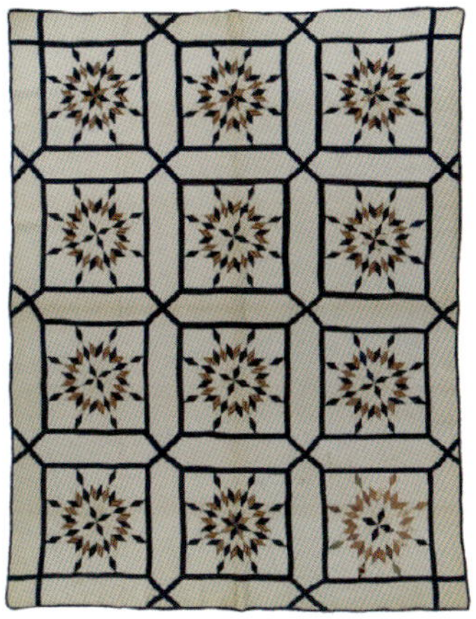

Garden Maze Star

Maker unidentified
Possibly made in Catskill, New York
1830 - 1850
99 x 74.5 in.

IQM 1997.007.0750

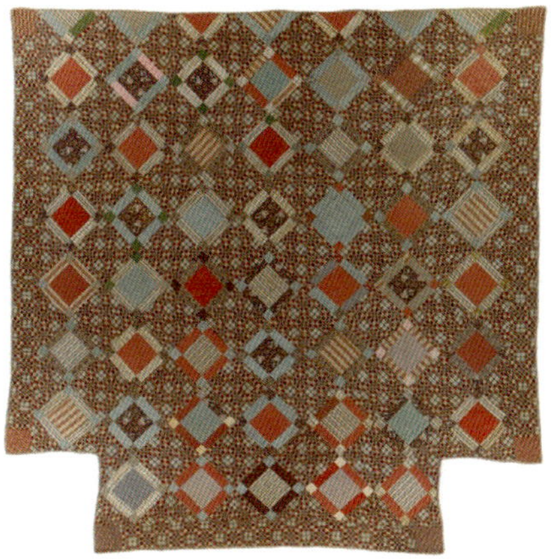

Nine Patch

Maker unidentified
Possibly made in Maine
1830 - 1850
92.5 x 91.5 in.

IQM 1997.007.0751

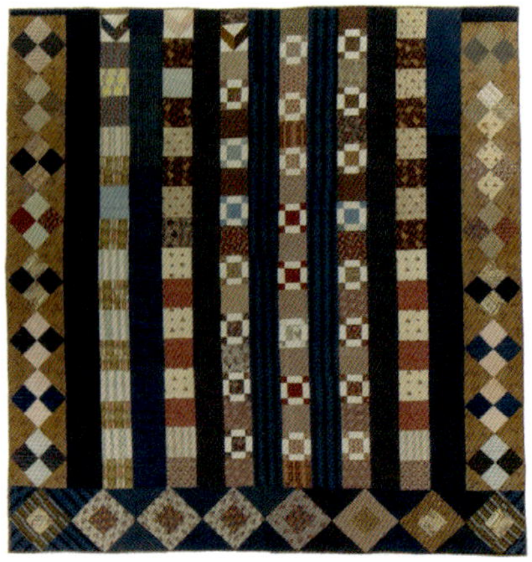

Nine Patch Bars

Maker unidentified
Possibly made in Orange, Connecticut
1830 - 1840
100 x 92.5 in.

IQM 1997.007.0752

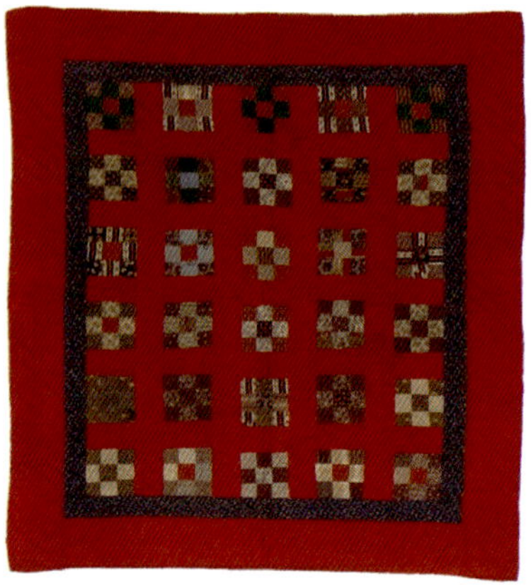

Nine Patch

Maker unidentified
Possibly made in Lancaster or Berks County, Pennsylvania
1860 - 1880
37 x 41 in.

IQM 1997.007.0753

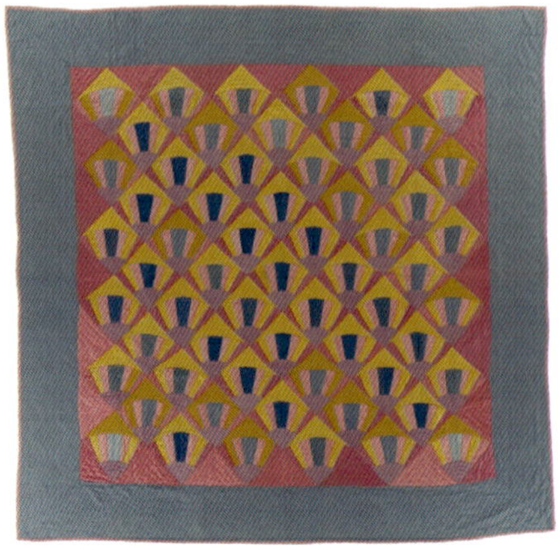

Fan

Maker unidentified
Possibly made in Ephrata, Pennsylvania
1920 - 1940
78 x 78 in.

IQM 1997.007.0754

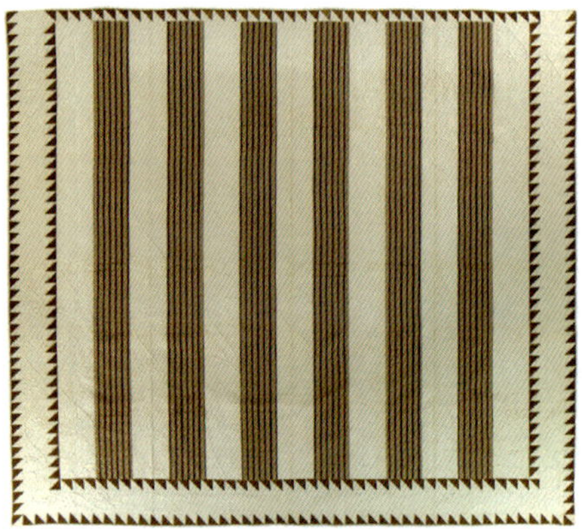

Bars

Maker unidentified
Made in United States
1850 - 1860
85 x 93 in.

IQM 1997.007.0757

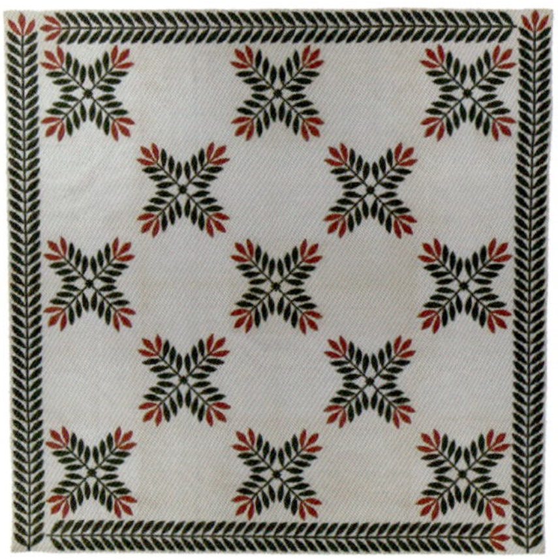

Laurel Wreath

Maker unidentified
Possibly made in Pennsylvania
1840 - 1860
106 x 105 in.

IQM 1997.007.0758

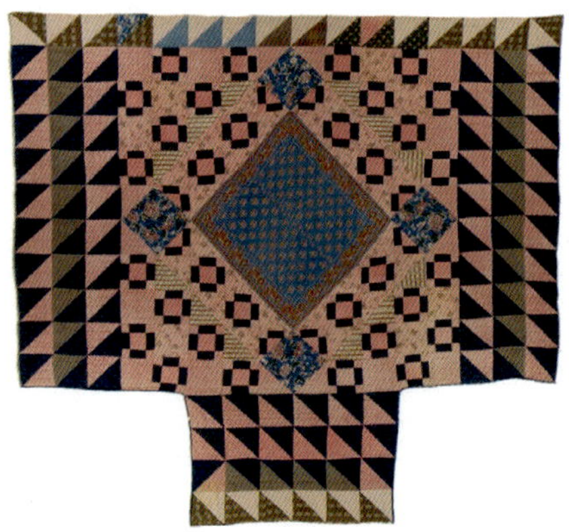

Nine Patch variation

Maker unidentified
Possibly made in New England
1810 - 1830
108.5 x 113.5 in.

IQM 1997.007.0759

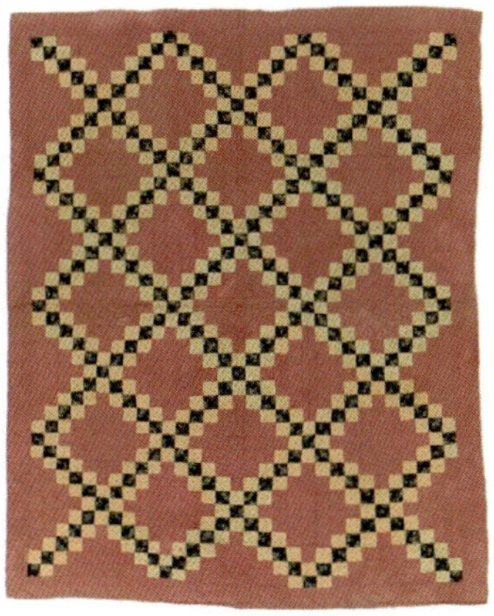

Double Irish Chain

Alice Sheirich
Probably made in Lancaster County, Pennsylvania
1875 - 1895
41.5 x 32.5 in.
IQM 1997.007.0760

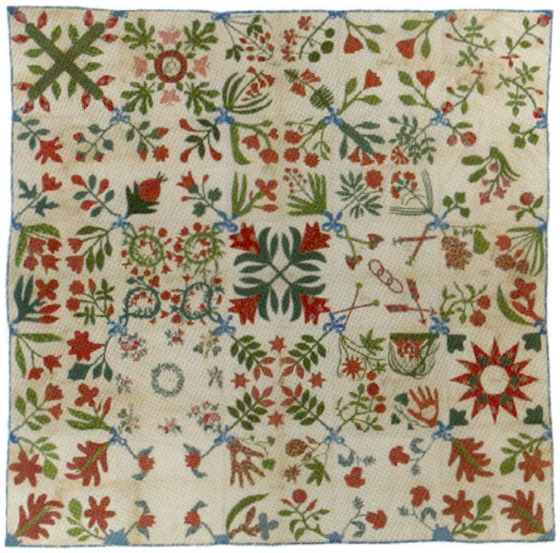

Album

Maker unidentified
Made in Philadelphia, Pennsylvania
Dated 1853
87 x 87 in.
IQM 1997.007.0761

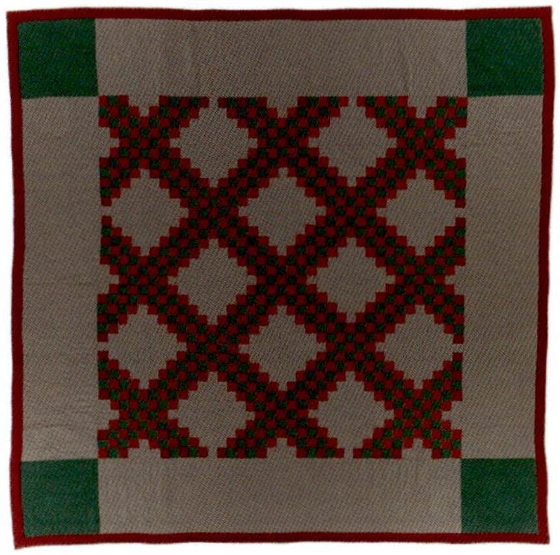

Triple Irish Chain

Maker unidentified
Possibly made in Lancaster County, Pennsylvania
1910 - 1930
86 x 86 in.
IQM 1997.007.0762

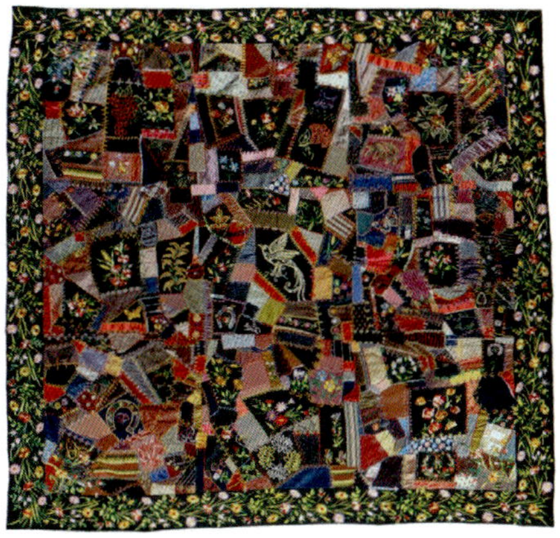

Crazy

Maker unidentified
Possibly made in Bucks County, Pennsylvania
1880 - 1900
80 x 79 in.
IQM 1997.007.0764

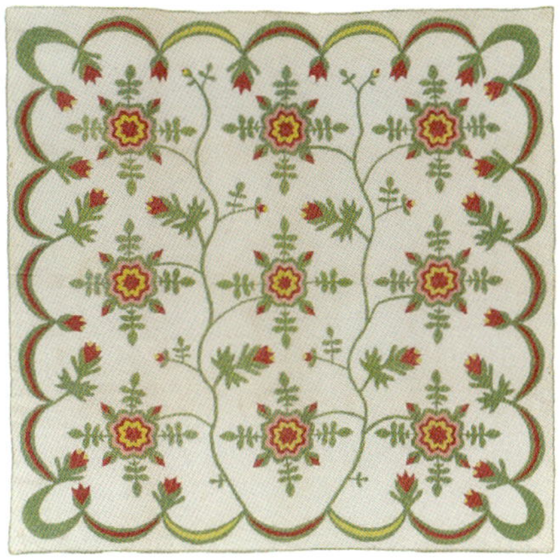

Rose of Sharon variation

Maker unidentified
Possibly made in Ohio
Dated 1851
80 x 80.5 in.
IQM 1997.007.0765

Love Apple

Maker unidentified
Possibly made in Morgantown, West Virginia
1850 - 1870
80.5 x 69 in.
IQM 1997.007.0766

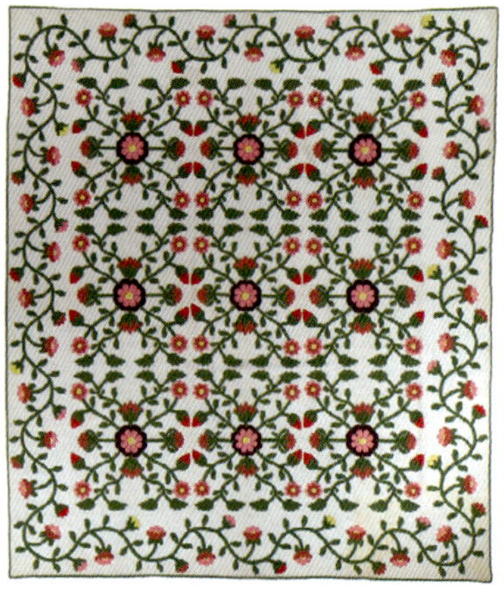

Floral

Maker unidentified
Possibly made in Pennsylvania
1850 - 1870
102 x 87 in.

IQM 1997.007.0767

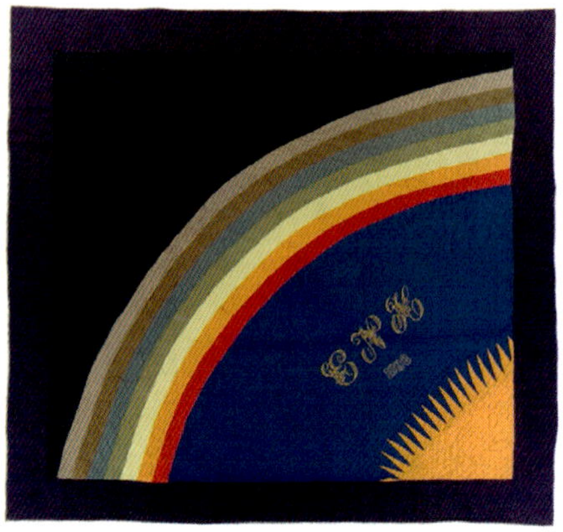

Rainbow Quilt

S.F. Schenck Habecker
Probably made in Pennsylvania
Dated 1898
87 x 82 in.

IQM 1997.007.0768

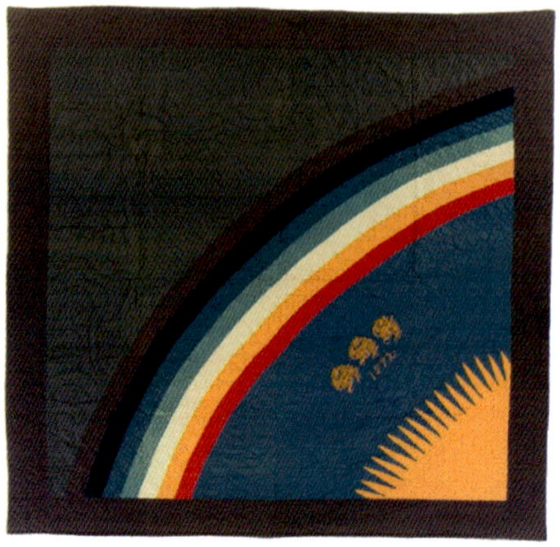

Rainbow Quilt

Brubaker or Habecker
Probably made in Pennsylvania
Dated 1892
78 x 77.5 in.

IQM 1997.007.0769

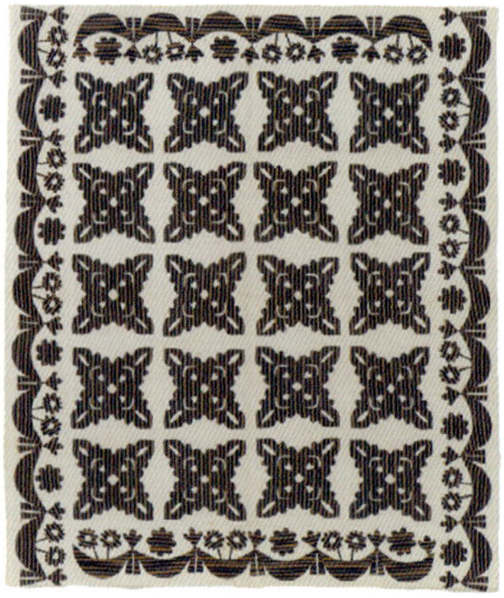

Papercut Appliqué

Maker unidentified
Possibly made in Berks County, Pennsylvania
1840 - 1860
101 x 85 in.

IQM 1997.007.0770

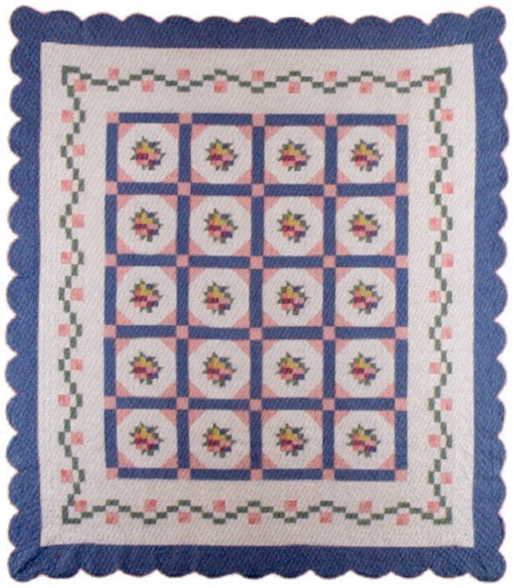

Dresden I

Maker unidentified
Possibly made in Dauphin County, Pennsylvania
Circa 1932
87 x 74 in.

IQM 1997.007.0771

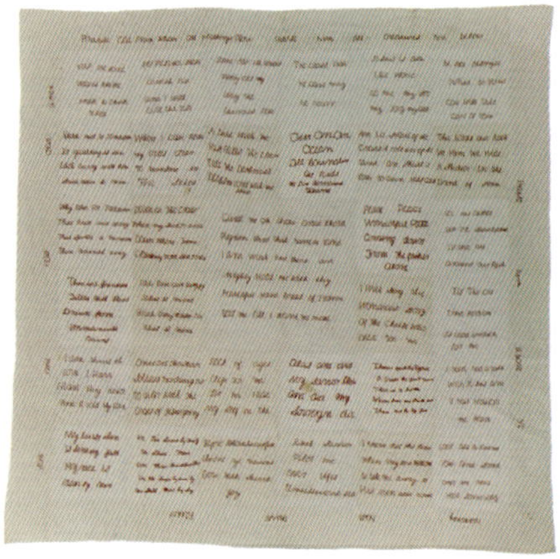

Original - Hymns

Maker unidentified
Possibly made in Johnstown, Pennsylvania
Circa 1925
80 x 79 in.

IQM 1997.007.0772

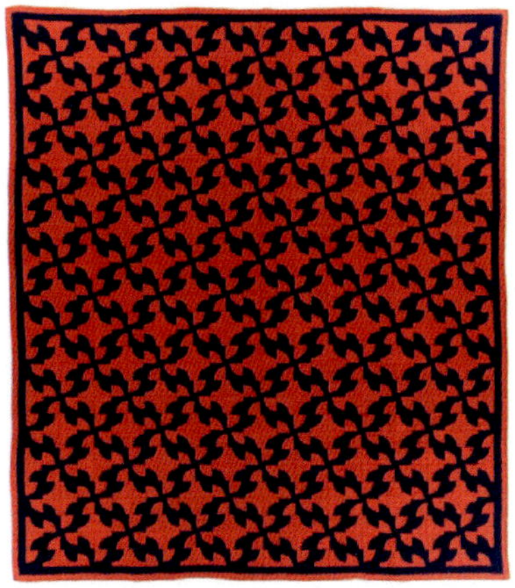

Drunkard's Path

Maker unidentified
Possibly made in Lancaster County, Pennsylvania
1870 - 1890
88 x 75 in.

IQM 1997.007.0773

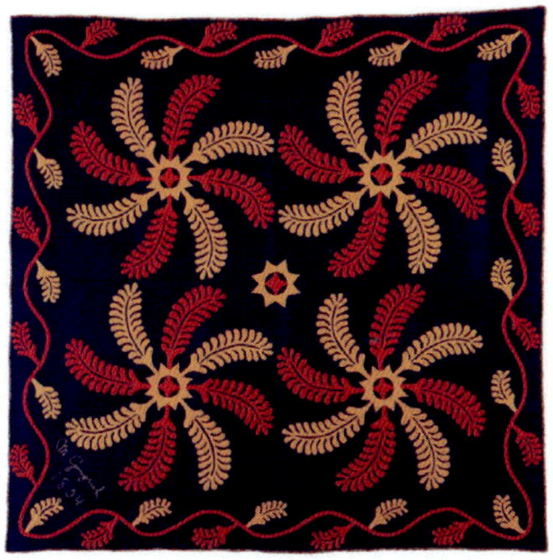

Princess Feather

M. Gingrich
Probably made in Dauphin County, Pennsylvania
Dated 1854
86 x 84.5 in.

IQM 1997.007.0774

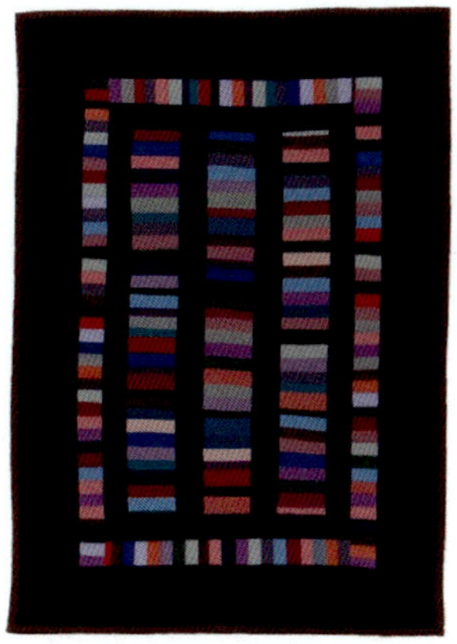

Chinese Coins

Possibly made by Yoder family member
Probably made in Holmes County, Ohio
1930 - 1950
46 x 31.5 in.

IQM 1997.007.0775

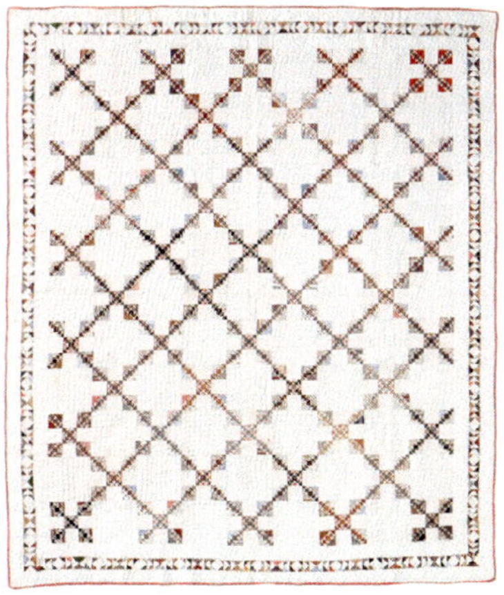

Irish Chain variation

Maker unidentified
Probably made in New England
1870 - 1890
80 x 66 in.

IQM 1997.007.0776

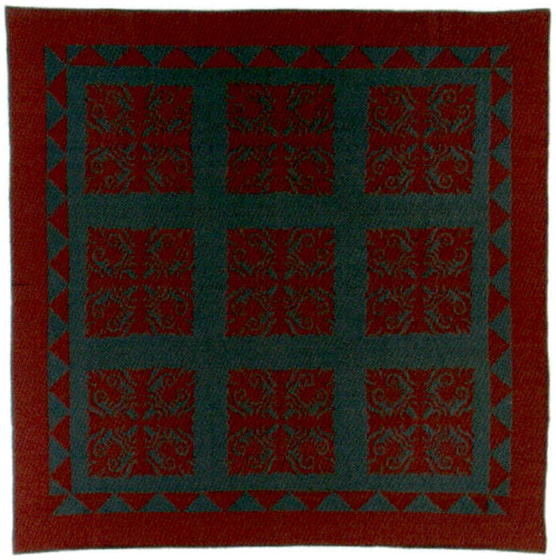

Appliqué

Possibly made by Lehman family
Probably made in Lancaster County, Pennsylvania
1870 - 1890
89 x 87 in.

IQM 1997.007.0777

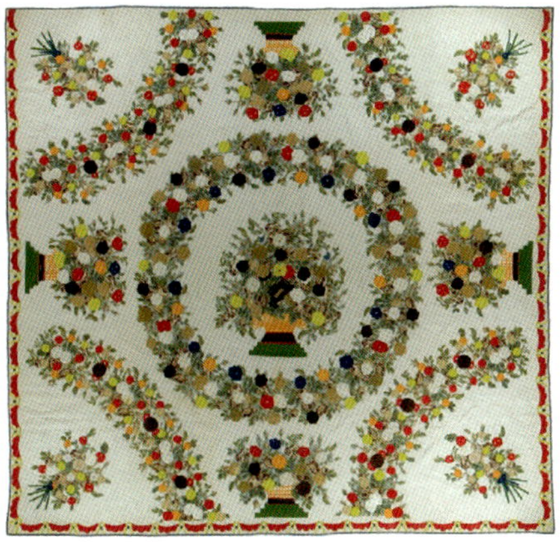

Medallion

Maker unidentified
Probably made in Pennsylvania
1840 - 1860
105 x 109 in.

IQM 1997.007.0778

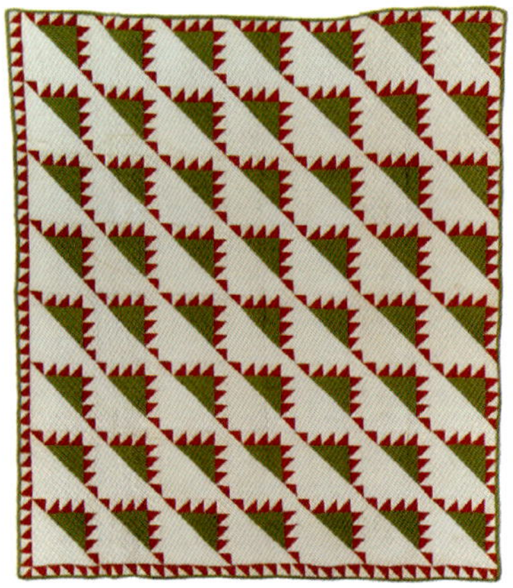

Sawtooth

Maker unidentified
Possibly made in Pennsylvania
1860 - 1880
76.5 x 66 in.

IQM 1997.007.0779

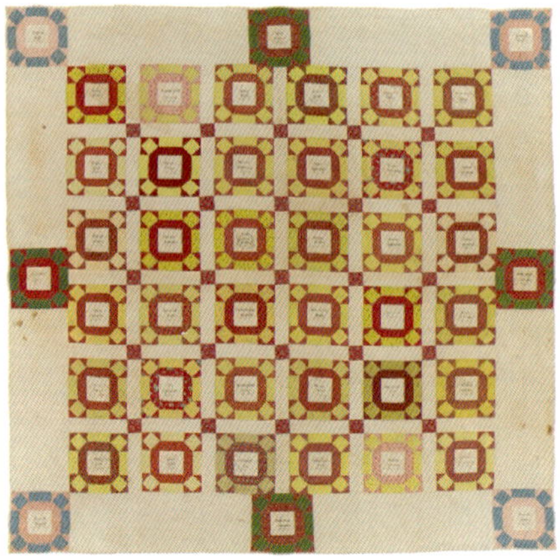

Rolling Stone

Probably made by Sarah Major
Made in Lehigh County,
Pennsylvania
Dated 1852
92 x 91 in.

IQM 1997.007.0780

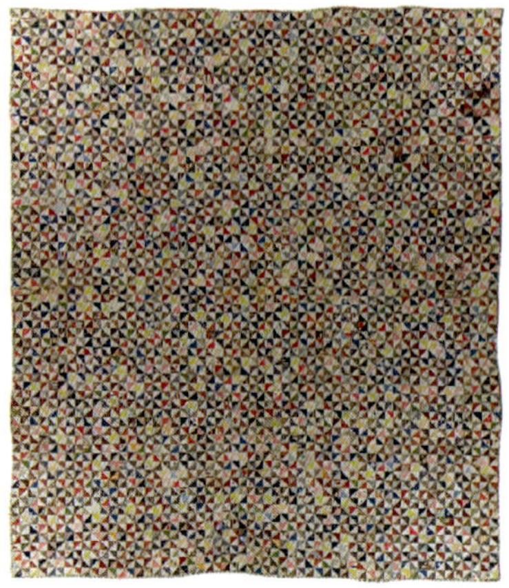

Birds in Air

Salome Thorpe
Made in Westport, Connecticut
1880 - 1900
88.5 x 77 in.
IQM 1997.007.07814

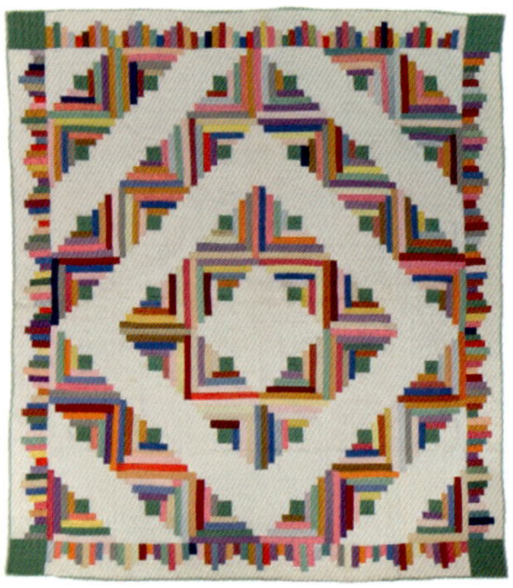

Log Cabin

Maker unidentified
Possibly made in Pennsylvania
1930 - 1950
80.5 x 71.5 in.

IQM 1997.007.0782

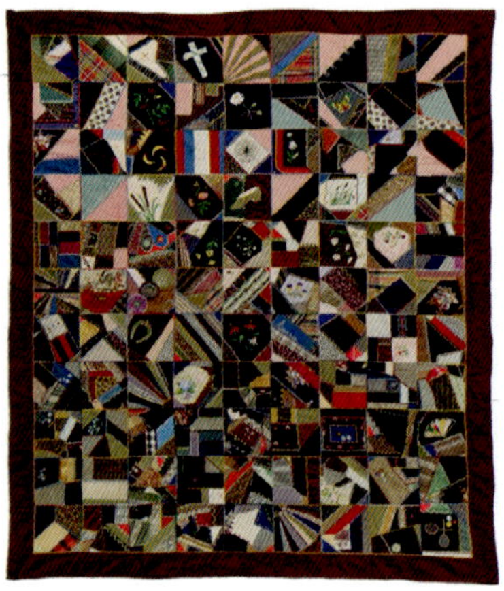

Crazy

Maker unidentified
Made in United States
Dated 1884
75 x 63 in.

IQM 1997.007.0783

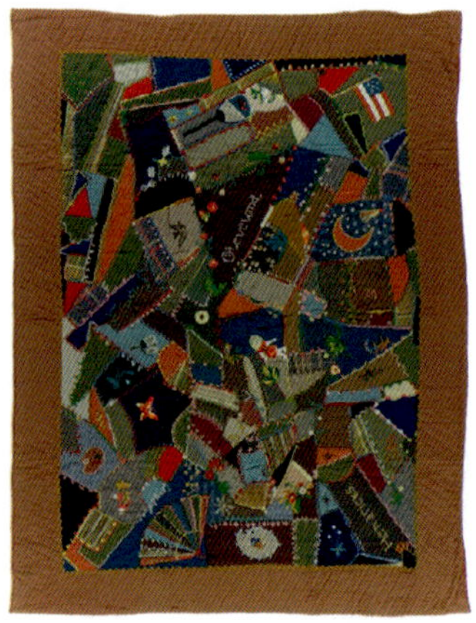

Crazy

Maker unidentified
Probably made in Cleveland,
Ohio
Dated 1885
76 x 59.5 in.

IQM 1997.007.0784

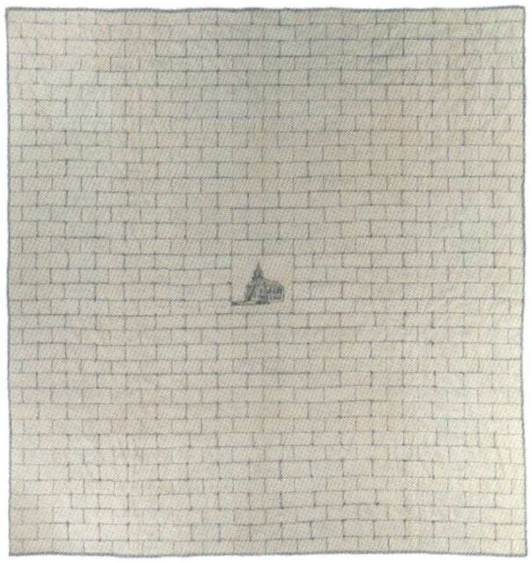

Original

Maker unidentified
Made in Ghent, New York
Dated 1924
87.5 x 81 in.

IQM 1997.007.0785

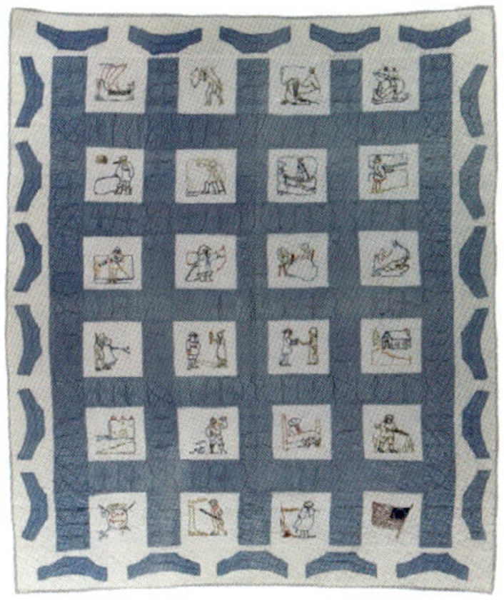

Colonial History

Paulina Mangold
Made in Bennington, Nebraska
Circa 1938
86 x 68.5 in.

IQM 1997.007.0786

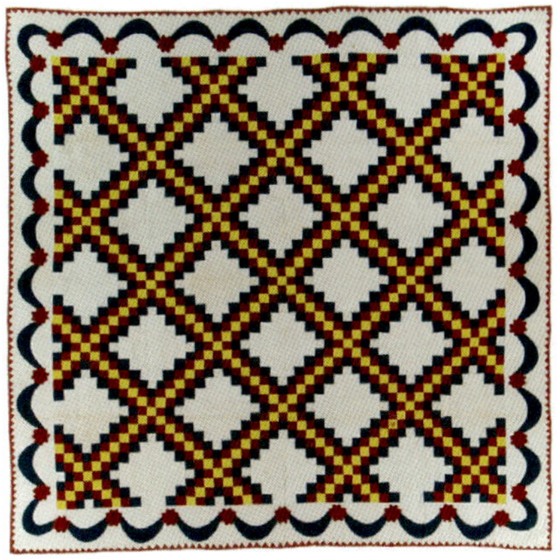

Triple Irish Chain

Maker unidentified
Possibly made in Pennsylvania
1880 - 1900
84 x 83 in.

IQM 1997.007.0787

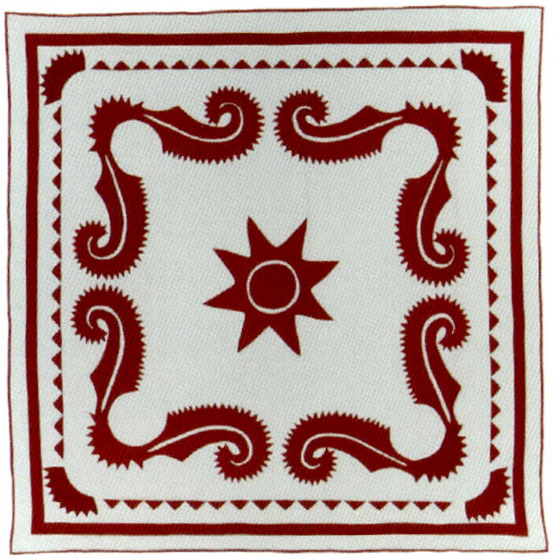

Princess Feather variation

Maker unidentified
Possibly made in Delaware
1900 - 1920
79 x 76.5 in.

IQM 1997.007.0788

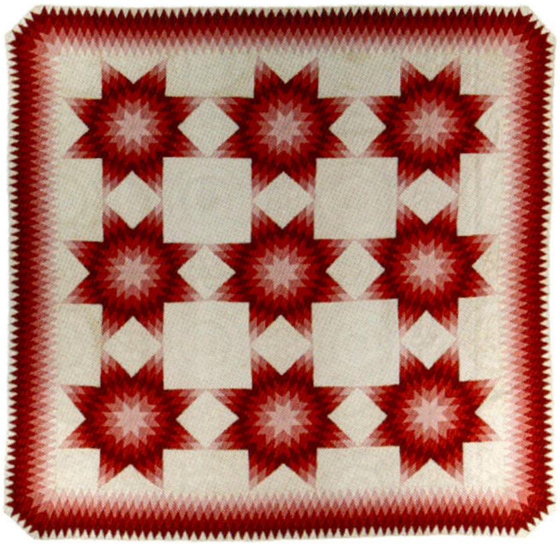

Blazing Star

Maker unidentified
Possibly made in Bremen, Indiana
1930 - 1940
90 x 83.5 in.

IQM 1997.007.0789

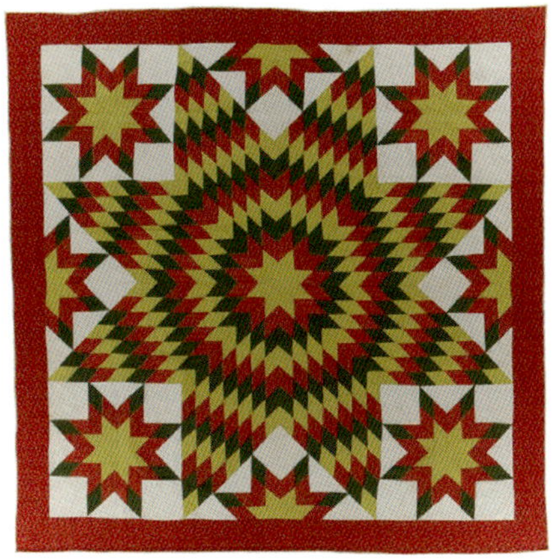

Star of Bethlehem

Maker unidentified
Possibly made in Lancaster or Berks County, Pennsylvania
1850 - 1870
81.5 x 80.75 in.

IQM 1997.007.0790

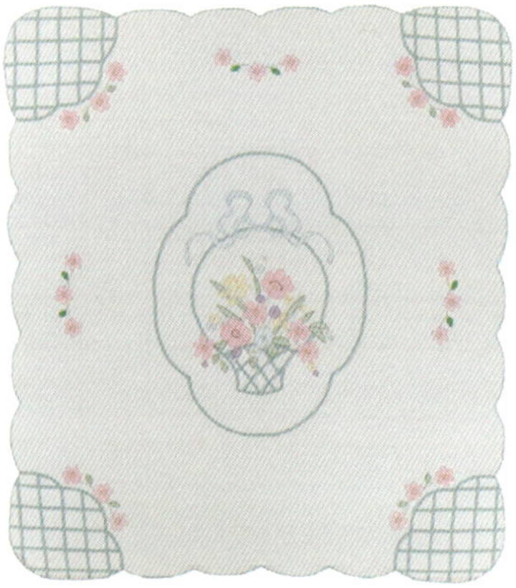

Floral Basket

Maker unidentified
Possibly made in Cleveland, Ohio
Circa 1932
87.5 x 76 in.

IQM 1997.007.0791

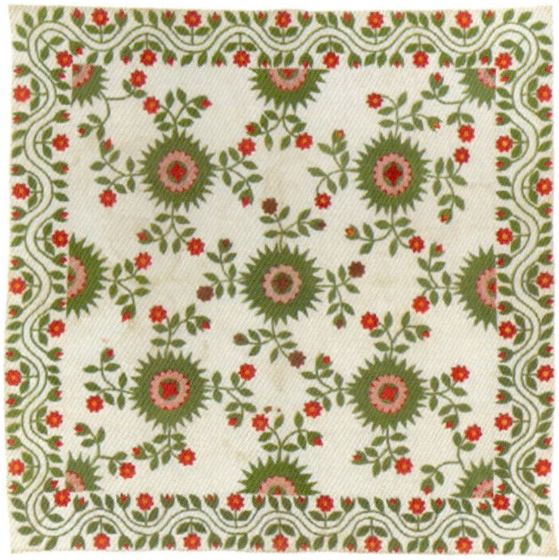

Rose of Sharon variation

Maker unidentified
Possibly made in Washington, Pennsylvania
Dated 1859
89.5 x 90 in.

IQM 1997.007.0792

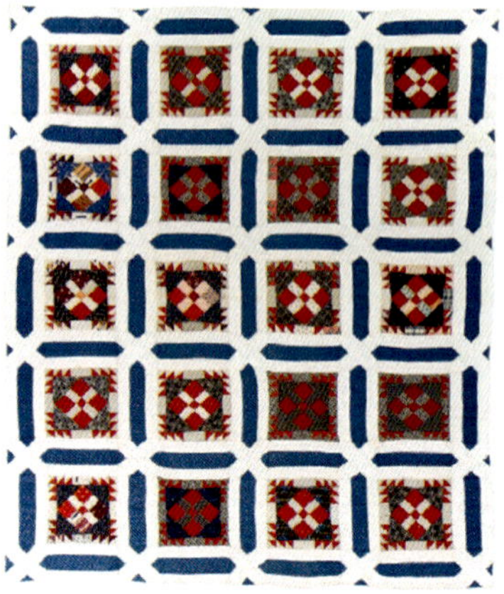

Four Patch

Maker unidentified
Possibly made in southern Indiana
1900 - 1920
85.5 x 70.5 in.

IQM 1997.007.0793

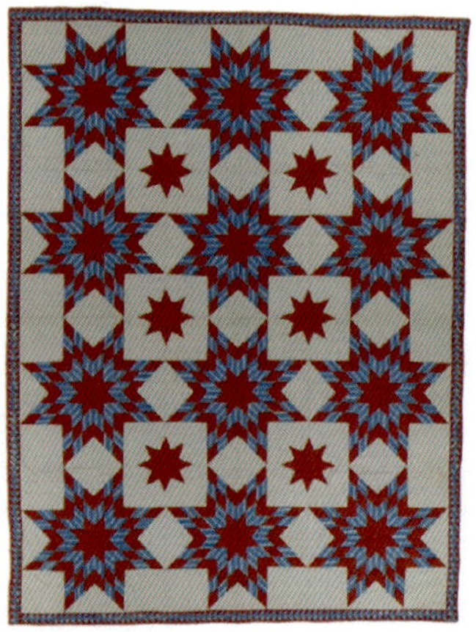

Touching Stars

Maker unidentified
Possibly made in Pennsylvania
1850 - 1870
108.5 x 81 in.

IQM 1997.007.0794

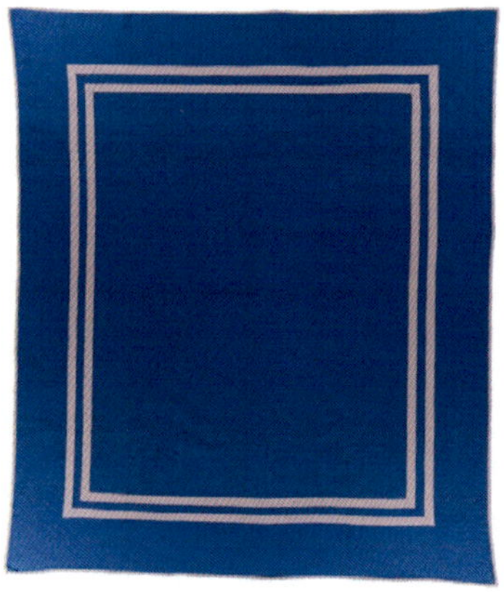

Plain Quilt

Maker unidentified
Possibly made in Holmes County, Ohio
1925 - 1945
80.5 x 70 in.

IQM 1997.007.0795

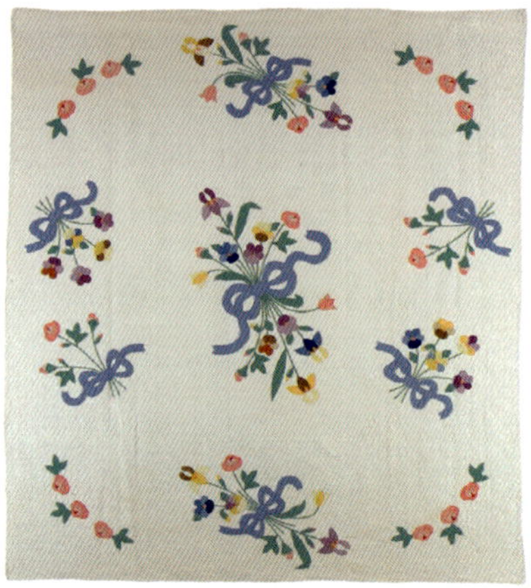

Bouquets

Maker unidentified
Possibly made in Pittsburgh, Pennsylvania
1925 - 1935
94 x 84 in.

IQM 1997.007.0796

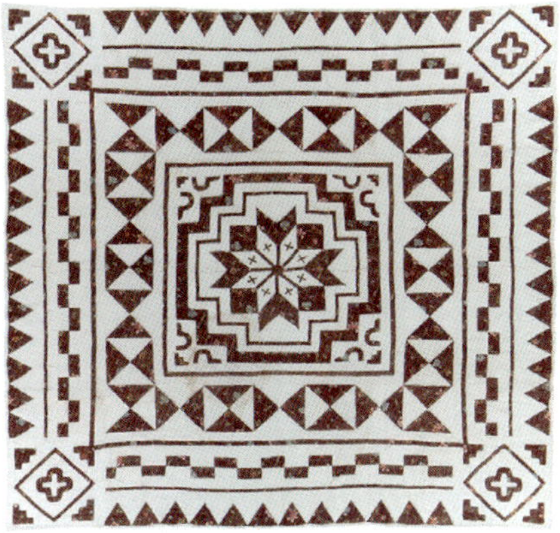

Medallion

Maker unidentified
Possibly made in Ohio
Circa 1850
79 x 81 in.

IQM 1997.007.0797

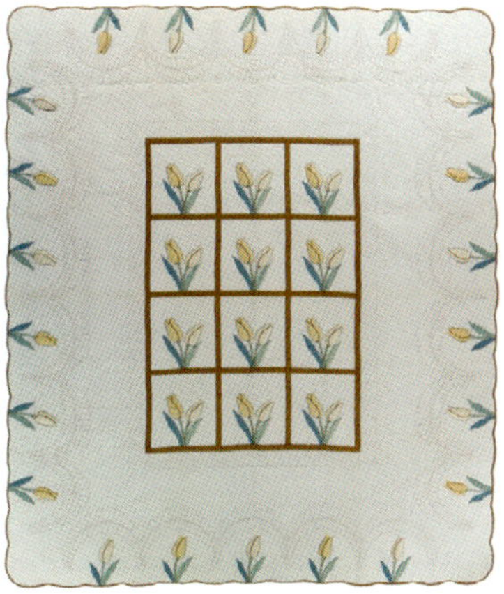

Tulip

Maker unidentified
Made in United States
Dated 1938
87.5 x 72.5 in.

IQM 1997.007.0798

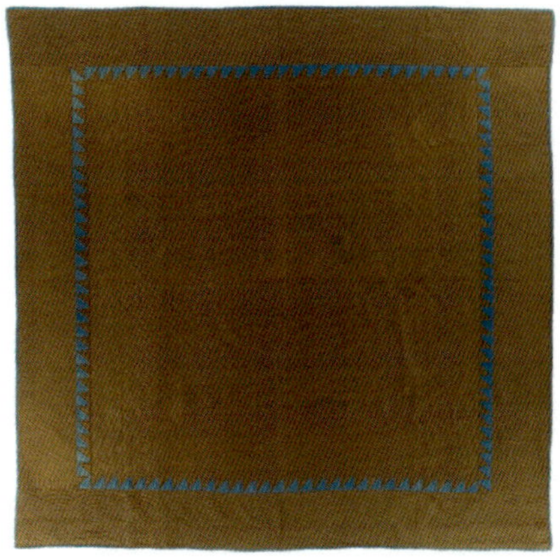

Plain Quilt

Maker unidentified
Probably made in Mifflin County, Pennsylvania
Circa 1915
75 x 75.5 in.

IQM 1997.007.0799

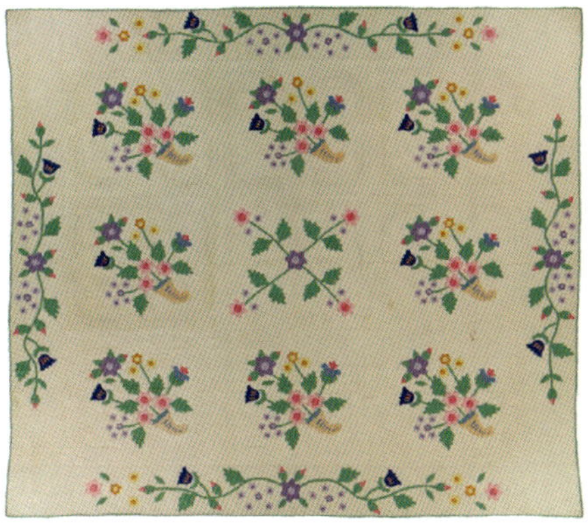

Horn of Plenty

Maker unidentified
Possibly made in Missouri
1920 - 1935
95 x 86 in.

IQM 1997.007.0801

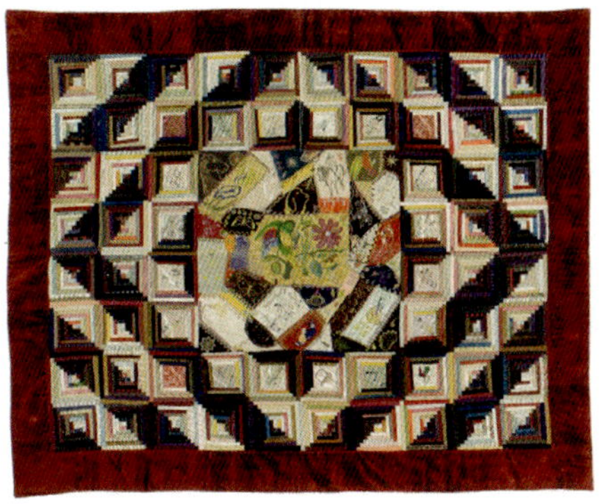

Log Cabin

Possibly made by Elizabeth Shelton
Possibly made in Coeur d'Alene, Idaho
1880 - 1900
77 x 63 in.

IQM 1997.007.0802

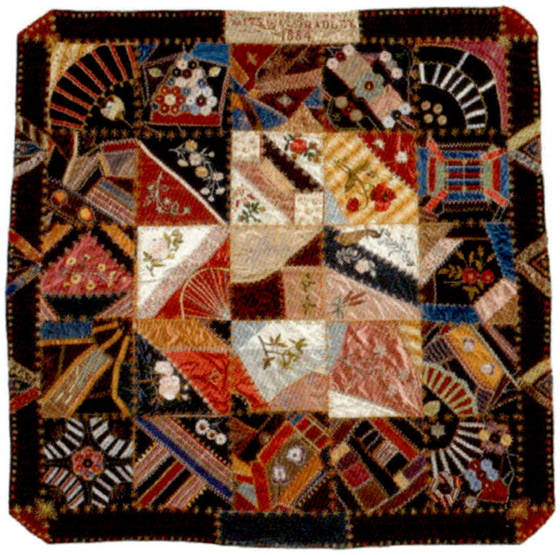

Crazy

Probably made by Lizzie M. Bradley
Probably made in George, Fayette County, Pennsylvania
Dated 1883 - 1884
67.5 x 67 in.

IQM 1997.007.0803

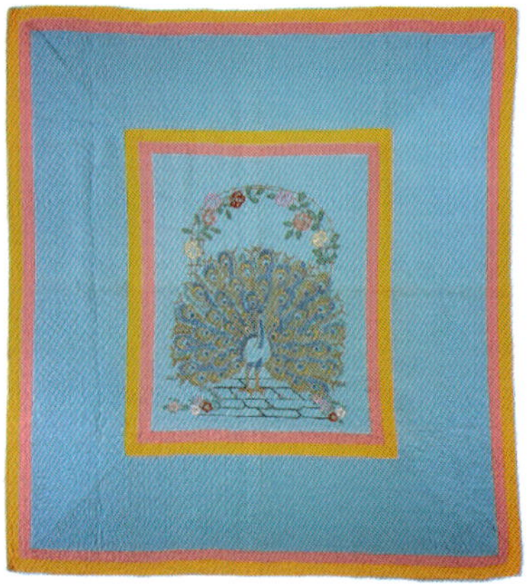

Peacock

Maker unidentified
Possibly made in Tennessee
1930 - 1950
86.5 x 77 in.

IQM 1997.007.0804

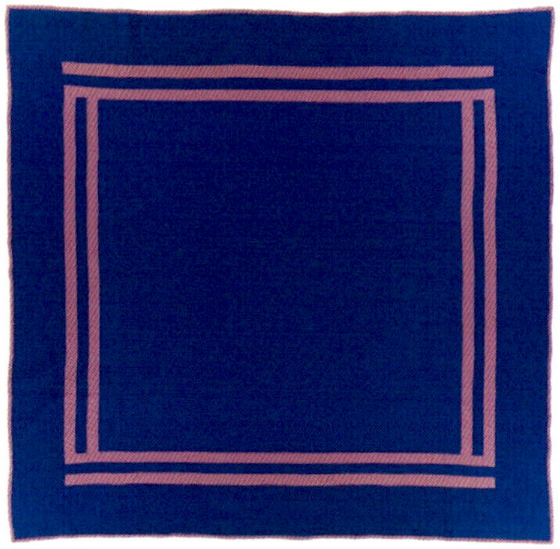

Plain Quilt

Susan Miller & mother
Probably made in Holmes County, Ohio
1925 - 1945
72.5 x 72.5 in.

IQM 1997.007.0805

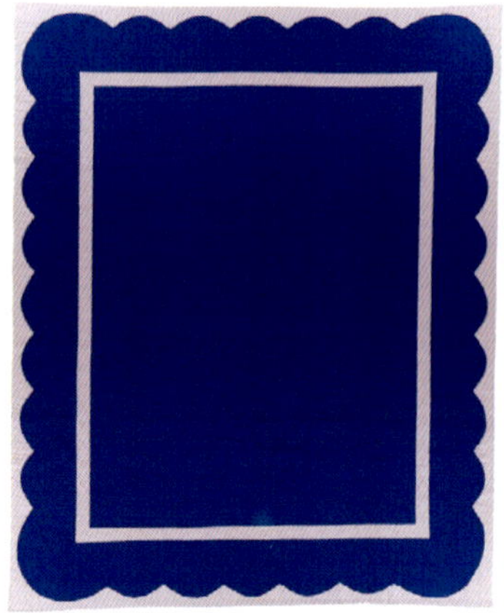

Plain Quilt

Maker unidentified
Possibly made in Ohio
1920 - 1940
90.5 x 71 in.

IQM 1997.007.0806

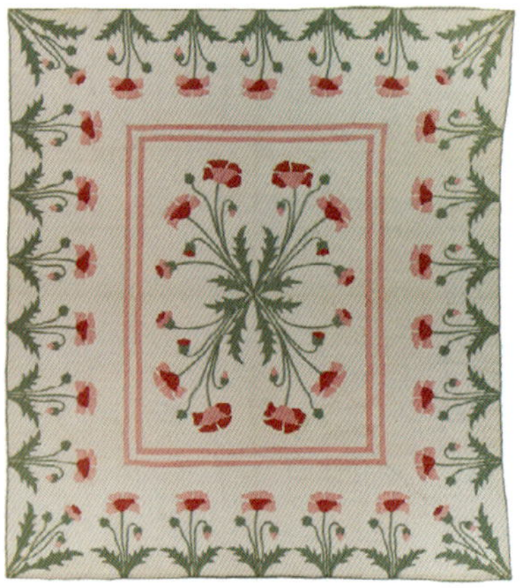

Poppy

Maker unidentified
Possibly made in Indiana
Circa 1912
93 x 81 in.

IQM 1997.007.0807

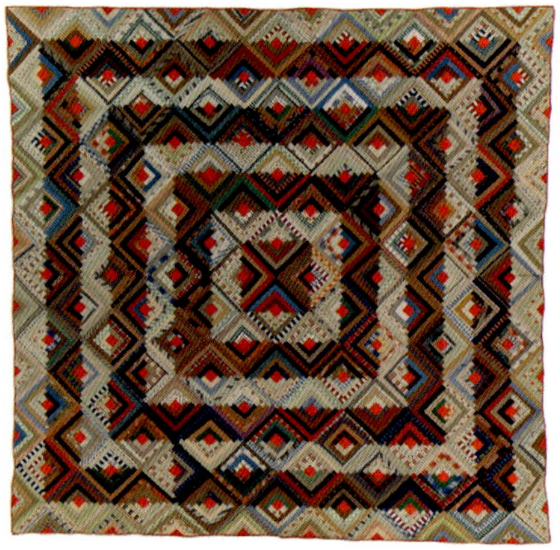

Log Cabin

Maker unidentified
Possibly made in Lancaster County, Pennsylvania
1870 - 1890
87.5 x 84.5 in.

IQM 1997.007.0808

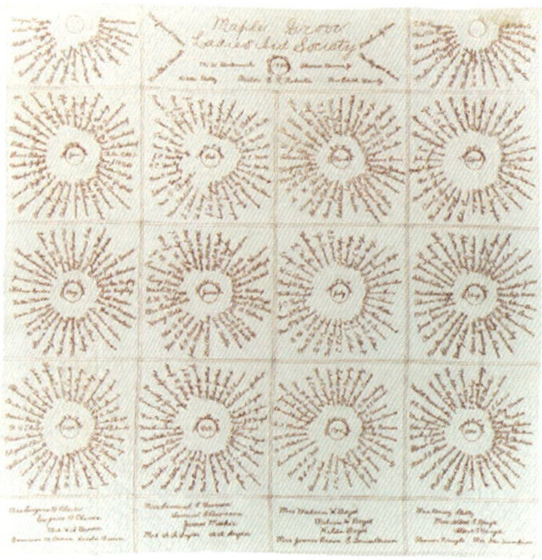

Original

Maker unidentified
Probably made in York County, Pennsylvania
Dated 1920
85 x 81.5 in.

IQM 1997.007.0809

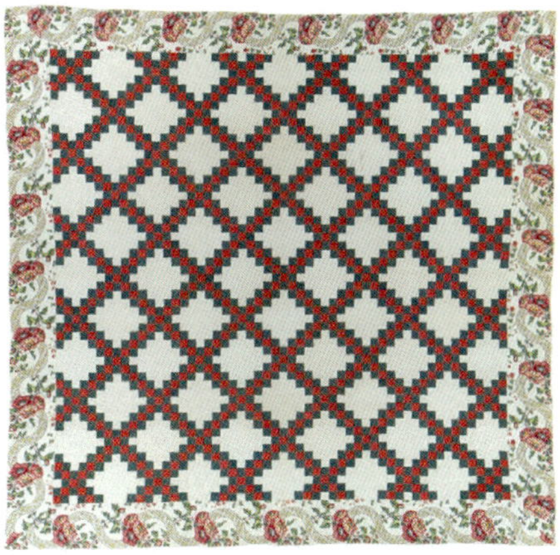

Double Irish Chain

Maker unidentified
Possibly made in Maryland
1820 - 1840
100 x 96.75 in.

IQM 1997.007.0811

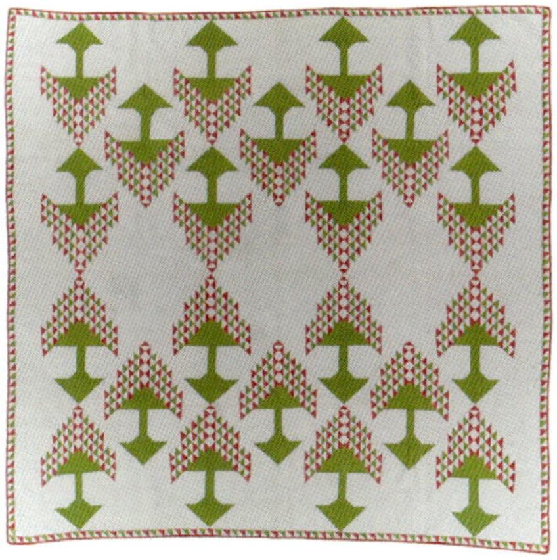

Pine Tree

Maker unidentified
Possibly made in Pennsylvania
1860 - 1880
83 x 82 in.

IQM 1997.007.0812

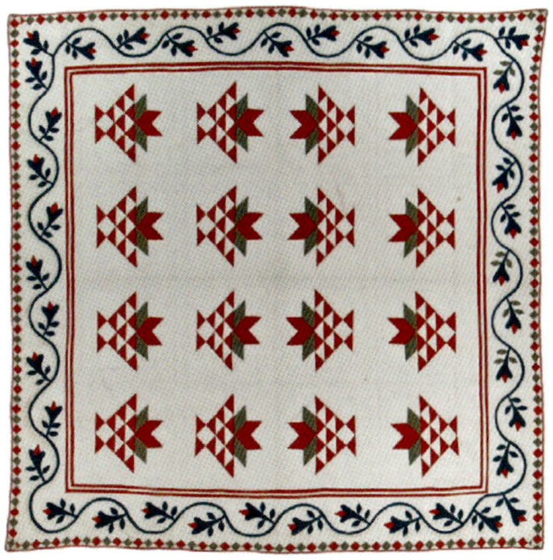

Basket

Maker unidentified
Possibly made in Ohio
1880 - 1900
89 x 85 in.

IQM 1997.007.0813

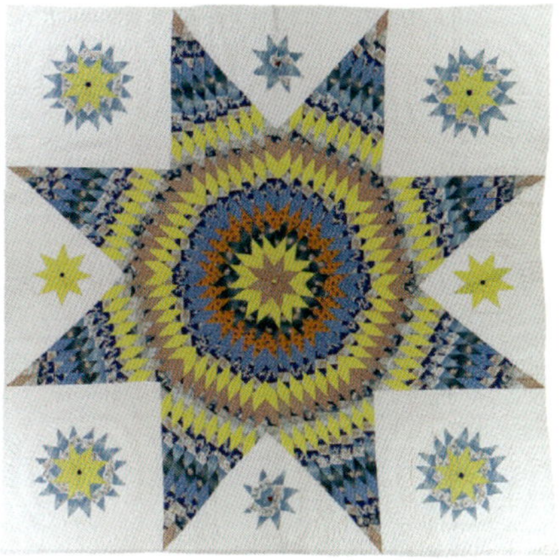

Star of Bethlehem

Maker unidentified
Possibly made in Harrisburg, Pennsylvania
1830 - 1850
87 x 84 in.

IQM 1997.007.0814

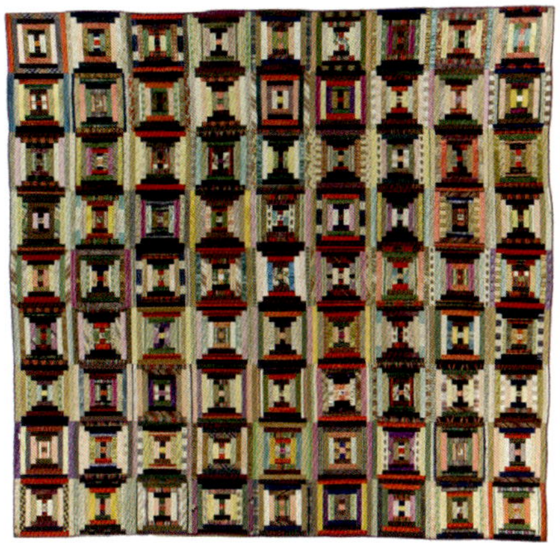

Log Cabin

Maker unidentified
Possibly made in eastern Pennsylvania
1870 - 1890
92 x 89.5 in.

IQM 1997.007.0815

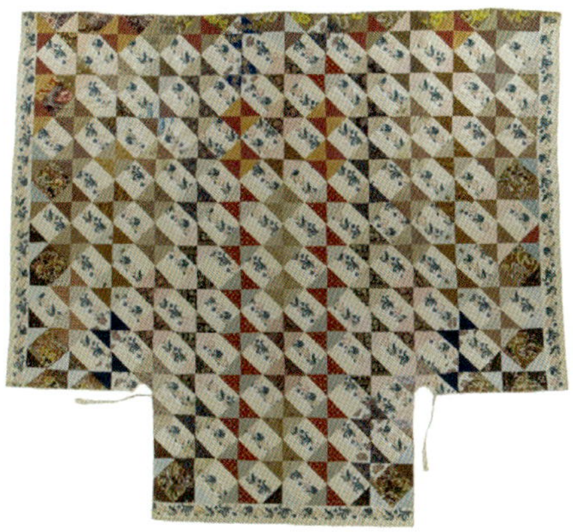

Broken Dishes variation

Maker unidentified
Possibly made in New England
1820 - 1840
106.5 x 111.5 in.

IQM 1997.007.0816

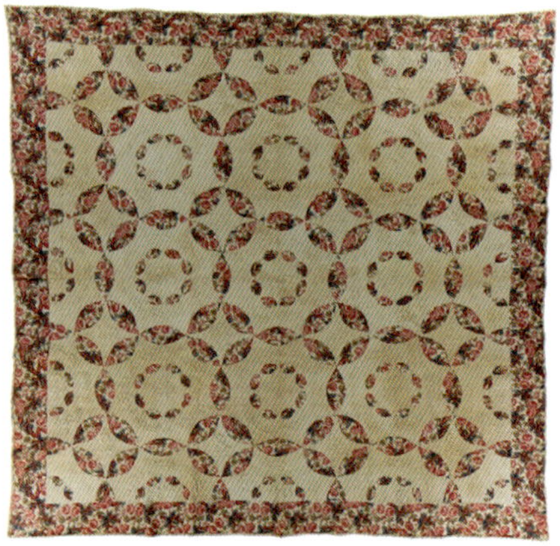

Orange Peel variation

Maker unidentified
Possibly made in New York
1820 - 1840
91.5 x 92 in.

IQM 1997.007.0817

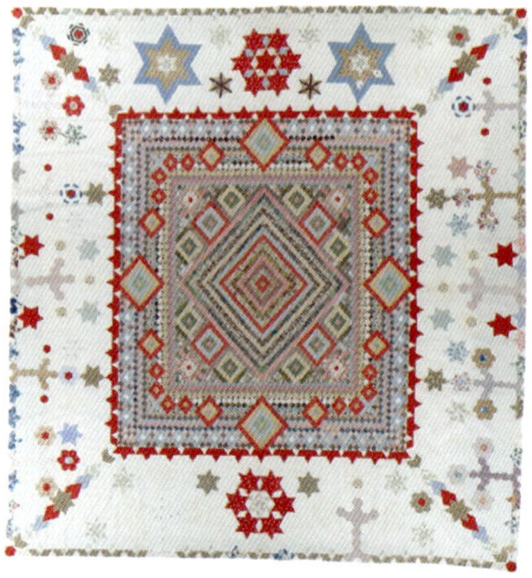

Medallion

Maker unidentified
Probably made in New Hampshire
1860 - 1880
88.5 x 81.5 in.

IQM 1997.007.0818

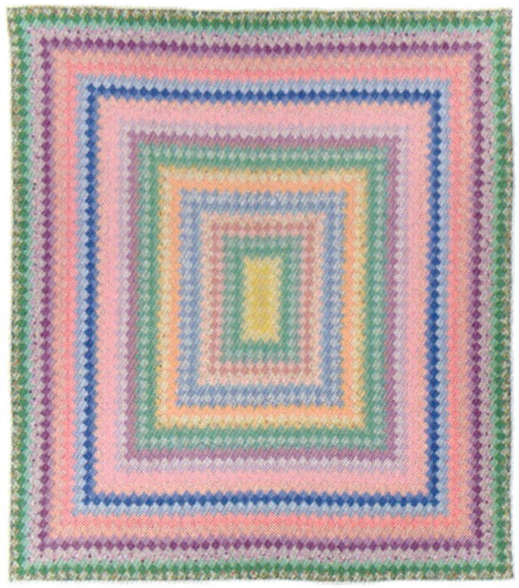

Trip around the World

Maker unidentified
Possibly made in Ohio
1930 - 1940
78 x 70 in.

IQM 1997.007.0819

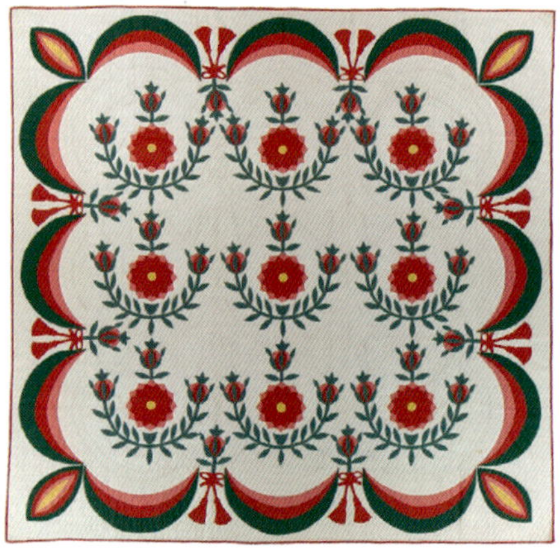

Prairie Rose

Maker unidentified
Possibly made in Indiana
Circa 1935
92 x 90 in.

IQM 1997.007.0820

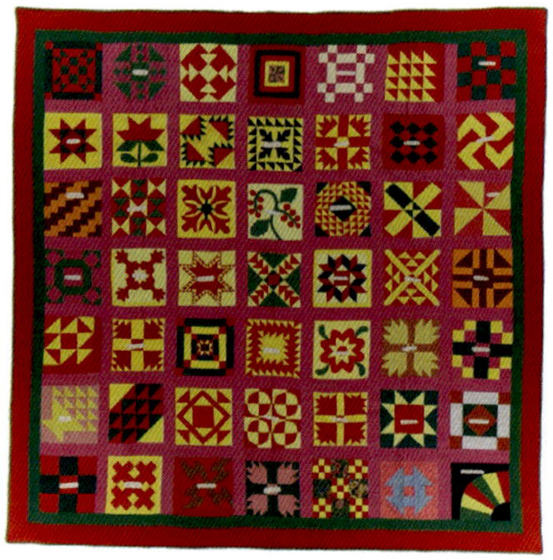

Album

Maker unidentified
Probably made in Lancaster County, Pennsylvania
Circa 1885
88.5 x 87 in.

IQM 1997.007.0821

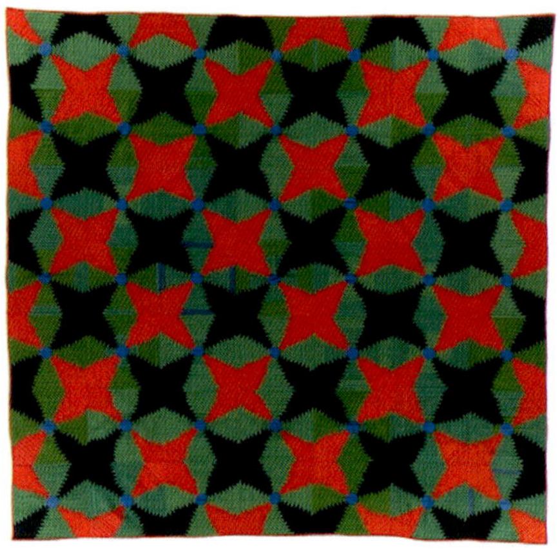

Log Cabin

Maker unidentified
Possibly made in Lancaster County, Pennsylvania
1865 - 1885
87.5 x 77 in.

IQM 1997.007.0822

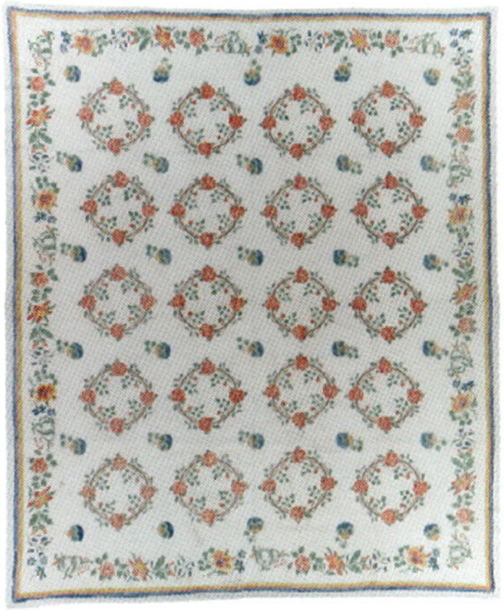

Wreath

Maker unidentified
Possibly made in Onondaga, New York
Dated 1867
87.5 x 72 in.
IQM 1997.007.0823

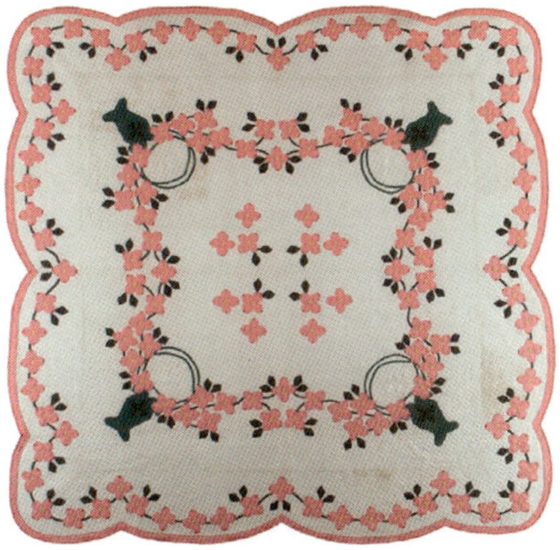

Pink Dogwood

Maker unidentified
Possibly made in Indiana
Circa 1930
84 x 83 in.
IQM 1997.007.0824

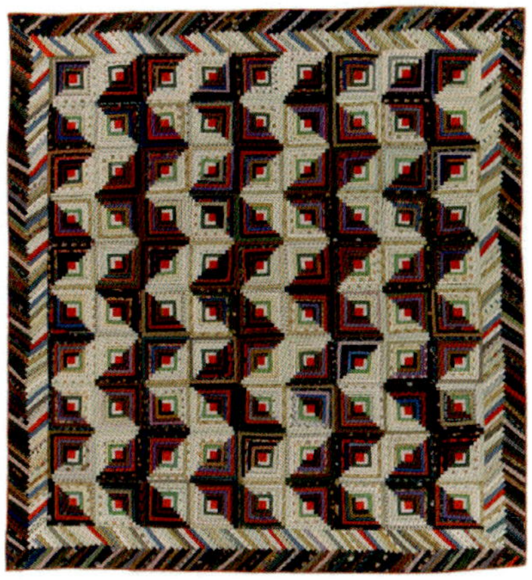

Log Cabin

Maker unidentified
Possibly made in Hagerstown or Franklin County, Maryland or Pennsylvania
1870 - 1890
87 x 79.5 in.
IQM 1997.007.0825

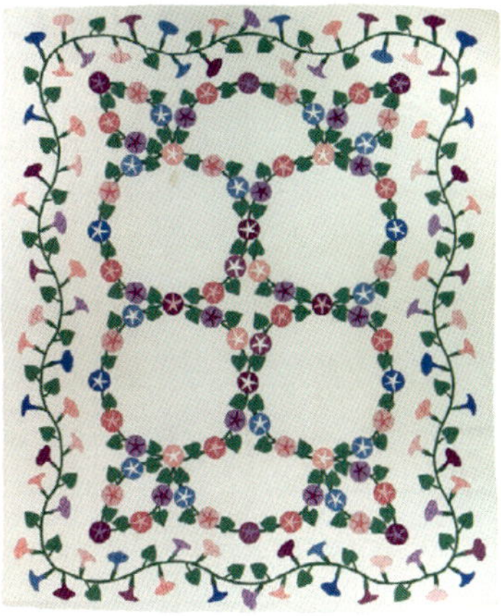

Morning Glory

Maker unidentified
Possibly made in Deerfield, Massachusetts
Dated 1935
89 x 70.75 in.
IQM 1997.007.0826

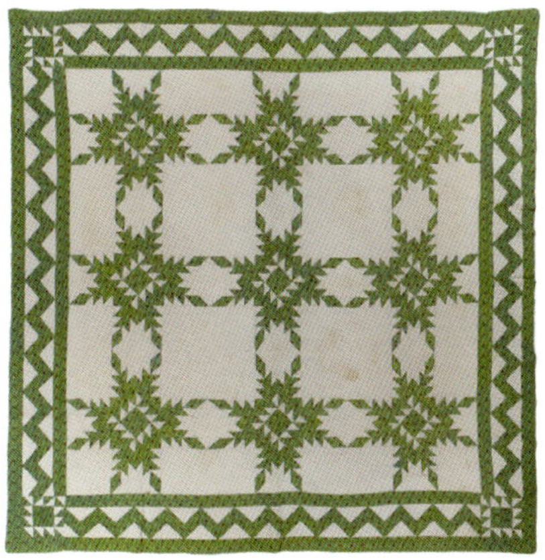

Feathered Star

Maker unidentified
Possibly made in Pennsylvania
1830 - 1850
84.5 x 86.5 in.
IQM 1997.007.0827

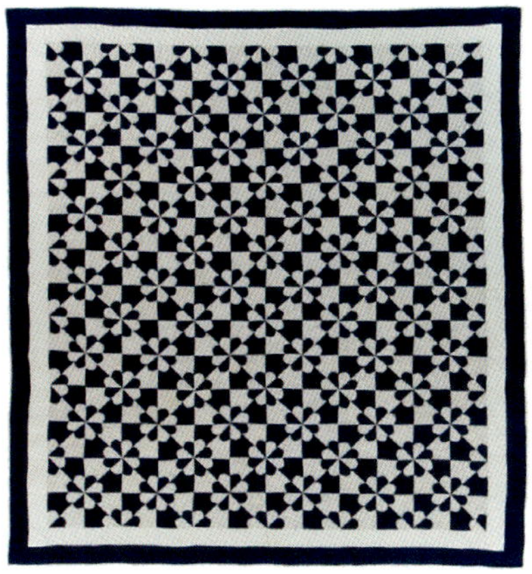

Hearts and Gizzards

Maker unidentified
Possibly made in central, Pennsylvania
Dated 1898
81 x 71 in.
IQM 1997.007.0828

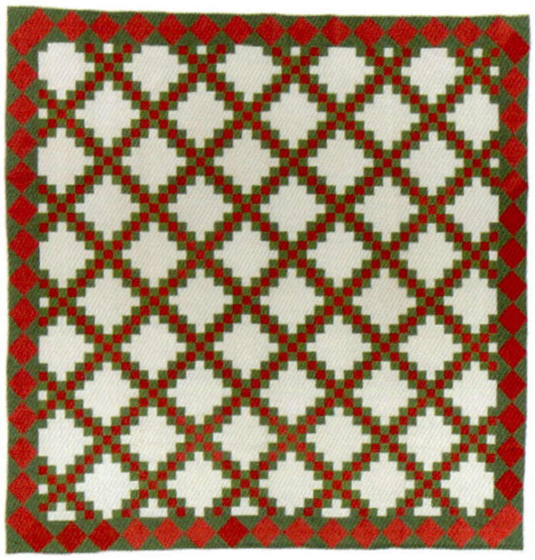

Double Irish Chain

Maker unidentified
Possibly made in Adams County, Pennsylvania
1840 - 1860
91.5 x 95.5 in.

IQM 1997.007.0829

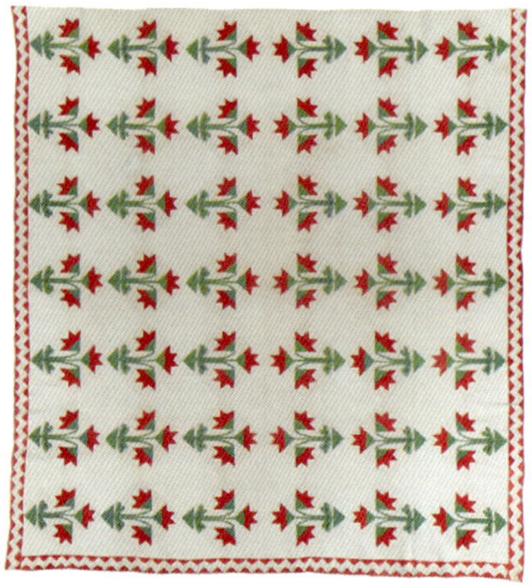

Lily

Maker unidentified
Possibly made in Mt. Somers County, Pennsylvania
1840 - 1860
98.5 x 90 in.

IQM 1997.007.0830

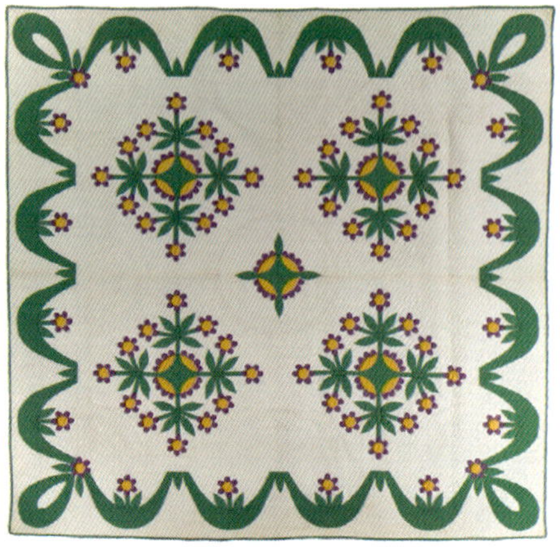

Whig Rose variation

Maker unidentified
Possibly made in Cleveland, Ohio
1920 - 1940
86 x 85 in.

IQM 1997.007.0831

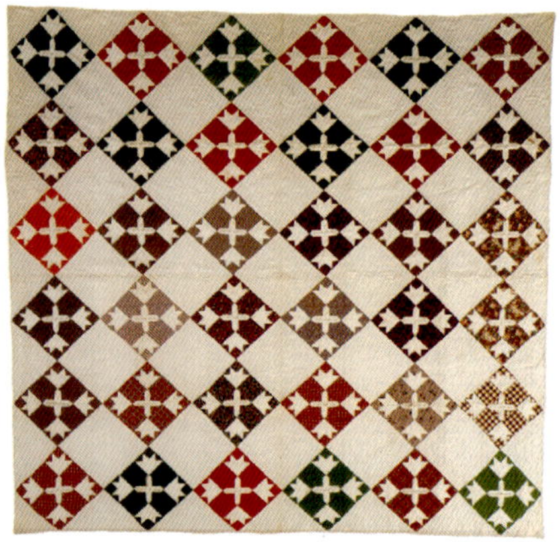

Bear's Paw

Maker unidentified
Made in Hilliar Township, Knox County, Ohio
Dated 1853
82 x 83.5 in.

IQM 1997.007.0832

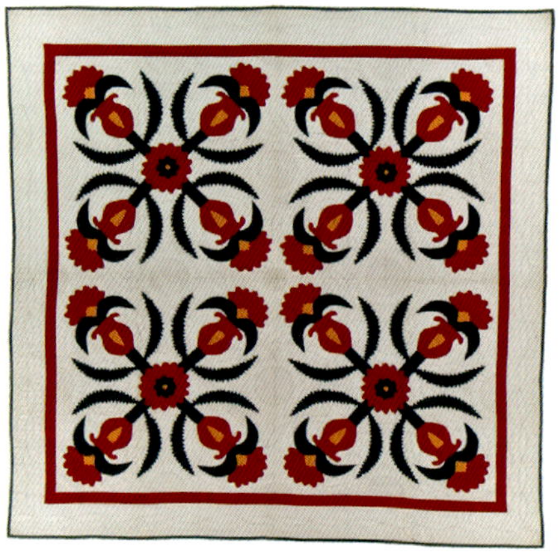

Coxcomb

Maker unidentified
Possibly made in southern Indiana
1880 - 1900
83 x 83 in.

IQM 1997.007.0833

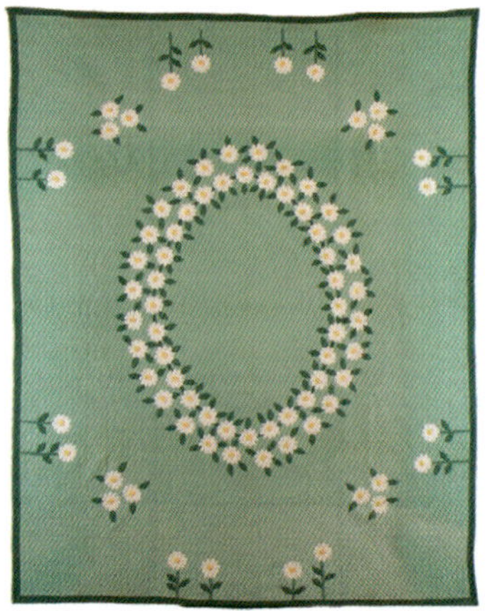

Daisy Chain

Maker unidentified
Possibly made in Shaker Heights, Ohio
Circa 1936
100 x 76.5 in.

IQM 1997.007.0834

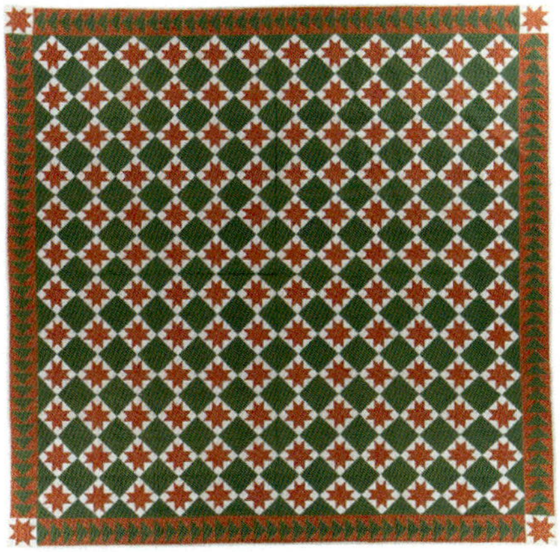

Sawtooth Star

Maker unidentified
Possibly made in Pennsylvania
1850 - 1870
88.5 x 86 in.

IQM 1997.007.0835

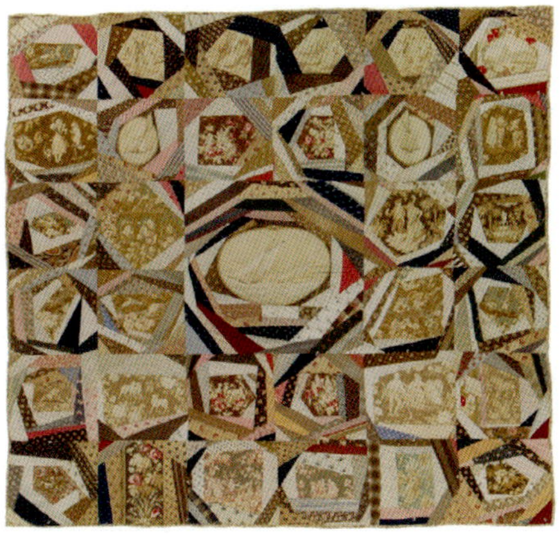

Crazy

Maker unidentified
Made in United States
Circa 1893
78 x 81 in.

IQM 1997.007.0838

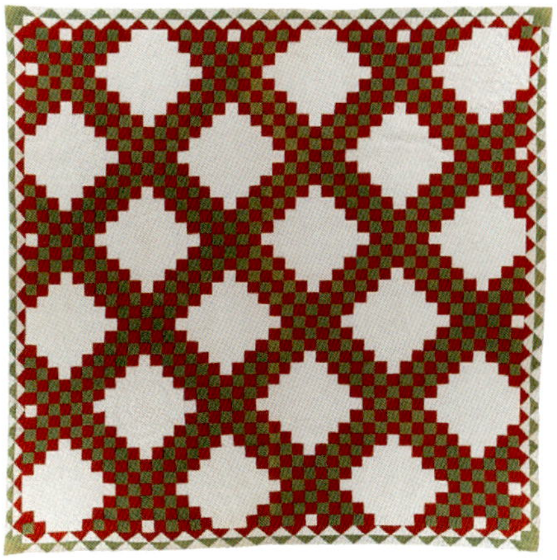

Triple Irish Chain

Probably made by Mary Elizabeth McCauley
Possibly made in Towson, Maryland
1860 - 1880
83 x 81.5 in.

IQM 1997.007.0839

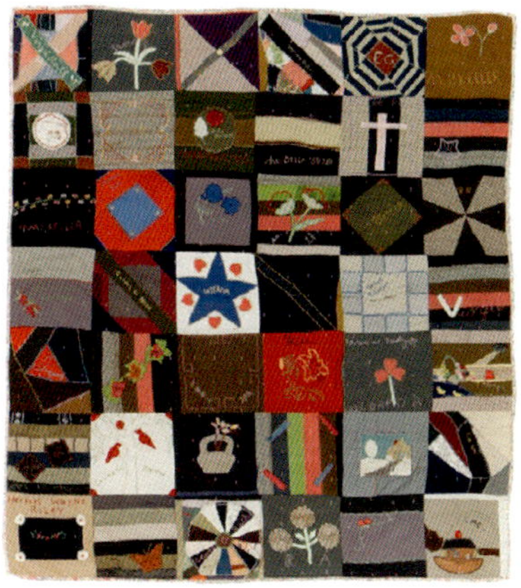

Album

Maker unidentified
Possibly made in Kentucky
Dated 1932
75 x 66 in.

IQM 1997.007.0840

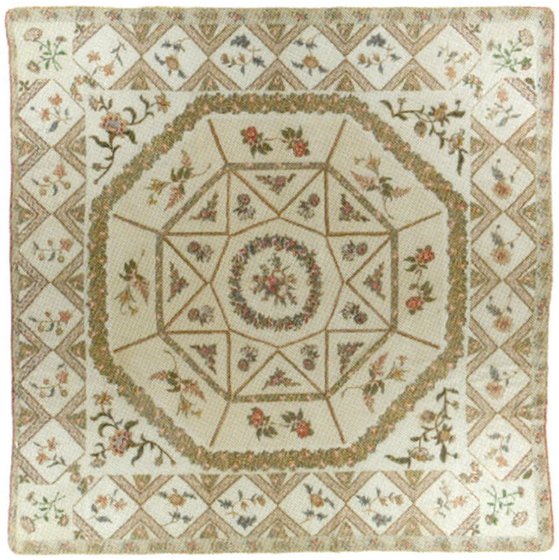

Medallion

Maker unidentified
Made in United States
1820 - 1840
104 x 102.5 in.

IQM 1997.007.0841

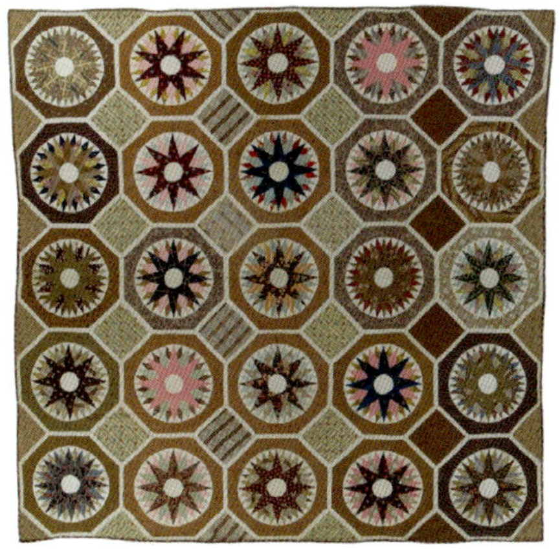

Rising Star

Maker unidentified
Possibly made in Pennsylvania
1810 - 1830
95.5 x 94 in.

IQM 1997.007.0842

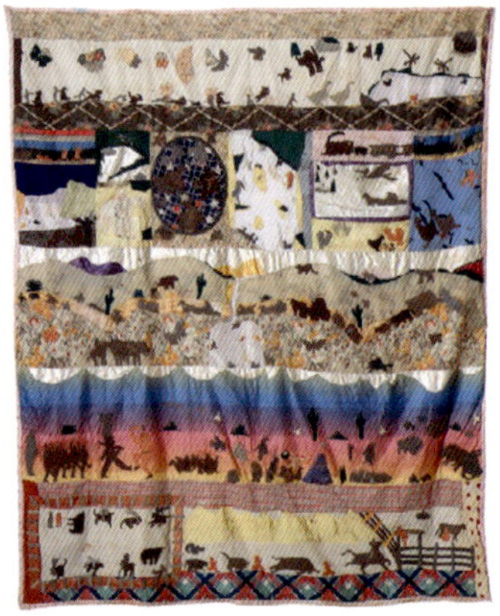

Uncle Clint's Quilt

Clinton R. Hamilton
Made in Washington, DC
Circa 1935
77 x 62.5 in.

IQM 1997.007.0843

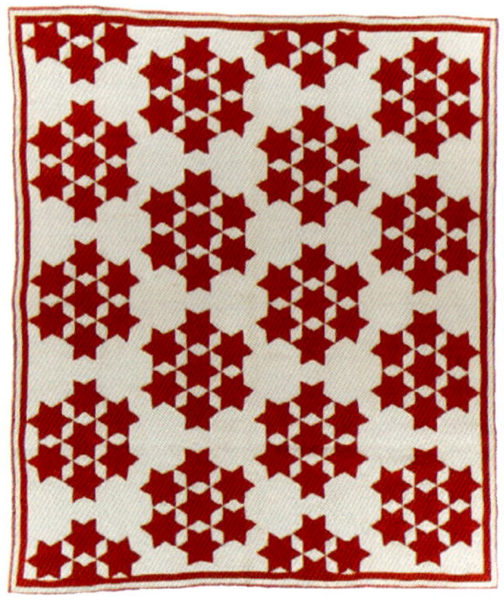

Seven Sisters

Maker unidentified
Possibly made in Indiana
1850 - 1870
80 x 66.5 in.

IQM 1997.007.0844

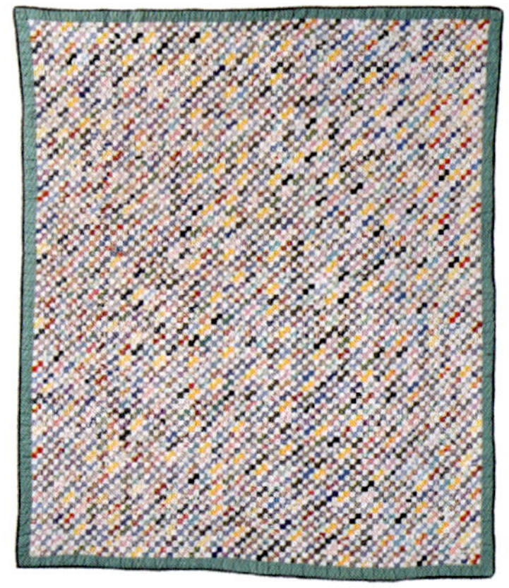

Bow Tie

Possibly made by Rachel Scofield
Possibly made in Indiana
1930 - 1950
81 x 67 in.

IQM 1997.007.0845

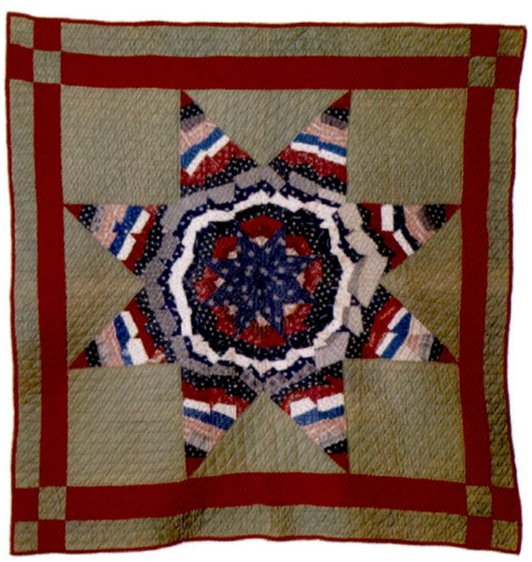

String Star

Maker unidentified
Possibly made in Indiana
1880 - 1900
74.5 x 72.5 in.

IQM 1997.007.0846

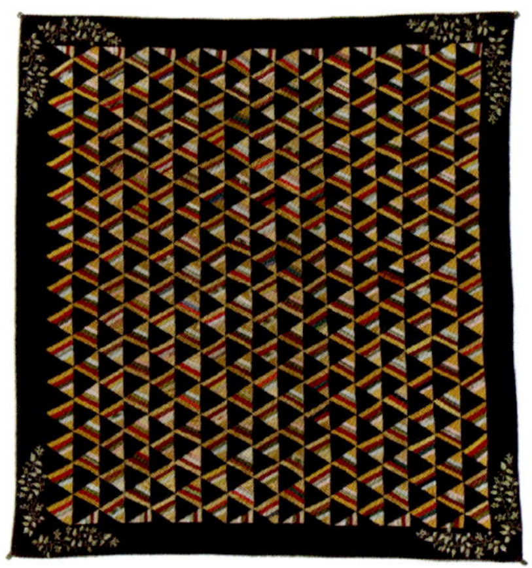

Roman Stripe

Maker unidentified
Possibly made in Knox County, Ohio
1880 - 1900
68 x 62.5 in.

IQM 1997.007.0847

Whole Cloth

Maker unidentified
Made in United States
1820 - 1840
88.5 x 88.5 in.

IQM 1997.007.0849

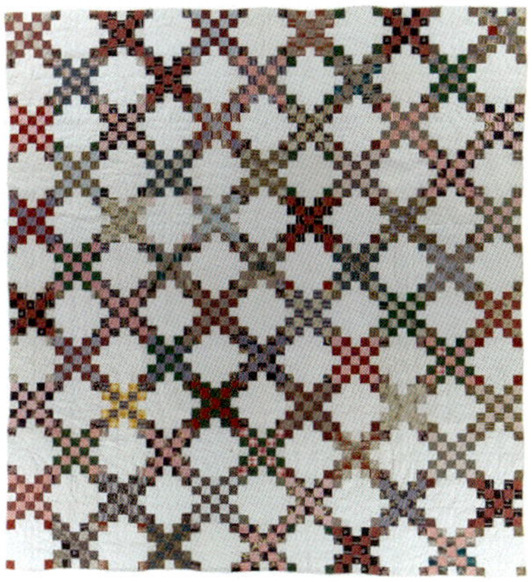

Double Irish Chain

Maker unidentified
Made in United States
1840 - 1860
93.5 x 84.5 in.

IQM 1997.007.0850

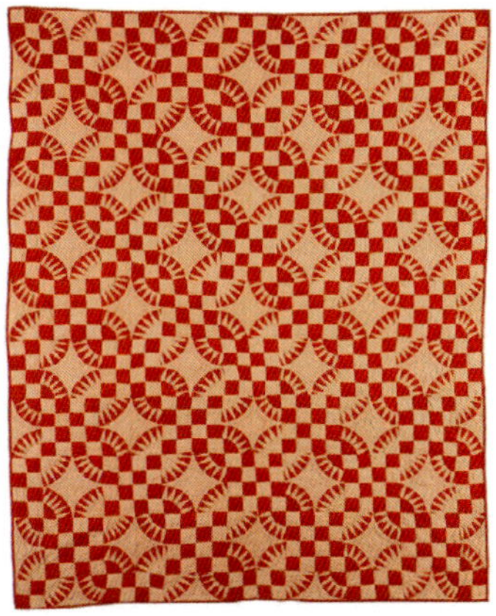

Dogwood Blossom

Maker unidentified
Probably made in midwestern United States
Circa 1928
88 x 67.5 in.

IQM 1997.007.0851

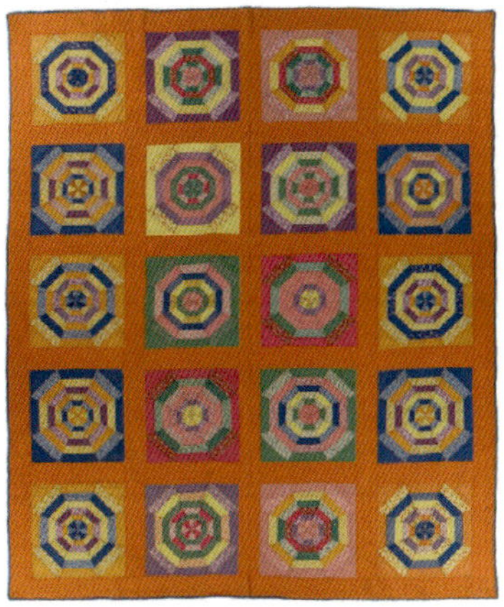

Spider Web

Maker unidentified
Possibly made in Ohio
1930 - 1940
104.5 x 81.5 in.

IQM 1997.007.0853

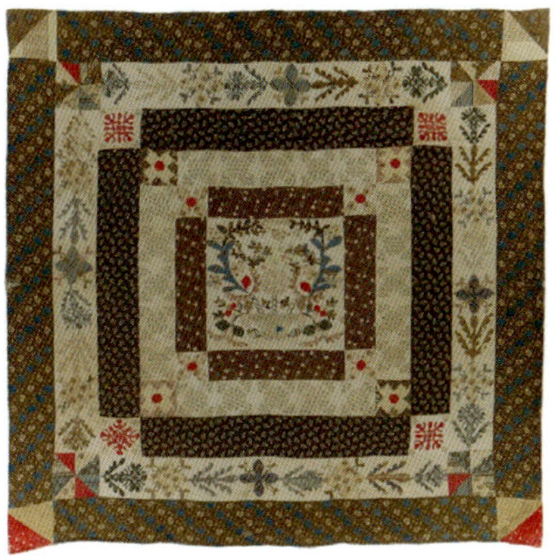

Medallion

Probably made by Bridget Hogan
Made in County Wexford, Ireland
Circa 1834
79 x 77.5 in.

IQM 1997.007.0854

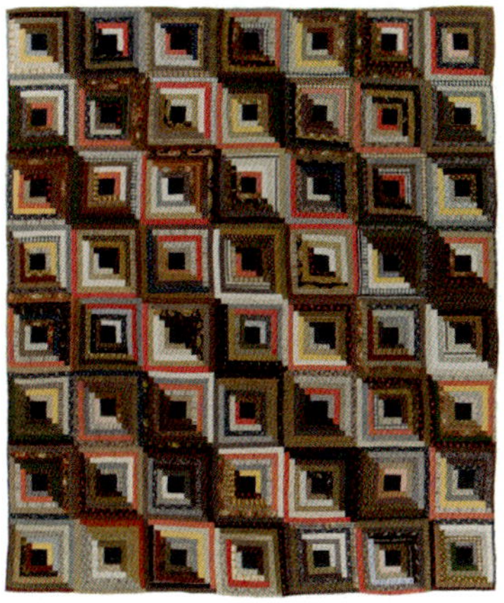

Log Cabin

Maker unidentified
Possibly made in Pennsylvania
1880 - 1900
83 x 71 in.

IQM 1997.007.0855

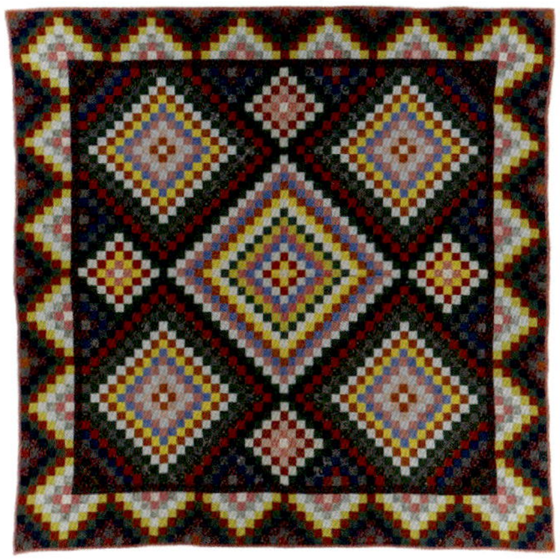

Philadelphia Pavement variation

Maker unidentified
Possibly made in Lancaster County, Pennsylvania
1880 - 1900
82 x 79 in.

IQM 1997.007.0856

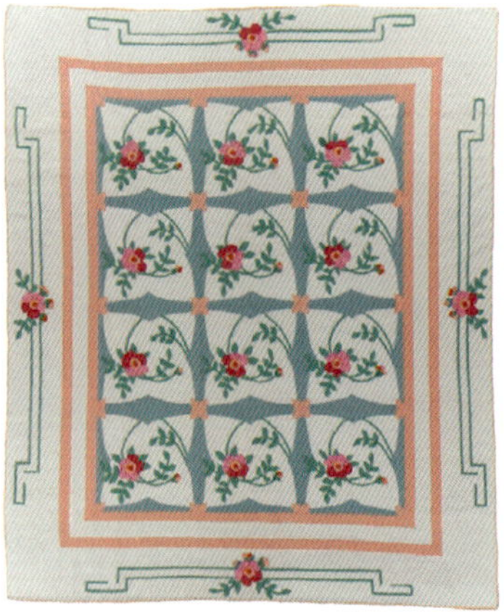

Plum Blossoms

Maker unidentified
Possibly made in Indiana
1935 - 1945
93.5 x 76 in.

IQM 1997.007.0857

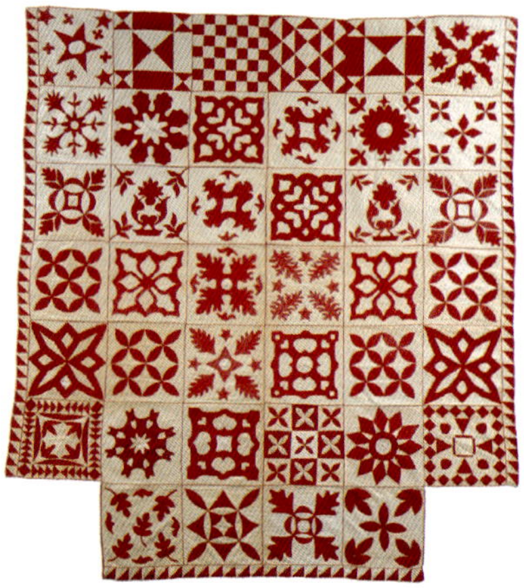

Album

Maker unidentified
Made in Boston, Massachusetts
Dated 1850 - 1851
93 x 83 in.

IQM 1997.007.0859

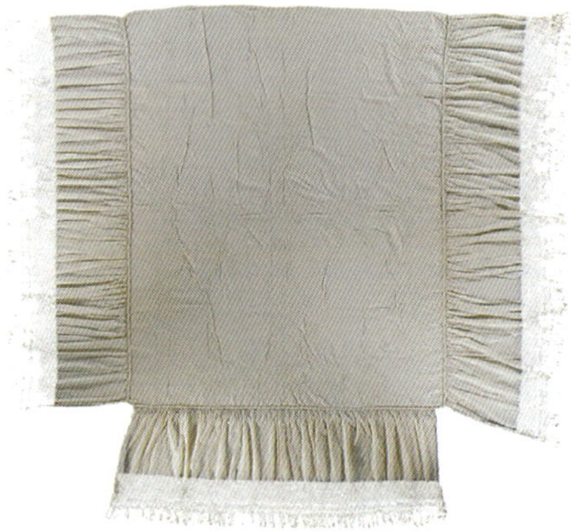

Whole Cloth

Maker unidentified
Made in United States
1800 - 1830
92 x 92 in.

IQM 1997.007.0860

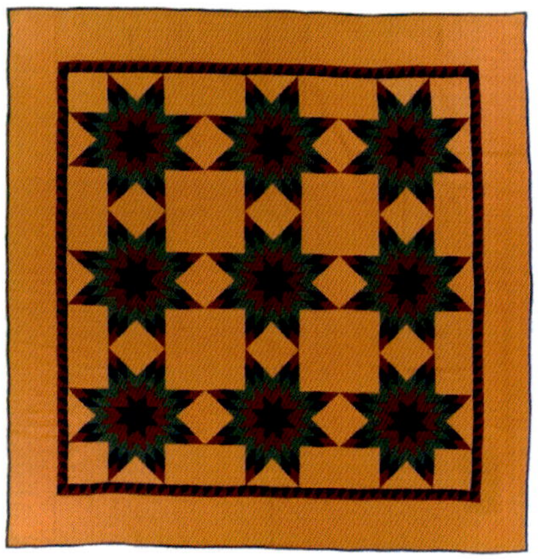

Touching Stars

Maker unidentified
Probably made in Pennsylvania
1880 - 1900
87.75 x 85 in.

IQM 1997.007.0861

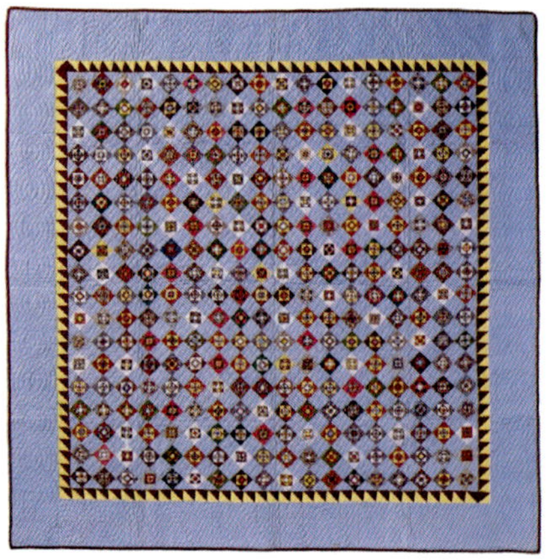

Square on Square

Probably made by Fianna Shafer Grabill
Made in Lancaster County, Pennsylvania
Dated 1882
79 x 78 in.

IQM 1997.007.0862

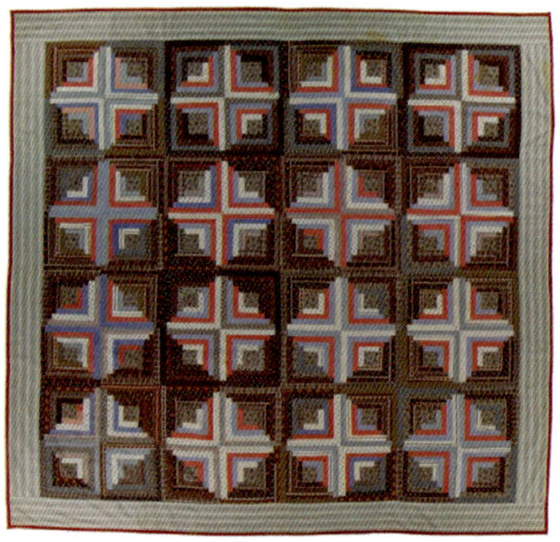

Log Cabin

Maker unidentified
Possibly made in Ephrata, Pennsylvania
1870 - 1890
94 x 96 in.

IQM 1997.007.0863

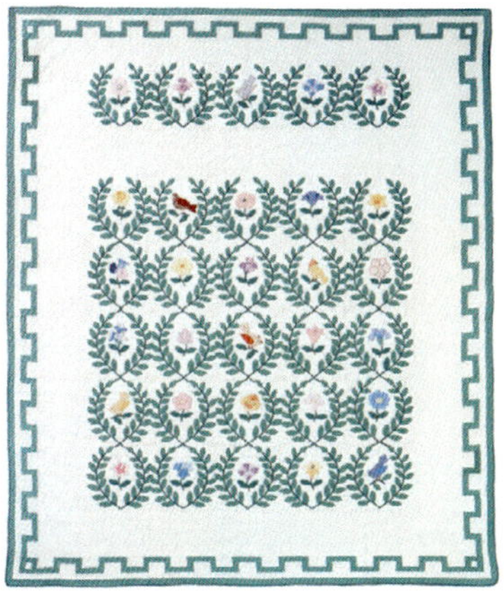

Laurel Wreath

Maker unidentified
Probably made in Ohio
1930 - 1950
93.5 x 76.5 in.

IQM 1997.007.0864

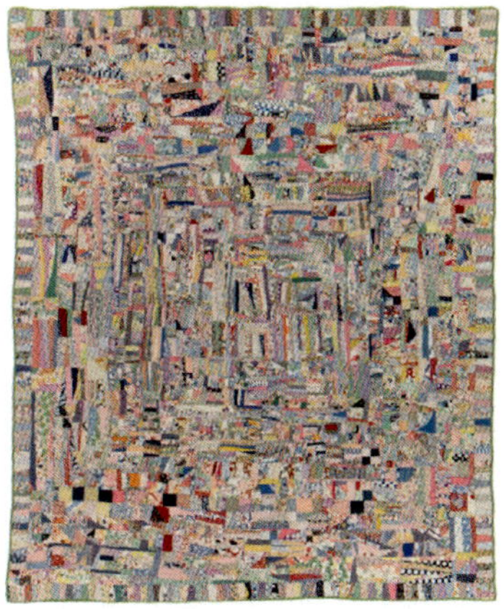

Crazy

Maker unidentified
Possibly made in Illinois
1930 - 1940
82.5 x 67.5 in.

IQM 1997.007.0866

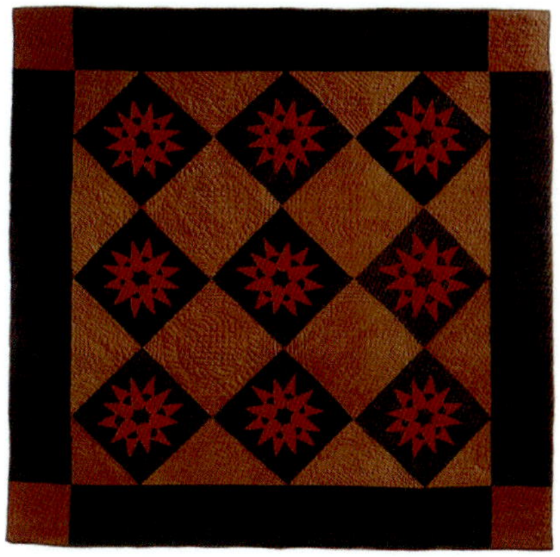

Cog Wheel

Maker unidentified
Probably made in Lancaster County, Pennsylvania
1890 - 1910
85 x 85 in.

IQM 1997.007.0867

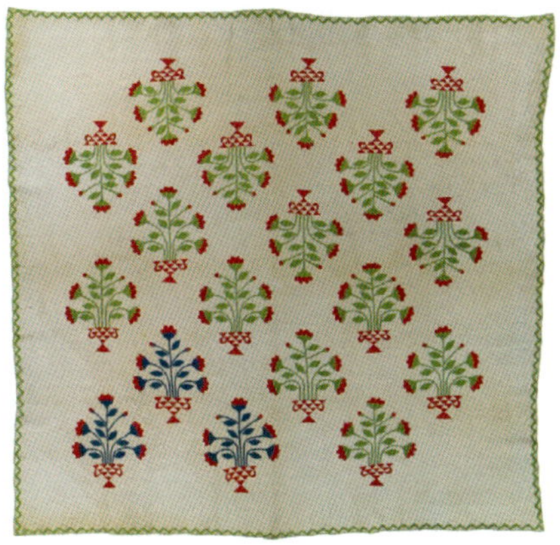

Pots of Flowers

Susan M. Lawrence
Possibly made in Greene County, Ohio
Dated 1853
94.25 x 93 in.

IQM 1997.007.0869

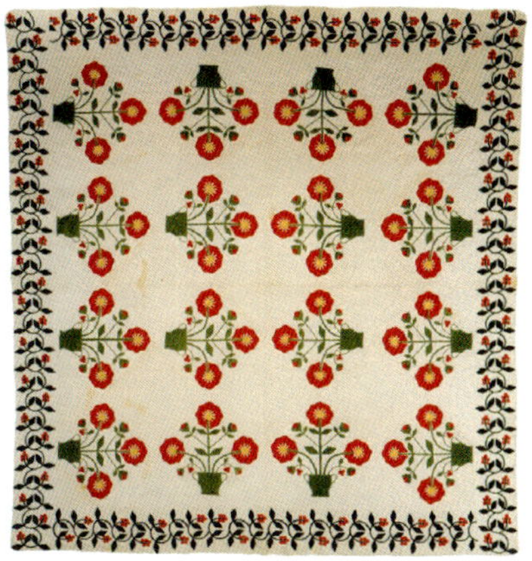

Pots of Flowers

Maker unidentified
Possibly made in Indiana
1850 - 1870
88 x 80 in.

IQM 1997.007.0870

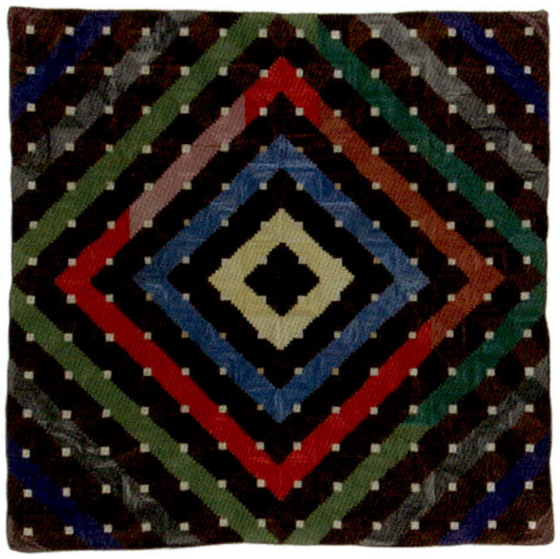

Log Cabin

Maker unidentified
Possibly made in eastern Pennsylvania
1865 - 1885
83.5 x 83.5 in.

IQM 1997.007.0871

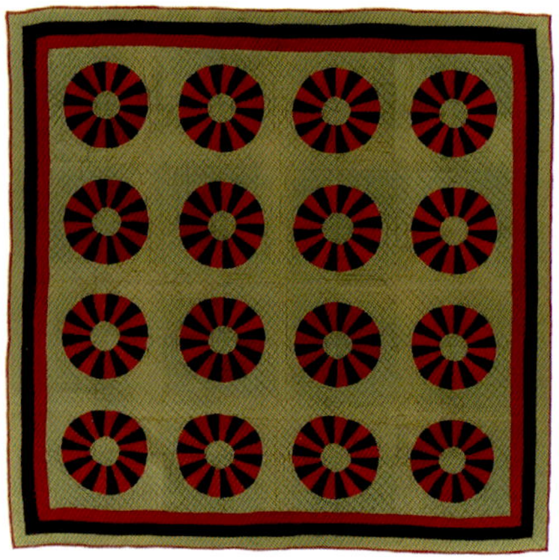

Wagon Wheel

Maker unidentified
Possibly made in Pennsylvania
1890 - 1910
78 x 78 in.

IQM 1997.007.0873

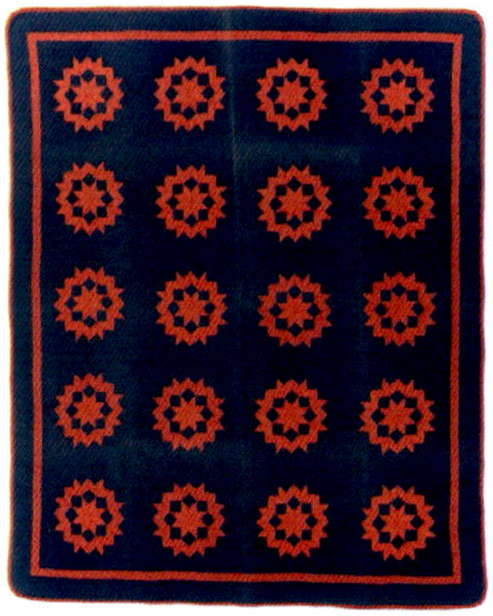

Carpenter's Wheel

Maker unidentified
Possibly made in Holmes County, Ohio
1890 - 1910
87 x 70 in.

IQM 1997.007.0874

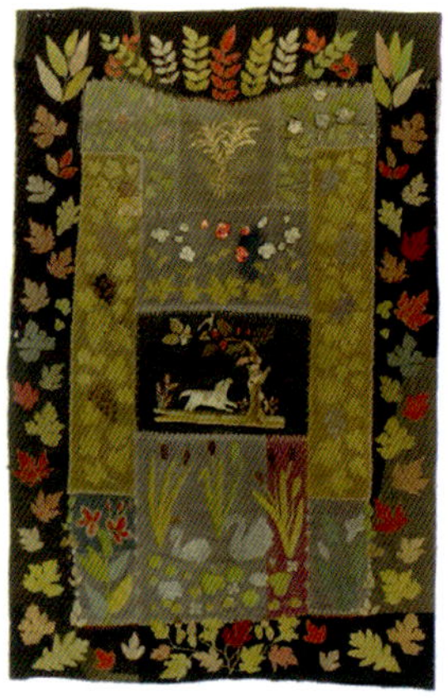

Original

Maker unidentified
Made in United States
1870 - 1890
85.5 x 52.5 in.

IQM 1997.007.0875

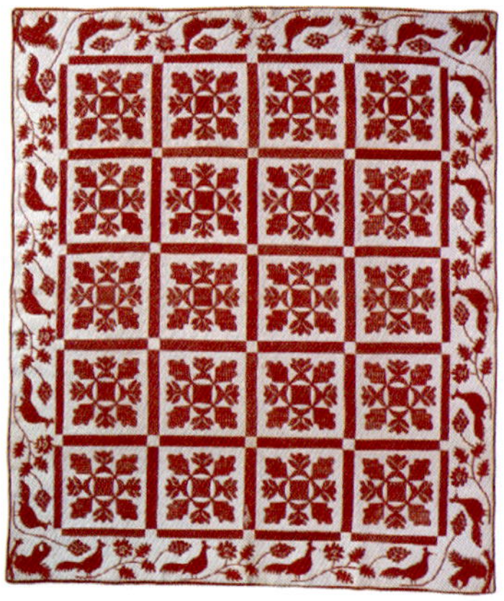

Oak Leaf

Sally Conklin
Possibly made in New York
Dated 1841
94.5 x 82 in.

IQM 1997.007.0876

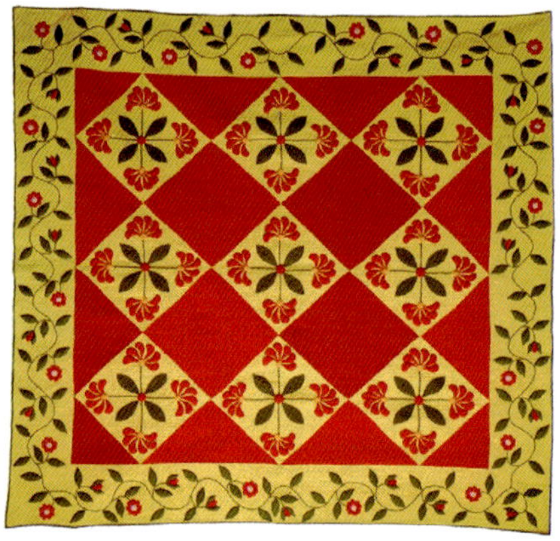

Mexican Rose

Maker unidentified
Possibly made in Pennsylvania
1860 - 1880
97 x 92.5 in.

IQM 1997.007.0877

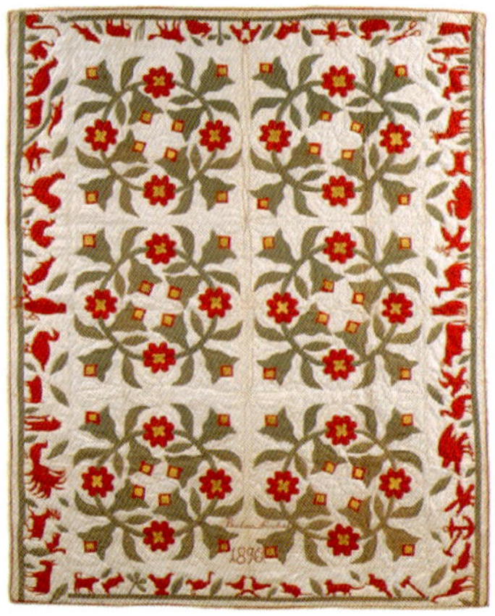

Wreath

Paulina Herdrich
Made in Sheboygan County, Wisconsin
Dated 1890
88.5 x 68.5 in.

IQM 1997.007.0878

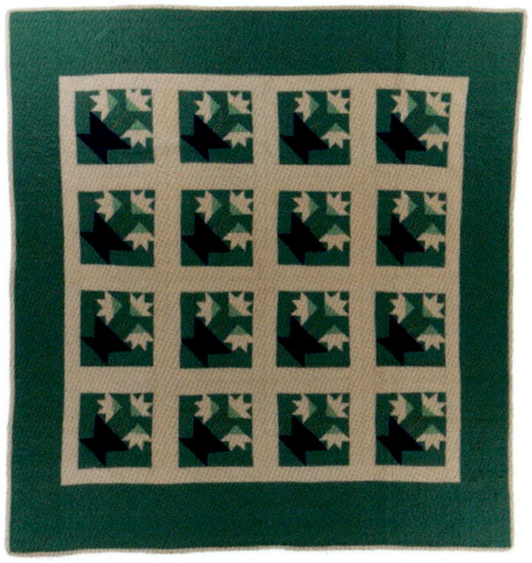

Lily

Maker unidentified
Possibly made in Ohio
1925 - 1945
74 x 80.5 in.

IQM 1997.007.0879

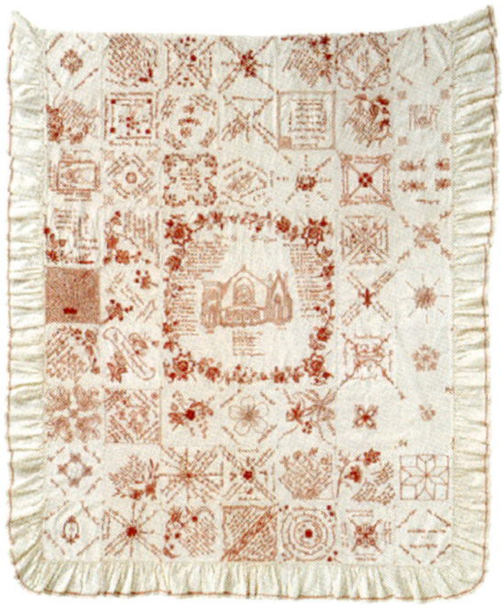

Original

Maker unidentified
Probably made in Louisville, Kentucky
Dated 1916
76.5 x 65 in.

IQM 1997.007.0880

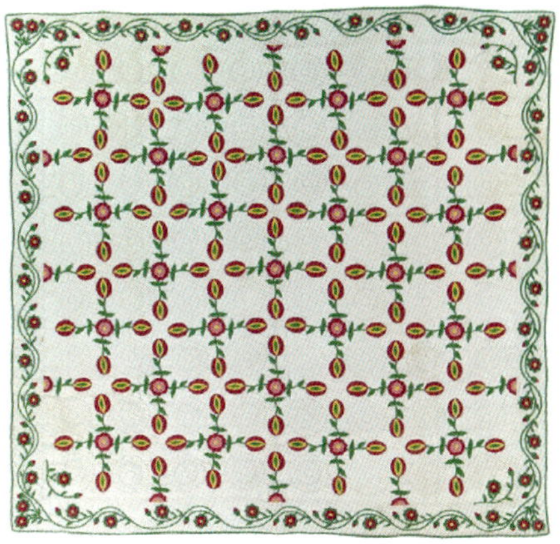

Love Apple

Maker unidentified
Possibly made in Pennsylvania
1920 - 1940
73 x 71 in.

IQM 1997.007.0881

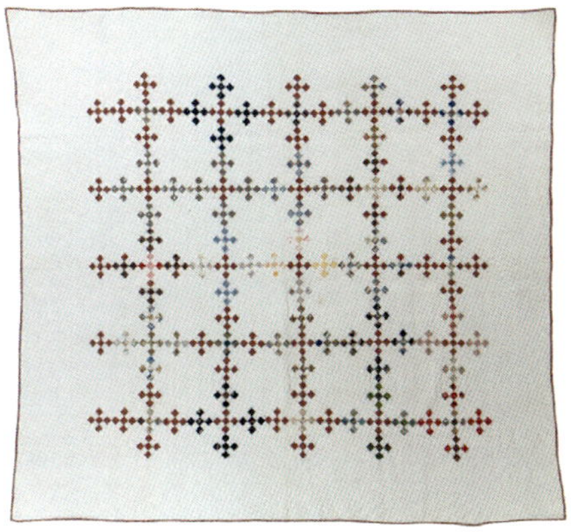

Double Nine Patch

Maker unidentified
Possibly made in Pennsylvania
1850 - 1870
75 x 72 in.

IQM 1997.007.0882

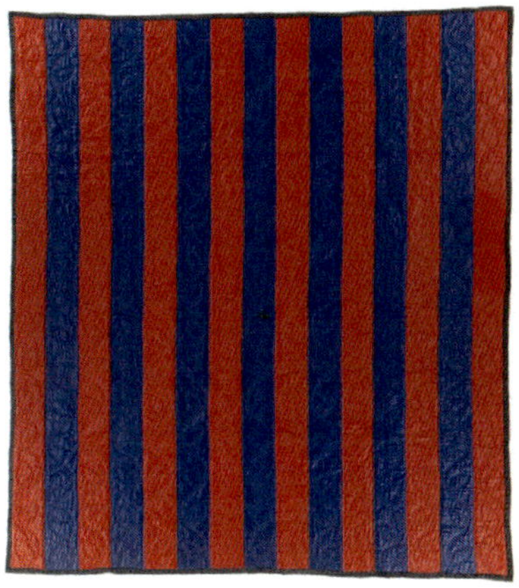

Bars

Maker unidentified
Possibly made in Kitchener, Ontario, Canada
1915 - 1935
82 x 73 in.

IQM 1997.007.0883

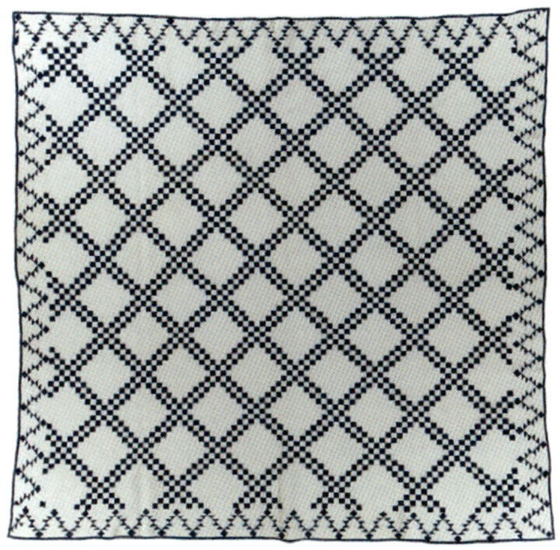

Double Irish Chain

Maker unidentified
Possibly made in Pennsylvania
1860 - 1880
79.75 x 81 in.

IQM 1997.007.0884

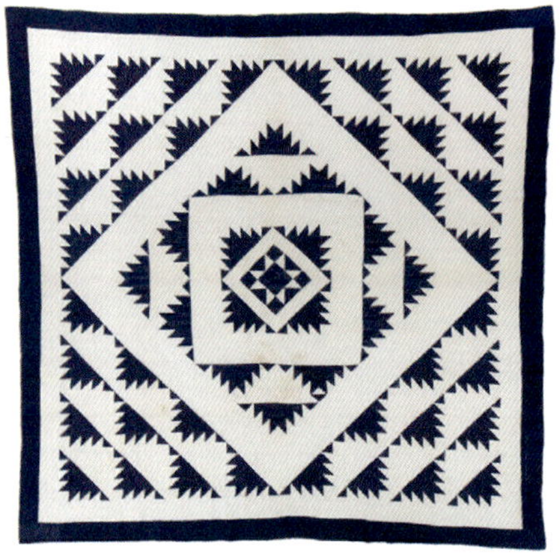

Delectable Mountains variation

Possibly made by Isabella McKearn Campbell
Made in Highland County, Virginia
1830 - 1850
92.5 x 92 in.

IQM 1997.007.0885

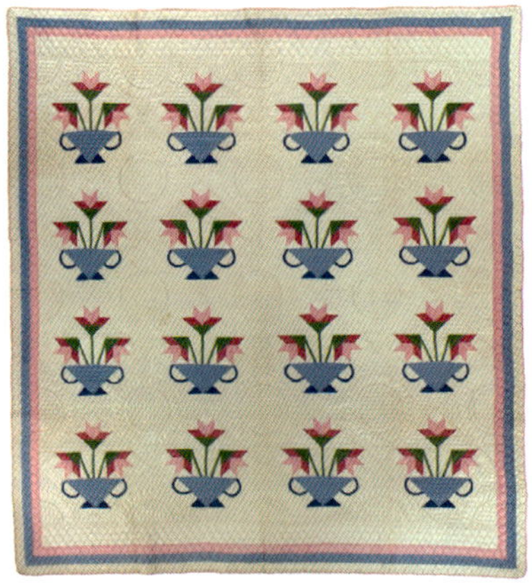

Lily

Maker unidentified
Made in United States
1925 - 1935
89 x 80 in.

IQM 1997.007.0886

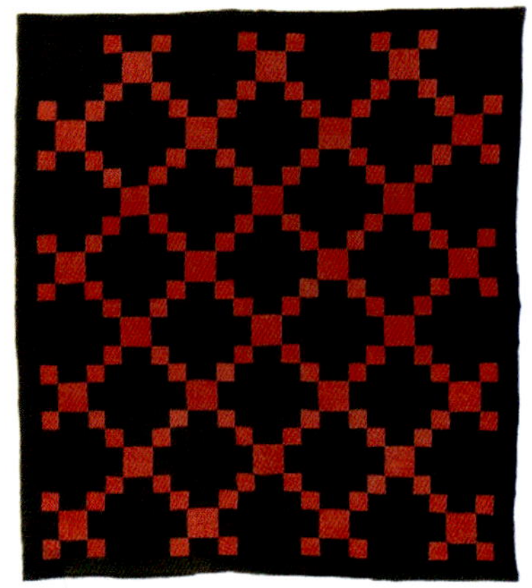

Nine Patch

Maker unidentified
Made in United States
1820 - 1840
95.5 x 83 in.

IQM 1997.007.0887

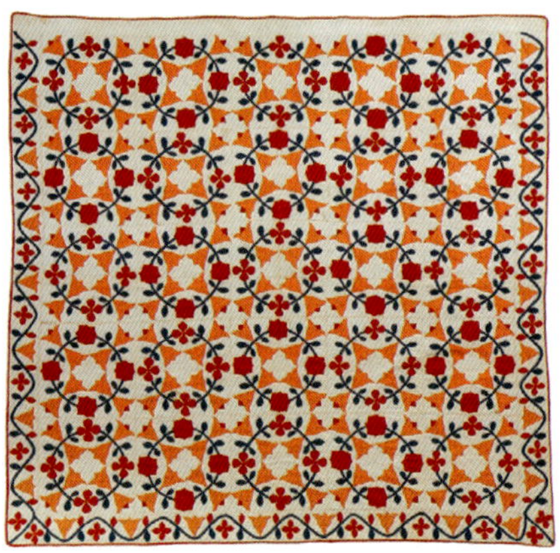

President's Wreath

Maker unidentified
Made in United States
1870 - 1880
72.5 x 71.5 in.

IQM 1997.007.0888

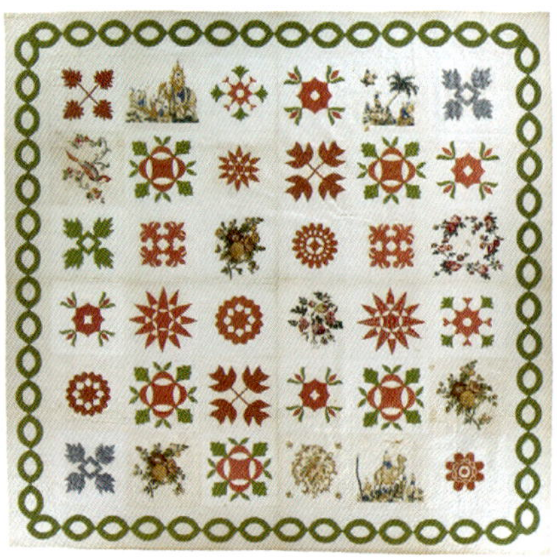

Album

Probably made by Elizabeth Stackhouse, A.C. Shreve, and Carrie
Possibly made in Pennsylvania
1840 - 1860
98 x 98 in.

IQM 1997.007.0890

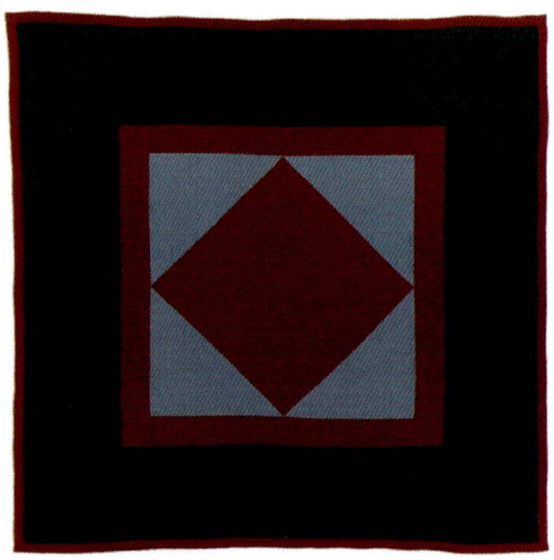

Center Diamond

Maker unidentified
Possibly made in Lancaster County, Pennsylvania
1915 - 1935
75.5 x 74.5 in.

IQM 1997.007.0892

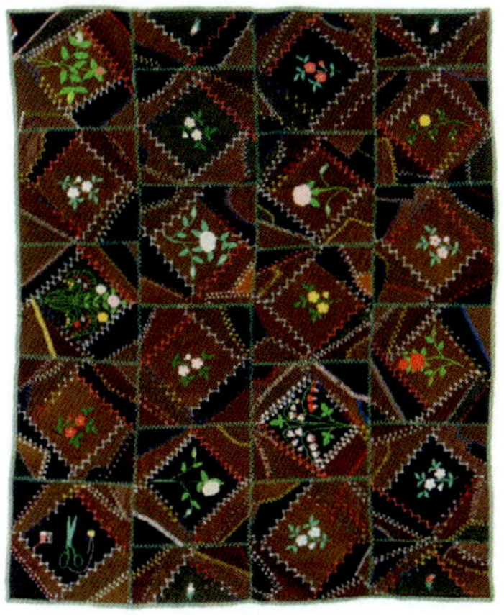

Crazy

Maker unidentified
Made in United States
1890 - 1910
80.25 x 65.5 in.

IQM 1997.007.0893

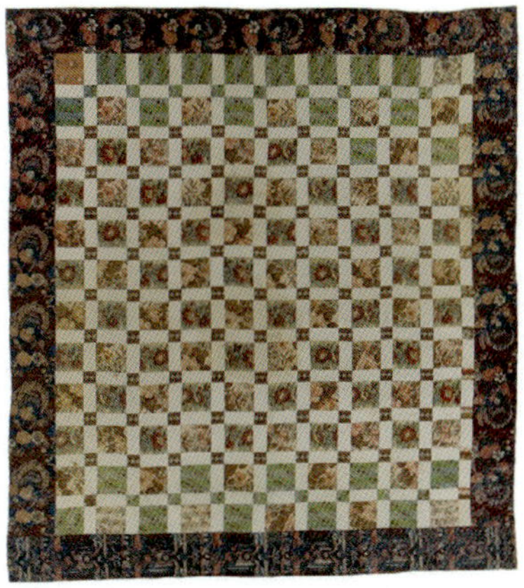

Nine Patch variation

Maker unidentified
Possibly made in New England
1840 - 1860
98 x 86 in.

IQM 1997.007.0894

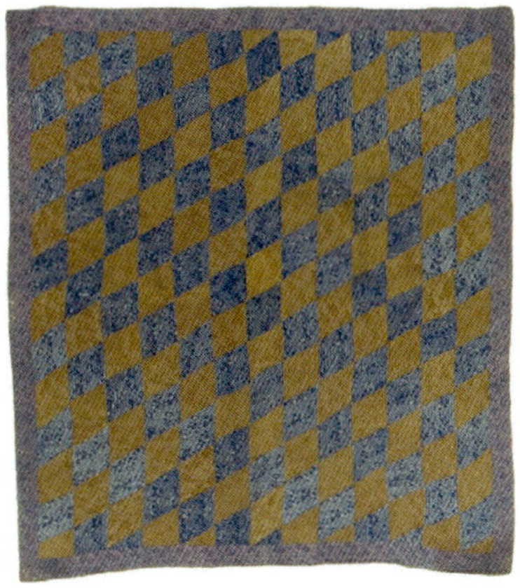

Diamonds

Maker unidentified
Made in United States
1840 - 1860
94.5 x 81 in.

IQM 1997.007.0895

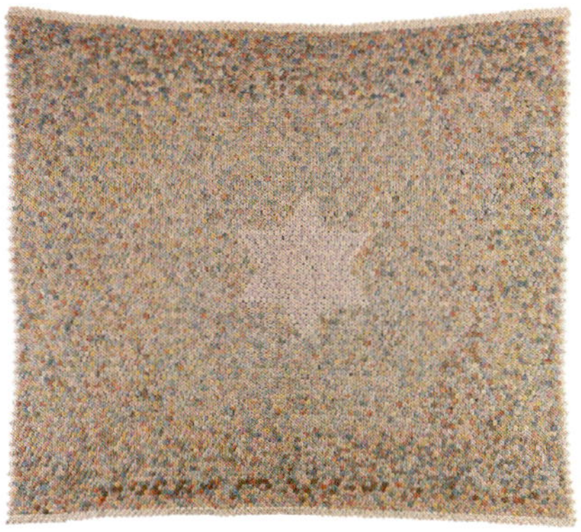

Yo-yo

Maker unidentified
Possibly made in midwestern United States
1930 - 1940
89 x 84.5 in.

IQM 1997.007.0896.1

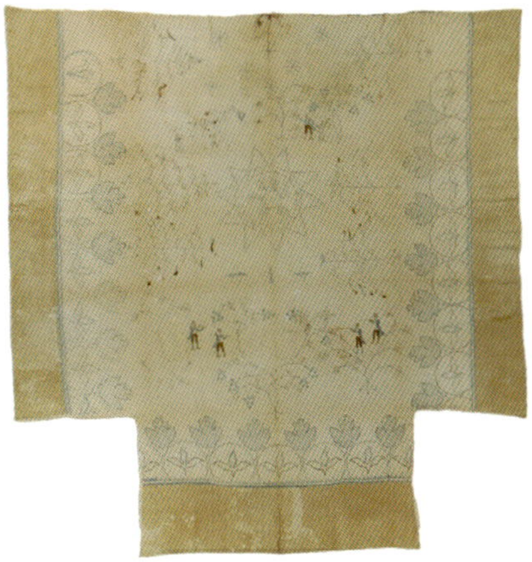

Medallion

Mary Beebe Strong
Made in Windsor, Connecticut
Circa 1815
97 x 92 in.

IQM 1997.007.0897

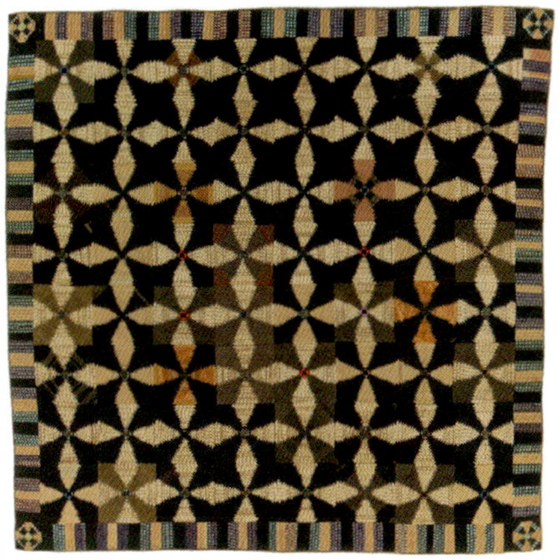

Log Cabin

Maker unidentified
Possibly made in Pennsylvania
1880 - 1900
82.5 x 83.5 in.

IQM 1997.007.0899

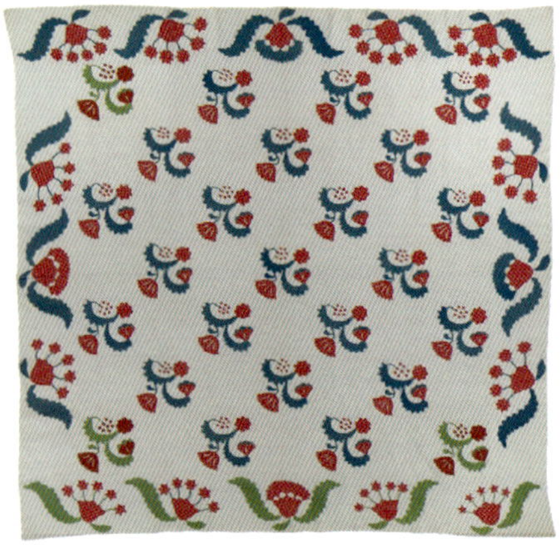

Coxcomb

Maker unidentified
Possibly made in Pennsylvania
1850 - 1870
99 x 96.5 in.
IQM 1997.007.0900

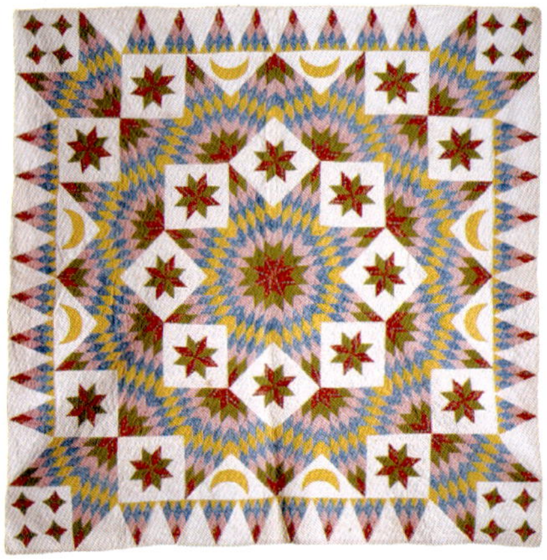

Broken Star

Emiline R. Miller
Probably made in Caroline, Tompkins County, New York
1830 - 1850
81.5 x 79 in.
IQM 1997.007.0901

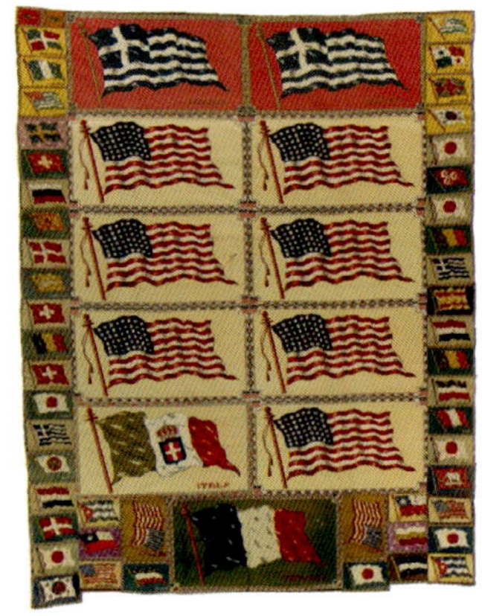

Tobacco Premium

Maker unidentified
Possibly made in North Carolina
1915 - 1925
96 x 70.5 in.
IQM 1997.007.0902

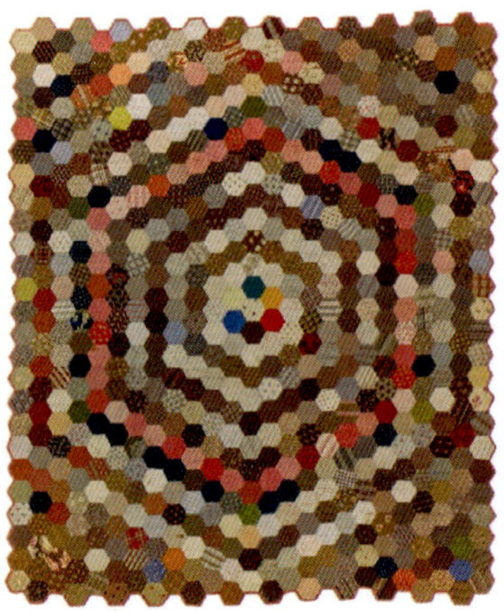

Hexagon

Mary Ann (Grosh) Stoner
Made in Paradise Hill, Ohio
Dated 1887
77.5 x 65.5 in.
IQM 1997.007.0907

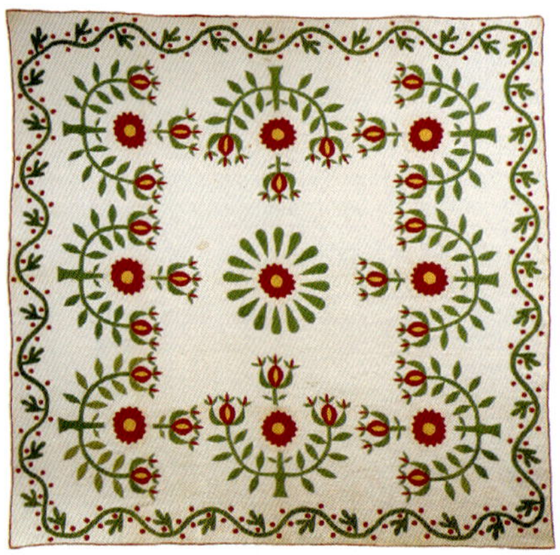

Prairie Rose

Eliza J. Herron
Made in Iowa
Dated 1857
90.5 x 90.5 in.
IQM 1997.007.0908

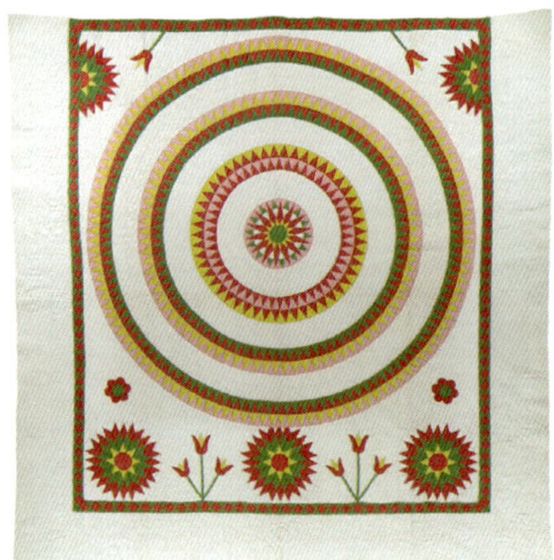

Mariner's Compass variation

Maker unidentified
Probably made in Lancaster County, Pennsylvania
1850 - 1870
93.5 x 88.5 in.
IQM 1997.007.0909

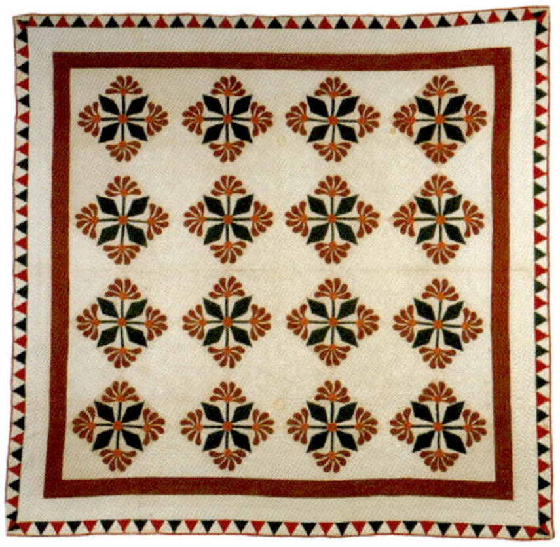

Mexican Rose

Maker unidentified
Possibly made in Ohio or Pennsylvania
1860 - 1880
100 x 99 in.
IQM 1997.007.0910

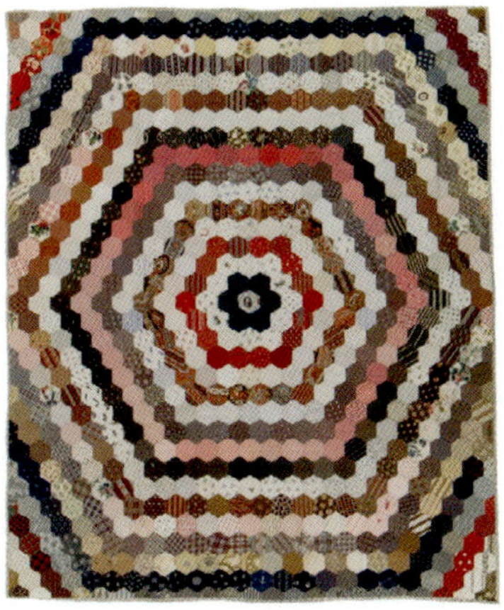

Hexagon

Maker unidentified
Possibly made in Pennsylvania
Circa 1876
77 x 64 in.
IQM 1997.007.0911

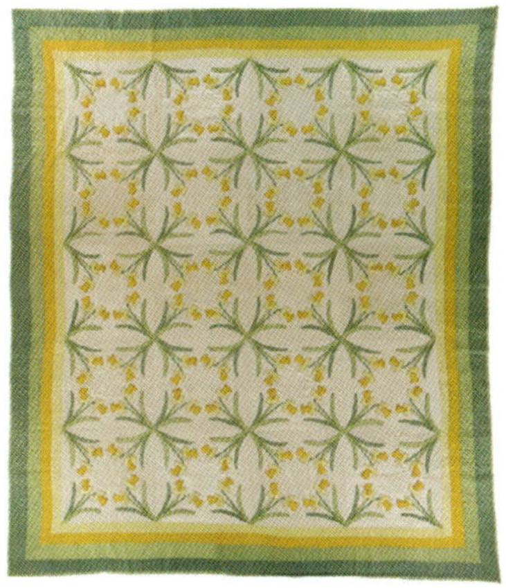

Dancing Daffodils

Maker unidentified
Possibly made in Pittsburgh, Pennsylvania
Circa 1931
98.75 x 85 in.
IQM 1997.007.0912

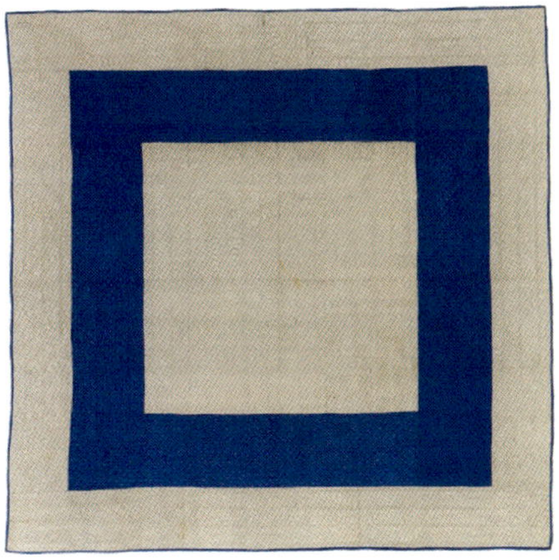

Framed Center

Maker unidentified
Possibly made in Pennsylvania
1850 - 1870
75 x 73.5 in.
IQM 1997.007.0913

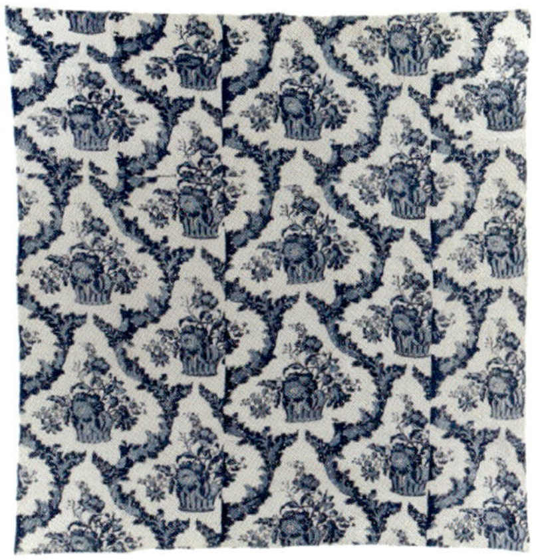

Whole Cloth

Maker unidentified
Probably made in eastern United States
1820 - 1850
95.5 x 87.5 in.
IQM 1997.007.0914

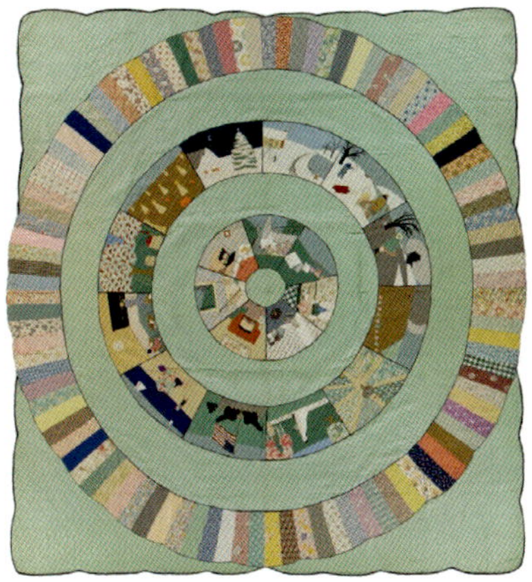

Calendar

Probably made by Lillian Smith Fordyce
Probably made in Greene County, Pennsylvania
Circa 1933
94 x 86.5 in.
IQM 1997.007.0915

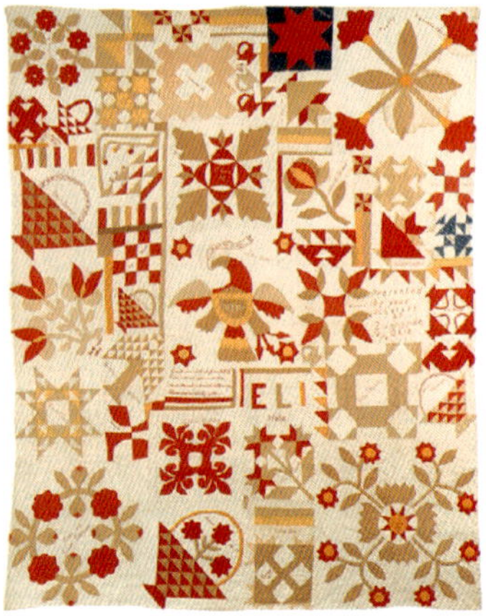

Album - Sunnyside Album

Sunnyside schoolchildren
Made in Miami County, Ohio
Dated 1894
88 x 66.5 in.

IQM 1997.007.0916

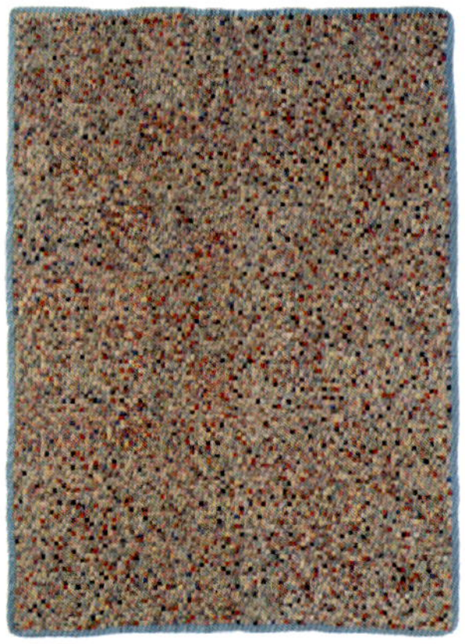

Yo-yo

Maker unidentified
Possibly made in Illinois
1930 - 1940
79 x 57 in.

IQM 1997.007.0917

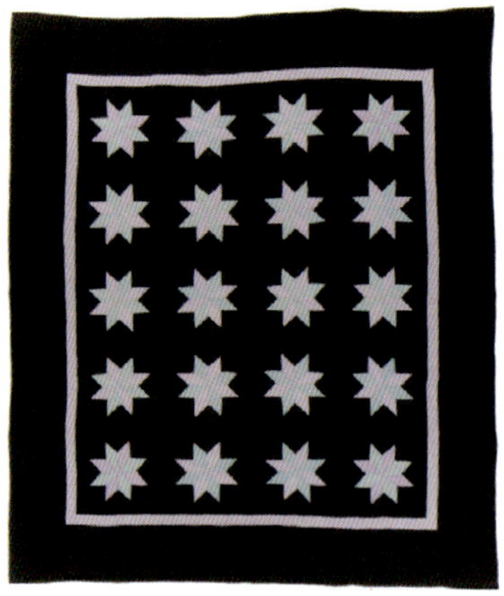

LeMoyne Star

Maker unidentified
Possibly made in Holmes County, Ohio
1920 - 1940
85 x 71.5 in.

IQM 1997.007.0921

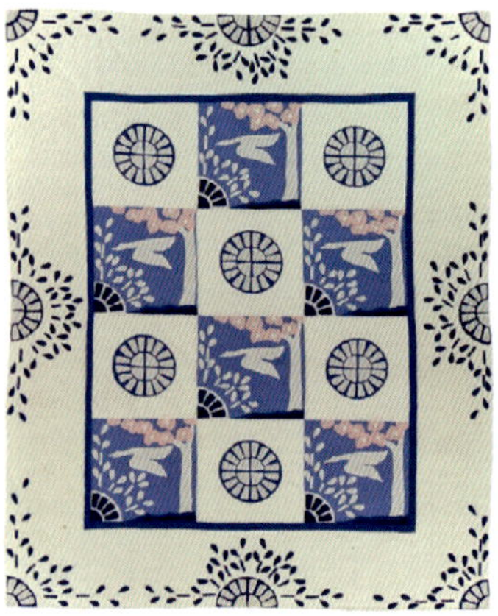

Wild Ducks

Maker unidentified
Possibly made in Ohio
Circa 1934
88 x 70 in.

IQM 1997.007.0922

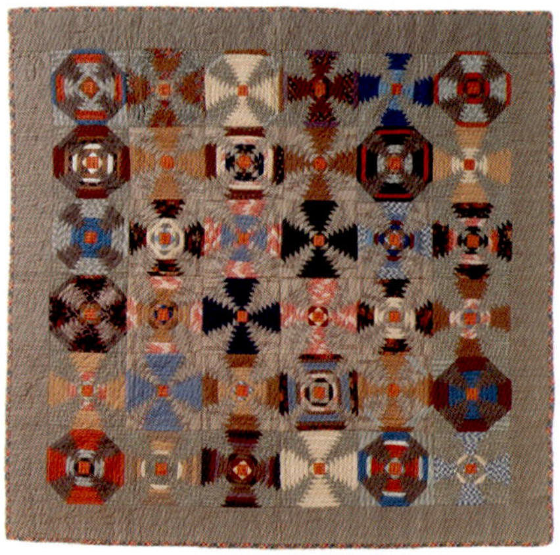

Log Cabin

Maker unidentified
Probably made in Pennsylvania
1880 - 1900
69.5 x 68.5 in.

IQM 1997.007.0923

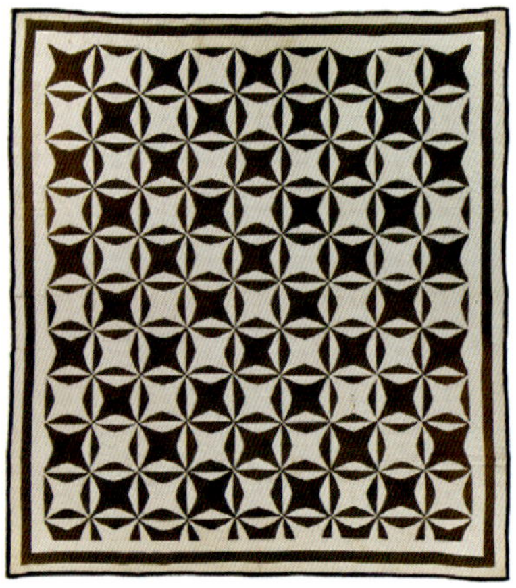

Rob Peter to Pay Paul

Maker unidentified
Probably made in Kansas
Dated 1892
83 x 72 in.

IQM 1997.007.0925

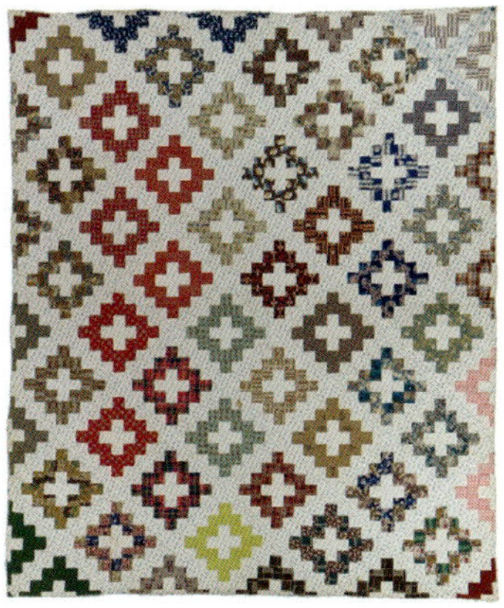

Chimney Sweep

Maker unidentified
Made in Delaware County, New York
1846 - 1849
95.5 x 79.5 in.

IQM 1997.007.0927

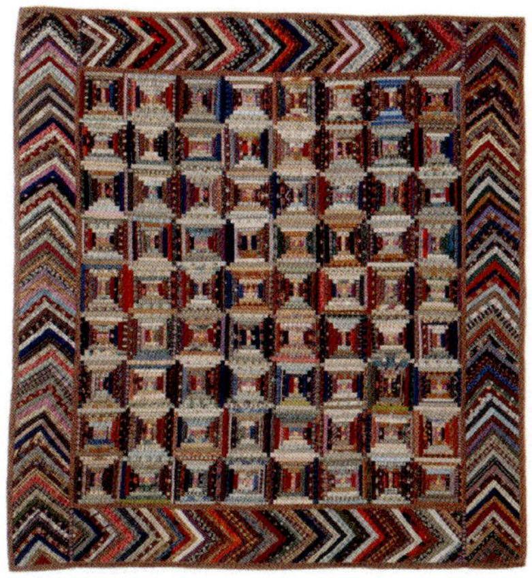

Log Cabin

Maker unidentified
Probably made in New York
1870 - 1890
97 x 86 in.

IQM 1997.007.0928

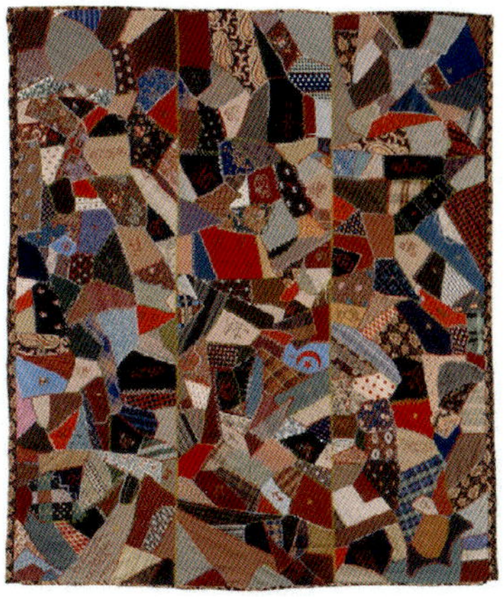

Crazy

Eva Wight
Made in Saline County, Kansas
Dated 1891
81.5 x 71 in.

IQM 1997.007.0929

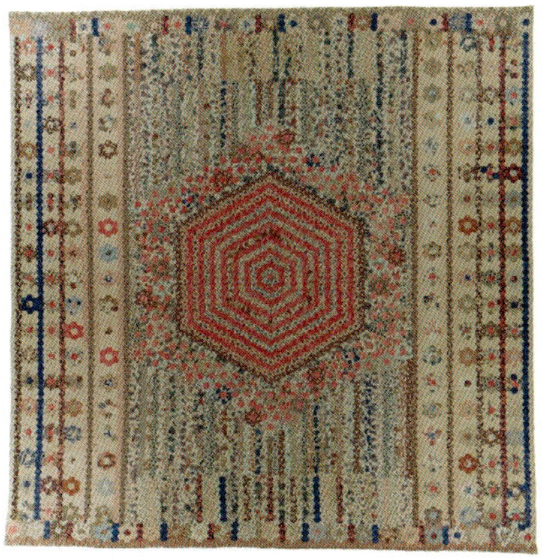

Hexagon

Maker unidentified
Probably made in Massachusetts
1820 - 1840
91.5 x 88 in.

IQM 1997.007.0930

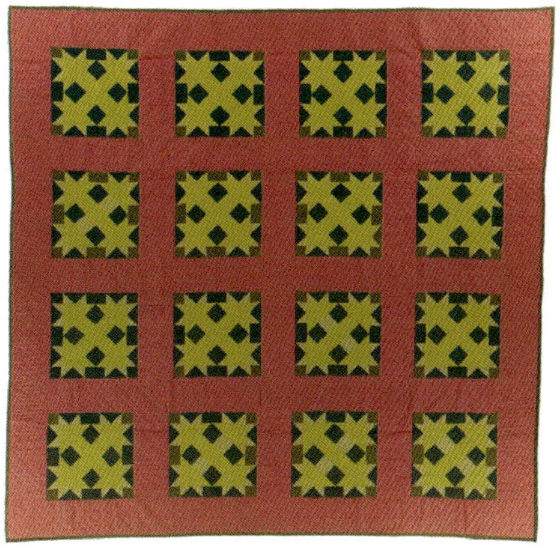

Cross and Crown

Maker unidentified
Possibly made in Pennsylvania
1860 - 1880
83 x 85 in.

IQM 1997.007.0931

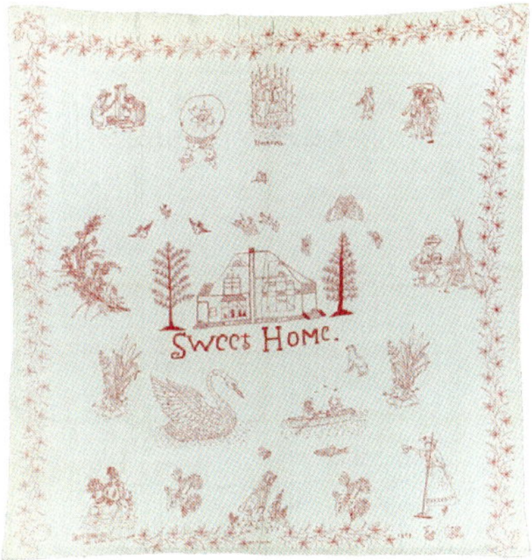

Album - Sweet Home

Maker unidentified
Possibly made in Massachusetts
Dated 1898
76.5 x 73 in.

IQM 1997.007.0932

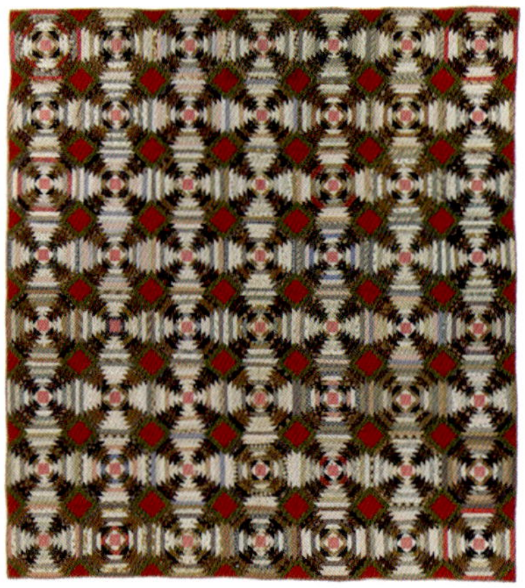

Log Cabin

Anna H. Burmeister
Made in Milwaukee, Wisconsin
Circa 1894
85 x 75.5 in.

IQM 1997.007.0933

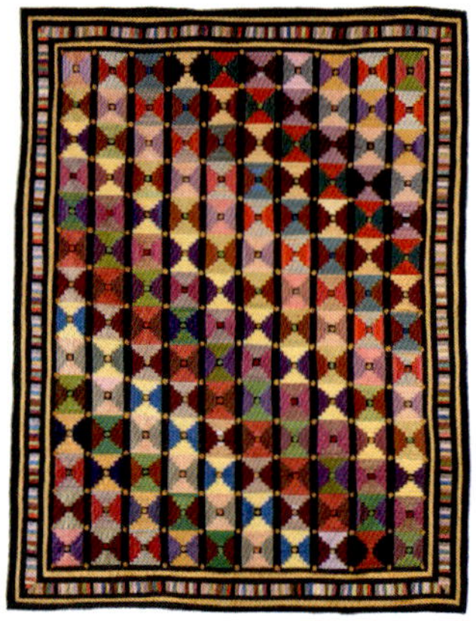

Log Cabin

Maker unidentified
Possibly made in Ohio
1870 - 1890
74 x 56 in.

IQM 1997.007.0934

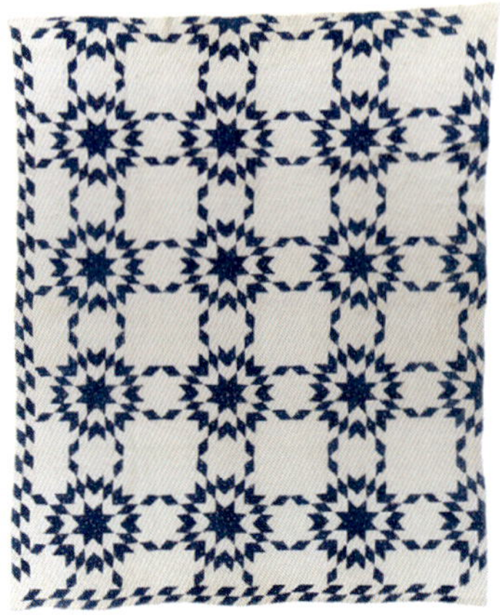

Touching Stars

Mary Ann Manwaring
Possibly made in Indiana
1840 - 1860
87.5 x 68.5 in.

IQM 1997.007.0935

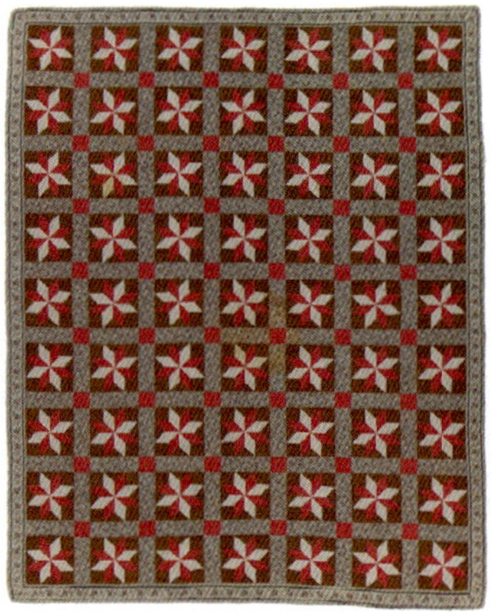

LeMoyne Star

Maker unidentified
Possibly made in New York
1870 - 1890
78 x 62 in.

IQM 1997.007.0936

Pineapple

Maker unidentified
Possibly made in Pennsylvania
1850 - 1870
93.5 x 81.5 in.

IQM 1997.007.0938

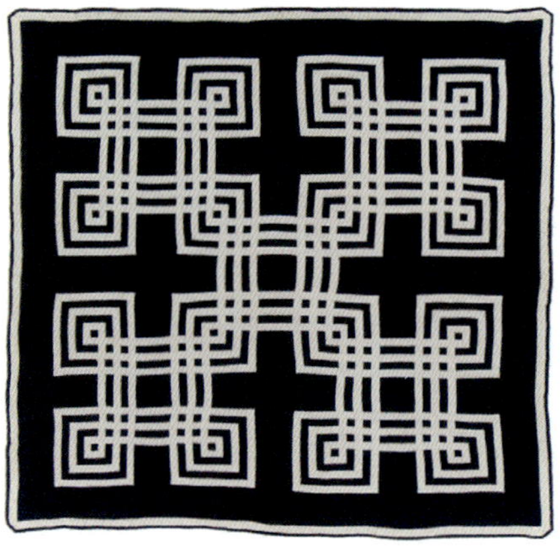

Carpenter's Square

Maker unidentified
Made in United States
1880 - 1900
75 x 75 in.

IQM 1997.007.0939

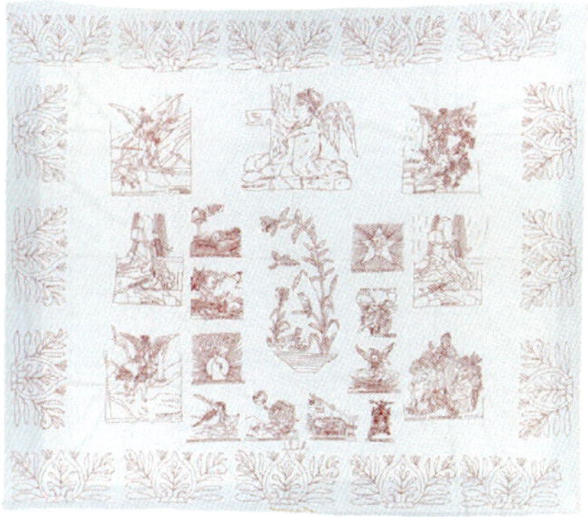

Album

Possibly made by Raymond D. Fry
Possibly made in Pennsylvania
Dated 1918
78.5 x 90 in.

IQM 1997.007.0940

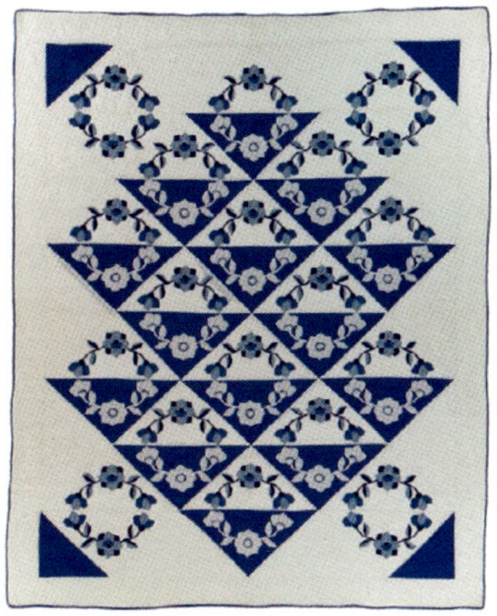

Shadow Wreath

Mary Anna McConahy Eckles
Made in Newcastle, Lawrence County, Pennsylvania
1940 - 1950
90 x 72.5 in.

IQM 1997.007.0941

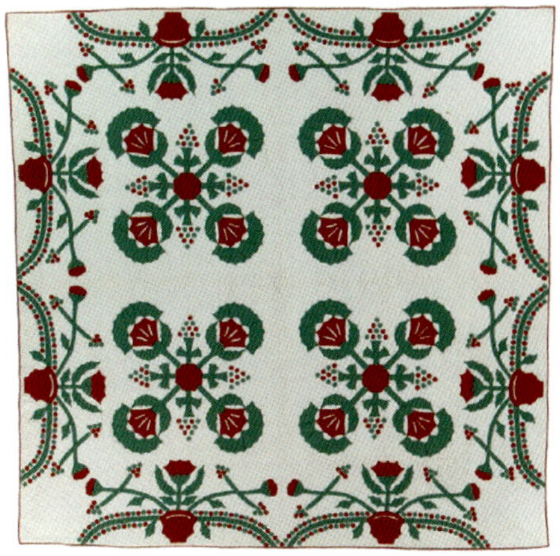

Coxcomb

Cora Arabelle Eckles Dinsmore
Made in Lawrence County, Pennsylvania
1925 - 1935
79 x 79.5 in.

IQM 1997.007.0942

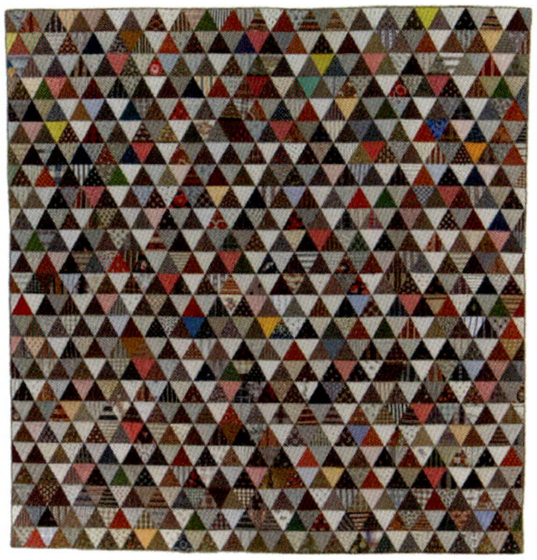

Thousand Pyramids

Maker unidentified
Possibly made in eastern Pennsylvania
1880 - 1900
79.5 x 76.5 in.

IQM 1997.007.0944

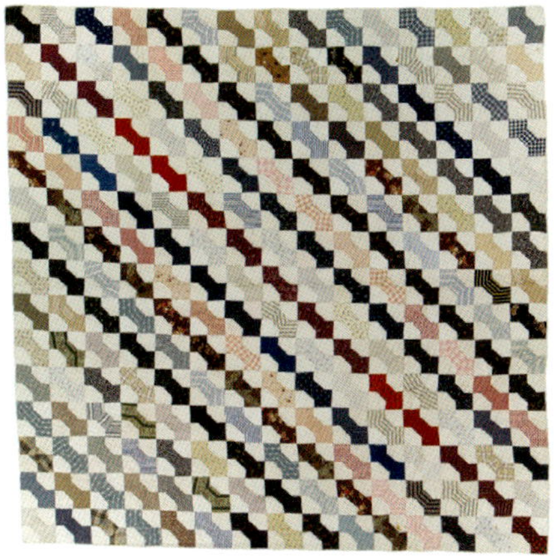

Bow Tie

Rebecca Alford Dinsmore
Made in Lawrence County, Pennsylvania
Dated 1891
84.5 x 84.5 in.

IQM 1997.007.0945

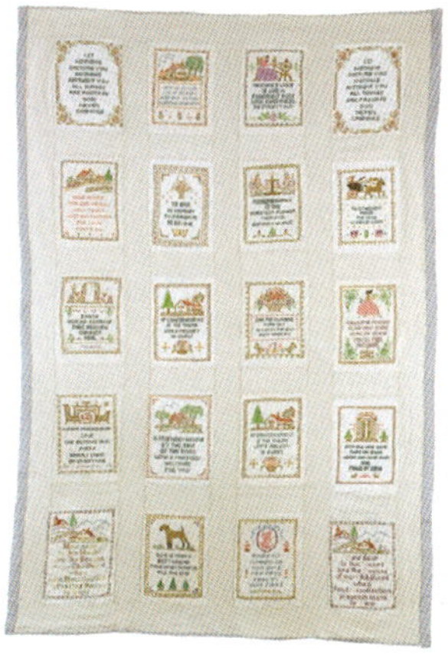

Album

Maker unidentified
Possibly made in eastern Pennsylvania
1930 - 1950
82 x 54 in.

IQM 1997.007.0946

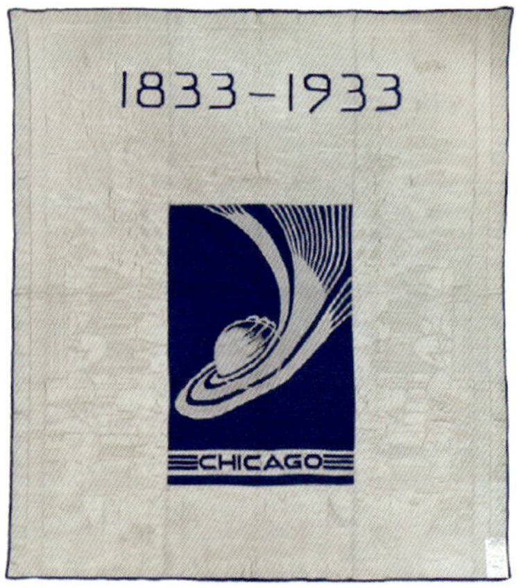

A Century of Progress

Ida Stow
Made in Park Ridge, Illinois
Dated 1933
91.5 x 76 in.

IQM 1997.007.0947

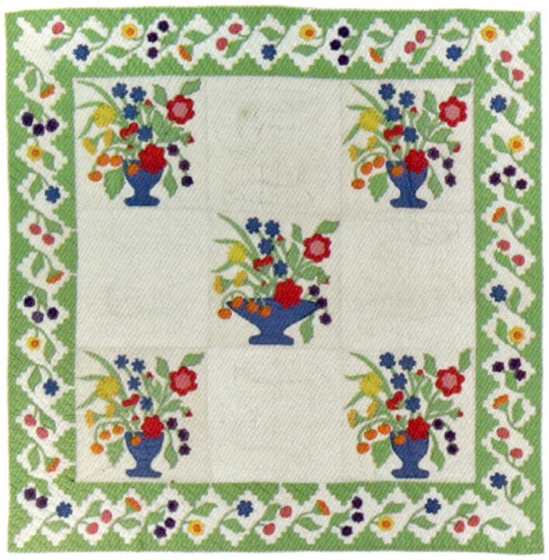

Pots of Flowers

Cora Eckles Dinsmore and
Mary Anna McConahy Eckles
Made in Lawrence County,
Pennsylvania
Circa 1941
72 x 71 in.

IQM 1997.007.0948

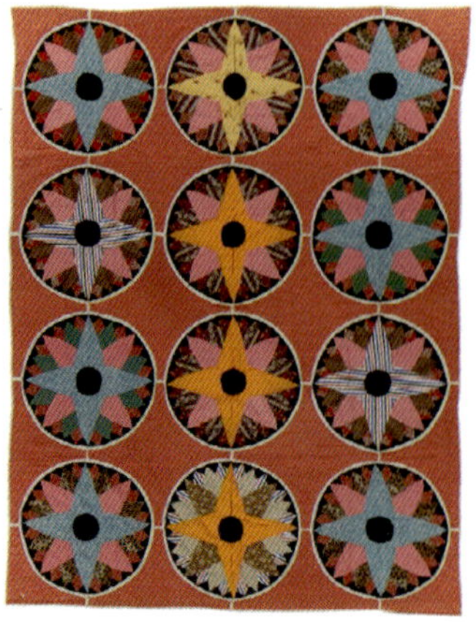

Compass

Maker unidentified
Probably made in Pennsylvania
1850 - 1870
86 x 65 in.

IQM 1997.007.0949

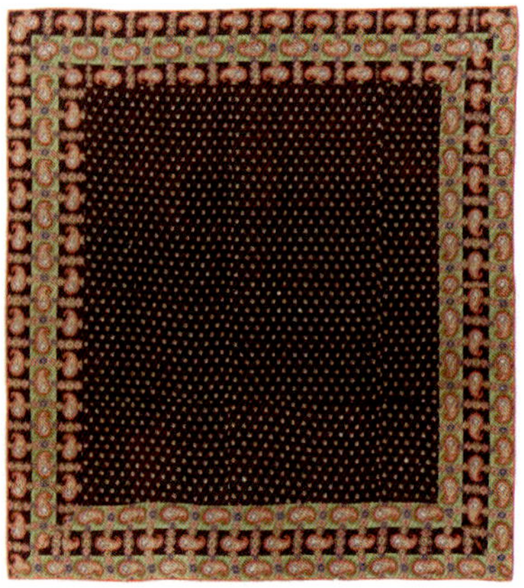

Framed Center

Maker unidentified
Possibly made in Pennsylvania
1840 - 1860
84.5 x 75 in.

IQM 1997.007.0950

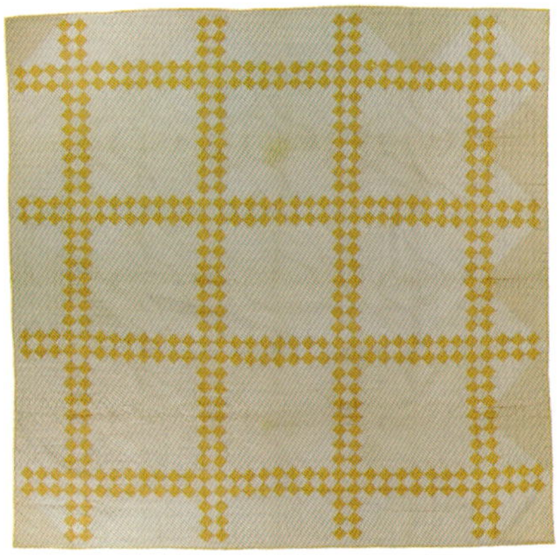

Double Irish Chain variation

Abbie Bell Dinsmore
Made in Lawrence County,
Pennsylvania
1920 - 1940
85 x 83.5 in.

IQM 1997.007.0951

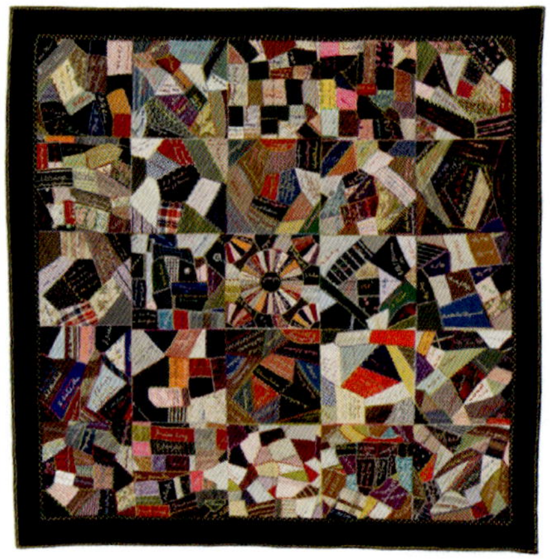

Crazy

Maker unidentified
Probably made in Turtle
Creek, Allegheny County,
Pennsylvania
Dated 1896
74 x 76 in.

IQM 1997.007.0952

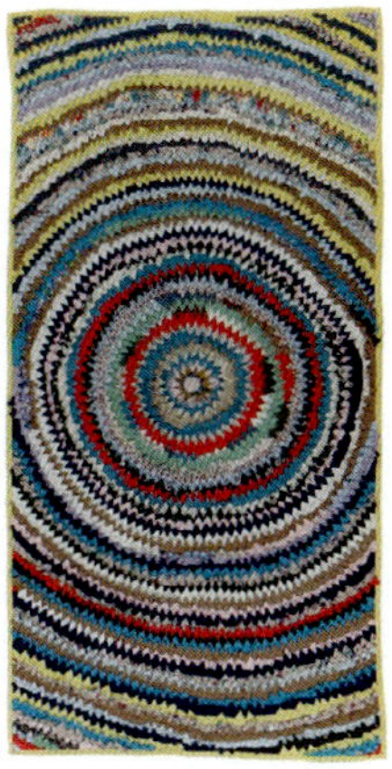

Petals

Maker unidentified
Made in United States
1940 - 1950
71 x 35.5 in.

IQM 1997.007.0953

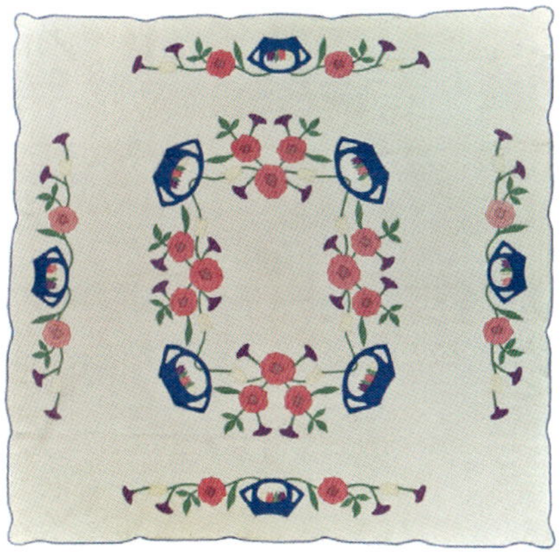

Dutch Basket

Maker unidentified
Made in United States
1930 - 1940
80.5 x 82 in.

IQM 1997.007.0954

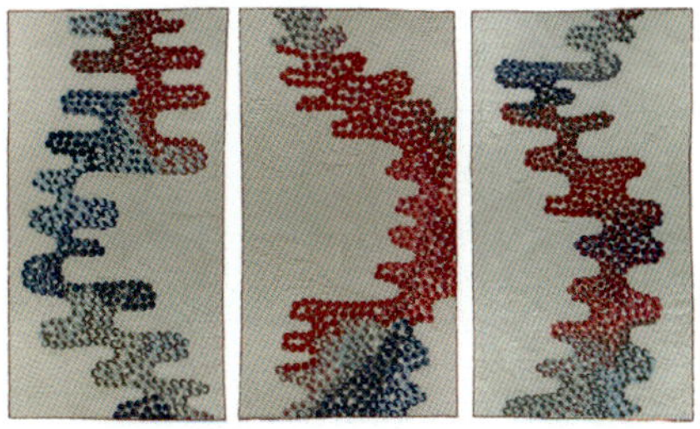

Bleu, Rouge, Marine (Triptyque)

Mariel Clarmont
Made in Paris, France
Dated 1980
100 x 110 in.

IQM 1997.007.1003

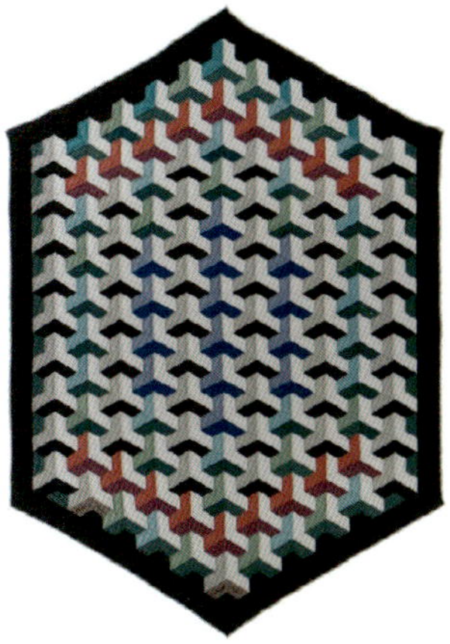

City of Chicago

Jon Cutrell
Made in Goshen, Indiana
Dated 1984
108.5 x 74.5 in.

IQM 1997.007.1004

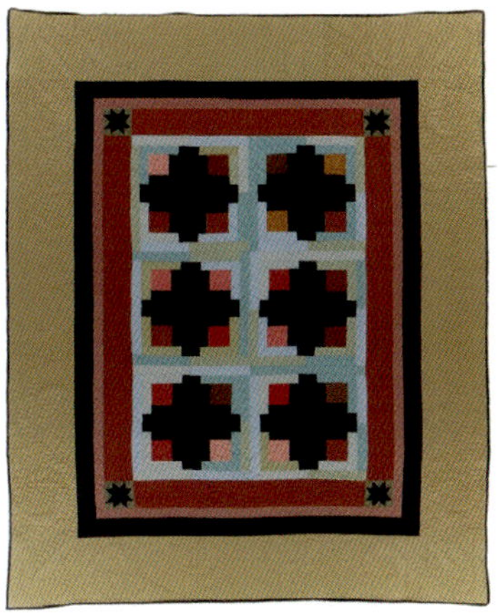

City of Black Crosses

Jon Cutrell
Made in Goshen, Indiana
Dated 1984
92.5 x 74 in.

IQM 1997.007.1005

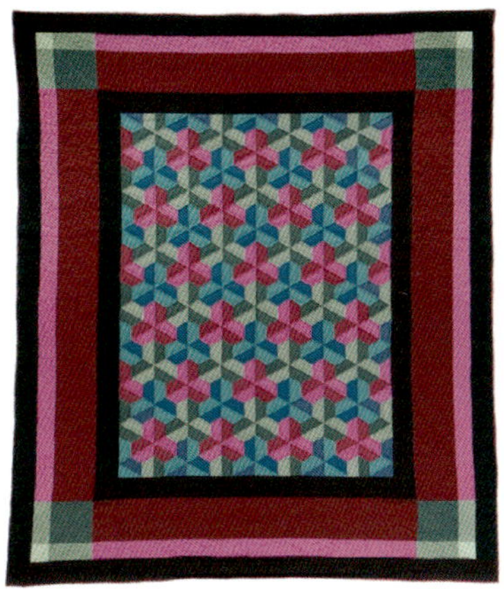

Cloverfield

Jon Cutrell
Made in Goshen, Indiana
Dated 1984
100 x 84.5 in.

IQM 1997.007.1006

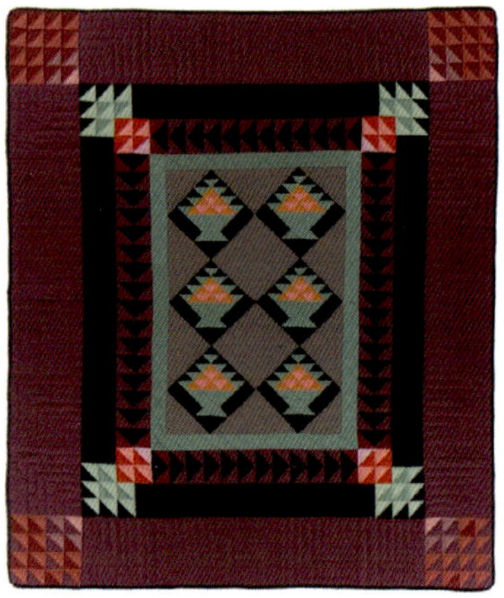

Basket of Coals

Jon Cutrell
Made in Goshen, Indiana
Dated 1983
85 x 72 in.

IQM 1997.007.1007

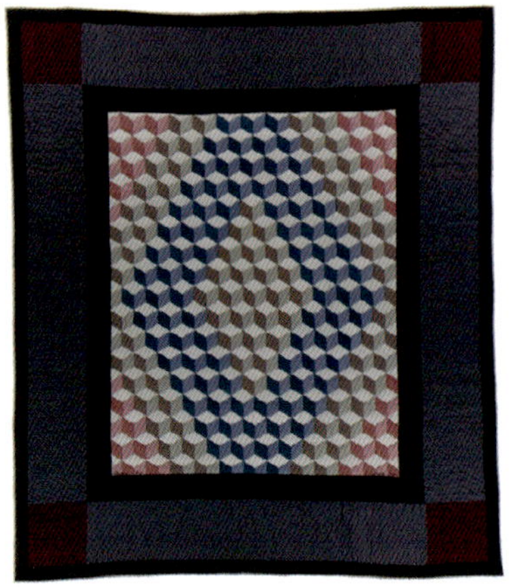

Tumbling Blocks

Jon Cutrell
Made in Goshen, Indiana
Dated 1984
95 x 81.5 in.

IQM 1997.007.1008

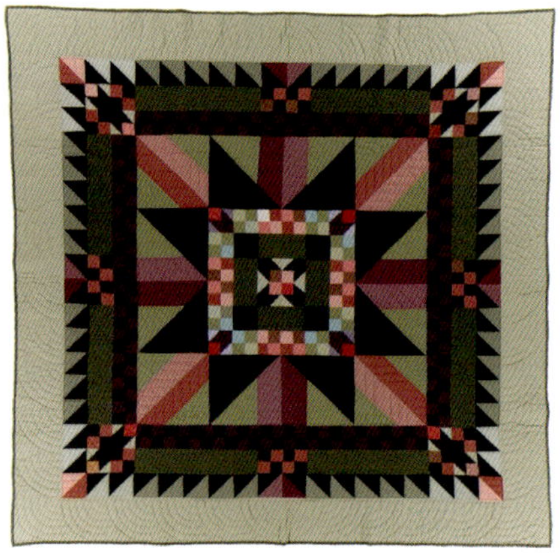

Star in Checkered Square

Jon Cutrell
Made in Goshen, Indiana
Dated 1984
88 x 86.5 in.

IQM 1997.007.1009

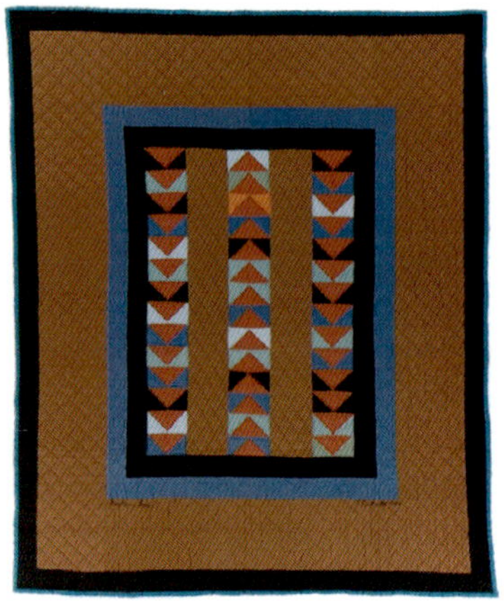

Wild Geese

Jon Cutrell
Made in Goshen, Indiana
Dated 1984
74.5 x 61 in.

IQM 1997.007.1010

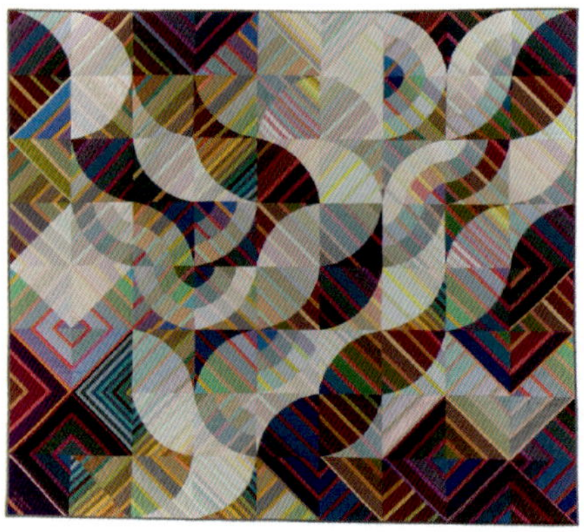

La Tempete

Michael James
Made in Somerset, Massachusetts
Dated 1983
77.5 x 86 in.

IQM 1997.007.1013

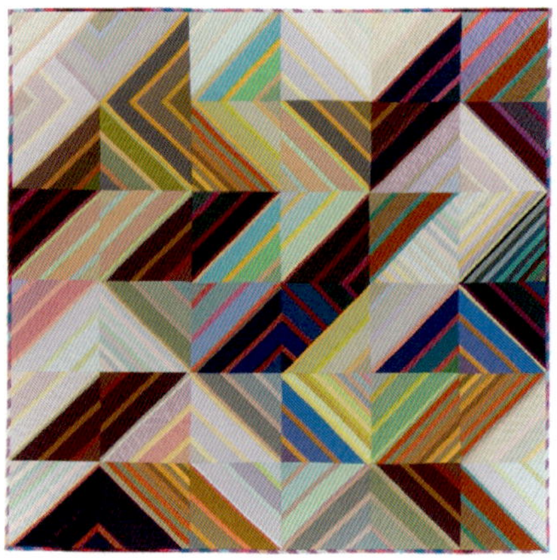

City Rhythms

Michael James
Made in Somerset, Massachusetts
Dated 1983
58 x 57.5 in.

IQM 1997.007.1014

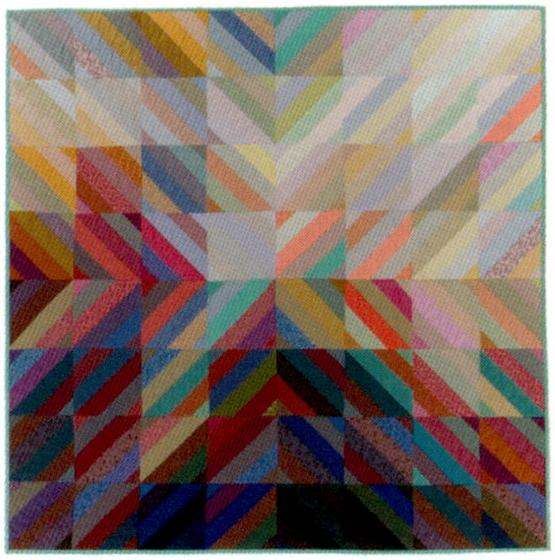

Interweave

Michael James
Made in Somerset,
Massachusetts
Dated 1982
48.5 x 48.5 in.

IQM 1997.007.1017

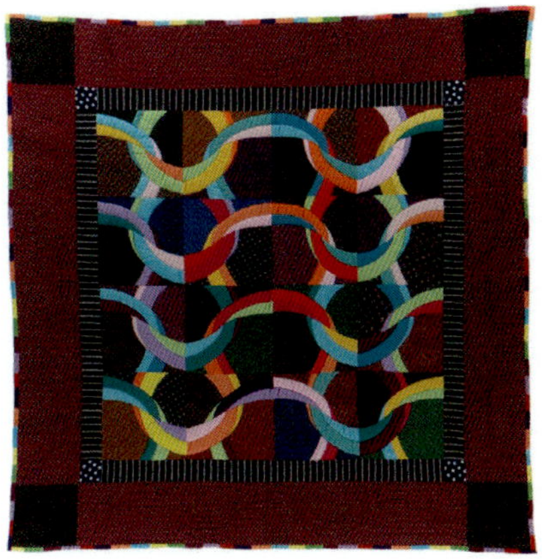

Knitted Neon

John Willard
Made in Ontario, Canada
Dated 1984
78.5 x 68 in.

IQM 1997.007.1018

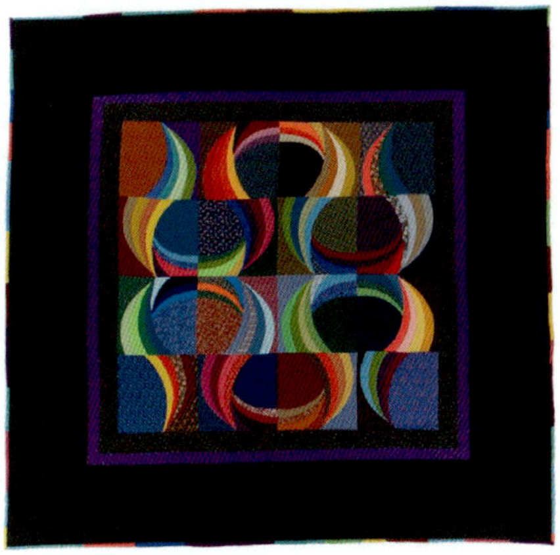

Ribbon Dancer

John Willard
Made in Ontario, Canada
Dated 1982
78 x 77.5 in.

IQM 1997.007.1019

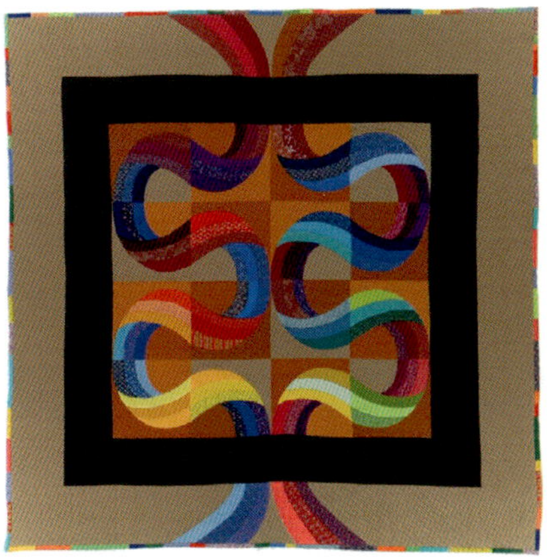

Ribbon Dancer Once Removed

John Willard
Made in Ontario, Canada
Dated 1983
77 x 78 in.

IQM 1997.007.1020

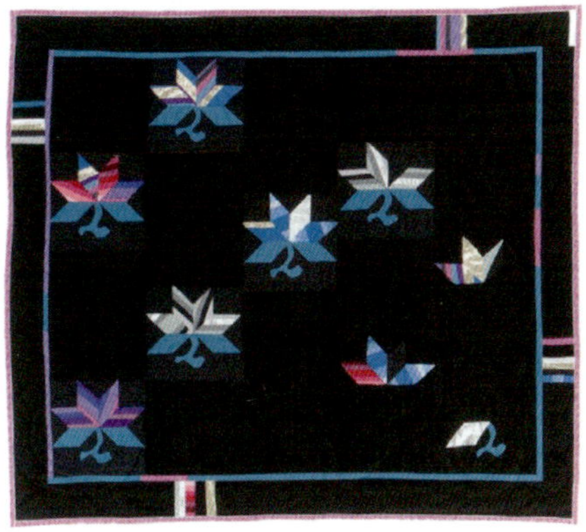

Leftover Lilies

Virginia Avery
Made in Porchester, New York
Dated 1984
56.5 x 50 in.

IQM 1997.007.1021

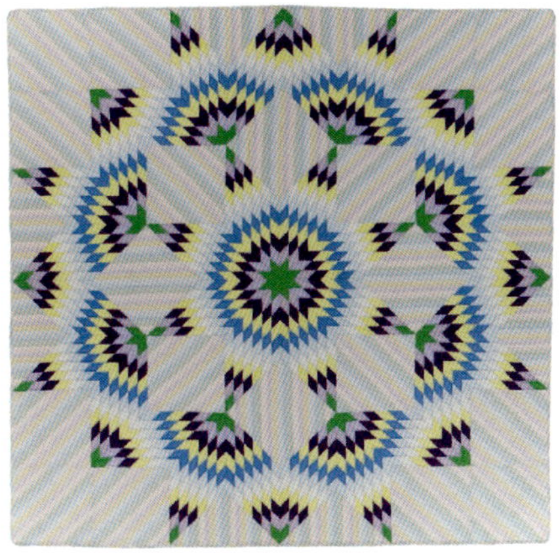

Kaleidoscope: Broken Star

John Mangiapane
Made in Waterbury,
Connecticut
Dated 1984
81 x 79.5 in.

IQM 1997.007.1022

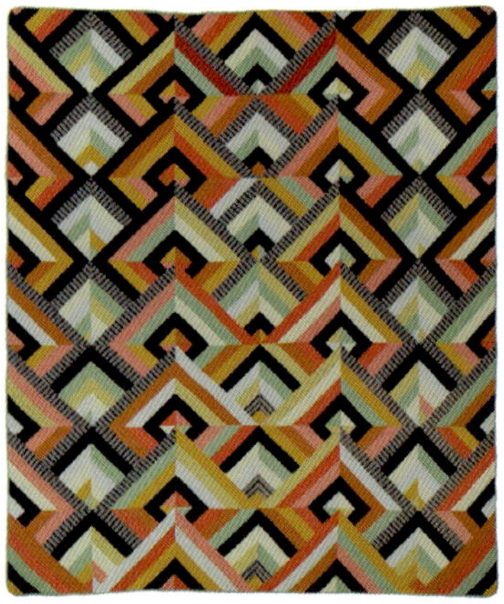

Art Deco

Francoise Barnes
Made in Ohio
Circa 1980
103 x 86 in.

IQM 1997.007.1023

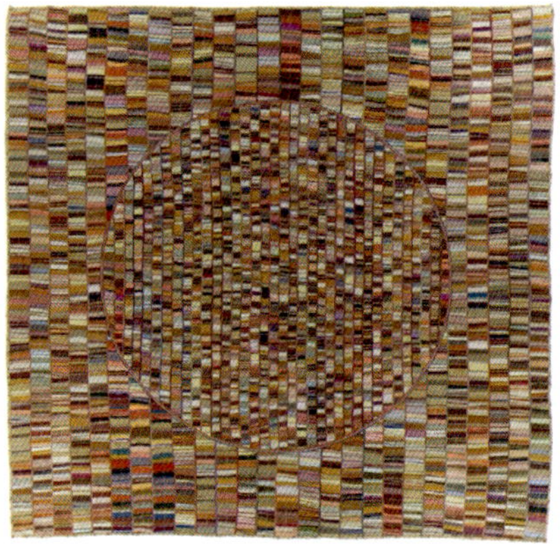

Circle on Square I

Lucy Wallis
Made in Merriott, Somerset, England, United Kingdom
Dated 1987
90.5 x 88.5 in.

IQM 1997.007.1025

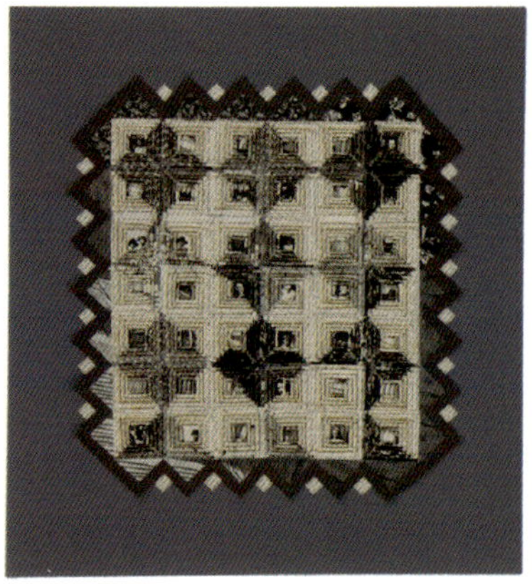

Chapter IX, The Pioneer Women, from Willa Cather's Oh! Pioneers

Christine Campbell
Made in Charlotte, North Carolina
Dated 1974
40 x 45 in.

IQM 1997.007.1026

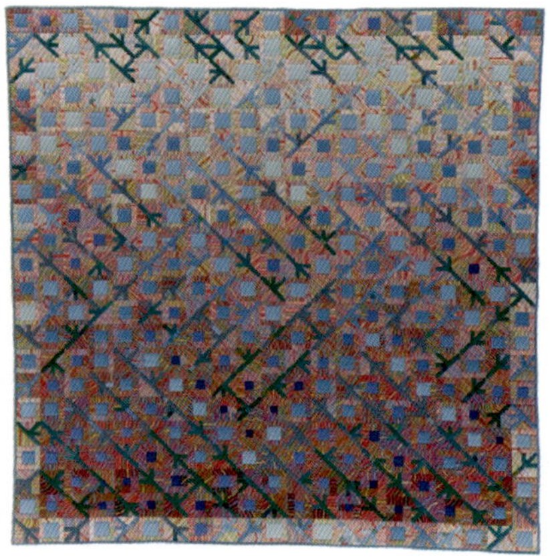

Number 41

Pamel Studstill
Made in Pipe Creek, Texas
Dated 1984
65.5 x 63.5 in.

IQM 1997.007.1029

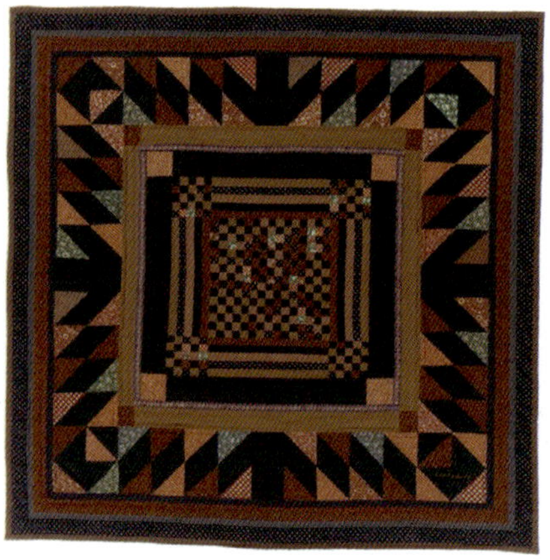

Heaven and Earth

Jean Ray Laury
Made in Clovis, California
Dated 1985
62.5 x 61.5 in.

IQM 1997.007.1030

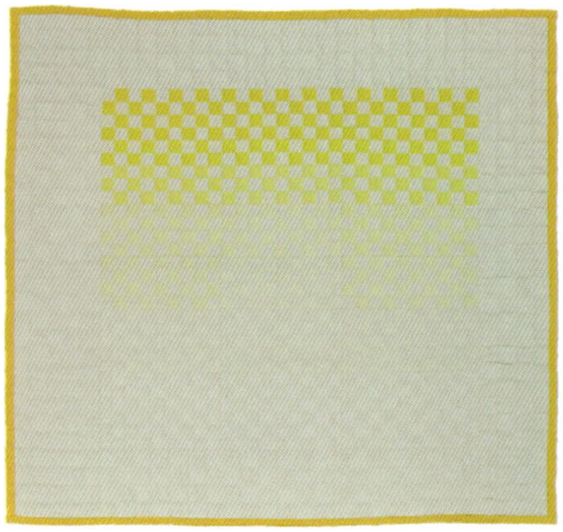

Light Shower

Jean Ray Laury
Made in Clovis, California
Dated 1984
28 x 29 in.

IQM 1997.007.1032

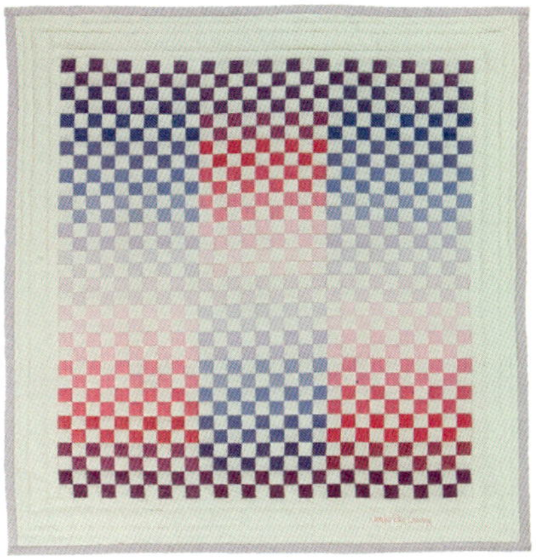

Doppler Effect #1

Jean Ray Laury
Made in Clovis, California
Dated 1984
27.5 x 26.5 in.

IQM 1997.007.1033

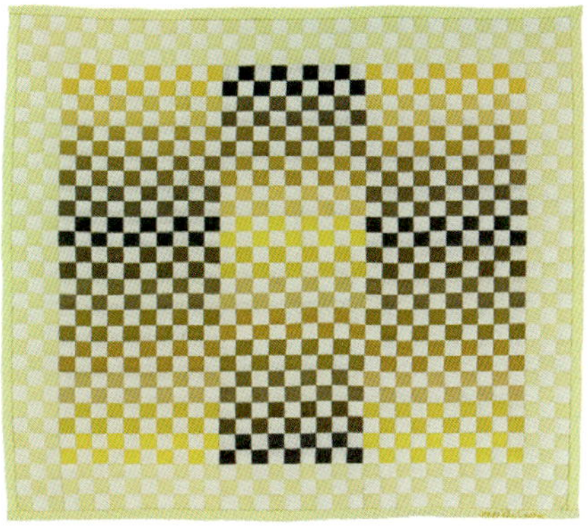

Doppler Effect #2

Jean Ray Laury
Made in Clovis, California
Dated 1984
23.5 x 25.5 in.

IQM 1997.007.1034

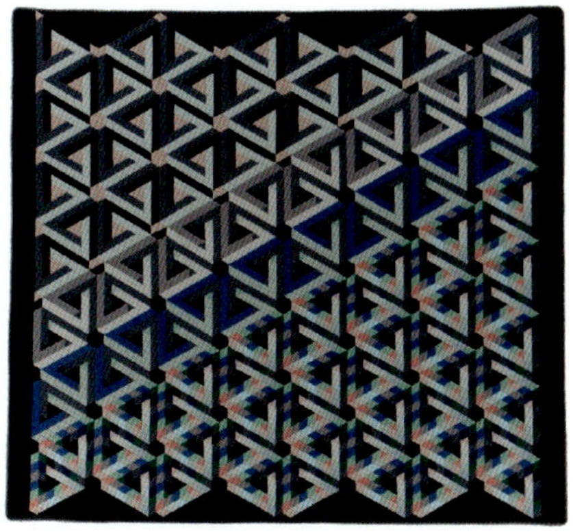

Eternal Triangle

Pauline Burbidge
Made in Nottingham, England, United Kingdom
Dated 1983
65 x 69 in.

IQM 1997.007.1036

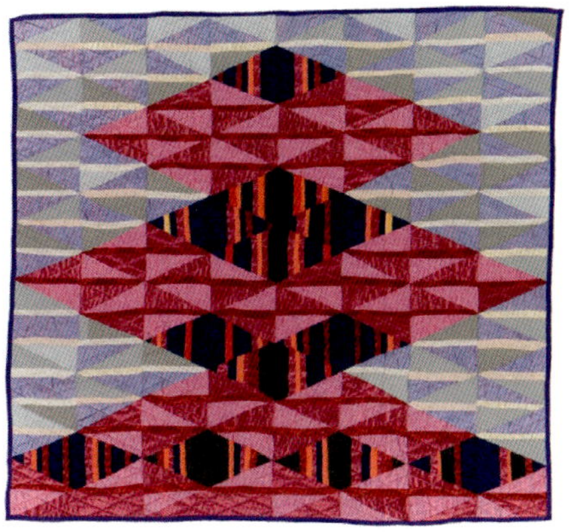

The Watcher

Judith Ann Larzelere
Made in Newbury, Massachusetts
Dated 1984
54 x 58 in.

IQM 1997.007.1037

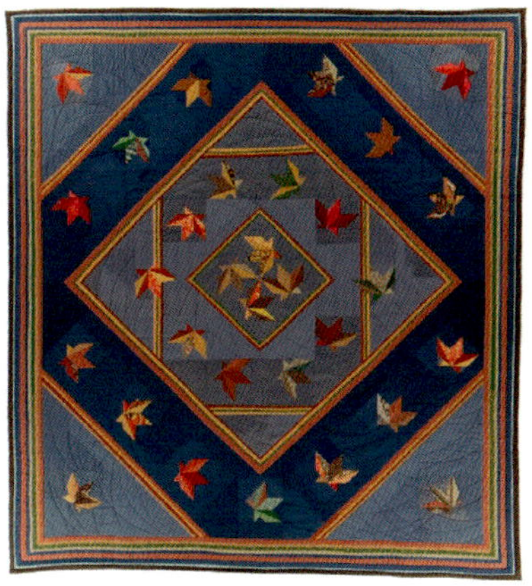

Autumn Leaves

Mathilde Salamon
Made in United States
Dated 1986
97.5 x 89 in.

IQM 1997.007.1039

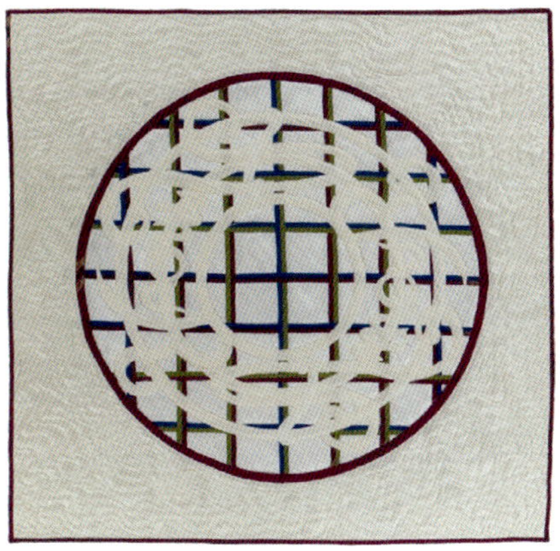

Amour Amour

Mariel Clarmont
Made in Paris, France
Dated 1983
48 x 47.5 in.

IQM 1997.007.1040

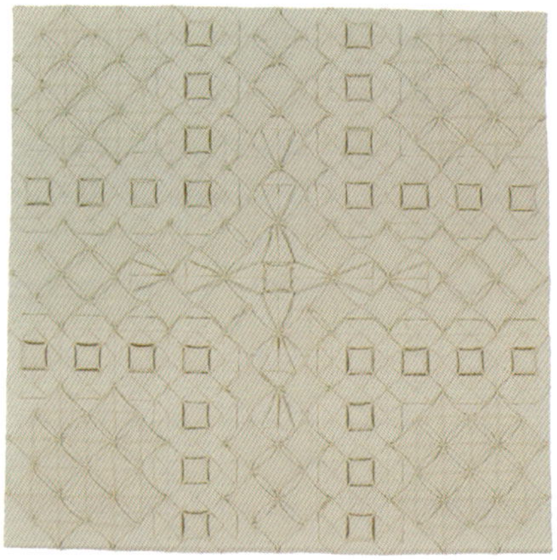

Contemplation

Margaret Stephenson Coole
Made in Ontario, Canada
Dated 1984
37 x 36.5 in.

IQM 1997.007.1045

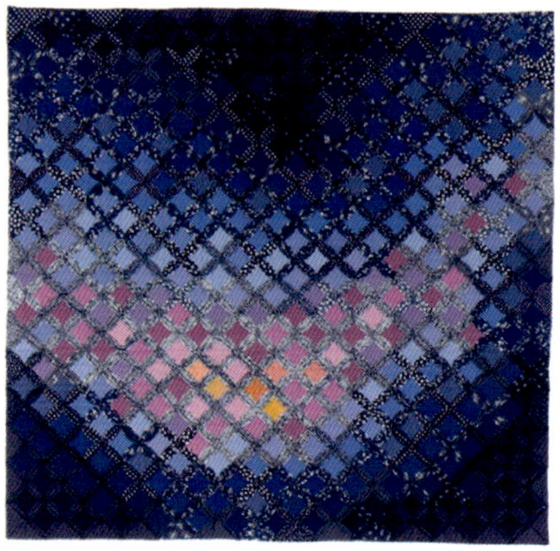

Night Shades

Margaret Stephenson Coole
Made in Ontario, Canada
Dated 1984
54 x 54 in.

IQM 1997.007.1046

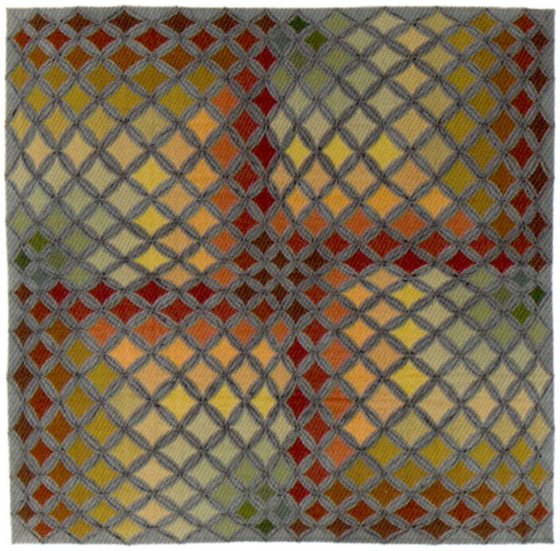

Quadrisphere

Margaret Stephenson Coole
Made in Ontario, Canada
Dated 1985
52.5 x 52.5 in.

IQM 1997.007.1047

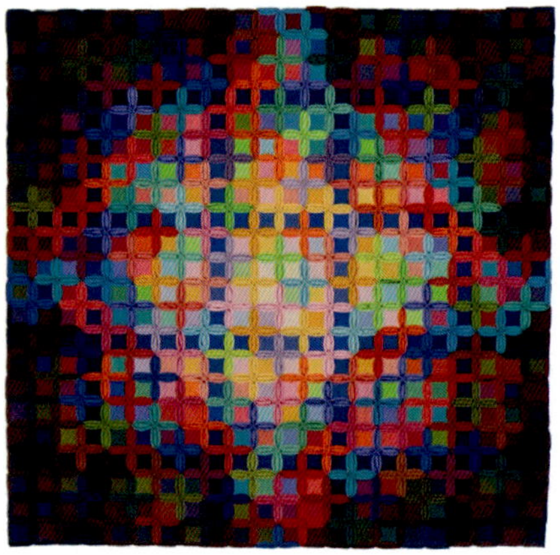

Rainbow Glazing

Margaret Stephenson Coole
Made in Ontario, Canada
Dated 1985
85 x 85 in.

IQM 1997.007.1048

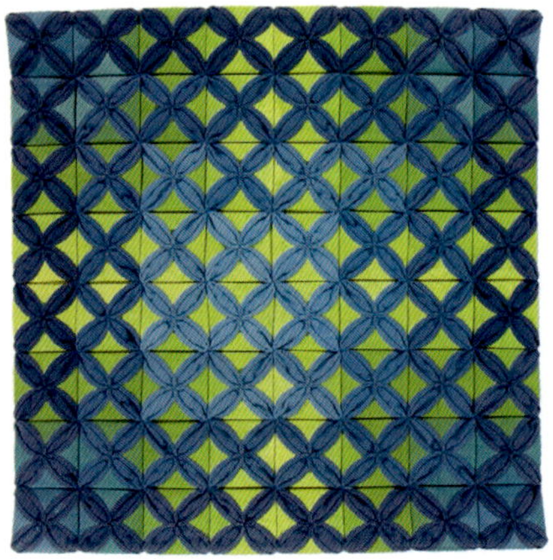

Double Green Glazing

Margaret Stephenson Coole
Made in Ontario, Canada
Dated 1982
30.5 x 31.5 in.

IQM 1997.007.1049

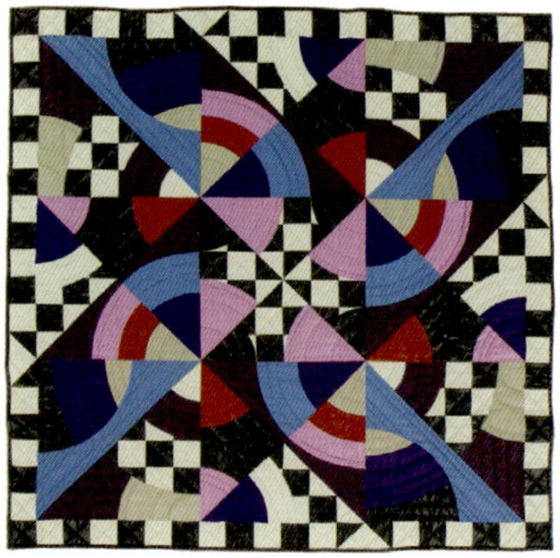

On the Boardwalk

Sonya Lee Barrington
Made in San Francisco, California
Dated 1984
39.5 x 39.5 in.

IQM 1997.007.1050

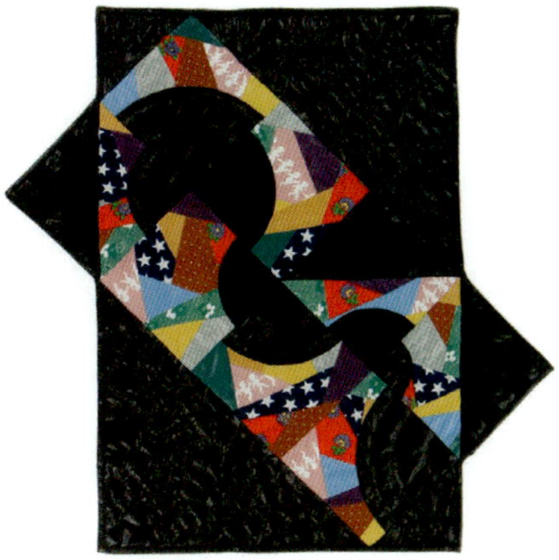

Bits & Pieces

Sonya Lee Barrington
Made in San Francisco,
California
Dated 1986
17 x 25.5 in.

IQM 1997.007.1051

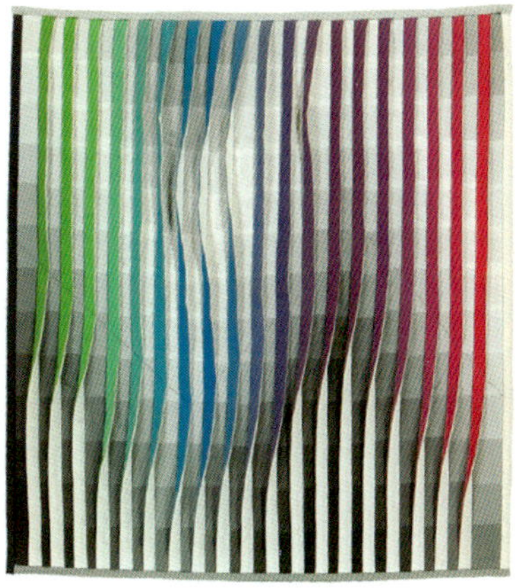

High Tech Tucks II

Caryl Bryer Fallert (Gentry)
Made in Oswego, Illinois
Dated 1986
22 x 19.5 in.

IQM 1997.007.1052

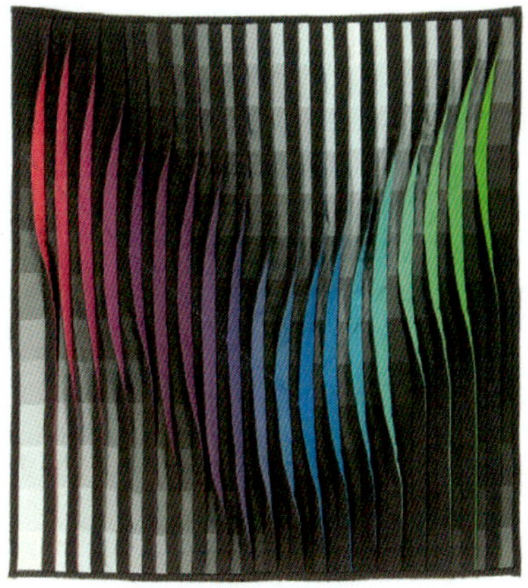

High Tech Tucks III

Caryl Bryer Fallert (Gentry)
Made in Oswego, Illinois
Dated 1986
22 x 20 in.

IQM 1997.007.1053

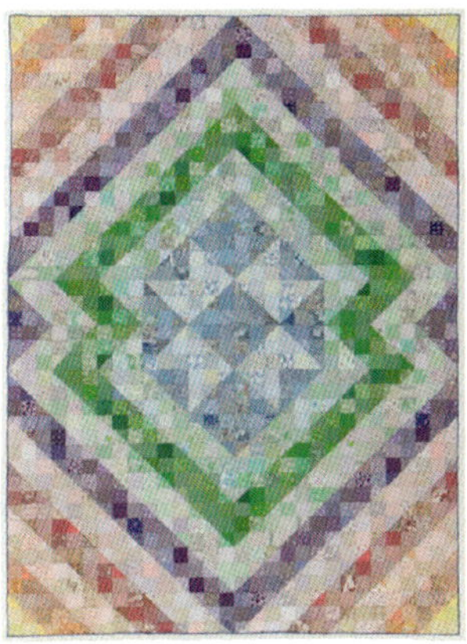

Nine Patch Log Cabin

Ardis James
Made in Chappaqua, New York
Dated 1982
86.5 x 62 in.

IQM 1997.007.1058

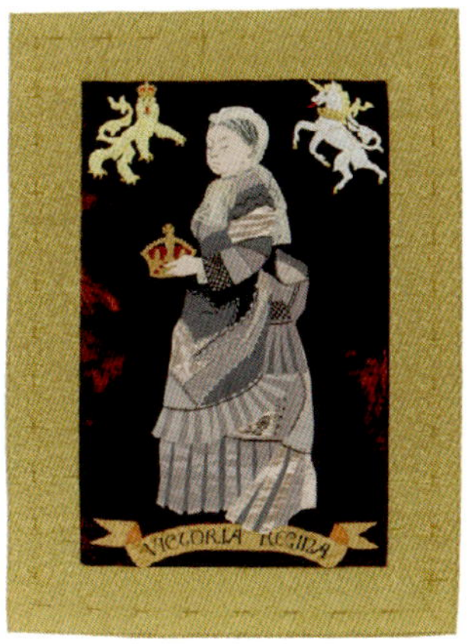

Jubilee

Helen Kelley
Made in Minneapolis,
Minnesota
Dated 1980
55 x 39.5 in.

IQM 1997.007.1059

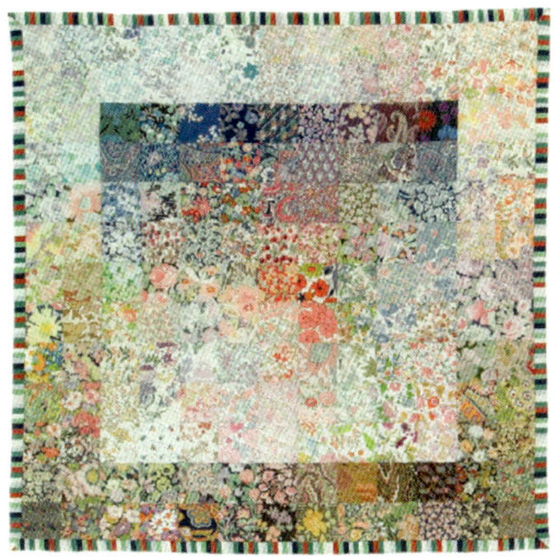

Colourwash Framed I

Deirdre Amsden
Made in Cambridge, England,
United Kingdom
Dated 1985
20 x 20 in.

IQM 1997.007.1064

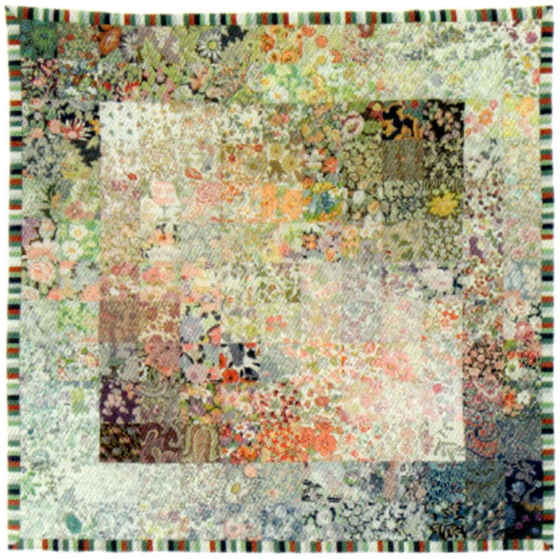

Colourwash Framed II

Deirdre Amsden
Made in Cambridge, England, United Kingdom
Dated 1986
20 x 20 in.
IQM 1997.007.1065

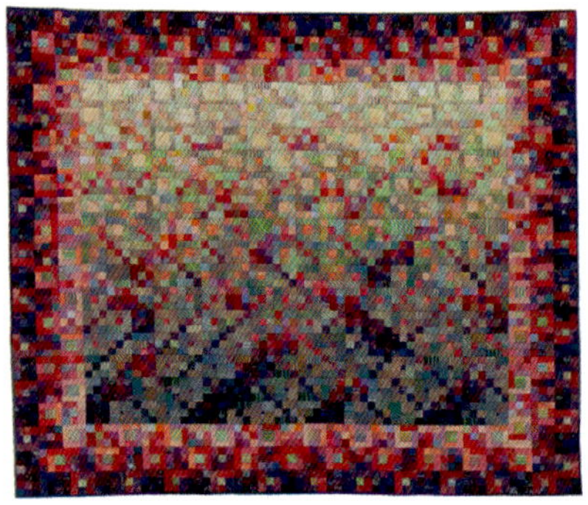

Number 63

Pamela Studstill
Made in Pipe Creek, Texas
Dated 1987
60 x 70 in.
IQM 1997.007.1067

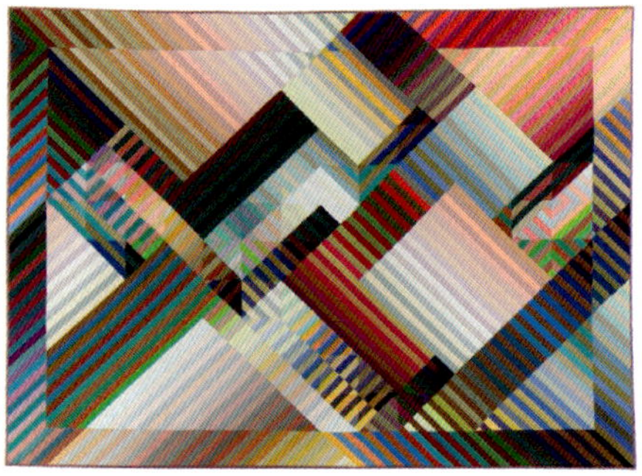

Bias Cut

Michael James
Made in Somerset, Massachusetts
Dated 1986
66.5 x 88 in.
IQM 1997.007.1068

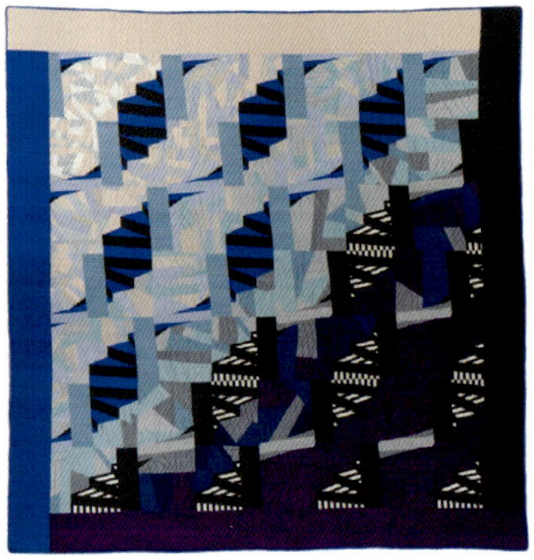

Spirals II

Pauline Burbidge
Made in Nottingham, England, United Kingdom
Dated 1985
88.5 x 83.5 in.
IQM 1997.007.1072

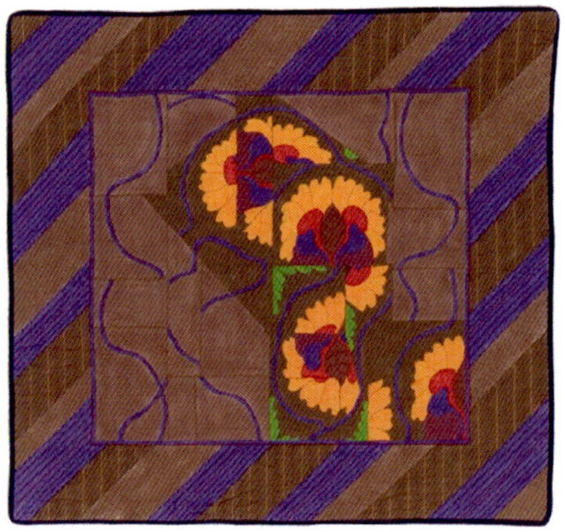

Fragments

Elizabeth Gurrier
Made in Hampton, New Hampshire
Dated 1986
38.5 x 41 in.
IQM 1997.007.1074

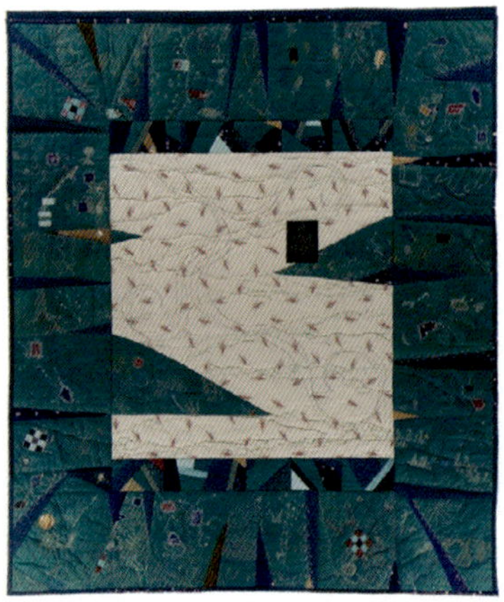

Lines from the Park

Damaris Jackson
Made in Minneapolis, Minnesota
Dated 1986
98.5 x 82.5 in.
IQM 1997.007.1075

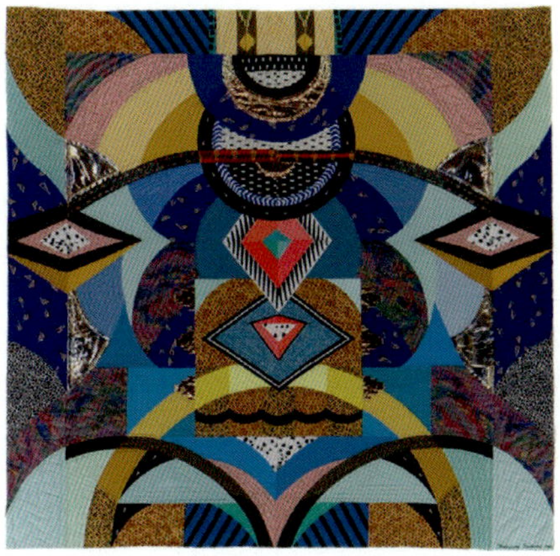

Voyages II:Casablanca

Francoise Barnes
Made in Colorado Springs, Colorado
Dated 1988
68.5 x 69 in.

IQM 1997.007.1077

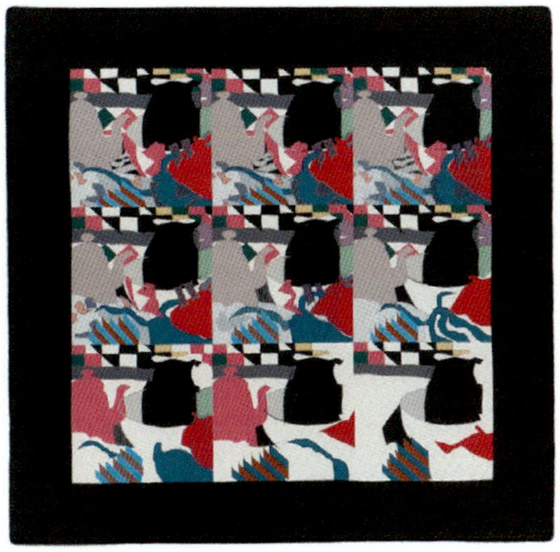

Pink Teapot

Pauline Burbidge
Made in Nottingham, England, United Kingdom
Dated 1987
69.5 x 62 in.

IQM 1997.007.1081

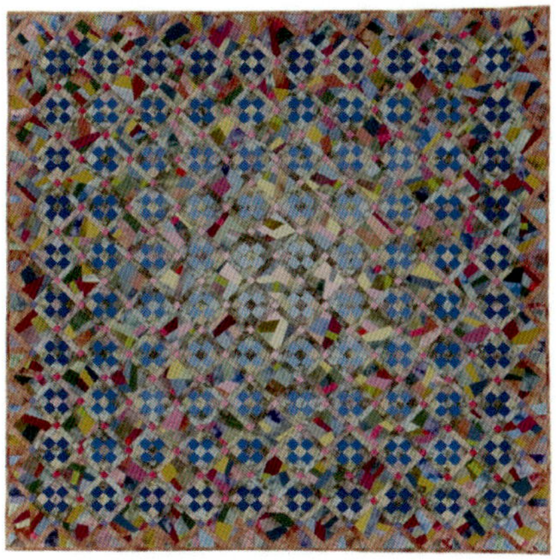

Crazy Ninepatch

Jan Myers-Newbury
Made in Minneapolis, Minnesota
Dated 1988
51.5 x 51 in.

IQM 1997.007.1085

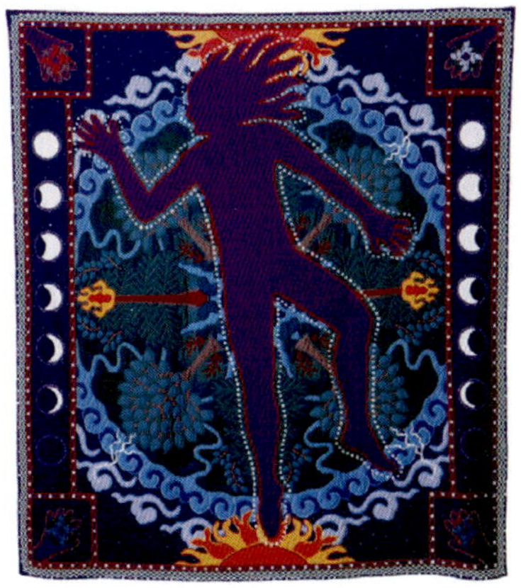

Revelation

Patrick Dorman
Made in Seattle, Washington
Dated 1986
92 x 81 in.

IQM 1997.007.1086

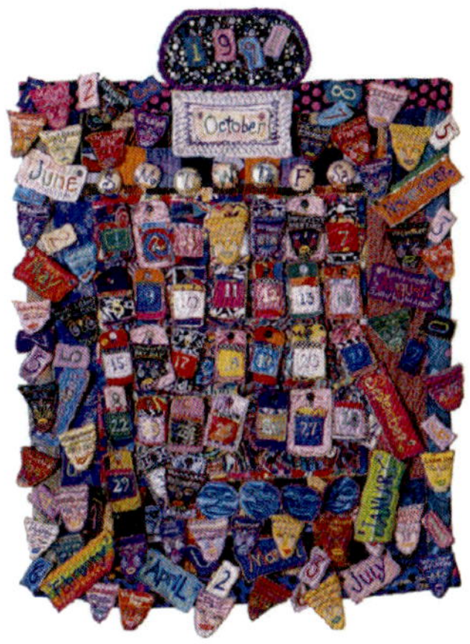

The Calendar Fetish:An Altar to Time

Susan Shie
Made in Wooster, Ohio
Dated 1989
79 x 61.5 in.

IQM 1997.007.1087

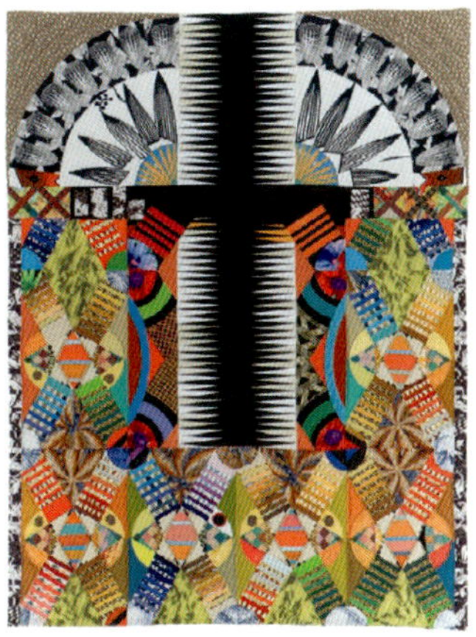

Lady of Guadelupe II

Nancy Crow
Made in Baltimore, Ohio
Dated 1987
82 x 61 in.

IQM 1997.007.1089

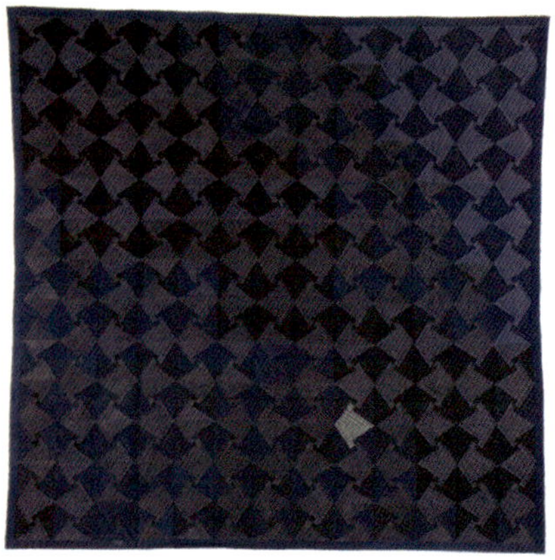

The Sea of Japan in Winter

Shizuko Kuroha
Made in Tokyo, Japan
Dated 1983
79 x 78 in.

IQM 1997.007.1091

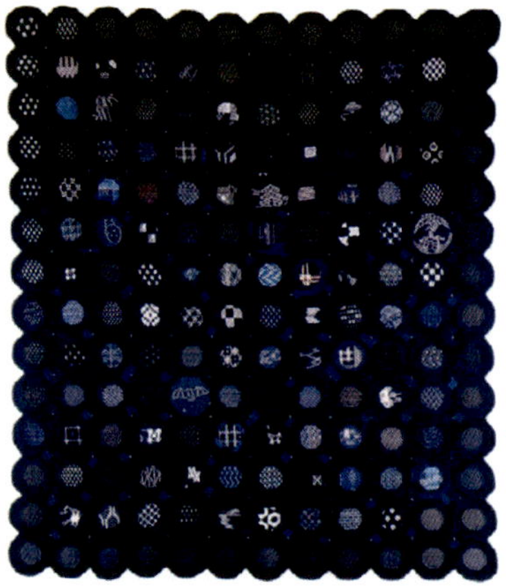

Poetry in Indigo III

Shizuko Kuroha
Made in Tokyo, Japan
Circa 1985
92 x 79.5 in.

IQM 1997.007.1092

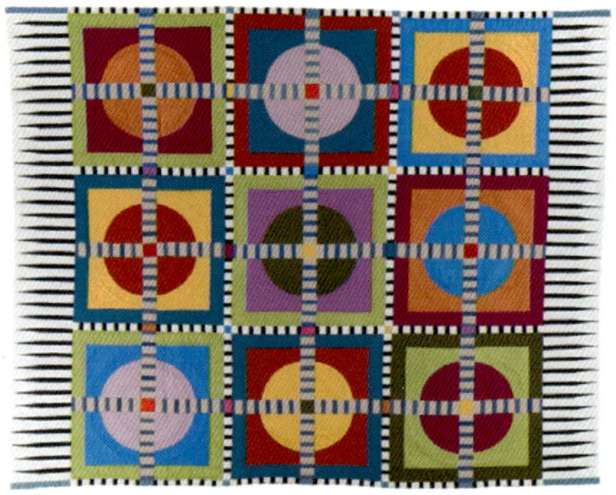

Manhattan Heat Wave

Elizabeth (Betsy) Cave
Made in Mansfield, Ohio
Dated 1987
66.5 x 81.5 in.

IQM 1997.007.1094

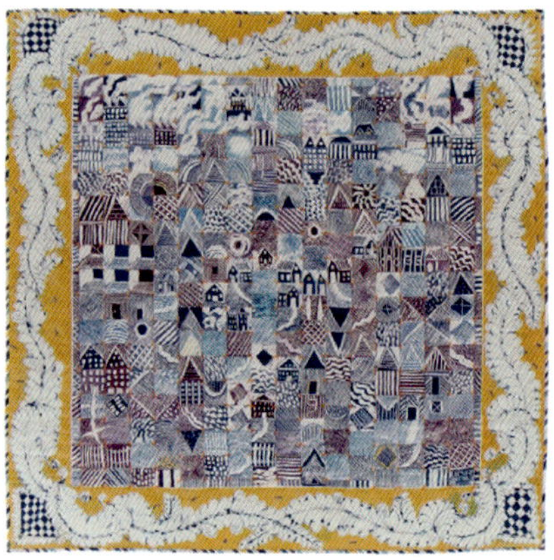

The Small City

Lenore Davis
Made in Newport, Kentucky
Dated 1990
68.5 x 68 in.

IQM 1997.007.1095

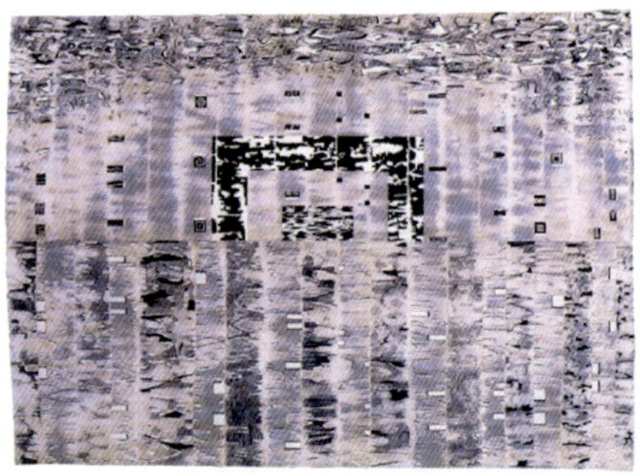

Opening Moves

Linda MacDonald
Made in Willits, California
Dated 1991
52 x 71 in.

IQM 1997.007.1096

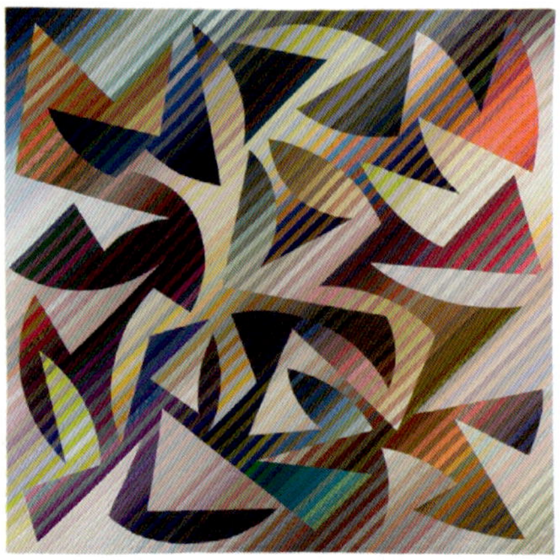

Suspended Animation

Michael James
Made in Somerset, Massachusetts
Dated 1992
89.5 x 88 in.

IQM 1997.007.1098

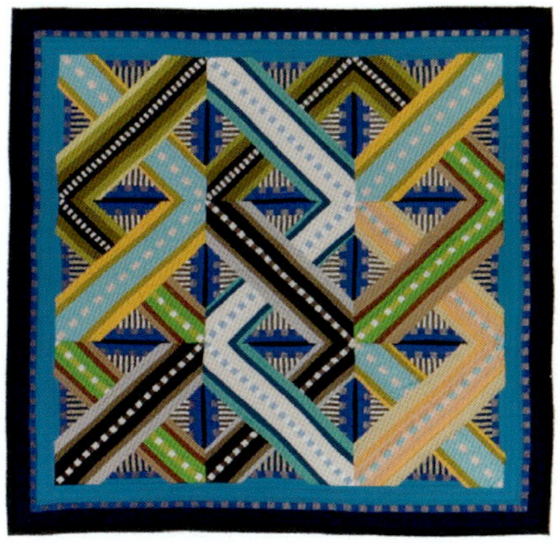

Bittersweet V

Nancy Crow
Made in Baltimore, Ohio
Dated 1980
42 x 41.5 in.

IQM 1997.007.1100

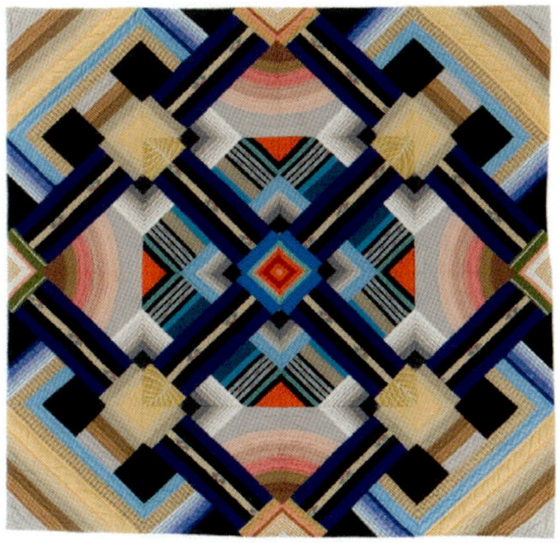

November Study #1

Nancy Crow
Made in Baltimore, Ohio
Dated 1980
59.5 x 61.5 in.

IQM 1997.007.1101

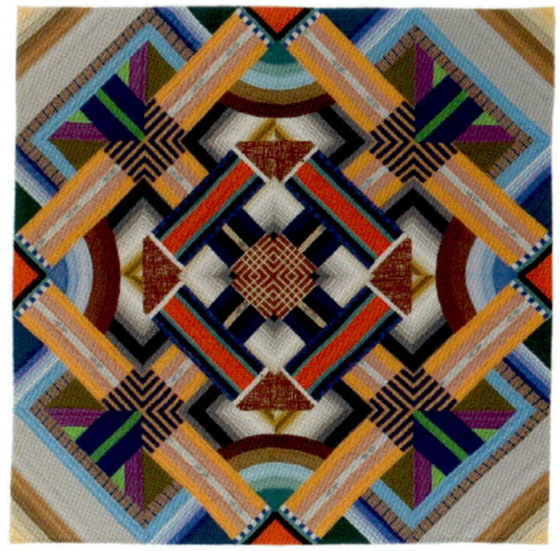

November Study #2

Nancy Crow
Made in Baltimore, Ohio
Dated 1980
60.5 x 60.5 in.

IQM 1997.007.1102

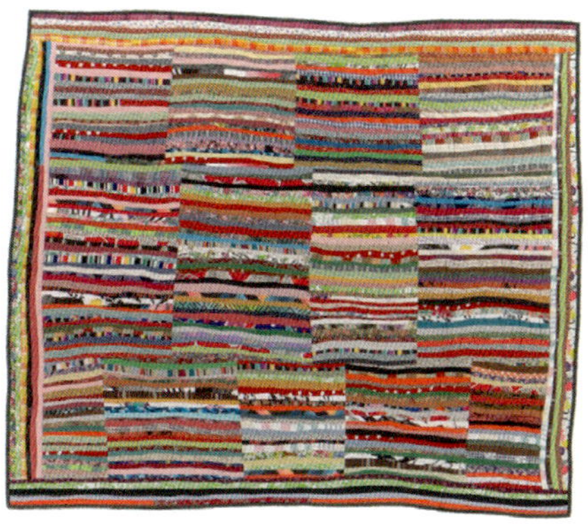

LII:Strip Quilts

Anna Williams
Made in Baton Rouge, Louisiana
Dated 1992
65 x 71.5 in.

IQM 1997.007.1103

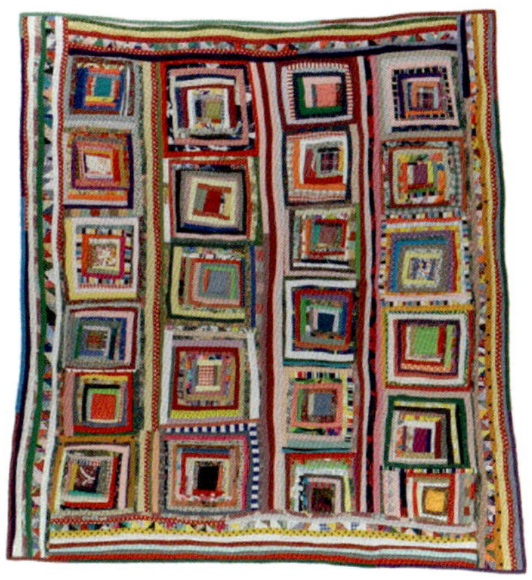

LIX:Log Cabin

Anna Williams
Made in Baton Rouge, Louisiana
Dated 1993
76 x 64.5 in.

IQM 1997.007.1104

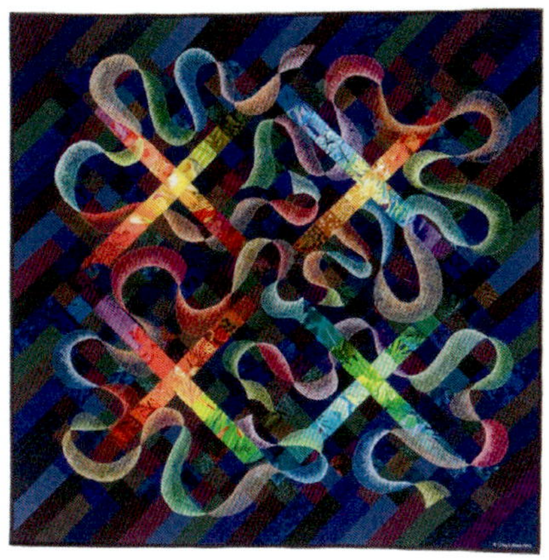

Ribbon Quartet

Libby Lehman
Made in Houston, Texas
Dated 1992
52 x 51 in.

IQM 1997.007.1105

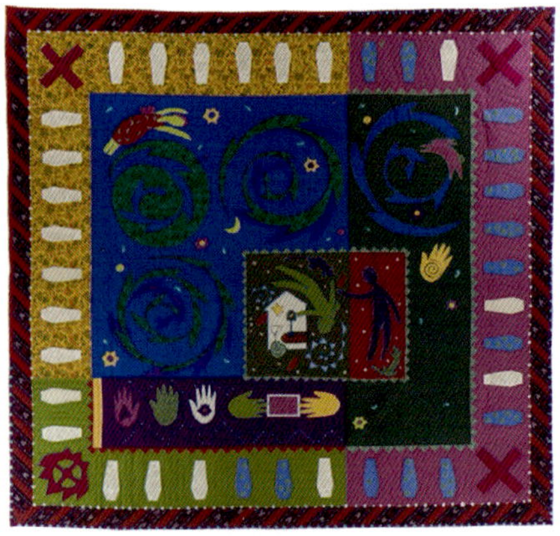

We Are Made of Dreams and Bones

Kimberly Stout
Made in Columbus, Ohio
Dated 1993 - 1994
85.5 x 89 in.

IQM 1997.007.1107

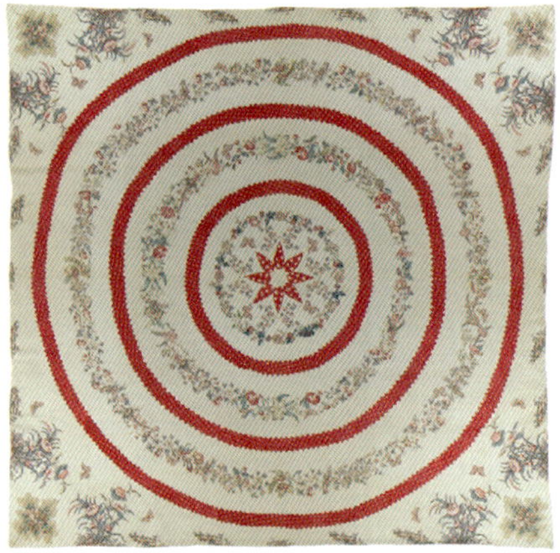

Medallion

Maker unidentified
Probably made in Salem, Massachusetts
1840 - 1850
103 x 101.5 in.

IQM 2006.003.0001

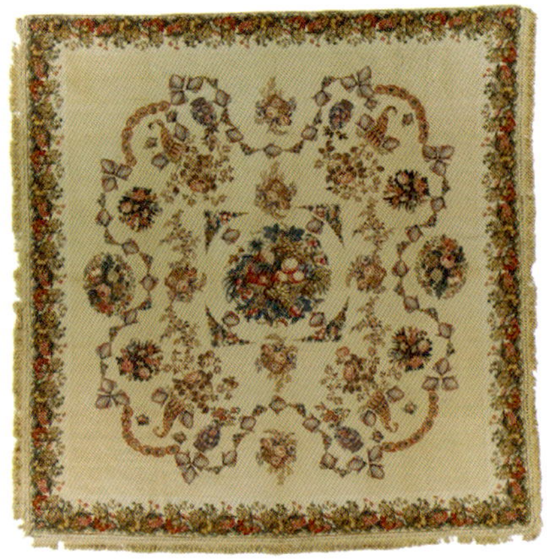

Medallion

Maker unidentified
Probably made in United States
1830 - 1850
101 x 98.5 in.

IQM 2006.003.0002

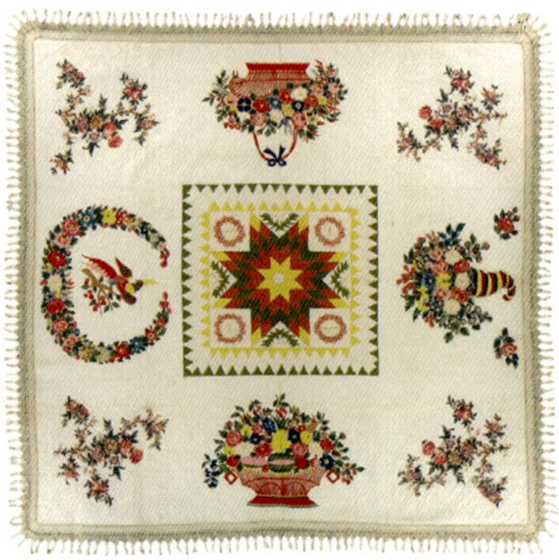

Album

T. Ann Hulls
Made in Baltimore, Maryland
Dated 1852
110 x 110 in.

IQM 2006.003.0003

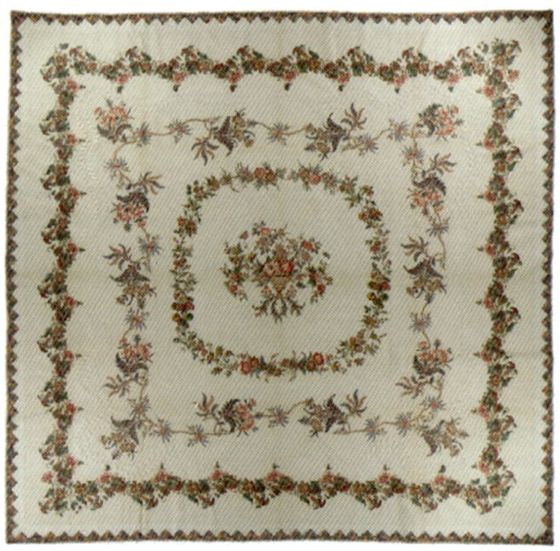

Medallion

Maker unidentified
Probably made in eastern United States
1820 - 1840
122.5 x 124 in.

IQM 2006.003.0004

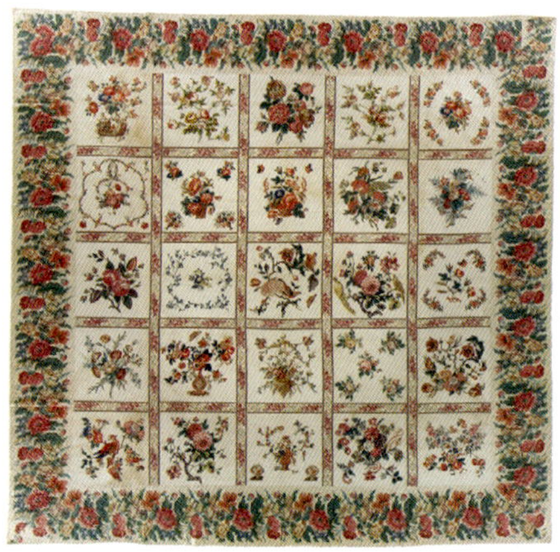

Album

Mary V. Yeadon
Probably made in Greenville, South Carolina
Dated 1848 - 1849
107.5 x 108 in.

IQM 2006.003.0005

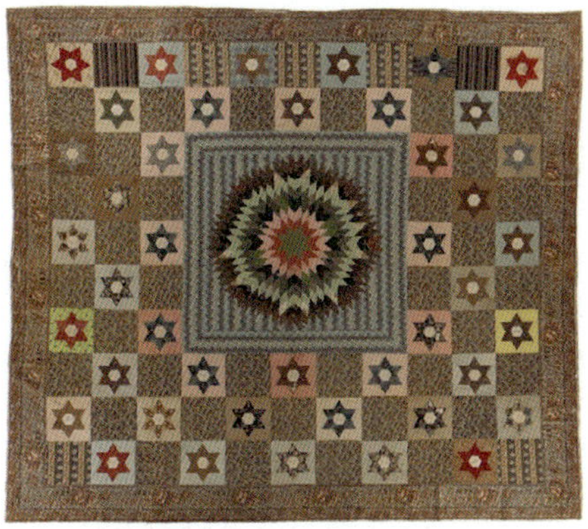

Medallion

Probably made by Rebecca Savery
Probably made in Philadelphia, Pennsylvania
1849 - 1850
104.5 x 115 in.
IQM 2006.003.0006

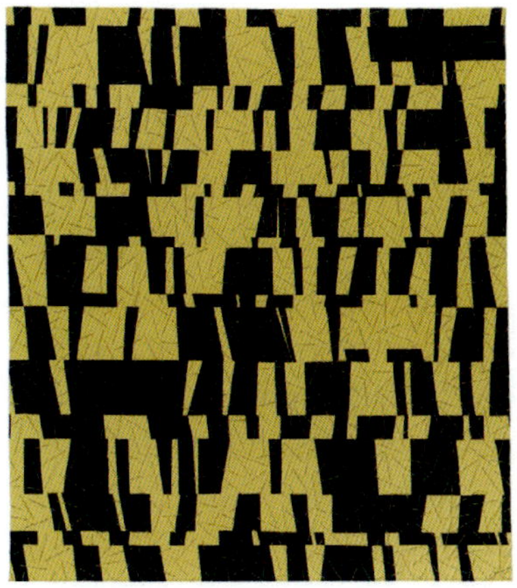

Yellow Brick Road

Michael James
Made in Somerset, Massachusetts
Dated 1996
88.5 x 72 in.
IQM 2006.043.0001

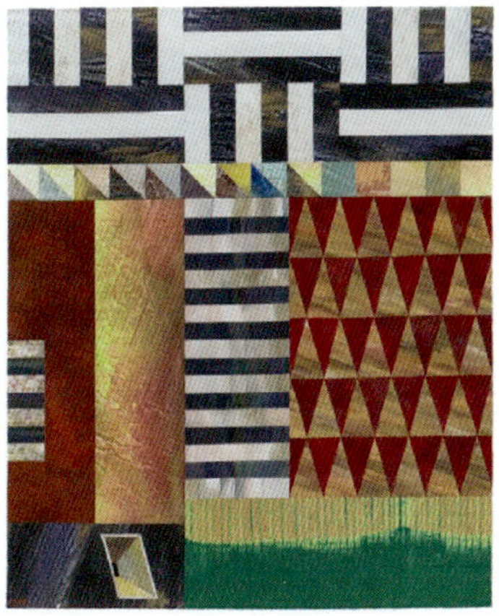

Wall 1

Michael James
Made in Somerset, Massachusetts
Dated 1999
68 x 55.5 in.
IQM 2006.043.0002

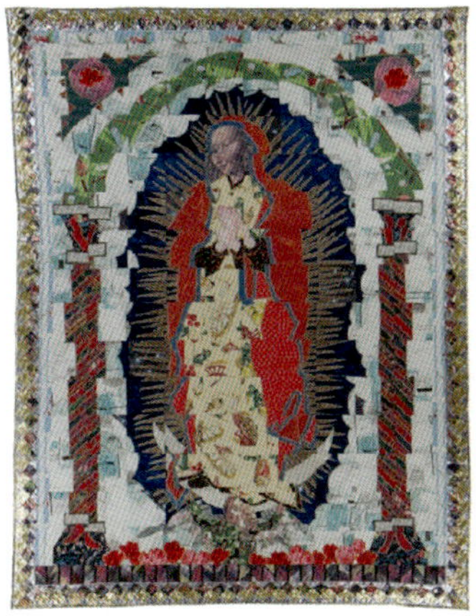

Guadalupe Reperceived

Mary Catherine Lamb
Made in Portland, Oregon
Dated 1992
102 x 76 in.
IQM 2006.043.0003

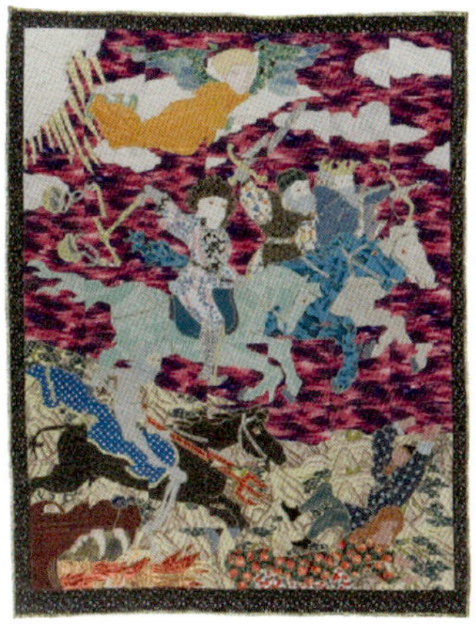

The Four Horsemen of Apocalypse

Mary Catherine Lamb
Made in Portland, Oregon
Dated 1995
80 x 60 in.
IQM 2006.043.0004

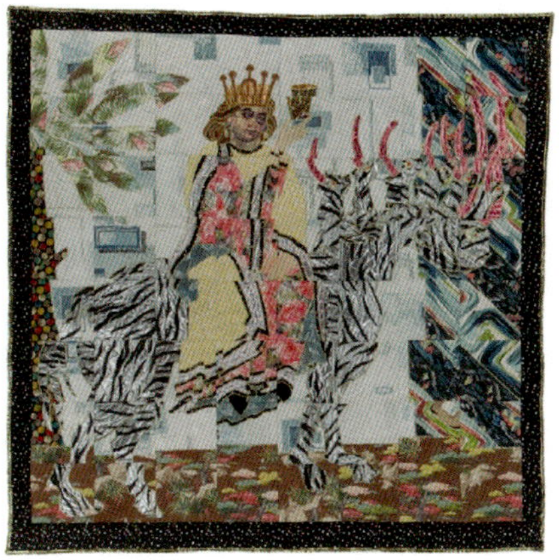

The Whore of Babylon

Mary Catherine Lamb
Made in Portland, Oregon
Dated 1997
65.5 x 64.25 in.
IQM 2006.043.0005

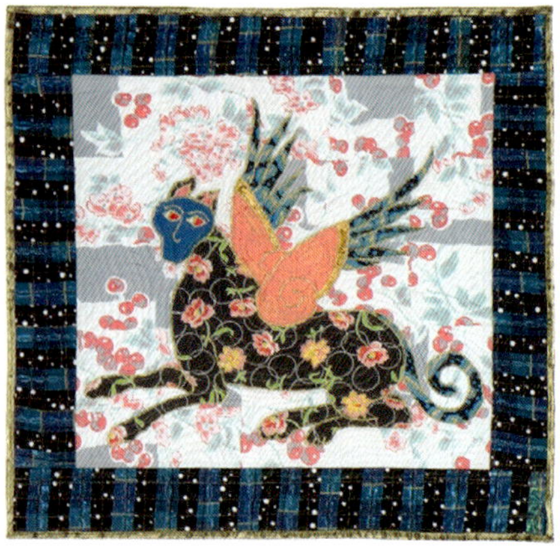

Winged Cheetah

Mary Catherine Lamb
Made in Portland, Oregon
1990 - 2000
23 x 24 in.

IQM 2006.043.0006

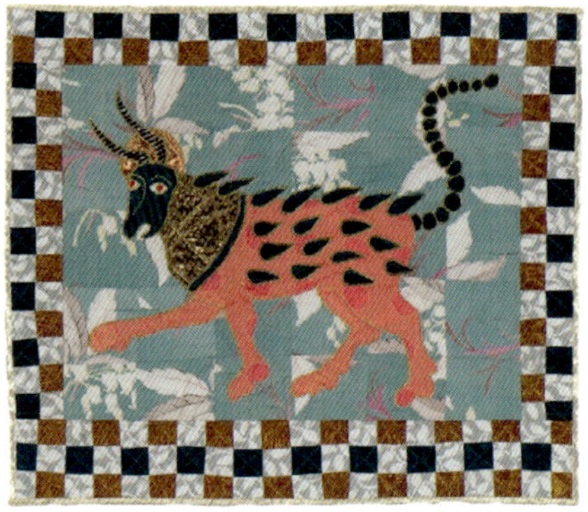

Scaley Beast

Mary Catherine Lamb
Made in Portland, Oregon
1990 - 2000
24.5 x 28 in.

IQM 2006.043.0007

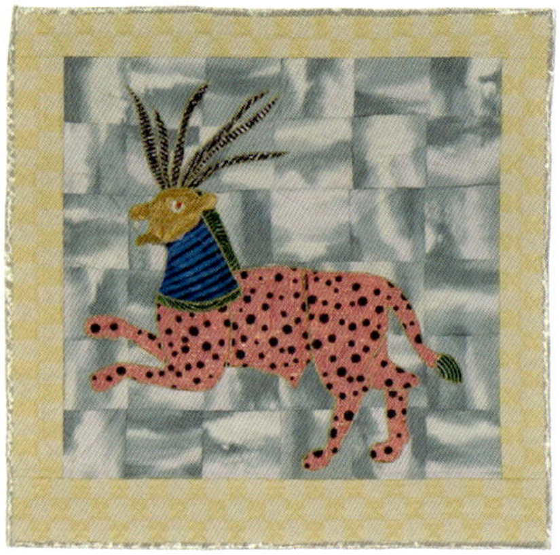

Spotted Beast

Mary Catherine Lamb
Made in Portland, Oregon
1990 - 2000
28.5 x 28 in.

IQM 2006.043.0008

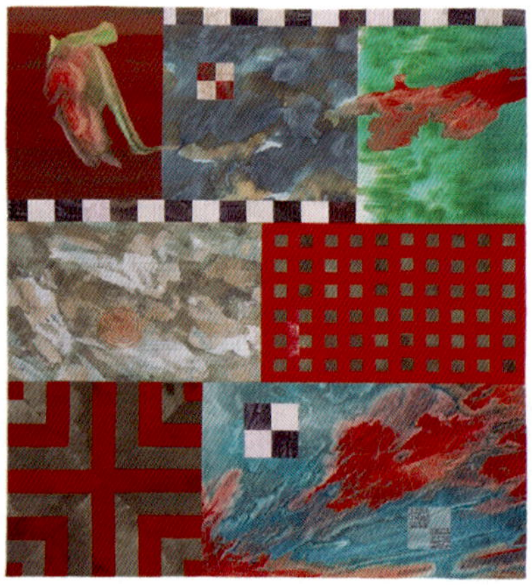

Spiritus Mundi

Michael James
Made in Lincoln, Nebraska
Dated 2000
55.5 x 61.5 in.

IQM 2006.043.0009

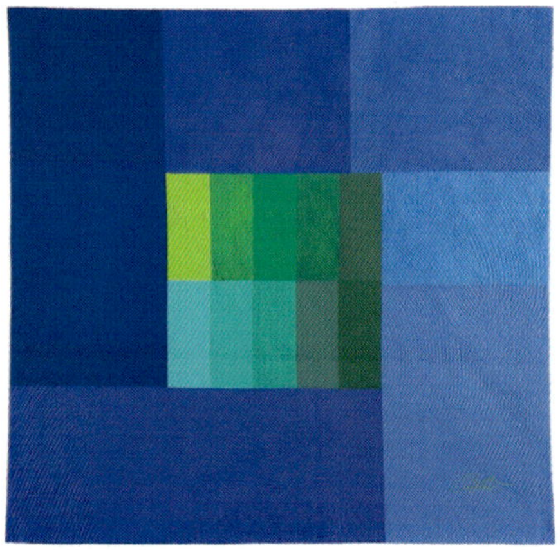

Atlantis

Ruth Eissfeldt
Made in Essen, Germany
Circa 2001
59 x 59 in.

IQM 2006.043.0010

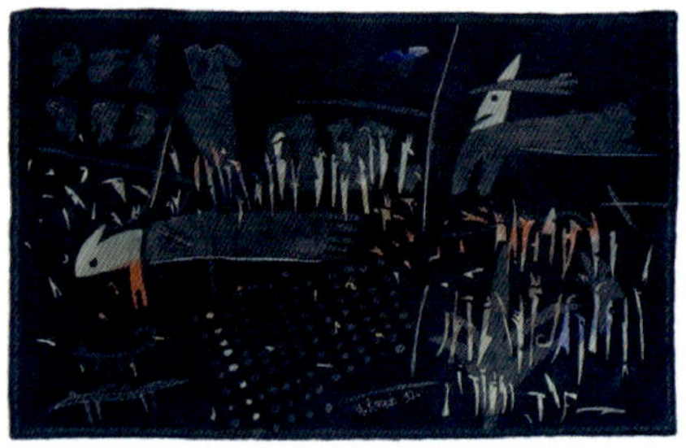

Judge and Victim

Ursula Rauch
Made in Weingarten, Germany
Dated 1992
81.5 x 56.5 in.

IQM 2006.043.0011

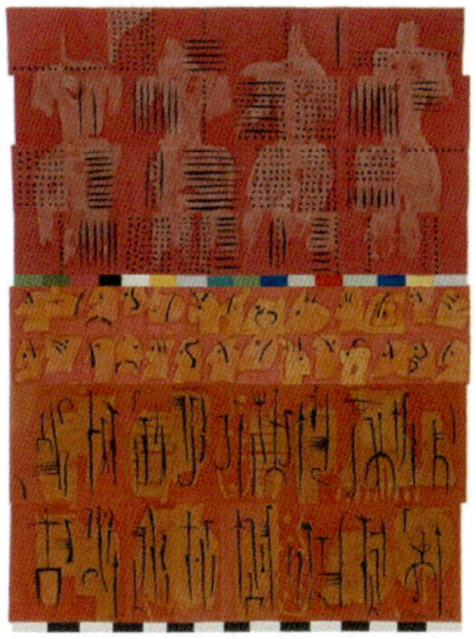

The Sorrow of the Black Woman

Ursula Rauch
Made in Weingarten, Germany
Dated 1996
75 x 54 in.

IQM 2006.043.0012

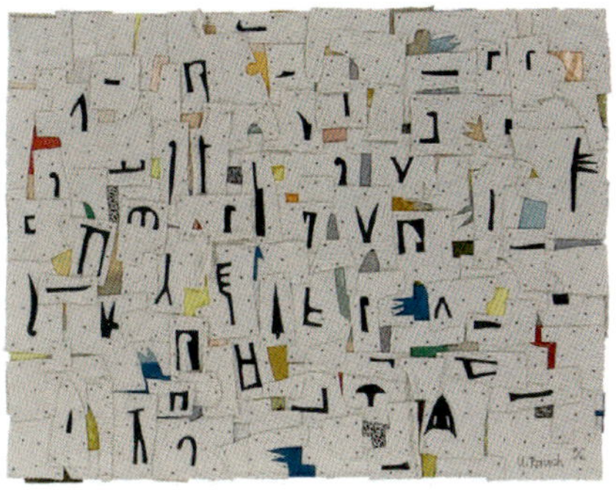

Maze

Ursula Rauch
Made in Weingarten, Germany
Circa 1995
75 x 58 in.

IQM 2006.043.0013

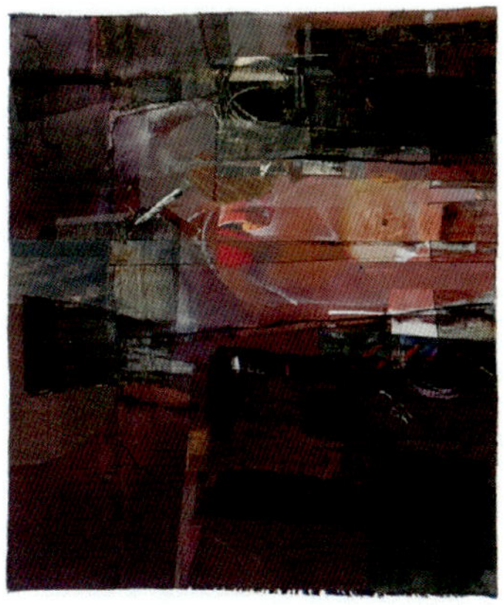

Red Landscape

Fran Skiles
Made in Plantation, Florida
Circa 1997
52 x 63 in.

IQM 2006.043.0014

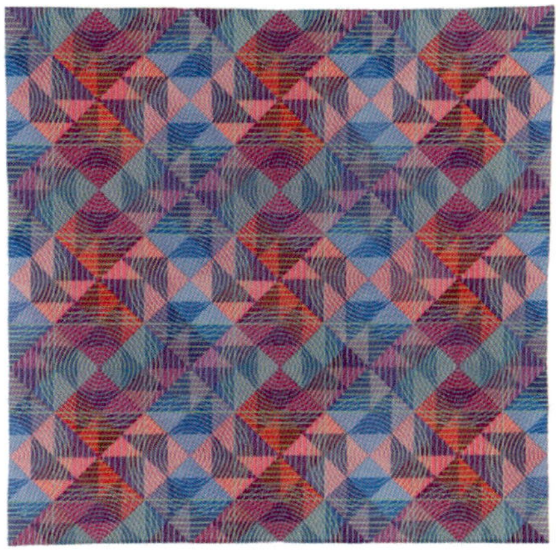

PW Block #4

Ellen Oppenheimer
Made in Oakland, California
Dated 2003
66 x 66 in.

IQM 2006.043.0015

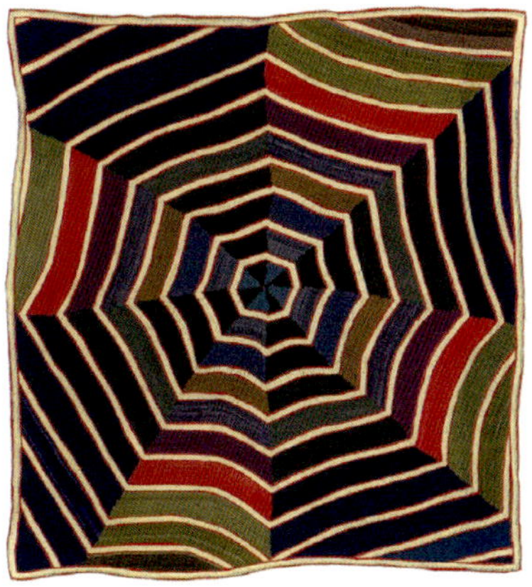

Spider Web

Maker unidentified
Probably made in Union County, Ohio
Dated 1936
78 x 70 in.

IQM 2006.043.0016

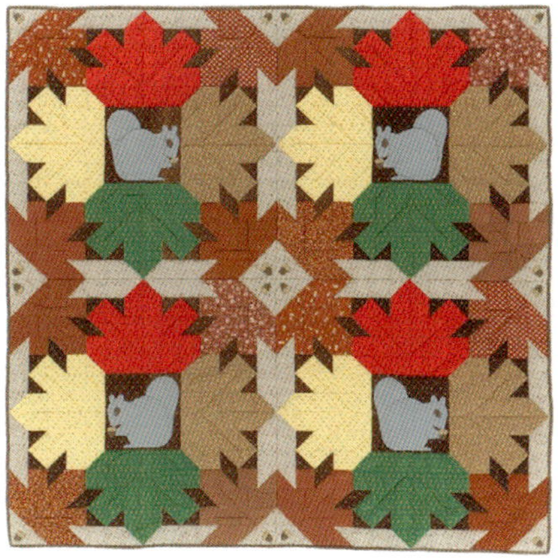

Squirrel and Acorn

Maker unidentified
Made in United States
Circa 1980
54 x 55 in.

IQM 2006.043.0018

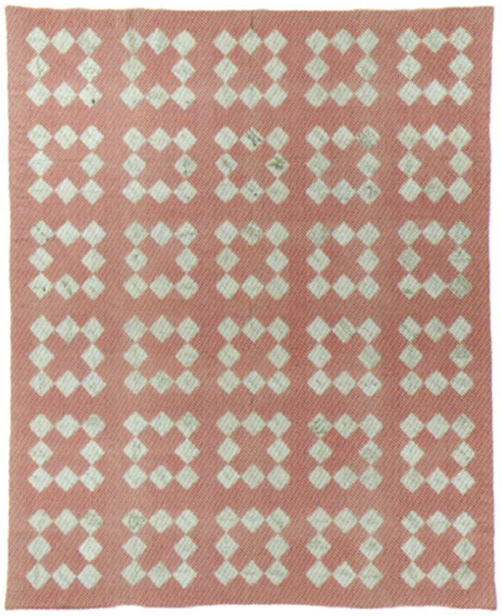

Album

Maker unidentified
Made in United States
Dated 1879 - 1891
90 x 74 in.

IQM 2006.043.0019

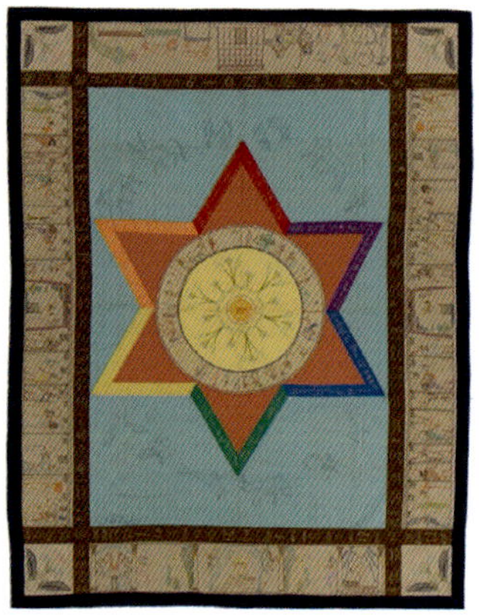

Original - Light of Egypt

Maker unidentified
Made in United States
Dated 1941
100 x 78 in.

IQM 2006.043.0020

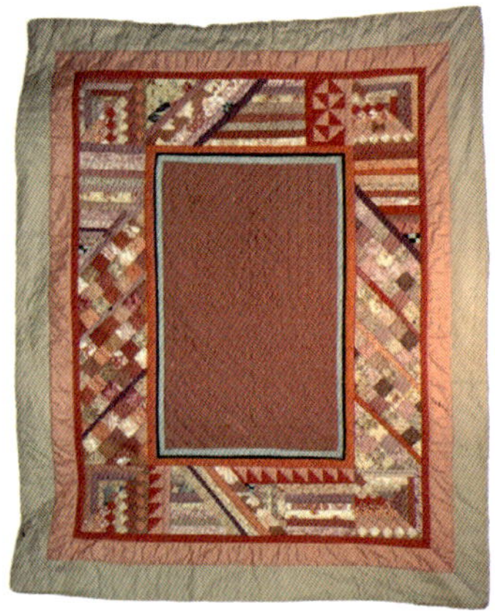

Nappe

Maker unidentified
Possibly made in New York
Dated 1983
60 x 48 in.

IQM 2006.043.0021

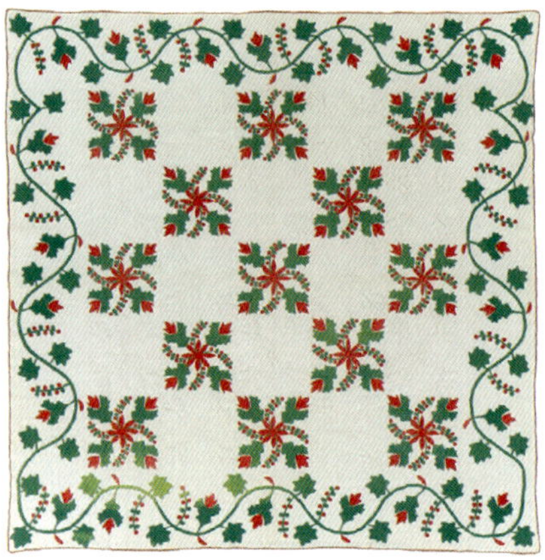

Currants and Coxcombs

Maker unidentified
Probably made in Jefferson County, Ohio
1850 - 1870
90 x 90 in.

IQM 2006.043.0023

Whole Cloth

Maker unidentified
Probably made in Wales, United Kingdom
1890 - 1910
77 x 82 in.

IQM 2006.043.0024

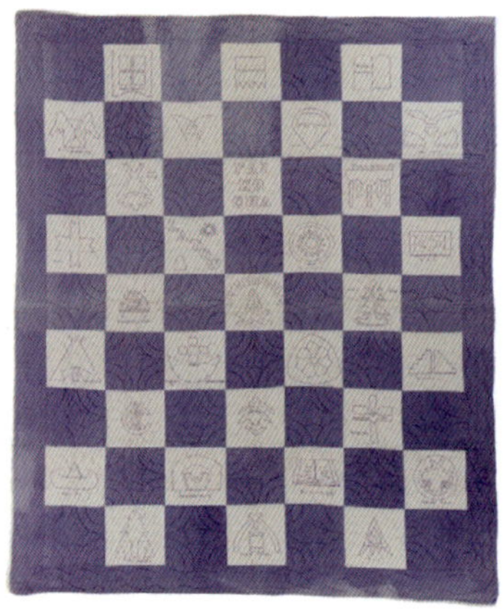

Girls Camp

Probably made by Thelma K. Greenert
Made in Pittsburgh, Pennsylvania
Circa 1950
79 x 65 in.

IQM 2006.043.0025

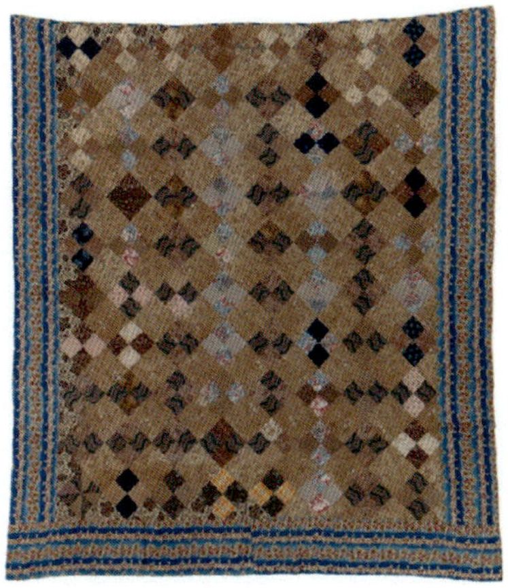

Four Patch

Maker unidentified
Made in United States
1830 - 1850
87 x 75 in.

IQM 2006.043.0026

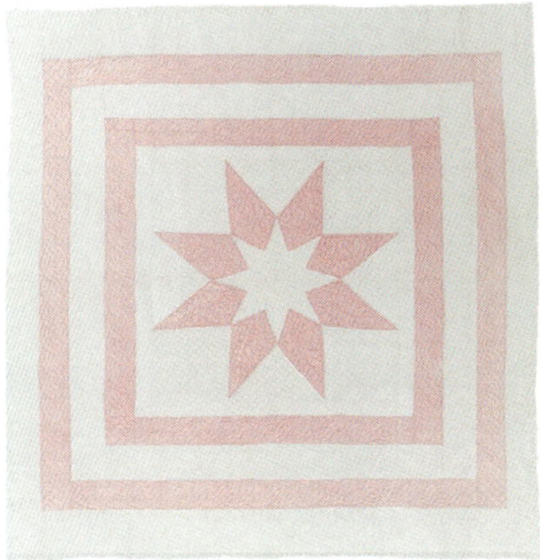

Star

Maker unidentified
Probably made in United Kingdom
Circa 1920
68 x 70 in.

IQM 2006.043.0027

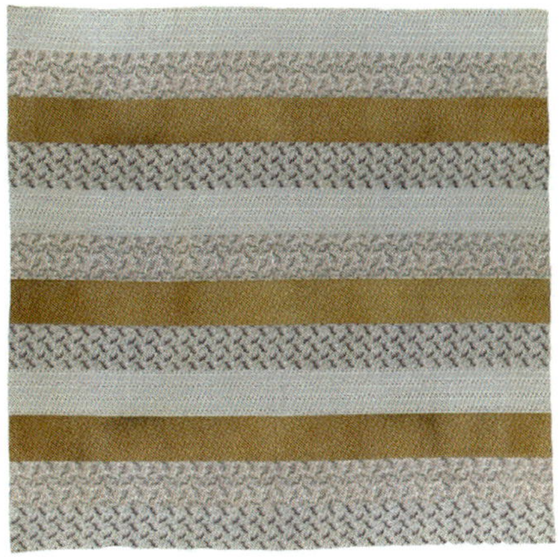

Bars

Maker unidentified
Probably made in Wales, United Kingdom
1860 - 1880
94 x 92 in.

IQM 2006.043.0028

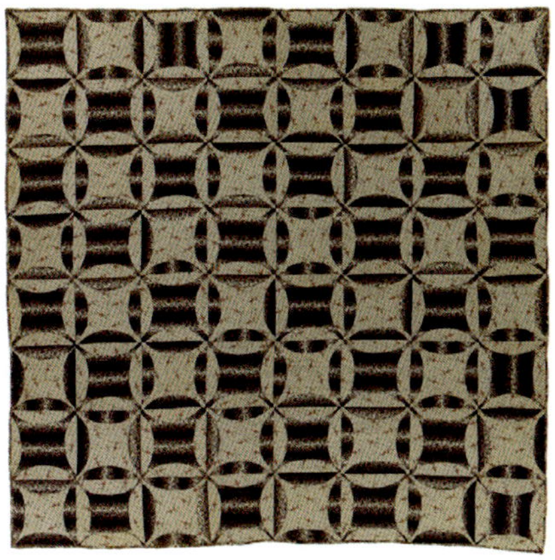

Rob Peter to Pay Paul

Possibly made by Rachel A. Clark Weed
Probably made in New York
1840 - 1850
84 x 82.5 in.

IQM 2006.043.0029

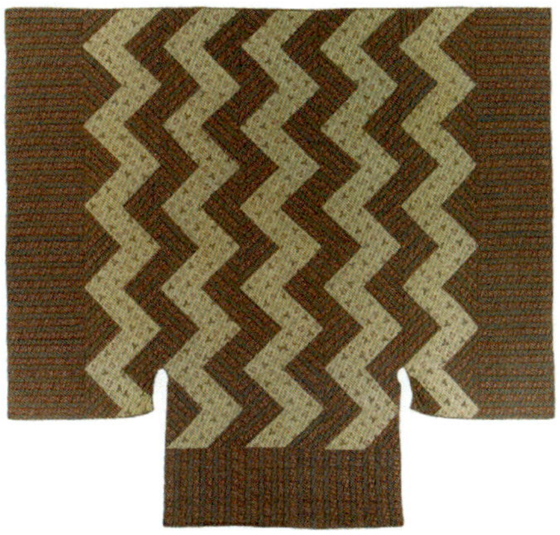

Streak of Lightning

Maker unidentified
Possibly made in New England
1840 - 1860
108 x 115 in.

IQM 2006.043.0030

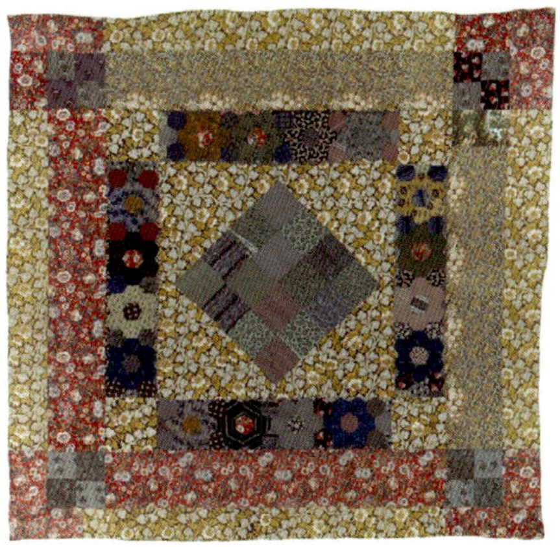

Center Diamond

Maker unidentified
Probably made in England, United Kingdom
1830 - 1850
90 x 93 in.

IQM 2006.043.0031

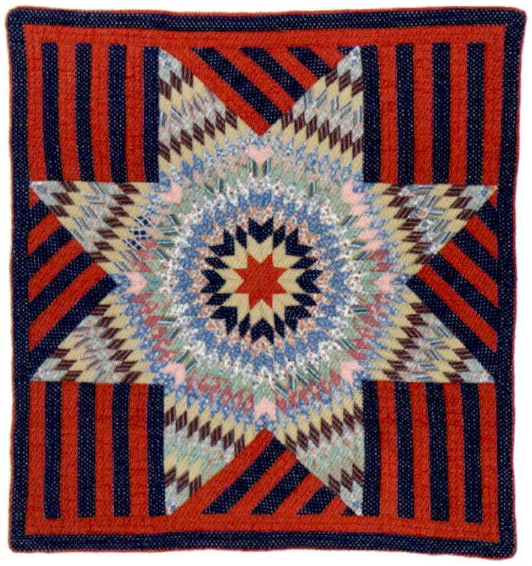

Star of Bethlehem

Maker unidentified
Made in United States
1920 - 1940
80 x 74 in.

IQM 2006.043.0032

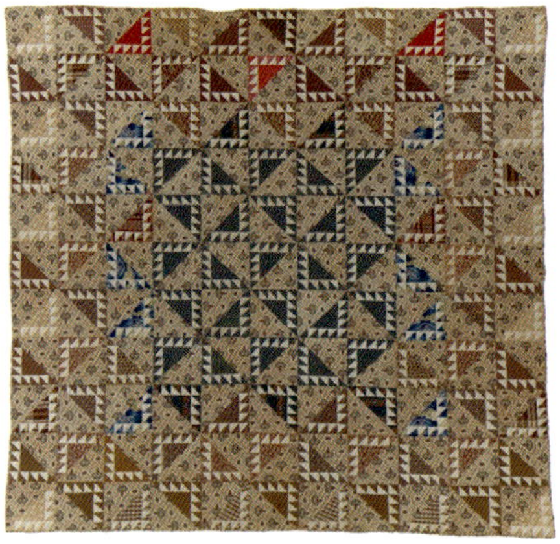

Delectable Mountains

Maker unidentified
Made in United States
1840 - 1860
89 x 87 in.

IQM 2006.043.0033

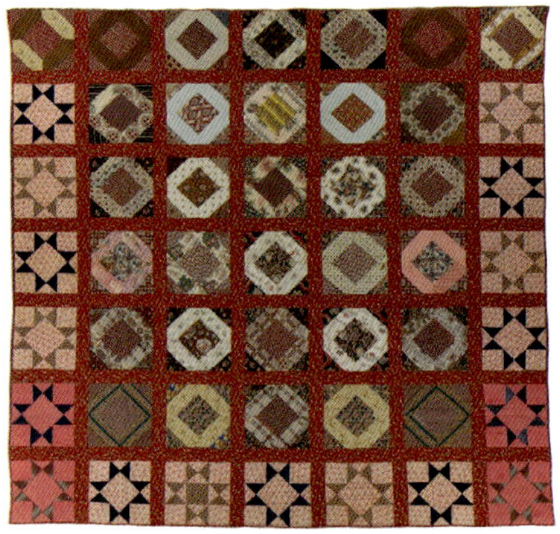

Variable Star

Possibly made by Mary B. Leonard
Made in United States
1850 - 1870
90 x 90 in.

IQM 2006.043.0034

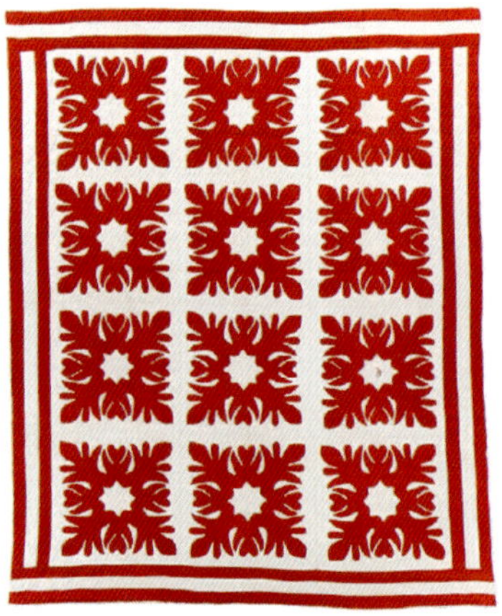

Appliqué

Maker unidentified
Made in United States
Dated 1897
88 x 72 in.

IQM 2006.043.0035

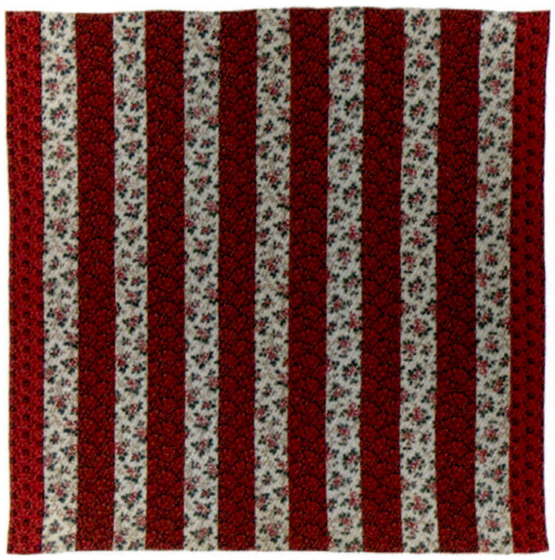

Bars

Maker unidentified
Made in United States
1870 - 1890
84 x 85 in.

IQM 2006.043.0038

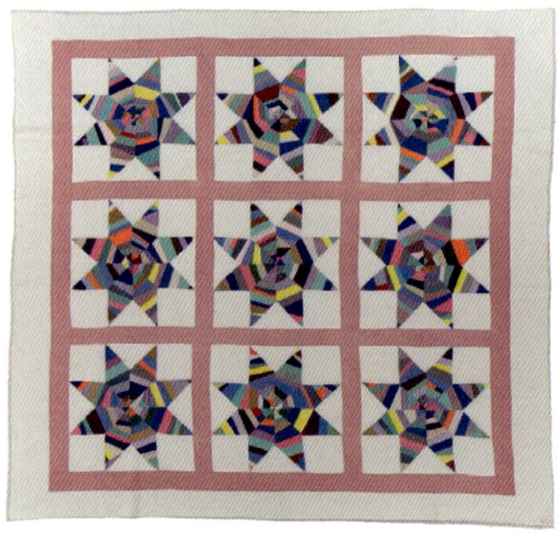

String Star

Probably made by Eunice Miller
Probably made in Iowa
Dated 1951
80 x 82 in.

IQM 2006.043.0041

Wreath of Roses

Maker unidentified
Possibly made in Indiana
Circa 1930
84 x 60 in.

IQM 2006.043.0042

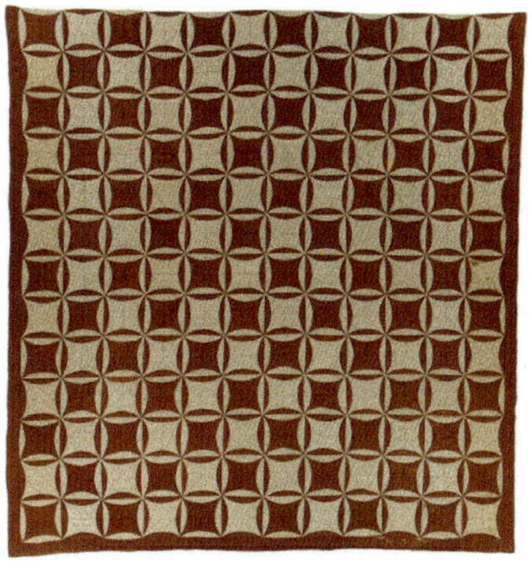

Rob Peter to Pay Paul

Maker unidentified
Made in United States
1820 - 1840
93 x 84 in.

IQM 2006.043.0043

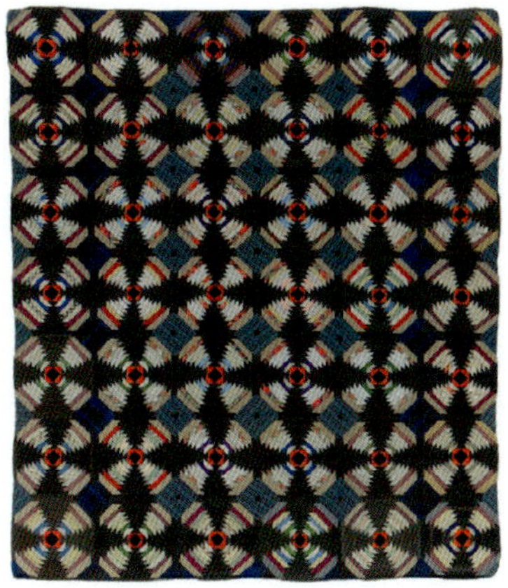

Log Cabin

Maker unidentified
Possibly made in Kentucky
Circa 1890
79.25 x 67.5 in.

IQM 2006.043.0044

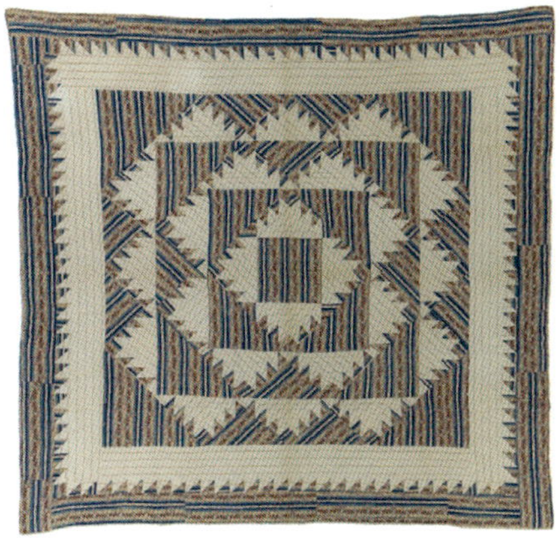

Delectable Mountains

Maker unidentified
Possibly made in Pennsylvania
1840 - 1850
83 x 80 in.

IQM 2006.043.0045

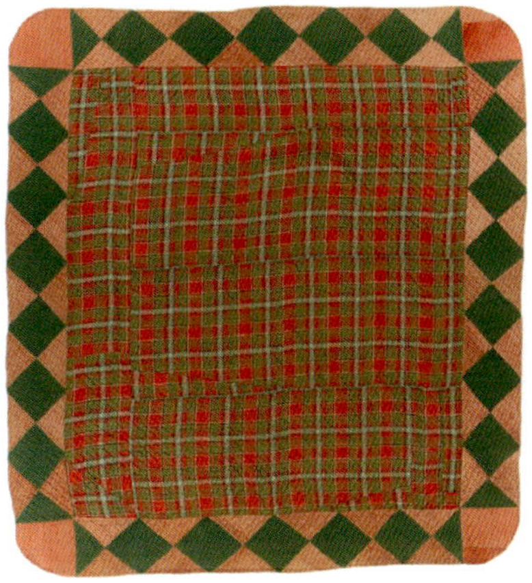

Framed Center

Maker unidentified
Made in Nova Scotia, Canada
Circa 1850
85 x 76 in.

IQM 2006.043.0046

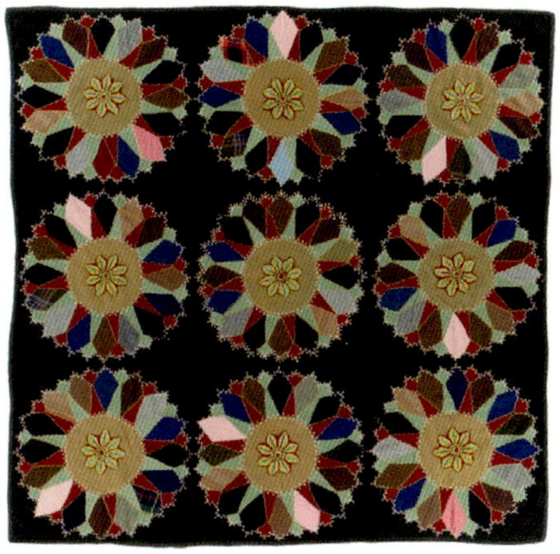

Wagon Wheel

Maker unidentified
Possibly made in Pennsylvania
1900 - 1920
73 x 72 in.

IQM 2006.043.0047

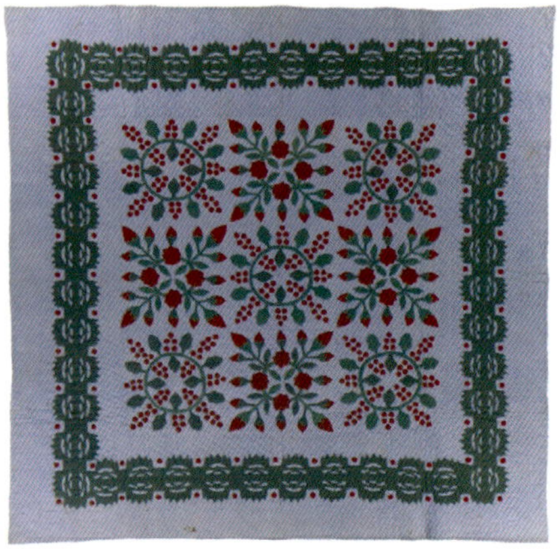

Flower Wreath

Maker unidentified
Made in United States
1870 - 1890
82 x 83 in.
IQM 2006.043.0048

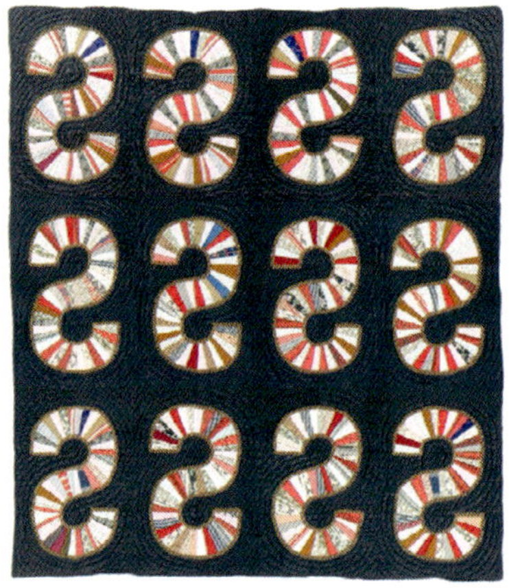

Fan

Maker unidentified
Possibly made in Pennsylvania
1900 - 1920
73 x 64 in.
IQM 2006.043.0049

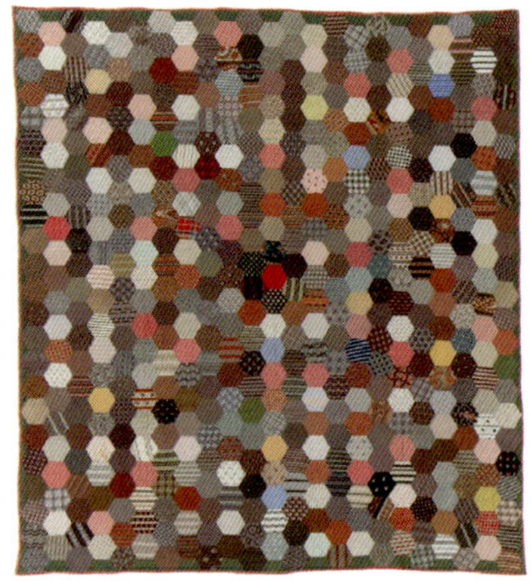

Hexagon

Maker unidentified
Made in United States
1880 - 1900
89.5 x 78.5 in.
IQM 2006.043.0051

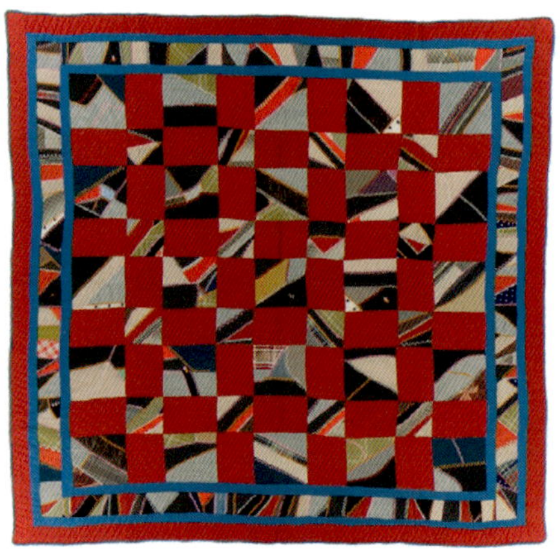

Crazy

Maker unidentified
Possibly made in Holmes County, Ohio
Circa 1890
76 x 80 in.
IQM 2006.043.0052

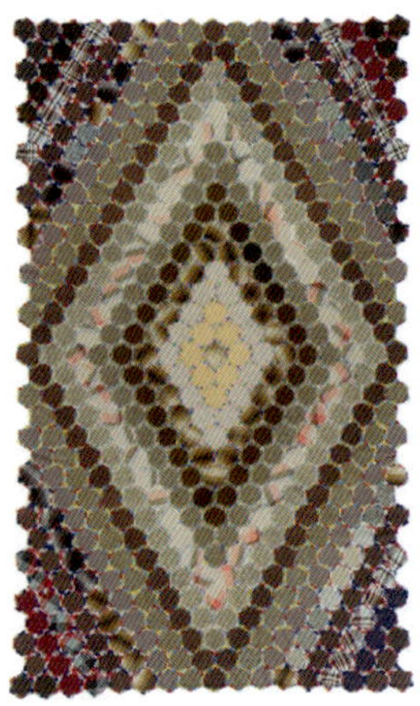

Hexagon

Maker unidentified
Possibly made in Vermont
1900 - 1920
99 x 56 in.
IQM 2006.043.0054

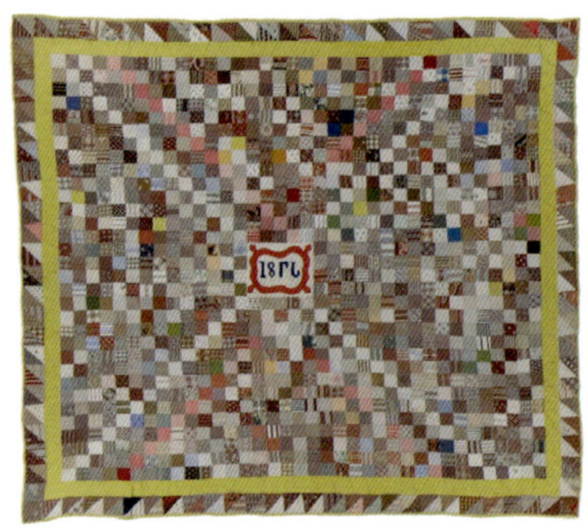

One Patch

Maker unidentified
Possibly made in western Pennsylvania
Dated 1876
86 x 78 in.
IQM 2006.043.0055

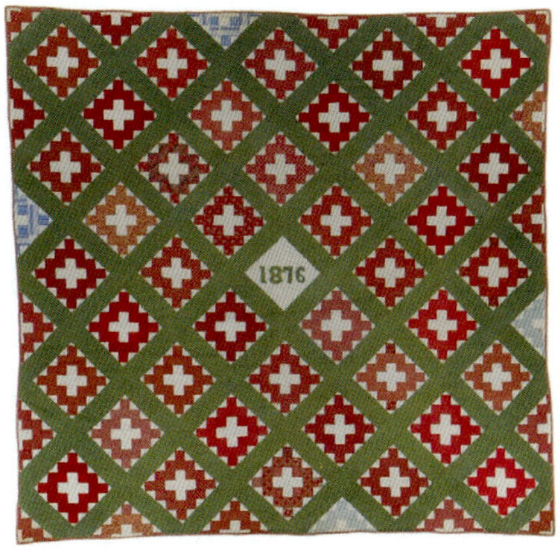

Chimney Sweep

Maker unidentified
Probably made in Connecticut
Dated 1876
90 x 82 in.

IQM 2006.043.0056

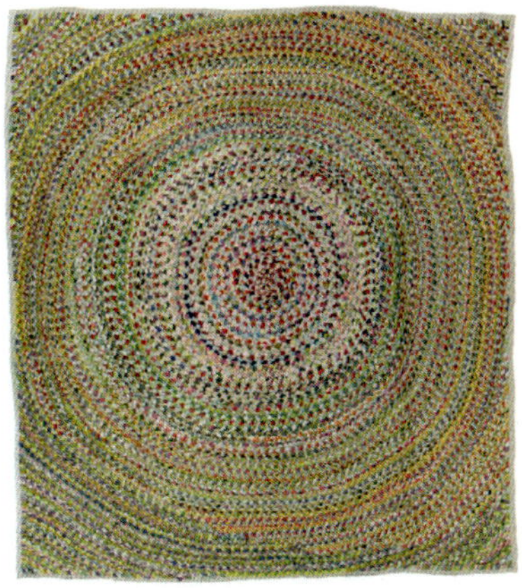

Target

Maker unidentified
Possibly made in Tennessee
1950 - 1970
85 x 75 in.

IQM 2006.043.0057

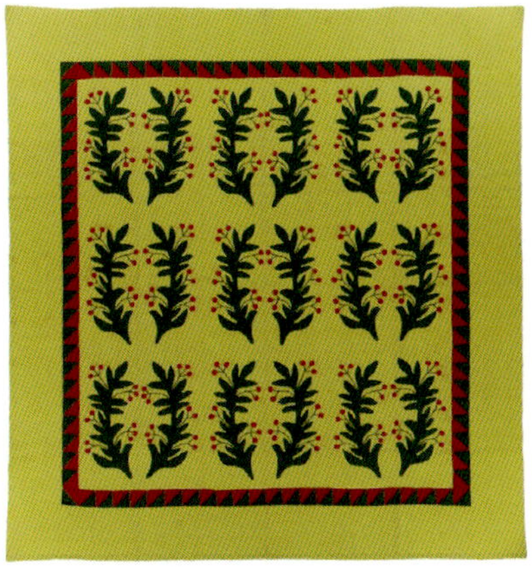

Laurel Wreath

Maker unidentified
Possibly made in Pennsylvania
1870 - 1890
89 x 85 in.

IQM 2006.043.0059

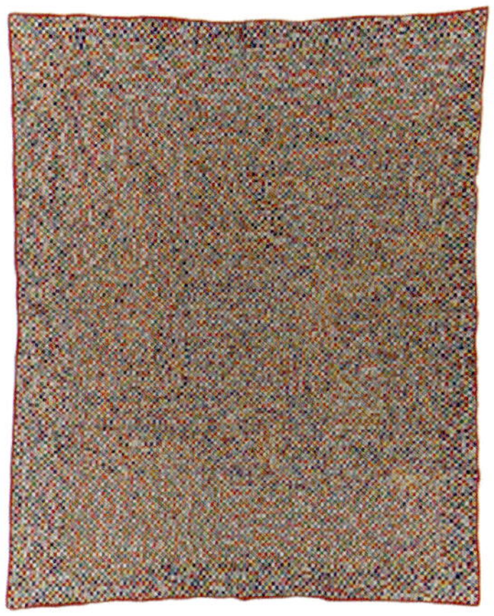

One Patch

Belle Ross
Possibly made in Coffeyville, Kansas
Circa 1950
92 x 72 in.

IQM 2006.043.0061

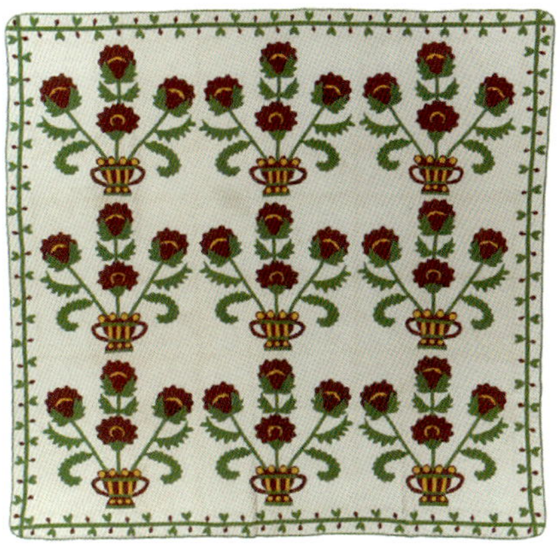

Urns of Flowers

Maker unidentified
Possibly made in Maryland or New York
1870 - 1890
82 x 82 in.

IQM 2006.043.0062

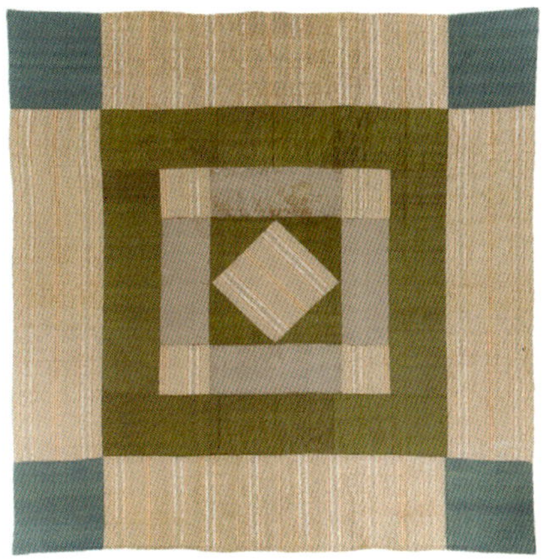

Center Diamond

Maker unidentified
Probably made in Wales, United Kingdom
Dated 1818
90.5 x 89 in.

IQM 2006.043.0063

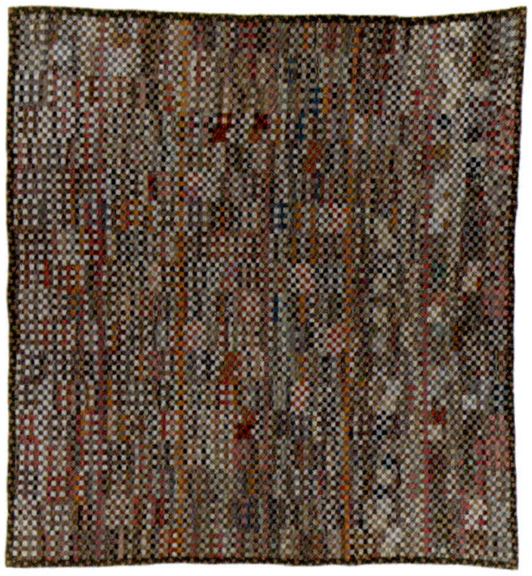

One Patch

Maker unidentified
Possibly made in Pennsylvania
1870 - 1890
86 x 77 in.

IQM 2006.043.0064

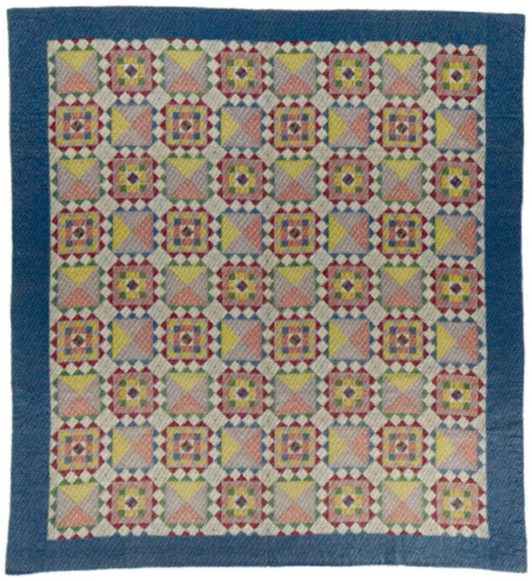

Framed Center

Maker unidentified
Possibly made in Pennsylvania
Circa 1940
81 x 70 in.

IQM 2006.043.0066

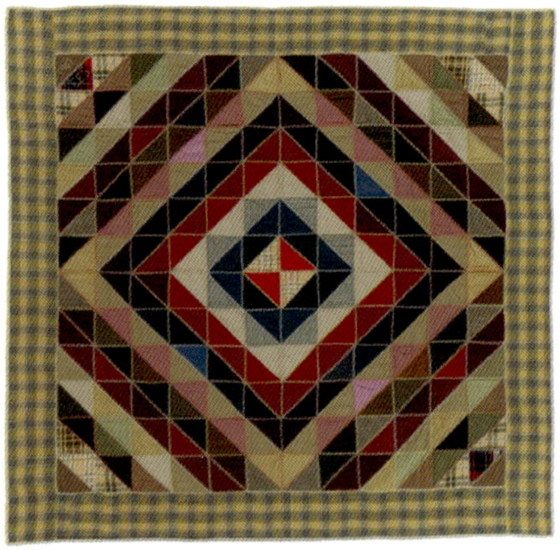

Barn Raising with Triangles

Maker unidentified
Possibly made in Hanover, Pennsylvania
Dated 1907
66 x 66 in.

IQM 2006.043.0070

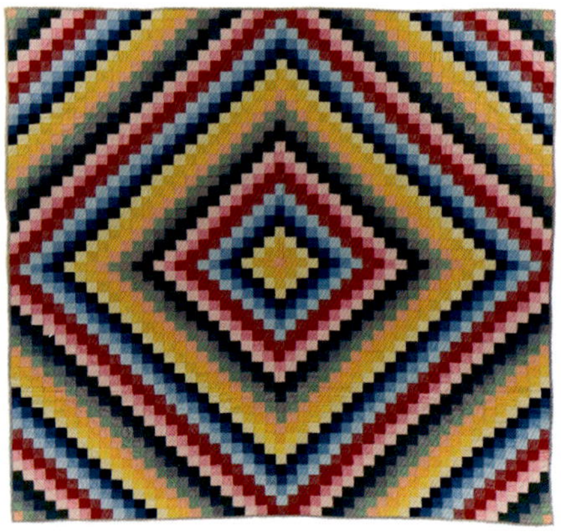

Sunshine and Shadow

Maker unidentified
Probably made in Lancaster County, Pennsylvania
1910 - 1930
77 x 77 in.

IQM 2006.043.0071

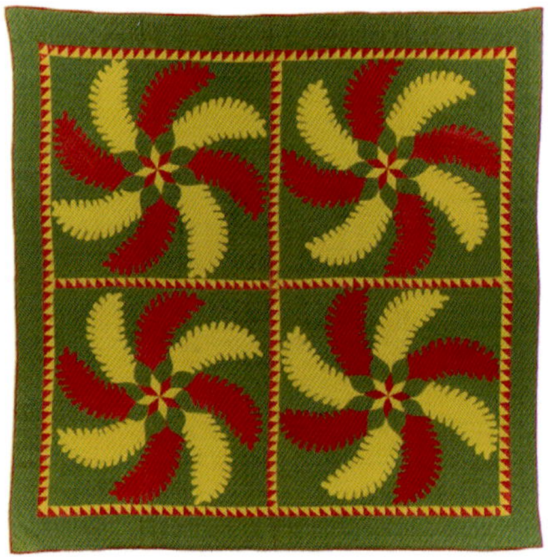

Princess Feather

Possibly made by Gladys Weininger
Probably made in Berks County, Pennsylvania
1860 - 1880
85 x 84 in.

IQM 2006.043.0072

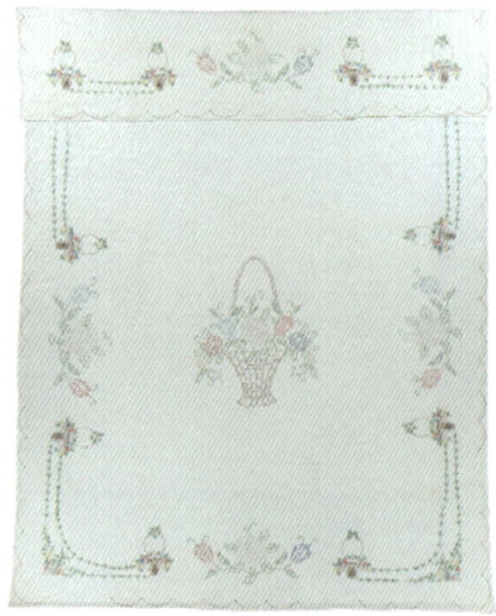

Bride's Quilt

Elsie Kosch Weis
Probably made in Humphrey, Nebraska
Dated 1928 - 1929
82 x 76 in.

IQM 2006.043.0073

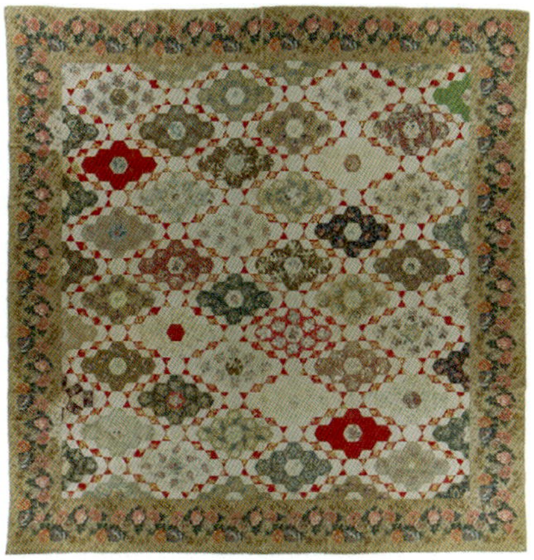

Diamond Field

Maker unidentified
Probably made in New England
1830 - 1850
124 x 106 in.

IQM 2006.043.0074

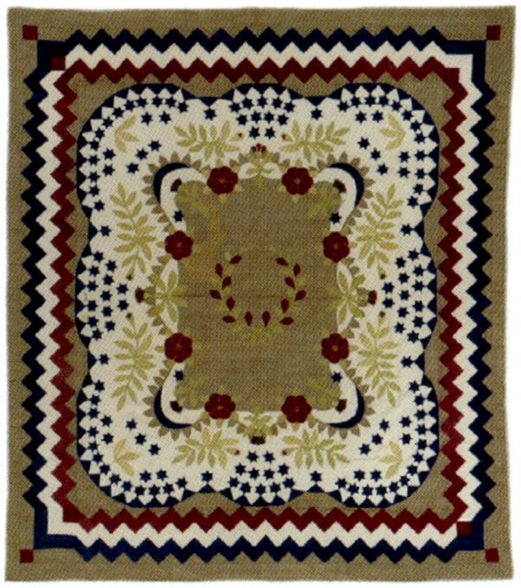

Floral and Swag

Maker unidentified
Made in United States
Dated 1896
78 x 70 in.

IQM 2006.043.0075

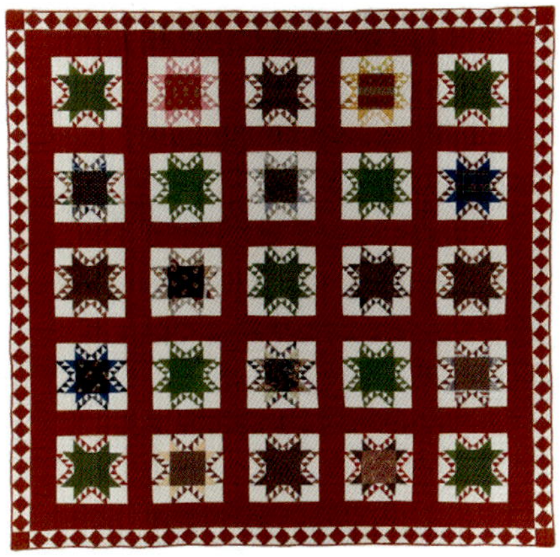

Feathered Star

Maker unidentified
Probably made in Lancaster County, Pennsylvania
1880 - 1900
80 x 80 in.

IQM 2006.043.0077

Pinwheel

J.O. Siddons
Made in Marion, Indiana
Dated 1862 - 1904
90.75 x 79.75 in.

IQM 2006.043.0078

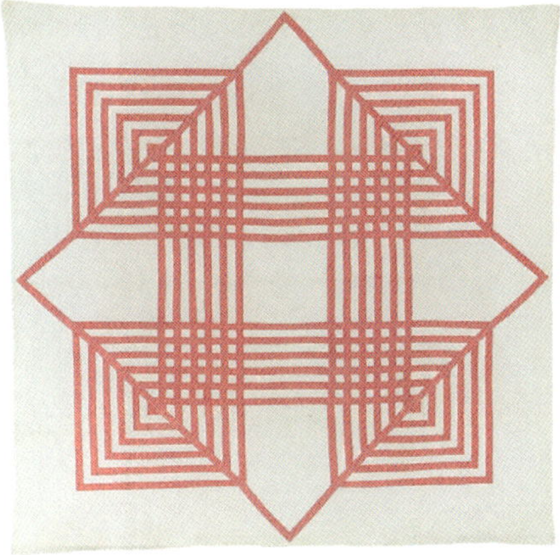

Carpenter's Square

Maker unidentified
Made in United States
Circa 1950
75 x 77 in.

IQM 2006.043.0080

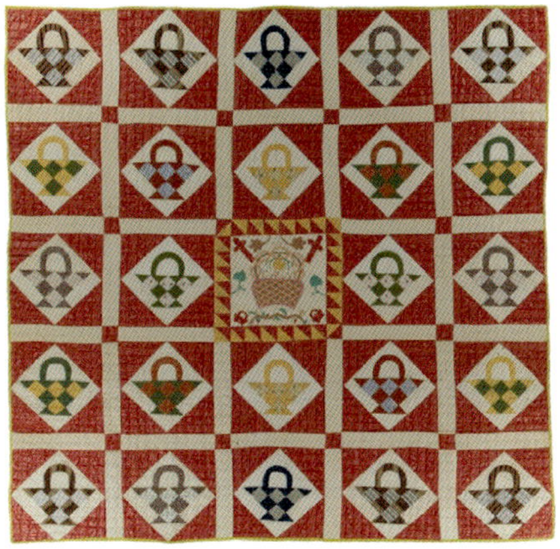

Basket

Maker unidentified
Possibly made in Toronto, Canada
Dated 1877
83 x 83 in.

IQM 2006.043.0082

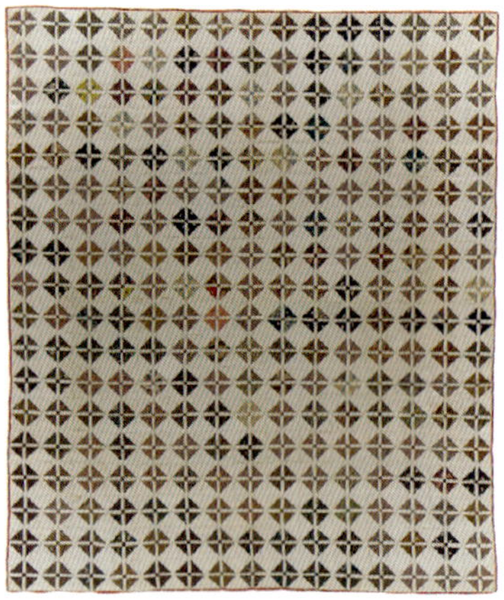

Devil's Puzzle variation

Maker unidentified
Made in United States
1840 - 1860
90 x 77 in.

IQM 2006.043.0083

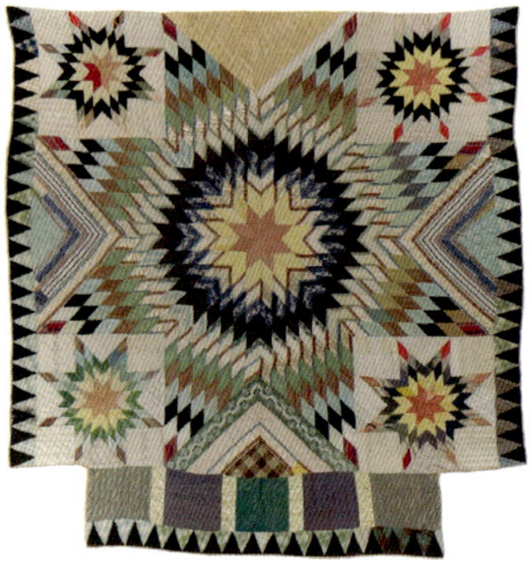

Star of Bethlehem

Probably made by Hannah Larrabee
Probably made in Phippsburg, Maine
Dated 1859
78 x 72.25 in.

IQM 2006.043.0084

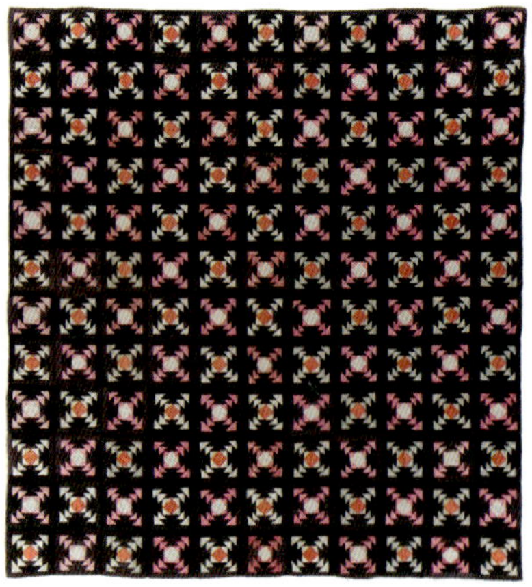

Log Cabin

Maker unidentified
Possibly made in western Ontario, Canada
Circa 1920
76 x 68 in.

IQM 2006.043.0085

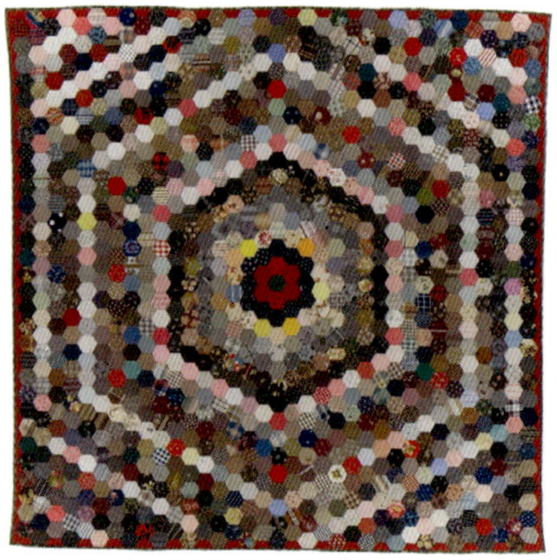

Hexagon

Maker unidentified
Made in United States
1890 - 1910
86 x 86 in.

IQM 2006.043.0086

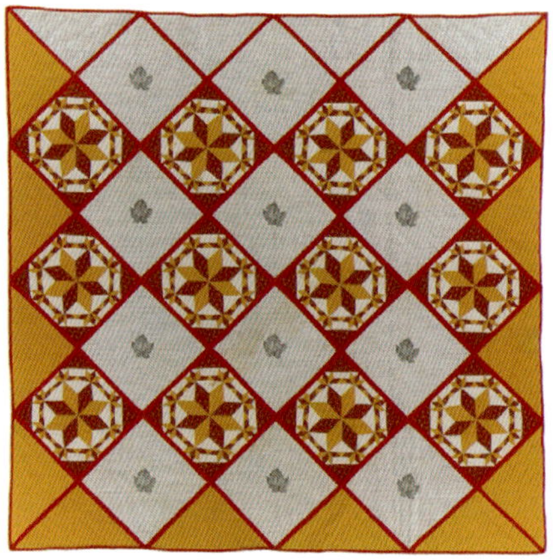

LeMoyne Star

Maker unidentified
Probably made in Lancaster County, Pennsylvania
1870 - 1890
66 x 66 in.

IQM 2006.043.0087

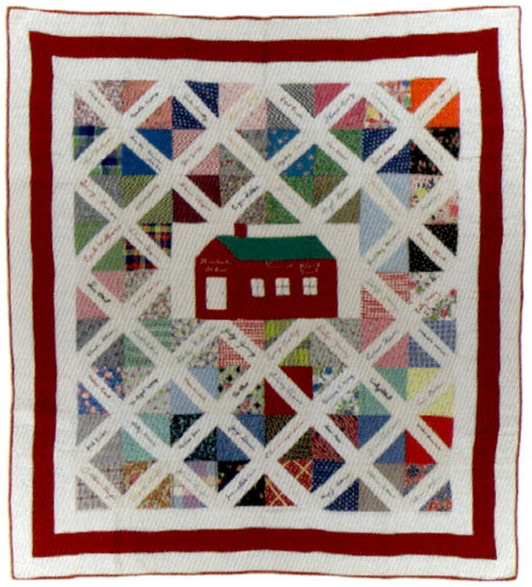

Schoolhouse

Probably made by Verna L. Black
Probably made in Pana, Illinois
Dated 1948 - 1955
86 x 80 in.

IQM 2006.043.0088

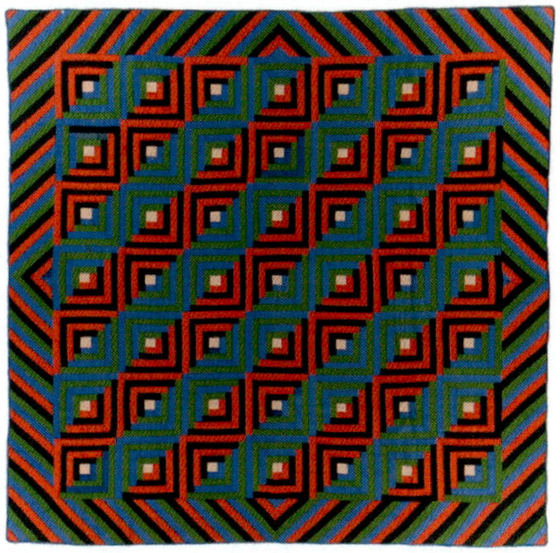

Log Cabin

Maker unidentified
Probably made in Lancaster or York County, Pennsylvania
1880 - 1900
85 x 85 in.

IQM 2006.043.0089

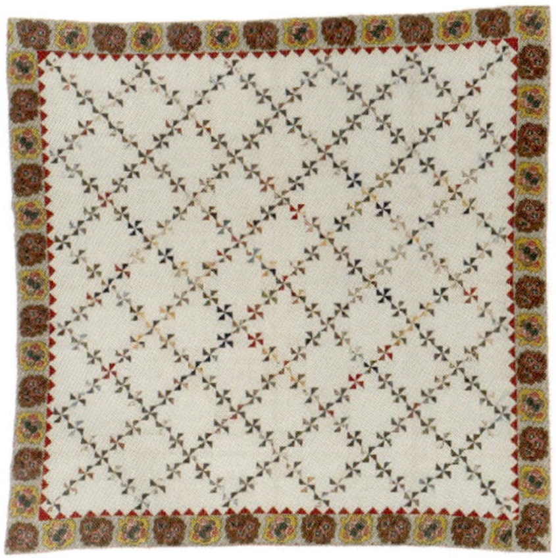

Double Nine Patch, Pinwheel

Maker unidentified
Probably made in Frederick County, Maryland
1840 - 1860
99.75 x 98 in.

IQM 2006.043.0090

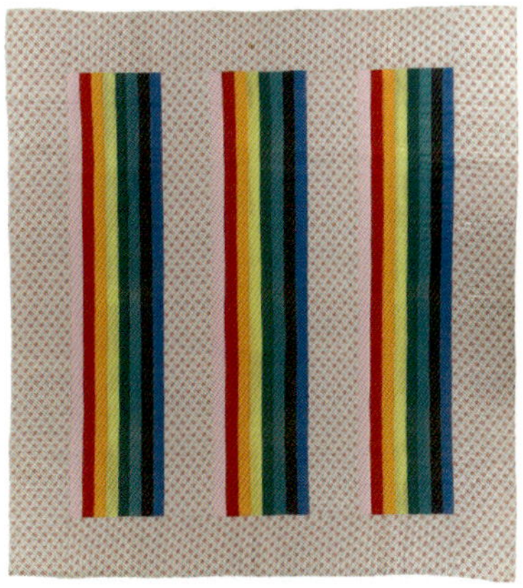

Roman Stripe

Maker unidentified
Made in United States
1890 - 1910
85 x 77 in.

IQM 2006.043.0091

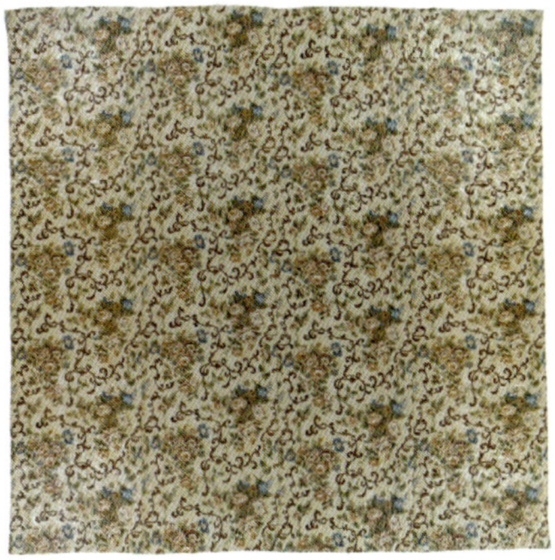

Whole Cloth

Maker unidentified
Made in United States
1830 - 1850
119 x 119 in.

IQM 2006.043.0092

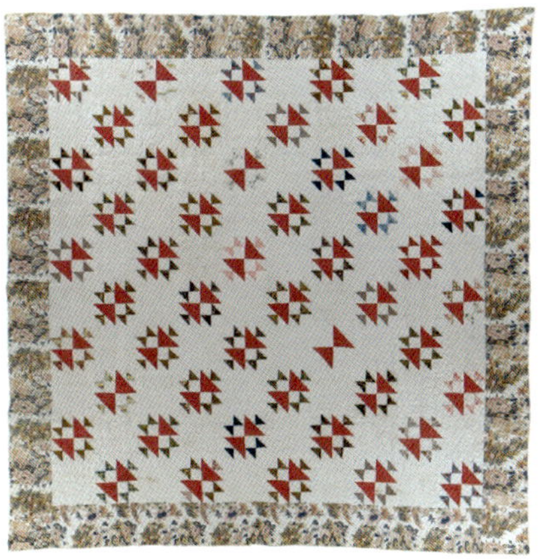

Double X

Maker unidentified
Probably made in Carroll County, Maryland
1830 - 1850
92 x 88 in.

IQM 2006.043.0094

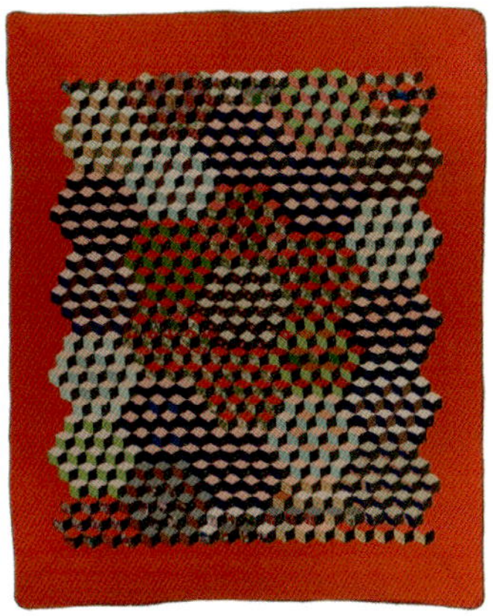

Diamond, Hexagon setting

Maker unidentified
Probably made in Kentucky
Circa 1855
84 x 66 in.

IQM 2006.043.0095

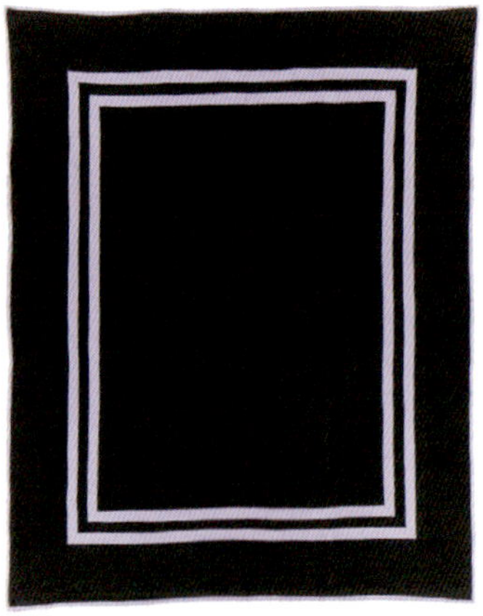

Plain Quilt

Maker unidentified
Probably made in Holmes County, Ohio
Circa 1930
83 x 65 in.

IQM 2006.043.0096

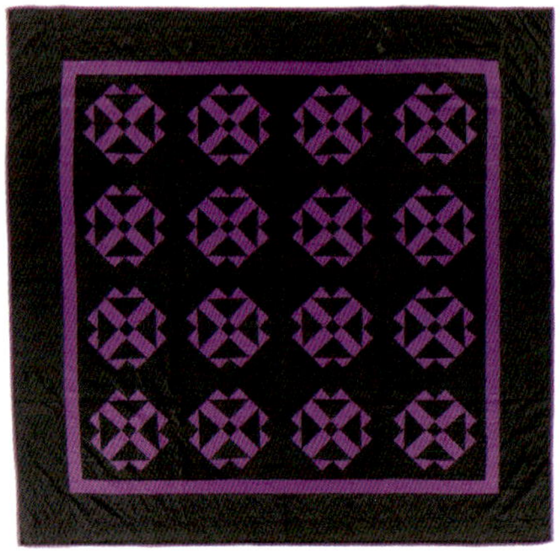

Crossed Ts

Maker unidentified
Probably made in Holmes County, Ohio
Dated 1928
80 x 80 in.

IQM 2006.043.0097

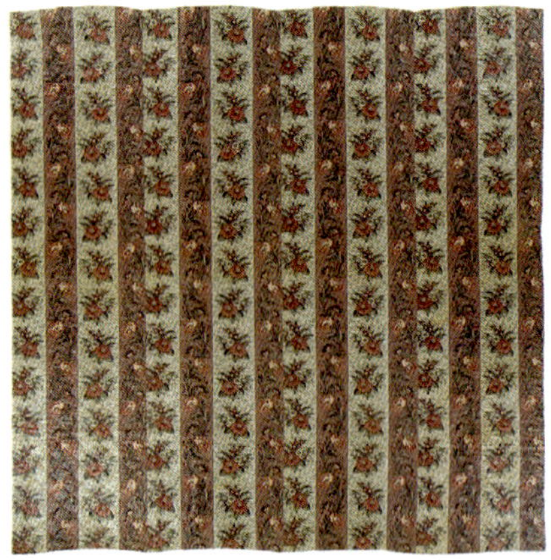

Whole Cloth

Maker unidentified
Made in United States
1830 - 1850
94 x 93 in.

IQM 2006.043.0098

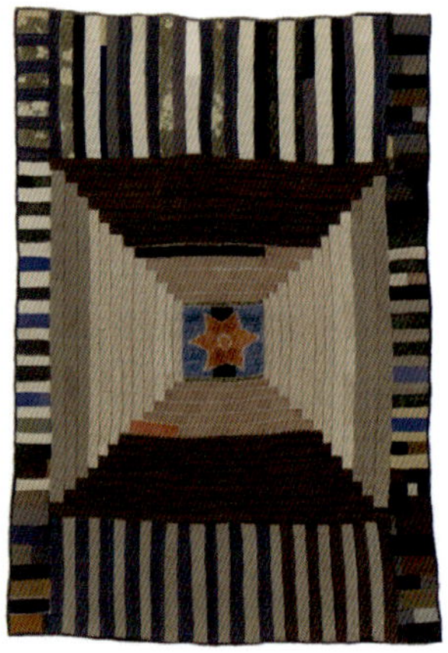

Log Cabin

Maker unidentified
Probably made in Knoxville, Tennessee
Circa 1900
80 x 52 in.

IQM 2006.043.0100

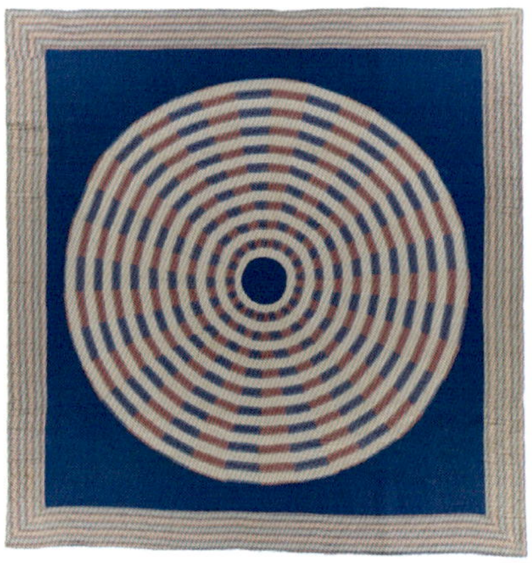

Rising Sun variation

Maker unidentified
Probably made in Gettysburg, Pennsylvania
Circa 1915
77 x 73 in.

IQM 2006.043.0101

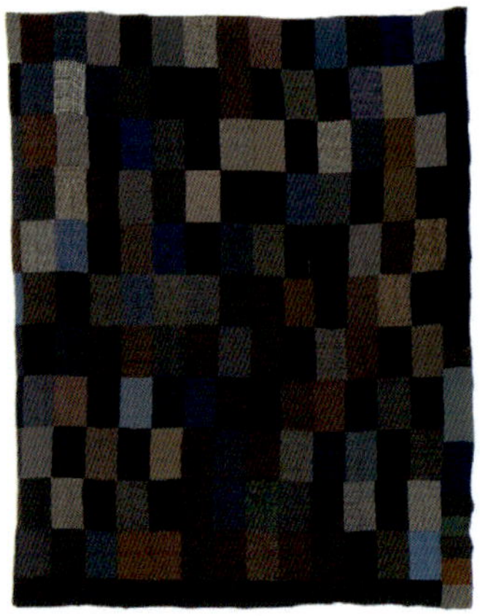

Rectangles - Kitchen Quilt

Probably made by Cora Gregory James
Probably made in Nebraska
Circa 1920
76 x 57.5 in.

IQM 2006.043.0102

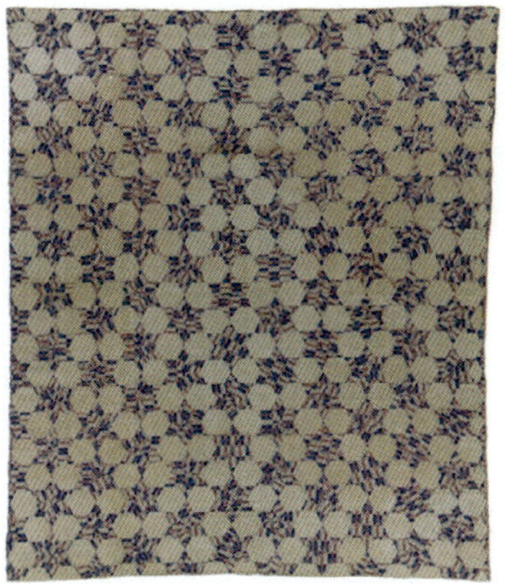

Six Pointed Star

Maker unidentified
Possibly made in Michigan
1830 - 1850
96.5 x 80.5 in.

IQM 2006.043.0103

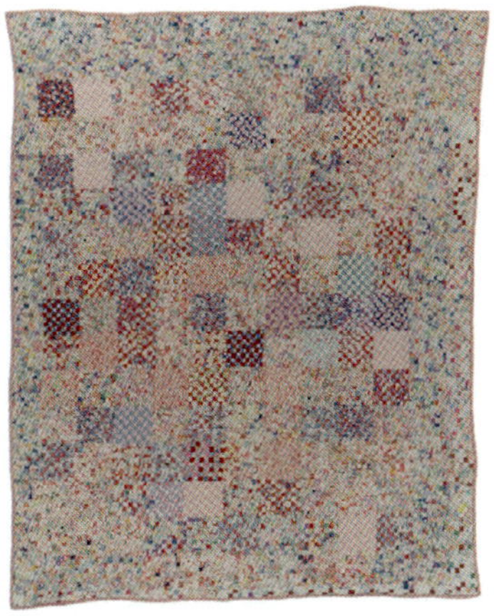

Sixty-four Patch

Maker unidentified
Probably made in Dallas, Texas
1920 - 1940
80 x 65 in.

IQM 2006.043.0104

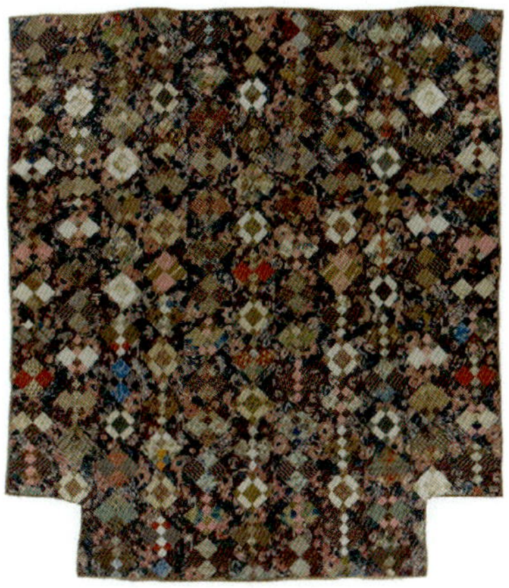

Nine Patch

Maker unidentified
Probably made in Lancaster County, Pennsylvania
1840 - 1850
88 x 75 in.

IQM 2006.043.0105

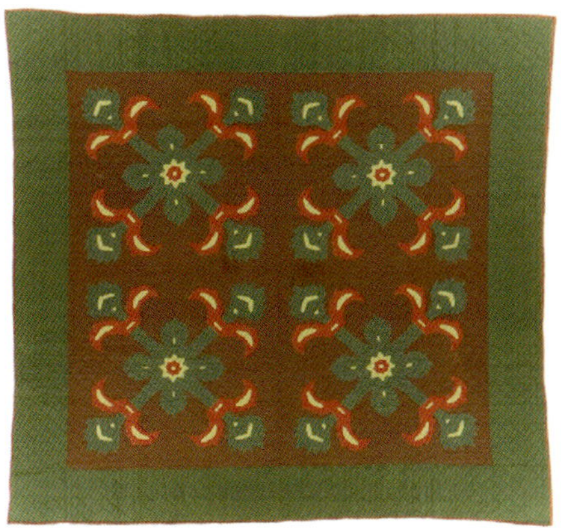

Appliqué

Maker unidentified
Probably made in Lancaster County, Pennsylvania
Circa 1880
91 x 88 in.

IQM 2006.043.0106

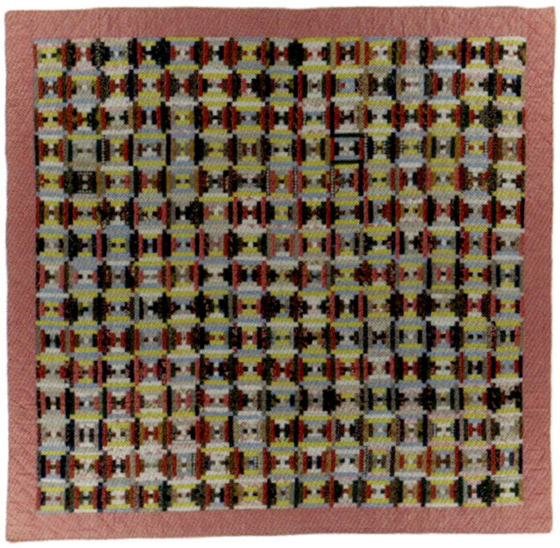

Log Cabin

Maker unidentified
Probably made in Pennsylvania
Circa 1880
82 x 80 in.

IQM 2006.043.0107

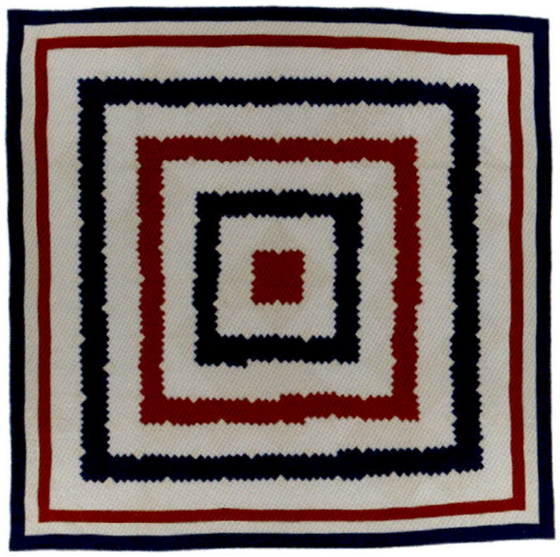

Log Cabin

Maker unidentified
Probably made in Lehigh Valley, Pennsylvania
Circa 1920
71 x 71 in.

IQM 2006.043.01083

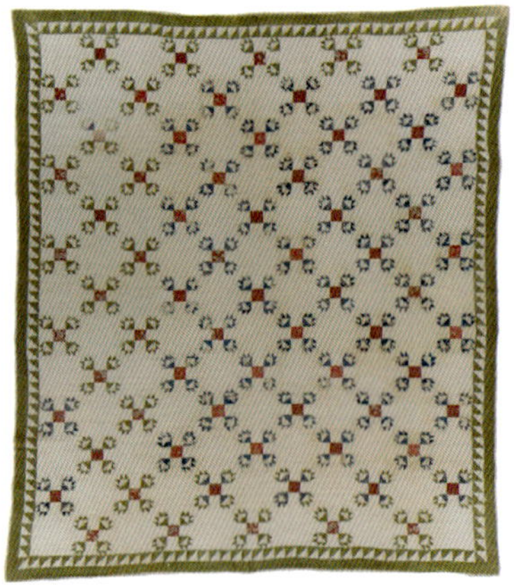

Bear's Paw

Maker unidentified
Probably made in New England
1830 - 1850
79 x 70 in.

IQM 2006.043.0109

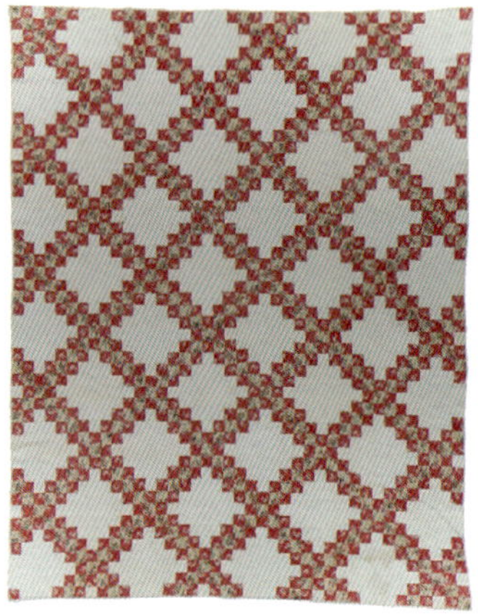

Double Irish Chain

Maker unidentified
Possibly made in Maryland
1840 - 1860
100 x 75 in.

IQM 2006.043.0110

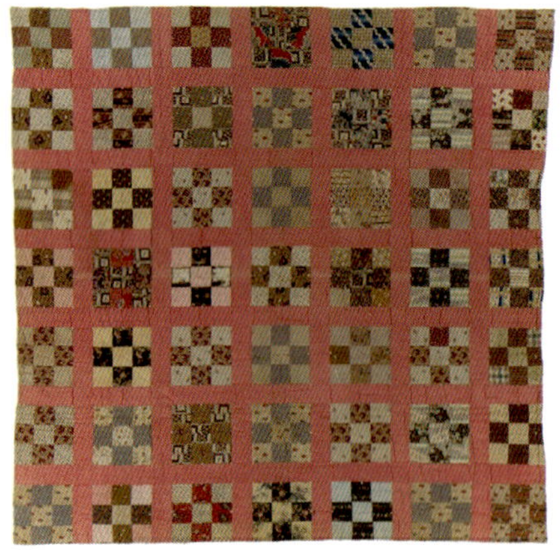

Nine Patch

Maker unidentified
Possibly made in Maryland
1860 - 1880
71 x 72 in.

IQM 2006.043.0111

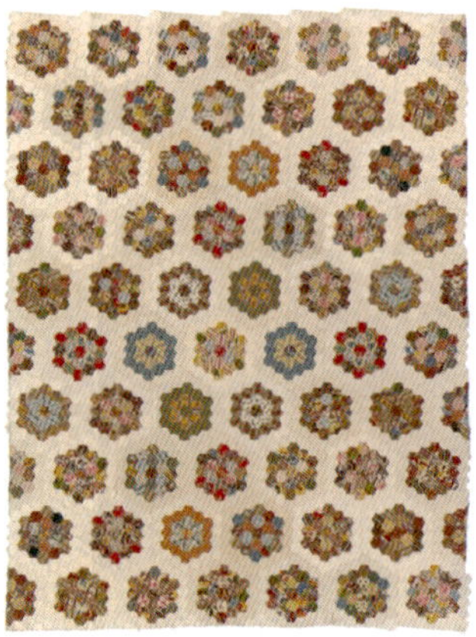

Hexagon

Maker unidentified
Made in England, United Kingdom
1820 - 1840
69 x 51 in.

IQM 2006.043.0112

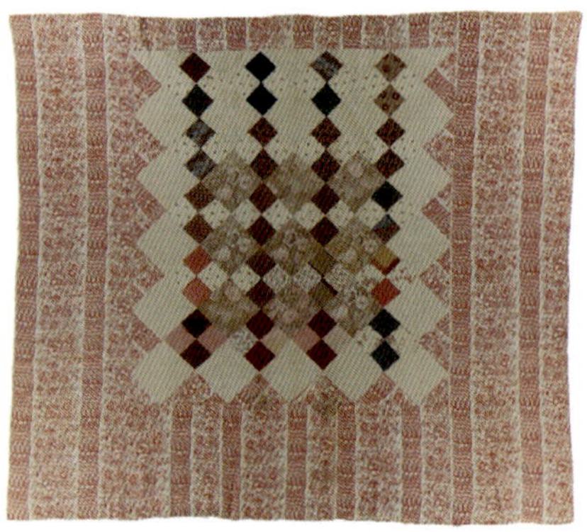

Four Patch

Maker unidentified
Possibly made in England, United Kingdom
1830 - 1850
102 x 88 in.

IQM 2006.043.0113

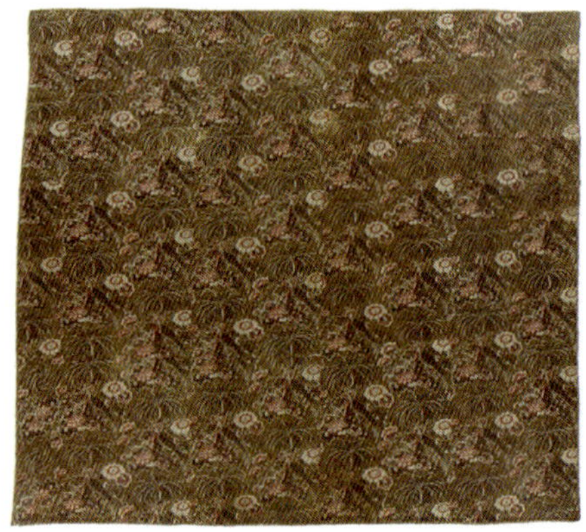

Whole Cloth

Maker unidentified
Probably made in New York
1820 - 1840
102 x 95 in.

IQM 2006.043.0114

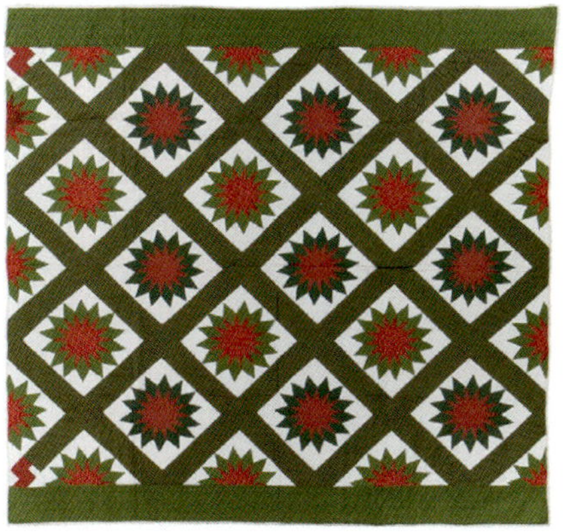

Sunburst

Maker unidentified
Possibly made in New York
Circa 1880
84 x 79 in.

IQM 2006.043.0115

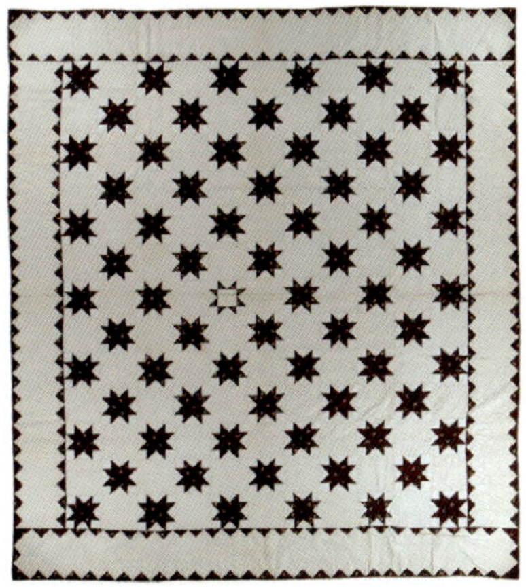

Sawtooth Star

Elisabeth C. Jones
Probably made in Allentown, Pennsylvania
1820 - 1840
113 x 101 in.

IQM 2006.043.0116

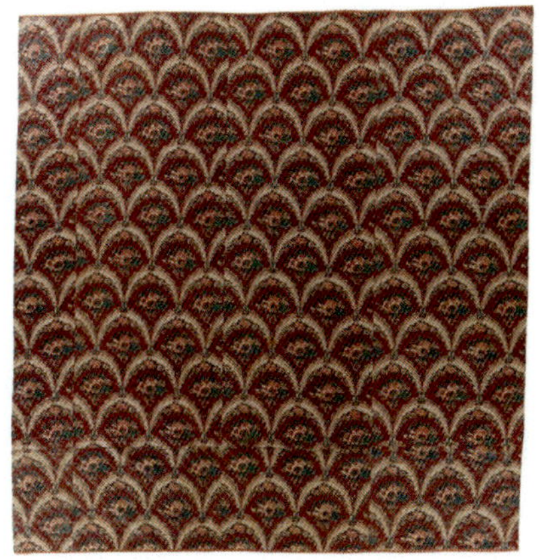

Whole Cloth

Maker unidentified
Probably made in Pennsylvania
1850 - 1870
88 x 82 in.

IQM 2006.043.0117

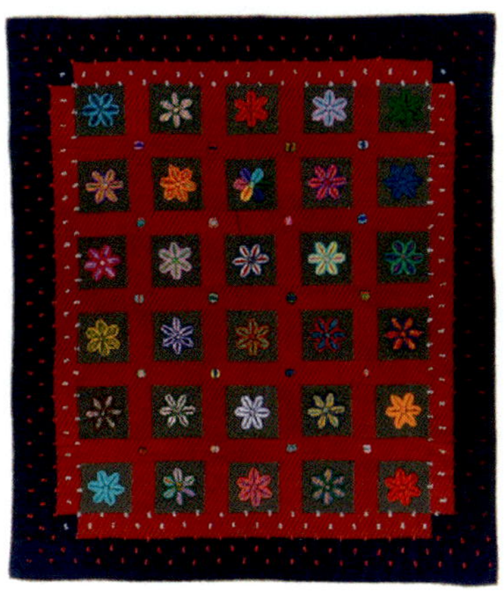

Original - Embroidered Flowers

Maker unidentified
Probably made in Lancaster County, Pennsylvania
1910 - 1930
83 x 68 in.

IQM 2006.043.0118

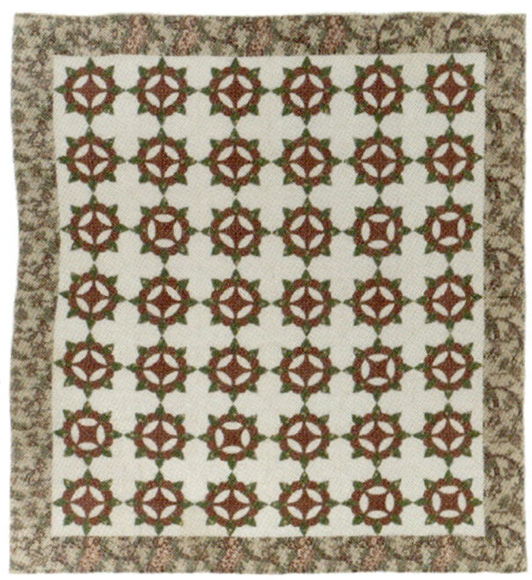

Crown of Thorns

Probably made by May E. Eckman
Probably made in Lancaster County, Pennsylvania
1830 - 1850
102 x 98 in.

IQM 2006.043.0120

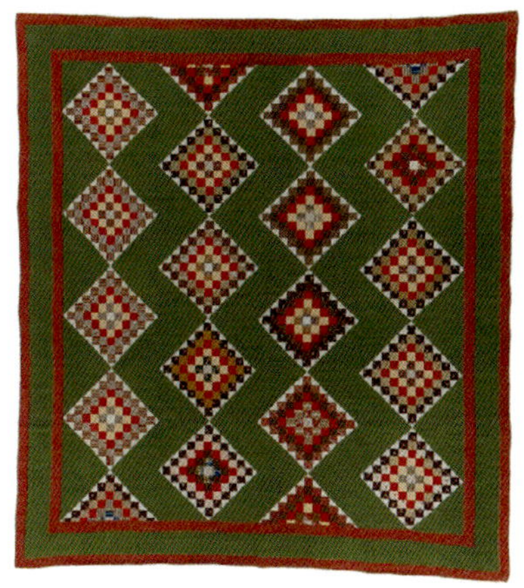

Six-patch

Maker unidentified
Probably made in Frederick, Virginia
1870 - 1890
86 x 78 in.

IQM 2006.043.0121

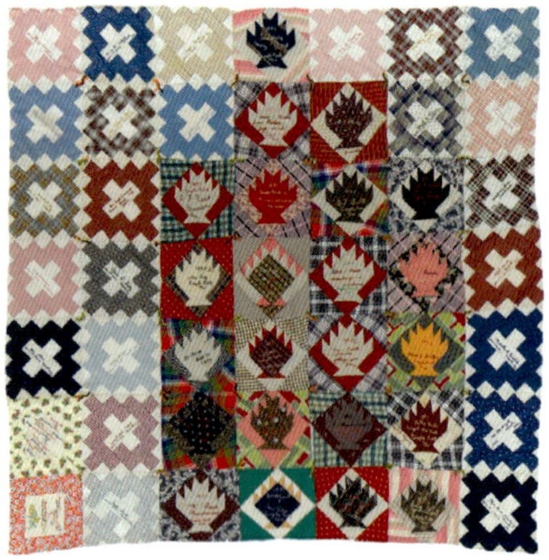

Basket

Sarah Russell, Opal Jewel Bower, and Mrs. Virgil Wood
Probably made in Meade, Kansas
Dated 1897 - 1976
80 x 76 in.
IQM 2006.043.0122

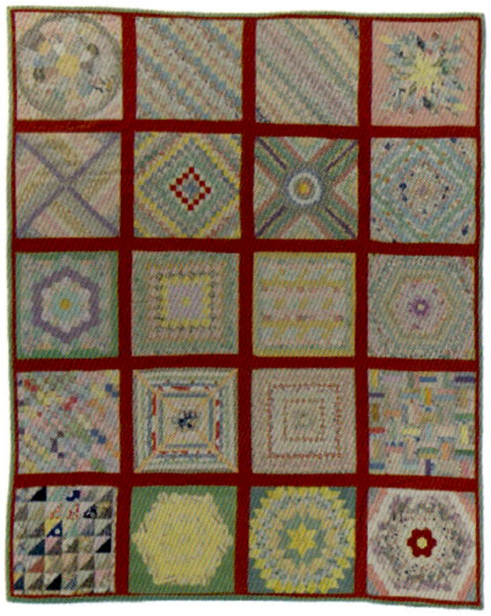

Sampler

Maker unidentified
Probably made in Indiana
1920 - 1940
94 x 74 in.
IQM 2006.043.0123

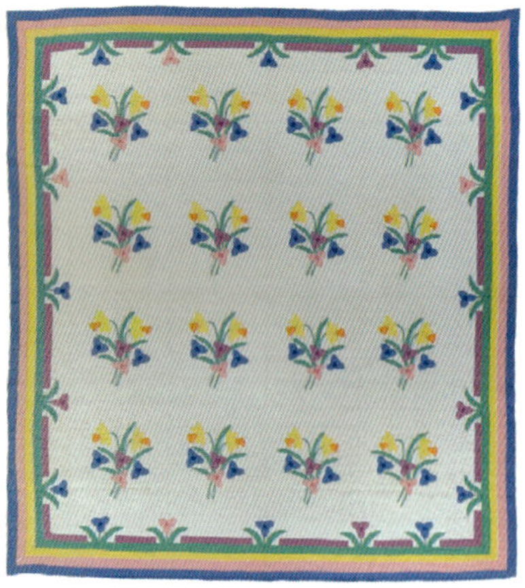

Rainbow

Maker unidentified
Probably made in Indiana
Circa 1920
90 x 82 in.
IQM 2006.043.0124

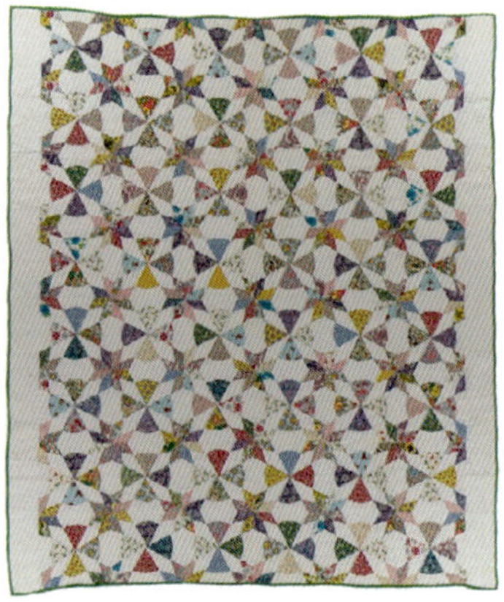

Original

Plotner, Gladys Overman
Made in Cass, Indiana
1950 - 1970
92 x 78 in.
IQM 2006.043.0125

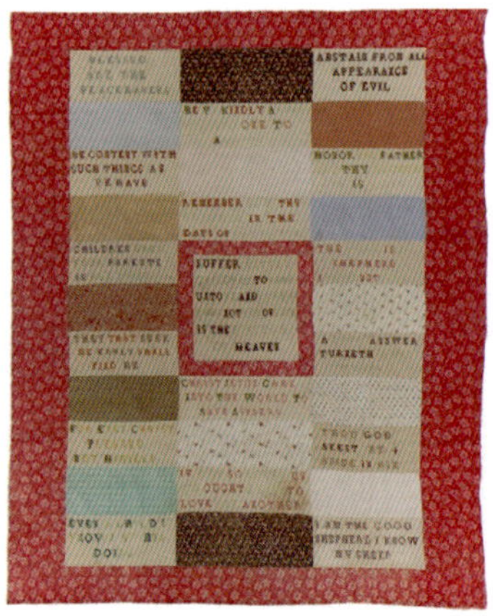

Bricks - Bible Quotations

Maker unidentified
Made in England, United Kingdom
Circa 1880
75 x 60 in.
IQM 2006.043.0126

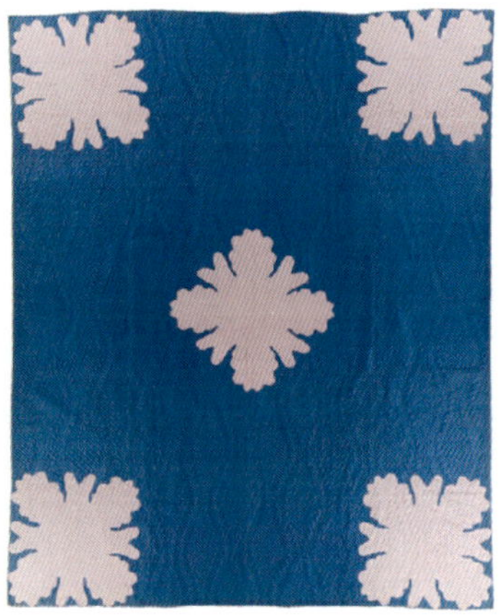

Appliqué

Maker unidentified
Made in Northumberland, England, United Kingdom
1920 - 1940
104 x 84 in.
IQM 2006.043.0127

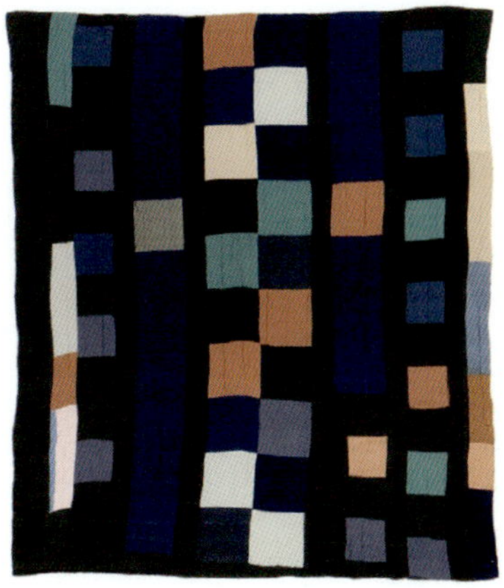

One Patch

Cora Gregory James
Made in Nebraska
Circa 1935
83 x 70 in.

IQM 2006.043.0128

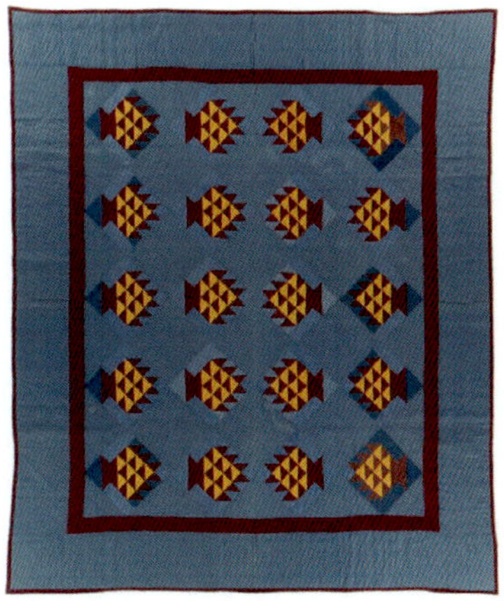

Basket

Probably made by Elizabeth J. Miller
Probably made in Elkhart County, Indiana
Dated 1922
88 x 74 in.

IQM 2006.043.0129

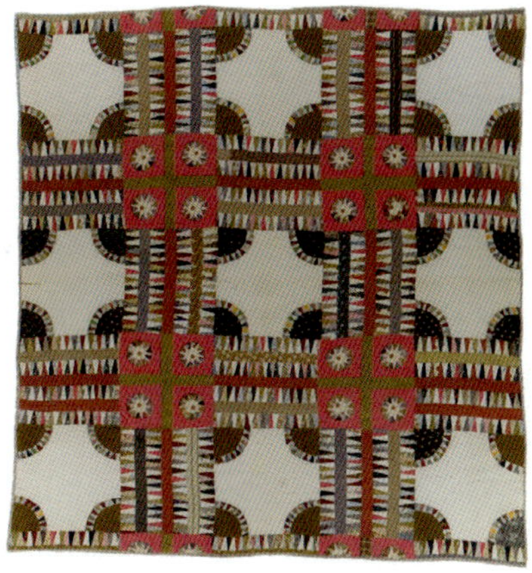

New York Beauty

Maker unidentified
Made in United States
1870 - 1890
85 x 80 in.

IQM 2006.043.0130

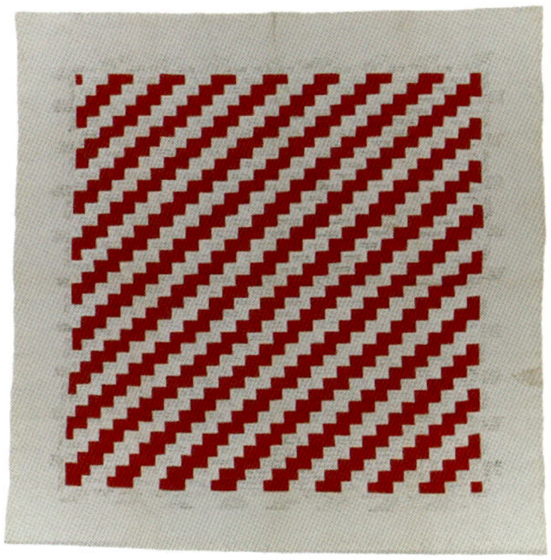

Bricks

Maker unidentified
Probably made in Pennsylvania
1870 - 1890
77 x 73.75 in.

IQM 2006.043.0132

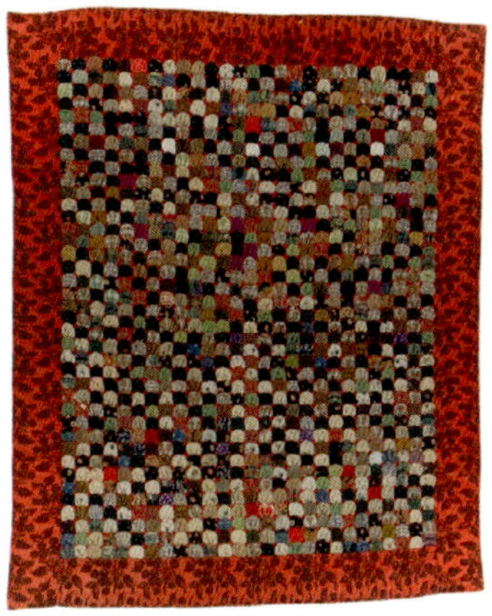

Puffed Squares

Maker unidentified
Probably made in Talbot County, Maryland
1880 - 1900
86 x 70 in.

IQM 2006.043.0133

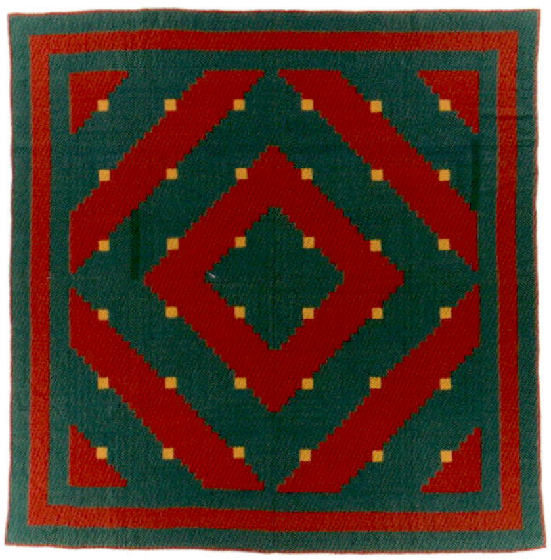

Log Cabin

Maker unidentified
Probably made in Pennsylvania
1890 - 1910
84 x 84 in.

IQM 2006.043.0134

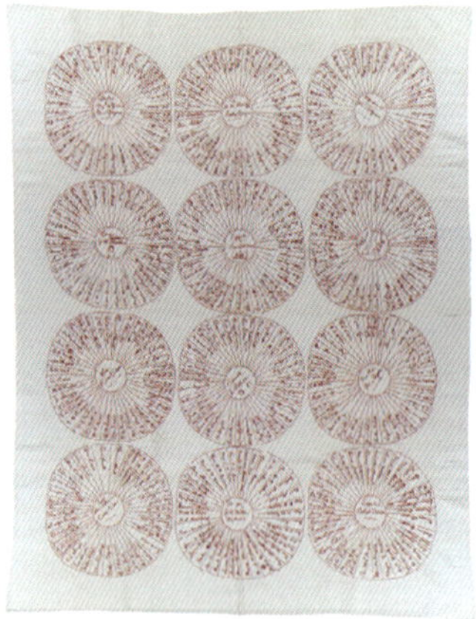

Original

Maker unidentified
Made in Henton, Shelby Cnty., Illinois
Dated 1924
83 x 63 in.

IQM 2006.043.0135

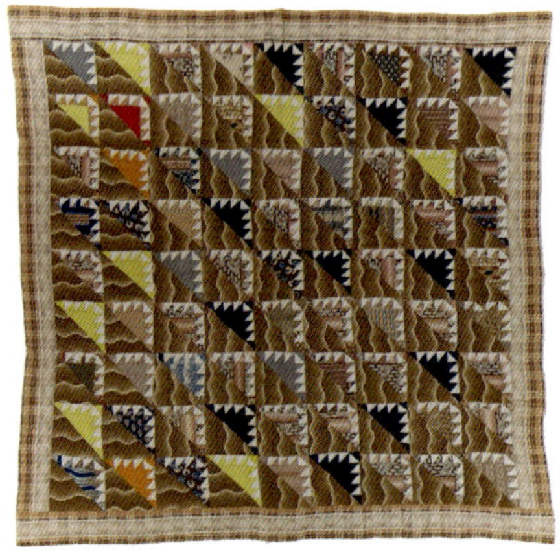

Delectable Mountains

Maker unidentified
Probably made in Pennsylvania
1840 - 1860
85 x 85 in.

IQM 2006.043.0136

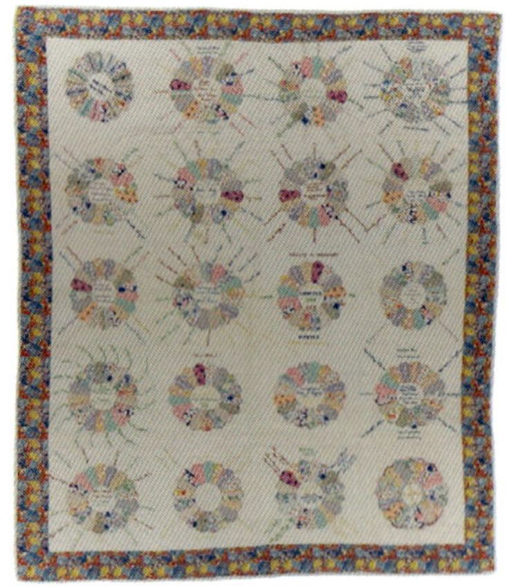

Dresden Plate

Maker unidentified
Made in United States
Dated 1933 - 1934
88 x 72 in.

IQM 2006.043.0138

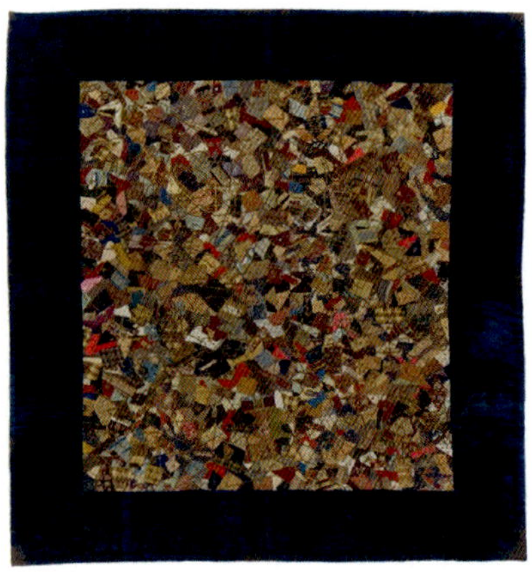

Crazy
Maker unidentified
Made in United States
1880 - 1900
65 x 60 in.

IQM 2006.043.0139

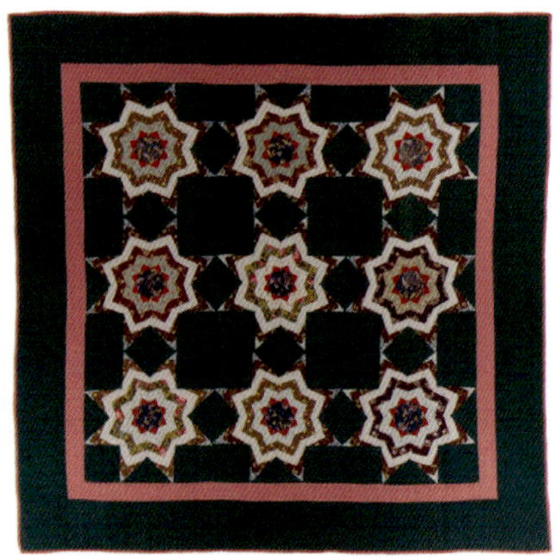

String Star
Maker unidentified
Possibly made in Pennsylvania
Circa 1885
88 x 83 in.

IQM 2006.043.0141

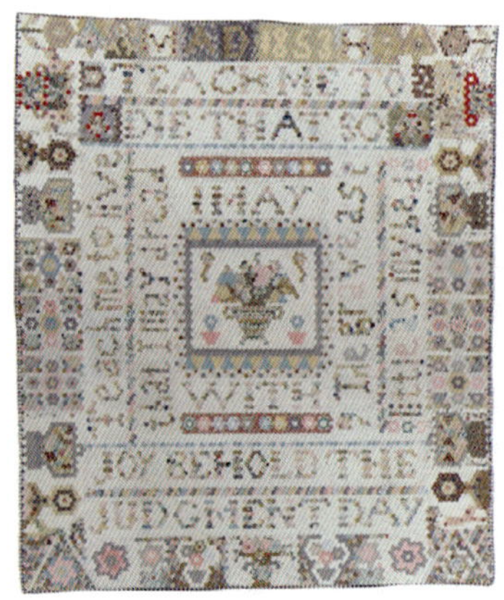

Hexagon
Maker unidentified
Possibly made in England, United Kingdom
Dated 1853
97 x 81 in.

IQM 2006.043.0143

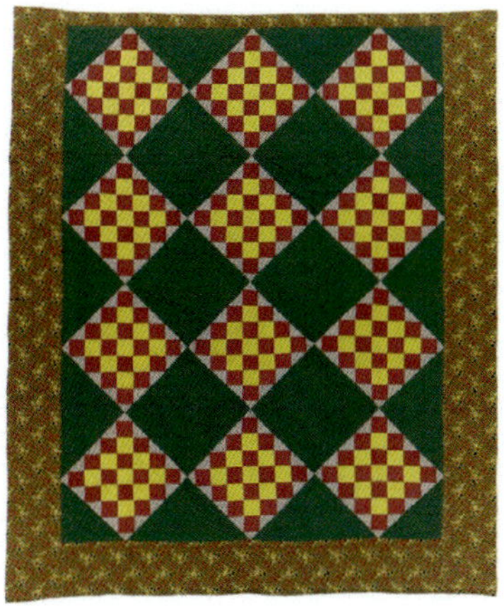

Checkerboard

Maker unidentified
Possibly made in Pennsylvania
1840 - 1860
88 x 74 in.

IQM 2006.043.0144

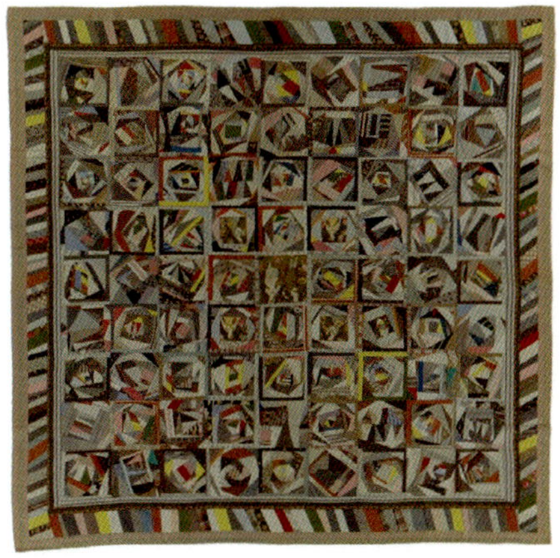

Crazy

Maker unidentified
Possibly made in New York
Circa 1875
83 x 81 in.

IQM 2006.043.0145

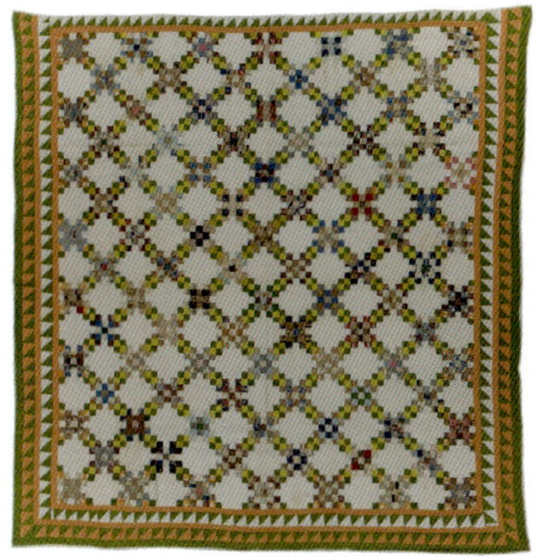

Double Irish Chain

Maker unidentified
Possibly made in Pennsylvania
1850 - 1870
74 x 71 in.

IQM 2006.043.0146

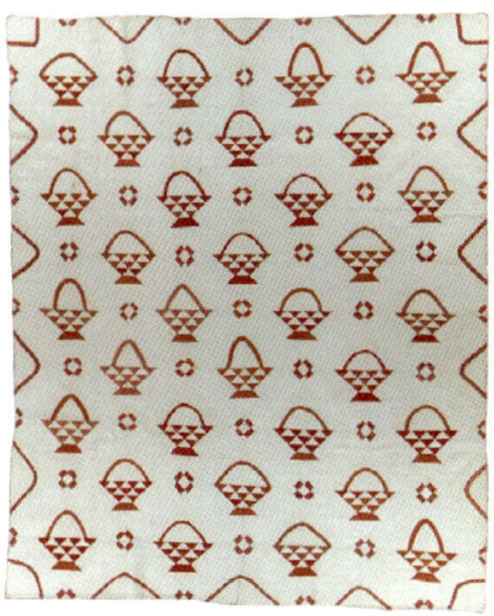

Basket
Maker unidentified
Possibly made in New York
1840 - 1860
100 x 80 in.

IQM 2006.043.0148

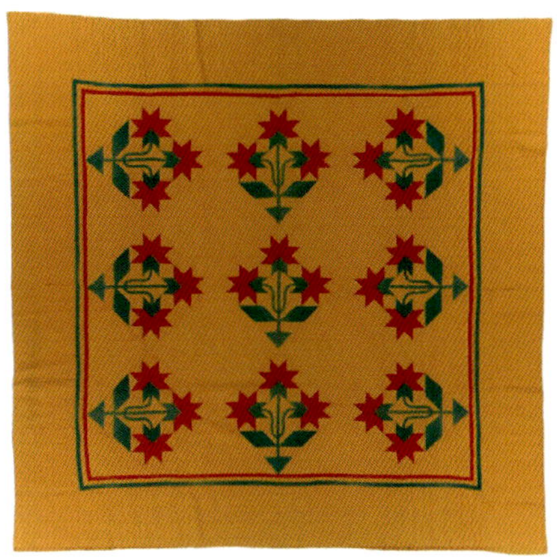

Lily
Maker unidentified
Possibly made in Pennsylvania
Circa 1890
88 x 88 in.

IQM 2006.043.0149

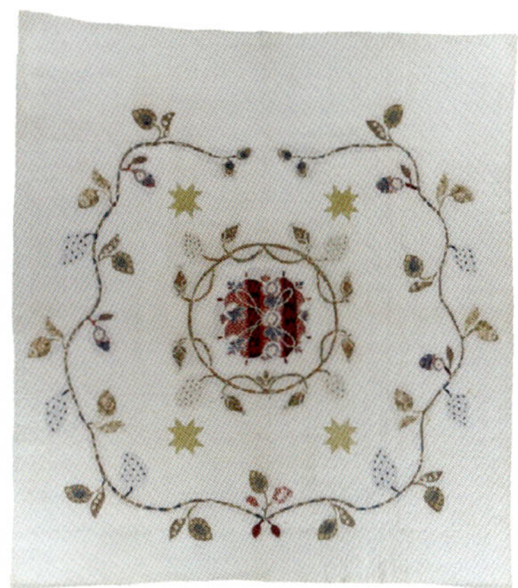

Medallion
Maker unidentified
Possibly made in Pennsylvania
1830 - 1850
94 x 84 in.

IQM 2006.043.0150

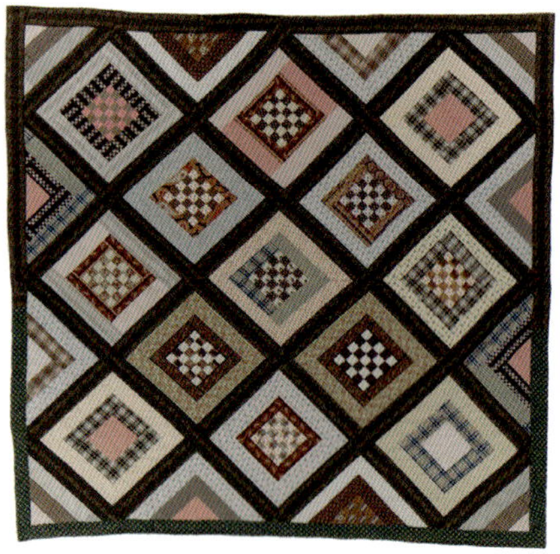

Twenty-five Patch

Maker unidentified
Made in United States
1870 - 1880
80 x 78 in.

IQM 2006.043.0153

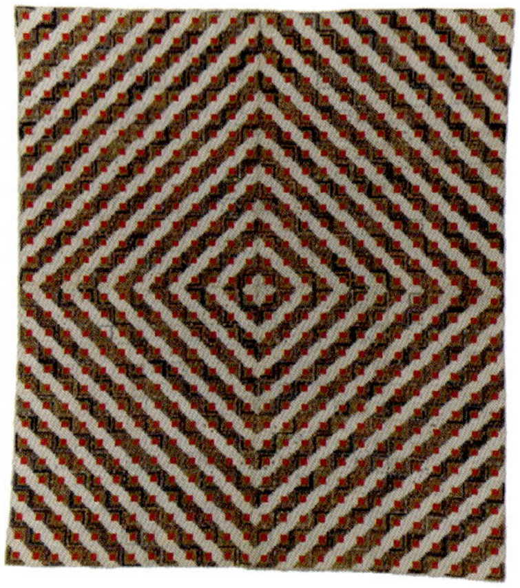

Log Cabin

Maker unidentified
Made in United States
1870 - 1890
80 x 70.5 in.

IQM 2006.043.0154

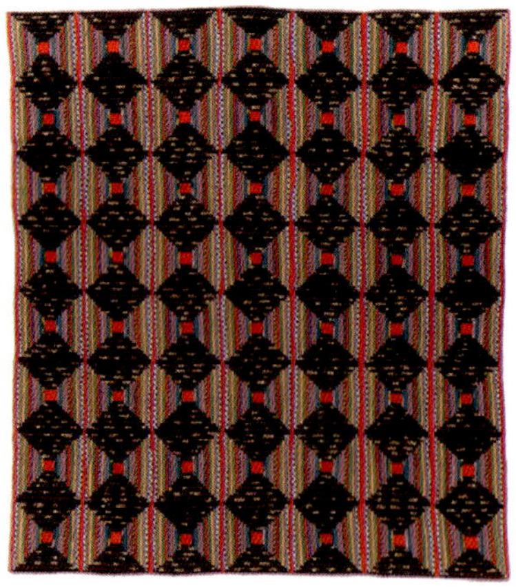

Log Cabin

Maker unidentified
Made in United States
1870 - 1890
84 x 72 in.

IQM 2006.043.01553

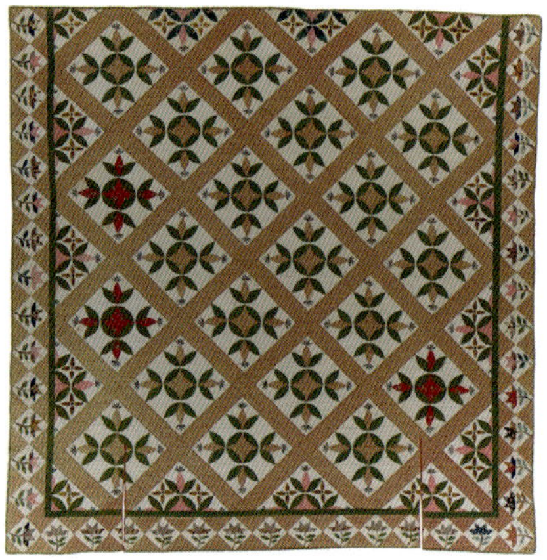

Turkey Tracks variation

Maker unidentified
Possibly made in New York
1840 - 1860
90 x 85 in.

IQM 2006.043.0156

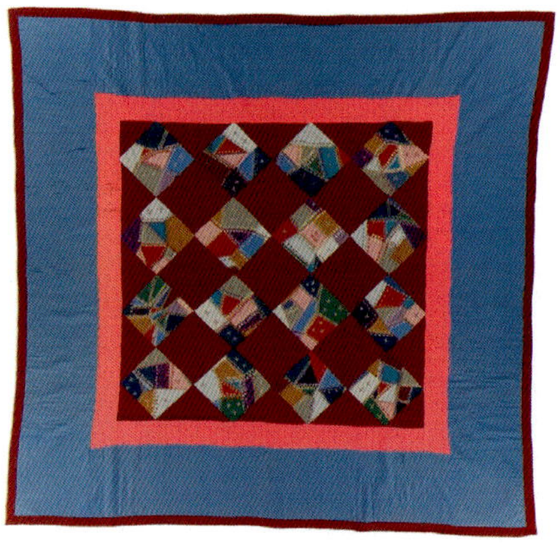

Crazy

Maker unidentified
Possibly made in Pennsylvania
Dated 1928
90 x 88 in.

IQM 2006.043.0158

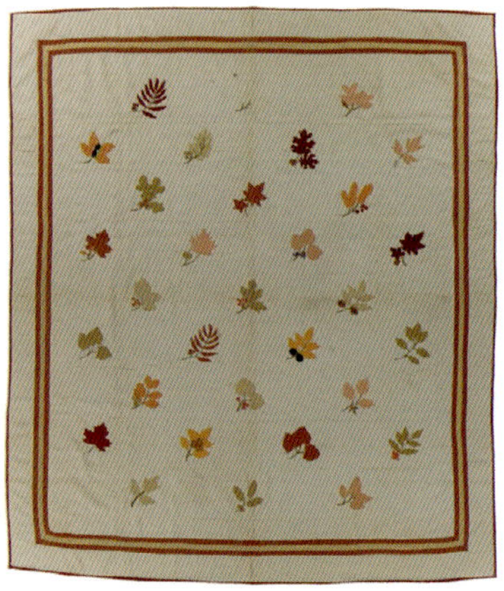

Autumn Leaves

Maker unidentified
Possibly made in Michigan
1910 - 1930
82 x 73 in.

IQM 2006.043.0159

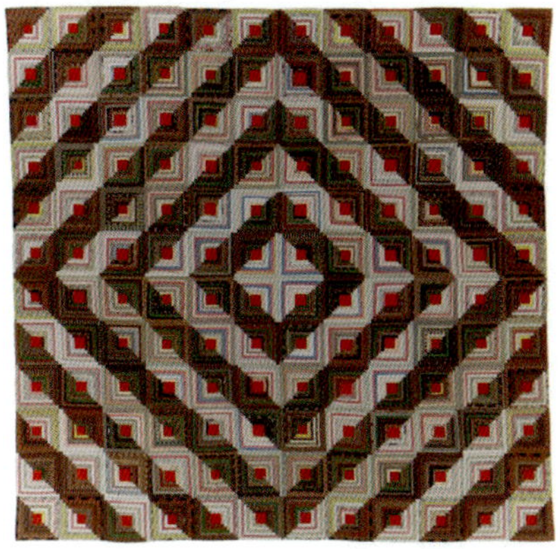

Log Cabin

Maker unidentified
Possibly made in Pennsylvania
1860 - 1880
92 x 86 in.

IQM 2006.043.0160

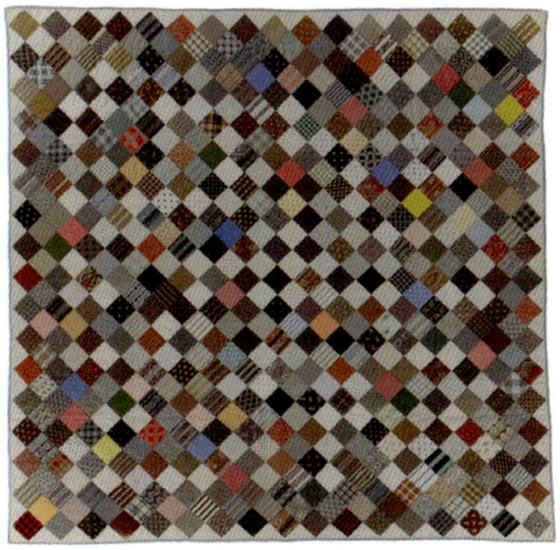

One Patch

Maker unidentified
Possibly made in Pennsylvania
Circa 1890
79 x 78 in.

IQM 2006.043.0161

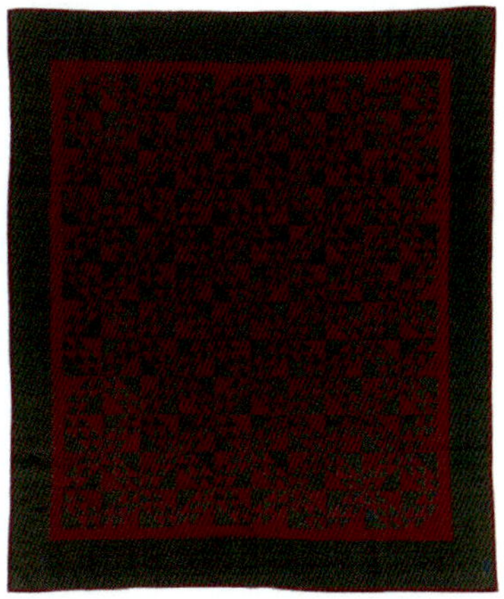

Ocean Waves variation

Kattren Yoder
Made in Sugarcreek, Ohio
1900 - 1920
82 x 73 in.

IQM 2006.043.0162

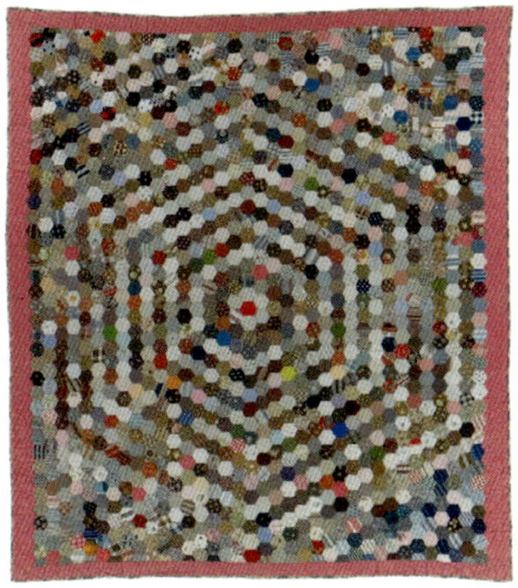

Hexagon

Maker unidentified
Made in United States
Circa 1880
85 x 73 in.

IQM 2006.043.0163

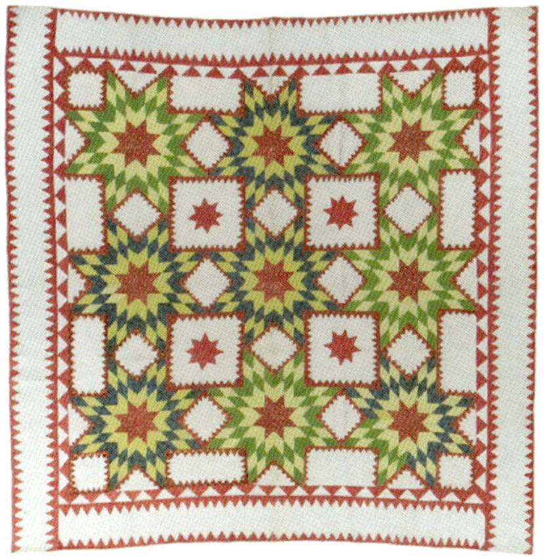

Touching Stars

Maker unidentified
Possibly made in New Jersey
1840 - 1860
108 x 102 in.

IQM 2006.043.01653

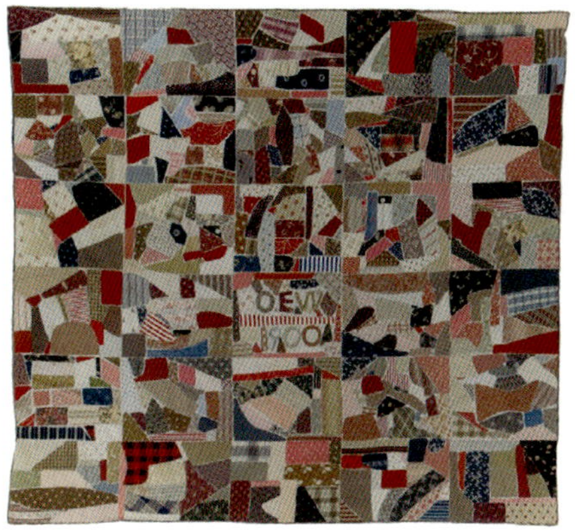

Tile Quilt

Maker unidentified
Probably made in Connecticut
Dated 1900
83 x 78 in.

IQM 2006.043.0167

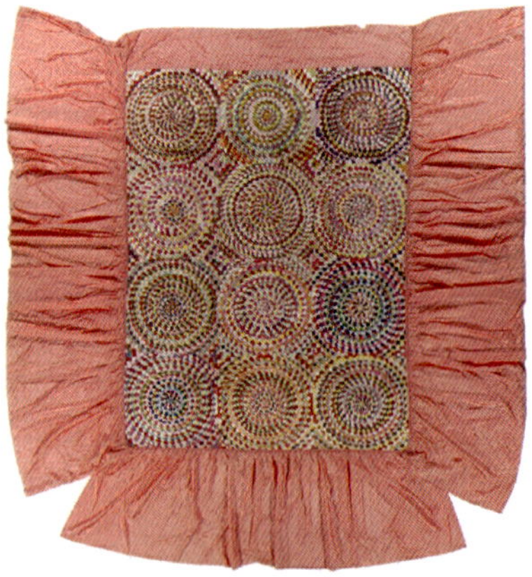

Target

Maker unidentified
Made in United States
Circa 1930 - 1950
71 x 63 in.

IQM 2006.043.0168

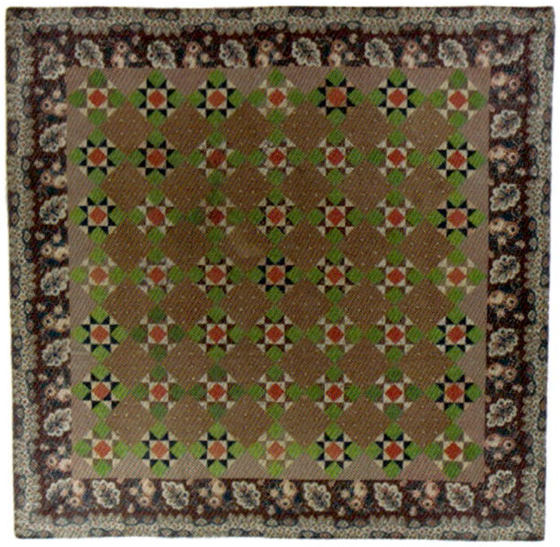

Variable Star

Maker unidentified
Made in United States
1840 - 1860
106 x 106 in.

IQM 2006.043.0169

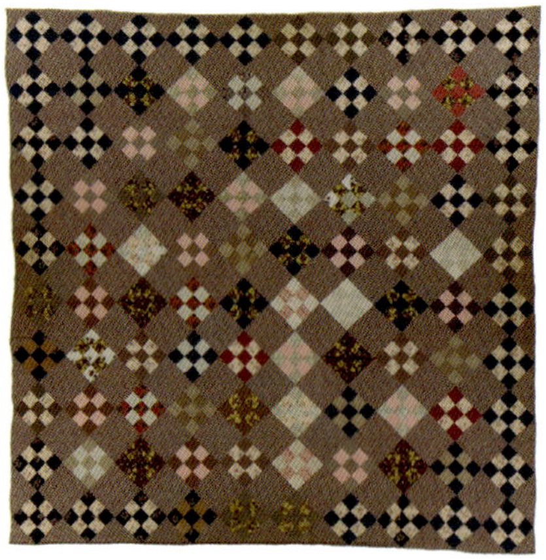

Nine Patch

Maker unidentified
Made in United States
1820 - 1840
90 x 87 in.

IQM 2006.043.0170

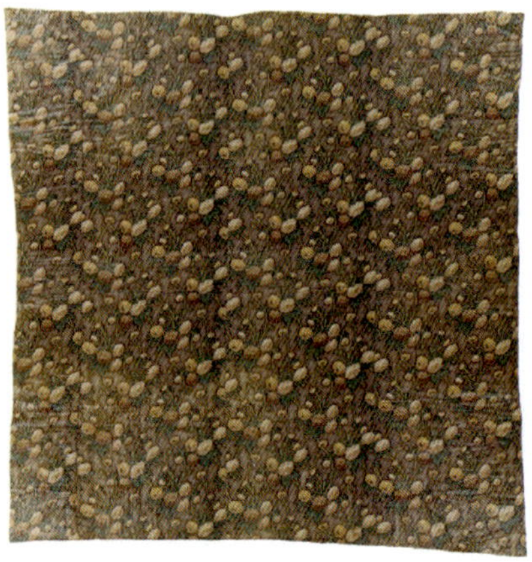

Whole Cloth

Maker unidentified
Made in United States
1870 - 1890
87 x 82 in.

IQM 2006.043.0171

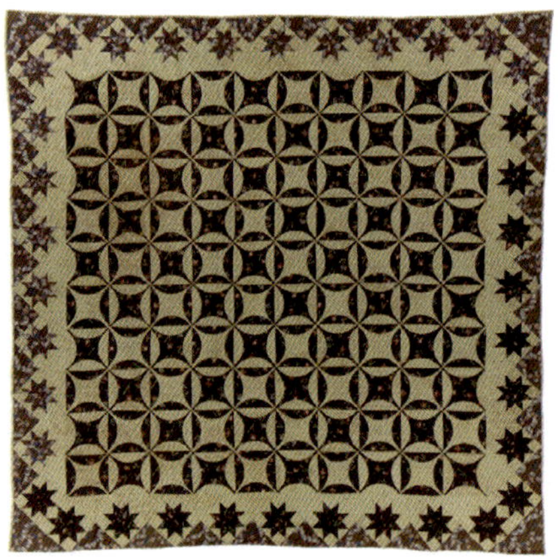

Rob Peter to Pay Paul

Maker unidentified
Made in United States
1830 - 1850
91 x 90 in.

IQM 2006.043.0172

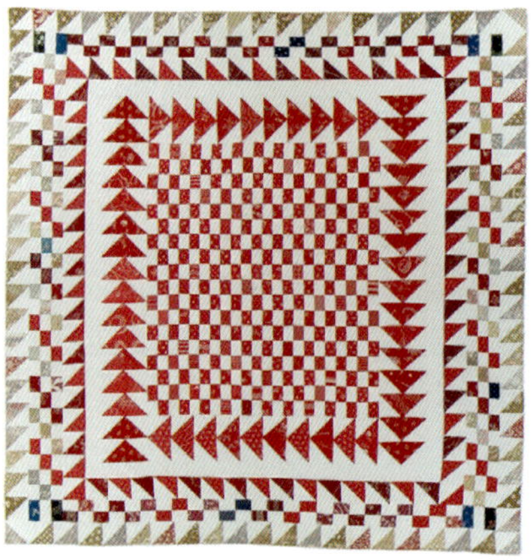

Bricks

Maker unidentified
Made in United States
1890 - 1910
81 x 76 in.

IQM 2006.043.0173

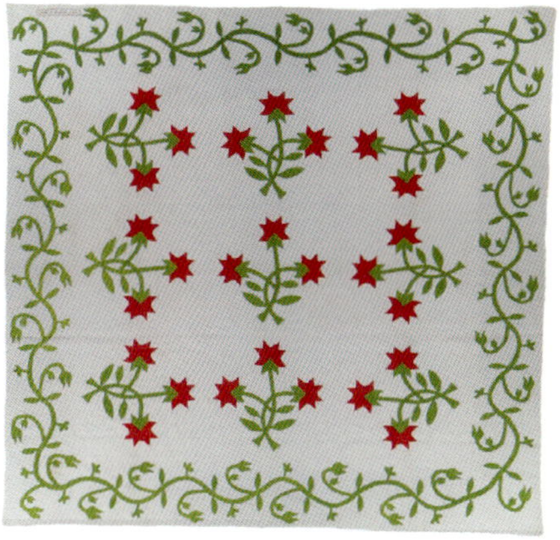

Lily

Probably made by Mary Kistler
Made in United States
Dated 1853
93 x 92 in.

IQM 2006.043.0174

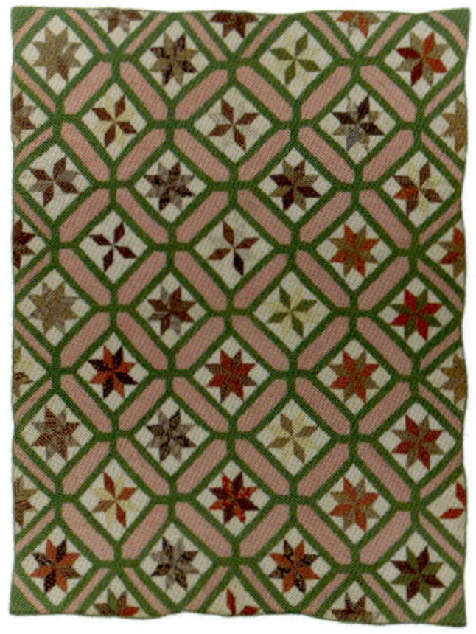

Garden Maze Star

Maker unidentified
Made in United States
1850 - 1870
102 x 76 in.

IQM 2006.043.0175

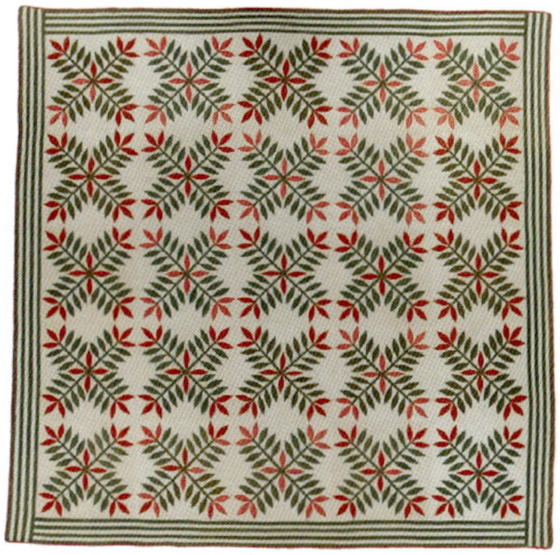

Sumac

Maker unidentified
Possibly made in Virginia
1840 - 1860
96 x 96 in.

IQM 2006.043.0176

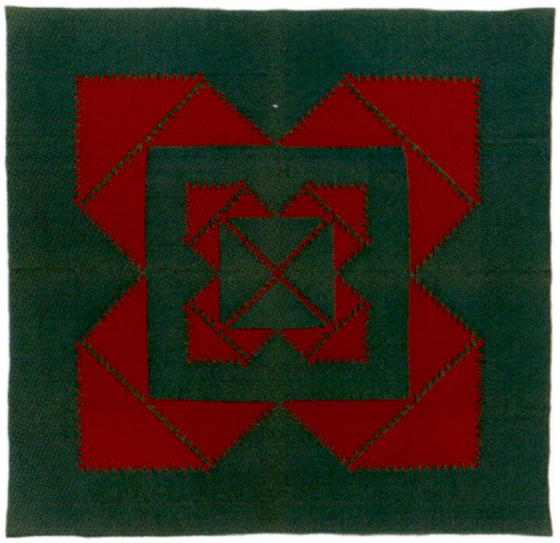

Delectable Mountains

Maker unidentified
Made in United States
1870 - 1890
81 x 80 in.

IQM 2006.043.0178

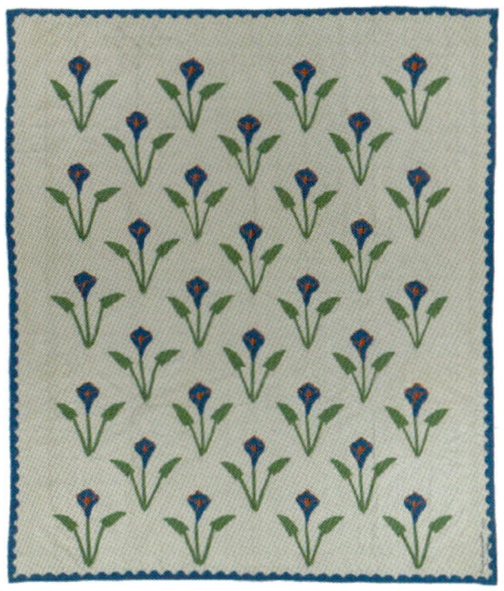

Calla Lily

Maker unidentified
Possibly made in Pennsylvania
Dated 1935
82 x 71 in.

IQM 2006.043.0179

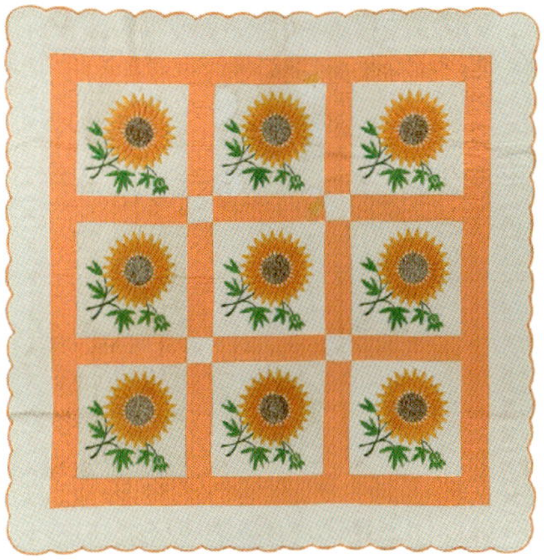

Sunflower

Maker unidentified
Possibly made in Pennsylvania
Dated 1938
79 x 79 in.

IQM 2006.043.0180

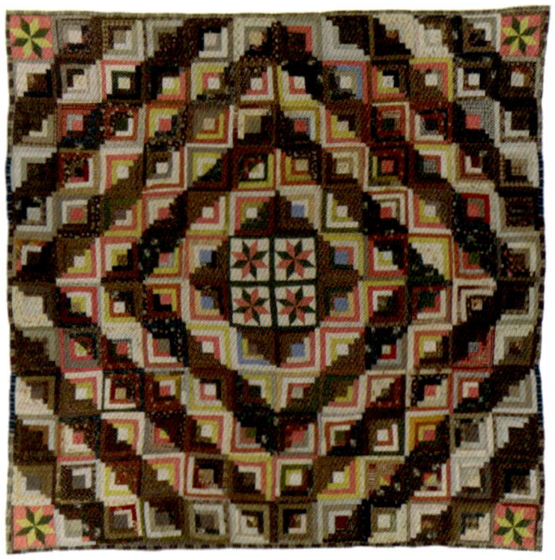

Log Cabin

Maker unidentified
Possibly made in Lancaster County, Pennsylvania
1870 - 1895
85 x 84 in.

IQM 2006.043.0181

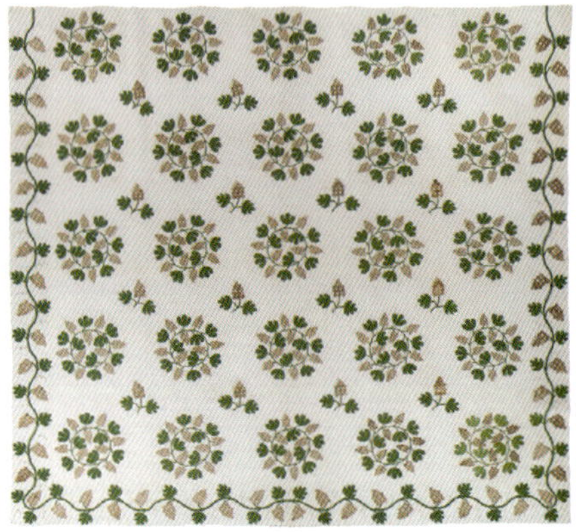

Appliquéd Grapes

Maker unidentified
Made in United States
1840 - 1860
101 x 95 in.

IQM 2006.043.0183

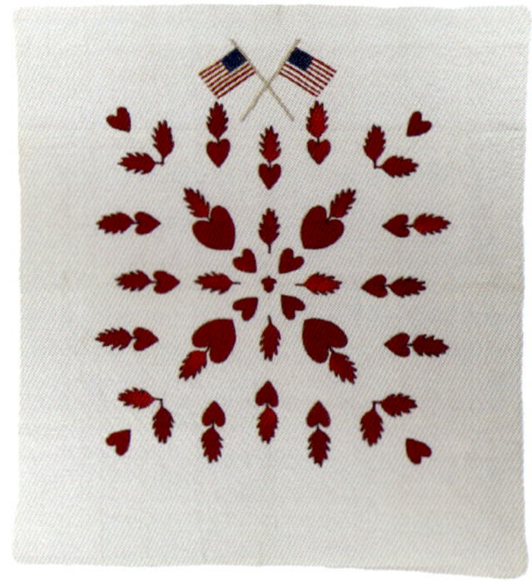

Hearts and Leaves

Maker unidentified
Made in United States
1912 - 1920
81 x 78 in.

IQM 2006.043.0184

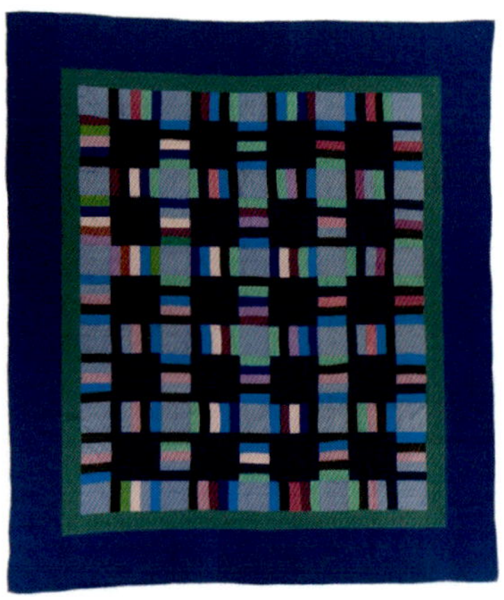

Railroad Crossing

Maker unidentified
Probably made in Iowa
1930 - 1950
84 x 72 in.

IQM 2006.043.0185

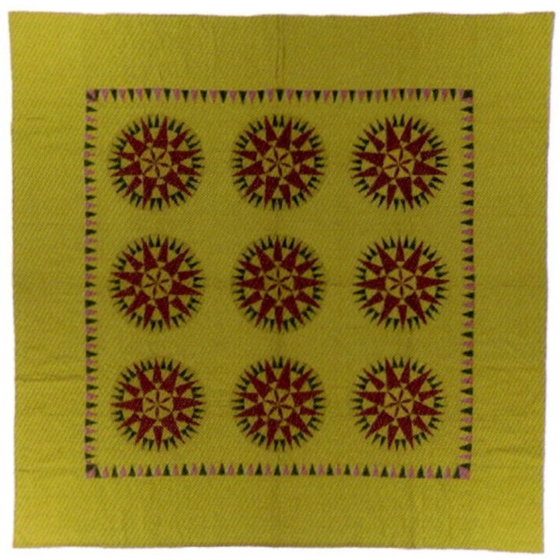

Mariner's Compass

Maker unidentified
Made in United States
1870 - 1890
88 x 86 in.

IQM 2006.043.01863

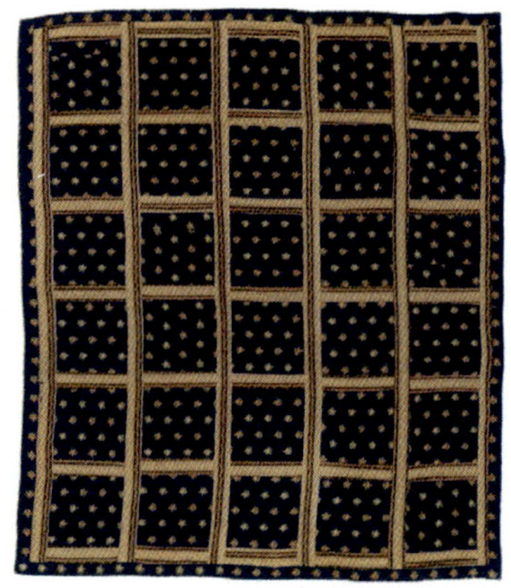

Squares

Maker unidentified
Made in United States
1860 - 1880
76 x 65 in.

IQM 2006.043.0187

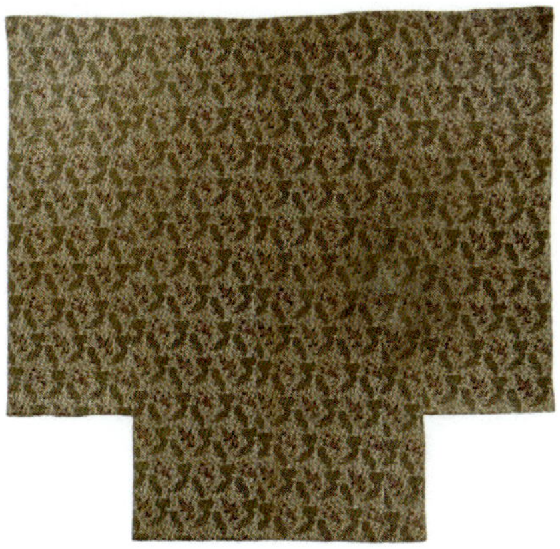

Whole Cloth

Maker unidentified
Probably made in New York
1830 - 1850
108 x 75 in.

IQM 2006.043.0190

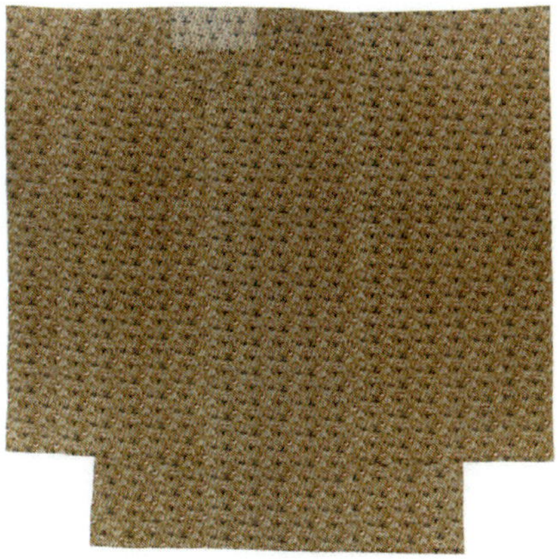

Whole Cloth

Maker unidentified
Possibly made in New York
Dated 1871
88 x 88.75 in.

IQM 2006.043.0191

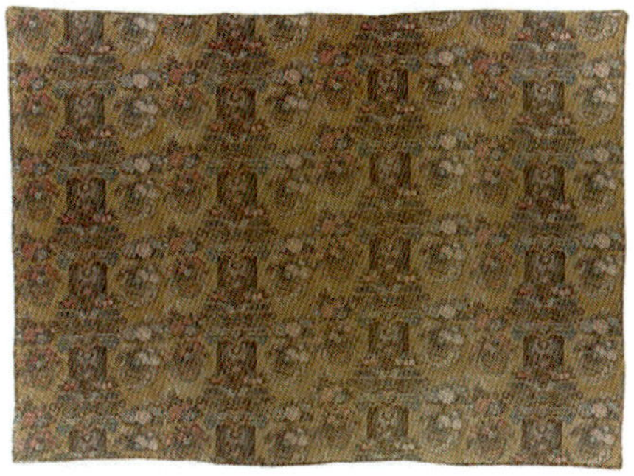

Whole Cloth

Maker unidentified
Probably made in New England
1830 - 1850
97 x 72 in.

IQM 2006.043.0192

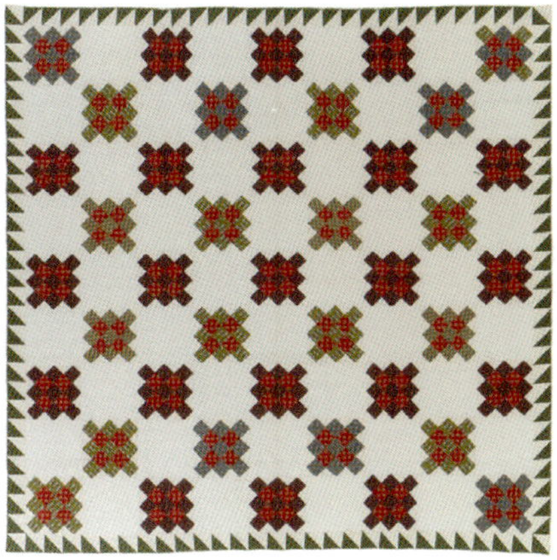

Thirteen Patch

Maker unidentified
Probably made in Lancaster County, Pennsylvania
1830 - 1850
100 x 98.875 in.

IQM 2006.043.0194

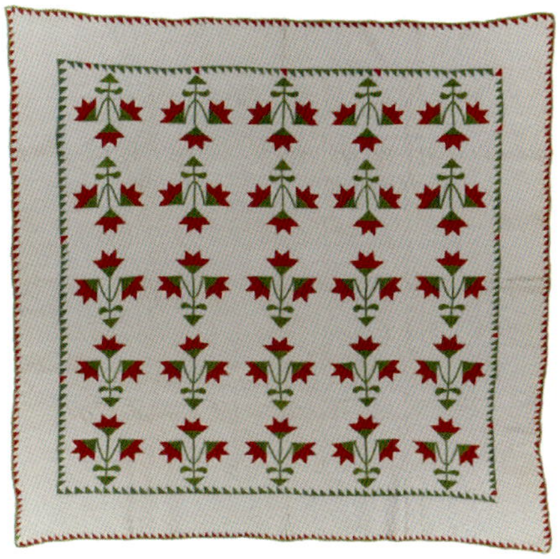

Lily

Maker unidentified
Probably made in Indiana
1850 - 1870
78 x 76 in.

IQM 2006.043.0195

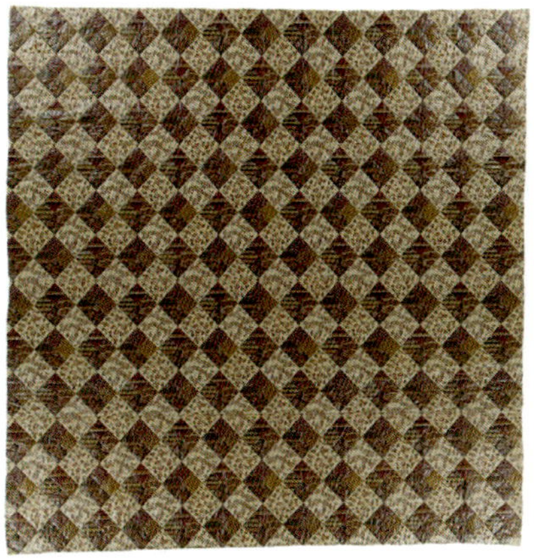

Whole Cloth

Maker unidentified
Possibly made in Pennsylvania
1840 - 1860
93 x 89 in.

IQM 2006.043.0196

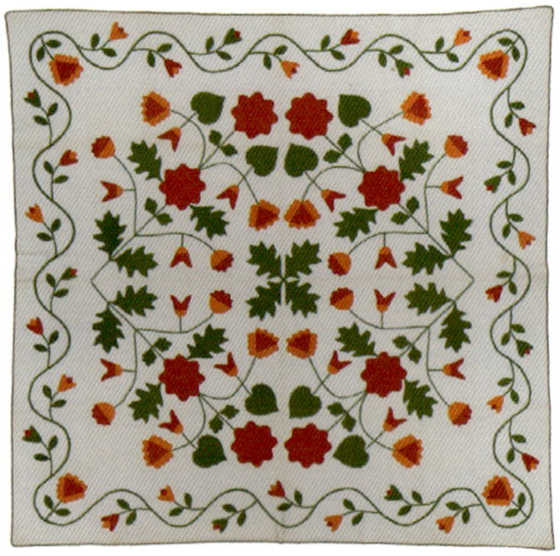

Leaves and Blooms

Maker unidentified
Probably made in Lancaster County, Pennsylvania
1840 - 1860
89 x 89 in.
IQM 2006.043.0197

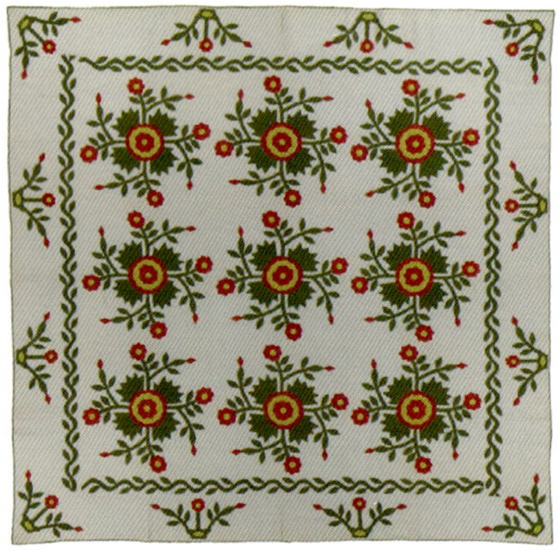

Whig Rose

Maker unidentified
Possibly made in Pennsylvania
1850 - 1870
87 x 87 in.
IQM 2006.043.0198

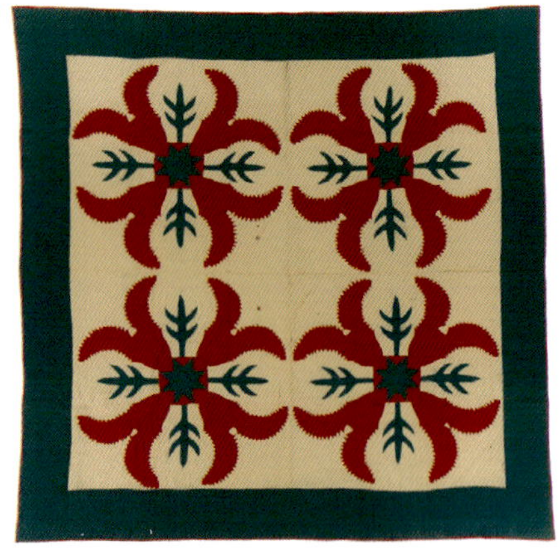

Princess Feather

Maker unidentified
Possibly made in western Pennsylvania
Circa 1890
83 x 84 in.
IQM 2006.043.0199

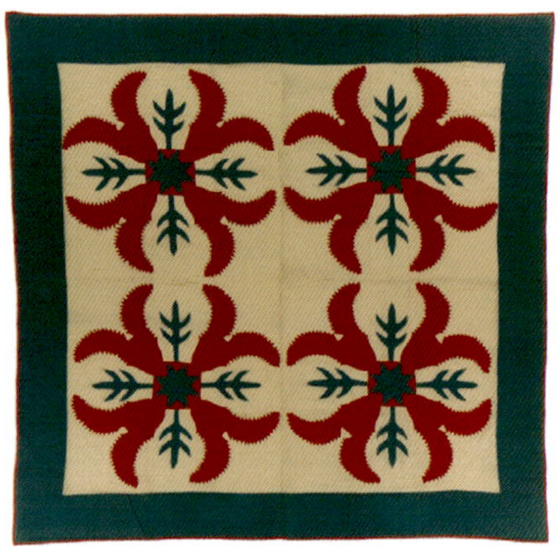

Princess Feather

Maker unidentified
Possibly made in western Pennsylvania
Circa 1890
85 x 84 in.
IQM 2006.043.0200

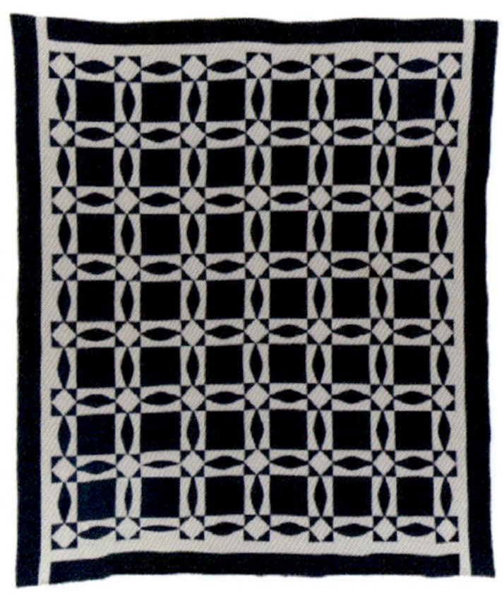

Storm at Sea

Maker unidentified
Made in United States
Circa 1870
78 x 67 in.
IQM 2006.043.0203

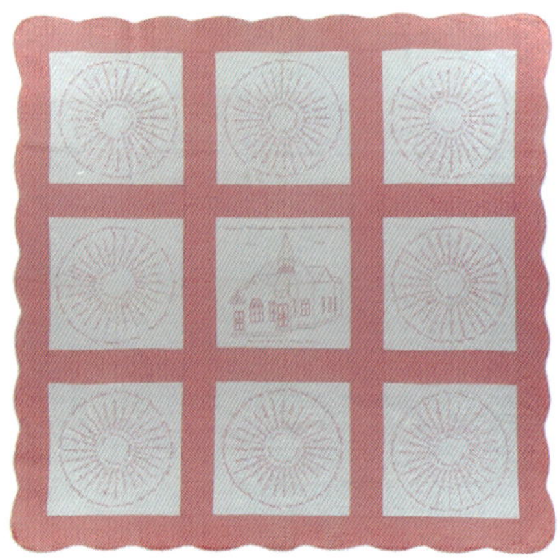

Original

Maker unidentified
Probably made in Smicksburg, Pennsylvania
Circa 1930
74 x 77 in.
IQM 2006.043.0204

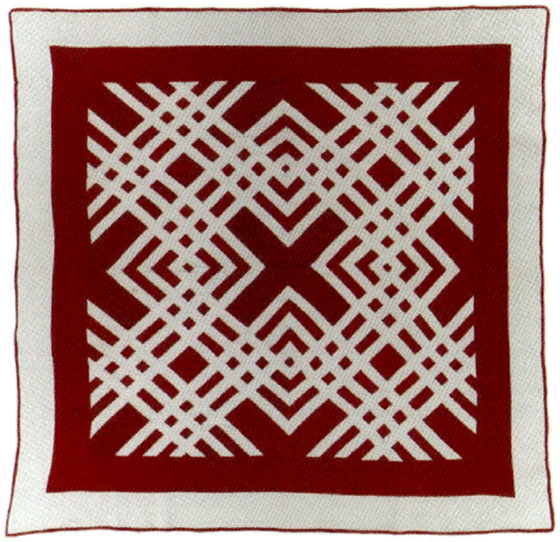

Carpenter's Square

Maker unidentified
Possibly made in Berks County, Pennsylvania
1890 - 1910
74 x 74 in.

IQM 2006.043.0205

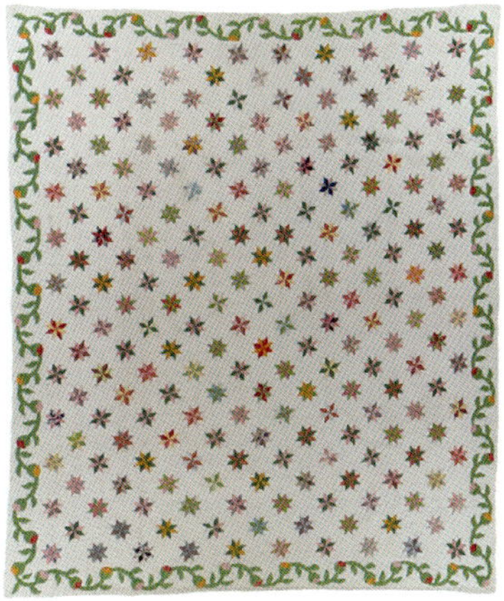

LeMoyne Star

Maker unidentified
Possibly made in Pennsylvania
1850 - 1870
90 x 75 in.

IQM 2006.043.0206

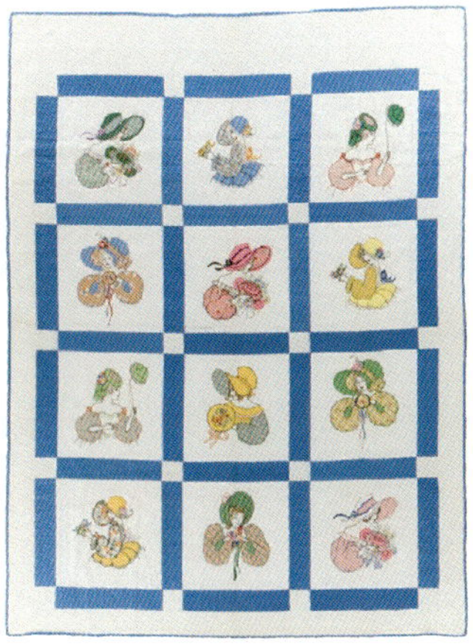

Pretty Ladies

Maker unidentified
Possibly made in York County, Pennsylvania
Circa 1940
80 x 60 in.

IQM 2006.043.0207

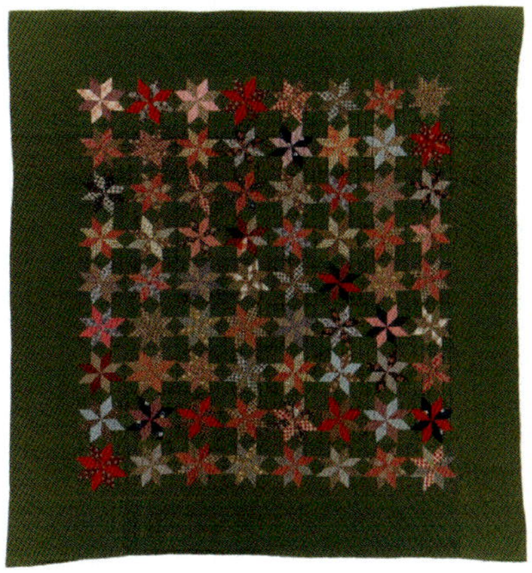

LeMoyne Star

Maker unidentified
Possibly made in Lancaster County, Pennsylvania
1895 - 1915
77 x 70 in.

IQM 2006.043.0208

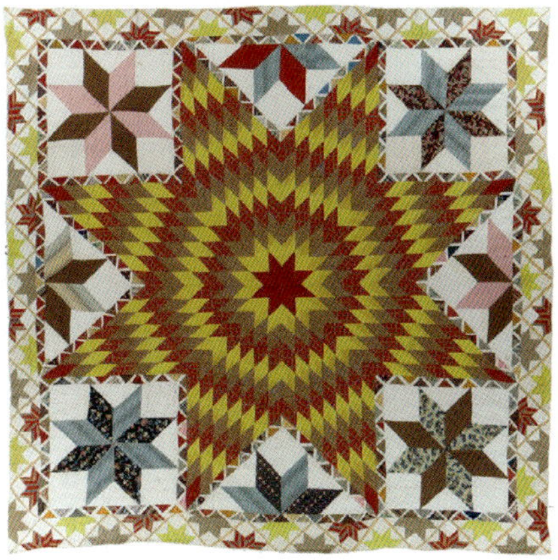

Star of Bethlehem

Maker unidentified
Possibly made in Philadelphia, Pennsylvania
1830 - 1850
95 x 93 in.

IQM 2006.043.0209

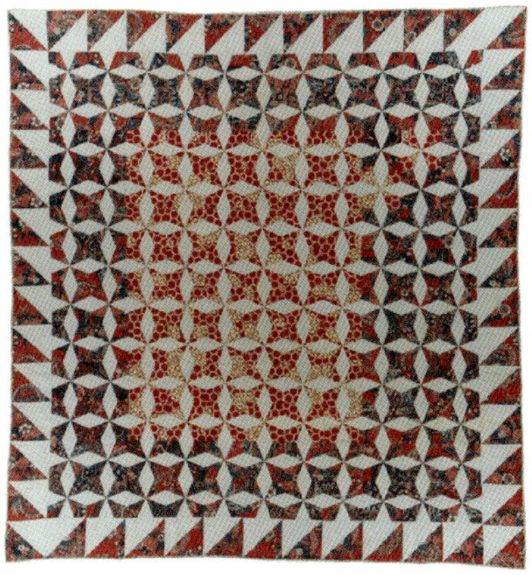

Four point star

Maker unidentified
Possibly made in Philadelphia, Pennsylvania
1830 - 1850
95 x 88 in.

IQM 2006.043.0210

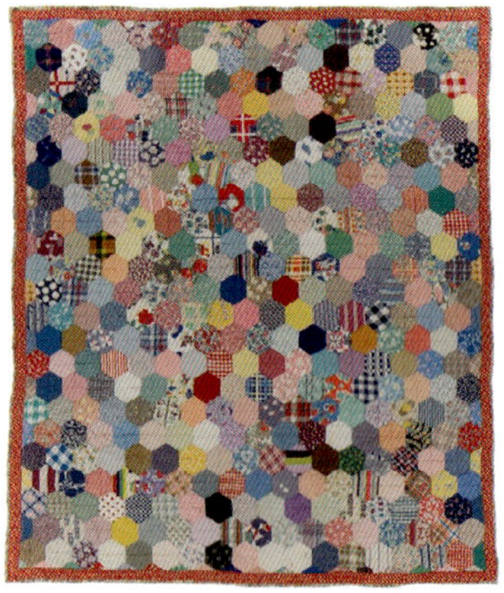

Hexagon

Maker unidentified
Possibly made in Tennessee
1930 - 1940
86 x 74 in.

IQM 2006.043.0211

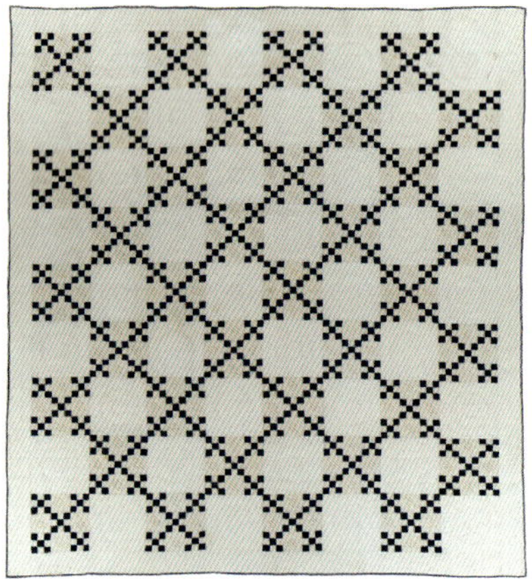

Double Nine Patch

Ladies Aid Society of Lordstown Evangelical Lutheran Church
Possibly made in Trumbull County, Ohio
1879 - 1882
84 x 76 in.

IQM 2006.043.0212

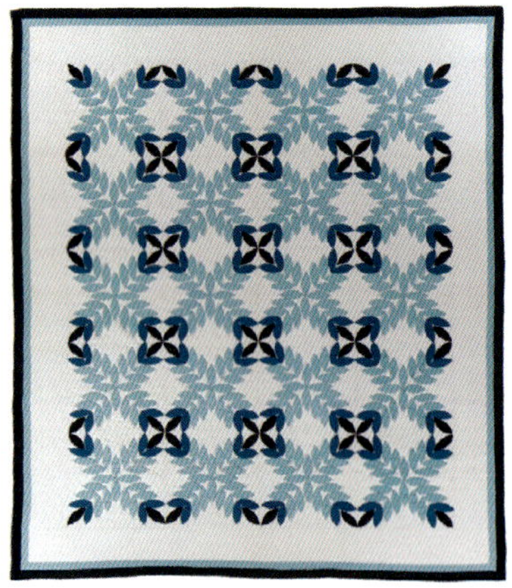

The Laurel

Betty Marsh
Possibly made in Brown County, Indiana
Circa 1940
95 x 82 in.

IQM 2006.043.0213

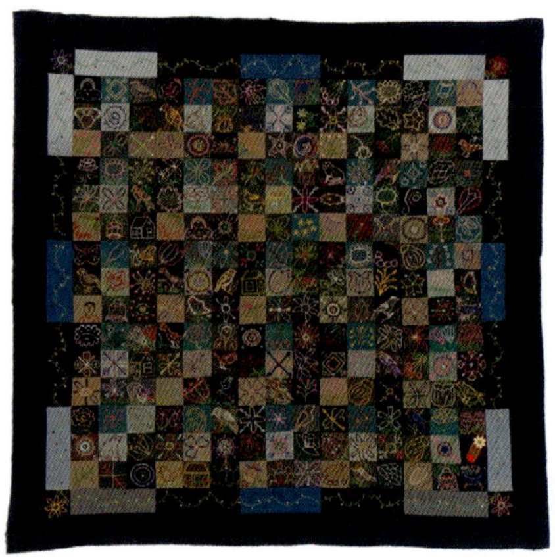

Album

Maker unidentified
Made in United States
Circa 1920
72 x 70 in.

IQM 2006.043.0215

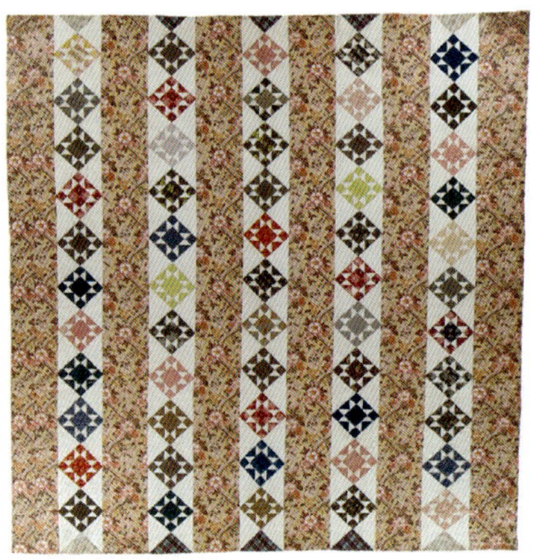

Eight Pointed Star Bars

Maker unidentified
Made in United States
1830 - 1850
105 x 100 in.

IQM 2006.043.0218

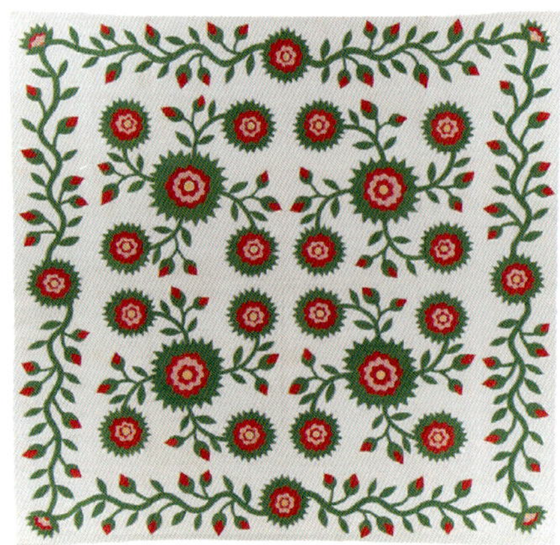

Rose of Sharon

Maker unidentified
Made in United States
1850 - 1870
84.25 x 83.75 in.

IQM 2006.043.0219

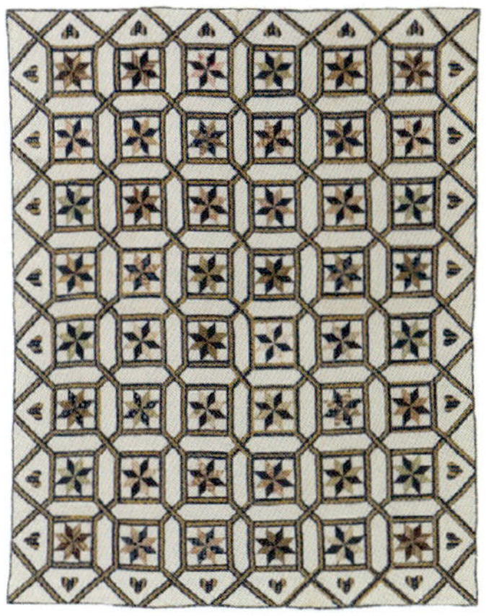

Garden Maze Star

Possibly made by Rebecca Snyder
Made in United States
1840 - 1860
95 x 74 in.
IQM 2006.043.0220

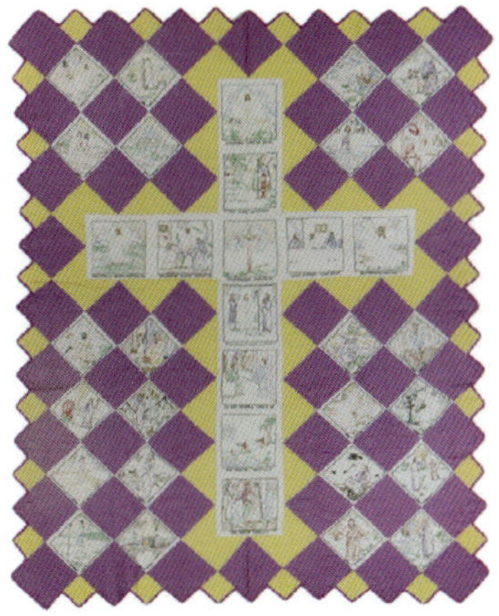

Bible Stories

Maker unidentified
Made in United States
1930 - 1940
95 x 80 in.
IQM 2006.043.0221

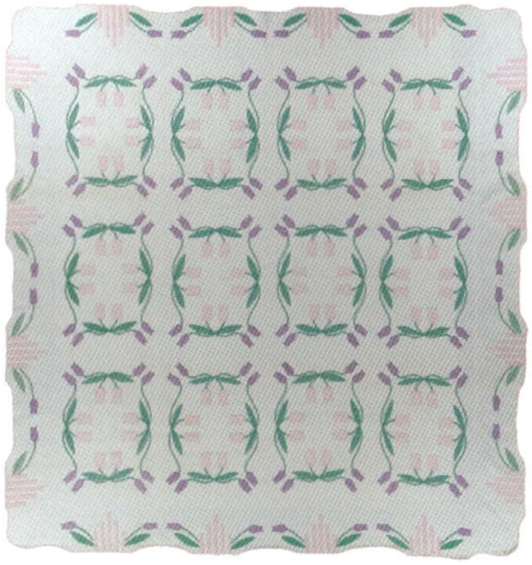

Tulip

Cora Gregory James
Made in Nebraska
1920 - 1930
86 x 85 in.
IQM 2006.043.0222

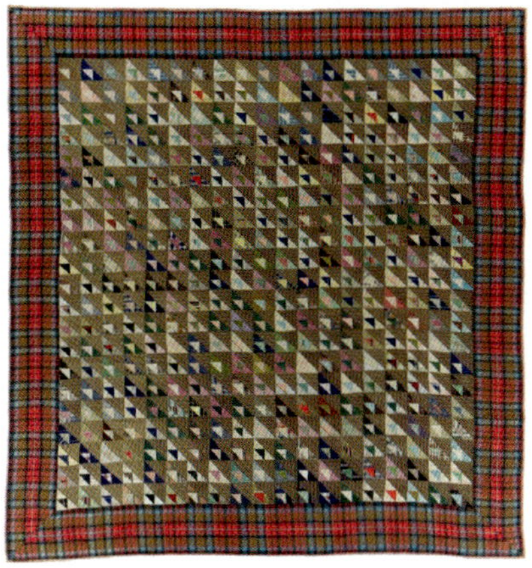

Flying Geese

Possibly made by Annie C. G. Thomas
Probably made in Maryland
1870 - 1890
90 x 84 in.
IQM 2006.043.0223

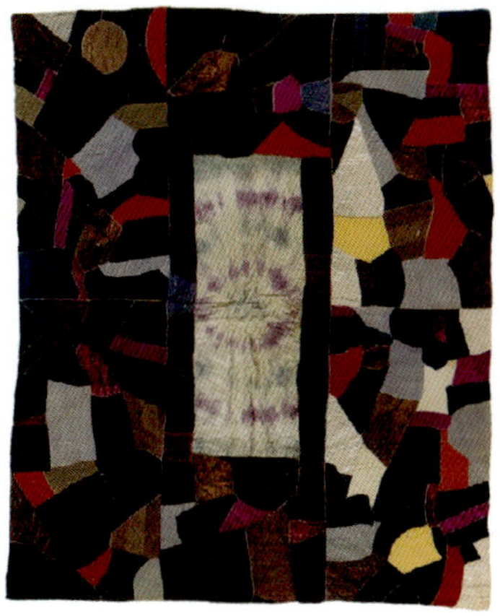

Crazy

Cora Gregory James
Made in Nebraska
1900 - 1920
84 x 65 in.
IQM 2006.043.0224

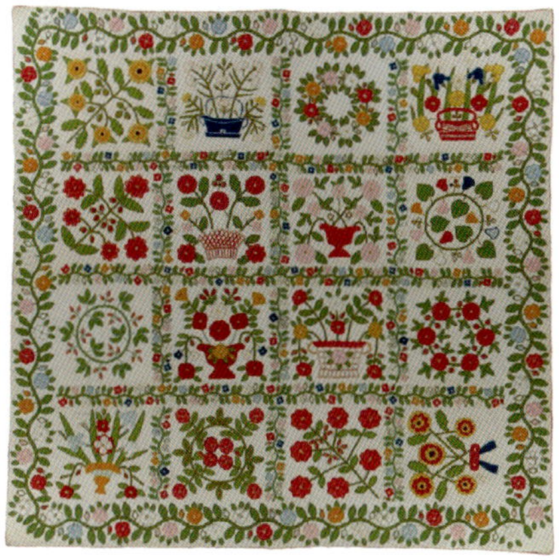

Album

Maker unidentified
Made in United States
1850 - 1870
94.5 x 93.5 in.
IQM 2006.043.0225

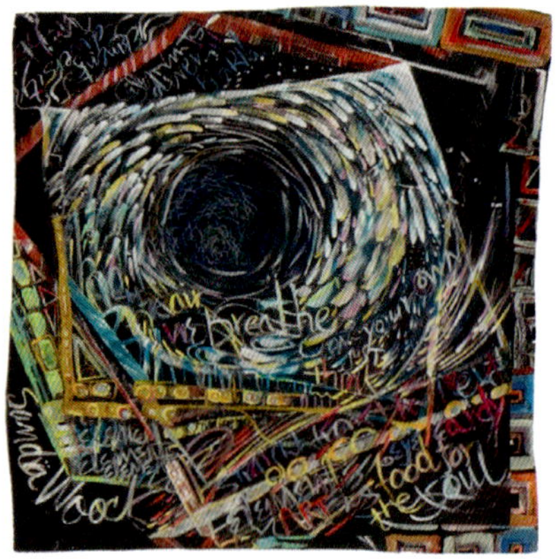

Elements #3: Existence

Sandra Woock
Made in Bethesda, Maryland
Dated 2003
41 x 40 in.

IQM 2006.043.0227

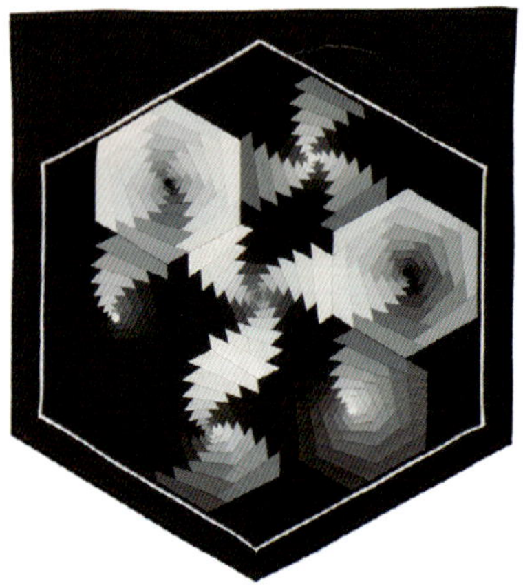

Gray Progressions

Carol Bryer Fallert (Gentry)
Made in Oswego, Illinois
Dated 1986
52.5 x 46.25 in.

IQM 2009.039.0001

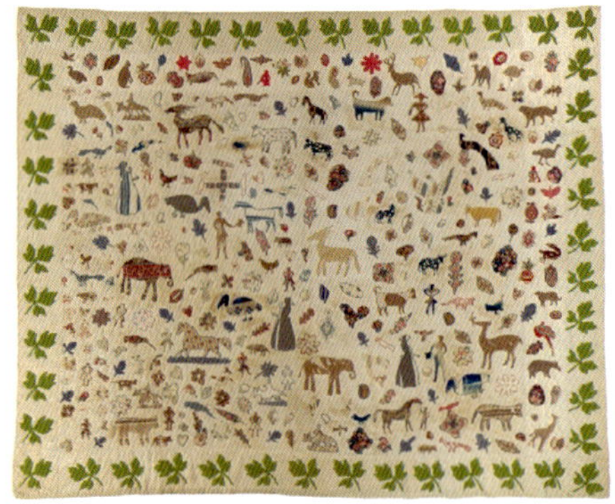

Original - Pictorial

Mary Eliza Trowbridge
Possibly made in Wisconsin
Dated 1869
66 x 77.75 in.

IQM 2009.039.0002

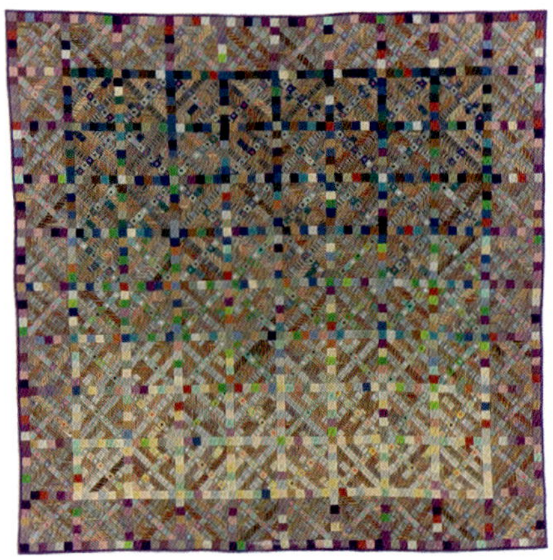

Number 25

Pamela Studstill
Made in Pipe Creek, Texas
Dated 1983
59.25 x 58.5 in.

IQM 2009.039.0003

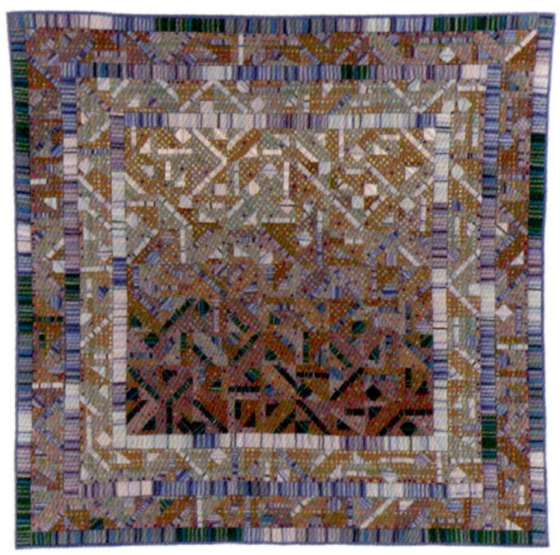

Number 43

Pamela Studstill
Made in Pipe Creek, Texas
Dated 1984
54.25 x 55 in.

IQM 2009.039.00043

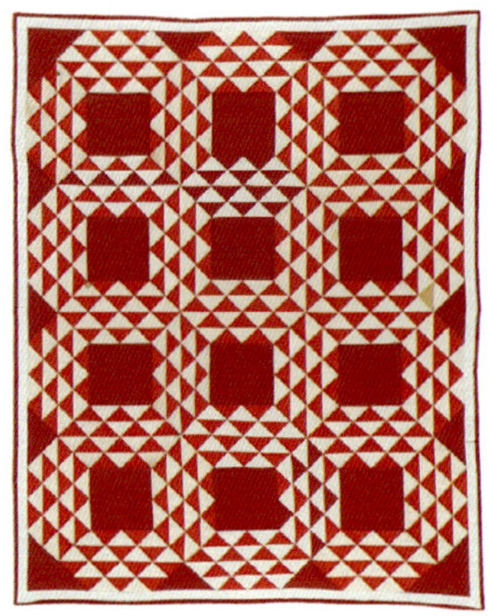

Ocean Waves

Blocks by Mrs. Kennedy,
finished by Ardis James
Made in Lincoln, Nebraska and
Chappaqua, New York
1840 - 1983
62 x 48 in.

IQM 2009.039.0005

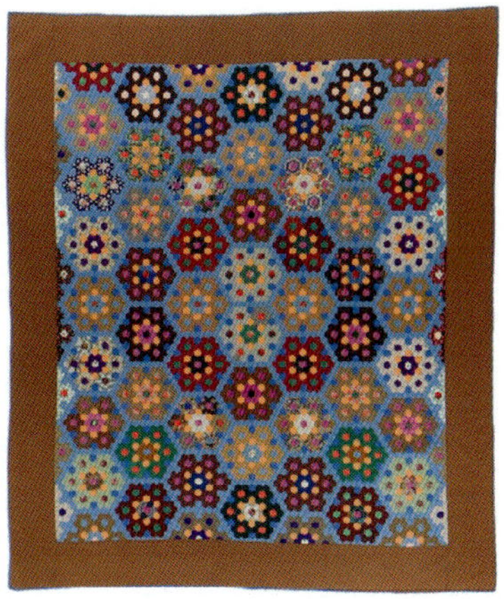

Hexagon

Maker unidentified
Possibly made in Ohio
Circa 1870
84.75 x 70.25 in.

IQM 2009.039.0008

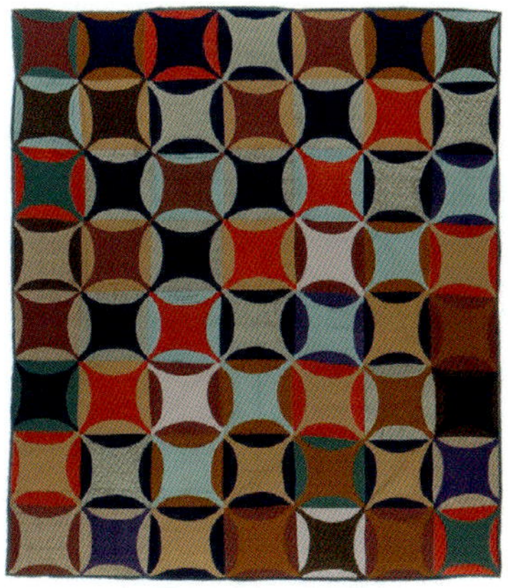

Rob Peter to Pay Paul

Maker unidentified
Possibly made in Pennsylvania
Circa 1880
80.25 x 69.5 in.

IQM 2009.039.0009

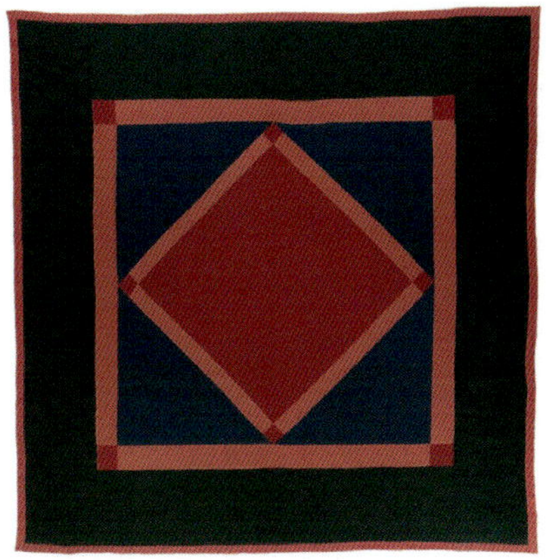

Diamond in Square

Maker unidentified
Probably made in Lancaster County, Pennsylvania
Circa 1900
79.5 x 77 in.

IQM 2009.039.0010

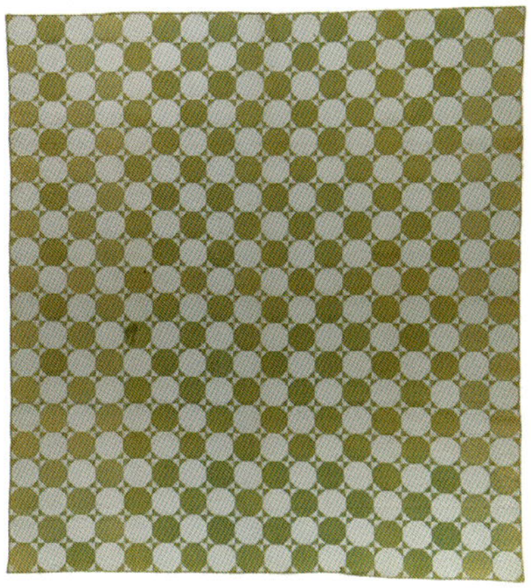

Snowball

Maker unidentified
Probably made in Tipton County, Indiana
1850 - 1870
91.5 x 82 in.

IQM 2009.039.0011

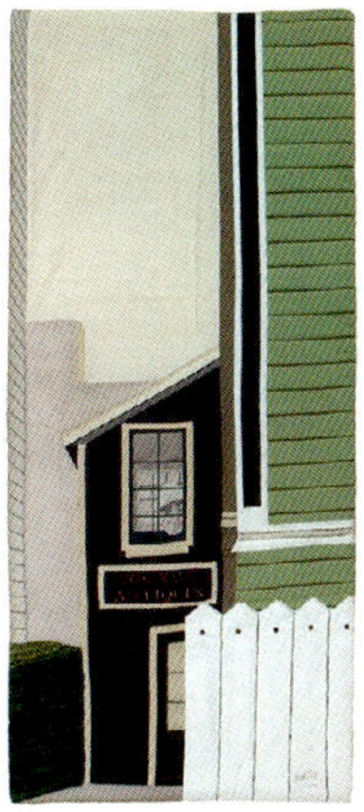

Tom Kaye Antiques

Nadine Ruse
Made in Paris, France
Dated 1981
58.25 x 25.5 in.

IQM 2009.039.00123

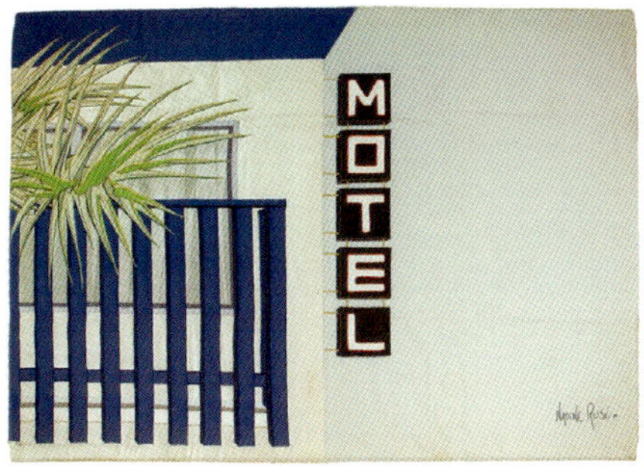

Motel

Nadine Ruse
Made in Paris, France
Dated 1981
43 x 59 in.

IQM 2009.039.0013

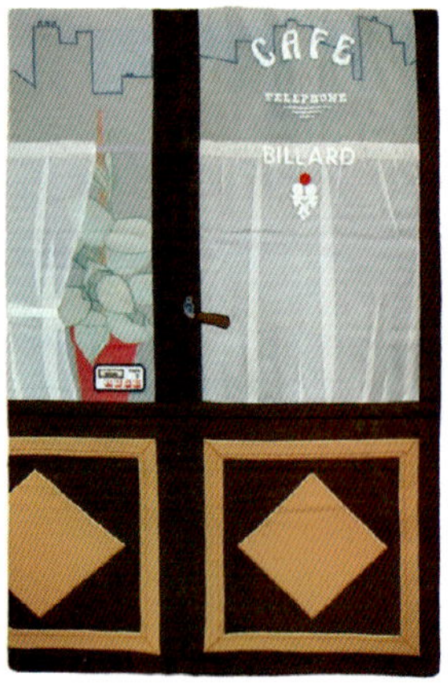

Cafe' Billiard

Nadine Ruse
Made in Paris, France
Dated 1984
55 x 35.5 in.

IQM 2009.039.0014

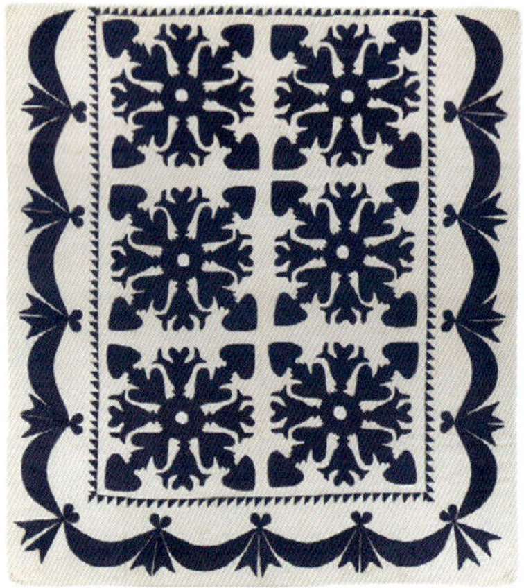

Hearts and Spades

Maker unidentified
Possibly made in New England or New York
Circa 1880
86 x 77.5 in.

IQM 2009.039.0015

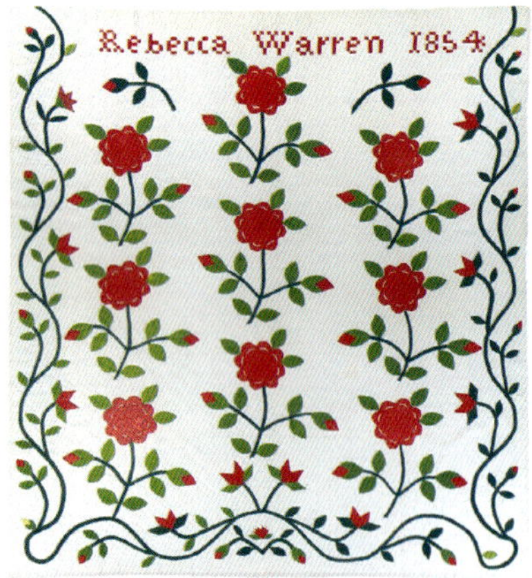

Rose

Possibly made by Rebecca Warren
Probably made in New York
Dated 1864
87.25 x 78.5 in.

IQM 2009.039.0016

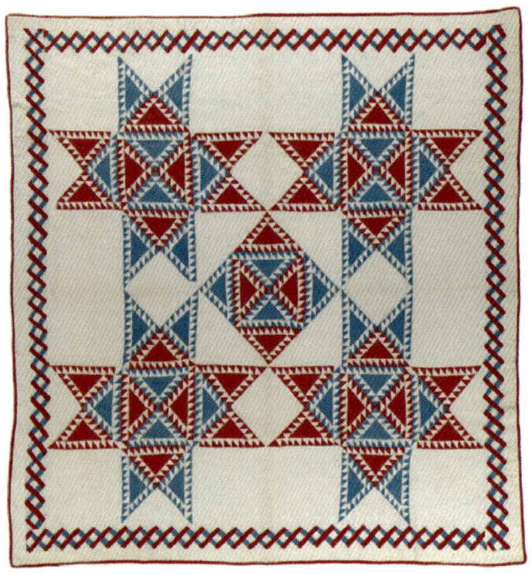

Feathered Star

Maker unidentified
Possibly made in Ohio
Circa 1920
79.25 x 74.25 in.

IQM 2009.039.0017

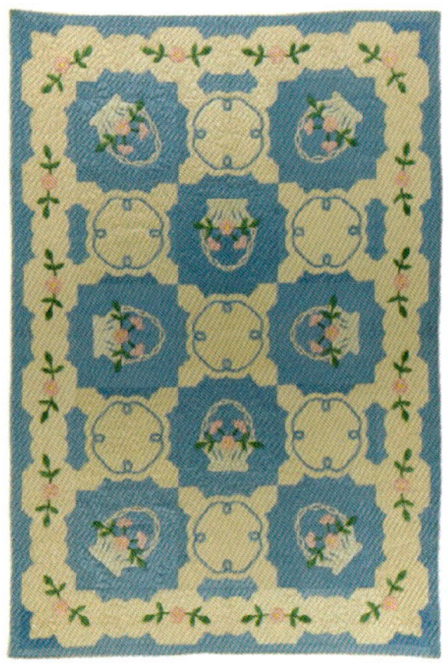

French Basket

Maker unidentified
Possibly made in Ohio
Circa 1925
92.75 x 63 in.

IQM 2009.039.0018

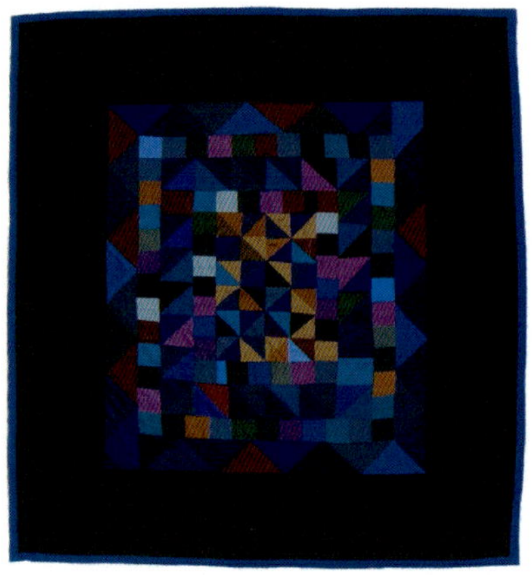

Broken Dishes

L. Miller
Probably made in Wayne County, Ohio
Circa 1975
32 x 29 in.

IQM 2009.039.0019

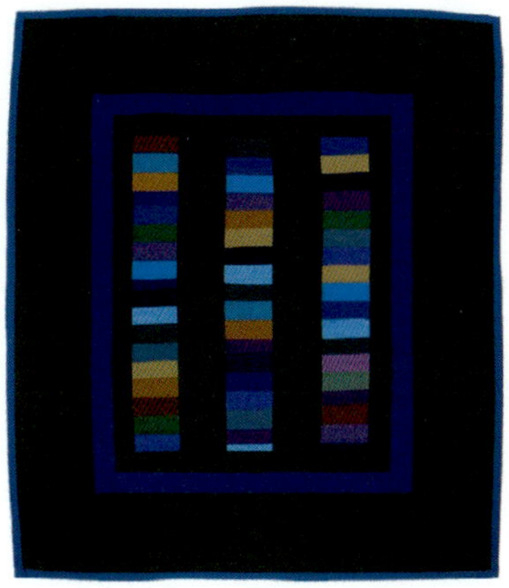

Chinese Coins

L. Miller
Probably made in Wayne County, Ohio
Circa 1975
35.25 x 31 in.

IQM 2009.039.0020

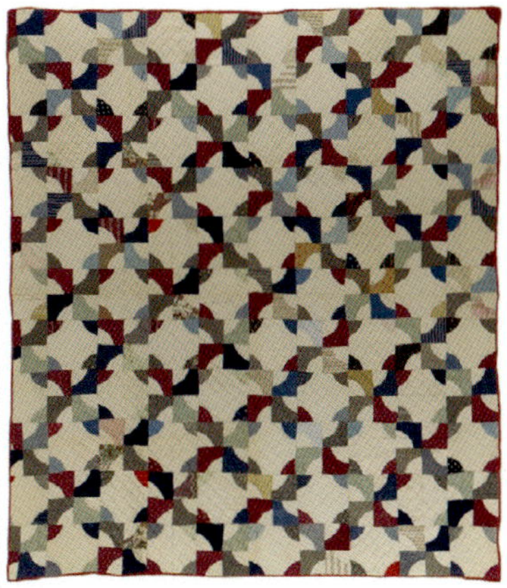

Drunkard's Path

Maker unidentified
Made in United States
Circa 1900
79.5 x 68.5 in.

IQM 2009.039.0021

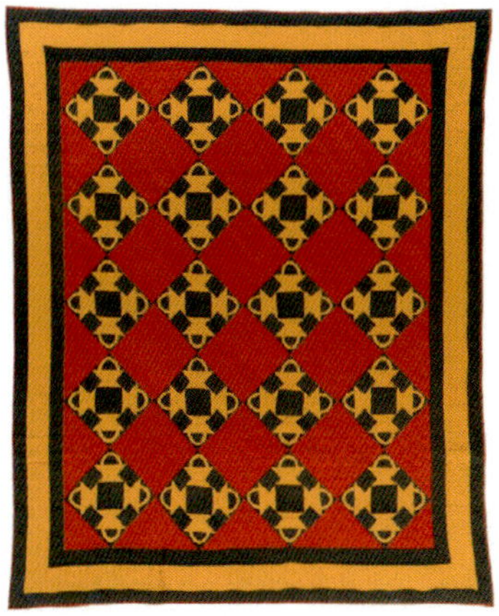

Basket

Probably made by Member of the Old Order River Brethren
Probably made in Chambersburg, Pennsylvania
1875 - 1885
84.25 x 70.5 in.

IQM 2009.039.0023

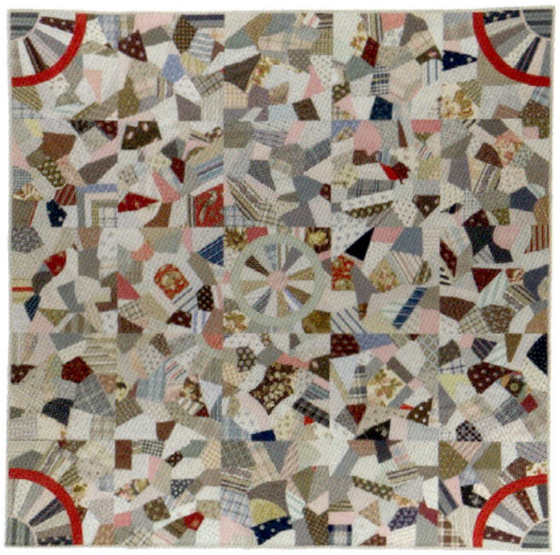

Crazy

Maker unidentified
Probably made in Egremont, Massachusetts
Dated 1893
85.5 x 86.25 in.

IQM 2009.039.0024

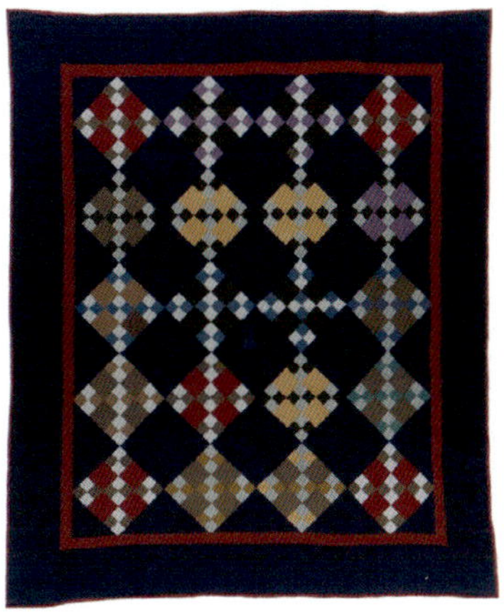

Four Patch

Maker unidentified
Probably made in Holmes County, Ohio
Circa 1900
88.25 x 74 in.

IQM 2009.039.0025

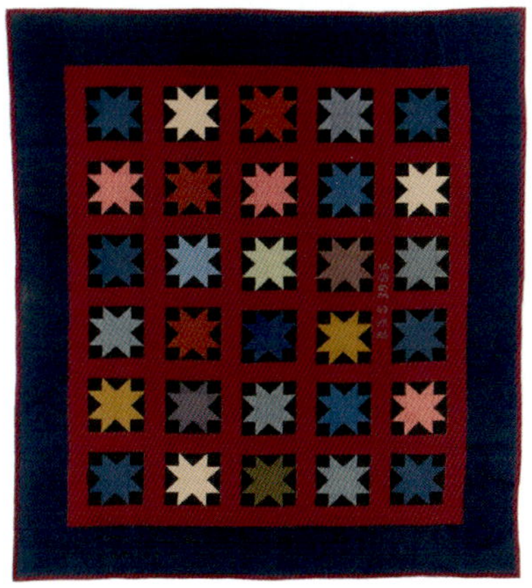

Star

Maker unidentified
Possibly made in Ohio
Dated 1906
71 x 79.25 in.

IQM 2009.039.0026

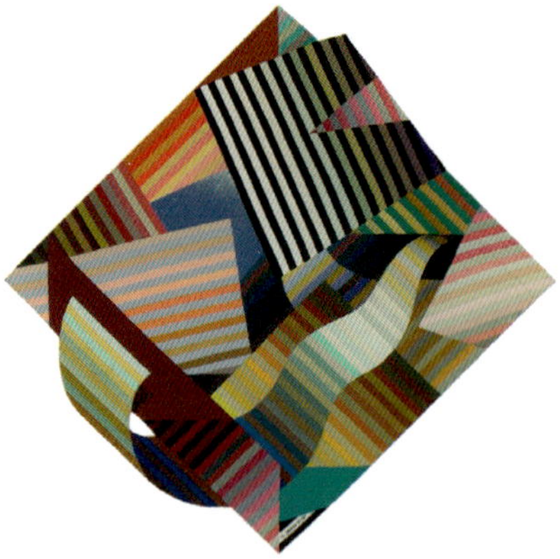

A View into Time/Motion

Michael James
Made in Somerset, Massachusetts
Dated 1987
35.5 x 42 in.

IQM 2009.039.0027

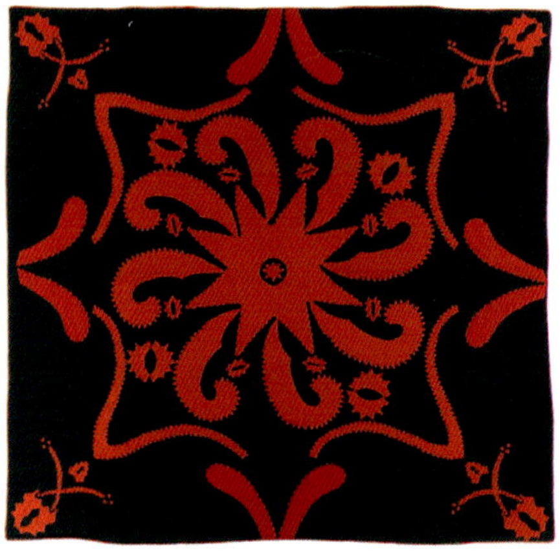

Princess Feather

Maker unidentified
United States
Circa 1870
77 x 77 in.

IQM 2009.039.0028

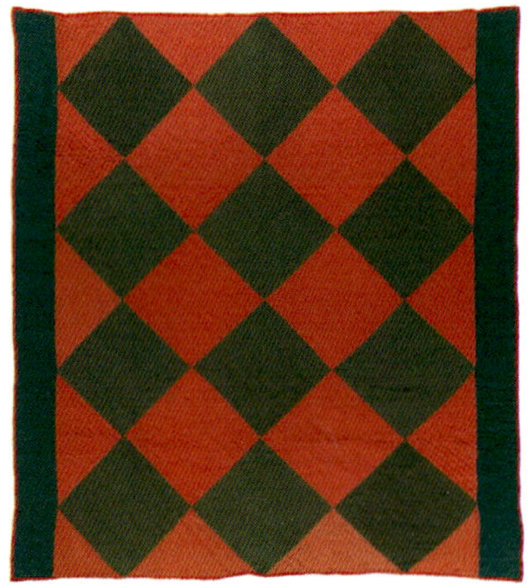

Diamonds

Maker unidentified
United States
Circa 1890
78 x 68.5 in.

IQM 2009.039.00293

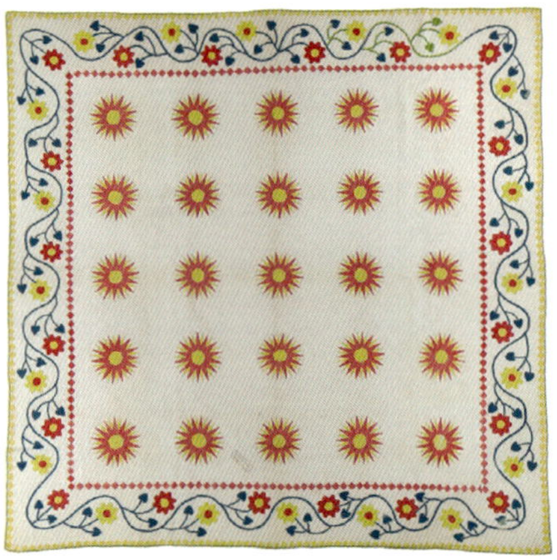

Sunburst

Possibly made by R. C. M. Story
Probably made in Perryton, Ohio
Dated 1851
89.25 x 89.5 in.

IQM 2009.039.0030

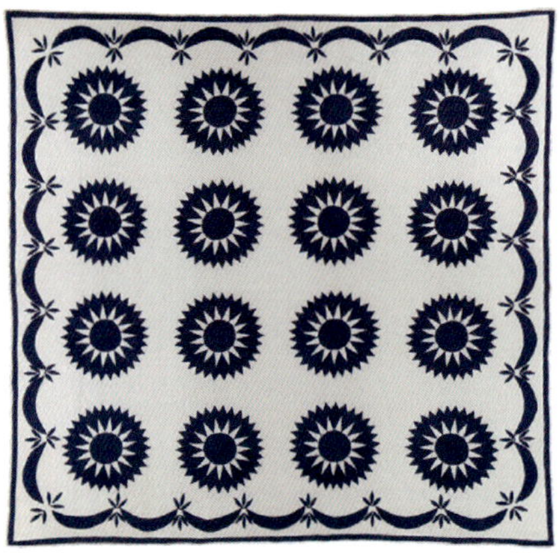

Rising Sun

Maker unidentified
Possibly made in Ohio
1840 - 1860
90 x 91 in.

IQM 2009.039.0031

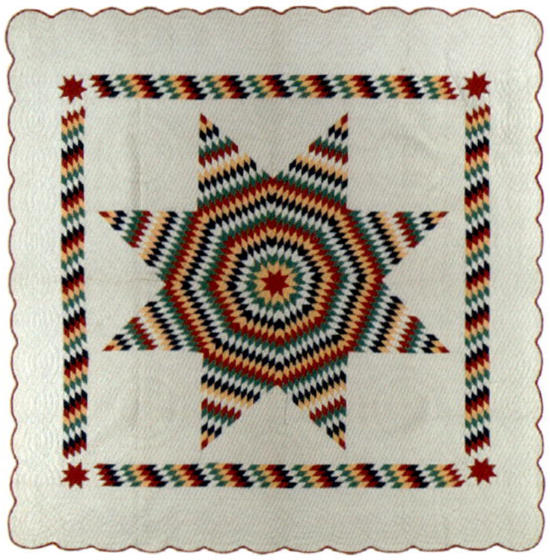

Star of Bethlehem

Maker unidentified
Probably made in Coshocton County, Ohio
Circa 1920
73.25 x 75.5 in.

IQM 2009.039.0032

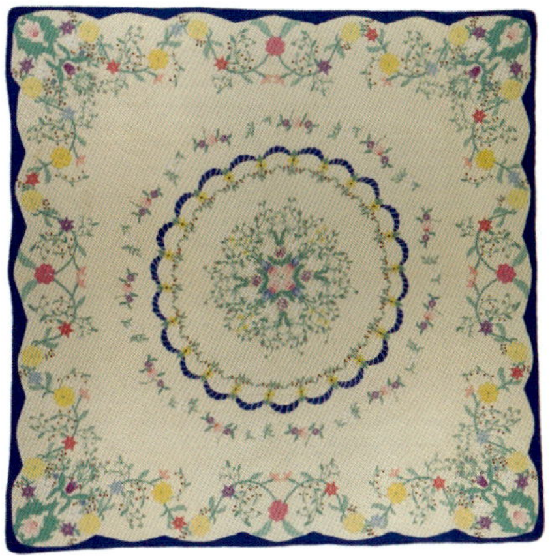

Medallion - Cottage Garden

Maker unidentified
Midwest
1930 - 1940
84.75 x 83 in.

IQM 2009.039.0033

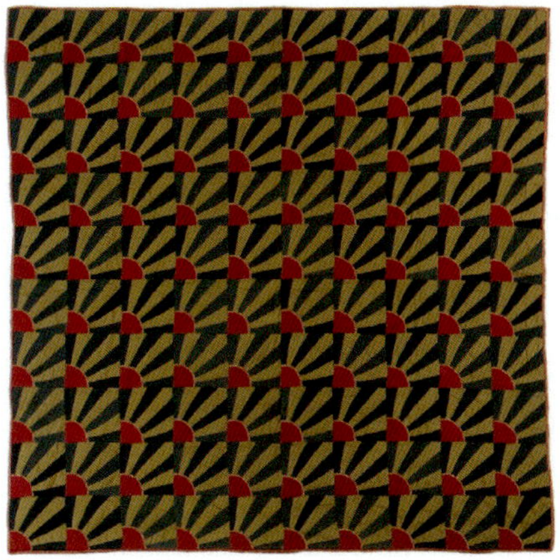

Fan

Maker unidentified
Probably made in Howard County, Indiana
Circa 1920
71 x 72.5 in.

IQM 2009.039.0034

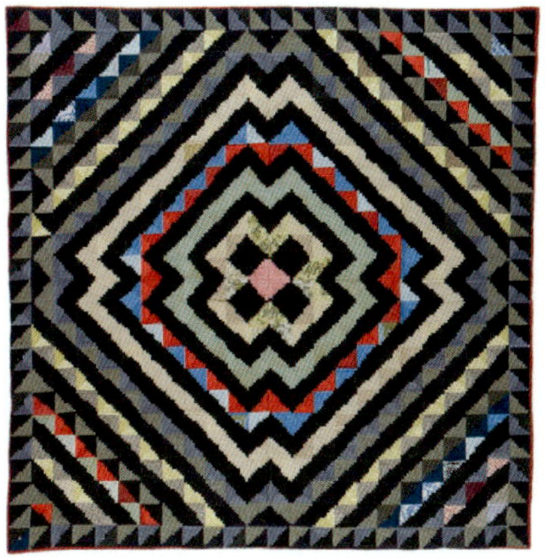

Log Cabin

Maker unidentified
United States
Circa 1880
74 x 73.5 in.

IQM 2009.039.0036

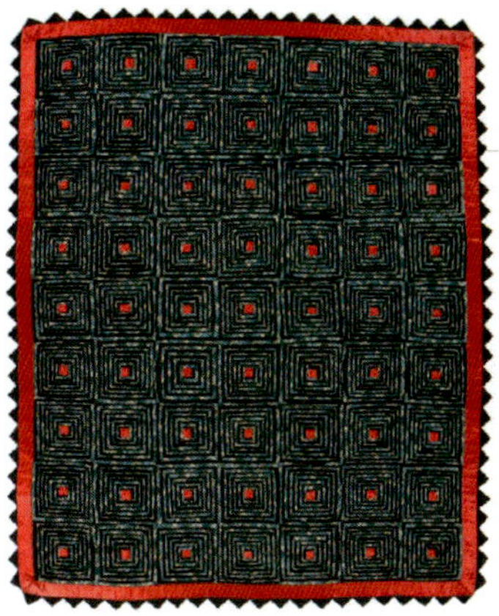

Log Cabin

Maker unidentified
United States
Circa 1925
48.25 x 39.25 in.

IQM 2009.039.0037

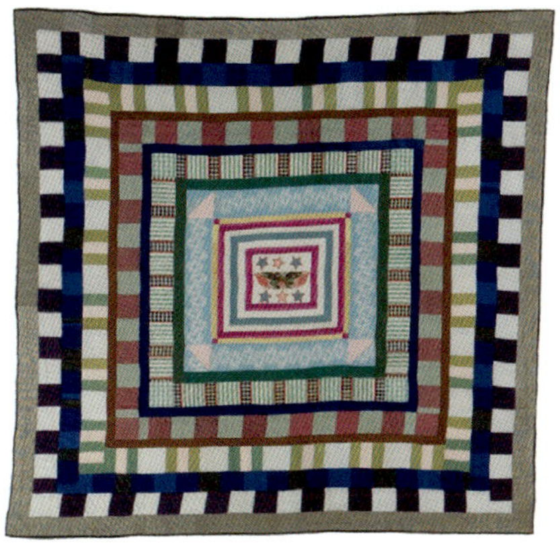

Medallion

Maker unidentified
Probably made in United States
1860 - 1880
78.75 x 78.75 in.

IQM 2009.039.0039

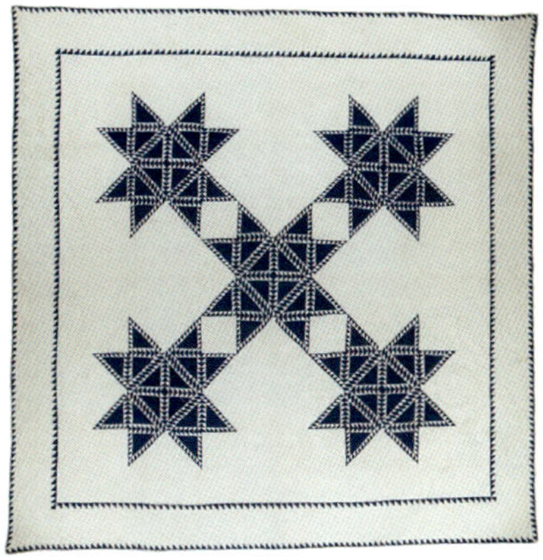

Touching Stars

Maker unidentified
Possibly made in Stark County, Ohio
1840 - 1860
85.75 x 84.25 in.

IQM 2009.039.0040

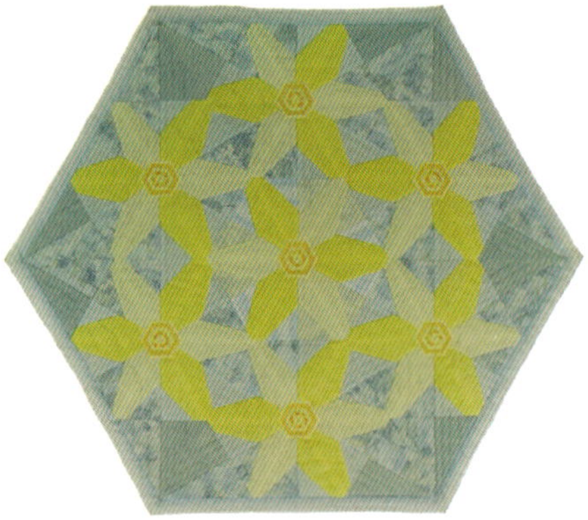

Daffodils

Ruth McDowell
Made in Winchester, Massachusetts
Circa 1983
40 x 47 in.
IQM 2009.039.0041

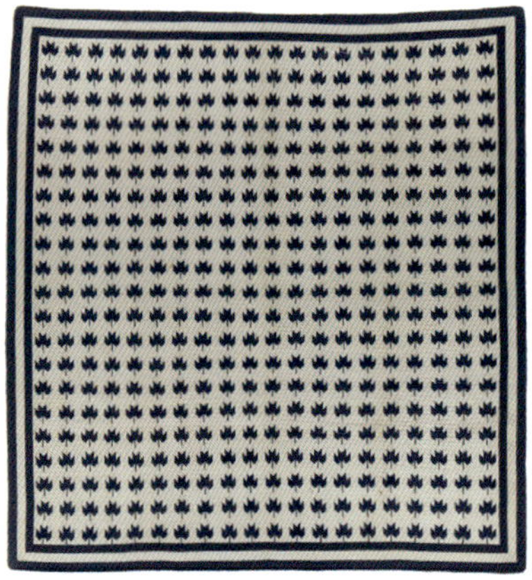

Tea Leaf

Possibly made by Mary Corrigan
Possibly made in western Virginia
Circa 1897
85.75 x 78.5 in.
IQM 2009.039.0044

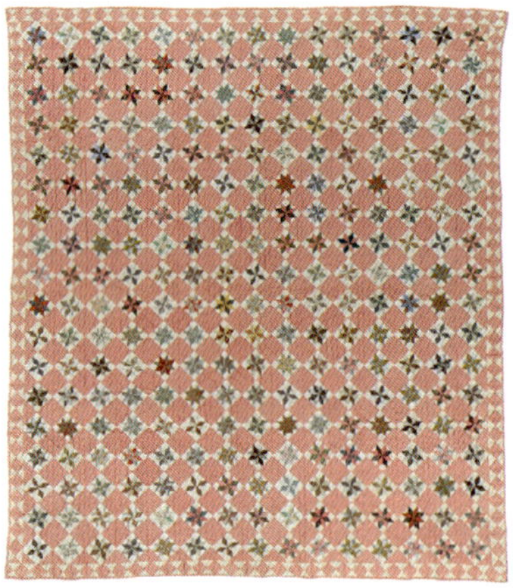

LeMoyne Star

Maker unidentified
Made in United States
Circa 1875
75.75 x 64.5 in.
IQM 2009.039.0045

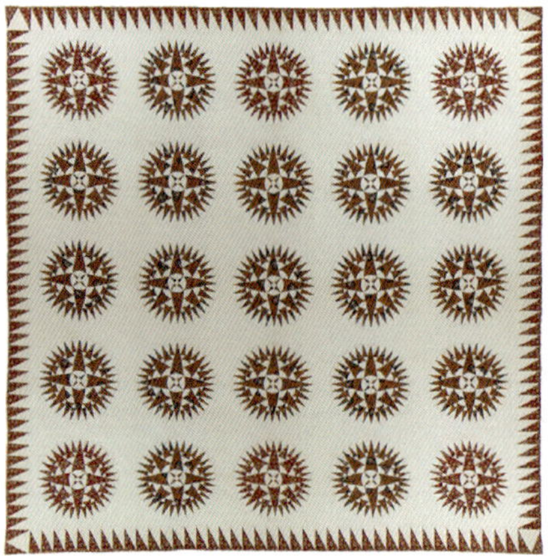

Mariner's Compass

Maker unidentified
Possibly made in Sharon, Pennsylvania
1820 - 1840
107 x 104.5 in.
IQM 2009.039.0046

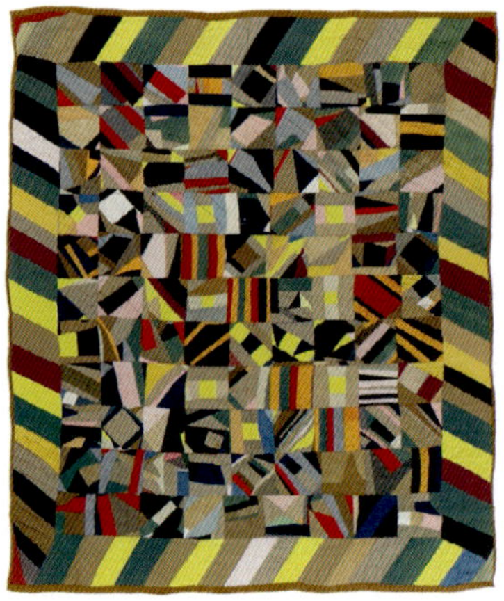

Crazy

Maker unidentified
Possibly made in Iowa
1925 - 1945
58.75 x 68.75 in.
IQM 2009.039.0047

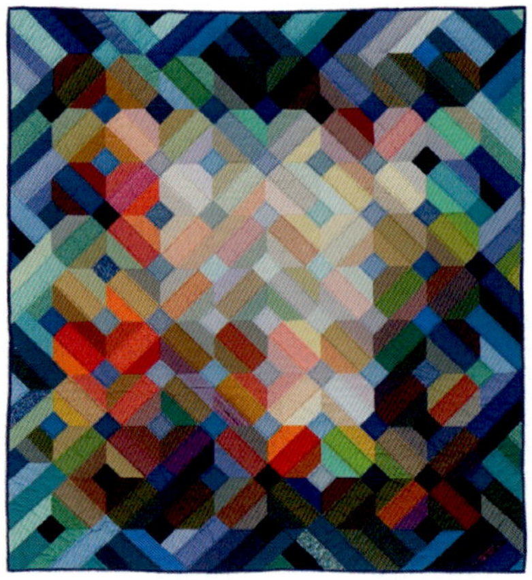

Pieces of Eight

Michael James
Made in Somerset, Massachusetts
1983 - 1984
56.25 x 50.25 in.
IQM 2009.039.0048

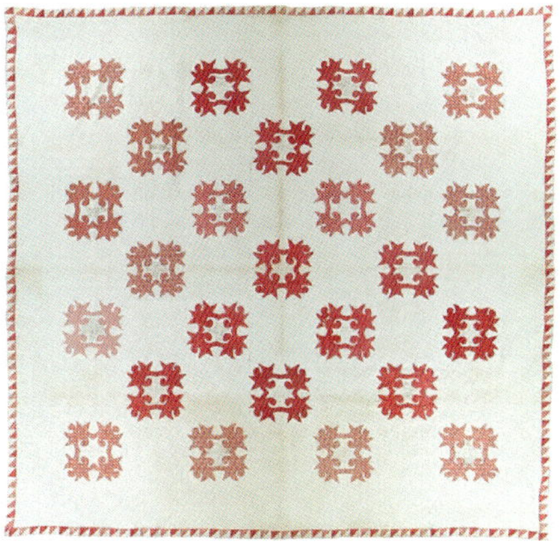

Papercut Appliqué

Friends and Relatives of Permelia Eavy
Probably made in Pennsylvania
Dated 1847
100.5 x 101 in.

IQM 2009.039.0050

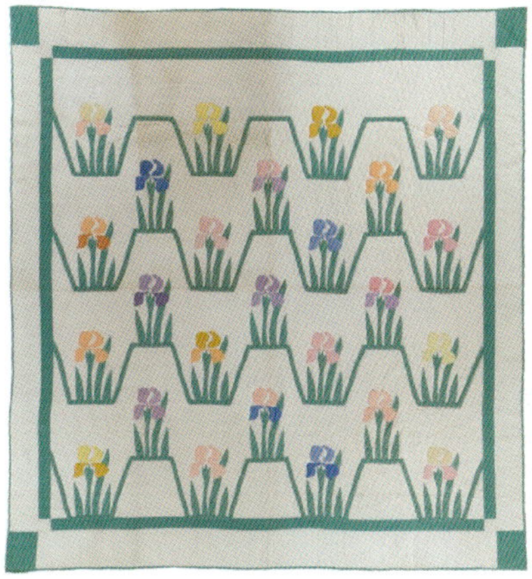

Iris

Maker unidentified
Made in United States
Circa 1940
94.75 x 86.5 in.

IQM 2009.039.0052

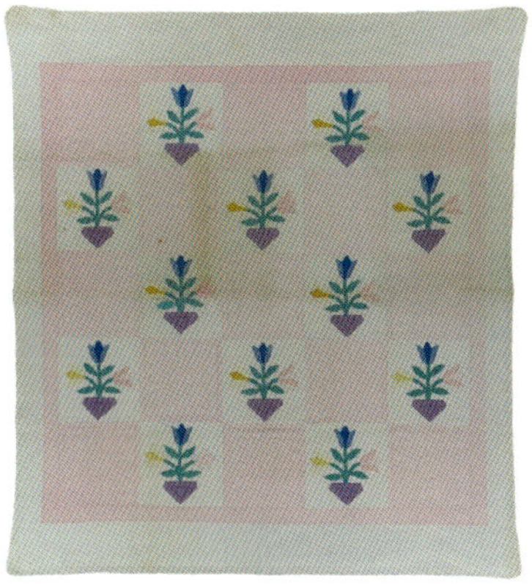

Tulip

Amelia Marie Frohn Bohl
Made in Lincoln, Nebraska
Circa 1940
80 x 72.5 in.

IQM 2009.039.0053

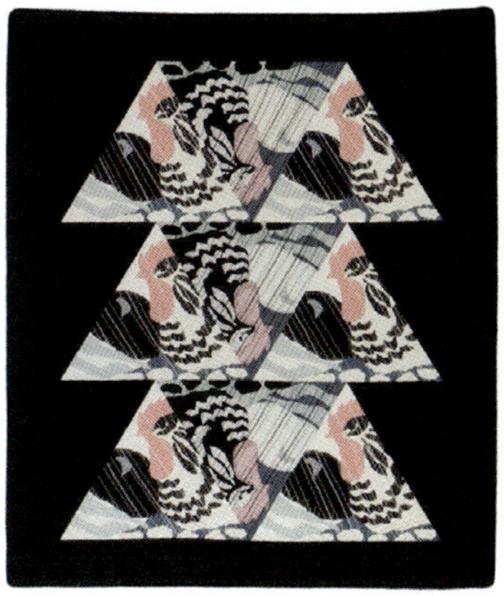

Hen Quilt

Pauline Burbidge
Made in Nottingham, England, United Kingdom
Dated 1986
48.75 x 41.5 in.

IQM 2009.039.0057

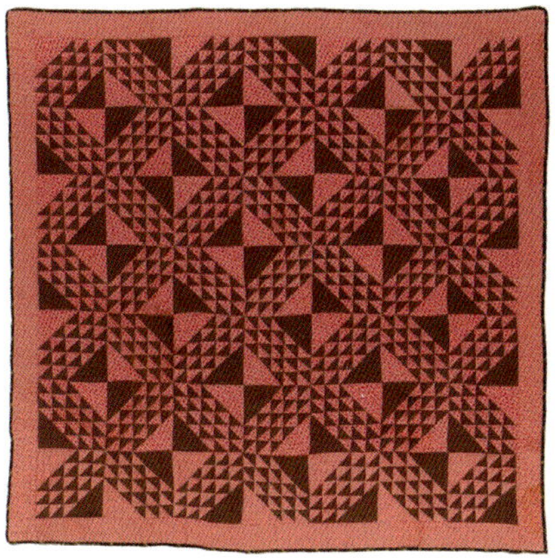

Lady of the Lake

Maker unidentified
Possibly made in Ohio
Circa 1880
66.75 x 66.5 in.

IQM 2009.039.0060

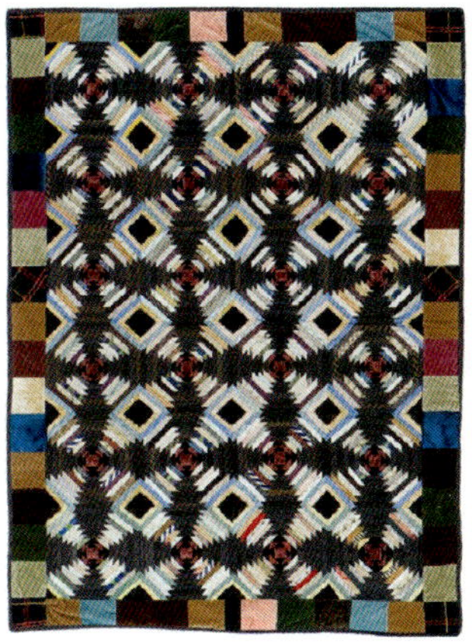

Log Cabin

Maker unidentified
Made in United States
Circa 1890
60.75 x 44.25 in.

IQM 2009.039.0061

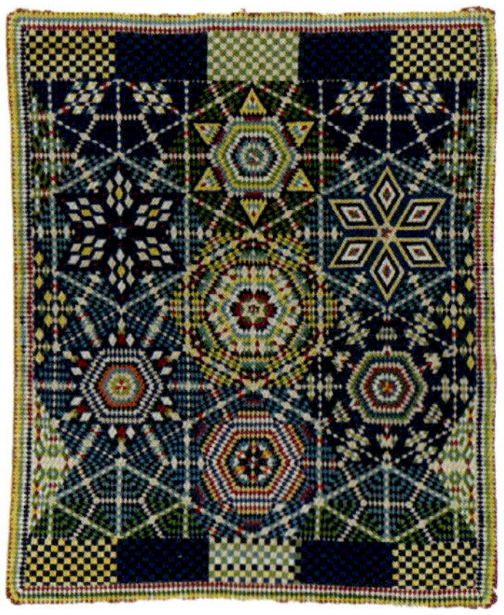

Mosaic Stars - Soldier's Quilt

Maker unidentified
Possibly made in Pennsylvania
1880 - 1900
77.25 x 62.75 in.

IQM 2009.039.0062

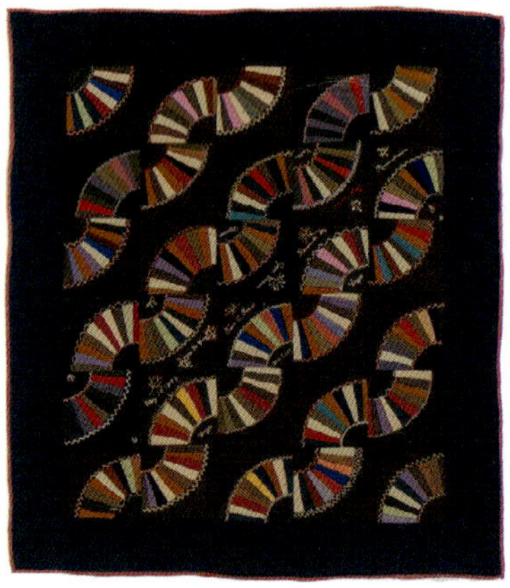

Fan

Maker unidentified
Made in Topeka, Indiana
Dated 1899
76.25 x 66.75 in.

IQM 2009.039.0064

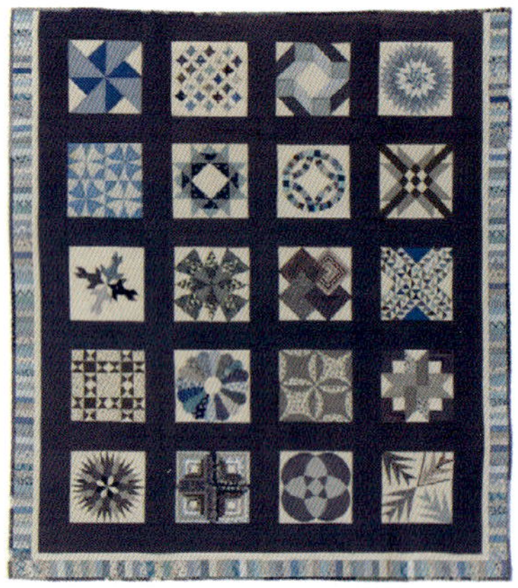

Big Blue

Ardis James
Made in Chappaqua, New York
Dated 1980
91.75 x 79.5 in.

IQM 2009.039.0065